James

D0070870

HANDBOOK OF AMERICAN HISTORY

Under the general editorship of

JOHN MORTON BLUM *Yale University*

HANDBOOK OF AMERICAN HISTORY

Donald B. Cole

Phillips Exeter Academy

HARCOURT BRACE JOVANOVICH, INC.

New York   Chicago   San Francisco   Atlanta

ALL MAPS: HARBRACE

© Harcourt Brace Jovanovich, Inc.

All rights reserved. No part of this publication may be reproduced or transmitted in any form or by any means, electronic or mechanical, including photocopy, recording, or any information storage and retrieval system, without permission in writing from the publisher.

ISBN: 0-15-530830-0

Library of Congress Catalog Card Number: 68-24778

Printed in the United States of America

To my mother and father

PREFACE

The *Handbook of American History* provides in one compact volume both a reference book and a chronological survey of American history. Since many instructors teach American history exclusively from paperbound monographs, students have at best only a vague notion of chronology. As a short, inexpensive reference textbook, the *Handbook* permits the instructor to assign a wide variety of supplementary reading. At the same time it assures him that his students have a complete reference to the relevant facts of American history. Although the *Handbook* was designed specifically for courses in American history, it is also a useful reference for students of American literature and government.

The *Handbook* is arranged chronologically, with primary emphasis on political and economic history; yet a considerable amount of data on social and cultural history is also included. Within the chronological order some subjects are grouped topically. For example, the important decisions of the Marshall Court appear together, as do facts relating to the history of immigration in the late nineteenth century and facts concerning the Negro in the early twentieth century. At the end of each of the nine parts there are brief biographies of important persons. In addition, there are statistical tables of economic and demographic data at the end of all but two of the parts; most of the economic and political data were derived from *Historical Statistics of the United States*. Maps illustrate the text throughout.

A word about dates: The *Handbook* follows New Style usage for all dates before 1752; thus it dates the sailing of the *Mayflower* from England as September 16, 1620 (New Style), rather than September 6, 1620 (Old Style). For events taking place across the International Date Line the book uses the date where the event occurred rather than the date in the United States. I give, for example, December 8, 1941—not December 7, 1941—as the date for the Japanese air attack on the Philippines. The *Handbook* dates acts of Congress on the day the act was signed by the President. Before 1845, when Congress established a uniform voting day, the book dates Presidential elections on the day the Presidential electors cast their ballots (hence December 3, 1828); after 1845 it uses the day on which the people actually voted (November 6, 1860).

Preparation of the book has taught me to be wary of factual exactness. It is impossible to determine, for example, the exact number who fell in most battles or to be certain about the exact vote cast for Presidential candidates. I have tried to avoid broad generalization, but selection and compression of a large body of data naturally involved a degree of generalization.

This book, begun at the Phillips Exeter Academy and completed while I was a visiting professor of history at the University of California, Los Angeles, during the academic year 1967–68, has taught me to respect the perception and kindness of many people. I am grateful to John M. Blum of Yale University for his constructive criticism of the entire work. As always, I am indebted to my colleague Henry F. Bedford for his friendship and advice. I wish also to thank Michael G. Kammen of Cornell University, William W. Freehling of the University of Michigan, G. Wallace Chessman of Denison University, and David W. Marcell of Skidmore College; each read parts of the manuscript. Zdenek Salzmann guided my thinking on the early Indian settlements in the New World, and Robert F. Brownell explained a number of scientific items and terms. Julius Milmeister's careful attention to detail alerted me to possible errors. Olive Hoxie was understanding and talented in typing the manuscript. And I owe much to my wife and children who bore up most patiently while I was writing the book.

Donald B. Cole

CONTENTS

4 THE JACKSON ERA, 1824–1848

5 CIVIL WAR AND RECONSTRUCTION, 1849–1877

6 THE RISE OF AN INDUSTRIAL WORLD POWER, 1865–1900

7 PROSPERITY, PROGRESSIVISM, AND WORLD WAR I, 1901–1929

8 DEPRESSION, NEW DEAL, AND WORLD WAR II, 1929–1945

9 THE COLD WAR, 1945–1967

LIST OF MAPS

THE AGE OF EXPLORATION AND COLONIZATION

PART 1

Discovery and Exploration of the New World

The American Indians

40,000–25,000 B.C. During the late ice age **Asian man** (fully developed modern man, or subspecies *Homo sapiens sapiens*) migrated across **Bering Strait** from Asia to North America.

18,000–10,000 B.C. The earliest human remains in America are of a woman whose skull, found in Midland, Tex., dates back at the most 20,000 years.

*c.*9,000 B.C. Early American Indians were of the **late stone age**; they hunted big game and used weapons and tools of chipped stone. Arrowheads or points found near Folsom, Col., and Clovis, N.M., date from *c.*9,000 B.C.

*c.*7,000 B.C. The Indians reached the tip of South America after moving down the west coasts of North and South America.

*c.*5,000 B.C. The earliest farming began in Central America.

*c.*2,000 B.C. Agricultural village life began in Central America.

2,000 B.C.–A.D. 900 Mayan Civilization developed on the Yucatan peninsula, Mexico, reaching its peak A.D. 300–900.

A.D. 900–1200 Toltecs built an empire in Mexico and invaded the Mayas.

1100–1300 Pueblo Culture in New Mexico, Arizona, and southern Colorado, led by the Zuñi and Hopi tribes, reached its height. These Indians were farmers and potters who lived in apartment-type masonry villages.

1200–1521 The **Aztecs** established an empire near Mexico City, supplanting the Toltecs. In 1521 Hernando Cortés overthrew the Aztec ruler Montezuma.

1200–1532 Inca Civilization reached its height in Peru, where the Incas developed an advanced stone architecture.

Other Indian Groups: Linguistic groups included the **Algonquian** (northeastern and central North America), **Siouan** (Great Plains), **Muskogean** (southeastern North America), **Athapascan** (northwestern North America and southwestern United States), **Iroquoian** (St. Lawrence River Valley). Their economy was one of hunting (especially buffalo on the Great Plains) and agriculture (plant cultivation and fishing elsewhere). The units of social organization were **clans** and tribes. Some tribes organized confederations, e.g., the **League of the Iroquois,** *c.*1570 (the Mohawk, Seneca, Oneida, Onondaga, and Cayuga tribes). The leading Algonquian tribes included the Abenaki (Maine), Cheyenne, and Blackfoot (Great Plains); Iroquoian tribes included the Huron; Muskogean included the Chickasaw, Choctaw, Creek, and Seminole; and Siouan included the Dakota and the Crow. Population at time of first contact with white men (*c.*1500): North America, *c.* one million; Central and South America, *c.* five million.

Viking Voyages

870 First Norse settlement in Iceland.

982–986 Eric the Red explored the coast of Greenland and planted the first settlement there.

986 Mainland of North America was sighted when the ship of **Bjarni Herjulfson**, a Norse trader, was blown off course.

1003 **LEIF ERICSON**, son of Eric, explored "Vinland" on the North American coast somewhere between Newfoundland and Virginia, probably **Nova Scotia. 1004–07 Thorvald Ericson**, brother of Leif, explored the coast of North America.

1010–13 **Thorfinn Karlsefni** and 150 others from Greenland spent two winters on the coast of North America.

1014–15 **Freydis**, Eric's daughter, made the last authenticated Norse voyage to the mainland of North America.

1355 Last expedition was sent from Norway to Greenland.

1440 World Map (known as the "Vinland" Map) included an accurate outline of Greenland and a rough outline of Vinland with perhaps the St. Lawrence River and either Hudson-Strait or Chesapeake Bay clearly indicated.

Portuguese Voyages

1410 Ptolemy's *Geography*, in translation, encouraged exploration by estimating the world at only ⁵⁄₇ its actual size. Although educated people realized that the world was round, they seem to have been unaware of the New World's existence.

1445 Portuguese explorers sent out by **Prince Henry the Navigator** reached Cape Verde, Africa. The Cape Verde Islands were discovered the next year.

1472 Portuguese voyage under João Vaz Corte-Real and Álvaro Martins Homem may have discovered Newfoundland.

1476–80 Expeditions sought the legendary land of Antillia in the Atlantic.

1487–88 **Bartholomew Dias** rounded the **Cape of Good Hope** and landed on the east coast of Africa.

1498 **Vasco Da Gama** reached **Calicut, India,** and returned home in 1499.

The Voyages of Columbus, 1492–1504

1451 **CHRISTOPHER COLUMBUS** was **born in or near Genoa.** Little is known of his early life until 1476, when he arrived in Portugal.

1477–78 Columbus made voyages for Portugal to England and Madeira.

1481–82 He may have sailed along the west coast of Africa.

1485–86 When the King of Portugal refused to finance a western voyage, Columbus moved to Spain. For several years he had

1-1 Voyages of Exploration

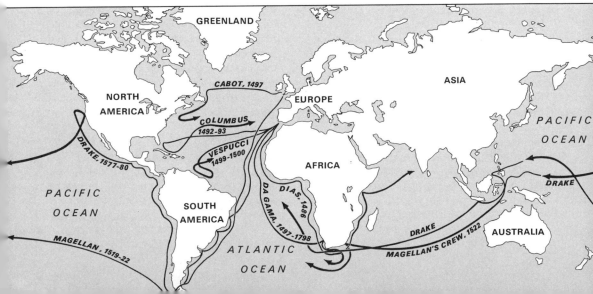

been in contact with geographers Martin Behaim in Nuremberg and Paolo Toscanelli in Florence. He spent several years seeking financial support, in Spain and in Portugal, for his proposed voyage to Asia.

1492 On Apr. 17, **Ferdinand and Isabella of Spain** titled Columbus "Admiral of the Ocean Sea" and together with private sources backed a voyage west to Asia. Columbus was to be governor of any territory he discovered.

1492–93 First Voyage: *Niña, Pinta,* and *Santa Maria* (Columbus' flagship) sailed Aug. 3 from Palos, Spain, with 90 men. The fleet reached the Canary Islands a week later and on Sept. 6 sailed west. Columbus narrowly averted a mutiny two days before first land was sighted (Oct. 12), which Columbus named **San Salvador** (now Watlings Island). Oct. 14–Dec. 5, explored the Bahamas and discovered and explored the coast of **Cuba**. Dec. 6–Jan. 15, 1493, he discovered and explored the northern coast of **Hispaniola (Santo Domingo)**, established a post. The fleet returned to Spain in March, 1493. In May, Papal bulls granted Spain all discoveries west of demarcation line 100 leagues west of Azores and Cape Verde Islands, and Portugal the land east of the line.

1493–96 Second Voyage: in September, Columbus sailed from Cadiz with 17 ships and about 1200 men. On Jan. 2, 1494, he planted the colony of **Isabella** on **Santo Domingo**. From late Apr. through Sept., he explored the remaining coasts of Santo Domingo, Jamaica, and Cuba. (The **Treaty of Tordesillas** of June 7 gave to Spain all discoveries west of line, 370 leagues west of Cape Verde Islands, and to Portugal all discoveries east of the line.) Return voyage, March–June, 1496.

1498–1500 Third Voyage: seven ships left Spain in May and reached Trinidad, July 31. Aug. 1–13, Columbus sighted the coast of South America and explored the mouths of the Orinoco. Columbus put down a rebellion at the Spanish colony at Santo Domingo, Aug. 31. Two years later, a new governor sent Columbus home in chains because of the unrest in Santo Domingo. Columbus was

freed but never recovered his authority in the New World.

1502–04 Fourth Voyage: began in May with four ships. Columbus explored the Central American coast from Honduras south to Panama and was shipwrecked on Jamaica in the summer of 1503. He returned to Spain the next year where he died in 1506, still believing that he had discovered the Coast of Asia.

Exploration of South America, 1499–1541

1499 AMERIGO VESPUCCI, sailing for Spain, sighted Cape Cassipore, South America, on June 27 and explored the coast past the mouth of the Amazon.

1499–1501 Expeditions to South America for Spain by Peralonso Niño and Cristóbal Guerra to Venezuela, by Vincente Pinzón to Brazil, by Rodrigo de Bastidas to north coast; for Portugal by Pedro Cabral to Brazil.

1501 Vespucci commanded Portuguese voyage to Cape São Roque, South America, and then sailed south to Argentina.

1502 Letter from Vespucci to Lorenzo di Pier Francesco de Medici, his former patron, announced that he had made two trips to a "New World."

1507 Martin Waldseemüller, the German geographer, proposed that the New World be called **America** for Amerigo Vespucci.

1529 In July, Spain made **Francisco Pizarro** Governor of New Castile, on the west coast of South America.

1531–41 Pizarro left Panama in January with three ships and 180 men and invaded Peru. He occupied Cuzco, Peru, in November, 1533. Incas besieged the Spanish at Cuzco, but the siege was raised (1536–37). Pizarro was murdered by colleagues in June, 1541.

Caribbean Exploration After Columbus

1508 Sebastián de Ocampo circumnavigated **Cuba**, proving it to be an island.

1508–09 Vincente Pinzón and Juan Diaz de Solis, sailing for Spain, explored the Honduran and Yucatán coasts.

1509–10 Spain conquered **Puerto Rico** and **Jamaica**.

1511 Diego de Velasquez subdued Cuba.

1513 **Juan Ponce de Leon**, governor of Puerto Rico, explored the coasts of the **Florida** peninsula.

1513 **Vasco de Balboa** crossed the Isthmus of Panama and discovered the **Pacific Ocean** (Sept. 25).

1519 Alvárez de Pineda explored coast of Gulf of Mexico.

1519–21 **Hernando Cortés** defeated Indians in Tabasco, Mexico, and was received by the Aztec king, Montezuma, at Mexico City. Cortés completed his conquest of Mexico in 1521.

Circumnavigation of the World

1519–22 **FERNANDO MAGELLAN** a Portuguese sailing for Spain, left (1519) in search of western passage to the Indies. He sailed south and west and wintered along the coast of South America. Discovered and sailed through the **Strait of Magellan**, Oct. 21–Nov. 28, 1520. Sighted Samar Island in the **Philippines** and was killed there by natives on April 27, 1521.

1522 **Sept. 6** One of Magellan's ships completed **first voyage around the world**.

1564 Spanish occupation of the Philippines began with an expedition under Miguel de Legaspi.

1577–80 **SIR FRANCIS DRAKE**, sailing for England, sailed to plunder Spanish shipping in the Pacific, passed through the Strait of Magellan and on Dec. 5, 1578, raided Valparaiso. He reached **San Francisco Bay** six months later (1579) and claimed it for England. After failing to find the western end of the so-called Northwest Passage to the Orient, (1579–80), he crossed the Pacific, arriving in England Sept. 26, 1580, with great amounts of plunder taken from Spanish shipping.

Voyages to North America

1497–98 **John Cabot** sighted either Cape Breton Island or Newfoundland in June, took possession for England, and then sailed south. Seeking passage to Japan, Cabot explored the North American coast from Newfoundland to Chesapeake Bay, May, 1498.

1504 French fishing vessels sailed to Newfoundland.

1509 Sebastian Cabot of England sailed to what he later claimed was Hudson Bay.

1524 Esteban Gomez sailed from Nova Scotia to Florida, thus completing Spanish exploration of the east coasts of North and South America.

1524 **Giovanni de Verrazano**, seeking a route to the Indies, entered the harbor of what is now New York and established French claim to North America.

1534–43 **Jacques Cartier** claimed Newfoundland and Prince Edward Island for France. He then entered the site of the **St. Lawrence River** in 1535 and went on to site of Quebec; he wintered there and returned to France in the spring. By 1540, France was able to control fishing off Newfoundland. Cartier again reached Quebec in 1541. His voyages helped establish French trade with the Indians, which began two years later.

1576–78 **Martin Frobisher** of England reached **Baffin Land** and **Frobisher Bay** in search of Northwest Passage and sailed through **Hudson Strait**.

1585–87 John Davis made three voyages to find the Northwest Passage.

Spanish and French Settlements in the New World, 1500–1700

Spanish Rule in Mexico, New Mexico, and California

1523 **Franciscans** sent first mission to the New World.

1533 Fortuno Ximenes discovered Lower California.

1535 Spain established the **viceroyalty system**, in which New Spain was ruled by a viceroy and a provincial governor.

1539 Francisco de Ulloa sailed into the Gulf of California.

1540–42 **Francisco de Coronado** explored New Mexico, Texas, and Kansas in search of the legendary treasures of the Seven Cities of Cibola.

1542 Juan Cabrillo sailed north along the California coast and took possession of the land for Spain.

1551 **University of Mexico** was founded as the Royal and Pontifical University of St. Paul.

1598 Don Juan de Onate founded San Juan near the site of Santa Fe and claimed New Mexico for Spain.

1602–03 San Diego and Monterey were discovered.

1609 **Santa Fe** was founded. From then until 1769, there was little additional Spanish expansion into New Mexico and California except where missions were founded.

1769–70 San Diego and Monterey were occupied as missions, and the Spanish discovered **San Francisco**. In the period until 1823, the Franciscans—initially under the leadership of Junipero Serra (d. 1784)—established 21 missions in California, the first at San Diego, the last at Sonoma.

Spanish Settlements in Florida

1521 **Ponce de Leon** landed at Charlotte Harbor.

1526 Vásquez de Ayllón established a settlement on the coast of North Carolina; the colony failed the next year after enduring a hard winter.

1528 **Panfilo de Narváez** landed at Tampa with 400 settlers, marched north to Tallahassee. They were shipwrecked, and almost all were lost on the way back to Mexico. In 1536, a lone survivor returned to Mexico.

1539–42 **HERNANDO DE SOTO** brought 600 soldiers to Tampa and journeyed to North Carolina. He later explored west to Mobile; discovered the Mississippi River near the site of Memphis, and explored west to Oklahoma where he died of fever.

1562 In competition with Spain, **Jean Ribaut** established an unsuccessful French Huguenot colony at Port Royal, near Charleston. Two years later, René de Laudonnière

1-2 Spanish and French Explorations

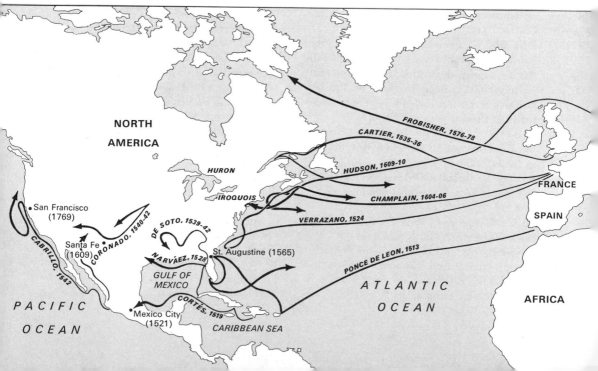

settled a French Huguenot colony at St. Johns River, Fla.

1565 **Pedro Menéndez de Avilés** of Spain was ordered to drive the French from Florida; he left Cadiz in June with 2600 soldiers and sailors; Ribaut went to Florida to reinforce Laudonnière. Menéndez founded **St. Augustine** in Sept. and directed the Spanish massacre of almost the entire French settlement.

1566–67 Menéndez established settlements at Charlotte Bay, Tampa Bay, Miami, and elsewhere.

1566–72 Jesuit missions were established in Florida.

1574 Spain abandoned west coast posts.

1595–1606 Franciscan missions were established in present-day Georgia; these were later abandoned, but the missions in Florida were retained.

1600 There were over 150,000 settlers in New Spain.

French Canada

1603 **SAMUEL DE CHAMPLAIN,** on first of 11 voyages to Canada, explored the **St. Lawrence** to the site of Montreal.

1604 The French set up a post at the mouth of the St. Croix River.

1604–06 Champlain explored the coast of North America as far south as Cape Cod.

1608–09 Champlain, on third voyage, founded **Quebec**. On a later campaign with the Algonquins, discovered **Lake Champlain**. In July, 1609, Champlain fired on the **Iroquois** near Ticonderoga, instigating two centuries of French-Iroquois hostility.

1615–16 Champlain joined the **Hurons** for an unsuccessful raid against the Iroquois in New York.

1615 The **Recollect Friars** arrived in Canada; they were followed by Jesuit missionaries in 1625.

1627 **Company of New France** was given control of French North America.

1627–32 As part of a war with France in Europe, the British captured Quebec and settled French **Acadia** (renamed Nova Scotia); they later returned both.

1634 **Jean Nicolet** pushed French exploration west to Green Bay, Wis.

1641 **Montreal** was founded, Oct. 14.

1642–53 The Iroquois drove the Hurons, who were supported by the French, back to Wisconsin.

1662 Finance Minister Colbert urged King Louis XIV to expand colonization. The king organized French Canada under governor, appointive council, and intendant, the King's personal representative. From 1663–72, **Jean Baptiste Talon** used his position as the "great intendant" to dominate the government of Canada and sent missions to the Indians as far west as Green Bay.

1665–66 The French defeated the Iroquois and British near Lake Champlain and established forts on the lake.

1669–70 **René Robert Cavelier, Sieur de la Salle** pushed French power south into Ohio.

1670 The British established **Hudson's Bay Company**, which challenged French control of the Hudson Bay region, 1670–83.

1672–82 Under the **Comte de Frontenac** as Governor of Canada, France conquered the Mississippi Valley. In 1673, the French built Fort Frontenac on Lake Ontario. The same year, **Père Jacques Marquette**, Jesuit, and **Louis Joliet**, trader, canoed through Green Bay to the Wisconsin River, reached the Mississippi River, and traveled down it. By 1681, Father Louis Hennepin had explored the upper Mississippi; in 1682 La Salle traveled by canoe down the river, discovered the mouth of the Mississippi, and claimed all of Louisiana for France.

1686 The French established a post at the mouth of the Arkansas River.

1687 La Salle was murdered by mutineers in Texas after a 3-year expedition to establish a base at the mouth of the Mississippi.

1698 The French sent an expedition under Pierre le Moyne, Sieur d'Iberville, by sea to colonize Louisiana. D'Iberville established a fort at Biloxi (Miss.) and another on the Mississippi River 40 miles above its mouth, 1699.

1714 The French made the first permanent settlement in Louisiana at Natchitoches and founded New Orleans in 1718.

English Settlements, 1600–1763

British Colonial Policies, 1588–1767

1558–1603   Queen Elizabeth followed an anti-Spanish policy with frequent raids on the Spanish treasure fleet until 1603.

1588   Defeat of the **Spanish Armada**.

1603–25   King James I began a policy of **mercantilism** in which he sought to establish a favorable balance of trade. Colonies would provide raw materials and markets for home manufacturing.

1606   Virginia Company was established. The earliest colonies were corporate, as in Massachusetts Bay, or proprietary, as in Maryland. In America, Virginia was the only royal colony until 1679.

1625–49   King Charles I struggled with Parliament over the powers of the crown.

1634–41   Commission for Foreign Plantations aided the Privy Council in its administration of the colonies.

1642–49   Civil War between King and Parliament—with the so-called Divine Right of Kings the central issue—resulted in a victory for Parliamentary forces.

1647–49   A radical army group known as the **Levelers** favored social equality, direct democracy through one representative body, and complete manhood suffrage, ideas that later had great influence on the American radicals, 1763–76.

1649   Charles I was tried by the army and beheaded, Jan. 30. This began the period of the **Commonwealth**, ostensibly government by Parliament, which continued under Oliver Cromwell until 1653. A Declaration of Parliament brought all colonies under its control; the Council of State set up a committee to handle trade and plantations.

1651   First Navigation Act was aimed at driving Dutch ships out of the colonial market. No goods from Asia, Africa, or America could be imported into England, Ireland, or the colonies except on English ships.

1652–54   First Dutch War, mostly on the seas.

1653–58   The **Protectorate**: rule by the Puritans under Oliver Cromwell after the Commonwealth proved unworkable. After Cromwell's death in 1658, his son was unable to continue the Protectorate.

1660   Restoration of the monarchy under **Charles II** (1660–85).

1660–75   Committee for Trade and Plantations of the Privy Council controlled colonies.

1660   NAVIGATION ACT: No goods could enter or leave English colonies except on English ships (including colonial ships). **Enumerated articles** (tobacco and sugar included) could be shipped from the colonies only to England or other colonies.

1663   NAVIGATION ACT: Most colonial imports from Europe had to travel on English ships and pass through England. These acts encouraged shipbuilding but tended to hurt the tobacco trade.

1673   NAVIGATION ACT: Duties were to be collected on enumerated articles at the port of departure to prevent evasion of duties. Customs Commissioners were appointed to enforce acts.

1675–96   Lords of Trade, a committee of the Privy Council, was put in charge of colonies.

1681–85   Tension between King and Parliament rose over the rights of the crown. Charles II ruled without Parliament until his death.

1685–88   Anti-Parliament and pro-Catholic policies of **James II** led to the **Glorious Revolution** of 1688. James II fled England in Dec.; was succeeded by William and Mary of Orange.

1689   Bill of Rights required free election of Parliament and Parliament's consent to taxation.

1689   John Locke's *Two Treatises on Civil Government* defended the sovereignty of the people and their right of revolution.

1696–1782   Board of Trade and Plantations was established to supervise the colonies.

1696   NAVIGATION ACT tightened the enforcement of earlier acts and set up **Vice-Admiralty Courts** in the colonies with jurisdiction over cases involving violations of the trade laws. These courts were unpopular because they did not use juries.

1699 Wool Act forbade the export of wool products from any colony in an effort to protect British producers from competition.

1701 Act of Settlement made royal ministers responsible to Parliament.

1705–74 Under various acts, bounties were paid for tar, hemp, turpentine, and indigo.

1732 Hat Act put restrictions on colonial manufacture of hats.

1733 Molasses Act put a high duty on rum (9d/gal.) and molasses (6d/gal.) imported from foreign West Indies to the mainland of North America. It was not enforceable.

1750 Iron Act forbade construction of slitting and other iron mills in the colonies and allowed colonial pig and bar iron into England duty-free.

1751 Money Act prohibited New England colonies from setting up land banks or issuing bills of credit (paper money) as legal tender.

1767 Non-enumerated goods destined for Europe north of Cape Finisterre had to be shipped to England first. By about 1763, Parliament controlled trade, while the colonial assemblies controlled taxation, appointed lower officials, raised troops, and maintained their rights as Englishmen.

Virginia

1584 Sir Walter Raleigh sent out a colonial expedition to North Carolina. From this came a settlement of 100 at Roanoke Island, N.C., that was abandoned in 1586 because of unrest among the Indians.

1587 "Lost Colony" of Roanoke was established under Raleigh's patent on Roanoke Island with John White as governor and 150 settlers. Virginia Dare was the first white child born in English America. White, who had gone to England for supplies, returned in 1591 to find the settlers had vanished, presumably killed in an attack by Indians.

1606 In April, James I authorized patents for two joint stock companies to colonize the New World; the **VIRGINIA COMPANY OF LONDON** received a grant to land between the 34th and 41st latitudes north, and the **VIRGINIA COMPANY OF PLYMOUTH**

was to settle farther north. Three ships of the London company, carrying 120 settlers, sailed for Virginia in December and landed at **Jamestown** in May, 1607. Indians, disease, famine, and internal dissension plagued the colony for several years.

1608 Capt. **JOHN SMITH** tried to rule the colony, but he was almost executed by the settlers and left Virginia in 1609.

1609 New charter gave control to a council chosen by the company. A governor and councillors replaced the old ruling council. Soon after, 400 new colonists arrived.

1609–10 Famine reduced the population from 500 to 60.

1610 Governor Thomas Lord De La Warr arrived and tried to establish order.

1612 The "Dale Code" of governor Sir Thomas Dale (1611–12, 1614–16) imposed a severe regime to check continuing disorder. The code was given up in 1619.

1612 John Rolfe started **tobacco cultivation.**

1619–23 The company gave 44 land patents to subsidiary corporations.

1619 A Dutch vessel brought the first 21 **Negroes** from Africa to Virginia as bound servants.

1619 General Assembly, the first in the New World, met in Jamestown in August with governor, council, and 22 **burgesses** from 11 towns, hundreds, and plantations present. It eventually became bicameral.

1620 King James I refused to allow the election of **Sir Edwin Sandys** as treasurer of the Virginia Company. The company rebuked the King by electing a Sandys supporter in his place.

1622 Indians massacred 347 settlers, and another 500 died of disease the following year, leaving a population in 1624 of 1,275. From then on Virginia followed a policy of relentless warfare against the Indians.

1624 Virginia became a **royal colony** when financial instability and the high death rate led to annulment of the charter. The government remained the same except that the governor was appointed by the crown, not the company. **Sir Francis Wyatt** continued as first royal governor until 1626 when Sir George Yeardley replaced him.

1629   House of Burgesses was called for the first time since 1624; Sir John Harvey became governor.

1635   When the council deposed Governor Harvey for his arbitrary actions, the King returned him to power. Hostility continued between governor and council.

1642–52   First administration of powerful royalist governor **Sir William Berkeley**, who introduced reforms and gained from the Indians the land between the James and York rivers (1644). During the Civil Wars, Virginia supported the crown and gave refuge to royalists.

1652–60   During the Protectorate, the House of Burgesses replaced Berkeley with Richard Bennett.

1660–77   Berkeley was reinstated by Charles II after the Restoration; his second administration was arbitrary and allowed no further elections until 1676. This was a period of hard times in Virginia. Taxes were raised to buy back royal grants in northern Virginia. Overproduction and the Navigation Act requiring that tobacco be sent to England led to a drop in its price. Losses of tobacco ships in wars with the Dutch and hard winters (1670–73) increased bitterness.

1676   **BACON'S REBELLION.** The immediate cause was Berkeley's refusal to send troops against the marauding Indians. Some accused him of protecting the fur trade for personal advantage. On May 10, **Nathaniel Bacon**, whose plantation had been attacked, led a force of settlers against the Indians without the governor's consent. Berkeley

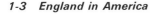

1-3   England in America

declared Bacon a traitor but later pardoned him. On June 23, Bacon led an army of about 500 men into Jamestown and forced Berkeley to make him general of the troops against the Indians. The governor could not raise a force sufficient to defeat Bacon, whose followers met in August and vowed loyalty to him against Berkeley and the crown. On September 18, Bacon drove Berkeley's men out of Jamestown and burned the town the next day. When Bacon died in October, Berkeley subdued Bacon's forces. In spite of his promise of amnesty he executed 23.

1677   Col. Herbert Jeffreys was sent to replace Berkeley as governor (April) and repudiated the voting reforms of 1676 that granted suffrage to all freemen.

1677–89   Struggle between House of Burgesses and governor over finances.

1698   Jamestown burned and was never rebuilt.

1710–22   Alexander Spotswood, as lieutenant governor, promoted the manufacture of iron. Friction developed between Spotswood and the assembly over heavy government expenses. Spotswood, who favored posts in the west to hold back the French, led a 1716 expedition into the Shenandoah Valley. By 1722, the Iroquois had agreed not to cross the Blue Ridge without permission of Virginia's governor.

1744   The Iroquois ceded land north of the Ohio River to Virginia, Maryland, and Pennsylvania.

Maryland

1632   Charles I made a proprietary grant (June 30) to **Cecilius Calvert**, son of George Calvert, **Lord Baltimore**, who had just died. The 2nd Lord Baltimore received the land between the Potomac and the 40th latitude on either side of Chesapeake Bay and called it Maryland. Baltimore was to appoint a governor and council but was supposed to consult the landowners. As a Catholic, he hoped to make the colony a refuge for **Roman Catholics**.

1633   About 200 sailed (Dec. 2) for Maryland with **Leonard Calvert**, brother of Lord Baltimore, as governor. The expedition founded

St. **Mary's**, near the Potomac River, Mar. 27, 1634. The settlers planted corn at once, and the colony did not suffer as had Jamestown.

1635   Assembly of all **freeholders** was established, and land was assigned according to a manorial plan.

1635–38   Maryland drove Virginians from Kent Island in Chesapeake Bay in a dispute over boundaries.

1649   Under the **TOLERATION ACT**, Maryland served as a refuge for Catholics and for Virginians not conforming to the Church of England.

1650   Assembly became bicameral.

1654   A Puritan parliamentary commission forced Governor William Stone out of office and repealed the Toleration Act.

1656   Lord Baltimore regained control and restored the Toleration Act.

1660   Charles Calvert, son of Cecilius, was named governor. He became the 3rd Lord Baltimore in 1675.

1661–76   Low tobacco prices, Indian attacks, and pro-Catholic policies caused dissatisfaction in the colony.

1676   In Sept., a revolt led by William Davyes and John Pate was put down.

1681   Revolt led by Josias Fendall against proprietary rule was crushed in April, and Fendall was banished.

1688   Baltimore sent **William Joseph**, an extreme royalist, to be deputy governor. When he prorogued the assembly, rumors spread that Maryland was to be given to the Catholics. In May, 1689, **John Coode** organized the **Protestant Association**, which in July ousted governor Joseph and recalled the assembly. As a result, the crown made Maryland a royal province in 1691 with Sir Lionel Copley first governor.

1692–1702   Church of England was established in Maryland. Catholic priests were not allowed to hold services, and Catholics were forbidden to educate their children. Additional anti-Catholic laws were passed in 1716–18.

1695   Capital was moved to **Annapolis** from St. Mary's.

1715   In May, the crown restored the government to Charles Calvert, 4th Lord Baltimore and a convert to the Church of England, under the charter of 1632.

1716–18 The province passed anti-Catholic laws.

1729 The city of **Baltimore** was founded.

Plymouth

PURITANISM originated in the 1560's when a group of men sought to "purify" the Church of England of bishops, church courts and other remnants of Catholicism. The English crown, which under Henry VIII had renounced Catholicism, was hostile to Puritanism and tried to establish conformity to Anglican practices. By 1600 the Puritans were divided into two groups: **Congregationalists** who were organized as small independent churches made up only of true believers, and **Presbyterians** who wanted a central authority and accepted all comers into the faith. Congregationalists were of two types: the **separatists** or **Pilgrims** who left the Anglican Church and went to Plymouth and the **Puritans** who wished to remain within the Church of England (but did not) and settled at Massachusetts Bay. Whatever the group, Congregational Puritans believed in the extreme power of God in the **predestination** of man to heaven or hell and in the teachings of the Bible. They believed also that a church member must have a religious experience in which God told him that he was saved.

1606 James I gave **PLYMOUTH COMPANY** rights to settle between the 38th and 45th parallels. Its first expedition built a temporary fort at the mouth of the Kennebec River (1607), but the colony was unsuccessful.

1608 Separatists from the Church of England (henceforth called **Pilgrims**) moved to Holland to avoid religious persecution.

1614 **Captain John Smith** explored the northeastern coast of present-day United States and named it **New England.**

1619 The Pilgrims set up a joint stock company with a Virginia Company patent to settle near Jamestown.

1620 July: 35 Pilgrims under **William Brewster** left Holland for England in the *Speedwell.* In Aug., they joined other English Separatists (and non-Pilgrims) in Plymouth and set forth for America on the *Speedwell* and the *Mayflower* but returned to port when the *Speedwell* sprang a leak. The *Mayflower* sailed for the New World, Sept. 16; Brewster led the Pilgrims, and Captain **Myles Standish** sailed as military leader. On Nov. 9, the *Mayflower* entered **Cape Cod Bay,** far north of its destination. Since the patent from the Virginia Co. was inoperative in the north, and since they were afraid that the non-Pilgrims would rebel, the Pilgrims persuaded 41 adults aboard to sign the **MAYFLOWER COMPACT,** Nov. 21. The signers agreed to follow laws "for the generall goode of the colonie." In Dec., an exploring party landed at **Plymouth**; on the 26th, the *Mayflower* anchored at Plymouth, and settlers went ashore.

1621 Over half the settlers died of disease during the first winter. In March, a treaty was made with the Wampanoag Indians, and in April, **WILLIAM BRADFORD** was elected governor. He was annually reelected (except for five years) until his death 1657. The government consisted of an annual assembly (the **General Court**) composed of governor, assistants, and all freemen (those granted the right to vote). The **Council for New England** (the Plymouth Co. reorganized to include land between the 40th and 48th parallels) granted the Pilgrims a patent to settle at Plymouth (June 1).

1623 The Pilgrims granted each family a parcel of land.

1626 The Company in London sold all rights to the settlers, who divided up the remaining land. Eight Pilgrims, including Bradford, took over the debts of the colony. Colony and corporation were merged, but Plymouth never received a royal charter.

1636 Representative system of government began. The General Court consisted of two deputies from each town, together with the governor and his assistants.

1691 Massachusetts Bay Colony absorbed the Plymouth Colony.

Massachusetts Bay

1626 The Council for New England put a fishing post at Cape Ann, north of Boston.

1628 New England Co. received a patent

from the Council for New England for land from three miles south of the Charles River to three miles north of the Merrimack River and sent 40 settlers to **Salem**.

1629 A Royal Charter merged New England Co. with **Massachusetts Bay Co.** (March 14), which sent its first group of settlers to Salem in July. The **Cambridge Agreement** (Aug.) came about when religious and economic difficulties led **John Winthrop**, Richard Saltonstall, and others of the Massachusetts Bay Co., most of them Puritans, to decide to migrate to the New World provided the charter and government of the Company went with them. The Company agreed to the Cambridge Plan, and Winthrop was elected governor.

1630 From March to Oct., over 1,000 settlers sailed for Salem in 17 ships and then founded **Boston**, Charlestown, and Watertown. The 12 freemen (company stockholders eligible to vote), consisting of **governor**, deputy governor, and **assistants**, ruled.

1631 May 28, the number of freemen (which came to mean landowners who could vote) was raised from 12 to 130, but only **church members** could be freemen. The governor was still elected by the assistants, who were chosen by the freemen. Direct election of the governor by all freemen began a year later.

1634 Each town gained the right to send deputies to the meeting of the **General Court**, which passed all laws for the colony.

1635 **Rev. Roger Williams** was banished in Sept. from Massachusetts Bay for preaching of his belief in the separation of church and state.

1636 **Antinomian** views of **Anne Hutchinson** and other Bostonians threatened orthodoxy. Antinomians stressed personal revelation, denied that Christians had to follow moral law, and questioned the power of the orthodox clergy.

1637 John Winthrop, orthodox leader, was reelected governor and continued to serve almost every year to 1649.

1638 Winthrop ignored a Privy Council order in April to give up the charter. The English Civil Wars prevented further action.

1641 The **Body of Liberties** made Massa-

chusetts Bay a Commonwealth or independent republic dominated by the church.

1644 The General Court became bicameral with a House of Deputies and a House of Assistants.

1646 **Rev. John Eliot** began to convert the Indians in eastern Massachusetts to Christianity. By 1663 he had translated the Bible into the Indian language.

1656 Massachusetts Bay banished two Quakers for religious non-conformity.

1658 Massachusetts established the death penalty for banished **Quakers** who returned and hanged four by 1661.

1664 Four royal Commissioners sent to investigate the governing of New England demanded that landowners be given the vote, that laws against the crown be repudiated, that all churches be recognized. Plymouth, Connecticut, and Rhode Island agreed with the Commissioners but Massachusetts refused to comply. No action was taken against Massachusetts.

1669 Massachusetts annexed Maine.

1676 Royal agent Edward Randolph accused Massachusetts of denying residents the right of appeal to the Privy Council and of failing to enforce the Navigation Acts.

1684 The charter of Massachusetts Bay was annulled by the crown because of the charges of Randolph.

1686 In Dec., the **DOMINION OF NEW ENGLAND**, with **Sir Edmund Andros** as governor, assumed authority over New England. In the period 1687–88, Andros irritated New Englanders by requiring Congregationalists to share churches with Anglicans, by trying to appropriate town land for the crown, and by limiting town meetings to one a year. Rev. John Wise of Ipswich, Mass., denounced Andros for taxation without representation. News of the Glorious Revolution reached Boston in April, 1689, and a mob forced Andros to surrender, charged him with misgovernment, and sent him to England for trial.

1691 Massachusetts became a **royal province** (Oct. 17) with a governor appointed by the crown, with property rather than religion as a qualification for voting, and with royal veto power over all legislation. Plymouth was absorbed into Massachusetts.

1692 Witchcraft Trials at Salem: Increase Mather's *Illustrious Providences* (1684) aroused interest in witchcraft. When Salem girls pretended to be bewitched, Governor **William Phips** (under clerical influence) set up a special court to try those accused of witchcraft. The province executed 20 and imprisoned 150.

1702–15 Governor **Joseph Dudley** battled with the General Court over its refusal to appropriate regular sums for the governor's salary.

1730–41 Governor Jonathan Belcher opposed the General Court's demand for paper money.

1740 Massachusetts organized a **land bank** to issue notes backed by mortgages, but Parliament destroyed it because it was inflationary.

1751 Parliament forbade New England to start new land banks.

New Hampshire and Maine

1622 The Council for New England granted **Sir Ferdinando Gorges** and **John Mason** the land between the Merrimack and the Kennebec rivers.

1623–24 Settlers arrived at Great Bay, N.H. (including **Portsmouth**) and at the Saco River and Casco Bay in Maine.

1629 New Hampshire and Maine were divided at the Piscataqua River.

1641–58 Many New Hampshire and Maine towns put themselves under the jurisdiction of Massachusetts because of the threat from Indian attacks.

1679 New Hampshire became a separate royal province and in 1692 was separated from the Dominion of New England. From 1698–1741 New Hampshire shared a governor with Massachusetts, getting its own governor, Benning Wentworth, in 1741.

Rhode Island

1636 Roger Williams and his followers founded the relatively democratic colony of **Providence.**

1638 Anne Hutchinson, after her expulsion from Massachusetts Bay, settled **Portsmouth.**

1640 Newport, founded 1639, united with Portsmouth.

1647 Providence, Newport, and Portsmouth formed the colony of Rhode Island. Governor and both houses of the legislature were elected annually by freeholders.

1663 Charles II granted Rhode Island a charter but allowed it to continue under its old independent rule. A statement was added about religious toleration, and Rhode Island continued to operate under this charter until 1842.

Connecticut

1631 Lord Say and Sele and others received a patent from the crown for Connecticut.

1633 Dutch laid claim to the area and built Fort Good Hope (at Hartford); in the same year, a party from Plymouth traveled the Connecticut River valley from its mouth north to **Windsor**.

1634 Settlers from Massachusetts Bay established **Wethersfield** and, in 1635, **Hartford.**

1635 Connecticut patent holders sent **John Winthrop the Younger** to settle at Saybrook, at the mouth of the Connecticut River.

1636–37 The Pequot Indians attacked Wethersfield and other settlements and were finally subdued by a combined force from Massachusetts, Plymouth, and Connecticut colonies.

1637 In May, settlers in Hartford, Windsor, and Wethersfield founded what became the **colony of Connecticut** with a representative General Court for the population of 800. In the same year, **Rev. John Davenport** and **Theophilus Eaton** sailed from England and founded **New Haven**.

1639 Hartford, Wethersfield, and Windsor agreed to the **Fundamental Orders,** which called for the governor and magistrates to be elected by "admitted inhabitants" (Trinitarian householders).

1643 Colony of New Haven was formed and was joined by two other towns.

1662 Connecticut requested from the crown and received a charter granting it autonomy under the Fundamental Orders and allowing it to absorb New Haven.

The New England Confederation and King Philip's War

1643 Massachusetts, Plymouth, Connecticut, and New Haven formed the **United Colonies of New England** to withstand the Dutch and Indians.

1675 The Wampanoags, Narragansetts, and Mohegans began to resist further expansion by settlers. When the colonists executed three Indians in June for alleged conspiracy, **King Philip** of the Wampanoags attacked Swansea (Mass.) and the war spread rapidly. In Sept., the Confederation declared war, although the Indians were victorious in the Connecticut Valley through Oct. By Nov., the Narragansett stronghold in South Kingston, R.I., was conquered by the colonists. Early in 1676, the Indians counterattacked in Massachusetts but were defeated by starvation, lack of supplies, and superior force. They began to surrender in May, and in Aug. Philip was betrayed and killed.

1684 The New England Confederation came to an end after a period of inactivity.

New Netherland

1609 **Henry Hudson** explored the Hudson River for the **Dutch East India Company** and established friendly relations with the Iroquois. The next year, the Dutch fur trade with the Indians began.

1613 Adriaen Block, Dutch sailor, explored Manhattan, Long Island, and Long Island Sound.

1614 The Dutch built Fort Nassau (later **Fort Orange**) near present-day Albany.

1621 Dutch West India Company was granted rights to establish colonies and trade in the New World and Africa.

1624 Some 30 families settled **New Netherland**, at Governor's Island, on the Delaware River, and at Fort Nassau.

1626–31 **Peter Minuit** was governor. The company operated New Netherland under a governor and a council but with no assembly. In 1626, Minuit bought **Manhattan Island** from the Indians for about $24 and named it **New Amsterdam**.

1628 Negro slaves from Africa were first brought to the colony.

1629 The company began to grant land to a few **patroons** who brought settlers to the colony and who governed their patroonships. It also monopolized the fur trade and maintained fairly good relationships with the Indians.

1633–38 The Dutch moved into Connecticut and Long Island.

1634 Indians destroyed a Dutch settlement on Delaware Bay.

1638 **New Sweden** was established along the Delaware River by Dutch and Swedish merchants.

1641–44 Indian attacks and English expansion forced governor **Willem Kiefft** to be more democratic.

1646–64 **Peter Stuyvesant** governor.

1647 Dutch householders elected nine men to advise the governor and council. He later called an occasional assembly of the towns near New Amsterdam. New Amsterdam and other towns gained a measure of self-government in the period 1652–61.

1650 Treaty of Hartford divided Dutch and English possessions at a line 10 miles east of the Hudson River. The Dutch were allowed to keep Fort Good Hope (Hartford), which was seized in 1653 by Connecticut during the **Anglo-Dutch War** (1652–54).

1655 New Sweden surrendered to New Netherland after an intermittent struggle (1643–55).

New York

1664 Charles II granted his brother **James, Duke of York**, Maine north of the Kennebec River and land from the western boundary of Connecticut to the eastern shore of Delaware Bay. In April, James named Col. **Richard Nicolls** deputy governor and ordered him to subdue New Netherland. By Sept., Stuyvesant surrendered New Netherland to Nicolls after a short siege. New Netherland became **New York**; Fort Orange became **Albany** and New Amsterdam became **New York City**.

1664–67 **Second Anglo-Dutch War** confirmed English possession of New York.

1665 The "**Duke's Laws**" provided a degree of self-government with elective officials on Long Island and were later extended to the rest of New York. New York City was granted self-government.

1673 New York surrendered to a Dutch fleet during the **Third Anglo-Dutch War** (1672–74) but was restored to England by the Treaty of Westminster.

1683 The first representative assembly drew up a **Charter of Liberties** (Oct. 30) calling for an assembly with the power to raise taxes.

1686 James II (former Duke of York) disallowed acts of the assembly, gave the governor full legislative power, and in 1687 dissolved the assembly.

1688 **Francis Nicholson** became lt. governor of New York under the Dominion of New England.

1689–91 **LEISLER'S REBELLION.** In May, news of the Glorious Revolution prompted **Jacob Leisler** and militia to take over New York; a convention in New York City appointed a committee of safety that made Leisler commander in chief of New York. Although Nicholson had fled for fear of the anti-Catholic sentiments resulting from the Glorious Revolution, the Privy Council ordered him to take over the government; Leisler intercepted the December order and declared himself lt. governor. In Feb., 1691, Maj. **Robert Ingoldesby** arrived in New York with a regiment, but Leisler refused to surrender. In March, Leisler surrendered to **Henry Sloughter,** who had been named the new governor, and was hanged for treason May 26. Sloughter called an **assembly,** which was the start of representative government in New York. Struggles between the Leisler and anti-Leisler factions, and between assembly and governor, continued for years.

1733 New York merchants and politicians who opposed governor **William Cosby** founded the *New York Weekly Journal*, edited by **John Peter Zenger,** who was arrested in 1734 for libel of the governor. Zenger's jury declared him innocent on the grounds that his statements had been accurate, an event considered a victory for freedom of speech.

New Jersey

1664 The Duke of York granted **John Lord Berkeley** and **Sir George Carteret** land between the Delaware and the Hudson rivers. Their "**Concessions and Agreements**" (1665) provided for a governor appointed by the proprietors, a council appointed by the governor, an elective assembly, and religious freedom. Governor **Philip Carteret** brought about 30 colonists to **Elizabethtown** in 1665.

1670–72 Protest against quit-rents (annual taxes paid to the proprietors) was put down.

1674 Berkeley sold his interest to two English Quakers, who later turned the land over to four Quaker trustees, including **William Penn**. In 1676, the colony was divided into **East Jersey** under Carteret and **West Jersey** under the Quakers.

1677 "**Laws, Concessions, and Agreements**," mostly by William Penn, granted religious liberty, jury trial, and representative government in West Jersey.

1681 Penn and eleven others bought East Jersey.

1683 The assembly in West Jersey took over the power of electing the governor and council from the trustees.

1688 Both Jerseys came under the Dominion of New England by decree of James II.

1702 In April, the crown **united** the two Jerseys as one **royal province**, which shared a governor with New York until 1738 when Lewis Morris became first governor of New Jersey.

Pennsylvania

1681 Charles II, who owed **WILLIAM PENN** £16,000, granted him in March the land between the 40th and 43rd latitudes. He put more restrictions than usual on the grant: Penn had to enforce the Navigation Acts; the King could disallow any law and reverse any court judgment; laws had to be approved by an assembly. Penn advertised widely for colonists, aiming at Quakers who were in the midst of their worst English persecution. In July, Penn's "**Conditions and Concessions**" set forth terms for land holding, and the first of Penn's settlers went to the New World in Oct.

1682 Penn's **Frame of Government** (May 5) called for a governor (normally the Proprietor) and a council and assembly elected by freeholders. Until 1696 the council initiated laws; after that, they were determined by both houses. The Frame included provisions for **religious toleration** and a **humane penal code.**

1683–84 **German Mennonites** led by **Francis Daniel Pastorius** settled Germantown, Pa.

1701 Penn granted the Charter of Privileges, which practically ended proprietary rule and which remained the government of Pennsylvania until the Revolution. At the same time, **Delaware** was granted a separate government but shared a governor with Pennsylvania.

1710–76 Pennsylvania received many immigrants from **Germany** (now known as the Pennsylvania Dutch) who served indentures and then moved west.

1712 A law was passed prohibiting importation of Negro slaves.

1714–17 **Scotch-Irish** (Presbyterians from northern Ireland) migrated to western Pennsylvania and moved south down the Valley of Virginia.

1731 First circulating library in America was founded in Philadelphia.

1756 Many Quakers withdrew from the assembly because they would not vote for military expenditures.

1776 Pennsylvania's population was ⅓ German, ⅓ Scotch-Irish, ⅓ others. A majority of the assembly was Quaker until 1755.

The Carolinas

1653 Virginians settled north of **Albemarle Sound** in what was later North Carolina.

1662 New Englanders arrived at **Cape Fear** to raise cattle but left the next year.

1663 Charles II granted (Apr. 3) land between 31st and 36th latitudes to eight proprietors including chancellor of the Exchequer **Sir Anthony Ashley Cooper,** later Lord Shaftesbury. Proprietors had power of govern-

ment with the consent of the freemen; religious liberty was to be granted.

1664–65 In Albemarle the government consisted of governor, a council, and an assembly of freeholders.

1669 The **Fundamental Constitutions** (March), calling for an aristocratic government, never went into effect. In practice Carolina was ruled by two governments (one north and one south). Each had a governor and a bicameral legislature with the lower house elective.

1670 **Charleston** was founded in what was later South Carolina.

1671 The government of southern Carolina met for the first time, in Charleston.

1677–80 **Culpeper's Rebellion** at Albemarle rose in opposition to the governor, to the Navigation Act (that taxed tobacco exports) and to quit-rents. John Culpeper set up a revolutionary government (Dec. 3), which was soon put down. Culpeper was acquitted of treason (1680).

1680 **French Huguenots** arrived at Charleston after religious persecution in France.

1681–85 Opposition to the governor in Albemarle continued until the assembly was dissolved.

1683 A Scotch colony was founded at Port Royal, S.C., which was overrun by the Spaniards in 1686.

1689 The Albemarle colony (called North Carolina after 1691) removed Governor Seth Sothel because of his harsh rule.

1708–11 Deputy Gov. **Thomas Cary** (N.C.) was ousted by Quakers and then staged a counter-revolt that was soon put down.

1715–16 Yamassee Indians rose against the white settlers in South Carolina but were finally defeated.

1716 Proprietors of the colony rejected an assembly law calling for voting in counties rather than at Charleston and ordered the governor to dissolve the assembly.

1721 South Carolina became a royal province, followed by North Carolina in 1729.

1734–52 In North Carolina, the assembly successfully opposed governor Robert Johnson's efforts to have quit-rents paid in hard money rather than in tobacco or in paper money.

1746 Rump assembly in North Carolina passed a law giving all counties the same representation as Albemarle, which was over-represented. The Privy Council rejected the law.

Georgia

1732   **James Oglethorpe** and others received (June 20) a grant to land between the Altamaha and Savannah rivers, named Georgia in honor of George II. Oglethorpe sought a refuge for convicts, especially debtors.

1733   **Savannah** was founded in Feb. Oglethorpe ruled as a benevolent despot with no assembly. Slavery was not allowed until 1749.

1739   Forts were set up on the Spanish border with Georgia and peace made with the Creeks.

1752   Georgia became a royal province with an assembly.

Colonial Wars Between France and England

1689–97   KING WILLIAM'S WAR (War of the League of Augsburg). In Europe, England and Holland combined to oppose French expansion in Europe. In 1690, French and Indians raided Schenectady, N.Y., and Falmouth (now Portland), Maine. Massachusetts soldiers under **Sir William Phips** captured **Port Royal**, which the French recaptured, 1691. From 1692–97 French and Abenaki Indians raided Wells, Maine; Haverhill, Mass.; and the Iroquois Confederacy. The **Treaty of Ryswick** (1697) restored the status quo in both Europe and the colonies.

1699–1703   French built forts at Cahokia (1699), Mackinac (1700), and Detroit (1701).

1701   Treaty of peace between the Iroquois and France removed a barrier to French expansion.

1702–13   QUEEN ANNE'S WAR (War of the Spanish Succession). England sought to prevent France from gaining control of Spain through inheritance.

1702   Carolina forces destroyed St. Augustine during border war against the Spaniards.

1704   Abenaki Indians destroyed **Deerfield, Mass.**

1710   New England and British soldiers captured **Port Royal.**

1713   **Treaty of Utrecht** gave Newfoundland, Acadia, and Hudson Bay to England, which also received **Gibraltar** from Spain as well as the right to send slaves to Spanish colonies. The **Iroquois** came under a British protectorate.

1713–39   The French built forts at **New Orleans** (1718), Kaskaskia (1720), Louisbourg on Cape Breton Island (1720), Vincennes (c.1724), and Crown Point on Lake Champlain (1731). Britain built forts at Columbia and Port Royal, S.C. (1718), and Oswego on Lake Ontario (1725).

1739–42   War of Jenkins' Ear between Spain and England. Inconclusive fighting occurred on the Florida border.

1740–48   KING GEORGE'S WAR (War of the Austrian Succession). England backed Austria against France, Spain, and Prussia in a continental war that spread to the colonies. New England militia under William Pepperrell captured **Louisbourg** (1745), but by the **Treaty of Aix-la-Chapelle** (1748) it was returned to France.

1749   The British founded **Halifax** to strengthen their hold on Nova Scotia.

1749–53   The French set up **Forts Niagara** and **Venango** and pushed into the Ohio Valley.

1753   Lt. Gov. Robert Dinwiddie of Virginia sent **George Washington** to investigate French expansion into the Ohio Valley.

1754–63   FRENCH AND INDIAN WAR (Seven Years' War). The French built **Fort Duquesne** (Pittsburgh) in 1754; on July 4, they forced Washington to surrender Fort

Necessity, near Fort Duquesne, and the war was underway. The Albany Congress met in June and July; commissioners from New England, New York, Maryland, and Pennsylvania gathered to discuss Indian affairs. On July 10, Franklin's **Plan of Union** was accepted at Albany but was later rejected by the colonies. It would have united the colonies under a President-General appointed by the King. A council of delegates from the colonies would have power to legislate, tax, raise armies, and deal with Indians, with veto power reserved for the President-General and King. By July, 1755, the British had gained control of the Bay of Fundy and proceeded to expel the French Acadians in order to prevent a revolt (the subject of Longfellow's *Evangeline*); General **Edward Brad-**

dock and 2,000 British troops were ambushed and defeated by French and Indians near Fort Duquesne. Braddock was killed in the battle. In the **Battle of Lake George** (Sept. 8), however, New Englanders under William Johnson defeated the French and Indians. **1756–63   Seven Years' War in Europe.** A realignment of powers pitted Britain and Prussia against France and Austria. **MARQUIS DE MONTCALM**, in command of French forces in Canada, took **Forts Oswego** and **George** (Aug.). In June, 1757, **William Pitt**, British Secretary of State and Prime Minister, started an all-out campaign to win the war. Despite this, Montcalm captured Fort William Henry on Lake George in Aug., and in Sept., the British failed to take Louisbourg. Montcalm also repulsed British attack

1-4   France in America

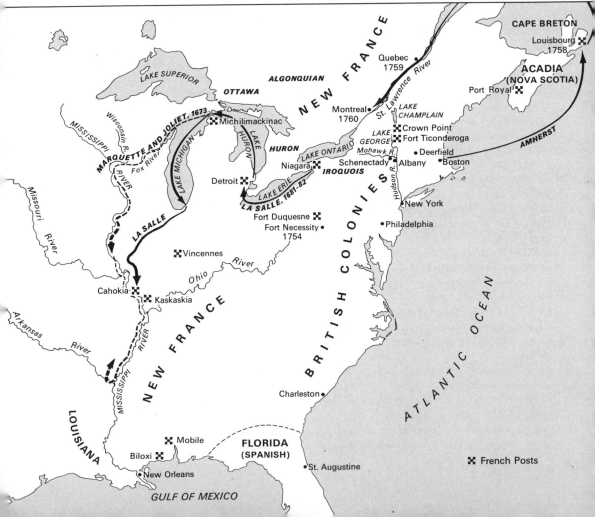

on **Ticonderoga** (July, 1758) and inflicted severe British losses. On July 26, Generals **Jeffrey Amherst** and **JAMES WOLFE**, with about 10,000 troops, took **Louisbourg**. The war began to go in favor of the British as they captured Fort Frontenac (Aug.) and took Fort Duquesne from the French. In July, 1759, the British captured **Fort Niagara**, and the French blew up Ticonderoga and Crown Point. At the same time, Wolfe landed troops near Quebec, and in early Sept. 4,500 of his troops climbed the cliffs west of **Quebec** to the Plains of Abraham. In the battle that followed, the French were badly beaten, and Wolfe and Montcalm were both killed. On Sept. 18, the French surrendered Quebec and a year later surrendered all of Canada. England declared war on Spain, which had sided with France, and took Havana and Manila (1762); by the secret **Treaty of Fontainebleau**, France ceded Spain all her territory west of the Mississippi River, as well as the Isle of Orleans, Louisiana. By the **PEACE OF PARIS** (Feb. 10, 1763), France ceded to England all of **Canada** and all land east of the Mississippi River except New Orleans. Spain ceded **East and West Florida** to England in exchange for Cuba. Manila was returned to Spain. When Pitt returned the two sugar islands of Martinique and Guadeloupe to France and took Canada, it marked a turn to territorial imperialism rather than commercial mercantilism.

Colonial Society

Labor and Slavery

1619–1776 **Indentured servants** bound themselves as servants for five to seven years to pay for their passage to America. Over half of the immigrants to America before the Revolution came this way. In addition, the British government sent a number of convicts and others who had been jailed for debt to the colonies.

1619 A Dutch ship brought the **first Negroes** to Virginia, where at first they probably served as bound servants.

1630–1770 **Negro population** in the American colonies rose from 60 in 1630, to 27,817 in 1700, and to 459,822 in 1770. In Virginia 5 per cent of the population was Negro in 1671, 24 per cent in 1715, and over 40 per cent in 1756.

1640–70 The institution of **slavery** emerged as Virginia and Maryland passed statutes that distinguished between white indentured servants and Negro chattel slaves.

1659, 1663 **Workers' strikes** for better working conditions took place in York County, Va., and Gloucester, Mass.

1680 Virginia enacted regulations severely restricting the activities of Negroes. By 1700 **discrimination against Negroes** was well established in the colonies.

1688 Francis Daniel Pastorius and German Friends attacked the institution of slavery as an unchristian institution.

1700–60 New England shippers and others began to import slaves from Africa by way of

1-5 North America, 1763

the West Indies; importation rose from an annual average of 2,500 in 1715–50 to 7,450 in 1760–70.

1712–41 The first **Negro uprising** was in New York City in 1712. Uprisings in South Carolina in 1739–40 resulted in over 100 deaths. In 1741 false rumors of a Negro plot in New York City led to over 30 Negro executions.

1775 Quakers organized the first **antislavery society** in the United States.

Education

1635 Boston Latin School was founded.

1636 Harvard College.

1647 Massachusetts Bay passed an act that required towns to provide a teacher or a school. Other New England colonies followed this example.

1693 College of William and Mary.

1697 William Penn Charter School in Philadelphia was typical of church-supported schools in the Middle colonies. In the South, the children of the planters were educated by tutors.

1701 Yale University.

1746 College of New Jersey (later Princeton).

1751 Franklin's Academy (later the University of Pennsylvania).

1754 King's College (later Columbia).

1764 Rhode Island College (later Brown).

1766 Queen's College (later Rutgers).

1769 Dartmouth College.

1769 American Philosophical Society was founded at Philadelphia.

Establishment of Colonial Churches

1609 The **Church of England** was established in Virginia and later in New York, Maryland, the Carolinas, and Georgia. James Blair, Commissary of the Bishop of London, was particularly important in the Anglican Church in Virginia after 1689.

1620–30 The **Congregational Church** was established in Plymouth and Massachusetts Bay. The power of the church began to decline somewhat with the establishment of

the Halfway Covenant, 1657–62. This doctrine permitted the baptism of the children of church members even though the children had not experienced conversion.

1628 The **Dutch Reformed Church** was started in New Amsterdam.

1634 The **Roman Catholic Church** was established in Maryland, where it was protected by the Toleration Act. The Act was later repealed, and Maryland passed anti-Catholic laws.

1636–37 Roger Williams, Anne Hutchinson, and others left the Massachusetts Congregational Church and founded separate congregations. Williams founded the first **Baptist Church**, which stressed the separation of church and state, in Providence, R.I., 1639.

1640 The **Lutheran Church** was started in New Sweden under Rev. Reorus Torkillus.

1654 **Jews** first arrived in New Amsterdam.

1681 **Quakers** in large numbers settled in Pennsylvania.

1706 The **Presbyterian Church** was organized in Philadelphia. William Tennent's Log College in Neshaminy, Pa. (1736), and the College of New Jersey (1746) promoted Presbyterianism.

Selected Writings

1608 John Smith, *A True Relation of . . . Virginia.*

1644 Roger Williams' *The Bloudy Tenent of Persecution* attacked Congregational theology.

1647 William Bradford, *History of Plimoth Plantation* (published in 1856).

1649 John Winthrop's *Journal* (published in 1790).

1693 Cotton Mather's *The Wonders of the Invisible World* defended the witchcraft trials. His *Magnalia Christi Americana* (1702) provided a theological interpretation of New England's history.

1705 Robert Beverley, *The History . . . of Virginia.*

1710 John Wise, *The Churches' Quarrel Espoused,* supported democratic Congregationalism.

1731–58   Jonathan Edwards' writings restored Calvinist theology (see p. 22).

1732–57   Benjamin Franklin, *Poor Richard's Almanack.*

Newspapers

1704   Boston *News-Letter,* the first regular newspaper in America.

1725   New York *Gazette,* first newspaper in New York.

1729   *Pennsylvania Gazette,* published by Benjamin Franklin.

1731   *South Carolina Gazette,* backed by Franklin.

1733   *New York Weekly Journal,* edited by John Peter Zenger.

1736   *The Virginia Gazette,* first in Virginia.

1741   *The American Magazine* (Philadelphia), first magazine in the colonies.

1755   Boston *Gazette,* patriot newspaper.

1756   (Portsmouth) *New Hampshire Gazette,* still published.

Architecture

1607–1776   The early colonists tried to duplicate European architecture. Spanish styles appeared in Florida and later in the Southwest, English styles along the Atlantic coast, French styles in New Orleans. Only the Swedes along the Delaware built log cabins, but later the Scotch-Irish introduced the log cabin to the frontier.

1607–1700   The earliest English houses were generally timber-framed. Jamestown, for example, had rows of two-story timber houses. Toward the end of the seventeenth century the English began to build more decorative frame houses of one- or one-and-a-half-stories with overhang, gables, and casement windows, such as the John Ward House in Salem, Mass. (1684). Bacon's Castle in Surrey County, Va. (*c.*1655), represents the English Jacobean style with its brick construction, gables, and clustered chimneys.

1700–1800   The colonists built more elaborate buildings following the English style of classical architecture loosely called "Georgian." Particularly significant were the large number of handsome domestic residences, generally rectangular with two or three stories and dormers. Westover in Charles County, Va. (*c.*1730), and the Longfellow House, Cambridge, Mass. (1759), are good examples. Among the public buildings are the Capitol at Williamsburg, Va. (*c.*1700), the Old State House, Boston (1728), and Independence Hall, Philadelphia (1741).

1750–1800   Before 1750 churches were generally simple rectangular structures without towers. By the middle of the century, however, the influence of the English architects Sir Christopher Wren and James Gibbs led to the construction of larger churches with towers.

Painting

1650–1750   Early American painting was often realistic and detailed. John Smibert held the first art exhibition in the English colonies in Boston in 1730 and founded a school of colonial portrait painters.

1760–74   **John Singleton Copley,** a student of Smibert's, was famous for his realistic portraits of Bostonians, such as those of John and Samuel Adams.

1765–81   Benjamin West, who left Philadelphia in 1760, trained many American artists at his London studio, including Copley, Gilbert Stuart, and John Trumbull.

Leading Figures of the Colonial Period

WILLIAM BRADFORD (Yorkshire, England, 1590–Plymouth Colony, 1657), colonial governor.

1606 Became a member of an English Separatist group that opposed the Church of England.

1609 Moved to Leyden, Holland, with members of his church. Was a weaver there until 1620.

1620 Sailed to America on the *Mayflower* and was one of the signers of the Mayflower Compact.

1621 Elected Governor of Plymouth Colony and continued in that office for every year except five through 1656.

1627 With seven other Pilgrims, took over responsibility for the investments of the original adventurers.

1636 Helped draft the laws that put Plymouth on a semi-constitutional basis.

1651 Completed his *History of Plimoth Plantation*, attributing the success of Plymouth to the hand of God.

WILLIAM BYRD II (Virginia, 1674–Westover, Va., 1744), planter and writer.

1674 Named for his father, William Byrd I, Virginia planter and merchant. The son was also known as William Byrd the Younger.

1684–91 Educated in London.

1692 Elected to Virginia House of Burgesses.

1697–1704 Returned to England as an agent for the colony of Virginia.

1709 Entered the Virginia Council, where he opposed efforts of Lt. Gov. Spotswood to remove its judicial power.

1720–44 Lived in his mansion at Westover, where he collected paintings and books; his *Diary* is a source of information about colonial Virginia. He was a member of the Royal Society, with a great interest in science.

1728 Acted as one of the commissioners to establish boundary line between Virginia and North Carolina, an experience described in his *The History of the Dividing Line*.

1733 Wrote *A Journey to the Land of Eden*, a diary of a trip to North Carolina.

JONATHAN EDWARDS (South Windsor, Conn., 1703–Princeton, N.J., 1758), theologian and writer.

1716 Entered Yale College, where he was influenced by the ideas of Locke and Newton. Came to believe that beauty had to be perceived independently of intellectual reason. Studied theology and became a Presbyterian minister.

1726 Congregational minister in Northampton, Mass. His preaching of belief in the majesty of God and in salvation through intuition or mystical experience rather than reason separated him from his parish.

1734–42 His "revivalist" preachings started the New England phase of the Great Awakening. Best-known of his sermons are *God Glorified in the Work of Redemption* (1731), *A Divine and Supernatural Light* (1734), and *Sinners in the Hands of an Angry God* (1741), which paints a picture of hellfire and damnation for the non-repentant.

1748–50 Fought with his church and was dismissed over question of admission to the sacraments.

1750–57 Missionary to the Mohegan Indians at Stockbridge, Mass.

1754 His major work, *A Careful ... Enquiry into ... Freedom of the Will*, reconciled Calvinist predestination and freedom of will.

1757 He became president of the College of New Jersey (Princeton) but died a few months later.

1758 Posthumous publication of *The Great Christian Doctrine of Original Sin Defended*.

BENJAMIN FRANKLIN (Boston, 1706–Philadelphia, 1790), statesman and publisher.

1723 Moved to Philadelphia as a printer.

1729 Bought *Pennsylvania Gazette* (editor until 1748).

1732 Published *Poor Richard's Almanack* annually until 1757.

1736 Founded first Philadelphia fire company.

1736 Served in Pennsylvania Assembly as clerk and, 1751–64, as a member.

1742 Invented the Franklin stove.

1753–74 Co-Postmaster General for the colonies.

1754 Delegate to the Albany Congress, where he drafted the Plan of Union that was later rejected.

1757–75 Represented Pennsylvania and other colonies in England. Helped gain repeal of Stamp Act in 1766.

1772–74 Was a party to publicizing the Hutchinson letters and suffered public censure.

1775 Delegate to 2nd Continental Congress.

1776 Served on committee to draft Declaration of Independence.

1776–85 Represented U.S. in France; signed treaty of alliance, 1778.

1782–83 Helped negotiate Treaty of Paris.

1785–88 President of Executive Council of Pennsylvania.

1787 Delegate to the Constitutional Convention; one of original signers of the Constitution.

1789 Completed his *Autobiography* through 1757.

WILLIAM PENN (London, 1644–England, 1718), colonial proprietor.

1644 His father, Admiral Sir William Penn, was a royal favorite to whom Charles II owed money.

1662 Expelled from Oxford for expression of Puritan beliefs.

1666 Attended Friends' meetings in Ireland; was converted and subsequently imprisoned.

1668–69 Wrote Quaker tracts—*The Sandy Foundation Shaken* and *No Cross, No Crown* —and was again imprisoned.

1670–80 Missionary tours in Europe to spread the Quaker religion.

1677 Wrote "Concessions and Agreements" for West Jersey.

1681 Received grant to Pennsylvania from the crown.

1682–84 Established colony in Pennsylvania. His "Frame of Government" (1682) was a humane document.

1684 Returned to England to assist Quakers suffering persecution.

1692–94 Governorship of Pennsylvania forfeited for two years.

1697 Proposed plan to the Board of Trade for uniting colonies; the plan was rejected.

1699–1701 Second trip to Pennsylvania.

1701 Issued Charter of Privileges in Pennsylvania, which reduced the power of the proprietor.

❡

JOHN SMITH (Lincolnshire, England, 1579–London, 1631), soldier and explorer.

1604 Returned to England after fighting against the Turks.

1607 Landed at Jamestown. Secured food from the Indians; was probably befriended by Pocahontas.

1608 Sentenced by his enemies to be hanged but was saved by the arrival of colonists from England.

1608 Governor of Virginia; wrote *A True Relation*, about settling the colony.

1609 Returned to England after much wrangling in Virginia.

1614 Explored the New England coast for English merchants and brought back a cargo of fish and furs that stimulated business interest in New England.

1624 Published *General Historie of Virginia*.

1630 Published *The True Travels . . . of Captaine John Smith . . . in America.*

JOHN WINTHROP (Suffolk, England, 1588–Boston, 1649), governor of Massachusetts.

1629 As an active lawyer and devout Puritan he was chosen governor of the Massachusetts Bay Colony and sailed to New England the next year. He served as governor until 1634.

1634 Defeated as governor by Thomas Dudley after revolt against his strict rule. He justified his arbitrary rule by belief that magistrates were guided by God.

1637 Led opposition to the Antinomian followers of Anne Hutchinson and once more became governor; drove Antinomians from the colony.

1638–49 Served total of eight years as governor.

1643 First president of New England Confederation. His *Journal* (1630–44) is a valuable source on Massachusetts.

Statistical Tables

Table 1.
Population of American colonies
(thousands)

	Total	Negro
1630	5	0.1
1650	50	2
1670	112	5
1690	210	17
1710	332	45
1730	629	91
1750	1,171	236

Table 2.
Population growth of the colonies
(thousands)

	1650	1690	1730
New Hampshire	1	4	11
Massachusetts Bay[a]	14	50	114
Rhode Island[a]	2	12	17
Connecticut	4	22	76
New York	4	14	49
New Jersy	—	8	38
Pennsylvania	—	11	52
Maryland	5	24	91
Virginia	19	53	114
Carolinas	—	12	60
Total	50	210	629

[a] Plymouth is included with Rhode Island in 1650 and 1690 and with Massachusetts Bay in 1730.

Table 4.
Pig iron exported to England
(tons)

1730	1,717	1750	2,924
1740	2,275	1760	3,265

Table 5.
Tobacco imported by England
(millions of pounds)

1700	38	1730	35
1710	23	1740	36
1720	35	1750	51

Table 6.
Slaves imported into Virginia

1619	21
1628	100
1639	46
1649	17
1662	80
1685	191
1699	349
1709	326
1720	1,368
1730	276
1740	1,646
1750	1,010
1760	1,158

Table 3.
Exports to and imports from England by American colonies
(thousands of £ Sterling)

	Total		New England		Virginia and Maryland	
	Export	Import	Export	Import	Export	Import
1700	395	344	41	92	317	173
1710	250	294	31	106	188	128
1720	468	320	49	129	331	111
1730	573	537	55	208	347	151
1740	718	813	72	171	342	281
1750	815	1,313	48	344	509	349
1760	761	2,612	38	600	504	606
1770	1,016	1,926	148	394	435	718

THE REVOLUTIONARY ERA, 1763–1789

PART 2

The Coming of the American Revolution, 1763–1775

New British Imperial Policies, 1763–1765

1763   In Feb., **Charles Townshend**, First Lord of Trade, was made responsible for the colonies. In April, **George Grenville** became Prime Minister (until 1765); his most immediate problem was a debt from the French wars in excess of £133 million. (For the **Proclamation of 1763**, see p. 44.)

1764   The **SUGAR ACT** of Parliament (Apr. 5) amended the unenforceable Molasses Act of 1733 by reducing the tax of 6*d* per gallon to 3*d* per gallon of molasses imported into the continental British colonies from foreign West Indies. Iron and hides were added to the list of enumerated goods that could be shipped only to England from the colonies. (See Navigation Act of 1660.) The Act was designed to raise £45,000 of the £300,000 annual cost of the colonial military establishment. Grenville also enforced **customs collection** by establishing a **vice-admiralty court** at Halifax with jurisdiction over all the colonies. Prosecutors could bring cases there and stand a better chance of getting convictions, and customs officials could not be sued for false arrest. Naval vessels especially assigned to enforce Navigation Acts could use **writs of assistance** (search warrants). The **CURRENCY ACT** (Sept.) forbade the issue of legal tender by colonies.

1765   **QUARTERING ACT** (in England, the Mutiny Act) required local civil authorities to provide quarters and supplies for British troops. A second act in 1766 required colonies to use taverns and uninhabited houses for troops. The **STAMP ACT** (March 22) called for a tax in the form of stamps affixed to newspapers, legal documents, and other papers and was designed to raise £60,000 annually in the colonies.

Colonial Reaction to the New Imperial Policies, 1763–1766

1763   In arguing the **Parson's Cause, Patrick Henry** used the theory of natural rights to deny the King's right to nullify a Virginia Act of 1755 that shifted payment of parsons' salaries from tobacco to money (thereby cutting salaries). After the Privy Council disallowed the act, Reverend James Maury sued for back pay. The royal judge granted Maury his salary, but after a speech by Henry opposing Maury's claim, the jury granted Maury only 1*d*. Henry's victory over clergy and crown made him a popular leader in Virginia.

1764   In his *Rights of the British Colonies* (July) **James Otis** of Boston argued that there could be **no colonial taxation without representation** in Parliament. In 1761 Otis had attacked the British use of writs of assistance.

1765

In *Considerations on . . . Taxes . . .* **Daniel Dulany** of Maryland denied the British theory of **"virtual representation"** by which every member of Parliament represented all parts of the empire. Dulany denied Parliament's right to levy internal taxes for revenue but allowed it the right to levy external taxes for trade regulation.

May 29–31   Patrick Henry introduced resolutions in the House of Burgesses denying the British any right to tax the colonies. When he suggested that King George III might suffer the fate of Caesar, he was accused of treason. The Burgesses passed only Henry's less extreme resolutions, expressing approval of the theory of no taxation without representation.

July   The **Marquess of Rockingham** replaced Lord Grenville as Prime Minister (1765–66).

Summer   SONS OF LIBERTY groups were formed in Boston, New York, and other towns to oppose the Stamp Act. In Aug., the Sons of Liberty all but destroyed the home of stamp agent Andrew Oliver in Boston. Oliver resigned, as did agents in every colony. In addition, the Sons almost destroyed the home of Chief Justice **Thomas Hutchinson** in Boston.

Oct. 7–25   STAMP ACT CONGRESS met in New York City with representatives from nine colonies. **Timothy Ruggles,** a Massachusetts moderate, was chosen president over the radical James Otis. The *Declaration of Rights and Grievances,* written by **John Dickinson** of Pennsylvania, conceded that Americans owed allegiance to the Crown but denounced the Stamp Act. Since colonists could not be represented, they could not be taxed by Parliament.

Nov. 1   As the Stamp Act went into effect, **non-importation** agreements in Boston, New York, and elsewhere brought colonial business temporarily to a standstill.

Dec. 6   *Memorial of Merchants of London Trading to North America* demanded repeal of the Stamp Act.

1766

Mar. 18   The Stamp Act was repealed. During the debate, Benjamin Franklin hinted that the colonists would accept an external tax. At the same time, the **DECLARATORY ACT** was passed, which stated that the Crown and Parliament had the right to make "laws" for the American colonies in "all cases whatsoever" but which avoided use of the word "tax."

Spring   The Sugar Act was modified so that the tax became 1*d* per gallon of molasses imported from both British and foreign West Indies.

July   William Pitt, Earl of Chatham, became Prime Minister; he shortly became ill and was replaced by the Duke of Grafton.

Aug. 10   After the New York assembly refused to appropriate money to support British troops, bitter feeling developed between the Sons of Liberty groups and the British soldiers who destroyed a "liberty pole." On Aug. 11, a clash between the Sons of Liberty and redcoats in New York City was led by **Isaac Sears.**

Dec. 19   The New York assembly was prorogued. In 1767, Parliament suspended the assembly's legislative powers.

The Townshend Acts and Colonial Reaction, 1767–1770

1767

Jan.   Charles Townshend, Chancellor of the Exchequer, took control of the Grafton government.

July 2   The **CUSTOMS COLLECTING ACT** replaced the Board of Customs Collection in England with a new one in Boston to regulate colonial trade. Four new vice-admiralty courts were established in the colonies. On the same day, the **TOWNSHEND REVENUE ACT** was passed to levy duties on the colonial imports of lead, paint, paper, glass, and tea. This external tax was estimated to raise from £35,000 to £40,000 a year. The purpose of the act was to defend the colonies, to pay for "the administration of justice," and to support the civil government in America.

Oct. 28   The Boston **non-importation** agreement was drawn up and was soon followed in other colonies.

Nov. 5   Board of Customs Commissioners arrived in Boston and began to enforce rulings on merchants; friction resulted.

Dec. 2–Feb., 1768 John Dickinson's *Letters of a Pennsylvania Farmer* were published. Dickinson, a Philadelphia lawyer, conceded that Parliament might regulate trade but might not raise revenue; he denied the difference between internal and external taxes.

1768

Lord North, Chancellor of the Exchequer, became the strongest man in the cabinet.

Jan. 20 The new office of Secretary of State for the Colonies was created, and Lord Hillsborough was appointed.

Feb. 11 **Massachusetts Circular Letter,** written by **Samuel Adams,** summarizing colonial opposition to British acts and urging united colonial action, condemned British taxation, insisted that representation in Parliament was impossible, and opposed British efforts to pay colonial governors.

Feb. 12 Customs commissioners in Boston asked England for military support.

Mar. 4 Governor Bernard dissolved the Massachusetts legislature because of the "seditious" Massachusetts Circular Letter. In that month, Boston merchants revived their policy of non-importation of British goods.

June 10 When customs commissioners seized **John Hancock's** sloop *Liberty,* a riot broke out in Boston, forcing the commissioners to flee to the frigate *Romney.*

June 15 Customs commissioners appealed again for troops. Not until Sept. did two regiments under General **Thomas Gage** arrive in Boston

July 1 Governor Bernard dissolved the new Massachusetts General Court when it refused to rescind the Circular Letter. In Aug., New York and Philadelphia joined Boston in non-importation. Seven colonies backed the Circular Letter.

1769

On Feb. 8, the House of Lords urged that the Massachusetts rebels be tried for treason, and the King concurred. The colonial reply came on May 16 in the form of the **Virginia Resolves,** written by **George Mason** and presented by **George Washington,** which denounced British taxation of the colonies. *Address to the King* of May 17 was drawn up by **Patrick Henry** and **Richard Henry Lee** in the House of Burgesses, which was then dissolved by Governor Botetourt. On May 18, the House of Burgesses met at Raleigh Tavern and drew up the **Virginia Association,** a non-importation agreement. For the rest of the year, the non-importation and association movement spread. Colonial imports dropped from £2.2 million in 1768 to £1.3 million in 1769, forcing the British to modify the Townshend duties.

1770

Jan. 17 British soldiers in New York cut down one of the "liberty poles" that had been erected to defy imperial authority. In retaliation, the Sons of Liberty, again led by Isaac Sears, staged a riot against British troops (the **Battle of Golden Hill**); there were only a few casualties on each side.

Jan. 31 **Frederick Lord North** became Prime Minister (1770–82).

Feb. 8 **Alexander McDougall,** leader of New York City Sons of Liberty, was arrested for criticizing the assembly for supplying British troops but was released on bail.

Mar. 5 The **BOSTON MASSACRE:** at 9 P.M. the main British guard under Captain **Thomas Preston** fired into a mob, killing four. To avoid rebellion the British removed the troops to islands in Boston harbor (Mar. 6); Preston and eight of his men were charged with murder. After a trial (Oct. 24–30) in which John Adams and Josiah Quincy defended them, Preston and six men were acquitted; the other two were branded and released.

Apr. 12 The Townshend duties, except those on tea, were repealed, and the Quartering Act was allowed to expire. The colonies, in turn, abandoned non-importation.

1771

The year was one of comparative peace in the increasing struggle between the colonies and Great Britain.

The Road to Revolution, 1772–1775

1772

June 9   Burning of the *Gaspée:* when the British revenue cutter *Gaspée,* which had been enforcing customs laws, ran aground in Narragansett Bay, Rhode Islanders set it on fire. A royal commission tried in vain to identify the culprits.

June and Sept.   The Exchequer took over salary payments for the Massachusetts governor and judges, thus rendering them immune from legislative control. In Oct., the Boston town meeting denounced this policy of paying colonial officials from the Exchequer.

Nov. 2   Boston established a standing **committee of correspondence** to communicate with other towns and colonies (**James Otis,** chairman), which drew up three radical statements that the Boston town meeting sent on to all towns in Massachusetts and to all colonial assemblies. These included Samuel Adams' *State of the Rights of the Colonists.*

1773

Mar. 12   House of Burgesses (Virginia) appointed a committee of correspondence that included **Patrick Henry, Richard Henry Lee,** and **Thomas Jefferson.** By Feb., 1774, all colonies but two had such committees.

May 10   TEA ACT was passed to save the East India Company from bankruptcy (it had 17 million pounds of tea on hand). The company was granted a drawback of all duties paid on tea reexported to the colonies and was to sell tea directly in the colonies instead of through English merchants. Even with the Townshend tax, the tea of the East India Co. would be the cheapest in the colonies. In Sept., the company decided to set up warehouses in Boston, New York, Philadelphia, and Charleston to sell to selected merchants. Other American importers, smugglers, and the Sons of Liberty united against the Tea Act.

Oct.   New York and Philadelphia merchants protested against the Tea Act, and the Massachusetts Committee of Correspondence asked all colonies to prevent East India tea from landing.

Nov. 27   When the *Dartmouth* and two other ships arrived in Boston with East India tea, Governor Hutchinson insisted that they be unloaded.

Dec. 16   The **BOSTON TEA PARTY**: a band of men disguised as Indians and led by Samuel Adams boarded the ships and threw 342 chests of tea into Boston harbor.

Dec. 16–20   Tea was landed in Charlestown, Mass., and stored in warehouses; it was sold during the war by the revolutionary government.

Dec. 25   Colonial patriots prevented tea from being landed in Philadelphia.

1774

Jan. 29   Benjamin Franklin was denounced in the Privy Council for his part in the **Hutchinson letters scandal.** In 1772 Franklin, as the Massachusetts agent in London, sent back home letters written by the then Chief Justice Thomas Hutchinson (of Mass.) urging a more restrictive British policy. The Massachusetts House called for Hutchinson's removal. Franklin was replaced as Deputy Postmaster General for America for his part in the affair.

Mar. 4   Parliament was summoned to punish Massachusetts for its defiance.

Mar. 31–June 2   Four **COERCIVE ACTS** were passed (called Intolerable Acts in America). The first, the **Boston Port Act** (Mar. 31), closed the port of Boston from June 1 until the East India Co. and the customs officers had been paid for their losses.

Apr. 19   Motion to repeal the Tea Act was defeated in Parliament despite a speech by Edmund Burke.

May 13   General Thomas Gage replaced Hutchinson as governor of Massachusetts, and troops returned from the harbor islands.

May 20   The 2nd Coercive Act, the **Massachusetts Government Act**, reduced the power of the people in Massachusetts. The council was to be chosen by the King, not elected; the governor would be able to appoint inferior judges and nominate superior judges for royal appointment; juries were to be chosen by the sheriff instead of being elected; town meetings other than annual election meetings were to be held only with governor's consent. The 3rd Act, the **Administration of Justice Act**, stated that trial of magistrates for capital offenses was to be held in Britain if the governor decided local courts would not give a fair trial.

May–Aug. All colonies except Georgia chose delegates for an intercolonial congress (the 1st Continental Congress) as protests rose against the Coercive Acts.

May 26 Gov. Dunmore dissolved the Virginia House of Burgesses, which met unofficially May 27, and called for an annual intercolonial legislature.

June 2 The 4th Act, the **Quartering Act** called for troops to be housed in occupied houses, not just in taverns and unoccupied houses as in the acts of 1765–66.

June 22 **QUEBEC ACT** (not one of the Coercive Acts) extended the Province of Quebec to include all land north of the Ohio River. Since the population was mostly French Roman Catholic, old **French civil law** was retained. Roman Catholics could sit in the assembly and **Catholicism** was **recognized**. Most power of taxation went to Parliament. Land speculators, especially in Virginia, opposed the act because they feared loss of land claims. Protestant New Englanders resented the benefits granted Catholics.

July Thomas Jefferson's *A Summary View of the Rights of British America* rejected the power of Parliament and claimed that colonists need obey only the King.

Aug. 17 **James Wilson** of Pennsylvania, wrote *Considerations on ... the Legislative Authority of ... Parliament*, describing the division of powers between Parliament and colonies as federalism.

Sept. 5–Oct. 26 **1st CONTINENTAL CONGRESS** met in Philadelphia with 55 delegates from all colonies but Georgia. Voting was by colony. Delegates were divided evenly among radicals, such as **Samuel** and **John Adams** (Mass.) and **Patrick Henry** and **Richard Henry Lee** (Va.); moderates, such as **James Duane** and **John Jay** (N.Y.) and **John Dickinson** (Pa.); and conservatives,

such as **Joseph Galloway** (Pa.). **Peyton Randolph** (Va.) was President.

Sept. 17 The Continental Congress endorsed **Joseph Warren's Suffolk Resolves**, adopted earlier by Suffolk County (Mass.) declaring the Coercive Acts unconstitutional and calling on the people of Massachusetts to arm themselves.

Sept. 28 The conservatives present offered **Joseph Galloway's** *Plan of Union*, calling for a separate American government consisting of a **President General** appointed by the King and a legislative council chosen by the assemblies. President and council would constitute an inferior branch of Parliament; Parliament and the American government could veto each other's colonial acts. The plan was barely defeated Oct. 22.

Oct. 14 DECLARATION OF RIGHTS AND RESOLVES was adopted by the Congress. It condemned the Coercive Acts, the revenue acts, and the standing army, and listed the rights of colonists including **"life, liberty, and property."** Britain, a "foreign power," could regulate only the external commerce of the colonies.

Oct. 20 The Congress established a **Continental Association** to pledge non-importation and non-consumption of British goods throughout the colonies.

Oct. 21 Congress adopted an address to the British people to explain colonial grievances.

Oct. 26 **Petition to the King** was loyal in tone but sought to limit the King's prerogative.

Fall Attacks on Loyalists increased—including tarring and feathering. Militiamen gathered in Cambridge. The Massachusetts House of Representatives met in Salem (later Concord) and made itself a **Provincial Congress**, the first revolutionary assembly in America. John Hancock was made head of the Committee of Safety with power to call out the militia known as **Minute Men**.

Dec. 10 First *Massachusettensis* weekly letter of **Daniel Leonard**, a Tory, was published in Boston, where it continued until April 3, 1775.

Dec. 14 New Hampshire patriots broke into Fort William and Mary in Portsmouth and carried away powder and arms.

1775

Jan. 19   Petition and Declaration of 1st Continental Congress were laid before Parliament, where a heavy majority supported the warlike policies of George III.

Jan. 23–Apr. 17   John Adams' *Novanglus* letters in reply to Leonard developed the idea of a federal empire with Parliament and colonies equal under a sovereign King.

Feb. 9   Parliament declared Massachusetts in a state of rebellion.

Feb. 26   British troops tried in vain to seize colonial military supplies at Salem.

Feb. 27   Lord North's Plan of Conciliation was adopted. Parliament would tax no colony that would help with imperial expenses.

Mar. 22   Edmund Burke's speech on conciliation with America failed to sway Parliament.

Mar. 23   Patrick Henry in his **"Liberty or Death"** speech in Virginia predicted war in Massachusetts.

Mar. 30   Act forbidding New England to trade with foreign nations and barring New England from the North Atlantic fisheries was passed in Parliament.

Apr. 14   General Gage was ordered to use force to break up rebellion in New England.

The American Revolution, 1775–1783

Congress and Independence, 1775–1776

1775

Apr. 19   BATTLES OF LEXINGTON AND CONCORD: when Lt. Col. **Francis Smith** and 700 British troops set out to seize supplies at Concord, Mass., **Paul Revere** and **William Dawes** spread the alarm. The British exchanged shots with Minute Men on **Lexington Green** and at **Concord Bridge,** killing 8 at Lexington. Americans pouring in from surrounding towns killed or wounded 247 British as they made their way back to Boston. There were only 95 American casualties.

May 10   Ethan Allen and **Benedict Arnold** with 83 men captured **Ft. Ticonderoga** on Lake Champlain.

May 10   The **2nd CONTINENTAL CONGRESS** met in Philadelphia with all colonies but Georgia represented. Radicals included **Samuel** and **John Adams** and **John Hancock** (Mass.), **Benjamin Franklin** (Pa.), **Thomas Jefferson** and **Richard Henry Lee** (Va.); moderates included **James Wilson** (Pa.) and **John Jay** (N.Y.).

May 24   John Hancock replaced Peyton Randolph as President of the Congress.

June 14   Congress voted to raise an army by requesting troops from the colonies.

June 15   GEORGE WASHINGTON was named commander-in-chief because of his military experience. **Artemas Ward** (Mass.), and **Charles Lee** (Va.) were second and third in command.

June 17   BATTLE OF BUNKER HILL: on the night of June 16–17 the Americans sent 1,200 troops to occupy Bunker Hill in Charlestown (near Boston) in order to prevent the British from seizing it. By mistake they built a redoubt on **Breed's Hill,** forcing the British into immediate attack. **Sir William Howe** led 2,200 men against Col. **William Prescott** and 1,600 Americans. After being turned back twice, the British took the hill when American gunpowder ran out. British casualties were over 1,000; American casualties were over 400.

July 3   George **Washington took command** of an army of 14,500 men in Cambridge and continued the siege of Boston.

July 5   Olive Branch Petition, by John Dickinson, urged George III to protect the colonies against Parliament and to call off the army.

July 6   DECLARATION OF CAUSES AND NECESSITIES OF TAKING UP ARMS, by

Jefferson and Dickinson, claimed that Americans were resisting tyranny but did not come out for independence.

Aug. 2   The Congress adjourned.

Aug. 23   George III proclaimed the colonies to be in open rebellion.

Sept. 12   The Congress reconvened in Philadelphia with all 13 colonies represented.

Nov. 8   **Benedict Arnold**, with over 600 men, reached the St. Lawrence River opposite **Quebec** after a difficult march through Maine.

Nov. 13   American expedition into Canada under Gen. **Richard Montgomery** seized **Montreal**.

Nov. 29   Congress appointed Committee of Correspondence to contact European nations.

Dec. 2   Montgomery joined Arnold at Quebec.

Dec. 11   Loyalist Gov. Dunmore of Virginia was defeated in battle by Virginians and North Carolinians at Great Bridge, Va.

Dec. 12   Congress asked Arthur Lee in London to sound out European nations.

Dec. 23   The Crown closed colonies to all external commerce effective Mar. 1, 1776.

Dec. 31   **Assault on Quebec** led by Montgomery and Arnold failed.

1776

Jan. 10   **Thomas Paine's** *Common Sense* called for an independent republic, and denounced King George as a tyrant. 120,000 copies were published within 3 months.

2-1   *The Revolutionary War*

Jan. George Washington declared himself in favor of colonial independence.

Jan. 24 Gen. **Henry Knox** arrived in Cambridge with 43 cannon from Ticonderoga.

Feb. 27 Patriots defeated Loyalists at **Moore's Creek Bridge**, N.C.

Mar. 17 The **British evacuated Boston** after Washington placed cannon on Dorchester Heights.

Apr. 6 Congress opened colonial ports to all nations save Great Britain.

June 7 Richard Henry Lee proposed a resolution in the Congress calling for independence from Great Britain.

June 11 Congress authorized a committee of Jefferson, Franklin, John Adams, Roger Sherman, and Robert Livingston to prepare a draft of a formal declaration. Jefferson then wrote the Declaration of Independence.

June 28 The British failed to capture the fort that guarded the mouth of Charleston harbor, S.C.

July 2 **Congress voted 12–0 for independence** with New York abstaining.

July 4 **Congress voted 12–0 to approve the DECLARATION OF INDEPENDENCE;** New York abstained.

2-2 Washington's Campaigns, New York and New Jersey, 1776–1777

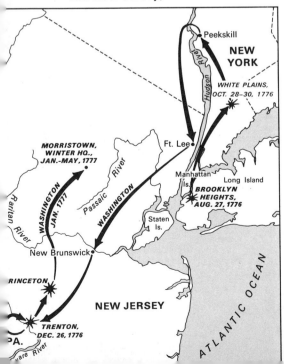

July 9 New York endorsed the Declaration of Independence.

Aug. 2 The signing of the Declaration by almost all of the 55 eventual signers. The Declaration held that man was created with the right to "life, liberty, and the pursuit of happiness." Governments were set up by the "consent of the governed," and could be overthrown if they did not protect the people's rights. Jefferson listed a "long train of abuses" by George III that justified independence.

The Northern Campaign, 1776–1779

1776

Apr.–Aug. Washington moved from Boston to New York, where he gathered 33,000 men.

July The British assembled 34,000 men at New York under General **William Howe** and his brother Admiral **Richard Howe**.

Aug. 27 **BATTLE OF LONG ISLAND:** Gen. Howe with 20,000 men badly defeated the Americans under **Israel Putnam** and **John Sullivan**.

Aug. 29–30 Washington evacuated the Americans from Long Island to Manhattan.

Sept. 11 **Staten Island Peace Conference:** American commissioners (Franklin, John Adams, and Edmund Rutledge) and Admiral Howe failed to make peace.

Sept. 15 Washington retreated to Harlem Heights.

Sept. 22 **Nathan Hale** was executed as a spy by the British.

Oct. 11–13 **Battle of Valcour Bay** on Lake Champlain: General Arnold's fleet was defeated but delayed the British.

Oct. 28 **BATTLE OF WHITE PLAINS:** Washington retreated again to White Plains, where he was defeated and was forced across the Hudson River into New Jersey.

Nov.–Dec. **Lord Cornwallis** drove Washington south through New Jersey.

Dec. 11 Washington crossed the Delaware River into Pennsylvania, and the British retired for the winter.

Dec. 19 Thomas Paine's first issue of **The American Crisis** appeared with the words,

"These are the times that try men's souls."
Dec. 26   BATTLE OF TRENTON: Washington recrossed the Delaware Christmas night and routed the Hessian garrison.

1777

Jan. 3   Battle of Princeton: Washington defeated Lord Cornwallis.

Mar. British Secretary of State for the colonies, **Lord Germain,** approved two contradictory plans: a three-pronged attack to isolate New England through invasion of New York from Canada by way of Lake Champlain and the Mohawk Valley together with a drive north from New York City by Lord Howe, and the seizure of Philadelphia by Lord Howe.

Summer Foreign officers **Marquis de Lafayette** and **Johann de Kalb** arrived from France and Germany to serve as generals in the American army. **Thaddeus Kosciusko** and Baron **Friedrich Wilhelm von Steuben** came from Poland and Prussia in 1776 and 1778. All served valiantly; Von Steuben was particularly helpful because of his skill in drilling troops.

June 17–Oct. 17   NEW YORK CAMPAIGN: Gen. **John Burgoyne** moved up Lake Champlain from Canada.

July 5 Burgoyne captured Ticonderoga for the British.

Aug. 3 Col. **Barry St. Leger,** aided by Loyalists and Indians, besieged Fort Stanwix on the Mohawk River.

Aug. 6   Battle of Oriskany, N.Y.: St. Leger ambushed and defeated Gen. **Nicholas Herkimer** and 800 Americans.

Aug. 16   Battle of Bennington: Gen. **John Stark** and 2,000 New Englanders defeated part of Burgoyne's force in southern Vermont.

Aug. 23   Benedict Arnold relieved **Ft. Stanwix** and forced St. Leger back to Lake Ontario.

Aug. 25–Oct. 4   PHILADELPHIA CAMPAIGN: William Howe and 15,000 troops landed at head of Chesapeake Bay. Washington with 10,500 blocked the road to Philadelphia. On Sept. 11, Howe defeated Washington at **Brandywine Creek,** Pa.

Sept. 26 Howe slipped around Washington to occupy Philadelphia.

Oct. 4 The British beat off Washington's attack on their lines at **Germantown,** Pa.

Sept. 19–Oct. 17   BATTLE NEAR SARATOGA: Burgoyne attacked Gen. **Horatio Gates,** in command of the American army, and was repulsed with heavy losses at Freeman's Farm near Bemis Heights, N.Y.

Oct. 7 Burgoyne was defeated again at **Freeman's Farm,** partly by **Benedict Arnold,** who fought without a command.

Oct. 17 Burgoyne and 5,700 men surrendered to Gates at **Saratoga.**

Dec. Washington moved into winter quarters at **VALLEY FORGE,** Pa., where his army suffered from shortages of supplies during the winter.

1778

June 28   Battle of Monmouth: when Gen. **Clinton** evacuated Philadelphia, Washington followed him across New Jersey to Monmouth, where they fought to a draw. Clinton entered New York City.

July 29   Comte d'Estaing and the **French fleet** arrived in New York harbor.

2-3   Northern Campaigns, 1775–1779

July 30   Washington took up headquarters at White Plains.

Aug. 29   American-French attack on **Newport**, R.I., failed.

1779

May   TREASON OF ARNOLD: Gen. Benedict Arnold, disgruntled because of his treatment by the Congress, started to send information to Clinton in New York City. In Sept., 1780, Arnold, in command of **West Point**, turned plans over to British major **John André**, who was captured and hanged by the Americans. Arnold then fled to the British.

Congressional Government and Diplomacy, 1776–1778

1776

Mar. 3   Silas Deane was sent to Europe to buy war materiel.

Mar.   Comte de Vergennes, French Foreign Minister, was assured of Spanish cooperation against Britain.

2-4   Central Campaigns, 1777-1779

May 2   Caron de Beaumarchais received money from the **French** government to give secret **aid** to the United States.

Sept. 26   Congress appointed **Franklin, Deane**, and Jefferson (**Arthur Lee** replaced Jefferson) as an official treaty commission to France.

Dec. 12   Congress fled from Philadelphia to Baltimore as the British marched through New Jersey. It returned Mar. 12, 1777.

1777

Apr. 17   Congress established a Committee for Foreign Affairs.

June 14   Congress adopted a flag with 13 stripes of red and white and 13 white stars on a blue field.

Sept. 19   Congress fled as Howe took Philadelphia.

Oct. 11   Gen. **Thomas Conway**, previously a colonel in the French army, wrote to Gen. Gates criticizing Washington for his handling of the war. Gates denied any effort to replace Washington and on Nov. 27 was appointed President of Board of War.

Dec. 14   Congress appointed Conway Inspector General. Historians once believed that a **Conway cabal** existed against Washington, but this theory has since been discredited.

Dec. 17   France recognized American independence after hearing news of Burgoyne's surrender at Saratoga.

1778

Feb. 6   FRANCO-AMERICAN ALLIANCE: France joined the United States against Great Britain. Neither side was to lay down arms separately. France renounced all claims east of the Mississippi River. Each of the two nations guaranteed the other's possessions in the New World.

Apr. 12   British Peace Commission was set up under **Lord Carlisle**. After spending the summer and fall of 1778 in the U.S., it returned to Great Britain unsuccessful.

June 17   Great Britain declared war against France.

The Southern Campaign, 1779–1781

1779

Apr.–June   Gen. Benjamin Lincoln failed to oust the British from Savannah, which they had seized in Dec., 1778.

Oct. 9–20   Siege of Savannah by Gen. Lincoln and the French fleet under d'Estaing was unsuccessful.

1780

Apr. 1–May 12   Gen. **Henry Clinton** captured Charleston, S.C., and more than 5,000 American prisoners.

July   The British under Lord Cornwallis moved north from Savannah.

Aug. 16   Cornwallis badly defeated the Americans under Gen. Gates at Camden, S.C.

Fall   American guerrillas in South Carolina under **Francis Marion** ("The Swamp Fox") and **Andrew Pickens** delayed Cornwallis in his march north.

Oct. 7   When American riflemen defeated British Loyalists on **King's Mountain**, S.C., Cornwallis was forced back into South Carolina.

1781

Jan. 17   The Americans under Gen. **Daniel Morgan** won a major victory at Cowpens, S.C.

Mar. 15   Cornwallis defeated Gen. Nathanael Greene, who had replaced Gates, at **Guilford Courthouse**, N.C., but suffered heavy losses and retreated to the seacoast.

Spring–Summer   Greene and Marion drove the British from the interior of South Carolina.

Apr. 25   Cornwallis led 1,500 men north into Virginia to secure reinforcements.

Aug. 1   Cornwallis established a base at **Yorktown**, Va., in order to maintain communications with Clinton in New York City.

Aug. 14   Washington received word from **DeGrasse** that the French fleet would be in Chesapeake Bay in September with 3,000 troops.

Aug. 21   Washington and French Commander **Comte de Rochambeau** decided to take advantage of French forces in Chesapeake Bay. They gave up plans to attack New York City and led French and American troops south to the bay.

Aug. 30–Sept. 24   French fleets arrived in Chesapeake Bay and transported 16,000 allied troops to Williamsburg.

Sept. 28–Oct. 19   The **SIEGE OF YORKTOWN**: after a three-week siege Cornwallis surrendered to Washington his force of about 8,000 men.

The War at Sea, 1775–1781

1775   On Oct. 30, Congress authorized a navy of four ships; in Dec., Congress commissioned **Esek Hopkins** first Commodore of the Navy.

1776   Congress gave permission in March for privateering.

1778   In April, **John Paul Jones** on the *Ranger* raided in the Irish Sea, attacked the fort at **Whitehaven**, England, and captured the sloop *Drake*.

1779   Jones on the ***Bonhomme Richard*** defeated the British warship *Serapis* (Sept. 23) in spite of heavy damage to his own ship. When asked to surrender, Jones replied, "I have not yet begun to fight."

2-5   Southern Campaigns, 1778-1781

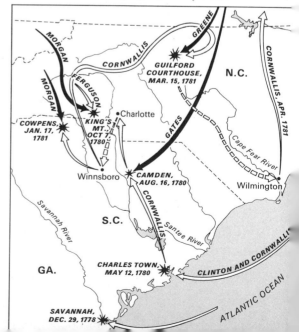

1781 In the spring, Capt. **John Barry** on the *Alliance* defeated four British ships. During the war American privateers captured about 600 British ships thereby reducing British foreign trade.

Peace Negotiations, 1779–1783

1779

June 16 Spain declared war on Great Britain but made no alliance with the U.S.

Nov. 3 Congress appointed John Adams to negotiate peace with Great Britain.

1780

John Jay, minister to Spain, offered Florida to Spain in return for an alliance and a promise that Spain would keep the Mississippi River open. No action was taken.

1781

June Adams was replaced by a **peace commission** made up of **Franklin, John Jay,**

2-6 North America, 1783

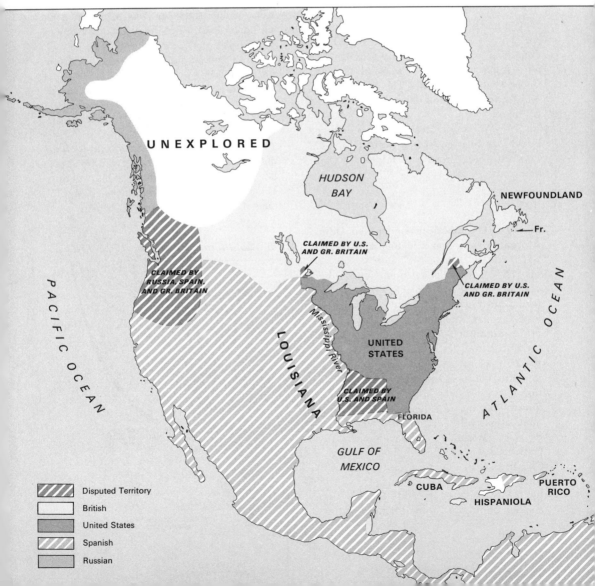

Disputed Territory

British

United States

Spanish

Russian

John Adams, Jefferson (who refused to serve) and Henry Laurens (who was a British prisoner).

1782

Mar. 4   The British House of Commons voted to end the war in America.

Mar. 20   The North Ministry resigned, and on Mar. 22, Rockingham became Prime Minister.

Apr. 12   The British sent **Richard Oswald** to Paris to start peace talks with Franklin.

Spring   The Comte de Vergennes, French Foreign Minister, promised Florida to Spain and tried to get the U.S. to accept a boundary east of the Mississippi River.

Spring   Anglo-American and Anglo-French negotiations were carried on separately in Paris.

July 1   Death of Rockingham. **Lord Shelburne** became Prime Minister on July 11.

Summer   Spain and France suggested to the British a settlement giving the old Northwest to Britain and Alabama, Mississippi and parts of western Kentucky and Tennessee to Spain. Jay and Franklin therefore determined to deal separately with Britain.

Sept. 19   The House of Commons tacitly admitted American independence by authorizing Oswald to deal with the U.S. commission.

Oct. 5   Oswald, Jay, and Franklin drew up a draft treaty granting the U.S. the Mississippi River as a boundary. The treaty collapsed when Britain refused to give the U.S. free trade in the British empire.

Oct. 26   John Adams arrived in Paris. The three commissioners agreed to ignore Congressional instructions to consult with the French because they suspected French treachery.

Nov. 5   Preliminary Peace Treaty with Great Britain. Concessions were granted to Britain in order to keep the Mississippi River boundary for the U.S.

1783

Jan. 20   Treaties between Britain and both France and Spain were agreed to. Florida was given to Spain.

Sept. 3   **PEACE OF PARIS** between Britain and the U.S. established 1.) **Independence** of the U.S.; 2.) **Boundaries:** in the north the St. Croix River, the St. Lawrence-Atlantic divide, and the 45th parallel; in the west the Mississippi River, in the south the 31st parallel and the Apalachicola and the St. Mary's Rivers; 3.) **Fishing rights** for the U.S. off Newfoundland and Nova Scotia; 4.) Payment of **debts** due both sides; 5.) Return of **slaves** captured by the British; and 6.) Promised recommendation from Congress that the states restore **property to Loyalists.**

Dec. 4   The British evacuated New York City and Staten Island. On that day, Washington took leave of his officers at Fraunces' Tavern, N.Y.

The Confederation Period, 1777-1789

The State Constitutions

1775-84   Writing the Constitutions: even before independence was declared the states established revolutionary governments that set about drawing up constitutions. These documents had a profound effect on both the Articles of Confederation and the U.S. Constitution.

1775   Mecklenburg (County, N.C.) **Resolutions** declared royal government "suspended" in that area (May 31). In Oct., Congress advised New Hampshire to set up whatever government "representatives of the people" desired.

1776   New Hampshire drew up the first revolutionary constitution. South Carolina followed in March, and by July Virginia and New Jersey had adopted permanent constitutions. Pennsylvania, Delaware, Maryland, and North Carolina had drawn up constitutions by Dec., and Rhode Island and Connecticut simply continued their provincial charters with references to the King omitted.

1777 Constitutions in Georgia and New York left only Massachusetts without a constitution.

1780 A convention in Massachusetts presented a constitution written by John Adams and declared it in effect after each article had been ratified by the towns.

1784 The New Hampshire constitution drawn up by a convention was ratified by the towns (June 13).

1776–84

Basic Provisions of the Constitutions

1. **Bill of rights** (the first was written by George Mason in Virginia).
2. An elective **legislature** (bicameral except in Pennsylvania). The legislatures were strong (originated money bills in nine states).
3. A **governor** elected by the voters or the legislature. He was generally weak (in nine states no veto power, one-year term).
4. Frequent **elections** (lower house annual or even semi-annual in all states but South Carolina).
5. **Suffrage** requirements: any taxpayer in five states, small poll tax in New Hampshire, land or other property required in the remaining states.
6. **Office-holding** requirements: property holders, the highest being £10,000 for governor in South Carolina.
7. **Judges** generally were appointed by the legislature (in eight states on good behavior).
8. **Voting districts** were arranged more evenly than before. Sectional favoritism was eased in Pennsylvania, Virginia, North Carolina, and Massachusetts but not in South Carolina.
9. **Individual constitutions**: South Carolina retained the most conservative constitution (50-acre freehold for voting, £2,000 estate to be a Senator, only Protestants granted civil rights). Pennsylvania was democratic (no governor or upper chamber, almost no qualifications for voting or holding office). Massachusetts had the strongest governor (veto power).

Social Reforms

Religious freedom:

1776–90 The Anglican Church was disestablished in all states south of Pennsylvania.

1776 Virginia Declaration of Rights called for the "free exercise of religion."

1786 The Virginia **STATUTE FOR RELIGIOUS FREEDOM** (Jan. 16), drawn up by Jefferson, stated that no one was to be "compelled to frequent or support any religious worship" nor "suffer on account of his religious opinions."

Abolition of slavery:

1775 Antislavery societies were formed in Philadelphia and (1785) in New York. There was southern opposition to slavery (Jefferson, Washington, and Henry) but no action took place.

1780–86 Gradual emancipation was provided in Pennsylvania, Connecticut, Rhode Island, New York, and New Jersey.

1783–84 Slavery was abolished in Massachusetts in 1783 (by the decision in the **Quock Walker Case**, which ruled that the Massachusetts constitution of 1780 made all men free) and in New Hampshire in 1784.

1786 The importation of slaves was ended in all states but South Carolina and Georgia.

Changes in landholding:
Quitrents were abolished during the revolution. **Entail** and **primogeniture** were abolished or made ineffective in all states by 1798. **Tory land** was confiscated and distributed by all states.

Humanitarian reform:
Treatment of debtors and prisoners improved in the states.

Increased "Americanism":
J. Hector St. John de Crèvecoeur, *Letters from an American Farmer,* 1782. Noah Webster, *American Spelling Book,* 1783.

The Articles of Confederation, 1776–1781

1776

June 12 Congress appointed a 13-man committee to draft the Articles of Confederation. Conservatives, especially **John Dickinson**, who wrote the Articles, dominated the committee.

July 12   The first Dickinson draft gave sovereignty to the central government, reserving only police power to the states, and called for a strong executive council of state.

1777

Apr.   Debate on a revised version of the Dickinson draft began in the Congress.

Oct. 7   Congress agreed to the principle of one vote per state.

Oct. 14   Congress decided to apportion taxes on the basis of land holdings in each state.

Oct. 15   Congress promised not to deprive states of western land.

Nov. 15   Congress adopted the Articles of Confederation. The Dickinson draft was amended so that sovereignty went to the states and the strong executive was changed to a weak "committee of the states."

Terms of the Articles of Confederation

1. Free inhabitants of one state were entitled to "**privileges and immunities**" in all states. States were to give "**full faith and credit**" to acts of other states.
2. Each state had one vote in the Congress.
3. States could not make treaties without consent of Congress.
4. No state could raise any army or navy except by permission of Congress.
5. **Money** and **armed forces** were to be raised from the states by **quotas**.
6. Congress had power to wage war, send ambassadors, make treaties, settle interstate disputes, issue money, manage Indian affairs, establish a post office, and set the value of coins.
7. Most major matters required 9 votes, amendments required all 13 votes.
8. Congress lacked the power to raise an army and to tax and it shared the power to regulate commerce and to coin money with the states.

Nov. 17   Congress sent the Articles to the states for ratification. Unanimous ratification was necessary.

1778–81

Ratifying the Articles of Confederation

1778   By July 8, eight states had ratified and two followed suit. Three states without western land claims (New Jersey, Delaware, and Maryland) refused to ratify until the other states ceded their western lands to the central government. Maryland land speculators had interests in land claimed by Virginia.

1779   Delaware ratified in Feb., leaving only Maryland.

1780   In Sept., Congress asked the landed states to surrender part of their western lands. The next month, Congress voted to make new states equal to the old out of the western land cessions.

Jan. 10–Feb. 6   Departments of Foreign Affairs, War, and Finance were set up. **Robert Livingston** became Secretary of Foreign Affairs and **Robert Morris** Superintendent of Finance.

1781   In Jan., Virginia agreed to cede its western land, and in Feb., Maryland ratified the Articles. On Mar. 1, the Articles went into effect.

Economic and Diplomatic Problems Under the Confederation, 1776–1789

During the war, the farmers, contractors, and commissaries prospered, but the clergy, workers, and soldiers suffered. Soldiers' pay was given in paper money ("Continental dollars") printed by the Congress and was often in arrears.

1776   Convention at Providence, R.I. (Dec.), provided price controls for New England. Middle States set up price controls in Jan., 1778.

1778   Four Continental Congress dollars equaled one gold dollar. A year later the ratio was as 100 to 1.

1780   Congress declared the maximum ratio between Continental and gold dollars to be 40 to 1, thereby wiping out $200 million in debt. The U.S. had $9 million in loans from France and Spain and had issued $200 million in Continental dollars and $100 million in quartermaster certificates and certificates given in place of pay. On Mar. 18, Congress retired $120 million in Continental bills by accepting them at $\frac{1}{40}$ of face value as payments due from states.

1781   Bank of North America was established (Dec. 31). As a private bank that loaned money to and received deposits from the government, it aroused opposition.

1781–83   Congress had an extremely difficult time raising money: in 1782–83, for example, Congress asked the states for $10 million but received only $1.5 million. James Madison and Edmund Randolph of Virginia, realizing the problem, in 1781 proposed amendments to the Articles giving Congress power to require states to fulfill their obligations, but none was passed. In 1782 Rhode Island blocked ratification of an amendment calling for a 5 per cent impost on imports.

1783

Jan. 25   Congress was unable to satisfy claims of army officers for back pay.

Mar. 10   Major **John Armstrong** called a meeting of officers at Newburgh, N.Y., to discuss grievances.

Mar. 11   Washington forbade the meeting and on Mar. 15 addressed his officers condemning Armstrong and urging patience. He prevented a mutiny.

Apr. 18   Congress proposed two amendments, a duty on imports and a tax on the basis of population (slaves to count $\frac{3}{5}$) instead of on land. Neither was ratified.

May 14   British Order in Council allowed American non-manufactured goods to enter Great Britain just as before the Revolution. Another order in Council (July 2) closed British West Indies to American shipping.

June 24   Congress moved from Philadelphia to Princeton and later to Annapolis to escape soldiers demanding back pay.

1784

Apr. 30   Congress asked the right to pass a navigation act, but no action was taken.

May 28   The Treasury Board replaced Morris as Superintendent of Finance.

Aug. 30   France closed her **West Indies** ports to American ships. Spain also closed

certain ports, but the restrictions were not well enforced. In 1766, 1,422 vessels entered U.S. ports from the West Indies; in 1788, 1,170 vessels. The drop in American shipping was partly compensated by the fact that the United States could export directly to Europe without going through Great Britain.

Dec. 23   Congress declared New York City the temporary national capital.

1784–87   A **depression** set in as **wholesale prices**, which were inflated during the war, dropped rapidly. The wholesale price indexes (1850–59 = 100) were as follows: 1775, 78; 1778, 598; 1782, 140; and 1785, 105. The foreign and domestic debt was $35 million and arrears of interest $3 million. The depression lasted until 1787, and prices reached the bottom in 1789 (94).

1784–89   **Foreign Trade**: the *Empress of China* sailed in Feb. from New York for Canton, thereby opening American trade with China. It returned in May, 1785, with a profitable cargo of tea and silks. Of 46 foreign vessels reported at Canton in 1789, 18 were American.

1785

Feb. 24   Congress appointed **John Adams** minister to Great Britain. Adams was unable to get a favorable trade treaty because the British realized that one state could negate any agreements. There was an unfavorable balance of trade with Great Britain in 1784–85: imports were equal to $6 million; exports were equal to $1.7 million.

May 15   Spanish Minister to the U.S. **Don Diego de Gardoqui** arrived. Spain kept American ships from using the lower Mississippi River, claimed land north of Florida, and intrigued with the Indians.

June 23   Massachusetts banned the export of American goods in British ships. Maryland, Pennsylvania, New York, North Carolina, New Hampshire, and Rhode Island also passed acts against British shipping to counter British trade restrictions.

July 20   Congress instructed **John Jay** to negotiate with Gardoqui and to insist on the American right to use the lower Mississippi River.

Nov. 30 Adams demanded that the British evacuate northwest posts such as Oswego, Niagara, and Detroit, but the British refused because Americans had not paid pre-war debts.

1786

Demand for the states to issue **paper money** arose from debtors who wanted their debt burden reduced by cheapening the value of the dollar. The demand was rejected in Virginia, Connecticut, Delaware, and Maryland. Paper money was issued in Pennsylvania, South Carolina, Rhode Island, North Carolina, Georgia, New York, and New Jersey in 1785–86.

May Rhode Island issued paper money and required creditors to accept it. In *Trevett v. Weeden* (Sept. 25, 1786) the Rhode Island supreme court used **judicial review** in declaring it illegal to require creditors to accept paper money.

June 28   Treaty with Morocco: American shipping in the Mediterranean was suffering losses from the Barbary pirates in Morocco, as well as in Tripoli, Tunis, and Algiers. The U.S. bought off the Moroccans but not the others.

Aug. 8 Congress adopted a **coinage system** based on the **dollar.** Counterfeiting continued to be a problem.

Aug. 29 Congress voted 7 to 5 to allow Jay to give up the Mississippi River in return for a Spanish trade treaty, but since nine votes were needed to ratify a treaty, no further action was taken. Southern states interested in the river blocked the treaty.

Aug.–Jan., 1787   SHAYS' REBELLION: protests arose in Worcester, Mass., against the number of foreclosures of farm mortgages. In July, the Massachusetts legislature had refused to issue paper money or pass a law staying these foreclosures, which threatened to ruin the farmers.

Aug. A convention of 50 towns in **Hampshire County** (Mass.) drew up **resolutions** complaining of high taxes, scarce money, and expensive legal aid and demanded that paper money be issued.

Aug. 31 Armed men prevented court in Northampton, Mass., from sitting.

Sept. A riot in support of paper money was put down in Exeter, N.H., by the state militia, and no money issued.

Sept. 5 An armed group broke up a court session in Worcester.

Sept. Gov. **James Bowdoin** sent 600 militiamen to protect the state supreme court in Springfield.

Sept. 26 **Daniel Shays** and a mob of almost 1,000 men forced the **Springfield** court to adjourn.

Oct. 20 Congress authorized Secretary of War Henry Knox to raise over 1,000 men to defend the federal arsenal at Springfield, but the army did not have to be used.

Nov. The Massachusetts legislature took no action to relieve debtors. On Nov. 5, Washington wrote to Madison about Shays' Rebellion and said that the U.S. was "fast verging to anarchy." Madison wrote back urging a new government.

1787

Jan. 25 Shays and over 1,200 men assaulted the arsenal at Springfield but were beaten off by the militia.

Jan. 27 A Massachusetts army of over 4,000 arrived in Springfield and drove Shays through deep snow to Petersham, where the rebellion ended. Shays escaped to Vermont and was later pardoned. The rebellion caused the legislature to lower court fees and to reject a proposed direct tax.

1788–89 Trade recovery: **British exports** to the U.S. were £400,000 a year less than in 1769–74; **imports** to Britain from the U.S. were over £800,000 less. **Ships** entering U.S. ports 1766: 2,300; 1785: 754; and 1788: 2,000. Exports from the U.S. regained their pre-war position by the end of the Confederation period:

	1771	*1790*
Exports		
Tobacco (hogsheads)	109,000	118,000
Rum (gallons)	300,000	383,000
Pig Iron (tons)	5,123	3,555
Wheat (bushels)	395,000	1,242,000

Framing the Constitution, 1785–1790

Steps Leading to the Philadelphia Convention, 1785–1787

1785

Mar. 28   A **convention** of Virginia and Maryland delegates at **Mount Vernon** called for a convention on commercial problems at Annapolis.

Oct.–Apr., 1786   Congress had a quorum on only three days. For months in 1786–87 there was no quorum as the delegates lost interest in the weak government.

1786

Aug.   New York blocked a proposal by a committee of Congress for an amendment allowing an impost on imports.

Sept. 11–14   At the **ANNAPOLIS CONVENTION**, delegates from New York, Pennsylvania, New Jersey, Delaware, and Virginia adopted an invitation to the 13 states, written by **Alexander Hamilton**, to meet in Philadelphia to discuss commercial matters and to draw up provisions necessary to make the government "adequate to the exigencies of the Union."

The Constitutional Convention, 1787

Feb. 21   Congress called a convention in Philadelphia "for the sole and express purpose of revising the articles of Confederation."

May 25   The convention opened at the Pennsylvania State House **(Independence Hall)** in Philadelphia. While all states but Rhode Island took part, only seven states were represented the first day. The 55 delegates averaged 42 years in age, 31 had college education, half were lawyers, the rest mostly merchants or planters. An average of 30 was present at meetings. **George Washington** was chosen President. Other leading figures were **Benjamin Franklin, Gouverneur Morris,** and **James Wilson** (Pa.), **James Madison** (Va.), **Alexander Hamilton** (N.Y.), **Roger Sherman** and **Oliver Ellsworth** (Conn.), **William Paterson** (N.J.), **Rufus King** and **Elbridge Gerry** (Mass.), **John Dickinson** (Del.), **Luther Martin** (Md.), and **Charles Cotesworth Pinckney, Charles Pinckney,** and **John Rutledge,** (S.C.). Madison's notes are the principal source on the convention.

May 29   **THE VIRGINIA PLAN,** composed by **Madison** and presented by **Edmund Randolph,** proposed a new government instead of revising the Articles:

1. It called for a **legislature,** with a lower house chosen by the people and an upper house chosen by the lower with representation in proportion to free population. The legislature would have all powers of the Confederation Congress as well as others that the states were incompetent to exercise.
2. It proposed an **executive** (chosen by the legislature) and a national judiciary.
3. State officials were bound to support the national government, which could veto state laws.
4. A **council of revision** made up of the executive and judiciary could veto acts of the legislature.

May 30–June 13   The convention discussed the Virginia Plan while meeting as a committee of the whole.

June 6–7   The committee of the whole voted to have the people elect members of the lower house and state legislatures elect members of the upper house.

June 13   The committee of the whole reported in favor of most of the Virginia Plan.

June 15   The **NEW JERSEY PLAN,** presented by **William Paterson,** gave the small-state alternative to the Virginia Plan:

1. It continued the Articles of Confederation but granted Congress power to levy duties on imports, to **regulate trade,** and to "direct the collection" of requisitions from the states.

2. Congress could name a plural executive and appoint a supreme court.
3. Acts of Congress and treaties were to be "the **supreme law of the respective States.**"
4. The executive was given power to enforce acts of Congress.

June 18   HAMILTON'S PLAN called for an assembly, elected by the people, a senate elected by electors chosen by the people, and an executive. Senate, executive, and judiciary were to be chosen for life tenure. Laws contrary to the constitution were to be void.

June 19   The Convention voted to support the Virginia Plan.

July 5   The **GREAT COMPROMISE**, proposed by **Roger Sherman** (Conn.), was adopted by the committee of the whole. Representation in the lower house was to be in proportion to population, and in the upper house there was to be an equal vote for each state. Bills to raise money would originate in the lower house. In determining representation five slaves would count the same as three free men.

July 12, 16   The Convention voted in favor of the Great Compromise, accepting the provisions for both the upper and the lower houses.

July 19–26   The Convention drew up a set of resolutions and agreed to a supreme law of the land clause.

July 26   A **committee of detail** made up of **Randolph, Wilson, Rutledge, Ellsworth, and Nathaniel Gorham** (Mass.) drew up a rough draft of a constitution drawing heavily on the Articles of Confederation and the New Jersey Plan.

Aug. 6–Sept. 10   The draft constitution was debated.

Aug. 16   Congress was granted the **power to regulate commerce.**

Sept. 4   A committee reported in favor of the **electoral system** for choosing the President.

Sept. 8   A five-man committee on style and arrangements was appointed, made up of **Hamilton, King, Madison, and Gouverneur Morris,** with **William Johnson** (Conn.) as chairman. Morris wrote the final draft.

Sept. 17   Each of the 12 state delegations approved the final Constitution. Of the 42 delegates remaining, 39 signed (**Gerry** of Massachusetts and **Randolph** and **George Mason** of Virginia refused).

Sept. 20   Congress received the Constitution and later submitted it to the states for special ratifying conventions. Ratification by nine states was necessary to put the Constitution into operation.

Ratification of the Constitution, 1787–1790

1787

During the Confederation Period those favoring a stronger central government were called "**nationalists,**" those for state sovereignty "**federalists.**" During the ratification struggle those for the Constitution usurped the name federalist leaving those opposed to ratification with the title "**antifederalists.**" In each state a special convention was held to ratify the Constitution.

Oct. 27–Apr. 2, 1788   Over 70 essays signed "Publius" in support of the Constitution appeared in New York newspapers. With eight additional essays, they were published in May as *The Federalist.* Written by Hamilton, Madison, and John Jay, *The Federalist* supported a strong yet republican government.

Dec. 7–Jan. 9, 1788   First five states ratified the constitution. Delaware, New Jersey, and Connecticut sought federal protection against New York City and so ratified without a struggle. Georgia needed the help of a strong central government against the Creeks. The Federalists won in Pennsylvania partly because the Philadelphia artisans wanted a strong government.

1788

Feb. 6   Massachusetts ratified 187 to 168. Samuel Adams was won over when the convention proposed amendments to the Constitution protecting the rights of the states against a strong federal government.

Mar. 24   Rhode Island rejected the constitution through a referendum.

Apr. 28   Maryland ratified 63 to 11, the seventh state to ratify.

May 23   South Carolina ratified the Constitution, 149 to 73.

June 21   The Constitution went into effect when New Hampshire became the ninth state to ratify (57 to 47).

June 25   After a convention that started on June 2, Virginia ratified by 89 to 79. **Patrick Henry** and **Richard Henry Lee** led the **antifederalists.** Lee was author of the *Letters from the Federal Farmer to the Republican,* the best expression of the antifederalist position. Washington and Madison led the supporters of the Constitution.

July 26   New York ratified 30–27 when news came of ratification by New Hampshire and Virginia.

July   North Carolina rejected the Constitution, 185–84.

Sept. 13   Congress set New York City as the site of the new government and Mar. 4, 1789, as the date for the first meeting of Congress. Presidential electors were to be chosen on the first Wednesday in January and were to vote on the first Wednesday in February, 1789.

Oct. 10   The Confederation Congress transacted its last business.

Dec. 23   Maryland ceded 10 square miles for a future federal capital.

1789

Nov. 21   North Carolina ratified 195–77 after the Bill of Rights was proposed by Congress.

1790

May 29   Rhode Island ratified by a majority of two.

The West, 1763–1789

1763

May 7   PONTIAC'S REBELLION, led by **Pontiac,** Chief of the Ottawa, began.

June–Nov.   All British posts west of Fort Pitt except Detroit were destroyed by Pontiac. **Detroit** was put under siege.

Oct. 7   PROCLAMATION OF 1763 closed all land south of Quebec, north of Florida, and west of the Appalachian divide to colonists.

Nov.   Pontiac gave up the siege of Detroit but continued his rebellion, which was not ended until a treaty was signed in 1766.

Dec.   PAXTON BOYS' REBELLION. Frontiersmen in Paxton and Donegal, Pa., angry at the colonial assembly's failure to protect them from the Indians, attacked Indians in western Pennsylvania. They then marched east to Philadelphia, where **Benjamin Franklin** convinced them to lay down their arms; in return, they were promised greater western representation in the Pennsylvania assembly.

1768

Mar.   Lord Hillsborough, Secretary of State for the colonies, established a new western policy that colonies could control the fur trade and that the Proclamation Line of 1763 could be moved west by means of treaties with the Indians.

Oct 14   Treaty of Hard Labor with the Cherokee, negotiated by the British Commissioner for the southwest, moved the border of Virginia west.

Nov. 5   The British **Treaty of Fort Stanwix** with the Iroquois gained all land south of the headwaters of the Susquehanna and south of the Ohio for the crown.

1769

Dec. 27   Grand Ohio Company secured 20 million acres to settle the colony of Vandalia (most of it in present-day West Virginia).

1770

Sept.   **Regulator War** broke out in western North Carolina, where settlers complained of lack of courts, under-representation, and inadequate protection against Indians. Vigilantes named Regulators (founded 1764) seized the court at Hillsborough. Gov. Tryon ordered the arrest of Regulator leaders under the Riot Act, classifying them as traitors. In May, 1771, Tryon defeated the Regulators at the **Alamance Creek**. Many Regulators became Loyalists during Revolution.

Oct. 18   **Treaty of Lochaber** with the Cherokee shifted the Virginia boundary further west. An expedition led by Daniel Boone entered central Kentucky by way of the Cumberland Gap and returned to North Carolina in 1771 with stories of a fertile blue-grass region.

1774

Jan.–Oct.   **Lord Dunmore's War**. When Virginia's Gov. Dunmore seized western Pennsylvania to strengthen the Virginia claim to the northwest, the Shawnee and Ottawa went on the warpath.

Oct. 10   Shawnee Chief Cornstalk was defeated at Point Pleasant in western Virginia. He granted free navigation of the Ohio and hunting rights in Kentucky to the settlers.

2-7   The West, 1763–1789

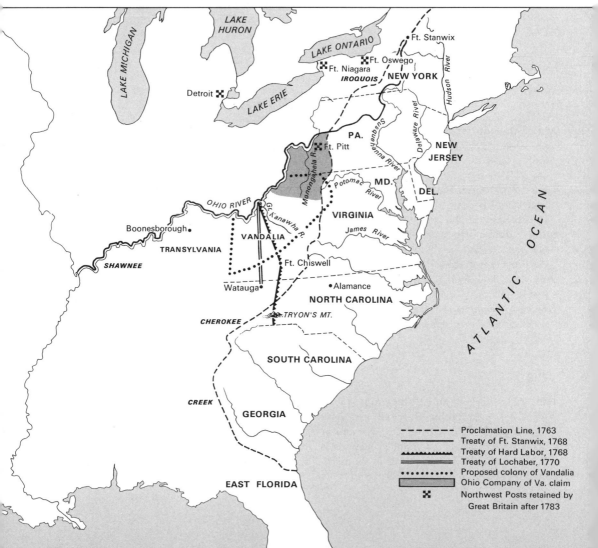

1775

Jan. The **Transylvania Company** sent Daniel Boone to blaze the Wilderness Road to its grant in Kentucky.
Mar. 17 By the Treaty of Sycamore Shoals, the Cherokee ceded much of present-day Kentucky to the Transylvania Company.
Apr. 6 Boonesborough was founded.

1776

Congress and the states offered land bounties to soldiers, ranging from 100 to 12,000 acres.
July–Oct. **Watauga** settlements in Tennessee stood off Cherokee attacks and retaliated.
Nov. North Carolina annexed the Watauga area.

1777

Kentucky settlements fought off Shawnee raids and were annexed to Virginia.

1778

May **Joseph Brant** led Iroquois in a raid on American settlements in the Mohawk Valley from the Tory-Iroquois base at Niagara, N.Y.
May 12 **George Rogers Clark** led 175 men from Virginia down the Ohio River to attack British bases in the Northwest.
June **John Butler** led Loyalists and Iroquois on a raid in the Wyoming Valley in eastern Pennsylvania.
July 4 Clark took the British post at Kaskaskia, Ill.
Nov. 11 Brant and Butler combined to attack American settlements at Cherry Valley, N.Y.

1779

Feb. 25 Clark captured **Vincennes, Ill.**
Aug. 29 Gen. **John Sullivan** and 5,000 men severely defeated the Loyalists and Indians under Butler and Brant at **Newtown, N.Y.**, and broke Indian power in the north. On the southern front, 20,000 frontiersmen

were able to move into Kentucky and Tennessee in 1779 as the Indian menace faded.

1780

Founding of Nashville, Tenn.

1781

Col. **John Sevier** and frontiersmen from Watauga attacked the Cherokee.
Jan. 2 Virginia ceded her claims north of the Ohio River.

1784

Apr. 23 An act was passed for the government of the northwest based on a draft by **Jefferson** but was not put into operation.
Aug. 23 The state of **Franklin** was organized in Tennessee but was not admitted to the union.

1785

May–Nov. **Creeks,** led by Alexander McGillivray, were defeated and ceded land to Georgia.
May 20 **LAND ORDINANCE** divided land in the northwest (north of the Ohio and east of the Mississippi rivers) into townships six miles square with 36 lots each of 640 acres. Minimum sale was 640 acres at $1 an acre. One lot was set aside for the support of public schools.

1787

July Congress granted the **Ohio Company,** led by Rev. **Manasseh Cutler,** 1.8 million acres in the Northwest Territory. The Scioto Company was given an option to 5 million acres in the northwest.
July 13 **NORTHWEST ORDINANCE** set up government for the Old Northwest:
1. The territory would be governed first by a **governor** appointed by Congress.
2. When the population reached 5,000 free adult males, the territory would elect a bicameral **legislature**.
3. When any part of the Northwest Territory

had 60,000 people, it could be **admitted to the Union** on an equal basis with the original states.

4. The Ordinance granted **freedom of religion,** habeas corpus, trial by jury, and **forbade slavery.** (Nathan Dane, the author of the bill, was influenced by Jefferson, Manasseh Cutler, and Rufus King of Massachusetts.)

1789

North Carolina ceded western land, leaving only Georgia (cession, 1802) holding land.

Leading Figures of the Revolutionary Period

JOHN ADAMS (Quincy, Mass., 1735–1826), 2nd President of the United States.

1755   Was graduated from Harvard.

1765   Wrote Braintree Instructions against the Stamp Act that were adopted in Braintree and in other towns.

1770   Defended British soldiers in the Boston Massacre.

1770–71   Served in General Court (legislature).

1774–75   Served in the Massachusetts Revolutionary Provincial Congress.

1774–75   Wrote "Novanglus" in Boston *Gazette.*

1774–78   Delegate to 1st and 2nd Continental Congresses.

1776   Helped draft Declaration of Independence; defended it to the Continental Congress.

1778   Commissioner to France.

1780   Wrote Massachusetts state constitution.

1782–83   Helped negotiate Paris peace treaty with Great Britain.

1785–88   Minister to Great Britain.

1789–97   Vice President of the U.S. under Washington.

1797–1801   President of the U.S.

1801–26   Retirement in Quincy.

SAMUEL ADAMS (Boston, 1722–1803), revolutionary patriot leader, cousin of John Adams.

1740   Was graduated from Harvard.

1756–64   Tax collector in Boston.

1765   Led Sons of Liberty in opposition to the Stamp Act; was elected to the General Court.

1766–74   Clerk of Massachusetts House of Representatives.

1768   Wrote Massachusetts Circular Letter and organized the Non-Importation Association.

1770   Used Boston Massacre for propaganda.

1772   Organized the Massachusetts Committee of Correspondence.

1772   Wrote *State of the Rights of the Colonists.*

1773   Organized Boston Tea Party.

1774   Represented Massachusetts at 1st Continental Congress.

1775–81   Delegate to 2nd Continental Congress.

1775   Spoke out in favor of immediate independence.

1776   Signed Declaration of Independence.

1779–80   Delegate to Massachusetts state constitutional convention.

1781   President of the Massachusetts Senate.

1788   Supported ratification of the federal constitution at the Massachusetts convention.

1789–93   Lt. Governor of Massachusetts.

1794–97   Governor of Massachusetts.

JOHN DICKINSON (Talbot County, Md., 1732–Wilmington, Del., 1808), statesman of the revolutionary period.

1750   Studied law in Philadelphia and London; began his practice in 1757.

1760–62   Member of Delaware assembly.

1762–65   Member of Pennsylvania assembly; also served again in 1770–76.

1765   Wrote *Late Regulations Respecting the British Colonies ... Considered* claiming that the Sugar and Stamp acts hurt British economic interests.

1765   Delegate to Stamp Act Congress and author of *Resolves.*

1767–68 His *Letters from a Farmer in Pennsylvania* attacked the Townshend Acts.

1774 Delegate to 1st Continental Congress; became increasingly conservative.

1775 Delegate to 2nd Continental Congress. Author of *Petition to the King* ("Olive Branch Petition") and with Jefferson of *Declaration of Causes and Necessities of Taking Up Arms.*

1776 Opposed Declaration of Independence, but headed Committee that drafted the Articles of Confederation.

1777, 1779–80 Delegate to Continental Congresses.

1781 President of Supreme Executive Council of Delaware.

1782–85 President of Pennsylvania.

1787 Delegate from Delaware to Constitutional Convention; supported ratification.

ALEXANDER HAMILTON (Nevis, British West Indies, 1755–New York City, 1804), financial expert and party leader.

1773 Arrived in New York as a student at King's College.

1774 Wrote the pamphlets *A Full Vindication of the Measures of Congress* and *The Farmer Refuted.* Was politically a moderate patriot.

1776 Commander of artillery in New York and New Jersey campaigns.

1777–81 Washington's aide-de-camp.

1781 Commanded troops at Yorktown.

1782–83 Served in Congress.

1783 Started law practice in New York City.

1786 Attended Annapolis Convention; wrote report calling for the Constitutional Convention.

1787 Delegate to Constitutional Convention; presented a plan for an aristocratic centralized government.

1787–88 Wrote about 50 of *The Federalist* essays; helped achieve constitutional ratification by New York.

1789–95 1st Secretary of the U.S. Treasury.

1790 1st *Report on Public Credit* proposed funding and assumption bills and the excise tax.

1791 Wrote *Report on the Bank,* in which he justified a national bank by doctrine of the "implied powers" of Congress.

1791 *Report on Manufactures* urged protective tariffs.

1792 Newspaper feud with Jefferson led to start of American political parties; Hamilton led the Federalists, Jefferson the Republicans.

1799–1800 Led opposition to John Adams within the Federalist party.

1801 Used his own influence in the House to help Jefferson defeat Aaron Burr for the Presidency.

1804 Thwarted Burr's chances of being elected Governor of New York. Later that year, he was killed by Burr in a duel at Weehawken, N.J.

PATRICK HENRY (Hanover County, Va., 1736–Charlotte County, Va., 1799), revolutionary war patriot.

1760 Started law practice.

1763 Argued "The Parson's Cause" case; gained great popular following.

1765 Took seat in Virginia House of Burgesses; represented frontier interests.

1765 Presented the seven "Virginia resolutions" against the Stamp Act. Supposedly closed with statement that King George III might suffer the fate of Caesar.

1774 Gathered Burgesses in Raleigh Tavern after Lord Dunmore had dissolved the assembly.

1774 Delegate to 1st Continental Congress; took radical side.

1775 Urged arming militia with statement, "Give me liberty or give me death!"

1775 Delegate to 2nd Continental Congress.

1776 Helped draft Virginia constitution and served as governor until 1779.

1778 Sent George Rogers Clark on western expedition.

1784–86 Governor of Virginia.

1788 Opposed ratification of Constitution as a violation of state sovereignty.

1789 Led movement for the Bill of Rights.

1790 Drafted the Virginia resolution opposing assumption of state debts, part of Hamilton's funding program.

JOHN JAY (New York City, 1745–Bedford, N.Y., 1829), diplomat and Chief Justice of the U.S. Supreme Court.

1764 Was graduated from King's College in New York City.

1768 Was licensed to practice law in New York.

1774 Member of 1st Continental Congress.

1775 Delegate to 2nd Continental Congress.

1776–77 Member of the New York Provincial Congress.

1777 Chief Justice of New York.

1778 President of the Continental Congress.

1780–82 Minister to Spain.

1782–83 Member of delegation to peace talks at Paris.

1784–90 Secretary for Foreign Affairs.

1785–86 Carried on fruitless Jay-Gardoqui negotiations for a trade agreement with Spain.

1787–88 Helped write *The Federalist,* essays supporting ratification of the Constitution.

1789–95 Chief Justice of the U.S. Supreme Court.

1794 Negotiated treaty with Great Britain ("Jay Treaty").

1795–1801 Governor of New York.

THOMAS JEFFERSON (Shadwell, Va., 1743– Monticello, Va., 1826), 3rd President of the United States.

1762 Was graduated from the College of William and Mary.

1767 Began to practice law.

1769–75 Delegate to Virginia House of Burgesses.

1774 Wrote *A Summary View of the Rights of British America.*

1775 Delegate to the 2nd Continental Congress. Author with Dickinson of *Causes of Taking up Arms.*

1776 Drafted Declaration of Independence.

1776–79 Member of Virginia House of Delegates.

1779–81 Governor of Virginia.

1783–84 Member of Continental Congress; wrote 1st definite plan to govern Western Territories.

1785–89 Minister to France; saw the outbreak of the French Revolution, 1789.

1785 Published *Notes on Virginia,* one of the 1st studies of natural history in America.

1786 Author of Virginia Statute for Religious Freedom.

1790–93 U.S. Secretary of State.

1791 Opposed constitutionality of the Bank of the U.S.

1792 Organized Republican opposition to Hamilton and the Federalists.

1797–1801 Vice President of the U.S. under John Adams.

1798 Author of 1st Kentucky resolution against the Alien and Sedition Acts.

1799 Author of 2nd Kentucky Resolution.

1800 Tied with Aaron Burr for the Presidency.

1801 Was chosen President by the House of Representatives.

1801–09 President of the U.S.

1803 Secured the Louisiana Purchase.

1803–06 Sent out the Lewis and Clark Expedition.

1807 Pressed for conviction in Burr treason trial.

1807 Supported the Embargo Act.

1819 Founded the University of Virginia at Charlottesville.

JAMES MADISON (Port Conway, Va., 1751– Montpelier, Va., 1836), 4th President of the United States.

1771 Was graduated from Princeton.

1775 Chairman, Committee of Public Safety, Orange County, Va.

1776 Helped draw up Virginia state constitution.

1776–77 Member of the Virginia legislature.

1778–79 Member of the Virginia state council.

1780–83 Member of the Continental Congress.

1784–86 Member of the Virginia House of Delegates.

1785 Helped call Mount Vernon Conference to discuss navigational rights on Chesapeake Bay.

1786 Secured passage of Jefferson's Statute for Religious Freedom.

1786 Took part in the Annapolis Convention on interstate commerce.

1787 A leading figure at Constitutional Convention, where he kept record of debates and drew up the Virginia Plan.

1787–88 Wrote 28 of *The Federalist* essays.

1788 Defended the Constitution at the Virginia Ratification Convention.

1789–97 Member of Congress.

1789 Proposed the Bill of Rights in the House of Representatives.

1790 Opposed Hamilton's funding bill and assumption of state debts.

1791 Opposed the national bank bill.

1791 Arranged publication of the *National Gazette,* opposing Hamilton's policies.

1792 Led Republican opposition to Hamilton's policies.

1798 Wrote the Virginia Resolution against the Alien and Sedition Acts.

1801–09 U.S. Secretary of State.

1809–17 President of the U.S.

1812 Presented war message to Congress.

1815 Vetoed 1st bank bill but in 1816 signed the 2nd bank bill.

1817 Vetoed the "bonus bill."

GEORGE WASHINGTON (Bridges Creek, Va., 1732–Mount Vernon, Va., 1799), revolutionary war commander, 1st President of the United States.

1753 Warned French against moving into Ohio Valley.

1759–74 Member of the Virginia House of Burgesses.

1754 Surrendered Fort Necessity (near Pittsburgh) to the French; start of French and Indian War.

1755 Was present at Braddock's defeat.

1758 Took part in capture of Fort Duquesne (Pittsburgh).

1774 Participated in a meeting of Virginia Burgesses at Raleigh Tavern after the assembly had been dissolved by the colonial governor.

1774–75 Member of 1st and 2nd Continental Congresses.

1775 Took command of Continental Army at Cambridge, Mass.

1776 Forced the British forces to evacuate Boston.

1776–77 Suffered many defeats in the New York, New Jersey, and Philadelphia campaigns but held the army together.

1777–78 Wintered at Valley Forge.

1777–78 Withstood congressional opposition to his command.

1781 Defeated the British at the Battle of Yorktown.

1783 Prevented mutiny of officers at Newburgh, N.Y.

1783 Farewell to officers at Fraunces' Tavern in New York. Returned to his home at Mount Vernon.

1786 Member of Annapolis Convention on interstate commerce.

1787 Presided over Constitutional Convention in Philadelphia.

1789–97 As first President, established many precedents including the Cabinet and the mode of drawing up treaties.

1793 Issued neutrality proclamation.

1794 Sided with Federalists.

1796 Farewell Address warned his countrymen of the dangers of permanent alliances and party strife.

1797 Retired to Mount Vernon.

Statistical Tables

Table 7.
Population of the 13 American colonies
(millions)

	Total	White	Negro
1760	1.6	1.3	0.3
1770	2.1	1.6	0.5
1780	2.8	2.2	0.6
1790	3.9	3.2	0.8

Table 8.
Nationality of white population, 1790[a]

English	61%	Dutch	3%
Scotch	8	French	2
Irish	10	Swedish	1
German	9	Unassigned	7

[a] Because of rounding, the percentages do not total to 100.

Table 9.
Iron Exported to England[a]
(thousands of tons)

	Bar Iron	Pig Iron
1760	0.1	3.3
1765	1.1	3.3
1770	1.7	4.2
1775	0.9	3.0

[a] Colonial iron production in 1775 was one-seventh of world iron production, more than England and Wales combined.

Table 10.
Tobacco exported by colonies to England
(millions of pounds)

1760	52.3
1765	48.3
1770	39.2
1775	56.0

Table 11.
Colonial exports to and imports from England
(millions of £ sterling)

	Exports	Imports
1760	0.8	2.6
1761	0.8	1.7
1762	0.7	1.4
1763	1.1	1.6
1764	1.1	2.2
1765	1.2	1.9
1766	1.0	1.8
1767	1.1	1.9
1768	1.3	2.2
1769	1.1	1.3
1770	1.0	1.9
1771	1.3	4.2
1772	1.3	3.0
1773	1.4	2.0
1774	1.4	2.6
1775	1.9	0.2
1776	0.1	0.1

Table 12.
Tea imported into colonies from England
(thousands of pounds)

1761	56	1768	874
1762	162	1769	229
1763	189	1770	110
1764	489	1771	362
1765	518	1772	265
1766	361	1773	739
1767	480	1774	73
		1775	22

Table 13.
Index of wholesale prices in the United States
(1850–59 = base 100)

1760	81.5	1775	78.0
1761	77.5	1776	108.0
1762	83.4	1777	329.6
1763	83.5	1778	598.1
1764	77.2	1779	2,969.1
1765	76.7	1780	10,544.1
1766	81.7	1781	5,085.8
1767	81.7	1782	139.6
1768	80.7	1783	119.1
1769	81.2	1784	112.7
1770	80.0	1785	105.0
1771	84.9	1786	105.1
1772	98.2	1787	103.9
1773	90.9	1788	97.4
1774	84.3	1789	94.0

Table 14.
Tax collections in America under new revenue acts

	Sugar Acts of 1764 and 1766	Townshend Act of 1767	Total (Thousands of £ sterling)
1765	14.1	—	17.4[a]
1766	26.7	—	26.7
1767	33.8	0.2	34.0
1768	24.7	13.2	37.9
1769	39.9	5.6	45.5
1770	30.9	2.7	33.6
1771	27.1	4.7	31.8
1772	42.6	3.3	45.9
1773	39.5	2.6	42.1
1774	27.1	0.9	28.0

[a] Including 3.3 under the Stamp Act.

Table 15.
Population of cities in America
(thousands)

	1760	1770	1790
Philadelphia[a]	20	28	42
New York	15	21	33
Boston	15	16	18
Charleston, S.C.	9	11	16

[a] In 1760 Philadelphia was the third largest city in the British empire.

Table 16.
Value of articles exported from
American colonies, 1770
(thousands of £ sterling)

Total	3,438
American goods	3,356
Reexports	82
Fish	375
Wheat	131
Indigo	132
Bread and Flour	505
Rice	341
Tobacco	907
Iron	67
Furs and Deer Skins	149
Naval Stores (Masts and Spars Included)	96

THE EARLY NATIONAL PERIOD, 1789–1825

PART 3

The Federalist Decade, 1789–1801

Organizing Government and Economy, 1789–96

1789

Feb. 4 **Presidential election: George Washington**, President, 69 electoral votes (the only man ever elected unanimously); **John Adams**, Vice President, 34 electoral votes. The two Washington Administrations are particularly significant because of the precedents set in both domestic and foreign affairs.

Mar. 4 **First Congress** met in New York City but lacked a quorum.

Apr. 6 Congress organized. Both houses were predominantly Federalist.

Apr. 30 **Washington** was inaugurated as President in **New York City.**

July 4 **Tariff Act,** primarily for revenue, levied duties averaging 8 per cent.

July 20 **Tonnage Act** taxed American shipping 6¢ a ton, foreign shipping 50¢ a ton. Hamilton blocked Madison's effort to discriminate further against British shipping.

July 27–Sept. 2 **Departments of State** (**Thomas Jefferson**, Secretary), **War** (**Henry Knox** of Massachusetts, Secretary), and **Treasury** (**Alexander Hamilton, Secretary**) were established. Congress gave the President power to remove an appointee without the consent of the Senate.

Aug. 22 Treaty making: Washington asked the Senate for advice and consent on a treaty with the Creeks. When the Senate delayed, Washington decided henceforth to submit signed treaties and ask only for consent.

Sept. 22 Office of **Postmaster General** was established.

Sept. 24 **Federal Judiciary Act** provided for a **SUPREME COURT** with a Chief Justice (**John Jay,** N.Y.) and five associates. It established three circuit courts (two Supreme Court justices per circuit) and 13 district courts. Cases could be appealed from state courts to the Supreme Court. The act also called for an **Attorney General** (**Edmund Randolph,** Va.).

Sept. 25 **Bill of Rights** was submitted to the states. Ten of the dozen amendments were ratified Dec. 15, 1791. Madison led the Bill of Rights movement in the House.

1790

Hamilton's financial program contributed to the rift that developed between his followers and those who supported Thomas Jefferson and James Madison. While Hamilton favored the merchant, the creditor, the federal government, and Great Britain, Jefferson preferred the farmer, the debtor, the state governments, and France.

Jan. 14 Hamilton's first *Report on the Public Credit* proposed **funding the U.S. debt** (foreign debt about $12 million; domestic about $44 million) at par value. The U.S. would also assume about $22 million in state debts. Creditors could exchange present securities for new bonds. Hamilton hoped to restore confidence in American credit and give creditors a stake in the government. In Feb., Hamilton's Report caused a wave of speculative buying in U.S. securities, leading to the charge that "insiders" were responsible. The real cause was faith in the economic strength of the new nation.

Feb. 22　**Madison** opposed paying the domestic debt at par value because it would benefit speculators who had bought up bonds from the original buyers. Congress rejected his proposal to discriminate in favor of the original buyer. Southerners disliked funding because most securities were held in the north and assumption of state debts because the northern states had the largest unpaid debts.

Apr. 12　Madison and others defeated the funding bill in the House.

July 16　Congress voted to put the national capital on the Potomac after Madison secured southern votes for the funding bill in order to get Hamilton's support for a southern capital.

Aug. 4　The **FUNDING ACT** (including the assumption of state debts) was passed. The House vote on assumption was (North) 24–9 in favor and (South) 18–10 against.

Dec. 6　Congress met in Philadelphia, where the capital remained until 1800.

Dec. 13　Hamilton's *Report on the Bank* proposed a **Bank of the United States** capitalized at $10,000,000 (80 per cent private, 20 per cent federal) to be the principal depository for federal funds. The bank's notes would be the nation's principal currency. As fiscal agent of the Treasury, the bank would assist the government in funding the debt.

Dec. 16　**Virginia Resolutions,** written by Patrick Henry, opposed the assumption of state debts.

1791

Feb. 8　In spite of Madison's opposition the bank bill passed the House. Northerners voted in favor of the bank 33–1; Southerners opposed it 19–6.

Feb. 15　Jefferson's *Opinion on the Bank* used strict construction of the Constitution to argue that the bank was unconstitutional.

Feb. 23　**Hamilton,** using loose construction, argued that the bank was justified by the "necessary and proper" clause.

Feb. 25　Washington signed the bank bill.

Mar. 3　**WHISKY TAX** passed amid great opposition from the frontier where surplus grain was distilled into whisky.

July 4　Stock in the B.U.S. sold within one hour. The government sold its $2 million worth of shares in 1802 and by 1811 foreigners held 18,000 of the 25,000 shares.

Nov. 26　The first cabinet meeting.

Dec. 5　*Report on Manufactures* by Hamilton urged protective tariffs to encourage manufacturing, bounties to help agriculture, and internal improvements to bind the nation together.

1792

Apr. 5　First Presidential **veto** (of the apportionment bill) was upheld by Congress.

Apr. 11　In the first **Hayburn Case,** a U.S. Circuit Court declared an act of Congress unconstitutional.

Aug. 21　Resistance to the Whisky Tax centered in North Carolina and western Pennsylvania. A Pittsburgh convention of farmers threatened to obstruct tax collections.

Dec. 5　**Presidential election: Washington** was reelected with the unanimous vote of 132 electors. **Adams** was reelected Vice President with 77 electoral votes. **George Clinton** (N.Y.), a supporter of Thomas Jefferson, received 50 votes as opposition to the Federalists began to arise.

1793

Jan. 23　Congressman **William Branch Giles** (Va.) proposed an inquiry into charges of corruption in the Treasury. After Hamilton's defense (Feb. 4 and 13) Giles' resolution to censure Hamilton failed.

Feb. 18　*Chisholm v. Georgia:* the Supreme Court decided in favor of two South Carolina citizens who sued Georgia for confiscated property.

1794

Mar. 5　State-rights opposition to the Chisholm decision led Congress to propose the **Eleventh Amendment**, which provided that a state could not be sued by a citizen of another state in federal courts. It was ratified Jan. 8, 1798.

July   WHISKY REBELLION in western Pennsylvania. Farmers protested against the whisky tax and against the law requiring those not paying the tax to stand trial in Philadelphia. Congress repealed the trial law in May but too late to prevent the rebellion; the rebels attacked excise officers and forced troops to surrender. A Presidential proclamation (Aug. 7) ordered the rebels to return to their homes and called out the militia from four states. In Sept., Washington ordered the suppression of the rebellion and accompanied the troops part of the way. The rebellion evaporated by Nov. as the troops approached.

1796   Land Act (May 18) called for rectangular survey, a minimum price of $2 an acre, and a minimum purchase of 640 acres for land west of the Appalachians.

Founding a Foreign Policy, 1789–1800

During the Washington and Adams Administrations the Federalists had to cope with problems stemming from the French Revolution, the war between France and Great Britain, and the American western frontier. The decisions made then set the pattern for American foreign policy in the nineteenth and early twentieth centuries.

1789   A Parisian mob stormed the **Bastille** (July 14). The French Revolution was inspired in part by the American example.

1791   An army under Gen. **Arthur St. Clair** was defeated by the Indians on the Maumee River in Ohio with heavy losses (Nov. 4). The defeat delayed settlement of the area.

1792   The French Republic was proclaimed on Sept. 21. Support for the Republic was strong in the United States.

1793

Jan. 21   The Reign of Terror followed the execution of Louis XVI in France; conservatives in America increasingly turned against the French Revolution.

Feb. 1   France declared war on Great Britain, Spain, and Holland as part of a campaign to spread the ideals of the Revolution and to gain her "natural" boundaries. Federalists tended to side with Britain, the Republicans with France.

Apr. 8   Citizen **Edmond Charles Genêt**, French minister to the U.S., arrived in Charleston, S.C. He travelled north through the back country amid great popular acclaim and intrigued with George Rogers Clark to attack Spanish Florida and Louisiana.

Apr. 22   Washington's **NEUTRALITY PROCLAMATION** established the American tradition of neutrality. Washington rejected Hamilton's proposal that the U.S. repudiate the Treaty of 1778, whereby the U.S. had agreed to defend French possessions in the New World.

May 18   Washington received Genêt, thereby recognizing the French Republic and initiating a policy of *de facto* recognition.

June 8, Nov. 6   British **Orders in Council** ordered seizure of neutral cargoes bound for France or for ports under French control.

Aug. 23   Washington asked that Genêt be recalled for violating American neutrality by fitting out privateers; Genêt was allowed to remain after the Jacobins came into power in France in 1794.

1794

Feb.   The British continued to refuse to return **northwest posts** on American soil and Canadian Governor-General **Lord Dorchester** made a warlike speech to Indians in the Northwest.

Spring   The British had seized about 300 American ships and Republicans began to cry for war. Federalists, however, wanted peace in order to preserve trade with Britain.

Apr. 16   Washington named **John Jay** as special envoy to Great Britain to negotiate differences.

Apr.   Non-intercourse act with Great Britain barely failed to pass the House.

Aug. 20   At the **BATTLE OF FALLEN TIMBERS**, Gen. **Anthony Wayne** defeated the Indians on the Maumee River and secured the American position in Ohio.

Fall   Jay negotiated with the British, who wanted peace but were unwilling to make concessions—partly because Hamilton had informed them that the U.S. had no intention of joining the Scandinavian **Armed Neutrality** against Great Britain.

Nov. 19   JAY TREATY provided that the U.S. could trade with the British Isles on a most favored nation basis and could trade without discrimination in the British East Indies; the British would evacuate the **northwest posts; claims** for debts and British seizures and the **northeast boundary** would be referred to commissions; and the British could continue to seize American foodstuffs bound for France. Concessions regarding the West Indies were so minor that they were later eliminated from the treaty; and nothing was said about Indian incitement.

1795

Spring   Public outcry arose against the Jay Treaty because Jay had failed to secure all the American goals, although the Senate ratified the treaty June 24 after Washington defended it.

July 22   Hamilton began his "Camillus" newspaper articles defending the treaty.

Aug. 3   By the **Treaty of Greenville**, the Indians ceded most of Ohio to the U.S.

3-1   The Treaty of Greenville, 1795

Lands Ceded by Indians

Oct. 27   PINCKNEY TREATY (Treaty of San Lorenzo, ratified Mar. 3, 1796) with Spain was negotiated by **Thomas Pinckney**, Minister to Great Britain. Spain recognized the **31st parallel** as the northern border of Florida, gave the U.S. free navigation of the **Mississippi River** and the right of **deposit** at New Orleans, and agreed to restrain the **Indians** of the south.

1796

Mar. 24   Washington refused to release papers on the Jay Treaty to the House on the grounds of executive prerogative.

Apr. 30   The House appropriation for carrying the Jay Treaty into effect passed.

Dec.   France, angry at the Jay Treaty, seized over 300 American ships in one year and refused to receive American minister **Charles Cotesworth Pinckney**.

1797

May 31   C. C. Pinckney, John Marshall, and **Elbridge Gerry** were appointed to secure a commercial treaty with France. On Oct. 18, the commissioners were approached by three French **agents** (designated **X, Y, and Z**) who demanded a bribe and were refused. No treaty was made.

1798

Spring   **Undeclared war** began with France because of French seizures of American shipping. The war ended with the Convention of 1800.

July 2   Washington was called out of retirement to command the army, with Hamilton his second in command.

July   The army and navy were greatly expanded. A faction in the Federalist Party led by **Timothy Pickering** urged war, but public opinion was divided.

1799

Feb. 18   Adams nominated **William Vans Murray, Oliver Ellsworth**, and Patrick Henry (replaced by **William R. Davie**) to make a treaty with France. The result was the **CONVENTION OF 1800** (Treaty of Morfontaine, Sept. 30, 1800), which abrogated the Treaty of 1778 with France. During his administration, Adams had rid the United States of an entangling alliance and had avoided war.

The Rise of Political Parties, 1791–1801

There is considerable dispute as to when political parties arose in the United States. As early as 1791, politicians supporting Hamilton began to call themselves **Federalists** and those backing Jefferson and Madison adopted the name **Republicans** (or **Democratic-Republicans**). Voting in Congress was generally on a sectional rather than a party basis, and not until late in the 1790's did the two-party system exist in most of the states.

1791

Oct. 31 Madison started the *National Gazette*, (**Philip Freneau**, editor) to attack Hamilton's program. Hamilton retaliated through the *Federalist Gazette of the United States*, founded in 1789 (**John Fenno**, editor). In 1792, even Washington was unable to reconcile Hamilton and Jefferson.

1793

Apr.–May About 40 **Democratic Societies** sprang up in support of the French Revolution and Citizen Genêt. The societies corresponded with each other but did not constitute a political party.
Dec. 31 Jefferson resigned as Secretary of State when Washington began to side with Hamilton.

1794

Jan. 3 Madison proposed trade discrimination against Great Britain in order to gain middle-state support. This marked the emergence of a party structure in Congress, with Madison the Republican leader.
Nov. Washington attacked the Democratic

Societies for sympathizing with the Whisky Rebellion, thereby establishing himself as a Federalist.

1795

Jan. 31 Hamilton retired as Secretary of the Treasury but continued to influence the government. Cabinet reorganization led to an all-Federalist Cabinet with **Timothy Pickering** (Mass.) the new Secretary of War.
Spring Opposition to the Jay Treaty helped the rise of the Republican Party.

1796

Mar. When Washington refused to release papers on the Jay Treaty to the House, Madison introduced a resolution calling the refusal unconstitutional.
Mar. 8 In *Hylton v. U.S.*, the Supreme Court declared that a federal tax on carriages was constitutional. This was the first time the Supreme Court had ruled on the constitutionality of an act of Congress.
Sept. 17 **WASHINGTON'S FAREWELL ADDRESS**, written with the aid of **Hamilton**, came out strongly against political parties and "permanent alliances." Washington declared that he would not run for a third term, thereby setting a precedent.

3-2 Pinckney Treaty, 1795

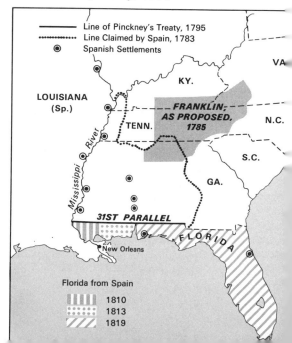

Dec. 7 Presidential election: John Adams, a Federalist, was elected President with 71 electoral votes to 68 for Jefferson, a Republican. It was the first election conducted even partially on a party basis. Parties, however, were still not organized in every state, and there were no party platforms.

1798

June–July The Federalists, fearful of French revolutionary ideas expressed by editors of Republican newspapers and concerned about the number of foreigners joining the Republican Party, passed four ALIEN AND SEDITION ACTS. The Naturalization Act (June 18) increased residence for naturalization to 14 years. It was repealed in 1802. The Alien Act (June 25) allowed the President to deport aliens suspected of being dangerous or treasonable. Never enforced, it expired June 25, 1802. The Alien Enemies Act (July 6) allowed deportation or imprisonment of enemy aliens. Since no war was declared, the act never went into effect. The Sedition Act (July 14)—proposed by Senator James Lloyd (Md.) and Rep. Robert G. Harper (S.C.) and approved by Adams—provided severe punishments for "false, scandalous, and malicious" statements against the government. It expired Mar. 3, 1801.

July Matthew Lyon, Republican Congressman from Vermont, made a libelous newspaper statement against President Adams. He was convicted in circuit court and sentenced to four months in jail and a $1,000 fine. Altogether 15 indictments and 10 convictions stemmed from the Sedition Act. Leading the prosecution were Secretary of State Timothy Pickering and Justice Samuel Chase.

Nov. 16–Dec. 24 The Alien and Sedition Acts united the Republicans. Jefferson and Madison drew up the KENTUCKY AND VIRGINIA RESOLUTIONS, which defended the state-rights theory of government and called the acts unconstitutional. The Kentucky Resolution (Jefferson) stated that unconstitutional acts of the government were void and that each state could determine its own course. The Virginia Resolution (Madison) simply said that the states could take action.

1799

June 15 New Hampshire passed a resolution against those of Kentucky and Virginia.

Nov. 22 SECOND KENTUCKY RESOLUTION (Jefferson) called for a state or states to nullify unconstitutional federal laws.

1800

May Federalist caucus nominated John Adams for President and Charles Cotesworth Pinckney for Vice President. Republican caucus selected Jefferson and Aaron Burr. A schism developed in the Federalist Party when Adams dismissed James McHenry, Secretary of War, and Timothy Pickering, Secretary of State, both Hamilton supporters. John Marshall was named Secretary of State.

May 10 Land Act reduced minimum purchase of public land to 360 acres and allowed purchases on credit.

Summer A two-party system went into operation. States such as Massachusetts and Virginia adopted a statewide system of voting for Presidential electors and thereby encouraged the rise of parties. There were Federalist and Republican parties in each state.

Nov. 17 Congress convened in Washington for the first time. Pierre Charles L'Enfant drew up the plan of the city; the White House and the Capitol were started in 1792–94, burned by the British in 1814, and completed after the War of 1812.

Dec. 3 Presidential election: the states cast their votes for electors at different times during the fall. New York went narrowly for Jefferson. When the Republicans carried South Carolina in Dec., they won the election. The vote was Jefferson and Burr, 73; Adams, 65; Pinckney, 64; Republicans swept the House 69–36.

1801

Jan. 20 Adams appointed John Marshall as Chief Justice of the Supreme Court.

Feb. 17 Hamilton used his influence in the House to turn the election from Burr to Jefferson.

Feb. 27 The **Judiciary Act**, designed to maintain Federalist control of the courts, reduced the Supreme Court to five justices and created 16 circuit judgeships. Adams made the final "midnight appointments" on Mar. 3, just before leaving office.

Republican Rule, 1801–1810

Jefferson in Office: Domestic Affairs, 1801–1805

1801

Mar. 4 **JEFFERSON'S INAUGURAL ADDRESS** sought to conciliate the opposition. In it, he called for a limited federal government, strong states, and economy in public expense. He recommended "honest friendship with all nations, entangling alliances with none." His Cabinet included **James Madison**, Secretary of State, and **Albert Gallatin**, Secretary of the Treasury. While President, (1801–05), Jefferson removed over 200 Federalists from office, thereby setting a precedent for the spoils system under Jackson. Although the Republicans reversed many of the steps taken by the Federalists, they also continued many Federalist policies.

Dec. 8 Jefferson, an advocate of simplicity, sent his first annual message to Congress in writing instead of appearing in person. Not until Woodrow Wilson did a President again deliver his annual message in person.

1802

Mar. 8 Repeal of Judiciary Act of 1801.

Mar. 16 A national military academy was established at **West Point**, N.Y.

Apr. 6 Excise duties, including the Whisky Tax, were abolished as part of Gallatin's policy of economy. The national debt dropped from $83 million to $45 million 1800–11.

Apr. 14 Naturalization Act reduced from 14 to 5 the years of residence required for naturalization.

Apr. 29 Judiciary Act restored the Supreme Court to six; six circuit courts were to be run by one Supreme Court justice and one district judge each.

1803

Feb. 24 **Marbury v. Madison**: President John Adams had appointed **William Marbury** justice of the peace in the District of Columbia (a "midnight appointment"). When Secretary of State Madison refused to deliver his commission, Marbury asked the Supreme Court for a **writ of mandamus** requiring Madison to give him the commission. Chief Justice Marshall declared that Marbury had a right to the commission but said that the Supreme Court could not issue a writ of mandamus. He thereby declared Section 13 of the Judiciary Act of 1789 unconstitutional, the first time the Supreme Court had taken such a step. The court would not call another act of Congress unconstitutional until the Dred Scott Case (1857).

Mar. 1 **Ohio** was admitted to the Union with the provision that the federal government retained its lands within the state but granted $\frac{1}{20}$ of the proceeds for roads to the Ohio Valley and $\frac{1}{36}$ for schools in Ohio. This system was followed with other states.

Dec. 12 The **Twelfth Amendment** (ratified Sept. 25, 1804) proposed a separate electoral vote for President and Vice President to avoid a tie as in 1800.

1804

Feb. 25 The first caucus of Republicans in the Congress chose a Republican ticket of **Jefferson** and **George Clinton**.

Mar. 12 Federal District Judge **John Pickering** of New Hampshire was impeached as part of the Republican attack on Federalists in the courts and removed from office on grounds of insanity.

Mar. 26 **Public Land Act** reduced the size of tract for minimum purchase of public land to 160 acres and the price to $1.64 per acre.

Apr. 25   Burr was defeated for governor of New York partly as a result of Hamilton's campaign against him.

Winter–Spring   The **Essex Junto**, made up of Federalists in Essex County, Mass., who feared loss of New England's power, and led by **Timothy Pickering**, made vague plans to set up a northern confederacy of New England, New York, and New Jersey. Their plans, which hinged on the election of Aaron Burr as governor of New York, who was to join them, collapsed when Burr killed Hamilton in a duel (July 12).

Dec. 5   Presidential election: Jefferson was reelected President with 162 electoral votes to 14 for **Charles C. Pinckney**.

1805

Mar. 1   Federalist Supreme Court Justice **Samuel Chase** was impeached by the House for his partisanship in the Sedition Act trials but was acquitted in the Senate. The trial was part of Jefferson's effort to curb the power of the Federalist court.

Summer   Republican split occurred between the supporters of Jefferson and Madison and the "**Quids**," led by **John Randolph** (Va.). The "Quids" considered Jefferson's national policies—such as the Louisiana Purchase—unconstitutional.

Jefferson in Office: Western and Foreign Affairs, 1801–1807

1801

Under Presidents Washington and Adams, the United States had paid tribute to the Barbary States (Algiers, Morocco, Tripoli, and Tunis) in order to secure immunity. On May 14, 1801, the **Pasha of Tripoli** declared war on the U.S., in order to get increased tribute, forcing Jefferson to give up plans of dismantling the fleet. A favorable peace treaty was signed June 4, 1805, after four years of naval fighting, but the U.S. paid tribute to the other Barbary states until 1816.

May   Jefferson heard of Spain's secret sale of Louisiana to France (by the Treaty of San Ildefonso, Oct. 1, 1800) and feared that France would threaten the western border of the U.S. The problem was resolved in 1803 by the **LOUISIANA PURCHASE**.

Oct. 1   Preliminaries to the **Peace of Amiens** between France and Great Britain left Napoleon free to build an empire in the New World.

1802

Napoleon sent an army to **Santo Domingo** to put down a Negro uprising led by **Toussaint L'Ouverture**. The failure of the expedition prompted Napoleon to abandon his imperial plans in the New World.

Oct. 16   Spain, still occupying Louisiana, suspended the American right to deposit goods at New Orleans before shipping them elsewhere. Though Spain restored the right in Apr., 1803, the action led to clamor in the U.S. for war.

1803

Jan. 12   Jefferson sent **James Monroe** to France to offer $10 million for New Orleans and West Florida.

Apr. 11   The day before Monroe arrived in Paris, **Talleyrand**, French Foreign Minister, offered all of Louisiana to U.S. minister **Robert Livingston**. Monroe and Livingston then agreed (Apr. 30) to buy Louisiana for $15 million (almost $4 million of it debts). Boundaries ran roughly along the continental divide and down the Mississippi River, but it was unclear whether the purchase, which doubled the size of the U.S., included Texas and West Florida.

June 20   Jefferson gave instructions to **Meriwether Lewis** and **William Clark** for an expedition to the west.

Oct. 20   The Senate approved the treaty in spite of strict-construction opposition from Federalists and old Republicans such as John Randolph.

Nov. 30   Spain ceded Louisiana to France, which in turn ceded it to the U.S. on Dec. 20.

1804

Mar. 26   District of Louisiana and Territory of Orleans were established.

May 14 Lewis and Clark began their ascent of the Missouri River. They wintered near Bismarck, N.D.

May 20 Jefferson established a collection district at Mobile as a first step in annexing West Florida. Monroe, in Spain, failed to buy West Florida.

1805

Apr. Lewis and Clark continued west, sighting the Pacific Ocean on Nov. 7 and returning to St. Louis on Sept. 23, 1806.

Aug. 9 Zebulon M. Pike set out to explore the sources of the Mississippi River. He returned to St. Louis in Apr., 1806, without finding the true source.

Dec. 3 Jefferson threatened war with Spain over West Florida.

1806

Aug. Pike set off to explore the Arkansas River. He reached Pueblo, Col., and sighted Pike's Peak. After nearly starving, he and his party were rescued by the Spanish.

Aug. Aaron Burr made plans for an expedition down the Mississippi River. When Jefferson issued an order against the expedition (Nov. 27), Burr fled and was arrested for treason. His plans are unknown, but he may have planned to take such states as Kentucky and Tennessee away from the Union.

1807

Aug. 3–Sept. 1 Burr Treason Trial at Richmond, Va., was heard by Chief Justice

3-3   The Louisiana Purchase and Western Exploration

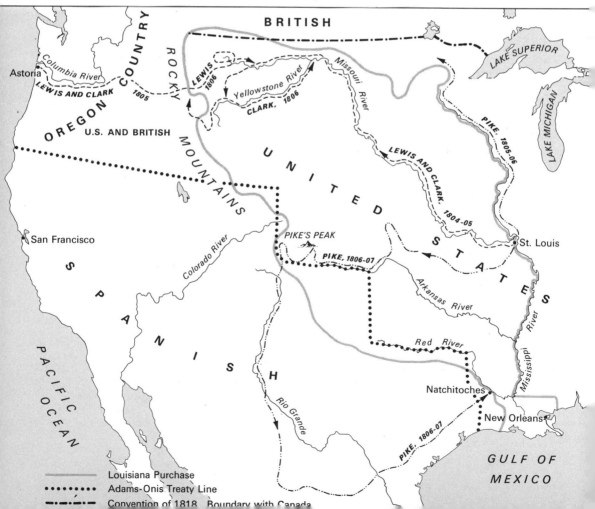

Louisiana Purchase
Adams-Onis Treaty Line
Convention of 1818 Boundary with Canada

Marshall in circuit court; he ordered Jefferson to testify, but the President refused. Marshall declared Burr innocent because he was not present when the overt act (the start of the expedition) took place.

American Neutrality, 1803–1810

1803

May 18   War between France and Great Britain was renewed. In the years that followed, Presidents Jefferson and Madison sought to preserve American neutral rights through economic pressure on the belligerents but in the end were unsuccessful.

1805

July 23   *Essex* **Case:** British Court of Appeals declared that an American vessel carrying goods from Spain to Spanish Cuba by way of the U.S. was violating the British **Rule of 1756**, according to which trade not open in peace was not open in war. (Spain had not allowed American ships to carry goods between Cuba and Spain during peace but allowed it in wartime because the British had driven the Spanish ships from the seas.) In the *Polly* **decision** (1800) the British had considered such a voyage legal because it was "broken" at the U.S. Now the British were calling it a continuous voyage.

1806

Jan. 25   Secretary of State Madison reported that British ships, often waiting outside U.S. harbors, seized many American ships after the *Essex* decision. He also attacked the British for **impressment** of American seamen. The British claimed the right to stop any American ship and seize any British subject aboard.

May 16   The British declared a blockade of the coast of Europe from the Elbe River to Brest.

Nov. 21   **Berlin Decree.** Napoleon, who controlled most of continental Europe, declared the British Isles under blockade.

Dec. 31   Treaty with Great Britain, signed by **James Monroe** and **William Pinckney,** made so few concessions to America's neutral rights that Jefferson refused to submit it to the Senate.

1807

Jan. 7   **British Order in Council** barred all shipping from the coastal trade of France.

June 22   The British warship *Leopard* asked permission to search the *U.S.S. Chesapeake* for deserters (the first attempt to impress seamen from an American warship). When the *Chesapeake* refused, the *Leopard* fired, killing three, then boarded the *Chesapeake* and removed four men. War loomed as indignation swept the U.S.

July 2   Jefferson ordered British warships out of U.S. ports.

Dec. 17   Napoleon's **Milan Decree** said that any ship that allowed itself to be searched by Great Britain would be treated as though it were British property.

Dec. 22   **EMBARGO ACT** prohibited U.S. or foreign vessels from leaving the U.S. for foreign ports. The act was opposed in New England, where merchants wanted to go on trading with Europe even though they lost ships.

1808

Apr. 17   Napoleon's Bayonne Decree ordered the seizure of all American ships in French harbors.

Dec. 7   **Presidential election:** hostility to the embargo brought Federalists back into power in New England. **James Madison** was elected President with 122 electoral votes to 47 for **Charles Cotesworth Pinckney,** a Federalist, and 6 for **George Clinton,** nominated by Eastern Republicans.

1809

Jan. 9   **Enforcement Act** authorized port collectors to seize goods apparently on their way to a foreign country. Hostility to the Embargo was strongest in the New England states.

Mar. 1   NON-INTERCOURSE ACT repealed the Embargo and opened trade with all nations except France and Great Britain. The President could resume trade with either of the latter if it repealed its acts violating American neutral rights.

Apr. 19   Encouraged by promises of the British minister to the U.S., Madison authorized trade with Great Britain.

Aug. 9   Madison reinstituted the Non-Intercourse Act against Britain when it failed to repeal the Orders in Council.

1810

Mar. 23   Napoleon's Rambouillet Decree ordered the seizure of U.S. ships entering French harbors.

May 1   MACON'S BILL NUMBER 2 allowed commerce with Great Britain and France but called for renewal of Non-Intercourse with either one if the other repealed its offensive decrees. Madison was continuing Jefferson's policy of economic pressure.

Aug. 5   Cadore Note: the French Foreign Minister, the Duc de Cadore, announced that France had repealed the Berlin and Milan decrees (effective Nov. 1, 1810) on the assumption that the British would repeal their Orders in Council or that the United States would "cause their rights to be respected."

Oct. 27   Madison announced the annexation of **West Florida**.

Nov. 2   Madison notified the British that Non-Intercourse would be restored in three months if the Orders were not repealed. He was too hasty, for France did not repeal its decrees and the British refused to repeal their orders.

The War of 1812, 1811–1815

The Coming of War, 1811–1812

1811

Mar. 2   The Non-Intercourse Act was applied to the British as impressment of Americans increased.

May 16   The American frigate *President,* ordered to protect American ships from impressment, badly defeated the British corvette *Little Belt* off the northeast coast of the U.S.

June–July   Indian raids increased in the west when Shawnee Chief **Tecumseh** and his brother the **Prophet** organized Indian resistance to white settlers.

Nov. 4   Congress convened. The House came under the control of young **"WAR HAWKS"** (as John Randolph called them) **Henry Clay** (Ky., Speaker), **John C. Calhoun** (S.C.), **Langdon Cheves** (S.C.), **Peter B. Porter** (N.Y.), **Felix Grundy** (Tenn.), and **Richard M. Johnson** (Ky.).

Nov. 7   BATTLE OF TIPPECANOE: William Henry Harrison, Governor of Indiana Territory, defeated the Indians at the junction of the Tippecanoe and Wabash rivers and destroyed their capital. Frontiersmen increasingly blamed the British for Indian trouble.

Nov. 29   Debate started over Porter's report in the House calling for military preparations for war with Great Britain with John Randolph ridiculing the "War Hawks" and Grundy, Clay, and Johnson speaking in their behalf.

1812

Feb. 6   Congress authorized a 50,000-man volunteer force in response to Madison's request for national defense.

Apr. 4   90-day embargo was placed on all ships in American harbors.

May 18   A Congressional caucus of Republicans nominated **Madison** for President.

May 29   New York antiwar Republicans nominated **DeWitt Clinton** for president.

June 1   Madison's war message listed four reasons for war: violation of the American flag, blockade of American shipping, impressment of seamen, and Indian raids instigated by the British.

June 16 Britain repealed the Orders in Council because of economic depression brought on by American trade restrictions.

June 18 Congress, unaware of the British action, **declared war**. The vote in the House was as follows:

	Yea	Nay
Maritime states: N.Y., N.J., Mass., Conn., and R.I.	11	33
Frontier New England and middle states: N.H., Vt., Pa., and Md.	28	8
Southern states: Va., N.C., S.C., and Ga.	31	8
Western states: Ohio, Ky., and Tenn.	9	0
	79	49

Historians have disagreed on the causes of the war: maritime rights (Henry Adams), Indian attacks (Julius W. Pratt), loss of western markets (George R. Taylor), and party politics and ideas of national honor (Bradford Perkins).

The Canadian Campaign, 1812–1814

1812

The Americans planned attacks on Canada from Detroit, Lake Ontario, and Lake Champlain.

Aug. 16 Gen. **William Hull** surrendered Detroit to Gen. Brock of the British. He was later convicted by a court martial of cowardice.

Oct. 13, Nov. 28 American attacks on Canada from Niagara failed.

Nov. 19 Gen. **Henry Dearborn** was unable to attack Canada from Lake Champlain when his militia refused to cross into Canada.

1813

Jan. 22 Gen. **William Henry Harrison**, in charge in the West, decided to wait for the

3-4 The War of 1812

U.S. to gain control of Lake Erie after heavy losses at the battle of Frenchtown.

Apr. 27 Americans burned **York** (Toronto), the capital of Upper Canada.

May 27 Col. **Winfield Scott** captured Fort George across the Niagara River, but the British prevented him from following up his success.

Sept. 10 In the **BATTLE OF LAKE ERIE**, Commodore **Oliver Hazard Perry** defeated six British ships at Put-in-Bay, Ohio, at the western end of the lake and sent the famous message: "We have met the enemy and they are ours." Lake Erie henceforth was in American hands.

Sept. 18 The British abandoned Detroit.

Oct. 5 **Battle of the Thames River**: Harrison moved into Ontario and defeated the British and Indians. When the Indian confederacy collapsed, the American northwest was secured.

Oct. 25 **Battle of Chateaugay River**: after advancing from Plattsburg, N.Y., the Americans skirmished with the British and fell back to Lake Champlain.

Nov. 11 **Battle of Chrysler's Farm**: after moving down the St. Lawrence River from Sacketts Harbor, Lake Ontario, Gen. John P. Boyd's regulars were routed by the British about 90 miles from Montreal. Gen. James Wilkinson then sent the American forces into winter quarters.

Dec. 30 The British burned Buffalo.

1814

July 5 Gen. Jacob Brown defeated British regulars at **Chippewa Plain** across the Niagara River.

July 25 **Battle of Lundy's Lane**, across the Niagara, ended in a draw. The Americans withdrew to the U.S. on Nov. 5.

Sept. 6 Gen. George Prevost and 11,000 British drove American forces into a defensive position at **Plattsburg**. At the **Battle of Lake Champlain** (Sept. 11), Capt. **Thomas MacDonough**, with a fleet of 14 ships, defeated the British fleet opposite Plattsburg. Henceforth Lake Champlain was under American control. Prevost was forced back to Canada.

Naval and Coastal Campaigns

1812

Since the U.S. Navy included only three first-class warships (the *President*, the *United States*, and the *Constitution*), it was decided to scatter and to harass the British.

Aug. 19 The ***Constitution*** destroyed the *Guerrière* off Nova Scotia.

Oct. 25 The *United States* captured the *Macedonian* off the Madeira Islands.

Dec. 29 The *Constitution* destroyed the *Java* off Brazil and received the name of "Old Ironsides."

1813

The British gradually extended a **blockade** to include the entire coast south of Rhode Island. Chesapeake Bay was a British naval base. The British exempted much of New England, hoping for secession, but when that failed they extended the blockade there in April, 1814.

June 1 The *Shannon* defeated the *U.S.S. Chesapeake* outside Boston Harbor. The last words of American Capt. **James Lawrence** "Don't give up the ship!" became the battle cry of the fleet.

1814

With the defeat of Napoleon in Europe the British were free to mount a major attack on the U.S.

Mar. 28 The *U.S.S. Essex* was captured by the British off Valparaiso after a year of raiding and destroying British merchantmen in the Pacific.

Aug. 19 Gen. Robert Ross landed 4,000 British troops near Washington. On Aug. 25, the British burned **Washington**.

Sept. 12 British troops landed near **Baltimore**.

Sept. 13–14 The British bombarded **Fort McHenry**, which defended Baltimore harbor. The strong defense inspired **Francis Scott Key**, detained on a British ship, to write *The Star-Spangled Banner*. On Sept. 15, the British withdrew.

The Southwest Campaign, 1813–1815

1813

Apr. 15   Gen. James Wilkinson captured **Mobile**.

Aug. 30   Creek Indians attacked Fort Mims, Ala., killing half the defenders.

Nov.   Gen. Andrew Jackson organized 2,000 Tennessee volunteers and attacked Creeks in eastern Alabama.

1814

Mar. 27   Jackson defeated the Creeks at **Horseshoe Bend** in eastern Alabama.

Aug. 9   By the Treaty of Fort Jackson, the Creeks agreed to leave most of Alabama.

Nov. 7   Jackson captured **Pensacola** in Spanish Florida and then returned to New Orleans.

Nov. 26   British fleet brought 7,500 regulars under Gen. **Edward Pakenham** to attack New Orleans.

1815

Jan. 8   **BATTLE OF NEW ORLEANS**: the British attacked **Jackson's** defensive position five miles below New Orleans and were defeated with losses of 2,000. American losses were less than 100. The battle made Jackson a national hero and contributed to American national spirit.

The Peace of Ghent

1812

Sept. 21   Czar Alexander I of Russia offered to mediate, but the British declined.

1814

Aug. 8   **Peace discussions** began at **Ghent**, Belgium, with **John Quincy Adams, Henry Clay, James A. Bayard, Jonathan Russell,** and **Albert Gallatin** representing the United States.

Dec. 24   **PEACE OF GHENT** was signed.

The U.S. failed to get any settlement of neutral rights issues, and Britain failed to get a neutral Indian state in the northwest. All territory was restored. A commission of arbitration was set up for the northeast boundary. The Senate ratified the Peace of Ghent on Feb. 15, 1815.

Opposition to the War, 1812–1815

1812

June 26   Fasts and protests were staged in Massachusetts against the war.

July 2   Connecticut refused to call out her militia for federal use; Massachusetts also refused on Aug. 5.

Aug. 5   "Rockingham (County, N.H.) Memorial" of **Daniel Webster** denounced the war.

Dec. 2   **Presidential election: Madison** defeated **DeWitt Clinton**, who was supported by Federalists and antiwar Republicans, by 128 electoral votes to 89. Clinton carried all of New England except Vermont, as well as New York, New Jersey, Delaware, and part of Maryland.

1813

Dec. 17   Congress passed an embargo to prevent New England from supplying the British in Canada. The embargo and the British blockade helped the rise of manufacturing in New England. New England had specie ($1.7 million in 1811 and $7.3 million in 1814) but refused to use it to purchase war bonds.

1814

Apr. 14   The embargo was repealed, but a protective tariff was established to help new industry.

Sept.   Massachusetts militia, which had been used briefly in the war, was formally withdrawn.

Dec. 15   **HARTFORD CONVENTION** met with representatives from Massachusetts, Connecticut, and Rhode Island and unofficial delegates from New Hampshire and Vermont.

The Convention adjourned on Jan. 15, 1815, and issued a report urging the states to resist unconstitutional acts of Congress (such as calling out state militia). It also asked for seven constitutional **amendments**:

1. **representation** and direct taxation to be in proportion to the number of free persons (which would end the ⅗ rule);
2. no **state** to be admitted to the Union without a ⅔ vote of Congress;
3. no **embargo** to be imposed for more than 60 days;
4. no **commercial interdiction** without a ⅔ vote of Congress;
5. no declaration of **war** without a ⅔ vote of Congress;
6. no **naturalized** citizen to hold federal office, and
7. no **President** to serve two terms and successive Presidents not to come from the same state.

Peace brought an end to the proposals of the Hartford Convention, which served further to discredit the Federalist party.

Postwar Nationalism, 1815–1825

Economic Policies

After the war, the Republicans began to adopt many of the national economic policies that had been used by the Federalists in the 1790's. Efforts in 1811 to recharter the first Bank of the United States were defeated by old Republican arguments that it was unconstitutional. Congress resented the fact that 18,000 of the 25,000 shares were owned abroad. In 1814, the wartime need for a national bank prompted Secretary of the Treasury Dallas to ask for a new B.U.S.

1815

Jan. 20   Madison vetoed a bill for a new B.U.S.

Mar. 3   Congress established a **standing army** of 10,000.

July 3   Convention with Great Britain kept American ships out of the West Indies.

Dec. 5   Madison called for a national bank, internal improvements, and a protective tariff. Republicans had modified their strict construction views and were called **National Republicans**.

1816

Jan. 8   **Calhoun** introduced a bill for a second B.U.S. capitalized at $35 million (⅘ from private funds, ⅕ from federal funds), a deposi-

tory for U.S. funds without paying interest, whose notes would serve as legal tender. It was to pay a bonus of $1.5 million to the government.

Apr. 10   The **B.U.S. BILL** passed Congress strongly supported by **Clay** but opposed by **Webster**. The combined vote of both houses was:

	Yea	Nay
New England and the middle states	44	53
Southern and western states	58	30

Apr. 27   **TARIFF ACT** established duties of 25 per cent on woolen and cotton goods and 30 per cent on iron products in order to counteract dumping of British goods on the American market. The primary goal of the tariff, however, was revenue, not protection. The vote in the House:

	Yea	Nay
Northeast (Pennsylvania and states north)	64	15
Southeast	16	35
West	13	4

Calhoun and some Southerners supported the tariff for nationalist reasons; **Webster** opposed it as hostile to the shipping interests of New England.

Dec. 4   **Presidential election: James Monroe** (Va. Republican) defeated **Rufus King** (N.Y. Federalist) 183 electoral votes to 34.

1817

Jan. 1   The second B.U.S. started operation. Its central office was in Philadelphia, and eventually there were 25 branches. **William Jones**, first president, ran the bank very ineptly.

Mar. 1   Calhoun's **BONUS BILL** passed Congress. It set aside the bonus and stock dividends from the B.U.S. for federal roads. New England opposed partly from fear of losing population; New York and Pennsylvania, which would benefit from east-west travel, were in favor of it; the rest of the country was divided.

Mar. 3   **Madison** vetoed the Bonus Bill as unconstitutional.

Mar. 4   Inauguration of James Monroe; **John Quincy Adams** was his Secretary of State and **William H. Crawford** his Secretary of the Treasury.

May–Sept.   Monroe's northern tour symbolized the **"ERA OF GOOD FEELINGS,"** a term coined by the Boston *Columbian Centinel*. There was little Federalist opposition to the Republican Party after 1816, but factions developed among Republicans.

July 4   Construction of the **ERIE CANAL** between Albany and Buffalo, N.Y., was begun. When completed in Oct., 1825, it helped open the northern part of the northwest and stimulated the growth of New York City.

1818

Apr. 18   **Navigation Act** closed American ports to British vessels arriving from the West Indies (in retaliation for British restrictions). Accordingly, British tonnage entering the U.S. shrank from 175,000 tons in 1817 to 36,000 tons in 1819.

Oct.   When the government demanded $2 million of its deposits in the B.U.S. to pay money due on the Louisiana Purchase, the bank began to call in its loans to state banks. The B.U.S. had loaned too freely to these banks, which had grown from about 200 in 1815 to over 300 in 1819, and they in turn had loaned too freely to speculators. (Money owed the government for land in 1815 was $3 million; in 1819, the sum was $22 million.)

1819

The **PANIC OF 1819** was caused fundamentally by overexpansion in land and manufacturing in 1816–18 and by loss of European markets. The immediate cause was the decision of the B.U.S. to call in loans. Hostility to the B.U.S. was extreme in the west, where **Thomas Hart Benton** (Mo.) called it "The Monster" and where state laws delayed debt payment.

1820

Apr. 24   **Land Act** abolished the credit system and reduced the minimum land price to $1.25 an acre and the minimum purchase to 80 acres.

Dec. 6   **Presidential election: Monroe** received all but one of the 232 electoral votes cast.

1821

Mar. 2   **Relief Act** was passed to make it easier for settlers to pay the government for western land.

1822

May 4   **Cumberland Road Tolls Bill** was vetoed by Monroe on grounds that it was unconstitutional. The bill called for repairs on the road to be paid for by tolls.

June 24   British West Indies trade was opened to American ships with certain restrictions. The next year, British West Indian vessels were allowed to trade with the U.S.

Nov. 25   **Nicholas Biddle** was elected president of the B.U.S. starting its "Golden Age," 1823–29.

1824

Mar. 30–Apr. 2   Tariff debate: in the House **Clay** defended his **"American System"** of protective tariffs and internal improvements. **Webster,** representing New England commercial interests, supported free trade. **Robert Hayne** (S.C.) argued that the tariff was unfair to the South, which imported manufactured goods. The vote in the House (Apr. 16) on the protective tariff was:

	Yea	Nay
New England	15	23
Middle states	57	9
South	4	56
Northwest (Kentucky included)	29	0
Southwest	2	14

Apr. 30   General Survey Act was passed to let the President make surveys for national roads and canals. The House vote:

	Yea	Nay
New England	12	26
Middle states	37	26
South	23	34
West	43	0

May 22   The first truly protective **TARIFF ACT** was passed, which put a duty of 33⅓ per cent on woolen and cotton goods.

The Marshall Court, 1801–1835

The decisions of the Marshall Court (**JOHN MARSHALL**, Va., Chief Justice) served to strengthen the national government.

1803   *Marbury v. Madison* (see p. 59) established judicial review.

1810   *Fletcher v. Peck* ruled that the Georgia legislature could not repudiate the corrupt **Yazoo land sale** of the previous legislature because such a repudiation violated the contract clause of the Constitution. It was the first time that the Supreme Court had declared a state act unconstitutional.

1816   In *Martin v. Hunter's Lessee,* the Court upheld the Judiciary Act of 1789 granting the Supreme Court the right to overrule state courts.

1819   In *The Trustees of Dartmouth College v. Woodward,* the Court held that New Hampshire had violated a **contract** when it changed a royal charter and put Dartmouth College under state control. The decision helped protect private corporations from adverse state actions.

1819   *Sturges v. Crowninshield* declared a New York **bankruptcy law** relieving debtors

a violation of the contract clause of the Constitution.

1819   *McCulloch v. Maryland* denied the right of a state to tax a branch of the B.U.S. Drawing on Hamilton's theory of loose construction, Marshall declared the Bank constitutional as "incidental" to the power to collect taxes and regulate commerce. Maryland might not tax the bank because the "power to tax" involved "the power to destroy."

1821   *Cohens v. Virginia* upheld a Virginia court ruling that convicted the Cohen brothers for selling lottery tickets. Marshall repudiated the extreme Virginia position—expressed by Judge **Spencer Roane**—that the Supreme Court could not review state court decisions.

1824   Aaron Ogden, who held a New York steamboat monopoly, tried to prevent Thomas Gibbons, who held a federal license, from running a steamboat from New York to New Jersey. In *Gibbons v. Ogden* the Court sided with Gibbons and argued that a federal law was superior to a state law. Marshall also gave a broad interpretation of the **commerce clause** of the Constitution, thereby helping free transportation from state monopoly grants.

The Missouri Compromise

1815–20   **Cotton production** spread from South Carolina to Alabama and Mississippi aided by the **cotton gin** (invented 1793) that made processing easier. Production rose from 178,000 bales in 1810 to 335,000 bales in 1820. The number of **slaves** increased from 1.2 million to over 1.5 million in the period 1810–20. Between 1816 and 1819, Indiana, Mississippi, Illinois, and Alabama were admitted to the Union. The number of slave and free states was 11 each, but free states outvoted slave 105–81 in the House.

1819

Feb. 13   Congressman **James Tallmadge** (N.Y.) proposed an amendment to a bill admitting Missouri to the Union. This amendment would have prohibited further importation of slaves into Missouri and would have freed slave children when they reached 25. After passing the House, the amendment was defeated in the Senate (Feb. 27).

Mar. 2 Arkansas Territory was organized with slavery in spite of efforts to prohibit slavery there, and the Missouri bill without the Tallmadge amendment passed the Senate but not the House.

1820

Jan. 3 Bill to admit **Maine** passed the House.

Feb. Senator **Rufus King** (N.Y.) argued that Congress could keep slavery out of Missouri under its power to regulate the territories. Republicans feared that Tallmadge, DeWitt Clinton, and King, all of New York, were plotting to form a Federalist-Republican anti-Southern party. There was actually no plot, but Martin Van Buren (N.Y.) was sufficiently alarmed to start seeking an alliance with the South.

Feb. 16 The Senate voted to consider the admission of Maine and Missouri in one bill.

Feb. 17 Senator **Jesse B. Thomas** (Ill.) proposed an amendment admitting Missouri as a slave state but prohibiting slavery in the Louisiana Purchase north of 36°–30′ latitude. It passed the Senate on Feb. 18.

Mar. 1 The House passed a bill to admit Missouri without slavery.

Mar. 2 The **Joint Committee**, partly selected by **Henry Clay**, Speaker of the House, agreed to accept the Thomas amendment. The House vote, by sections, was:

	Yea	Nay
Northeast	14	79
Southeast	59	0
Northwest	0	8
Southwest	17	0
	90	87

Mar. 3 The **Missouri-Maine bill** was signed into law.

July 19 The **Missouri constitution** included a provision to exclude free Negroes from the state.

3-5 *The Missouri Compromise, 1820–1821, and Admission of States, 1791–1821*

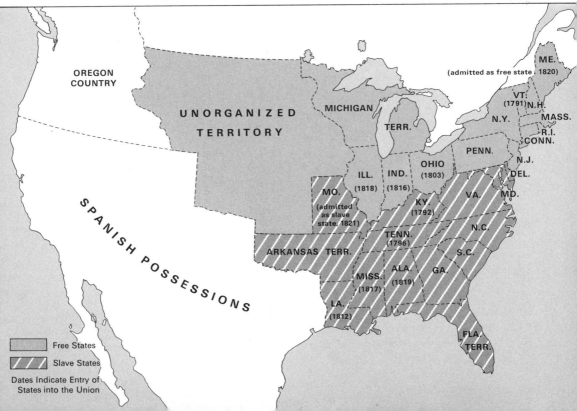

Dec. 12   The Senate evaded the issue raised by the Missouri constitution by accepting it with the provision that the Senate did not assent to any clause that violated the right of citizens of each state to the privileges and immunities of citizens of the several states.

1821

Feb.   Henry Clay arranged a similar evasion in the House.

Mar. 2   The "Second Missouri Compromise" passed both the House and the Senate. On June 26 the Missouri Legislature agreed to the compromise, and on Aug. 10 Missouri was admitted to the Union. However, in 1825, Missouri repudiated the second compromise by refusing to admit free Negroes.

Foreign Affairs, 1815–1825

1815

May 10–Aug. 5   An American fleet under Capt. **Stephen Decatur** forced the **Barbary states** to stop molesting American ships in the Mediterranean. Foreign policy in this period tended to be nationalistic and expansionist.

1817

Apr. 28–29   RUSH-BAGOT AGREEMENT: Acting Secretary of State **Richard Rush** and British minister to the U.S. **Charles Bagot** exchanged notes agreeing to limit American and British vessels on the Great Lakes to one or two small ships. The agreement was ratified by the Senate.

Dec. 26   Monroe empowered Gen. **Andrew Jackson** to pursue hostile Indians across the border into Florida. When Jackson wrote Secretary of War Calhoun asking for Presidential permission to seize Florida, Monroe was silent; Jackson interpreted this to mean approval.

1818

Apr. 7   Jackson seized St. Mark's and later Pensacola (May 24) in Florida, executing two British traders suspected of inciting disorder among the Indians.

May 10   Henry Clay urged the U.S. to recognize the newly independent Latin American republics, but Secretary of State John Quincy Adams delayed because he did not want to irritate Spain while he was negotiating for Florida.

Oct. 20   By the **CONVENTION OF 1818** with Great Britain, Americans could land to cure fish on Labrador and Newfoundland. The northern boundary of the U.S. was to run along the **49th parallel** to the Rocky Mountains. **Joint occupation of Oregon** was arranged for 10 years.

Nov. 28   The Spanish were outraged at Jackson's actions, but Adams blamed Spain for not controlling Florida.

1819

Jan. 18–Feb. 8   Congress debated whether to censure Jackson for his Florida expedition, but no action was taken. All Cabinet members but Adams wanted Monroe to discipline Jackson, but he refused. The public considered Jackson a hero.

Feb. 22   ADAMS-ONÍS TREATY (Transcontinental Treaty): Adams signed a treaty with Spanish minister Don **Luis de Onís** in which Spain ceded East and West Florida to the U.S., the U.S. gave up all claims to Texas, and Spain gave up its claim to Oregon; the western boundary of the Louisiana Purchase was defined; and the U.S. assumed $5 million of American claims against Spain. The treaty was ratified on Feb. 22, 1821.

1821

Mar. 6   Greek War for Independence from the Ottoman Empire began. Enthusiasm in the U.S. for Greece was high.

Sept. 16   Russian Ukase warned foreign vessels not to come within 100 miles of Alaska north of the 51st parallel, thus extending Russian claims to land within Oregon. Russia had earlier established Fort Ross north of San Francisco. The U.S. did not protest the Ukase until July, 1823.

1822

June 19　The U.S. recognized Colombia and later Mexico (Dec. 12). Chile, Argentina, Brazil, and Peru received diplomatic recognition in 1823–26.

Oct. 20　At the Congress of Verona, France asked the rest of the **Quadruple Alliance** (or "Holy Alliance"—Austria, Russia, and Prussia) to intervene in the New World to restore the Spanish and Portuguese empires and in Spain to restore the monarchy.

1823

Spring　When France invaded Spain to restore the monarchy, the U.S. was afraid that the Quadruple Alliance would next invade the New World. In Great Britain, Foreign Secretary **George Canning** was alarmed at possible French economic rivalry in South America.

Aug. 16–20　Canning proposed to Richard Rush, U.S. minister in London, a joint Anglo-American action against the Quadruple Alliance with both nations renouncing future possession of new Latin American republics.

Oct. 9　Despairing of an American agreement, Canning secured the **Polignac Memorandum** from the French ambassador to Great Britain in which France promised not to intervene in Spanish America. Jefferson and Madison urged Monroe to accept Canning's proposal. John Quincy Adams, however, feared British designs on Cuba and convinced Monroe to take an independent stand.

Nov. 27　Adams sent a note warning Russia that the U.S. would not allow the transfer of Spanish colonies (i.e., California) to Russia or to any other power.

Dec. 2　**THE MONROE DOCTRINE**: Adams wrote much of the statement, but Monroe was thought responsible for including it in his annual message. The Doctrine said:

1. the American continents were not "subjects for **future colonization** by any European powers";
2. the U.S. would not **intervene** in European matters (Greece);
3. the U.S. would consider any attempt by Europe to **extend its "system** to ... this hemisphere as dangerous to our peace and safety";
4. the U.S. would not **intervene** in "existing colonies"; and
5. the U.S. would consider any attempt to **control the new republics** as unfriendly to the U.S.

The Monroe Doctrine summarized ideas that had grown up since 1789—two hemispheres, no transfer, non-intervention, and non-entanglement. Canning was annoyed and felt rightly that the Polignac Memorandum had more influence on Latin America than the Monroe Doctrine.

1824

Apr. 17　**U.S.–Russian Treaty** set the boundary of Alaska at 54°–40′ latitude rather than 51° latitude and withdrew the 100-mile restriction of 1821.

Leading Figures of the Early National Period

JOHN QUINCY ADAMS (Braintree, Mass., 1767–Washington, D.C., 1848), sixth President of the United States. Son of President John Adams.

1778–80　Studied abroad.

1781–83　Served as a secretary to Francis Dana in Russia and then to his father in Great Britain.

1787　Was graduated from Harvard.

1794　Minister to the Netherlands.

1797　Minister to Prussia.

1801　Practiced law in Boston.

1803　Was elected to the U.S. Senate as a Federalist.

1804–08　Adopted Republican views and resigned from the Senate.

1809　Minister to Russia.

1814　Served on peace commission at Ghent.

1815 Minister to Great Britain.

1817–25 Secretary of State.

1819 Negotiated Adams-Onís Treaty.

1823 Helped write the Monroe Doctrine.

1825 Was elected President by the House of Representatives.

1825–29 As President, called in vain for a nationalist program.

1828 Defeated for the Presidency by Jackson.

1831–48 Congressman.

1836–44 Opposed the gag rule, which prevented debate on slavery.

1848 Collapsed on the floor of Congress and died two days later.

ALBERT GALLATIN (Geneva, Switzerland, 1761–Astoria, N.Y., 1849), Secretary of the Treasury.

1780 Emigrated to the U.S.

1784 Set up a store on the Pennsylvania frontier.

1788 Contributed radical ideas to the Harrisburg Convention called to consider revisions of the U.S. Constitution.

1790–92 Served in the Pennsylvania legislature.

1793 Was elected to the Senate but was ousted by Federalists because he had not been a citizen nine years.

1794 Sympathized with the Whisky Rebellion but counselled moderation.

1795–1801 Democratic-Republican Congressman and party leader. Helped create Ways and Means Committee in the House.

1801–14 Secretary of the Treasury. Wars thwarted his efforts to cut expenses; tried in vain to save the B.U.S.

1814 Served as a peace commissioner at Ghent.

1815 Negotiated U.S.-British Trade Treaty.

1816–23 Minister to France.

1826–27 Minister to Great Britain.

1831–39 President of the National Bank of New York.

JOHN MARSHALL (Germantown, Va., 1755–Philadelphia, 1835), Chief Justice of the Supreme Court.

1772–76 Self-educated in the law.

1776–81 Rose to Captain in the revolutionary army.

1782 Was elected to the Virginia assembly.

1783 Began law practice.

1788 Defended the Constitution at the Virginia ratifying convention.

1789–97 A leading Federalist in Virginia.

1797 One of the XYZ commissioners to France.

1799 Was elected to Congress.

1800 Secretary of State.

1801–35 Chief Justice of the U.S. Supreme Court, whose decisions dominated. His constitutional views were that the Constitution emanated from the people, that the courts were to be used to enforce the Constitution, that national power was supreme, and that property was to be defended.

1803 Established the court's power of judicial review in *Marbury v. Madison.*

1807 In the Burr treason trial he interpreted treason narrowly.

JAMES MONROE (Westmoreland County, Va., 1758–New York City, 1831), fifth President of the United States.

1774–76 Attended the College of William and Mary.

1776–78 Served as an officer in the Revolution and was wounded at Trenton.

1780–83 Studied law with Jefferson.

1782 Member of the Virginia legislature. Served again in 1787–90.

1783–86 Served in the Confederation Congress.

1786 Delegate to the Annapolis Convention.

1788 Opposed the Constitution at the Virginia ratifying convention.

1790–94 U.S. Senator; supported Jefferson and opposed Hamilton.

1794–96 Minister to France.

1799–1802 Governor of Virginia.

1803 Cooperated with Robert R. Livingston in securing the Louisiana Purchase.

1804 Failed to secure Florida from Spain.

1805–06 Negotiated the Monroe-Pinkney Treaty with Great Britain, although it was never submitted to the Senate.

1808 Was defeated by Madison for the Republican Presidential nomination.

1811 Governor of Virginia.

1811–17 U.S. Secretary of State. Served concurrently as Secretary of War, 1814–15.

1817–25   President of the U.S.

1819   Acquired Florida through negotiated treaty.

1822   Vetoed the Cumberland Road bill.

1823   Monroe Doctrine was issued.

1829–30   Chairman of Virginia constitutional convention where he supported the conservatives.

Statistical Tables

Table 17.
Population
(thousands)

	1790	1800	1810	1820
Total	3,929	5,297	7,224	9,618
Negro	757	1,002	1,378	1,772
Negro Slaves	698	893	1,191	1,538
Free Negroes	60	109	186	234
New England	1,009	1,233	1,472	1,660
Middle Atlantic	959	1,403	2,015	2,700
Old Northwest	—	51	272	793
South Atlantic	1,852	2,286	2,675	3,061
Southwest	109	335	786	1,358

3-6 Population, 1800

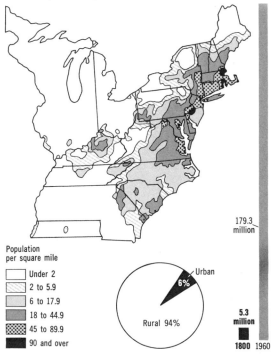

Population per square mile

- Under 2
- 2 to 5.9
- 6 to 17.9
- 18 to 44.9
- 45 to 89.9
- 90 and over

Urban 6%

Rural 94%

179.3 million

5.3 million

1800 1960

Table 18.

Exports

(millions of dollars)

	Total exports including re-exports	United States merchandise	Finished manufactures[a]	Cotton[a]	To Europe including re-exports	General imports
1791	19	19	—	—	10	23
1795	48	40	—	—	31	70
1800	71	32	—	—	41	91
1805	96	42	2	9	61	121
1810	67	42	2	15	47	85
1815	53	46	2	18	38	113
1816	82	65	—	24	59	147
1818	93	74	—	31	68	122
1820	70	52	3	22	48	74
1825	91	67	6	37	59	90

[a] United States merchandise only

Table 19.

Banks

(millions of dollars)

1820	Capital	Circulation	Deposits
Bank of the U.S.	35.0	3.6	6.6
State Banks[a]	102.1	40.6	31.2

[a] Number of state banks: 30 in 1801, 88 in 1811, 208 in 1815, and 307 in 1820.

Table 21.

U.S. government expenditures

(millions of dollars)

	Total	Interest on Debt
1792	5.1	3.2
1795	7.5	3.2
1800	10.8	3.4
1805	10.5	4.1
1810	8.2	2.8
1815	32.7	5.8
1820	18.3	5.1
1825	15.9	4.4

Table 20.

U.S. government debt

(millions of dollars)

1791	75
1795	81
1800	83
1805	82
1810	53
1815	100
1820	91
1825	84

Table 22.

U.S. government receipts

(millions of dollars)

	Total	Customs
1792	3.7	3.4
1795	6.1	5.6
1800	10.8	9.1
1805	13.6	12.9
1810	9.4	8.6
1815	15.7	7.3
1820	17.9	15.0
1825	21.8	20.1

Table 23.
Wholesale commodity price index
(1900–1914 = 100)

1790	90
1795	131
1800	129
1805	141
1810	131
1815	170
1820	106
1825	103

Table 24.
Public land sales
(thousands of acres)

1800	68
1805	582
1810	286
1815	1,306
1818	3,491
1820	814
1825	999

Table 25.
Number of vessels entered in U.S. ports
(selected years, 1790–1825)

1790	606
1795	637
1800	804
1805	1,010
1808	586
1810	989
1813	351
1815	918
1818	917
1820	880
1825	974

Table 26.
Manufactures

1788	First jenny power cotton mill at Beverly, Mass.
1790	First Arkwright cotton mill set up by Samuel Slater at Pawtucket, R.I.
1813	Boston Manufacturing Co. at Waltham, Mass. the first to combine all cotton manufacturing in one factory.
1815–20	Cotton manufacturing was hard hit by British imports after the War of 1812. Most Arkwright mills failed.
1822	Lowell, Mass., cotton manufacturing mills were started. Factory workers were drawn in from farms.

1810	Value of all manufactures	$127 million
	Textiles manufactures	47
	Iron manufactures	14
	Manufactures of hides and skins	18
	Distilled and fermented liquors	17
	Pennsylvania	32
	Massachusetts	18
	New York	15
	Virginia	11
	Cotton spinning mills	87 mills
	Woolen mills	14 mills
	Cotton consumed (1805)	500 bales
1816	Capital invested in manufacturing	$100 million
	Cotton manufacturing	40
	Woolen manufacturing	12
	Value of woolen manufactured goods	19
	Cotton consumed (1815)	90,000 bales

THE JACKSON ERA, 1824–1848

PART 4

The Rise of the Democratic Party, 1822–1828

The Election of 1824

1821 In late Dec., **Calhoun** announced his candidacy for President.

1822 The Tennessee legislature nominated **Andrew Jackson** for President (July). The Kentucky legislature nominated **Henry Clay,** while New England rallied behind the candidacy of Secretary of State **John Quincy Adams.**

1823–25 Jackson served as U.S. Senator from Tennessee.

1823 **William Crawford** of Georgia, Secretary of the Treasury, was in the lead for the Presidential nomination until he was struck by paralysis in Sept.

1823 Clay was chosen Speaker of the House (Dec.).

1824

Feb. 24 The Republican Congressional caucus, only a minority present, nominated Crawford for President.

Mar. 4 The Pennsylvania convention nominated Jackson. Calhoun withdrew and became Vice Presidential candidate on both the Jackson and the Adams tickets. Both Jackson and Adams supported the protective tariff and internal improvements. Jackson had voted for the tariff of 1824 and the Survey Bill, and Adams backed Clay's American System.

Dec. 1 **Presidential Election: Jackson** received 153,544 popular votes (99 electoral—mostly from the South, the West, Pennsyl-

vania, and New Jersey). **Adams** had 108,740 (84 electoral—from New England and most of New York); Crawford had 46,618 (41 electoral—from Georgia and Virginia); and Clay had 47,136 (37 electoral—from Ohio, Kentucky, and Missouri).

1825

Jan. 9 Since no candidate had a majority, the election went to the House, which was to select among the three leading candidates. Clay, who had been eliminated, promised to support Adams. Representative George Kremer (Pennsylvania) accused Adams and Clay of making a "**corrupt bargain,**" a charge that became more plausible later when Adams appointed Clay as Secretary of State. The charge was probably unfounded—Adams was more sympathetic to Clay's American System than was Jackson—but Jackson used the charge as a campaign issue, 1825–28.

Feb. 9 The House elected Adams President, **Adams** carried 13 states, **Jackson** 7, and **Crawford** 4. Clay helped swing Kentucky, Ohio, and Missouri over to Adams.

The Adams Administration, 1825–1828

1825

Mar. 4 Adams' cabinet included **Henry Clay** as Secretary of State and **Richard Rush** as Secretary of the Treasury. Adams refused to use his power of patronage and removed only 12 men from federal posts while he was in office.

Dec. 5   Congress convened with four political groups in evidence: 1. the **administration** bloc led by Webster and Clay; 2. the **Jacksonians** such as Senators **Thomas Hart Benton** (Mo.) and **John H. Eaton** (Tenn.); 3. the **Calhoun** followers; and 4. the **Jeffersonians** led by **Martin Van Buren** (N.Y.), and **John Randolph** (Va.). Adams' national proposals drove the Calhoun and Van Buren blocs toward the Jacksonians. Vice-President Calhoun and Postmaster General John Mc-Lean appointed anti-Administration men to office. In Jan., 1826, Calhoun and others established the **United States Telegraph,** edited by **Duff Green** in Washington as an anti-Administration newspaper.

Dec. 6   Adams' **first annual message,** strongly nationalistic, called for federal roads and canals, a national university, an astronomical observatory and a standardized system of weights and measures.

Dec. 26–Apr. 22, 1826   The **PANAMA DEBATE.** President Adams nominated two delegates to an inter-American Congress to be held in Panama. He and Clay believed that the U.S. should strengthen its position in the western hemisphere.

1826

Jan. 11   The Senate Committee on Foreign Relations disapproved the plan to send delegates to Panama. In the debate that ensued, Van Buren and others reunited the old **New York–Virginia alliance** against Adams. They argued that participation in the Congress would be an "entangling alliance" that might involve the U.S. in efforts to free Cuba or in antislavery discussions. The opposition to Adams included future Jacksonian Democrats Thomas Hart Benton, John Eaton, Hugh L. White (Tenn.), and Levi Woodbury (N.H.), as well as Calhoun and Van Buren.

Mar. 14   The Senate ratified the appointments of Richard Anderson and John Sergeant to attend the Congress, which met in June and July with only Colombia, Mexico, Peru, and Guatemala represented. Anderson had died enroute, and Sergeant had not yet

reached Panama when the Congress adjourned.

Dec. 26   Van Buren promised to bring the Jeffersonians of New York and Virginia (the latter led by **Thomas Ritchie**) over to Jackson, who had gained control of Congress in the fall elections.

1827   ORGANIZATION OF THE DEMOCRATIC PARTY: correspondence among Van Buren, Calhoun, Ritchie and Major William Lewis, who represented Jackson in Nashville, Tenn., led to the rise of the Democratic Party. A chain of **Democratic newspapers** was organized, including the *United States Telegraph,* Ritchie's Richmond *Enquirer,* Amos Kendall's *The Argus of the West* (Ky.), and Isaac Hill's *New Hampshire Patriot.* The organization was called variously "the Jacksonians," "the Opposition," or (rarely) "the Democratic Republicans." The term "Democratic Party" did not emerge until Jackson was President, and even then the Jacksonians claimed the title "Republican."

July 30   Harrisburg, Pa., **Convention on Tariff Protection** demanded higher tariffs on textiles, other manufactured goods, and raw materials such as hemp.

1828

Jan. 31   Jacksonians introduced a high tariff bill in the House. They reasoned that the South would reject the bill because of its high rates on manufactured goods and the Northeast would reject it because of the high rates on raw materials. The bill would not pass, but the middle states, which favored tariff protection, would be grateful to the Jacksonians and would support Jackson in 1828. Since the Democrats felt sure of the South, middle-state support would assure Jackson's victory.

Apr. 23   The Jacksonian **"TARIFF OF ABOMINATIONS,"** passed the House. The regional distribution of the vote was:

	Yea	Nay
Northeast	71	29
Southeast	5	48
Northwest	17	0
Southwest	12	17
	105	94

May 13 The Tariff passed the Senate. New England, led by Daniel Webster, supported the bill because manufacturing was now more important there than shipping. The South, led by Calhoun, opposed tariff protection. On May 19, the tariff became law.

Dec. 19 *South Carolina Legislative Resolves* declared the tariff unconstitutional, and the *South Carolina Exposition and Protest,* written secretly by Calhoun to accompany the *Resolves,* called the tariff unconstitutional, defended the compact or state-rights theory of government, and recommended state nullification of acts of Congress. Calhoun, who expected to follow Jackson as President, was unwilling to join the radicals who were talking of disunion.

The Election of 1828

1816–30 By **DEMOCRATIC VOTING CHANGES,** many states abolished property qualifications for voting. Ten states either revised their constitutions or wrote new ones. Indiana, Illinois, Alabama, Maine, and Mississippi granted white manhood suffrage. Missouri, New York, Massachusetts, and Connecticut extended the vote to taxpayers (very close to manhood suffrage). The New York constitutional convention of 1821 enlarged the number of eligible voters by 30 per cent in spite of **Chancellor James Kent,** who spoke eloquently against liberalizing the suffrage. Historians in the past, however, exaggerated the broadening of democracy— in many states most adult males had been able to vote even before 1816. Nor did an increase in the number of voters necessarily realign parties.

1824–28 POPULAR ELECTION OF THE PRESIDENT: Between 1824 and 1828 the number of states where the legislature chose presidential electors dropped from six to two (Delaware and South Carolina). Party organization became easier as most states chose electors on a statewide ticket rather than by districts: seven states used districts in 1824; only four did so in 1828.

1824–28 INCREASED POPULAR VOTE: The number voting for President rose from 0.4 million in 1824 to 1.2 million in 1828. The percentage of white adult males voting in 1828, however, was not particularly high. In 16 states out of 22 the percentage was actually lower than it had been at some earlier election. The increase was caused by population growth, the added number of states with popular choice of electors, and renewed interest in politics. The truly great increase in voting took place in the election of 1840.

1825 The Tennessee legislature nominated Jackson for President (Oct.). Vice President John C. Calhoun became the Vice Presidential candidate on that ticket.

1828 The **National Republicans** nominated **Adams** for President and **Richard Rush** for Vice President (Jan.).

1828 Presidential campaign: The Democrats were well organized in Ohio, Indiana, Kentucky, Missouri, Illinois, Virginia, North Carolina, New Hampshire, Pennsylvania, and New York. The "Albany Regency" under Van Buren, the "Richmond Junto" under Ritchie, and the New Hampshire machine under Isaac Hill were particularly effective. Mudslinging was extreme. **Jackson** won the Presidential election (Dec. 3) with 647,286 popular votes (178 electoral) to 508,064 (83) for **Adams.** Jackson's 56 per cent of the popular vote was not equaled until the twentieth century. Jackson carried New York, Pennsylvania, the South and the West. While Democrats claimed that the National Republicans were simply old-time Federalists, both parties had support from former Federalists.

The Age of Jackson, 1829–1837

The New Administration

1829

Feb. Jackson arrived in Washington. As Jacksonians poured into the capital, Democratic editors such as Isaac Hill, Gideon Welles (Conn.), Mordecai M. Noah (N.Y.), and Amos Kendall (Ky.) laid plans for the coming administration.

Mar. 4 The **Inauguration of Jackson** attracted 15,000–20,000, many of whom stampeded through the White House. In his inaugural address Jackson vaguely promised to safeguard the rights of states. Principal members of the Cabinet were **Van Buren**, Secretary of State, **Samuel D. Ingham** (Pa.), Secretary of the Treasury, and **John H. Eaton** (Tenn.), Secretary of War. The **"KITCHEN CABINET,"** an unofficial body to advise Jackson, became more important than the regular Cabinet. Van Buren was the leader; other important members were **Amos Kendall,** fourth auditor of the Treasury, **Isaac Hill,** second comptroller of the Treasury, Maj. **William B. Lewis** (Tenn.), and **Francis P. Blair,** Sr., who later became editor of the Washington *Globe.*

1829–37 Jackson demonstrated the **power of the Presidency** by vetoing 12 bills, more than all his predecessors combined and more than any President until Andrew Johnson. He became a symbol for the Democratic Party, whose members were known as Jacksonian Democrats.

Mar. SPOILS SYSTEM: Jefferson had appointed party faithfuls to office but the practice had lapsed by 1829. Jackson, who believed in **"rotation in office,"** used the spoils system on a large scale, but in eight years removed only 10 per cent–20 per cent of all federal office holders. The spoils system came into use at the state level, notably in New Hampshire and New York, where U.S. Senator **William Learned Marcy** coined the phrase "to the victor belongs the spoils."

Spring PEGGY EATON AFFAIR: on Jan. 1, 1829, John H. Eaton married Margaret (Peggy) O'Neale Timberlake, formerly a barmaid and the wife of a naval purser who had committed suicide supposedly because of Peggy's affair with Eaton. When the Calhouns and others refused to entertain the Eatons, a Cabinet rift developed with Jackson and Van Buren (both widowers who defended Peggy) on one side and the Calhoun forces on the other. This affair helped cause a reorganization of the Cabinet.

Dec. 8 In his first annual message Jackson promised to distribute surplus revenue and questioned the constitutionality of the B.U.S.

1830

Jan. 13–27 WEBSTER–HAYNE DEBATE: Senator Samuel A. Foot's (Conn.) resolution to limit the sale of western land (proposed Dec. 29, 1829) was taken up for debate, and Senator Thomas Hart Benton (Mo.) replied that the plan would restrict the growth of the west. On Jan. 19, Senator **Robert Y. Hayne** (S.C.) backed Benton and accused the East of wanting to check the growth of the West. Senator **Daniel Webster (Mass.)** denied Hayne's charge in his first reply to Hayne (Jan. 20). Hayne's first reply (Jan. 21) was to defend state-rights and nullification and accuse New England of disloyalty during the War of 1812. In his famous second reply (Jan. 26) Webster denied the state-rights theory and maintained that only the federal government exercised sovereign power over the people. He ended with the statement, "Liberty and Union, now and forever, one and inseparable." In his second reply (Jan. 27) Hayne expounded the compact, state-rights theory of government; Webster, in a final rebuttal, maintained that the government rested on the people, not on the states. The Foot resolution was finally tabled May 21. The debate marked the failure of a possible Southeast-Northwest alliance against the Northeast.

Apr.–May The Senate rejected the appointments of editors **Henry Lee, Mordecai M. Noah,** and **Isaac Hill.** The attack led by John Tyler and Calhoun contributed to the split between the Calhoun and Van Buren wings of the Democratic Party.

Apr. 13 Since the **Jefferson Day Dinner** was planned to glorify Jefferson's state-rights position, Jackson's toast shocked everyone: "Our Union: It must be preserved." Calhoun replied: "The Union, next to our liberty, most dear." In May, Jackson learned that in 1818 Calhoun had wanted to punish him for his conduct in Florida, and the party rift grew wider.

May 27 **MAYSVILLE ROAD VETO:** Jackson vetoed a bill authorizing federal funds for a road to be built in Kentucky on the grounds that it was a local road. By the end of 1830 Jackson had vetoed four internal-improvement bills, but nonetheless his administration spent more money on such improvements than any previous administration.

May 28 **INDIAN REMOVAL ACT** called for moving Indians westward across the Mississippi River. The removal policy, started by Secretary of War Calhoun in 1823, was now vigorously carried out. By 1835 all Indians except the Seminoles had ceded their lands east of the Mississippi: the **Choctaw,** 1830; **Sauk** and **Fox** tribes, 1831; **Creeks,** 1832; **Chickasaw,** 1832; and **Cherokee,** 1835. The Indian removal involved great fraud and cruelty. The **Seminoles,** who resisted, went to war in 1835 and were not subdued until 1843. The **Bureau of Indian Affairs** was set up in 1836.

May 29 **Preemption Act,** proposed by Benton, allowed settlers ("squatters") on public land to secure 160 acres at $1.25 an acre. Benton's **Graduation Act,** calling for a gradual reduction of the price of unsold public land until it was free, passed the Senate but was tabled in the House in May, 1830. Preemption was in effect until 1842. Meanwhile, Thomas Skidmore and George Henry Evans, speaking for eastern workingmen's groups, demanded free land for the eastern worker.

May 31 Jackson approved $130,000 in federal funds for the **Cumberland Road** because it was a "national" project.

Oct. 5 **West Indies trade** was reestablished when the British removed tonnage restrictions. In 1825 the British had closed the West Indies carrying trade to American ships. Secretary of State Van Buren, who used a softer line toward the British than had Adams and Clay, achieved an important trade victory.

Dec. 7 **The Washington _Globe_** (Francis P. Blair, Sr., editor), backed by Van Buren and the Kitchen Cabinet, began to publish in order to offset the _U.S. Telegraph,_ which was pro-Calhoun.

1831

Apr.–Aug. Reorganization of the Cabinet: when Van Buren and Eaton resigned over the Peggy Eaton affair, Jackson called for the resignation of the entire cabinet. The new cabinet, under the influence of Van Buren, included **Edward Livingston** (La.), Secretary of State, **Roger B. Taney** (Md.), Attorney General, **Levi Woodbury** (N.H.), Secretary of the Navy, **Lewis Cass** (Mich.), Secretary of War, and **Louis McLane** (Del.), Secretary of the Treasury. When Calhoun blocked the appointment of Van Buren as minister to Great Britain (Jan. 25, 1832), it led to Van Buren's nomination for Vice President.

1830–32 **GEORGIA INDIAN AFFAIR:** for many years the Cherokee Indians in Georgia had been recognized as an independent nation. Settlers in Georgia, however, wanted the land, so the state began to push the Cherokee out. On Dec. 20, 1828, Georgia passed a law declaring Cherokee laws null and void after June 1, 1830. In Dec., the Supreme Court issued a writ of error to the state of Georgia declaring the state court decision to execute an Indian named **Tassel** illegal. (Tassel had murdered a fellow Cherokee within Cherokee territory.) Georgia ignored the writ and executed Tassel two days later. This was a form of nullification.

1831 **_Cherokee Nation v. Georgia:_** when the Cherokee asked the U.S. Supreme Court for an injunction restraining Georgia from exercising sovereignty within their land, Marshall refused on the grounds that the

Supreme Court lacked jurisdiction since the Cherokee were a "domestic dependent nation" and not a foreign state. Marshall, however, ended with the statement that the state had inflicted wrongs on the Indians.

1832 *Worcester v. Georgia:* a state law of 1830 ordered whites residing in Cherokee territory to obtain a state license. Samuel A. Worcester and Elizur Butler, missionaries, refused and were sentenced to jail. On appeal, Marshall declared the Georgia law unconstitutional because the federal government had exclusive jurisdiction in Indian territory. When Georgia defied the court, Jackson sided with the state.

Sept. 26 The **Anti-Masonic Party convention** in Baltimore nominated **William Wirt** (Va.) for President. This was the first third party in the U.S., it held the first political party convention, and it adopted the first party platform. The Anti-Masonic movement began with the disappearance of **William Morgan** in western New York after he had written an exposé of Freemasonry. By 1830 an Anti-Masonic Party had arisen in New York to oppose Jackson, who was a Mason.

Dec. 12 The **National Republican Convention** met in Baltimore and nominated **Henry Clay** (Ky.) for President and **John Sergeant** (Pa.) for Vice President.

1832

Apr. 6–Aug. 2 The **Black Hawk War** began when Chief Black Hawk led the dispossessed Sauk Indians back across the Mississippi River into northern Illinois. Abraham Lincoln served in the war, which ended with the final removal of the Sauk across the Mississippi River.

May 21–22 **Democratic Convention** in Baltimore nominated **Jackson** for President and **Van Buren** for Vice President. In order to prevent opposition to Van Buren the convention adopted the **⅔ rule**, which required that each nominee received ⅔ of the total vote of the convention. The rule was in effect until 1936.

Dec. 5 **Presidential election: Jackson** defeated **Clay** by 687,502 votes (219 electoral)

to 530,189 votes (49). **William Wirt**, the Anti-Masonic candidate, carried only Vermont (7 electoral votes). South Carolina gave its 11 votes to **John Floyd** of Virginia.

Nullification in South Carolina

In the struggle over nullification, the Jackson Administration had to choose between nationalism and state rights. See also the chronologies of the "Tariff of Abominations" and the South Carolina *Exposition and Protest* (pp. 78–79).

1830 The Democratic House rejected George McDuffie's (S.C.) bill to reduce the tariff (Feb.).

1831

July 4 Thomas Mitchell (S.C.), a strict constructionist, opposed nullification. He represented many Jeffersonian Republicans who were unwilling to support nullification.

July 26 Calhoun's **Fort Hill Address** (from his home in S.C.), defended the right of state interposition against federal laws (nullification).

1832

July 14 **Tariff Act**, still protective but slightly lower than that of 1828, was passed. Southern states were angry because the act was permanent and because it increased the duty on manufactured woolens and admitted cheap raw wool and flax free.

Aug. 28 Calhoun in a letter to James Hamilton, Jr., governor of South Carolina, reaffirmed his doctrine of nullification.

Oct. 22 Gov. Hamilton called a special session of the South Carolina legislature, which in turn called a special convention to consider the tariff.

Oct. 29 President Jackson alerted the forts in Charleston harbor, S.C.

Nov. 24 **SOUTH CAROLINA ORDINANCE OF NULLIFICATION** was passed by the State convention. It declared the tariffs of 1828 and 1832 null and void in South Carolina after Feb. 1, 1833, and threatened secession if the federal government used force. In Nov., the state legislature passed laws to enforce nullification.

Dec. 4   Jackson declared himself in favor of tariff reduction.

Dec. 10   Jackson's **PROCLAMATION TO SOUTH CAROLINA** (drafted by Edward Livingston) called the federal government supreme, nullification absurd, and "disunion by armed force" treason. Jackson assured members of Congress that he would use force to enforce the tariff.

Dec. 12   Calhoun was elected United States Senator from South Carolina.

Dec. 17   South Carolina resolutions denounced Jackson's proclamation. The state legislature also called for a meeting of the states to consider the federal-state relationship. Because most states, north and south, condemned nullification, the meeting was never held.

1833

Jan. 8   Administration bill calling for 50 per cent tariff reduction was proposed in the House.

Jan. 21   **Force Bill** in the Senate gave the President power to enforce his proclamation.

Jan. 21   South Carolina suspended the Ordinance of Nullification in anticipation of tariff reduction.

Feb. 12   Clay introduced a compromise tariff bill and secured Calhoun's support.

Feb.   Webster defended the Force Bill against Calhoun.

Mar. 1   **Clay's compromise tariff**, which passed the Senate, called for gradual rate reduction to 20 per cent by 1842. The South was for the bill, the North-central states were split, and the New England and Middle-Atlantic states opposed it. Webster, who opposed the bill, turned against Clay. The next day, the Compromise Tariff and the Force Act were signed into law by Jackson.

Mar. 3   Jackson used the pocket-veto to kill Clay's bill that would have distributed to the states proceeds from the sale of land.

Mar. 15   South Carolina rescinded the Ordinance of Nullification and three days later nullified the Force Act.

The Bank War, 1829–1837

The eight-year struggle over the B.U.S. revealed important political and economic conflicts in the U.S. and helped promote and form the American two-party system. It began in July, 1829, with the so-called New Hampshire Bank War. Isaac Hill and Levi Woodbury, leading Jacksonians there, complained to Secretary of the Treasury Samuel Ingham of mismanagement of the B.U.S. branch at Portsmouth. Criticism also was voiced against the branches in Louisiana and Kentucky. In his first annual message (Dec.), Jackson questioned the constitutionality of the B.U.S. An 1830 report of the House Ways and Means Committee, however, defended the B.U.S.

1832

Jan. 9   President **Nicholas Biddle** of the B.U.S. applied for recharter of the Bank even though the existing charter would not expire until 1836.

Jan.–July   Congressional debate over the B.U.S.: those defending the B.U.S. included Congressmen **George McDuffie** (S.C.) and **John Quincy Adams** (Mass.) and Senators **Daniel Webster** (Mass.) and **Henry Clay** (Ky.). They argued that the Bank had helped the U.S. reduce its debt, had sold U.S. bonds, and had checked inflation. The B.U.S. branches, they pointed out, provided an easy means of circulating money throughout the country. They denied that the Bank was a monopoly: it controlled only $\frac{1}{5}$ of the note circulation of the nation and $\frac{1}{3}$ of the deposits. Congressmen **Augustin S. Clayton** (Ga.), chairman of the House committee investigating the Bank, and **Churchill C. Cambreleng** (N.Y.) and Senators **Benton** (Mo.) and **Hill** (N.H.) led the attack on the B.U.S. They argued that the Bank was an unconstitutional monopoly that influenced politics and the press and had too many foreign stockholders. Western and debtor groups opposed the Bank because it curtailed loans to state banks, while hard money men, whose spokesman was **William M. Gouge,** a writer and editor on financial matters, argued that the Bank was inflationary.

June 11   The recharter bill passed the Senate 28–20.

July 3   The recharter bill passed the House. The sectional vote was:

	Yea	Nay
Northeast	66	30
Southeast	18	35
Northwest	11	5
Southwest	12	16
	107	86

July 10   Jackson vetoed the recharter bill. Aided by Amos Kendall, Roger B. Taney, and Levi Woodbury, he wrote a strong political document, calling the Bank a monopoly that took power away from the states and had too many foreign stockholders. Jackson, who argued that each branch of the government could determine constitutionality, called the B.U.S. unconstitutional and an agent of the "rich and powerful" against the people.

July 11   Webster spoke out against the veto, but the Senate failed to pass the bill over the veto.

Nov.   Jackson, backed by Kendall and Taney, suggested removal of the federal deposits from the B.U.S.

1833

Mar. 2   Clay and Calhoun supporters in the House put through a resolution calling for the continuation of federal deposits in the B.U.S.

Mar. 19   Jackson asked the Cabinet for opinions on the removal of the deposits, which was opposed by Secretary of the Treasury McLane.

June 1   Jackson appointed **William J. Duane** Secretary of the Treasury, but he also opposed the removal.

June 6–July 1   Jackson's tour of the Atlantic states went as far north as Concord, N.H.

Sept. 18   Jackson told the Cabinet that he planned to remove the deposits and on Sept. 23 replaced Duane with **Roger B. Taney.**

Oct. 1   Removal of deposits began. The Union Bank of Baltimore, the Girard Bank of Philadelphia, three banks in New York City, and two banks in Boston were the first "pet banks" to receive deposits. In all, 22 were selected to recieve deposits by the end of 1833, there was a total of 37 by 1836. Almost all "pet banks" were controlled by Jacksonians.

Oct.   Biddle began a contraction policy by calling in notes. A **business recession** followed, partly as a result of the removal of the deposits and partly as a result of Biddle's contraction policies. Business recovered by the spring of 1834.

Dec. 26–Mar. 28, 1834   Senate debate took place over Clay's **resolution to censure Jackson** for removing the deposits. Benton led the defense, but the resolution passed on Mar. 28.

1834

Apr. 15   Jackson protested the censure, which was finally expunged by the Senate on Jan. 16, 1837.

June 24   The Senate refused to ratify Taney's appointment as Secretary of the Treasury. **Levi Woodbury** then became Secretary of the Treasury, and **Taney** became Chief Justice in 1836.

June 28   Coinage Act raised the ratio between gold and silver from 15–1 (1792) to 16–1. Silver, undervalued, was driven out of circulation.

1836   On Feb. 18, the B.U.S. received a Pennsylvania charter, and on March 1 its federal charter expired.

The Final Jackson Years, 1834–1837

1834

Apr.   WHIG PARTY: *Niles' Weekly Register* and Henry Clay used the name Whig to describe the Anti-Democratic party, which was a coalition of **Anti-Masons** (William Wirt), **National Republicans** (John Quincy Adams), and **state-rights Democrats** (Calhoun and John Tyler of Virginia); it included **northeastern industrialists** and **merchants** (led by Webster), **western businessmen** and supporters of internal improvements (led by Clay), and **southern planters** and **urban moneyed interests.** Clay's American System best represented the Whig economic program.

Dec. 1   Jackson recommended reprisals on French property if the French continued to delay payment of claims by American citizens dating back to the Napoleonic Wars.

1834–36   Boom in land sales: federal land sales for 1831–36 totaled 46,394,000 acres compared to only 9,796,000 for 1821–30. Sales for 1835 were almost 13,000,000 acres and for 1836 were over 20,000,000 acres.

1834–36   Expansion of currency: currency in circulation, which totaled $124 million in 1834, exceeded $200 million in 1836 as western banks over-extended themselves.

1835

Apr. 25   France agreed to pay the claims if Jackson would tender a diplomatic apology.

May 20   Democratic National Convention named Van Buren for President and **Richard M. Johnson** (Ky.) for Vice President.

Oct. 29   The radical wing of the Jackson party received the name **"Loco-Focos"** when regular Democrats in New York City tried to break up a radical meeting by turning off the gas lights, at which point the radicals used the new-style matches ("loco-focos") to light candles. The Loco-Focos were urban eastern Democrats who took over the program of the Workingmen's Party: a 10-hour day, abolition of imprisonment for debt, opposition to the chartering of banks, and free public schools. Leaders included **Thomas Skidmore, Robert Dale Owen, George Bancroft, William Leggett.**

1836

Jan. 15   Jackson again urged reprisals against France and called for an expanded navy.

May 10   Jackson announced that the French had begun to pay their claims. British mediation was partly responsible.

Apr. 22   Benton's resolution demanding hard money for western land was rejected in the Senate.

July 11   The **SPECIE CIRCULAR** (ordered by Jackson, drafted by Benton, and issued by Woodbury) required gold or silver in payment for public land. The Circular reduced the sale of land and lowered confidence in western banks.

June 23   Distribution Act, introduced by Henry Clay, provided for the temporary deposit of surplus federal revenue with the states. In 1837 payments were discontinued because of the financial panic.

Fall   Presidential campaign: the **Whigs** held no convention but put up regional candidates: **Daniel Webster** (Mass.) and **Hugh L. White** (Tenn.). The **Anti-Masons** nominated **William Henry Harrison** (Ohio).

Dec. 7   Presidential election: Van Buren won with 765,483 votes (170 electoral from 15 states); **Harrison** had 549,567 (73 electoral from seven states, mostly Middle-Atlantic and western); **White** had 145,396 votes (26 electoral from Tennessee and Georgia); **Webster** had 41,287 votes (14 electoral from Massachusetts); **Willie P. Mangum** (N.C.) carried South Carolina with its 11 electoral votes. Richard M. Johnson failed to get a majority vote but was elected Vice-President by the Senate (the only Vice President so elected).

1837

Mar. 4   Jackson's **Farewell Address,** drafted by Taney, called for national unity, a limited federal government, and hard money, while opposing the B.U.S., monopoly, and privilege.

Democrats and Whigs, 1837–1848

Van Buren and the Panic of 1837

1837

Jan. The **Panic of 1837** started in the winter of 1836–37 after a two-year boom in land, railroads, canals, housing, slaves, and securities. The Specie Circular drained money from the East, and an English depression led English investors to withdraw American loans. The result was tight money and financial panic. The land and real-estate market collapsed, and by March, the price of cotton in New Orleans had fallen by almost one-half. Unemployment was heavy in New York City.

May 10 New York City banks suspended specie payments, setting off a wave of bank failures (over 600 in 1837).

1837–43 In the **depression**, the wholesale commodity price index fluctuated widely from 90 in 1834 to 114 in 1836; 110 in 1838, 75 in 1843, and 83 in 1845.

Sept. 4 **Special session of Congress:** in his message Van Buren blamed the depression on speculation and overextension of bank credit. He proposed that the government print temporary notes to pay its debts and give up depositing its funds in banks.

Sept. 14 **INDEPENDENT TREASURY BILL,** introduced in the Senate by **Silas Wright** (N.Y.), called for withdrawal of government funds from pet banks to federal depositories. Radical (Loco-Foco) Democrats supported the bill. Calhoun returned to the Democratic Party by supporting the bill. It was opposed by conservative Democrats and Whigs.

Oct. 12 Congress voted to issue up to $10 million in temporary Treasury notes.

Oct. 14 The House tabled the Independent Treasury bill, which was later rejected (June 25, 1838).

1838

May 21 The Specie Circular was repealed. To gain western support for the Independent Treasury Van Buren backed Benton's pre-emption and graduation plans. Whigs opposed the easy land policy.

1839

Dec. 6 **Whig Convention** in Harrisburg, Pa., nominated **William Henry Harrison** for President and **John Tyler** (Va.), formerly a state-rights Democrat, for Vice President.

1840

Mar. 31 Van Buren established a 10-hour working day for federal employees.

Apr. 1 The **Liberty Party,** which was abolitionist, nominated **James G. Birney** (N.Y.) for President and **Thomas Earle** (Pa.) for Vice President at its convention in Albany, N.Y.

May 5 **Democratic Convention** in Baltimore renominated **Van Buren** for President but left the Vice Presidential nomination up to the states. The platform opposed federal internal improvements, tariff protection, the B.U.S., and interference with slavery.

July 4 The **Independent Treasury System** was passed.

Fall **Presidential campaign:** the election of 1840 was the first modern election. For the first time each party was well-established throughout the nation, held a national convention, and rallied behind a single leader. The two-party system was better balanced than before; many conservative Democrats had joined the Whigs, and Calhoun was back with the Democrats. The Whigs in particular used modern political techniques: parades, placards, floats, and rallies. Capitalizing on Harrison's frontier background, they used the log cabin and the cider jug as campaign symbols and sang **"Tippecanoe and Tyler, too."** The percentage of adult white males voting shot up from about 56 per cent in 1828–36 to 78 per cent in 1840.

Dec. 2 **Presidential election:** Harrison won with 1,274,624 votes (234 electoral) to 1,127,781 for **Van Buren** (60) and 7,059 for the Liberty Party candidate, **James G. Birney.**

1841

Mar. 4   Harrison took office and appointed **Daniel Webster** as Secretary of State. The Cabinet was under the influence of Clay and Webster.

Apr. 4   After the **death of Harrison** from pneumonia, debate arose as to whether Vice President **John Tyler** would become President or merely assume the duties of the office. Tyler set a precedent by considering himself actually President.

The Tyler Administration, 1841–1845

1841

May 31   Special session of Congress began.

June 7   Clay outlined his program, which included repeal of the Independent Treasury, reestablishment of the B.U.S., and an increased tariff.

Aug. 6   Henry Clay's **Fiscal Bank bill** passed Congress. It called for a central bank, similar to the B.U.S., in the District of Columbia with branches in the states.

Aug. 13   Repeal of the Independent Treasury Act: for the next five years the government kept its money in state banks.

Aug. 16   Tyler vetoed the Fiscal Bank bill because it called for branches without state consent. The Senate failed to overcome the veto on Aug. 19.

Aug. 19   Bankruptcy Act (to replace the act of 1800) allowed debtors voluntarily to declare themselves bankrupt.

Sept. 4   Distribution-Preemption Act made preemption permanent. A squatter on government land could buy 160 acres without competition when the land was put on sale. Ten per cent of the proceeds from land sales went to the states in which the land was situated; the rest was to be distributed to all the states. Distribution would be repealed if tariff rates exceeded 20 per cent. Since the tariff soon went above 20 per cent, distribution never went into effect.

Sept. 9   Tyler vetoed a second Bank bill.

Sept. 11   The **Cabinet,** except Webster, **resigned** out of loyalty to Clay. The new Cabinet included strong state-rights men such as Abel P. Upshur of Virginia, Secretary of the Navy. Webster stayed on as Secretary of State. The rest of the Tyler Administration was marked by a struggle between Tyler and Clay and by frequent Cabinet shifts.

Oct.   The **Dorr Rebellion** was caused by a reform convention at Providence that set up a new Rhode Island constitution granting white manhood suffrage. Since 1663 Rhode Island had been ruled by the original charter, which granted suffrage to freeholders, or only one-half of the white adult males. In Mar., 1842, freeholders rejected proposals to enlarge the franchise. The reformers set up a new government with Thomas W. Dorr as governor. The freeholders thereupon called out the militia to put down the rebellion. Both sides appealed to President Tyler, who promised to intervene to support the regular government. Dorr's efforts to seize the state arsenal failed and the revolt collapsed in May. In Apr., 1843, the state relaxed its voting requirements. Dorr was sentenced to life imprisonment but was later released. The Supreme Court in *Luther v. Borden* (1849) upheld the use of militia to put down the rebellion.

Aug. 30   Tariff Act raised duties back to the 1832 level, partly to pay the national debt.

1843

May 8   Webster retired as Secretary of State and was replaced by **Abel Upshur.**

June   American Republican Party was formed in New York with a nativist program. In 1844 the American Republicans united with the Whigs and defeated the Democratic candidate for mayor of New York City. In Philadelphia severe Catholic-Protestant riots took place in 1844. The Native American Party held a national convention in July, 1845, but the movement waned until the 1850's.

Aug. 30   Liberty Party met in Buffalo, N.Y., and nominated **James G. Birney** for President and Thomas Morris (Ohio), for Vice President. The platform ignored Texas but opposed the extension of slavery.

1844

Mar. 6 **Calhoun** was named Secretary of State after Upshur was killed by an explosion on the *Princeton;* the appointment demonstrated the strong southern influence in the Democratic Party.

Apr. 27 Letters from **Henry Clay** and **Van Buren** were published in Washington, both opposing the annexation of Texas because it would mean war with Mexico. It was assumed that the two had come to a prior agreement to keep Texas and slavery out of the 1844 campaign. When Jackson heard of the Van Buren letter, he turned away from Van Buren and supported Polk for the Democratic nomination.

May 1 **Whig Convention** met in Baltimore and nominated Clay for President and **Theodore Frelinghuysen** (N.J.), for Vice President; there was no mention of Texas or of expansion.

May 27 **Democratic Convention** met in Baltimore. Van Buren led on the first ballot, but the ⅔ rule prevented his nomination. George Bancroft (Mass.), and Gideon J. Pillow (Tenn.), led the swing to **James K. Polk** (Tenn.), an expansionist Jacksonian, who was nominated on the ninth ballot. **George M. Dallas** (Pa.) was nominated for Vice President. Though Polk had been Speaker of the House, he was considered a dark-horse candidate. The platform called for the "reoccupation of Oregon and the reannexation of Texas."

May 27 Tyler Democrats in Baltimore nominated Tyler on a third party ticket, but he withdrew Aug. 20 and brought his followers back into the Democratic Party.

Fall **Presidential campaign:** the Democrats called for Texas and for "54°–40' or fight" on Oregon. Clay claimed that he did not oppose the annexation of Texas but wanted to avoid war and any sectional conflict over slavery.

Dec. 4 **Presidential election: Polk** won with 1,338,464 votes (170 electoral) to **Clay's** 1,300,097 (105) and **Birney's** 62,300. Birney took enough votes away from Clay in New York to give the state and the election to Polk.

1845

Jan. 23 Congress declared the Tuesday following the first Monday in November the uniform election day for Presidential elections.

Mar. 3 Congress for the first time passed a bill over a Presidential veto.

The Polk Administration, 1845–1848

Democratic party politics: Polk ignored the Van Buren wing of the Democratic Party in his Cabinet and appointed William L. Marcy, an anti-Van Buren Democrat from New York to be Secretary of War. He also set up a new party newspaper, the *Union,* in Washington. Patronage in New York went to conservative Democrats, known as "Hunkers" (because they "hungered" after office) rather than to the radical "Barnburners" (so uncompromising they would burn down the barn to get rid of the rats), who allied with the Loco-Focos. Secretary of the Treasury **Robert J. Walker** (Miss.) dominated the Cabinet as the Democratic Party came under the control of Southerners.

Dec. 2 In his annual message Polk called for a return to low tariffs and the independent treasury.

1846

July 30 The **Walker Tariff** reduced rates to about 25 per cent.

Aug. 3 Polk vetoed an important rivers and harbors bill on the grounds that the projects were mostly local. (He vetoed a similar bill in 1847.)

Aug. 6 The **INDEPENDENT TREASURY ACT** was passed. The government would henceforth put its money in depositories rather than state banks and would accept only gold, silver, or Treasury notes in payment of debts. The Independent Treasury remained in effect until 1920.

The Taney Court

Chief Justice of the Supreme Court **ROGER B. TANEY** (Md., 1836–64) presided over a court composed largely of agrarian Democrats appointed by Democratic Presidents. The Taney Court tended to defend the right of the popular majority to regulate private property —a shift from the Marshall Court, which had defended property rights.

1837 *Charles River Bridge v. Warren Bridge:* the Charles River Bridge Company had a Massachusetts charter to operate a toll bridge. When the legislature granted a charter (1828) to the Warren Bridge Company to build a competing bridge, the Charles River Company claimed its contract had been impaired. Taney ruled in favor of the second bridge, arguing that the legislature could do what was best for the **welfare of the community**. The decision helped business growth by encouraging new corporations.

1839 *Bank of Augusta v. Earle:* Taney ruled that a corporation chartered in one state could ordinarily do business in another, but that a state could exclude or regulate a "foreign" corporation if it wished to. Thus a state could exercise some control over interstate commerce. Other major decisions were *Prigg v. Pennsylvania* (1842, p. 99), *Luther v. Borden* (1849, p. 87) *Dred Scott v. Sandford* (1857, p. 123), *Ableman v. Booth* (1859, p. 124), and *Ex Parte Merryman* (1861, p. 136).

Manifest Destiny, 1790–1850

The Rocky Mountains and Oregon

1792 Capt. **Robert Gray** (U.S.) discovered the Columbia River.

1805 British North West Company founded a fort in the interior of Oregon, and the **Lewis and Clark** expedition reached the Pacific Ocean.

1811 **John Jacob Astor,** head of the **American Fur Company,** set up a fur post at **Astoria** at the mouth of the Columbia River but sold it in 1813 to the North West Co.

1818 Great Britain and the U.S. agreed to the joint occupation of Oregon for 10 years. It was renewed indefinitely in 1827.

1819 Spain gave up all claim to Oregon.

1821 **Hudson's Bay Co.** took over the North West Co.

1823–24 **Jedediah S. Smith** led the first expedition through the Rocky Mountains by way of **South Pass,** later used by pioneers on the Oregon Trail.

1824 Hudson's Bay Co. built **Ft. Vancouver** on the Columbia River.

1825 William H. Ashley, from Missouri, established the **"rendezvous system"** whereby trappers exchanged their beaver furs each summer at a central point in the mountains for goods brought from the East.

The great period of the Rocky Mountain fur trade came to an end in 1840.

1826–29 Jedediah Smith explored the Colorado River, and parts of California, and Oregon.

1834 Methodist missionary **Jason Lee** founded a mission in the **Willamette Valley,** Ore., which soon attracted American settlers.

1836 Presbyterian mission under Dr. **Marcus Whitman** brought the first white women across the Rockies to Oregon.

1843 Heavy migration to Oregon began over the **OREGON TRAIL** running from Independence, Mo., to Astoria, Ore.

1843 American settlers in Oregon set up a provisional government (May 2). By 1844, 5,000 Americans lived in the Willamette Valley.

1844–46 The U.S. and Great Britain negotiated the boundaries of **Oregon territory,** which extended from the 42nd parallel to 54°–40', although the British were willing to concede the territory south of the Columbia River. Democrats in Congress demanded the "reoccupation of Oregon", and President Polk asked for power to end the joint occupation. He also expanded the **Monroe Doctrine** by warning European nations not to interfere with North American nations (Dec., 1845). By 1846, the British were ready to compromise for several reasons: 1. the Hudson's Bay Co. had been removed to Vancouver Island, 2. the beaver trade had declined, and 3. the British wanted to import grain from the U.S. after repeal of the Corn Laws, which had restricted such imports. In May, Polk warned that in one year the U.S. would end the joint occupation of Oregon, and the British offered to divide it at the **49th parallel**. In spite of his pledge to occupy Oregon to 54°–40′ Polk submitted the **OREGON TREATY** (the 49th parallel treaty) to the Senate, which ratified it June 15.

Relations with Great Britain

1837   The *Caroline* Affair: a rebellion led by William L. Mackenzie was put down in Upper Canada. When the American steamer *Caroline* was engaged to carry supplies to Mackenzie on Navy Island in the Niagara River, the British destroyed it. War threatened briefly.

1839   The **Aroostook War** broke out when Canadian lumbermen began operations in the disputed border area of Maine. Both Maine and New Brunswick called out militia, but a truce was arranged in 1840.

1840   **McLeod Affair**: Alexander McLeod, a Canadian, was arrested in New York for murder in connection with the *Caroline* affair. Once again war threatened, but in 1841 McLeod was found not guilty.

1841   *Creole* Affair: slaves on the American ship *Creole* mutinied and took the ship to Nassau in the Bahamas, where the British

4-1   The Westward Movement

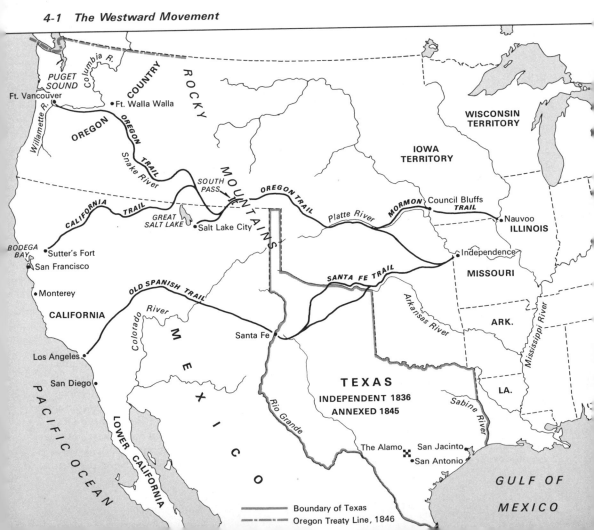

Boundary of Texas
Oregon Treaty Line, 1846

freed them. The British rebuffed Webster's efforts to have the slaves returned to their American owners.

1842   WEBSTER-ASHBURTON TREATY: Lord Ashburton of Britain began discussions of the disputed northeast boundary with Secretary of State Webster in the U.S. on June 13. The treaty, signed on Aug. 9 and ratified in the U.S. on Aug. 20, fixed the **northeast boundary** along its present line (7,000 of the disputed 12,000 square miles went to the U.S.). The boundary along the 45th parallel in New York was moved one-half mile north to let the U.S. keep a fort on Lake Champlain. The boundary from Lake Superior west to the **Lake of the Woods** was adjusted north giving the U.S. an additional 5,000 square miles, including the Mesabi iron range. A **joint squadron** was set up off Africa to enforce laws against the slave trade.

The Mormons

1827   JOSEPH SMITH announced that he had dug up golden plates at Manchester, N.Y., on which were inscribed *The Book of Mormon.*

1830   The **Church of Jesus Christ of Latter-Day Saints** (Mormons) was founded at Fayette, N.Y. A cooperative society ruled by an oligarchy, it was constantly in conflict with the community. *The Book of Mormon* was published that year and it described the establishment of an American colony from the Tower of Babel.

1831   The Mormons moved to **Kirtland,** Ohio, to escape persecution.

1839   Smith founded the independent city of Nauvoo, which in five years was the largest city in Illinois.

1844   Smith and his brother were killed at Carthage, Ill. (June 27), by a mob of anti-Mormons, who particularly objected to the rise of **polygamy** among the Mormons.

1846   15,000 Mormons under **BRIGHAM YOUNG** began to migrate westward.

1847   The first band of Mormons reached the Great Salt Lake on July 22.

1848   Young's plan for the **Mormon Settlement at Salt Lake City** involved a government run by the Church, with Brigham Young as president. Land, owned and irrigated by the community, would be assigned on the outskirts of the city. About 22,000 Mormons lived near the Great Salt Lake by 1856.

1849   The Mormon State of **Deseret,** Brigham Young governor, was established as Utah became part of the U.S. At the same time, the Gold Rush brought prosperity and non-Mormons to Salt Lake City.

1850   Utah Territory was established by Congress with Young as governor.

1857–58   The **Mormon War** was brought on by Mormon refusal to use the federal courts; President Buchanan sent troops to Utah.

1858   The Mormons accepted U.S. jurisdiction under a new governor.

California

1697   Jesuit missionaries entered Lower California.

1769   San Diego was occupied and **San Francisco Bay** was discovered by the Spanish. In this "Mission Period," which lasted until 1823, the Franciscans, led by **Junipero Serra,** established 21 missions.

1812–41   The Russians held a trading post at Fort Ross.

1827   Ocean trade between New England and California began. Ships sailed around Cape Horn and traded for hides at Monterey before setting forth across the Pacific to China. Partly because of this trade, Americans began to settle in California.

1833–34   Joseph R. Walker expedition explored the route along the Humboldt River to California later called the **CALIFORNIA TRAIL.**

1839–43   JOHN A. SUTTER built **Fort Sutter** near present-day Sacramento. Sutter became a Mexican subject and his post was the goal of migrants to California.

1841   The first group of settlers reached California over the California Trail.

1841   British minister to Mexico Richard Pakenham proposed a British colony in California, reviving American fears of Britain.

Efforts by Webster to buy California failed, as had Jackson's efforts in 1835.

1842 U.S. Commodore **Thomas C. Jones,** believing that the U.S. and Mexico were at war, seized **Monterey** for two days (Oct. 19–21).

1843–44 **John C. Frémont** explored parts of Oregon and California and stirred up further interest in the West.

1845

Oct. 17 Polk sent a dispatch to **Thomas O. Larkin,** U.S. consul at Monterey (received Apr. 17, 1846), urging him to stir up a revolt and apply for annexation to the U.S.

Dec. 9 A 60-man American party under John C. Frémont arrived at Sutter's Fort.

Dec. 16 The Slidell mission to Mexico to buy California and the Southwest was rejected.

1846

Mar. 9 Frémont headed north after being ordered out of California by the Mexicans, who feared insurrection.

May 8 At the Oregon border, Frémont was overtaken by a messenger from Washington who told him that war was about to break out with Mexico. He turned south and reached Sutter's Fort May 30.

June 14 Americans at **Sonoma** raised the **Bear Flag** and declared California independent.

June 23 Frémont began to take part in the California revolt.

July 7 Commodore **John D. Sloat,** U.S. naval commander, seized **Monterey** and claimed California for the U.S.

July 9 The U.S. Navy captured San Francisco and Sonoma and raised the American flag.

Aug. 17 Commodore **Robert F. Stockton** declared California annexed to the U.S. and himself governor.

Sept. 22–30 **Los Angeles revolt** brought southern California back into Mexican hands.

Nov. 25 Brig. Gen. **Stephen W. Kearny** arrived in California from Sante Fe.

1847

Jan. 13 Mexican southern California surrendered to Stockton, who suspended Kearny when he tried to organize a government. Stockton appointed Frémont governor.

Feb. 13 New instructions made Kearny governor, but Frémont refused to give up his position.

Nov.–Jan., 1848 Frémont was court-martialed for disobedience and found guilty.

1848

Jan. 24 **Gold was discovered** by **James W. Marshall** on a branch of the American River, on the property of John Sutter, and a gold rush developed. In 1849, 25,000 "**Forty-niners**" came from the east coast by way of Panama or Cape Horn and twice as many came overland. The mines in 1849 yielded $10 million; in 1851 $55 million. The population of California rose during 1849 from 25,000 to almost 100,000; by 1852 it was over 200,000.

Texas and the Southwest

1821 In Jan., Spain granted **Moses Austin** of Missouri a charter to settle families in Texas. Austin soon died but his son **STEPHEN F. AUSTIN** brought in Americans who settled between the Brazos and Colorado Rivers. A month later, Mexico became independent of Spain. In 1823, Austin confirmed his grant with Mexico and was authorized to bring in 300 families.

1821–22 **William Becknell** made the first trading expedition to Santa Fe, which had been closed under Spanish rule, and opened the **SANTA FE TRAIL.**

1825 Coahuila-Texas **land law** granted 885 acres of farm land and 22,130 acres of grazing land to each **empresario** (colonizer) for every 100 families he brought in. Each family would receive 177 acres of farm land and 13,098 of grazing land.

1829 Jackson failed in an effort to buy Texas.

1829 "**Old Spanish Trail**" from Santa Fe to Los Angeles was explored by Antonio

Armijo. Caravans soon moved over the trail. That year, **slavery was abolished** in all Mexico, including Texas.

1830   Over 4,000 Americans lived in Texas. By 1836 Anglo-American settlers outnumbered Mexicans in Texas by 10 to 1.

1832   Gen. **Antonio López de Santa Anna** seized control of Mexico.

1833   Austin went to Mexico City to demand Texan independence but was refused and jailed.

1835

June 30   Texans seized the garrison at **Anahuac**.

Oct. 2   Texans defeated Mexican cavalry at the Battle of Gonzalez.

Nov. 3   Convention of settlers at San Felipe de Austin voted for local self-government.

1836

Jan.   Santa Anna marched into Texas.

Feb. 23–Mar. 6   **Siege of the Alamo** mission at San Antonio. Less than 200 Texans held off 3,000–4,000 Mexicans, but in the end all the Texans were killed including **Jim Bowie** and **Davy Crockett**. "Remember the Alamo" became the Texans' rallying cry.

Mar. 2   **Texas declared its independence,** and **SAM HOUSTON** took command of the Texan army.

Mar. 27   Santa Anna executed about 350 Americans at the **Goliad**.

Apr. 21   **BATTLE OF SAN JACINTO**: after retreating eastward, Houston turned and defeated the Mexicans, killing 630.

May 14   Santa Anna signed a treaty (later repudiated) promising Texan independence with the Rio Grande River as a boundary.

July 1, 4   Resolutions in Congress called for annexation of Texas, but Jackson took no action.

Oct. 22   **Sam Houston** became the first **president** of the Republic of Texas. The constitution guaranteed slavery.

1836–50   American and European immigration increased the population of Texas from 30,000 to 212,000.

1837   The U.S. granted recognition to Texas but refused to annex it.

1838–41   **Mirabeau B. Lamar,** President, secured French and British but not Mexican recognition for Texas.

1841   **Sam Houston** was again elected President.

1842   Mexico staged raids against San Antonio and promised to recapture Texas.

1843   Texans broke off annexation discussions and developed close relations with Great Britain, which wanted an independent Texas as a buffer against U.S. expansion. Santa Anna warned that American annexation would lead to war.

1844

Mar. 6   **John C. Calhoun** became Secretary of State determined to annex Texas to keep it away from British abolitionists.

Apr. 12   Calhoun negotiated an **annexation treaty** with Texas.

Apr. 18   Calhoun wrote to British Minister Pakenham defending slavery.

June 8   The Senate rejected, 35–16, a treaty to annex Texas.

Dec. 4   Polk was elected President on a platform calling for the annexation of Texas.

1845

Feb. 25–28   A **JOINT RESOLUTION TO ANNEX TEXAS** passed both houses of Congress and was signed by Tyler on Mar. 1.

July 4   Texas ratified the annexation.

Dec. 29   Texas was admitted to the union with slavery, and the state government was set up Feb. 19, 1846.

War with Mexico, 1845–1846

1845

July   "MANIFEST DESTINY" was a phrase used by **John L. O'Sullivan** in the *U.S. Magazine and Democratic Review.* Robert C. Winthrop (Mass.) used it on the floor of Congress (Jan. 3, 1846), and it became a popular slogan.

Mar. 28 Mexico **broke off diplomatic relations** with the U.S. because of the annexation of Texas, which she still claimed. The U.S. demanded more than $2 million in payment for claims against Mexico for lives and property lost during Mexican outbreaks. Both sides were extremely belligerent.

Nov. 10 President Polk sent **John Slidell** to Mexico to offer $30 million for California, New Mexico, and the acceptance of the Rio Grande as the boundary of Texas.

June 15 Polk ordered Gen. **ZACHARY TAYLOR** to a point near the Rio Grande. The area between the **Nueces River** and the **Rio Grande** was in dispute because the boundary of the state of Coahuila–Texas had been the Nueces, but Texas had claimed up to the Rio Grande.

July 31 Taylor occupied **Corpus Christi**, south of the Nueces.

Dec. 16 The Mexican government **rejected** the Slidell mission.

1846

Jan. 12 Polk received word of Slidell's rejection and ordered Gen. Taylor to march to the north bank of the Rio Grande, where he and 4,000 men arrived Mar. 28.

Apr. 24–25 Gen. **Mariano Arista** at Matamoros sent 1,600 men across the Rio Grande, where they attacked a small body of American troops.

Apr. 30–May 1 Mexicans in large numbers crossed the Rio Grande.

May 8 Slidell, who had returned from Mexico, urged immediate action.

May 9 Polk told the Cabinet that he planned to ask Congress for war. After the Cabinet meeting he received word of the Apr. 25 skirmish.

May 11 Polk's **war message** accused Mexico of having "shed American blood on American soil." The Senate and House voted for war 40–2 and 174–14. All antiwar votes were from northern Whigs. Calhoun and two other Senators abstained. At this time, the American army had only 7,200 men—compared to a Mexican army of 32,000—but about 100,000 Americans took part in the war before it ended.

1846 TAYLOR'S CAMPAIGN ACROSS THE RIO GRANDE was one of the two major successful campaigns of the war. In the battles of **Palo Alto** and **Resaca de la Palma** (May 8–9), north of the Rio Grande, Taylor defeated Arista, who retreated south.

May 18 Taylor crossed the Rio Grande. Polk put Taylor in charge of the campaign instead of Commander-in-Chief Winfield Scott partly because Scott was a potential Whig Presidential candidate for 1848.

July 7 **Santa Anna**, exiled in Cuba, promised the U.S. peace if allowed to slip through the lines into Mexico. When he had done this (Aug. 16), he immediately laid plans to carry on the war.

Sept. 20–24 Taylor **captured Monterrey**, allowed the Mexicans to withdraw, and promised not to advance for eight weeks. Polk disapproved of the armistice.

Oct. 8 Santa Anna moved north to San Luis Potosi with over 20,000 troops. On Feb. 22–23, 1847, the forces met in the battle of **Buena Vista** near Monterrey. Taylor repulsed Santa Anna, who then withdrew to Mexico City.

1846 The **SOUTHWESTERN CAMPAIGN** of Gen. **Stephen W. Kearny** began in June when he led 1,700 men west from Fort Leavenworth and captured **Santa Fe** on Aug. 18. In Sept., an American territorial government was set up in New Mexico with Charles Bent as governor.

Dec. 25–28 Col. **Alexander W. Doniphan** and American frontiersmen defeated the Mexicans at **El Brazito** and took **El Paso**.

1847 In The **Battle of the Sacramento** (Feb. 28) near Chihuahua, the Americans won a great victory by defeating 4,000 Mexicans while suffering no casualties.

1847 SCOTT'S ASSAULT ON MEXICO CITY was the second major campaign. In Nov., 1846, Polk agreed to send a land-sea expedition against Vera Cruz under Gen. **Winfield Scott** who took 9,000 men from Taylor's army for his expedition.

Feb. 19 Scott issued **General Order No. 20** establishing rules for administering parts of Mexico, the first American program for rule of conquered territory.

Mar. 9 Beachhead was set up at Vera Cruz

after the **first amphibious landing** in U.S. history. The city surrendered on Mar. 27.

Apr. 17–18 Scott reached the plateau leading to Mexico City by defeating Santa Anna in battle at the pass of **Cerro Gordo.** Captains George B. McClellan and Robert E. Lee, later opponents in the Civil War, took part in the battle.

May 15 Scott stopped at Puebla to rebuild his forces.

Aug. 19–20 In the battles of **Contreras** and **Churubusco,** the Americans suffered heavy casualties but captured Santa Anna's defensive positions five miles outside Mexico City.

Aug. 27–Sept. 6 Nicholas Trist Negotiations: Trist, Chief Clerk in the State Department, had arrived in Vera Cruz on May 6 with instructions from President Polk to buy New Mexico and California for up to $30 million. He was not to communicate with Scott, whom Polk still considered a potential Whig candidate. After a bitter battle with Scott, Trist carried on negotiations, which failed.

Sept. 8–14 American forces defeated the Mexicans at **Molino del Rey** and at the hill of Chapultepec and broke through into **Mexico City,** which they captured.

Oct. 12 Fighting ceased.

4-2 The Mexican War, 1846–1848

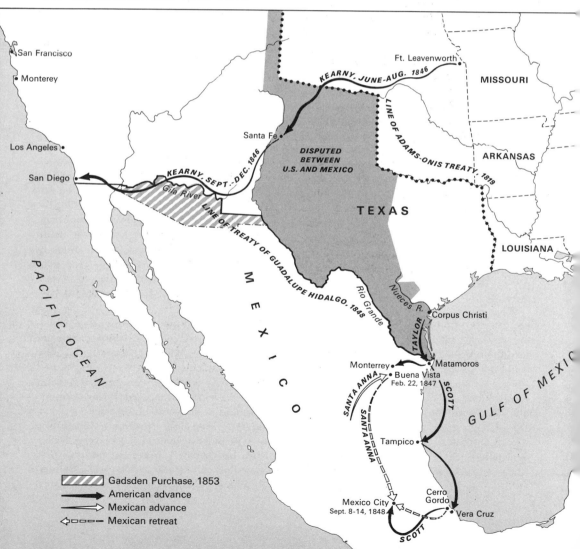

Dec. 12   Trist ignored Polk's order to return and started peace negotiations. Since war fever was high in the U.S., Trist may have prevented the conquest of all Mexico.

1848   By the **TREATY OF GUADALUPE HIDALGO** (Feb. 2), Mexico ceded California and New Mexico to the U.S. and agreed to the Rio Grande as the border of Texas in return for $18,250,000 ($3,250,000 in claims). The treaty was ratified Mar. 10, 1848. U.S. **war casualties** were 1,721 dead and 4,102 wounded; almost 12,000 died of disease.

Slavery in the Territories, 1846–1848

1846

Enthusiasm for the Mexican War was high in the West, but many in New England opposed it, calling it a conspiracy to "strengthen the 'Slave Power'."

Aug. 8   WILMOT PROVISO: David Wilmot, a Democratic congressman from Pennsylvania, introduced an amendment to a bill to appropriate $2 million to acquire territory from Mexico. The Proviso stated that slavery would never exist in any territory so acquired and was adopted by the House on Aug. 8, but the Senate rejected the appropriation bill two days later. On Mar. 3, 1847, Congress passed a bill to appropriate $3 million for territorial negotiation with no Wilmot Proviso.

Nov.   In Congressional elections, the Whigs made gains because of opposition to the war and won a majority in the House.

1847

Feb. 19–20   Calhoun Resolutions defending slavery: Calhoun argued that since the territories belonged to the states, Congress could not abolish slavery in them, nor could Congress dictate to any state regarding its constitution.

Dec. 22   Abraham Lincoln, recently elected Whig Congressman from Illinois attacked the war by introducing his **"spot resolutions"** demanding that Polk prove that the spot where war started was actually American soil.

1848

Jan.–Aug.   Debate over slavery in the Oregon Territory: on Jan. 10, Senator **Stephen A. Douglas** (Democrat, Ill.) introduced a bill in which Oregon would retain its laws excluding slavery until the territorial legislature saw fit to change them. A month later, a bill was introduced in the House to extend to Oregon the Northwest Territory restrictions on slavery. Senator **Jesse D. Bright** (Ind.) introduced on June 27 an amendment extending the Missouri Compromise line to the Pacific. If passed this would have extended slavery to New Mexico and parts of California, where it had been excluded by Mexican law. Calhoun opposed any restrictions on slavery, insisting that the Mexican laws were not valid. On July 27, the Senate voted for a compromise that legalized Oregon laws on slavery and left slavery in California and New Mexico up to the Supreme Court. The House voted for a **territory of Oregon** with restrictions on slavery. It passed the Senate and was signed by Polk on Aug. 14. There was no decision on California and New Mexico.

May 22   The **Democratic Convention,** which met at Baltimore, was split between the Administration wing and independent Democrats, who opposed slavery in the territories. With Polk pledged not to run, the nomination went to Gen. **Lewis Cass** (Mich.) with **William O. Butler** (Ky.) as the nominee for Vice President. Cass, an expansionist, favored **"squatter sovereignty,"** the right of local government to decide on slavery. The platform opposed congressional debate over slavery.

June 7   The **Whigs,** meeting at Philadelphia, nominated Gen. **Zachary Taylor** for President and **Millard Fillmore** (N.Y.) for Vice President. Northern **"Conscience" Whigs** such as **William H. Seward** (Senator from N.Y.) in vain opposed Taylor's nomination because he was a slaveowner.

Aug. 9   Free-Soil National Convention met at Buffalo. Radical (antislavery) Democrats had begun to leave the party in 1845 including **John Parker Hale** (N.H.), **Salmon P. Chase** (Ohio), **Hannibal Hamlin** (Me.), and **Charles Sumner** (Mass.). On June 17 the New York Barnburners, who had bolted the Democratic Convention, had nominated Martin Van Buren for President. The **Liberty Party** on Oct. 21, 1847, had nominated Senator Hale for President. Radical Democrats, Barnburners, Liberty Party supporters, "Conscience" Whigs, land reformers, and Workingmen formed the Free-Soil Party at Buffalo and nominated **Van Buren** for President and **Charles Francis Adams**, a Whig from Massachusetts for Vice President. The platform called for internal improvements, free homesteads, the Wilmot Proviso, and "free soil, free speech, free labor, and free men." Hale later withdrew in favor of Van Buren.

Nov. 7   Presidential election: Taylor won with 1,360,967 popular votes (163 electoral), to 1,222,342 (127) for **Cass**, and 291,263 (no electoral) for **Van Buren**. The Van Buren vote threw New York to Taylor but also gave Indiana and Ohio to Cass.

Slavery and Abolition, 1810–1850

The Southern Nation

Population in the South, 1810–60
(in millions)

	1810	1820	1830	1840	1850	1860
Total	3.5	4.4	5.7	7.0	9.0	11.1
White	2.2	2.8	3.5	4.3	5.6	7.0
Free Colored	0.1	0.1	0.2	0.2	0.2	0.3
Slaves	1.2	1.5	2.0	2.4	3.1	3.8

Agricultural production: cotton production, which was concentrated in South Carolina and Georgia before 1800, spread to Tennessee and Mississippi by 1800 and to Louisiana, Alabama, and Texas in the early nineteenth century. Production rose from 178,000 bales (1810) to 732,000 (1830) to 2,136,000 (1850) and 5,387,000 (1859). In 1859 Mississippi led in cotton production with 1,203,000 bales; then came Alabama with 990,000; Louisiana with 778,000; and Georgia with 701,000. **Tobacco** production spread west to Kentucky and Tennessee. Total production rose from 110,000 hogsheads in 1790 to 160,000 in 1860. **Corn, wheat, sugar, and rice** were also important crops in the South.

The slave system: slaves were most numerous in a lowland belt running from central Virginia south and west through the Carolinas and from Georgia to Texas. In 1860 the leading slave states were Virginia with 472,000 slaves; Georgia, 462,000; Mississippi, 437,000; Alabama,

435,000; and South Carolina, 402,000. In 1850 perhaps 300,000 of the 5.6 million white population of the south were **slaveowners**. Together with their families they made up about one-fourth of the southern whites. Most slaveowners had only a few slaves; in 1850 only 11 owned 500 or more, 243 owned 200–499, and less than 8,000 owned 50–199. Most white farmers were small planters with less than 20 slaves or yeomen farmers with no slaves.

Plantation life was neither as ideal as southerners portrayed it nor as harsh as abolitionists painted it. Historians debate about the degree of cruelty. Nonetheless, the slave lived in a society in which he had no rights: slave families were broken at the whim of the owner, slave marriages had no legal status, and slavery was permanent. The slave's diet, clothing and housing were poor by modern standards but often no worse than those of the poor white farmer. **Occasional slave revolts** took place, and there was much day-to-day resistance. Slavery was **profitable** to a degree: the value of a male field hand, for example, rose from $300 in the 1790's to $1,000 in 1840 and to over $1,200 in 1860. With so much capital tied up in land and slaves the plantation owner was unable to diversify or to alter his investment. Large-scale industry failed to develop in the South as the planter put his profits back into land and slaves. The system also contributed to the rise of a poor white class.

The Antislavery Movement

1790 Petitions began to arrive in Congress demanding the abolition of slavery.

1808 Slave importation into the U.S. became illegal.

1814 More petitions to Congress demanded the abolition of slavery in the District of Columbia.

1817 The American Colonization Society was founded to resettle Negroes in Africa; its program was moderate in that it did not propose abolition of slavery.

1821 Benjamin Lundy (Ohio) founded his abolitionist newspaper, *The Genius of Universal Emancipation,* and led an antislavery petition campaign in 1828.

1822 Slave uprising led by **Denmark Vesey** was crushed in Charleston, S.C., June 16 before it could get underway.

1829 The House adopted a resolution condemning slavery in the District of Columbia.

1829 Walker's Appeal in Four Articles, written by **David Walker,** a free Negro in Boston, called on slaves to kill their masters.

1831 The Liberator, an abolitionist newspaper in Boston edited by **WILLIAM LLOYD GARRISON,** began publication on Jan. 1.

1831 The Aug. 21 **NAT TURNER REBELLION** in Southampton County, Va., was put down after 55 whites were killed.

1831–32 A Virginia convention narrowly voted against emancipation of ·slaves. The convention, *Walker's Appeal,* the *Liberator,* and the Nat Turner Rebellion marked a turning point in the history of slavery. Henceforth the South tightened its control over Negroes.

1831–60 Free colored population in the U.S. rose from 108,000 in 1800 to 488,000 in 1860, 230,000 of them in the North. By 1840, 93 per cent of the free northern Negroes lived in states that disenfranchised them. Extralegal codes segregated them into "Jim Crow" sections of stagecoaches, railroad cars, and theaters; they could not enter most hotels. In the case of *Roberts v. the City of Boston* (1849) Chief Justice **Lemuel Shaw** of the Massachusetts Supreme Court enunciated the doctrine of "**separate but equal**" educational facilities.

1831 **John Quincy Adams,** newly-elected Congressman from Massachusetts, presented 15 petitions for abolition of slavery in the District of Columbia.

1832 Thomas R. Dew's *Review of the Debate in the Virginia Legislature* contained his summary of the pro-slavery arguments. From this point on the South began to present slavery as a positive good, a humane institution sanctioned by history and by the Bible. **George Fitzhugh** in *Sociology for the South* and *Cannibals All!* (1854, 1857) compared the allegedly miserable conditions in northern mill cities with supposedly idyllic conditions in the South.

1832 New England Antislavery Society, founded by William Lloyd Garrison, demanded the immediate abolition of slavery.

1833 The American Antislavery Society was founded in Philadelphia by **Lewis and Arthur Tappan, Garrison, William Jay,** and **Theodore Dwight Weld.**

1833 Oberlin College was founded in Ohio, the first college to admit Negroes.

1835

In one of his lectures the evangelist **Charles G. Finney** declared slavery a sin, thereby linking revivalism and abolition.

July 30 Charleston, S.C., citizens burned antislavery pamphlets. Postmasters were allowed to impound such pamphlets to avoid such disturbances.

Oct. 21 A Boston mob, strongly opposed to abolition, seized William Lloyd Garrison and dragged him through the streets.

1836

In the **Med Case** Chief Justice Shaw of Massachusetts declared that a slave taken to a free state was free. The first slave rescue took place in Boston in 1836.

Jan. 7–Mar. 11   Antislavery petitions were presented to the Senate. Calhoun argued that the Senate should not receive petitions to end slavery in the District of Columbia. His motion lost, but the Senate adopted a policy of receiving petitions and rejecting them.

May 18   Congressman Henry L. Pinckney (S.C.) proposed the **"gag resolution"** to lay all antislavery petitions to the House on the table. In spite of the opposition of John Quincy Adams, the "gag resolution" passed (May 26) along with two others that stated: 1. Congress had no power over slavery in the states; and 2. It was inexpedient to interfere with slavery in the District of Columbia.

June 8   Calhoun's proposal to prohibit the circulation of antislavery pamphlets through the mails was defeated in the Senate.

1837

There were over 600 abolition societies in Massachusetts, New York, and Ohio alone, and membership throughout the North reached 150,000 by 1840. Prominent abolitionists included **John Groonleaf Whittier, Wendell Phillips**, and **James Russell Lowell**, of Massachusetts, **Lucretia Mott** of Philadelphia, the **Grimké sisters**, originally from South Carolina, and **Frederick Douglass**, an escaped slave. In spite of the abolitionists the vast majority of Northerners showed no interest in abolition.

Nov. 7   **Elijah P. Lovejoy**, an abolitionist editor, was murdered by a mob in Alton, Ill.

Dec. 19   The House adopted a stricter "gag rule," which was renewed every year until 1844.

1838

Jan. 3–12   **Calhoun's Resolutions** stating that Congress was not to interfere with slavery in the states, the District of Columbia, or the territories, passed the Senate. When

Senator Allen of Ohio proposed a resolution to the effect that nothing in Calhoun's Resolutions should be construed to abridge freedom of speech, the vote in favor of tabling revealed how sectional interests had overshadowed party loyalty. Of the 23 votes to table, 20 were from slave states; 19 of the 21 votes against the motion were from free states.

Feb. 14   John Quincy Adams introduced in the House over 300 petitions against slavery and the annexation of Texas.

Dec. 3   Joshua R. Giddings, a Whig, from Ohio, took his seat in the House, the first abolitionist Congressman.

1839   An antislavery meeting of the **Liberty Party** in Warsaw, N.Y. (Nov. 13), decided in favor of political action, thereby departing from the extremist policies of Garrison and Weld. Weld that year published *Slavery As It Is*, an indictment of its excesses.

1840   **Fugitive slave laws** in Vermont and New York provided defense attorneys for escaped slaves. The **American and Foreign Antislavery Society** under Weld broke away from Garrison's American Antislavery Society.

1840   The House voted not even to receive antislavery petitions.

1841   *Amistad* **Case**: the Supreme Court declared that the slaves who had mutinied on the Spanish ship *Amistad* and come ashore on Long Island were free in spite of efforts to return them to Spain.

1842   *Prigg v. Pennsylvania:* the Supreme Court ruled that the states had no power over cases arising under the Fugitive Slave Act. States were thus prevented from either helping or hindering fugitive slaves. As a result, northern states began to pass personal liberty laws to help runaway slaves.

1842   Congressman Joshua Giddings was censured by the House for antislavery resolutions. He resigned but was reelected in April.

1844   Adams' motion to strike out the "gag rule" passed the House (Dec. 3).

UNDERGROUND RAILROAD: this was a term used to describe a loose network of hiding places for Negroes escaping from the South, often to Canada. **Levi Coffin** (N.C.), Rev.

Theodore Parker (Mass.), and **Harriet Tubman,** an escaped slave, were leaders in this organization that had stations in Maryland, Pennsylvania, New York, Ohio, and New England. The importance of the movement, which started before 1800, has been exaggerated, but it probably rescued as many as 50,000 slaves in the period 1830–60.

Economic Development, 1790–1860

Transportation, 1790–1860

1790–1820   TURNPIKE BOOM helped speed settlement and economic development. Philadelphia to Lancaster, Pa., turnpike was built, 1790–94, and in 1795 the **Wilderness Road** was opened to wagons. The **National Road** was started in 1811; it reached Wheeling by 1818 and Vandalia, Ill., by 1838.

1815–40   CANAL BUILDING. The **Erie Canal** (built 1817–25) linked the Hudson River and Lake Erie. It made accessible northern Ohio, Indiana, Illinois, and Michigan, helped make New York the leading city of the U.S., and started the canal boom. Value of goods shipped west on the Canal

rose from $10 million in 1836 to $94 million by 1853. Pennsylvania Portage and Canal System linked Philadelphia and Pittsburgh (1826–40), and the Chesapeake and Ohio Canal linked Georgetown and the District of Columbia with Cumberland, Md. (1828–50). Portsmouth and Cleveland were linked by the Ohio Canal (1825–32) as were Lake Michigan and the Illinois River by the Illinois and Michigan Canal (1836–48). Canals in the U.S. increased from 100 miles in 1816 to 3,326 miles in 1840.

1837   The financial panic brought an end to the canal boom, though completion of canals continued into the 1840's.

1807–60   STEAMBOAT ERA began when

4-3   Roads and Canals about 1840

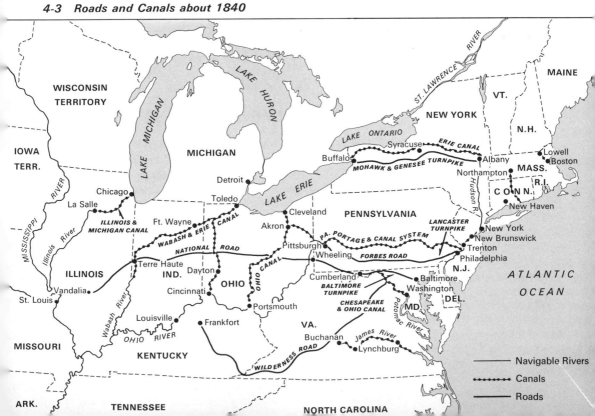

Robert Fulton's *Clermont* made the first successful steamboat run—from New York City to Albany and back. In 1815, the first steamboat run on the Mississippi River from the Ohio River to New Orleans and back took place. The next year, steam navigation started on the **Great Lakes**. The number of U.S. steamboats rose from 9 in 1817 to 770 in 1855.

1790–1860 The **MERCHANT MARINE**: the gross tonnage of American ships in foreign trade rose from 127,000 tons in 1789 to 981,000 tons in 1810. American vessels in overseas traffic rose from 125,000 tons to over a million tons from 1789–1810, and the percentage of the nation's commerce carried in U.S. ships rose from about 25 per cent to over 90 per cent. Beginning in 1818, transatlantic **packet lines** operated out of New York City, and in 1819, the *Savannah* made the first transatlantic voyage under steam.

1843–60 The era of the **Clipper Ship**: these graceful sailing ships made the passage from Boston around Cape Horn to San Francisco in less than 100 days. The gold rush brought the clipper-ship era to its peak in 1848–54.

1848–60 Atlantic steamship boom. U.S.

ocean steamship tonnage rose from 5,631 in 1847 to 97,296 in 1860.

1827–60 The first of many **RAILROADS**, from Quincy to the Neponset River, Mass., was built in 1827. Construction of the **Baltimore and Ohio** began in 1828; by 1853 it ran from Baltimore to Wheeling, Va. The Lexington (Ky.) and Ohio railroad opened in 1832, followed in 1835 by the Boston and Worcester. The Vicksburg to Jackson (Miss.) road was completed in 1840, bringing railroad mileage in operation to 2,818 miles; canal mileage was 3,326.

1850 Congress authorized **grants of land** to railroads in Illinois, Mississippi, and Alabama. Railroad mileage in operation was 9,021; canal mileage was 3,698.

1851 Railroads connecting Albany and Lake Erie later became the New York Central. Philadelphia and Pittsburgh were connected by rail in 1852, and New York City was linked to Chicago by direct rail transportation in 1855.

1860 Railroad mileage in operation was 30,626. The leading states in miles of road were Illinois, 2,799; Ohio, 2,946; New York, 2,682; Pennsylvania, 2,598; and Indiana, 2,163.

4-4 The Growth of Railroads, 1850–1860

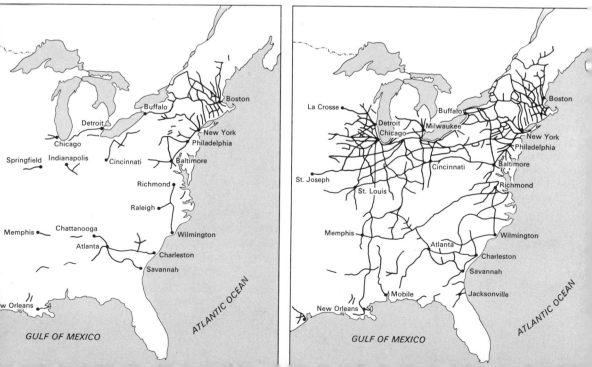

1816–50 SPEED IN TRANSPORTATION.

In 1816, it took 103 hours to travel from Philadelphia to Quebec by steamboat and stage; by 1860 the journey took 31 hours by railroad. Between 1817 and 1850, shipping time between New York and Cincinnati was reduced from 50 days by wagon and keelboat to 6–8 days by railroad.

1860 Five **EXPRESS COMPANIES** controlled most long-distance business: American, Wells Fargo, Adams, United States, and National.

1860 The **Pony Express** made its first trip, from St. Joseph, Mo., to Sacramento, Calif. The service was replaced after 18 months by the telegraph.

The Rise of the West

Westward expansion increased the financial resources and power of the area across the mountains.

1796 **Cleveland** was founded.

1820 The frontier line moved from the Appalachian Mountains (1790) to St. Louis (1820) to Independence, Mo. (1840).

1830 From 1790–1830 the western population increased as follows: Ohio, 46,000 to 938,000; Kentucky, 74,000 to 688,000; Tennessee, 106,000 in 1800 to 682,000; Indiana, 6,000 in 1800 to 343,000.

1833 **Chicago** was founded.

1840 The largest western cities were Cincin-

U.S. Economic Statistics

(all monetary sums in millions of dollars)

	1820	1830	1840	1850	1860
Population (in millions)	10	13	17	23	32
Urban population (% of total)	7	9	11	15	20
Immigration (by thousands)	8	23	84	370	154
Percentage of population in the Northeast	50	47	43	40	37
South	30	29	28	27	26
West	19	23	29	33	38
Value of manufactures			483	1,055	1,886[a]
Value of agricultural products				994	1,910
Value added by manufacturing (1879 prices)			190	490	860
Value added by agriculture (1879 prices)			790[b]	990[b]	1,490[b]
Railroad miles in operation			2,818	9,021	30,626
Net U.S. international liabilities		75	261	217	377
Banks; number	307	330	901	824	1,562
value of deposits			120	146	310
Wholesale commodity price index[c]	106	91	95	84	93
Exports (excluding gold, silver, or reexports)	52	59	112	135	316
Cotton exports	22	30	64	72	192
Agricultural exports			95		259
Imports (value)	74	63	98	174	354
Cotton and woolen manufactures imports	13	12	12	32	69
Percentage of imports made up by cotton and woolen manufactures	29[d]	23	13	19	20

[a] 1859. [b] 1839, 1849, and 1859. [c] 1910–14 = 100. [d] 1821.

nati (population 46,000), Louisville (21,000), and St. Louis (16,000). By 1860, the largest western cities were Cincinnati (161,000), St. Louis (161,000), and Chicago (109,000).

Business Cycles and Industrial Growth

1789–1815 **Economic boom** took place except for recessions in 1802 and 1808.

1815–19 **Heavy importation from Great Britain** hurt the economy, with wholesale commodity prices dropping from 182 in 1814 to 147 in 1818. The westward movement led to a boom in public land sales (median annual sale 1800–14 was 386,000 acres; median annual sale 1815–19 was 1,886,000; median annual sale 1820–28 was 814,000.

1819–34 **The Panic of 1819** was followed by years of sluggish business growth. Wholesale commodity prices dropped from 125 in 1819 to 98 in 1824 and then fell again during the bank crisis to 90 in 1834.

1834–37 **Financial boom** brought the wholesale commodity price index to 115 in 1837 as public land sales reached 20.1 million acres for 1836 and bank deposits rose from $102 million in 1834 to $190 million in 1837. Foreigners invested so heavily in state internal improvements that net international liabilities of the U.S. rose from $75 million in 1830 to $240 million in 1837.

1837–43 **Panic and Depression**: by 1843 wholesale commodity prices sagged to 75, bank deposits dropped to $78 million, U.S. net liabilities reached $189 million (1847), and public land sales fell to 1.1 million acres (1842).

1844–57 Large-scale **industrial growth** began as westward expansion, foreign loans, cotton exports, railroad construction, immigration, and gold discovery contributed to the "takeoff" of the American economy. Net international liabilities were $381 million and bank deposits $288 million in 1857; land sales were worth $12.8 million in 1854. Annual railroad construction, which had dwindled to 180 miles in 1844, reached 1,056 miles in 1848 and 3,442 miles in 1854. Immigration rose from 52,496 in 1843, to 234,968 in 1847, and to 427,833 in 1854.

1857–58 Overexpansion in land and railroads led to a **financial panic** from which the nation recovered by 1860.

1860 Railroads were vital to U.S. industrial growth before the Civil War; **railroad capitalization** in 1860 was *one-fourth* of the total U.S. capitalization of $6 billion.

Manufacturing

1800–60 The number of **corporations** increased rapidly with peaks in the growth cycle, in 1814, 1837, and 1857.

1813–60 The **textile manufacturing** factory system started in Massachusetts at **Waltham** in 1813 and was extended to **Lowell** (1822), Chicopee (1823), and **Lawrence** (1845). The number of spindles in cotton manufacturing increased from 220,000 in 1820, to 800,000 in 1825, to 1,750,000 in 1835, and to 2,280,000 in 1840. Woolen manufacturing also expanded rapidly after 1830. While labor in Lowell consisted partly of farmgirls from northern New England, Lawrence from the start turned to immigrant labor.

1840–60 **Iron industry** (cast, forged, rolled, and wrought iron) expanded rapidly in the Middle-Atlantic states, 1840–50. The value of bar, sheet, and railroad iron more than doubled, 1850–60. Production of **pig iron** rose from 54,000 long tons in 1810 to 821,000 long tons in 1859.

Leading manufactures in the U.S., 1860
(millions of dollars)

	Value added by manufacturing
Cotton goods	54.7
Lumber	53.6
Boots and shoes	49.2
Flour and meal	40.1
Men's clothing	36.7
Iron	35.7
Machinery	32.6
Woolen goods	25.0
Carriages, wagons, and carts	23.7
Leather	22.8

Manufacturing by sections, 1860
(millions of dollars)

	Value added by manufacturing
Middle states	358.2
New England	223.1
West	159.0
South	69.0
Pacific states	42.7
Total	854.3

By 1860 the U.S. ranked second in world value of manufactures with $1.9 billion behind the United Kingdom with $2.8 billion.

Immigration

1820   Significant **Irish** immigration began.
1830   Significant **German** immigration began.

1840   **Scandinavian** immigration grew rapidly with heaviest settlements in Wisconsin and Minnesota.
1846   **Potato Famine** in Ireland brought Irish immigration to a peak of over 220,000 in 1851.
1848   The **Revolution of 1848** in Germany brought a flood of German refugees to America, especially to New York, Cincinnati, St. Louis, and Milwaukee. The peak years were 1852–54.

Foreign-born population, 1860

Total	4,138,697
England	433,494
Scotland	108,518
Ireland	1,611,304
France	109,870
Germany	1,276,075
Canada	288,285

American Life, 1790–1860

The Reform Impulse

Beginning in the 1820's, Americans, who had always considered theirs a divine mission, sought perfection on earth through many exciting **communities** and **reform movements**. Most of the communities had failed or were in decline by the time of the Civil War.

Religious groups (such as Rappites, Shakers and Mormons) sought freedom to follow their particular creeds. The **Rappites**, German Pietists led by George Rapp, founded New Harmony, Ind., in 1815, where they practiced celibacy and devoted themselves to work and to religious services. The **Shakers**, former Quakers led by Ann Lee, settled near Albany, N.Y., in 1776 and by 1824 had established 18 communities in the Northeast and the old Northwest.

Owenist societies followed the teachings of **Robert Owen**, humanitarian textile-mill owner in Scotland. Owen bought **New Harmony, Ind.,** 1824, but it soon failed. His son, **Robert Dale Owen,** was active in a wide variety of reform movements.

Fourierist societists were influenced by the phalanx system of Charles Fourier of France, outlined to Americans by Albert Brisbane in the New York *Tribune*. Among the 40 phalanxes (farming communities of about 1,500 members) was **Brook Farm, Mass., (1841–60)** run by Transcendentalists.

John Humphrey Noyes established a community in **Oneida**, N.Y., in 1848 to carry out his perfectionist and free love doctrines.

Social Reform

Prison reform and treatment of the insane: imprisonment for debt gradually disappeared. **Dorothea Dix**, Mass., travelled widely, 1841–44, and promoted humane treatment of those confined to state asylums.

Temperance: in 1840 the **Washington Temperance Society** was organized in Baltimore and began to urge men to take the cold water pledge. In Maine **Neal Dow** succeeded in getting the first statewide prohibition law passed in 1851.

Feminism: in 1848 **Elizabeth Cady Stanton** and **Lucretia Mott** called the **Seneca Falls, N.Y., convention** of women, which adopted resolutions demanding equality for women. Women did not receive the right to vote before the Civil War, but they increasingly gained the right to control their own property. **Emma Willard** founded the first women's secondary school at Troy, N.Y., 1821. Oberlin College admitted women in 1833, the first college to do so. **Mary Lyon** founded Mt. Holyoke Female Seminary, the first woman's college, in 1837.

Peace movement: in 1828 **William Ladd** (N.H.) founded the **American Peace Society** in New York City. Pacifists considered the Mexican War pro-slavery aggression; Henry David Thoreau refused to pay taxes for its support; James Russell Lowell called it murder in the *Biglow Papers.*

The Labor Movement

1794–1815 The **Journeymen Cordwainers** of Philadelphia, one of the first trade unions, joined other trade unions in a series of strikes for higher wages and shorter hours. Unions were generally unsuccessful because the courts considered them illegal conspiracies.

1827–28 In Philadelphia the **Mechanics' Union of Trade Associations** was formed, journeymen carpenters struck for a ten-hour day, and the **Workingmen's Party** organized to seek equality for workers.

1829 Workingmen's Party was organized in New York City; it favored free public education, a 10-hour day, mechanics lien laws, and free land in the west. By 1834 these organizations had been absorbed by the Loco-Foco Democrats and the Whigs.

1834 President **Jackson sent troops** to put down a **strike** on the Chesapeake and Ohio Canal, the first such federal intervention (Jan. 29).

1834 **National Trades Union** was organized and presented a memorial to Congress calling for the **10-hour day**.

1836 The Philadelphia Navy Yard established the 10-hour day.

1840 Van Buren ordered the **10-hour day** in all **federal public works**.

1842 Chief Justice **Lemuel Shaw** of Massachusetts ruled in *Commonwealth v. Hunt* that trade unions and strikes were legal.

1847 New Hampshire became the first state to pass a 10-hour law for workers, and seven states followed by 1858. Escape clauses, however, weakened the laws.

1852–60 National trade unions were established by the printers, hat finishers, stone cutters, iron moulders, and others.

1860 **Shoemakers** of Lynn and Natick, Mass., struck for higher wages, the largest pre-Civil War strike.

Education

1789–1860 Perhaps 500 **denominational colleges** and universities were founded before the Civil War, but many of them closed by 1900.

1795 North Carolina opened the first state university; other such universities were established before 1819 in Vermont, South Carolina, Georgia, and Virginia.

1820–30 Other than in New England, there was no free primary education in the U.S. Children went to private schools, pauper schools, or none at all.

1821 Boston established the first **public secondary school**.

1827 Massachusetts required every large town to establish a secondary school.

1832 New York City established its first **free primary school**, followed by Philadelphia in 1836.

1834 Pennsylvania set up the **first free school act** outside of New England, but free primary education was not widespread until after the Civil War.

1836–57 *Eclectic Readers,* by **William H. McGuffey,** were published for elementary schools.

1837–48 **HORACE MANN,** first secretary

of the Massachusetts Board of Education, carried out a series of reforms including a minimum six-month school year, higher salaries for teachers, revised curricula, and regular teacher training. Mann promoted free public education as necessary to a democracy. He travelled widely in Europe and the U.S., and his reforms had a great influence on American education.

1839   Mann established the **first state normal school** to train teachers in the U.S. at Lexington, Mass.

Religion

1789-1800   **Deism**, popular with rationalists, was associated with those supporting the French Revolution. Deists, like **Jefferson** and **Ethan Allen**, believed that nature proved the existence of God and considered formal religion unnecessary or even harmful. **Tom Paine's** *The Age of Reason* (1794) was a major deist tract.

1796, 1798   Missionary societies were formed in New York and Connecticut to convert the Indians to Christianity.

1797-1810   **Revivalism** on the frontier started with the meetings of **James McGready**.

1802   A religious revival led by President Timothy Dwight began at Yale College, and similar awakenings followed at other colleges.

1810   American Board of Commissioners for Foreign Missions was organized by the Congregational Church, the start of the American foreign missionary movement.

1816   The **African Methodist Episcopal Church** was founded, part of the movement for separate Negro churches.

1818-33   **Disestablishment** of the Congregational Church in Connecticut, New Hampshire, and Massachusetts marked the end of church establishment in the U.S.

1815-20   **UNITARIANISM**: attacks on the doctrine of the Trinity began before the American Revolution, and King's Chapel in Boston became the first Unitarian Church in 1785. The large-scale separation of Unitarian churches from Congregationalism, however, began in Boston in 1815. **William Ellery**

Channing of Massachusetts became the acknowledged leader of Unitarianism after his Baltimore address of 1819 openly condemning orthodoxy. Unitarians refused to believe in the Trinity or in the depravity of man.

1824   **Charles G. Finney** began his career as a revivalist in the East, mostly in New York.

1830   Mormon Church was founded.

1834   The Ursuline Convent in Charlestown, Mass., was burned by an anti-Catholic mob, part of the anti-Catholic sentiment of the day.

1836-50   **TRANSCENDENTALISTS**, led by **Ralph Waldo Emerson**, revolted against Unitarianism. They believed in the divinity of man, in an oversoul that unified mankind, and in the discovery of truth through mystical experiences outside of any church.

1843-45   **Millerism**: after predicting the second coming of Christ for 1843-44, **William Miller** founded the **Adventist Church**, 1845.

1843-47   Baptist, Methodist, and Presbyterian churches split over the issue of slavery.

1847   **Horace Bushnell's** *Christian Nurture* stressed the divity of man and the role of intuition rather than doctrine in salvation.

Literature

1772-1822   The **HARTFORD WITS** were conservatives who supported Calvinism and Federalism and praised the rise of American independence. **John Trumbull** satirized the Tories in the epic *McFingal* (1775-82). **Joel Barlow** expanded his patriotic poem *The Vision of Columbus* (1787) into the epic *Columbiad* (1807). **Timothy Dwight** defended Calvinism in his *Triumph of Infidelity* (1788).

1809-60   The **New York School: Washington Irving** (1809-59) was famous for his satirical *A History of New York* (1809), *The Sketch Book* (including "Rip Van Winkle" and "The Legend of Sleepy Hollow," 1820), *The Conquest of Granada* (1829), *Astoria* (1836), and *The Life of Washington* (1859). **William Cullen Bryant** (1817-60) at first wrote such poems as *Thanatopsis* and *To a Waterfowl* (*1817-1818*) and then turned to journalism. **James Fenimore Cooper** (1820-46) idealized the American Indian and depicted the clash of nature and civilization in his *Leatherstocking Tales,* including *The Last of the Mohicans* (1826) and *The Deerslayer* (1841). Cooper, a New York aristocrat, was a conservative Jacksonian Democrat who resented the rise of financial interests. His *Home as Found* (1838) severely criticized American democracy.

1836–60   The **New England Renaissance: Ralph Waldo Emerson,** (Concord, Mass., 1836–60), outlined the doctrines of Transcendentalism in his essay *Nature* (1836). In *The American Scholar,* an address at Harvard (1837), Emerson called for a body of native American scholarship and literature. His poems included "The Rhodora" and "Concord Hymn," his essays enlarged on his Transcendental beliefs, and his *Journal* provided him with material for his hundreds of lectures. Other Transcendentalists were **Margaret Fuller, Henry David Thoreau, Bronson Alcott, Theodore Parker,** and **Orestes Brownson. Nathaniel Hawthorne** (1837–63, born in Salem, Mass.) probed deeply into the problem of evil. His early stories were collected in *Twice-Told Tales* (1837), his experiences at Brook Farm became *The Blithedale Romance* (1852), and his powerful examination of sin and guilt in Puritan life appeared in *The Scarlet Letter* (1850). **Henry David Thoreau** (1845–62) spent two years in isolation at Walden Pond, near Concord; *Walden* (1854) was his diary of that time. Because he disapproved of the Mexican War, he went to jail rather than pay his Massachusetts poll tax; he defended his actions in "Civil Disobedience." Essayist **Oliver Wendell Holmes,** who thought Boston "the hub of the Universe," wrote "The Autocrat of the Breakfast-Table" (1857–58).

1838–83   Poetry: Henry Wadsworth Longfellow, though not very original, was popular for *Evangeline* (1847), *Song of Hiawatha* (1855), *The Courtship of Miles Standish* (1858), and *Tales of a Wayside Inn* (1863, including "Paul Revere's Ride"). **James Russell Lowell** satirized the Mexican War in his *Biglow Papers* (1848). **John Greenleaf Whittier,** the Quaker abolitionist poet, described New England life in poems such as "Barefoot Boy,"

"Maud Muller" (1856), and "Snowbound" (1866); he attacked slavery in *Poems Written During the Progress of the Abolition Question* (1838) and Daniel Webster in "Ichabod" (1850).

1827–91   Writers in the Middle States: Edgar Allan Poe (1827–49), grew up in the South but spent most of his career in New York and Philadelphia writing horror tales, mysteries, and haunting poetry. *Tamerlane and Other Poems* (1827), *Tales of The Grotesque and Arabesque* (1840) and *The Raven and Other Poems* (1845) were among his best works. He died of alcoholism in 1849. **Herman Melville** (1846–91) wrote novels based on his experiences as a seaman—*Typee* (1846), *Omoo* (1847), and his great study of man and evil, *Moby Dick* (1851). After 1865, he turned to poetry. **Walt Whitman** (1855–91), who started his career as a newspaperman in Brooklyn, N.Y., published his first poetry in *Leaves of Grass* (1855). His devotion was to democracy and mankind, and his grief on the death of Lincoln is expressed in "When Lilacs Last in the Dooryard Bloom'd" and "O Captain! My Captain!" (1865); his faith in democracy is apparent in "Song of Myself" (1855).

1834–60   Southern Writers: William Gilmore Simms (1834–55) wrote poetry and romances about the South—*Guy Rivers* (1834) and *The Yemassee* (1835)—and excellent novels about the American Revolution—*The Partisan* (1835) and *The Forayers* (1855).

1835   Augustus B. Longstreet published *Georgia Scenes,* describing the backwoods area. **Joseph Baldwin,** in *The Flush Times of Alabama and Mississippi* (1853), also portrayed rural life.

1860   Henry Timrod published a volume of poetry but did most of his writing after the Civil War. For southern writing on the slavery question see p. 98.

1834–92   Historians: George Bancroft (1834–89), Democratic Party leader in Massachusetts, published a 10-volume *History of the United States* based on original sources covering the years to 1782. Patriotic and extremely democratic, Bancroft believed that God was presiding over the rise of America. **Francis Parkman** (1849–92), a Bostonian, described a journey west in *The Oregon Trail* (1849) and then set to work on his history of the French and Indian Wars—*The History of the Conspiracy of Pontiac* (1851), *Montcalm and Wolfe* (1884), *A Half-Century of Conflict* (1892), and five other volumes. His use of original sources, his knowledge of the terrain, and his dramatic narrative style made Parkman a great historian. **William H. Prescott** (1838–58), also from Boston, wrote accurate narrative accounts of Spanish history, including *History of the Reign of Ferdinand and Isabella* (1838) and *History of the Conquest of Mexico* (1843). **John L. Motley** (1856–67) wrote *The Rise of the Dutch Republic* (1856) and *History of the United Netherlands* (1860–67), both of which gloried in the triumph of freedom over despotism.

1800–60 Other important writing: Mason L. Weems, *Life of Washington* (1800); *The Tales of Peter Parley* (children's books, 1827–60); Maria Monk, *Awful Disclosures* (an anti-Catholic work, 1836); William H. McGuffey, *Eclectic Readers* (1836–57); Richard H. Dana, Jr., *Two Years Before the Mast* (1840); Harriet Beecher Stowe, *Uncle Tom's Cabin* (1852); Timothy S. Arthur, *Ten Nights in a Bar-Room* (1854); Frederick Law Olmsted, *The Cotton Kingdom* (1856–61); and Ann S. Stephens, *Malaeska* (the first dime novel, 1860).

Newspapers

1800 *National Intelligencer* (Washington, D.C.), Whig, edited by Joseph Gales, Jr., and (1812–64) William W. Seaton.

1801 New York *Evening Post*, Federalist, Alexander Hamilton; Democratic under William Cullen Bryant (1829–78).

1804 *Richmond Enquirer* (Virginia), Democratic, Thomas Ritchie.

1808 *Argus of Western America* (Frankfort, Ky.), Amos Kendall (1816–29).

1809 *New Hampshire Patriot* (Concord), Democratic, Isaac Hill.

1811 *Niles' Weekly Register* (Baltimore), Whig, Hezekiah Niles.

1815 *Western Journal* (St. Louis), later the *Enquirer*.

1826 *United States Telegraph* (Washington, D.C.), Democratic, Duff Green.

1829 *Working Man's Advocate* (New York City), **labor**, George H. Evans.

1830 *Globe* (Washington, D.C.), Democratic, Francis Blair, Sr.

1833 *Sun* (New York City), **first penny paper, Benjamin H. Day**.

1834 *Staats-Zeitung* (New York City), **German**, Jacob Uhl.

1835 *Morning Herald* (New York City), stressed crime and sex, **James Gordon Bennett**.

1841 *Tribune* (New York City), was seriously concerned with important issues, **Horace Greeley**.

1846 *Oregon Spectator* (Oregon City), first newspaper in the Pacific Coast.

1847 *Daily Tribune* (Chicago), backed Lincoln in 1860.

1851 *Daily Times* (New York City), Whig, Henry J. Raymond. In 1857 became *The New York Times*, Republican.

Magazines

1815 *North American Review* (Boston), intellectual journal.

1827 *Youth's Companion* (Boston).

1830 *Lady's Book* (Philadelphia), later *Godey's Lady's Book*.

1834 *Southern Literary Messenger* (Richmond), leading southern journal.

1837 *U.S. Magazine and Democratic Review* (Washington, D.C.), Democratic, John O'Sullivan.

1839 *Dial* (Boston), Transcendentalist, Margaret Fuller, Ralph Waldo Emerson.

1839 *Graham's Magazine* (Philadelphia), Edgar Allan Poe, literary editor.

1844 *Littell's Living Age* (Boston).

1846 *Commercial Review of the South and West* (New Orleans), later *De Bow's Review*, social and economic.

1850 *Harper's New Monthly Magazine* (New York City).

1857 *Atlantic Monthly* (Boston), James Russell Lowell.

Science, Medicine, and Inventions

1793 Yellow Fever Epidemic in Philadelphia.

1793 **Eli Whitney** invented the cotton gin.

In 1799, he invented interchangeable parts for firearms.

1797 Charles Newbold invented the cast-iron plow.

1799 Nathaniel Bowditch published his *Practical Navigator*, the first American navigation book.

1802 Smallpox vaccination was proved effective by Benjamin Waterhouse.

1806 **Benjamin Silliman** the elder founded the first school of geology, at Yale.

1807 **Robert Fulton** sailed the first successful steamboat, the *Clermont*, from New York City to Albany.

1818 Benjamin Silliman the elder founded the *American Journal of Science and Arts*.

1826 John Stevens designed the first railroad locomotive.

1827–38 **John James Audubon**, *Birds of America*.

1830 Peter Cooper built the first locomotive in the U.S.

1831–32 Joseph Henry published papers on magnets.

1831 **Cyrus H. McCormick**, reaper.

1835 **Samuel Colt**, revolver.

1836 Asa Gray published his *Elements of Botany*.

1839 **Charles Goodyear**, vulcanizing of rubber.

1840 Astronomical observatory was established at Harvard.

1842–46 **Anesthesia:** Dr. Elijah Pope used ether in a tooth extraction in 1842, and **William T. G. Morton** first administered ether in a surgical operation in 1846. Dr. Horace Wells, Charles T. Jackson, and Dr. Crawford W. Long also claimed to have discovered anesthesia.

1844 **Samuel F. B. Morse**, telegraph.

1846 Louis Agassiz, prominent Swiss zoologist, arrived in America to take a professorship at Harvard.

1846 Smithsonian Institution was founded.

1846 **Elias Howe** invented and patented the sewing machine.

1846 Richard M. Hoe, rotary printing press.

1851 William Kelly, process for converting pig iron to steel, similar to the Bessemer process in England.

1859 **Edwin L. Drake**, drilled the first oil well, at Titusville, Pa.

1860 **Oliver F. Winchester**, repeating fire rifle.

Painting and Sculpture

1785–1860 **Historical painting: John Trumbull's** *The Battle of Bunker's Hill* and *The Declaration of Independence* started a period of historical panoramic painting. Others who followed included **Washington Allston** (*Belshazzar's Feast*) and **Emanuel Leutze** (*Washington Crossing the Delaware*).

1792–1828 **Portraiture: Gilbert Stuart,** in his American period, painted famous portraits of Washington, Jefferson, and many others. **Charles Willson Peale** painted portraits and nature subjects.

1830–60 **Hudson River school** of landscape painting was led by Thomas Cole, Asher Brown Durant, and George Inness.

1830–60 Early American **sculpture** emphasized statues of American leaders (often equestrian): **Horatio Greenough**, Statue of Washington on the U.S. Capitol grounds; **Hiram Powers**, *Greek Slave*.

Architecture

1789–1820 **Roman Revival** began with Thomas Jefferson's plans for the Virginia capitol at Richmond (1789), based on the Maison Carée at Nîmes, France. He utilized various Roman architectural orders in his plans for the University of Virginia at Charlottesville.

1789–1830 Samuel McIntire, who was a carpenter-builder rather than an architect, built many mansions in the **American Federal** style for the merchants of Salem, Mass. **Charles Bulfinch** followed the dignified Federal style for his state capitols in Boston (Mass.) and Augusta (Maine) and in the Massachusetts General Hospital, as well as in many other buildings in New England.

1793–1830 Major **Pierre Charles L'Enfant**, who designed the city of Washington, chose **William Thornton** as the architect for the **Capitol Building** at Washington, D.C. **Benjamin Henry Latrobe** modified Thornton's original plans as he worked on the building, 1803–17, during which time the

British burned it (the War of 1812). Bulfinch completed the Capitol, 1817–30. Latrobe and **James Hoban** were responsible for the construction of the White House.

1820–60 Benjamin Henry **Latrobe** used a **Greek Revival** style for the Bank of Pennsylvania in Philadelphia as well as for the Capitol in Washington. His pupil **Robert**

Mills built the United States Treasury Building and started the Washington Monument (1836). Another pupil, **William Strickland,** used Greek design in the Tennessee state capitol at Nashville.

1840–60 **Gothic Revival** began with St. Patrick's Cathedral (completed 1879) and Trinity Church in New York City.

Leading Figures of the Jackson Era

GEORGE BANCROFT (Worcester, Mass., 1800–Washington, D.C., 1891), historian.

1817 Was graduated from Harvard.

1820 Received doctorate at University of Göttingen.

1822–31 Taught at Harvard, wrote poetry, and founded a boys' school.

1830–40 Rose in the Massachusetts Democratic Party.

1834–40 Published first three volumes of his *History of the United States,* which reflected his faith in democracy.

1844 Helped swing the Democratic convention to Polk.

1845–46 Secretary of the Navy. Established the U.S. Naval Academy.

1846–49 Minister to Great Britain.

1852–66 Issued six more volumes of the *History.*

1867–74 Minister to Prussia.

1874 Brought out the final volume of the *History,* which covered the years to 1782.

THOMAS HART BENTON (Hart's Mill, N.C., 1782–Washington, D.C., 1858), U.S. Senator.

1798–99 Attended the University of North Carolina.

1800 Moved to Nashville, Tenn., where he became a lawyer.

1809 State senator.

1812 Served in the War of 1812 but saw no combat.

1813 Engaged in a tavern brawl with Andrew Jackson.

1815 Moved to St. Louis.

1817 Killed U.S. district attorney Charles Lucas in a duel.

1819 Editor of the Missouri *Enquirer.*

1821–51 U.S. Senator from Missouri. He opposed the B.U.S., which he called "The Monster," favored hard money, hence his nickname "Old Bullion," and opposed Clay's American System.

1824 Introduced his graduation bill.

1825–28 Led the Democratic Party campaign to elect Jackson President.

1830 Opposed the Foot Resolution at the start of the Webster-Hayne Debate.

1831 His speech against the B.U.S. reopened the Bank War.

1832 Led the anti-Bank forces in the Senate.

1833 Supported the removal of the B.U.S. deposits.

1834 Secured a change in the ratio of gold to silver from 15–1 to 16–1.

1836 Wrote the Specie Circular.

1837 Had the Senate censure of Jackson expunged.

1840–41 Supported the Independent Treasury and preemption.

1844 Opposed the annexation of Texas.

1846 Supported war with Mexico.

1846 Favored compromise with Great Britain over Oregon.

1847 Refused to follow pro-slavery Missouri instructions.

1850 Did not support the Compromise of 1850. Was defeated in election for the Senate.

1852 Was elected to the House of Representatives.

1854 Opposed Kansas-Nebraska Act and was defeated in Congressional election.

1856 Refused to join the Republican Party even though his son-in-law John C. Frémont was the Presidential candidate.

NICHOLAS BIDDLE (Philadelphia, 1786–1844), banker.
1801 Was graduated from the College of New Jersey.
1804–07 Served on U.S. missions to France and Great Britain.
1806–14 Edited the *Port Folio*, a literary magazine.
1809 Was admitted to the bar in Philadelphia.
1810–11 Served in the Pennsylvania legislature.
1814 Published a history of the expedition of Lewis and Clark.
1814–18 Served in the Pennsylvania senate.
1819–22 A director of the second B.U.S.
1823–36 President of the second B.U.S. Fought the Bank War against Jackson.
1832 Applied for the recharter of the B.U.S.

JOHN C. CALHOUN (Abbeville District, S.C., 1782–Washington, D.C., 1850), U.S. Senator.
1804 Was graduated from Yale.
1807 Started law career in Charleston, S.C.
1808–09 Served in the South Carolina legislature.
1811–17 U.S. Congressman; was acting chairman of the Foreign Affairs Committee; supported the War of 1812.
1815–17 Supported national legislation including the second B.U.S., internal improvements, and a high tariff.
1817–25 Secretary of War.
1825–32 Vice President.
1828 Wrote *South Carolina Exposition* in opposition to the tariff.
1830 Broke with Jackson and Van Buren over state-rights issue.
1832 His Fort Hill Address expounded nullification.
1832 Resigned as Vice President to become a senator from South Carolina.
1832–44 U.S. Senator.
1833 Left the Democratic Party and joined the Whigs.
1837 Returned to the Democratic Party in support of Van Buren's Independent Treasury bill.

1837 Supported slavery as a positive good.
1844–45 Secretary of State; secured the annexation of Texas.
1845–50 U.S. Senator.
1846 Opposed war with Mexico and the Wilmot Proviso.
1849 Denounced Northern "acts of aggression" against Southern slave interests.
1850 In his final Senate speech, he opposed the Compromise of 1850.
1850 Died. His *Disquisition on Government* and *Discourse on the Constitution and Government of the United States,* published after his death, outlined his theories of a dual executive and a concurrent majority to enable one section to check another.

HENRY CLAY (Hanover County, Va., 1777–Washington, D.C., 1852), U.S. Senator.
1797 Moved to Lexington, Ky., where he practiced law.
1803–06 Served in the Kentucky legislature.
1806–07 Finished an unexpired term in the U.S. Senate.
1807–09 Speaker of the Kentucky House of Representatives.
1809–10 Filled a second unexpired term in the Senate. Opposed the recharter of the B.U.S.
1811–21, 1823–25 U.S. Congressman (Speaker of the House except in 1820–21).
1811–12 Led War Hawks in support of War of 1812.
1814 Member of U.S. peace commission at Ghent.
1816 Supported B.U.S. and internal improvements for transportation.
1817 Favored recognition of South American republics.
1820–21 Took part in the two Missouri compromises.
1824 Outlined his "American System" of protective tariff, internal improvements, and the B.U.S.
1824 Unsuccessful candidate for President.
1825 Helped Adams win the Presidential election and was accused of a "corrupt bargain" when he became Secretary of State.
1831–42 U.S. Senator.
1832 Supported the recharter of the B.U.S.
1832 Was defeated for the Presidency.

1833 Arranged the compromise tariff.

1834 Led in censuring Jackson for his removal of the deposits from the B.U.S.

1841–42 Failed to get his "American System" passed. Retired from the Senate.

1844 Opposed annexation of Texas.

1844 Was defeated for the Presidency.

1846 Supported Mexican War.

1849–52 U.S. Senator.

1850 Helped arrange the Compromise of 1850.

RALPH WALDO EMERSON (Boston, 1803–Concord, Mass., 1882)

1821 Was graduated as class poet from Harvard.

1821–25 Taught school in Boston.

1825 Entered Harvard Divinity School.

1829–32 Served as a Unitarian minister.

1832–33 Made a tour of England and other countries in Europe during which he met Coleridge, Carlyle, and Wordsworth. These contacts and his exposure to German idealism formed the basis for his Transcendentalist thought.

1835 Moved to Concord, Mass., where he associated with Thoreau, Alcott, and other Transcendentalists. Began his lecture career and gave up the pulpit.

1836 His first published work, *Nature*, outlined Transcendentalism.

1837 His Phi Beta Kappa address at Harvard, *The American Scholar*, urged American artists and scholars to rely on themselves rather than on Europe.

1838 His Harvard Divinity School address said the church was dead.

1840 Began to contribute to the Transcendentalist journal *The Dial* (and was its editor 1842–44).

1841, 1844 Published his *Essays*.

1847 Published his first volume of poems.

WILLIAM LLOYD GARRISON (Newburyport, Mass., 1805–New York City, 1879), abolitionist.

1818 After brief schooling was apprenticed to the Newburyport, Mass., *Herald*.

1826 Became editor of the Newburyport *Free Press*.

1829 Delivered his first address against slavery, in Boston.

1829 In Baltimore, helped Benjamin Lundy edit *The Genius of Universal Emancipation*.

1830 Spent seven weeks in jail for libel.

1831 Published the first issue of the Boston *Liberator* on Jan. 1. His manifesto ended with the statement: "I will not retreat a single inch—and *I will be heard*." The paper was published continually for 35 years.

1831 Helped draft the constitution of the New England Antislavery Society.

1832 Wrote *Thoughts on African Colonization* in which he attacked the idea of sending Negroes back to Africa.

1833 Helped draw up the declaration of principles of the American Antislavery Society, pledging non-violent means to free the slaves.

1835 A Boston mob hostile to the abolitionists dragged Garrison through the streets.

1840 Opposed political action to secure abolition.

1843 Was elected president of the American Antislavery Society and served for 22 years.

1841 Came out in favor of disunion.

1847 Made a western lecture tour with Negro abolitionist Frederick Douglass.

1854 Publicly burned the U.S. Constitution at Framingham, Mass.

1862 Supported Lincoln after the President issued the Emancipation Proclamation.

WILLIAM HENRY HARRISON (Charles City County, Va., 1773–Washington, D.C., 1841), 9th President of the United States.

1773 Was born on a plantation, the son of Benjamin Harrison, who was later governor of Virginia.

1787 Entered Hampden-Sidney College.

1790 Studied medicine.

1791 Was commissioned as an ensign in the United States infantry.

1794–95 Acted as aide-de-camp to Anthony Wayne at the Battle of Fallen Timbers and during the Treaty of Greenville.

1798 Was appointed secretary of the Northwest Territory. In 1799, served as the territory's first delegate to Congress.

1800 Helped draw up the Land Act of 1800 and was appointed first governor of the Indiana Territory. While governor (1800–13), he secured land cessions from the Indians.

1811 Defeated the Shawnee Indians at the settlement of Tippecanoe, Indiana.

1812 Was appointed Supreme Commander of the Army of the Northwest with the rank of brigadier general. In 1813, he reoccupied Detroit and defeated the British and Indians on the Thames River, Ontario.

1814 Resigned from the army with the rank of major general; took up farming.

1816–19 Served as a representative from Ohio to Congress.

1819 Was elected to the state senate.

1825–28 Served as United States Senator from Ohio.

1828–29 Was Minister to Colombia.

1836 Was one of the Whig and Anti-Masonic candidates for President.

1839 Won the Whig Party nomination for President.

1840 Won the Presidential election on the slogan "Tippecanoe and Tyler too." His symbols were the log cabin and the cider barrel.

1841 Died of pneumonia one month after taking office.

ANDREW JACKSON (Waxhaw, S.C., 1767–Nashville, Tenn., 1845), 7th President of the United States.

1781 Fought in the Revolutionary War.

1787 Was admitted to the bar in North Carolina.

1788 Moved to Nashville, Tenn., where he became U.S. prosecuting attorney.

1791 Married Mrs. Rachel Robards, who did not actually receive her divorce until 1793.

1796 Member of Tennessee's constitutional convention.

1796–97 U.S. Congressman.

1797–98 U.S. Senator.

1798–1804 Superior Judge of Tennessee.

1804 Retired to private life on his plantation "The Hermitage."

1806 Killed Charles Dickinson in a duel.

1812–1815 Commanded Tennessee militia in War of 1812.

1814 Defeated the Creeks at Horseshoe Bend, Ala.

1815 Defeated the British at New Orleans.

1818 Invaded Spanish Florida.

1821 Served as governor of Florida territory.

1822 Was nominated for the Presidency by the Tennessee legislature.

1823–25 U.S. Senator.

1824 Received highest vote in the Presidential election but not an electoral majority.

1825 Was defeated by John Quincy Adams when the Presidential election went to the House.

1825–28 Campaigned for President, claiming a "corrupt bargain" between Clay and Adams.

1828 Was elected President.

1829 Reintroduced spoils system.

1832 Vetoed bill to recharter the B.U.S.

1832 Issued proclamation against South Carolina nullification.

1833 Removed deposits from the B.U.S.

1834 Was censured in the Senate for removal of the deposits. Censure was expunged, 1837.

1836 Issued Specie Circular.

1837 Gave his farewell address and retired to "The Hermitage."

JAMES K. POLK (Mecklenburg County, N.C., 1795–Nashville, Tenn., 1849), 11th President of the United States.

1806 Moved to Tennessee.

1818 Was graduated from the University of North Carolina.

1820 Was admitted to the bar in Tennessee.

1823–25 Served in the Tennessee legislature.

1825–39 U.S. Democratic Congressman; Speaker of the House, 1834–39.

1832 Opposed the B.U.S.

1839–41 Governor of Tennessee.

1844 Nominated as the Democratic "dark horse" candidate for President.

1845–49 President. Carried out territorial expansion, lowered the tariff, and set up the Independent Treasury.

1846–48 War with Mexico.

1848 Did not seek reelection.

ROGER B. TANEY (Calvert County, Md., 1777–Washington, D.C., 1864), Chief Justice of the Supreme Court.

1795 Was graduated from Dickinson College.

1799 Began to practice law.

1799–1800 Federalist member of Maryland legislature.

1816–21 State senator.

1823 Moved to Baltimore.

1825 Became a supporter of Andrew Jackson.

1827–31 Attorney general.

1832 Helped write Jackson's veto message on the recharter of the B.U.S.

1833 Secretary of the Treasury; removed deposits from the B.U.S.

1834 Retired.

1836–64 Chief Justice of the U.S. Supreme Court. His court supported state rights, strict construction of the Constitution, and the rights of the people.

1861–64 Opposed the use of force in the Civil War.

MARTIN VAN BUREN (Kinderhook, N.Y., 1782–1862), 8th President of the United States.

1803 A Republican lawyer in New York State.

1812–20 State senator in New York.

1816–19 Attorney general of N.Y.

1821 Served as a delegate to state constitutional convention.

1821–28 U.S. Senator. Headed the "Bucktail" Republican faction. His organization soon became known as the "Albany Regency."

1824 Supported Crawford for President.

1826 Organized a New York–Virginia alliance in support of Jackson, which marked the start of the Democratic Party.

1829 Governor of New York for two months, then was appointed U.S. Secretary of State.

1831 Cabinet reorganization brought Van Buren men into the Cabinet. Van Buren, himself, resigned as Secretary of State.

1832 His nomination as minister to Great Britain was rejected by the Senate.

1833–37 Vice President.

1837–41 President. The Panic of 1837 made him an unpopular President.

1840 Independent Treasury bill passed.

1840 Was defeated for reelection.

1844 Lost the Presidential nomination when he opposed the annexation of Texas.

1845 Member of the radical Barnburner wing of the Democratic Party in New York.

1848 Presidential candidate for the Free Soil Party.

1852 Rejoined the Democratic Party.

DANIEL WEBSTER (Salisbury, N.H., 1782– Marshfield, Mass., 1852), U.S. Senator.

1801 Was graduated from Dartmouth.

1801–05 Taught school and read law.

1805 Was admitted to the Boston bar.

1807 Moved to Portsmouth, N.H., where he practiced law and became a Federalist.

1812 His "Rockingham Memorial" speech opposed the War of 1812.

1813–17 U.S. Congressman. Opposed the War of 1812 and the tariff of 1816.

1816 Moved to Boston.

1819, 1824 Appeared before the Supreme Court for Dartmouth College in *Dartmouth College v. Woodward*, for the B.U.S. in *McCulloch v. Maryland*, and for Gibbons in *Gibbons v. Ogden*.

1823–27 U.S. Congressman from Massachusetts. Opposed the protective tariff and supported John Quincy Adams.

1827–41 U.S. Senator.

1828 Supported the protective tariff.

1830 Webster-Hayne debate.

1832 Spoke against Jackson's veto of the B.U.S. recharter.

1833 Attacked Jackson for his removal of the deposits.

1836 Massachusetts Whig candidate for President.

1841–43 Secretary of State.

1842 Webster-Ashburton Treaty.

1843 Resumed law practice.

1845–50 U.S. Senator. Opposed the Mexican War.

1850 Defended the Compromise of 1850.

1850–52 Secretary of State.

Statistical Tables

Table 27.
Ten largest cities in the U.S.
(thousands)

1820		1840		1860	
Philadelphia[a]	137	New York[a]	349	New York[a]	1,072
New York[a]	135	Philadelphia[a]	258	Philadelphia[a]	585
Baltimore	63	New Orleans	102	Baltimore	212
Boston	44	Baltimore	102	Boston	178
New Orleans	27	Boston	93	New Orleans	169
Charleston	25	Cincinnati	46	Cincinnati	161
Washington	13	Albany	34	St. Louis	161
Albany	13	Charleston	29	Chicago	109
Richmond	12	Washington	23	Buffalo	81
Salem, Mass.	11	Providence	23	Newark	72

[a] Philadelphia includes all of Philadelphia County; New York includes Brooklyn.

4-5   Population, 1850

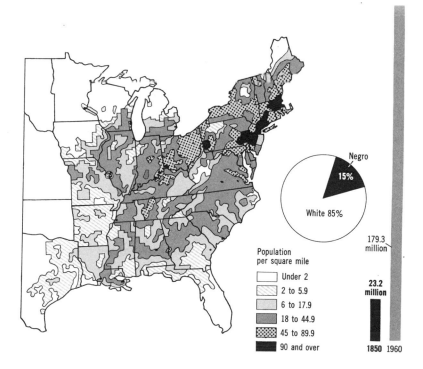

Negro
15%

White 85%

Population
per square mile

☐ Under 2
▨ 2 to 5.9
▨ 6 to 17.9
▨ 18 to 44.9
▨ 45 to 89.9
■ 90 and over

179.3
million

23.2
million

1850 1960

Table 28.
U.S. population
(thousands)

	1830	1840	1850	1860
Total	12,901	17,120	23,261	31,513
Negro	2,329	2,874	3,639	4,442
Negro Slave	2,009	2,487	3,204	3,954
Free Negroes	320	386	435	488

Table 29.
Regional population
(thousands)

	1820	1840	1860
New England	1,660	2,235	3,135
Middle Atlantic	2,700	4,526	7,459
Old Northwest	793	2,925	6,927
Northwest across Miss. River	67	427	2,170
South Atlantic	3,061	3,925	5,365
Old Southwest	1,190	2,575	4,021
Southwest across Miss. River	168	450	1,748
Mountain			175
Pacific			444

Table 30.
Total population, 1860

Grand Total	31,443,321
Urban	6,216,518
Rural	25,226,803
White, total	26,922,537
White, native	22,825,784
White, foreign-born	4,096,753
Negro, total	4,441,830
Negro, slave	3,953,760
Negro, free	488,070
Other races	78,954

Table 31.
Wholesale commodity price index
(1900–14 = 100)

1830	91
1835	100
1840	95
1845	83
1850	84
1855	110
1860	93

Table 32.
Public land sales
(thousands of acres)

1830	1,930
1835	12,565
1840	2,237
1845	1,844
1850	1,406
1855	11,960
1860	2,543

Table 33.
U.S. government expenditures and receipts
(millions of dollars)

	Expenditures	*Receipts*	*Debt*
1830	15.1	24.8	48.6
1835	17.6	35.4	.04
1840	24.3	19.5	3.6
1845	22.9	30.0	15.9
1850	39.5	43.6	63.5
1855	59.7	65.4	35.6
1860	63.1	56.1	64.8

Table 34.
Vessels entering U.S. ports

1830	1,099
1835	1,994
1840	2,289
1845	2,946
1850	3,749
1855	5,945
1860	8,275

PART 5

The Road to War, 1849–1861

The Compromise of 1850

1849

The Growing Crisis

Jan. 22   48 Southern Congressmen signed **Calhoun's "address"** attacking the North for interfering with slavery.

Nov. 13   California ratified a constitution prohibiting slavery.

Dec. 3   Congress convened with 112 Democrats, 105 Whigs, 12 Free-Soilers, and one Native-American in the House, and 35 Democrats and 25 Whigs in the Senate. A new generation of Senators—such as Whig **William H. Seward** (N.Y.), and Democrats **Stephen A. Douglas** (Ill.) and **Jefferson Davis** (Miss.)—joined Clay, Calhoun, Webster, and Benton, who were serving their last terms. In the House, Alexander H. Stephens and Robert A. Toombs, Whigs of Georgia, bitterly opposed the Whig nomination of Robert C. Winthrop (Mass.) as Speaker. Party lines collapsed as North turned against South, and it took almost three weeks and 63 ballots to elect Democrat Howell Cobb (Ga.) as Speaker.

Dec. 4   President Taylor outraged Southerners in Congress by urging the immediate admission of California as a free state and the eventual admission of New Mexico with no preliminary territorial status.

1850

The Great Debate

Jan. 29   **Henry Clay** introduced resolutions for the Senate (1) to admit California as a free State; (2) to organize the rest of the territory acquired from Mexico without any decision on slavery; (3) to compensate Texas for giving up its claim to part of New Mexico; (4) to prohibit the slave trade in the District of Columbia but not to abolish slavery there without compensation for and the consent of its residents and those of Maryland; and (5) to pass a more rigorous fugitive slave act and announce that Congress could not interfere with the slave trade.

Feb. 5–6   Clay spoke for his resolutions and for the Union.

Feb. 13   Jefferson Davis rejected Clay's proposals in a bitter speech attacking the North.

Mar. 4   **Calhoun,** too ill to speak (he died Mar. 31), made his last appearance in the Senate as Sen. James M. Mason (Va.) delivered his final speech for him. Calhoun, refusing to compromise, said that the only way to save the Union was for the North to give the South equal rights in the new territories and to cease agitation on the slavery question.

Mar. 7   **Webster,** speaking not "as a Northern man, but as an American," defended the resolutions, arguing that nature had already made it impossible for slavery to flourish in the new territories and pointing out that both North and South had just grievances. Abolitionists and Free-Soilers bitterly attacked Webster (Whittier in his *Ichabod* called Webster "So fallen! so lost!"), but northern Whigs rallied to his support.

Mar. 11   **William H. Seward,** speaking for the antislavery North, opposed the compromise and called on "a higher law" than the

Constitution to keep slavery out of the territories.

Mar. 13   Stephen A. Douglas supported popular sovereignty in the territories. He was already making plans to carry out the compromise.

Apr. 18   The Senate referred Clay's resolutions to a select committee with Clay as chairman.

May 8   The Senate committee reported an **Omnibus Bill** containing the substance of the Clay Resolutions. A four-month debate followed.

June 10   Nashville (Tenn.) **Convention** of nine slave states rejected the extremist position of Robert B. Rhett (S.C.) and called for the extension of the Missouri Compromise line to the Pacific.

July 9   President Taylor died in the White House. Though Taylor had opposed Clay's resolutions, his successor, **Millard Fillmore,** favored compromise.

Aug. 13–23   While Clay was vacationing, **Douglas** broke the Omnibus Bill into several separate bills that passed the Senate.

Sept. 9–20   Five acts constituting the "Compromise of 1850" were enacted:

1. Congress admitted **California** as a **free** state (Sept. 9).
2. The Texas and New Mexico Act defined the boundaries of Texas, compensated Texas for land surrendered to New Mexico, and organized the New Mexico Territory. **New Mexico** was to be admitted into the Union **"with or without slavery"** as its constitution prescribed (Sept. 9).
3. The Utah Act established the Territory of **Utah** (separated from New Mexico by the 37th parallel) with the same provisions as for New Mexico (Sept. 9).
4. The **Fugitive Slave Act** provided for special federal commissioners empowered to issue warrants for the arrest of fugitives. While affidavits by the claimants were sufficient proof of ownership, the fugitives were denied the right of trial by jury and their testimony was not admitted as evidence. The vote for the Act in the Senate was 27–12. Among the nay votes were those of eight northern Whigs, three northern Democrats, and one Free-Soiler.

5. Congress abolished the **slave trade** in the **District of Columbia** (Sept. 20).

1851

Acceptance of the Compromise

The North supported the Compromise with a number of mass meetings. In New York, however, a majority of the Whigs backed Seward's radical position and forced conservative Whigs to bolt the party and eventually join the Know-Nothing Party. In addition, northern opposition to the fugitive slave law led to the passage of **personal liberty laws.** The Massachusetts law (1855), which virtually nullified the Fugitive Slave Act, was particularly stringent. Several **rescues of fugitive slaves** took place in 1851, such as those of Shadrach in Boston and Jerry in Syracuse. A majority in the South accepted the Compromise, and only a few delegates appeared at the second Nashville Convention on Nov. 11–18. A state convention in **Georgia** on Dec. 10 resolved to abide by the Compromise but warned that it would resist further northern attacks on slavery. Southern secessionists lost state elections in Mississippi, South Carolina, and Alabama in 1851. Northern refusals to abide by the Fugitive Slave Law soon undermined the Compromise of 1850.

Dec. 1   Charles Sumner (Mass.) and Benjamin F. Wade (Ohio), both opponents of slavery, took their seats in the Senate.

1852

Mar. 20   Harriet Beecher Stowe published the book version of *Uncle Tom's Cabin,* a powerful novel attacking the evils of slavery. It had first been serialized in an antislavery newspaper and had then appeared on the stage. Over a million copies were published by early 1853.

June 1   The **Democratic Convention** met in Baltimore and nominated **Franklin Pierce** (N.H.) for President and **William R. King,** (Ala.) for Vice President on a platform that supported the Compromise of 1850.

June 16   The **Whig Convention** met in Baltimore and nominated Gen. **Winfield Scott** (La.) for President and **William A.**

Graham (N.C.) for Vice President on a platform that accepted the Compromise of 1850.

Aug. 11 The **Free-Soil Party** met at Pittsburgh and nominated **John P. Hale** (N.H.) for President and **George W. Julian** (Ind.) for Vice President on a platform that attacked slavery as a sin.

Nov. 2 Presidential election: Pierce was elected with 1,601,117 votes (254 electoral) to 1,385,453 (42 electoral) for **Scott** and 155,825 for **Hale**.

American Imperialism, 1844–1860

1844 After the Opium War (1839–42) the British negotiated treaties with China in which they secured favorable trading rights in special treaty ports. Caleb Cushing secured similar rights for the United States in the **Treaty of Wanghia.**

1846 By treaty, the **Republic of New Granada** (Colombia) granted the United States right of transit across the Isthmus of Panama.

1850 Alarmed by British expansion in Central America, Presidents Polk and Taylor negotiated treaties in 1848–49 that granted the U.S. exclusive right of way across the isthmus at Nicaragua in return for protecting Nicaraguan sovereignty, but the treaties were never submitted to the Senate. Negotiations between Secretary of State John M. Clayton and British Minister to the U.S. Sir Henry Lytton Bulwer led to the **Clayton-Bulwer Treaty,** in which both nations agreed that neither would obtain exclusive control over any Central American canal or fortify it nor would either obtain dominion over any part of Central America.

1850 When President Taylor in 1849 promised to recognize the revolutionary government that resulted from the Hungarian Revolution (1848), the Austrian government protested. Secretary of State Webster replied that the United States had every right to take an interest in European revolutions, which had their origins in American ideas. Americans, particularly **"Young America"** expansionists led by Stephen A. Douglas, applauded Webster's nationalism. American enthusiasm for the revolutions of 1848

reached its peak in the reception given the Hungarian patriot Louis Kossuth in 1851.

1851 American expansionists, especially Southerners seeking more slave territory, looked eagerly toward Cuba after the Mexican War, but Polk was unable to buy the island from Spain. In 1850 General Narciso López, a Venezuelan, organized Cuban refugees and American adventurers in New Orleans for an unsuccessful invasion of Cuba. He landed near Havana in 1851 with 400 men, but the revolt was snuffed out. When the Spanish government executed him and 51 others (all American southerners), the U.S. government protested and gained the release of the rest of the Americans.

1853 Gadsden Purchase: James Gadsden, U.S. minister to Mexico, signed a treaty with Mexico on Dec. 30 that sold to the United States for $10 million the land south of the Gila River in present-day southern Arizona and southern New Mexico. Southerners led by Secretary of War Jefferson Davis wanted the land for a southern transcontinental railroad.

1854

Feb. 28 When the Spanish in Cuba seized an American merchant vessel on a technicality, Pierre Soulé, the American minister to Spain and an expansionist, demanded satisfaction. The resulting **Black Warrior affair** caused war fever to break out in the United States, but the matter was settled peacefully.

Mar. 31 Perry's Reopening of Japan: in Nov., 1852, President Fillmore sent an expedition under Commodore Matthew C. Perry from Norfolk, Va., to Japan, which had been closed to foreign trade since 1638. Perry sailed into Yedo (Tokyo) Bay in July, 1853, delivered a letter for the Emperor, and then sailed away. He returned in March, 1854, and signed the **Treaty of Kanagawa,** which allowed the United States to trade at two ports. Other western powers soon followed the U.S. into Japan.

June 5 Reciprocal Fishing Treaty with Canada gave the United States fishing rights along the shores of Canada, Nova Scotia, and elsewhere, and the British similar rights along the United States coast.

Oct. 18   The **Ostend Manifesto** resulted from a brief meeting at Ostend, Belgium, among John Y. Mason, U.S. minister to France, James Buchanan, minister to Great Britain, and Soulé; they sent a memorandum to Secretary of State William L. Marcy recommending that the United States either buy Cuba or consider "wresting it from Spain." Southerners and expansionists were delighted, but Northerners forced Pierce to repudiate Soulé, who resigned on Dec. 17.

1854   President Pierce made a treaty to annex **Hawaii** but failed to get it through the Senate. American traders had begun to stop in Hawaii in the early nineteenth century and missionaries had arrived in the 1830's.

1855   American railroad across the Isthmus of Panama was completed.

1855–57   **William Walker** of the United States, on an expedition into Central America, gained control of Nicaragua but was ousted in 1857. The U.S. Navy blocked his second expedition later in 1857. When he did get back in 1860, he was captured and shot in Honduras.

1858   **Harris Treaty** with Japan: Townsend Harris, first American consul-general to Japan, signed a treaty on July 29 by which Japan opened to American trade three more ports and called for an exchange of ministers.

The Kansas-Nebraska Act and the Rise of the Republican Party, 1853–1856

1853

Mar. 4   In his Inaugural Address, Franklin Pierce urged further expansion. During his Administration Pierce, who was a weak President, allowed power to shift to Secretary of War Jefferson Davis and Senator Stephen A. Douglas.

Summer   Anti-immigrant and anti-Catholic sentiment, which had arisen in the 1830's and 1840's, revived with the great increase in immigration, 1847–53. By 1853 nativist organizations had coalesced into one known first

as the Order of the Star Spangled Banner and then as the **Know-Nothing Party** because its members answered all questions about the organization with the phrase, "I know nothing." It demanded the exclusion of Catholics from national office and a 21-year residence requirement for naturalization.

1854

The Kansas-Nebraska Act

Jan. 4   Senator Stephen A. Douglas introduced a bill to organize the territory of Nebraska "with or without slavery." On Jan. 17 an amendment was offered in the Senate to repeal the Missouri Compromise of 1820.

Jan. 23   Douglas offered a new bill to organize the territories of Kansas and Nebraska with or without slavery and to **repeal the Missouri Compromise**.

Jan. 24   **Salmon P. Chase**, Free-Soil Party Senator from Ohio and five other abolitionists or freesoilers in Congress published the **"Appeal of the Independent Democrats,"** written by Chase. The Appeal attacked the Kansas-Nebraska Act as a plot to keep free labor out of the territories and to populate them with slaves.

Jan. 30   Douglas defended the Kansas-Nebraska bill as a continuation of the Compromise of 1850. Historians have argued variously that Douglas was selfishly seeking Southern support for the 1856 nomination, that he wanted to organize the territories to promote a central transcontinental railroad that would help develop Chicago, or that he was supporting the reelection of Sen. David R. Atchison of Missouri, who had promised his constituents a proslavery plan for the territories. It is more likely that as a "Young America" expansionist he wanted to people the territories and that he considered his bill the best way to unify his party and the nation. Whatever his motive, Douglas, who had no moral repugnance for slavery, underestimated the depth of a northwestern opposition to slavery in the territories.

May 22   The **Kansas-Nebraska Act** passed the House, 113–100, after having been passed by the Senate. The House vote broke down party lines as follows:

	Yea	*Nay*
Northern Democrats	44	42
Southern Democrats	57	2
Northern Whigs	0	45
Southern Whigs	12	7
Others	0	4

May 30   President Pierce signed the Kansas-Nebraska Act into law.

Feb.–June   Northern opposition to the Kansas-Nebraska Act erupted at countless mass meetings at which speakers such as Chase, Sumner, Seward, Horace Greeley, and others—Whigs, Democrats, and Free-Soilers —joined in condemning the bill. Democrats suffered great losses in the spring elections, and the Whig Party split into northern and southern wings.

Feb.–July   Organization of the REPUBLICAN PARTY: the first meeting to combine "**Anti–Kansas-Nebraska**" Whigs and Democrats into a new party took place in Ripon, Wis., Feb. 28, and the movement spread rapidly throughout the North. On May 9 Massachusetts fusionists agreed on the name "Republican," which was formally adopted at Jackson, Mich., on July 6. While other places have claimed the honor of creating the title "Republican Party," the name sprang up spontaneously. Republicans agreed on repealing the Kansas-Nebraska Act and preventing the spread of slavery to the territories.

The Kansas Struggle, 1854–1856

Apr. 26   Eli Thayer incorporated the Massachusetts Emigrant Aid Society to encourage free settlers to migrate to Kansas. Soon reorganized as the **New England Emigrant Aid Society,** it gave moral impetus to freesoil

5-1   The Kansas-Nebraska Act, 1854, and Admission of States, 1836–1863

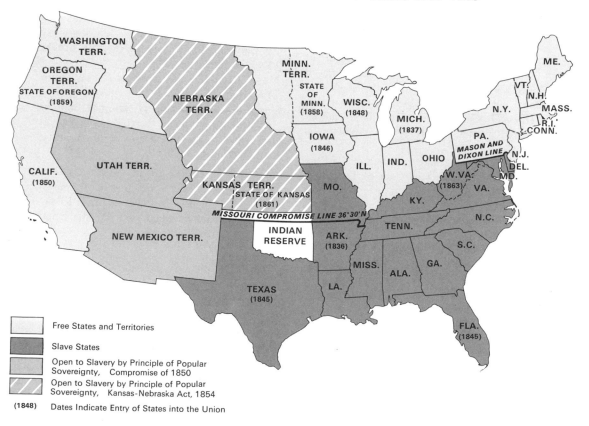

Free States and Territories

Slave States

Open to Slavery by Principle of Popular Sovereignty,   Compromise of 1850

Open to Slavery by Principle of Popular Sovereignty,   Kansas-Nebraska Act, 1854

(1848)   Dates Indicate Entry of States into the Union

settlers but managed to send west only 1,240 settlers in 1854–55.

June 29 Andrew H. Reeder became the first territorial governor of Kansas.

Summer The Massachusetts Emigrant Aid Society, established **Lawrence, Kan.**, as a free town.

Summer Slaveholders from Missouri settled **Leavenworth, Kan.**, as a slave town.

Oct. 4 **Abraham Lincoln**, still a Whig, spoke in Springfield, Ill., in answer to Stephen A. Douglas, who had spoken there the day before. He denounced the injustice of slavery and opposed its spread to the territories. Delivered again at Peoria, Ill., the speech became known as the **Peoria Address**.

Nov. 29 **First election** in Kansas. Over 1,700 Missourians crossed over into Kansas, voted illegally, and elected a proslavery delegate to Congress.

1855

Mar. 30 In the territorial election, Missourians again voted illegally and elected a proslavery legislature, which drew up a proslavery body of statutes. Violence broke out as freesoilers and proslavery elements moved into Kansas.

Sept. Wilson Shannon became the new governor of Kansas; President Pierce had removed Reeder on July 28 for opposing the legislature.

Sept. 5 A free-state convention led by Reeder and James Lane met at Lawrence, Kan.

Oct. 23–Nov. 11 Freesoil men met at Topeka, Kan., and drew up a constitution to abolish slavery in Kansas by 1857. Freesoil voters ratified the constitution on Dec. 15.

Nov. 21–Dec. 7 In the **Wakarusa War** proslavery forces in Kansas, supported by "Border Ruffians" from Missouri, moved against the freesoil stronghold at Lawrence, but war was averted.

1856

Jan. 15 A freesoil governor and legislature were elected in Kansas.

Jan. 24 President Pierce recognized the proslavery legislature in Kansas.

Mar. The freesoil legislature asked Congress for admission of Kansas as a free state. In Congress, Seward proposed admission of Kansas under the freesoil constitution; Douglas proposed delaying admission, meanwhile supporting the proslavery government.

"Bleeding Kansas" As proslavery and freesoil elements poured into Kansas, savage acts of violence occurred on both sides.

May 19–20 In the Senate, **Charles Sumner** delivered his **"Crime Against Kansas"** speech in which he extravagantly condemned "slave power" in general and Senator Andrew P. Butler (S.C.) in particular.

May 21 Proslavery forces captured and sacked Lawrence as civil war broke out in Kansas.

May 22 Congressman **Preston S. Brooks** (S.C.), angered by Sumner's assault on his uncle, Senator Butler, attacked Sumner in the Senate chamber and injured him so severely that he was absent from the Senate (except for one day) until Dec., 1859.

May 24–25 **John Brown**, a fanatical antislavery leader, and six others murdered five proslavery settlers at **Pottawatomie Creek, Kan.**

May Civil war continued in Kansas. **John W. Geary**, newly appointed governor, used federal troops to stop an army of "Border Ruffians" and brought the civil war to an end on Sept. 15. Perhaps 200 were killed during the fighting in 1856.

Presidential campaign of 1856: as political parties broke apart over the Kansas-Nebraska Act, the Republican and Know-Nothing parties emerged, and the Whig and Free-Soil parties vanished.

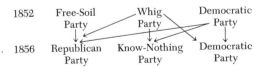

1852	Free-Soil Party	Whig Party	Democratic Party
1856	Republican Party	Know-Nothing Party	Democratic Party

Feb. 22 The **American (Know-Nothing) Party** convened at Philadelphia and nominated **Millard Fillmore** (N.Y.) for President and **Andrew J. Donelson** (Tenn.) for Vice President. Northern delegates withdrew in protest.

June 2   The **Democratic Party** met in Cincinnati and nominated **James Buchanan** (Pa.) for President and **John C. Breckinridge** (Ky.) for Vice President. The party refused to nominate Pierce or Douglas because they were too well known for their proslavery views. Buchanan, who had been absent in Great Britain, seemed best qualified to unite northern and southern Democrats.

June 16   The antislavery seceders from the American Party convention met to nominate Nathaniel P. Banks (Mass.) for President, but a few days later they joined the Republican Party and accepted the nomination of John C. Frémont.

June 17   The Republican Party met in Philadelphia. By this time Whigs such as William H. Seward and Abraham Lincoln had joined the party. The Republicans nominated **John C. Frémont** (Calif.) for President and **William L. Dayton** (N.J.) for Vice President on an antislavery platform.

Sept. 17   Remnants of the Whig Party endorsed the American Party ticket.

Nov. 4   Presidential election: Buchanan was elected President with 1,832,955 votes (174 electoral) to 1,339,932 (114 electoral) for **Frémont** and 871,731 (8 electoral) for **Fillmore.** The election was noticeably sectional with Frémont's vote confined generally to northern states. His failure to carry Pennsylvania, Indiana, and Illinois cost him the election.

Slavery and Politics, 1857-1858

1857

Mar. 4   Buchanan's Inaugural Address supported "popular sovereignty" in the territories but also recommended that the decision on the issue be left to the Supreme Court. Buchanan, of course, knew then what the decision would be.

Mar. 6   DRED SCOTT DECISION: Chief Justice Taney, speaking for the majority on most points, declared that **Negroes could not be citizens,** that Congress could not keep slavery out of the territories, and that the **Missouri Compromise** was therefore **unconstitutional.** Since all nine justices rendered briefs, the exact terms of the deci-

sion were never clear. The slave **Dred Scott** had been taken by his master, Dr. John Emerson, from Missouri—first to **Illinois** and then to **Wisconsin** Territory. Dr. Emerson brought Scott back to Missouri just before he died, whereupon Scott became the property of the doctor's widow and then of her brother, **John F. A. Sanford** of New York. Aided by Henry T. Blow, a son of his former owner, and others, Scott first sued for his freedom in Missouri courts by arguing that his residence in free territory (Illinois under the Northwest Ordinance and Wisconsin under the Missouri Compromise) had made him a free man. When he was unsuccessful there, he sued in the federal district court as a citizen of Missouri against his master, John Sanford, a citizen of New York. *Dred Scott v. Sandford* was reargued on appeal before the Supreme Court beginning in Dec., 1856; by Mar., 1857, the whole country was awaiting the decision. Three justices argued that no Negro of slave ancestry could be a citizen, hence Scott could not sue in a federal court; six justices argued that residence in free territory did not make him free, because his status depended on the laws of Missouri. Six justices argued that Congress could not keep slavery from a territory, thereby declaring the Missouri Compromise unconstitutional. Only two justices, **John McLean** (Ohio) and **Benjamin R. Curtis** (Mass.), argued for the minority that Scott was a citizen and that Congress could bar slavery from a territory. The decision marked the first time since *Marbury v. Madison* that the court had declared an act of Congress unconstitutional and set a precedent for later cases of judicial review. It also widened the sectional rift.

Mar.-May, 1858   Kansas

Mar. 4   Gov. Geary was forced to resign after vetoing an attempt to set up a proslavery constitution without submitting it to the people.

Mar. 26   Buchanan appointed former Secretary of the Treasury **Robert J. Walker** of Mississippi as the new governor of Kansas. Realizing that slavery was doomed in Kansas (only 200 slaves remained), Walker was determined to bring Kansas into the Union as a free state.

Oct. 5–6 Freesoil candidates won the first all-Kansas election after Gov. Walker threw out many fraudulent ballots.

Oct. 19–Nov. 8 Proslavery convention at Lecompton, Kan., drew up a constitution guaranteeing the right to slave property. The delegates voted not to submit the details of the constitution to the people but to allow the people to vote on accepting the constitution with or without slavery. Slaves presently in Kansas would remain whichever way the vote came out. Gov. Walker opposed the **Lecompton Constitution**.

Dec. 8–May, 1858 **The Congressional battle over Kansas: President Buchanan**, fearing southern secession, urged Congress to admit Kansas under the Lecompton Constitution.

Dec. 9 **Senator Douglas** broke with Buchanan and opposed the Lecompton Constitution when the legislature submitted it for ratification. This time freesoilers voted.

1858

Apr. 1 The House of Representatives blocked the Administration's Senate bill to admit Kansas under the Lecompton Constitution.

Apr. 23 Democrat **William D. English** (Ind.) proposed a compromise bill in the House to admit Kansas under the Lecompton Constitution after it had been resubmitted to the people.

May 4 In spite of Douglas' opposition, the English bill became law. Kansas again rejected the Lecompton Constitution, and the Kansas issue faded.

June–Nov. **Congressional campaign:** in a speech accepting the Illinois Republican nomination for the U.S. Senate, Abraham Lincoln spoke strongly against slavery and predicted a crisis. He continued, "'A house divided against itself cannot stand.' I believe this government cannot endure permanently half slave and half free." This **"House Divided" speech** attracted national attention to Lincoln.

Aug. 21–Oct. 15 **The LINCOLN-DOUGLAS DEBATES**

When Lincoln challenged his opponent for the Senate, Stephen A. Douglas, to a series of debates, seven took place in various Illinois towns.

At **Freeport** on Aug. 27 Lincoln began by outlining his own position:

1. continuance of the Fugitive Slave Act;
2. gradual abolition of slavery in the District of Columbia;
3. Congressional prohibition of slavery in the territories;
4. the ultimate extinction of slavery.

He then asked Douglas how he could reconcile popular sovereignty and the Dred Scott decision. Douglas replied that in spite of the Dred Scott decision the people in a territory could exclude slavery by denying it police protection. Known as the **Freeport Doctrine**, this answer helped Douglas win the election and the Democratic nomination in 1860 but lost him much southern support. Throughout the debates Lincoln declared slavery a moral wrong, though he did not support its abolition. Douglas never considered it a moral issue. Lincoln lost the election in the Illinois legislature, 54–41.

Oct. 25 At Rochester, N.Y., **William H. Seward**, denounced slavery and called the struggle over slavery an **"irrepressible conflict."**

Fall In **Congressional elections**, the Republicans scored heavy gains in the North, picking up 28 seats in Congress, where the Administration lost control of the House.

The Coming of War, 1858–1861

1858

From Dec. until May, 1860, **friction over the issue of slavery increased**. On Dec. 20–21, **John Brown** raided in Missouri, seized 11 slaves, and carried them to freedom.

1859

Mar. 7 *Ableman v. Booth:* when the Wisconsin Supreme Court freed abolitionist editor Sherman M. Booth from a charge of violating the Fugitive Slave Act on the grounds that the act was unconstitutional, U.S. Marshall Ableman appealed to the U.S. Supreme Court, where the decision of Chief Justice Taney reversed that of the Wisconsin court. The Wisconsin legislature then passed resolutions defending the sovereignty of the states in such matters. Like the South, the North was willing to resort to the state-rights doctrine over vital issues.

May 12   Southern Commercial Convention at Vicksburg, Miss., demanded the opening of the foreign slave trade.

May 24   A Cleveland mass meeting, with Gov. Salmon P. Chase the chief speaker, declared the Fugitive Slave law null and void. At the same time federal courts released from Oberlin and Wellington, Ohio, men who had rescued slaves escaping from Kentucky the preceding fall.

July 5   Kansas constitutional convention at Wyandotte completed a constitution, ratified on Oct. 4, prohibiting slavery.

Summer   **Robert B. Rhett** (S.C.), **William L. Yancey,** (Ala.), and other radicals intensified their southern campaign for secession.

Oct. 16–18   **JOHN BROWN'S RAID:** backed by abolitionists such as Theodore Parker, Gerrit Smith and Frederick Douglass, John Brown led 18 men in a raid on the federal arsenal at Harper's Ferry, Va. He hoped to start a slave rebellion that would spread throughout the South. Brown seized the arsenal but two days later surrendered to U.S. marines under Col. **Robert E. Lee.**

Oct. 25–31   The Circuit Court of Virginia convicted Brown of treason against the state and of conspiracy to incite a slave rebellion.

Dec. 2   John Brown was hanged at Charles Town, Va.; six of his band were hanged later. Brown's raid brought war closer: Southerners blamed abolitionists; while many Northerners agreed with Emerson that Brown had made the "gallows glorious like the cross."

Dec. 5   A two-month struggle began over the election of the Speaker of the House. Southerners blocked Republican John Sherman of Ohio because he and other Republicans had endorsed **Hinton R. Helper's** book *The Impeding Crisis of the South.* The book, published in 1857, had attempted to prove by statistics that slavery had debased the condition of the poor whites in the South. It enraged southern leaders, who considered it insurrectionary. Emotions were so high in the House that many members came armed. William Pennington, formerly a Whig from

New Jersey was elected Speaker on Feb. 1, 1860, as a compromise candidate.

1859–60   The South tightened its restrictions on Negroes (slave and free). Alabama, for example, forbade the manumission of slaves. During this period, the governors of South Carolina, Mississippi, and Alabama exchanged letters planning a radical southern convention for June, 1860, but the convention was never held. Threats of secession were frequent.

1860

Feb. 2   The **Davis Resolutions,** offered by Jefferson Davis in the Senate, outlined the southern radical position by stating that attacks on slavery violated the Constitution; that the national government should protect slavery in the territories; and that state laws interfering with the recovery of runaway slaves were unconstitutional. A bitter debate over slavery continued until the resolutions were adopted on May 24.

Feb. 27   Lincoln brought his speaking tour in the Northeast to a climax with his **Cooper Union speech** in New York City. After refuting Douglas' popular sovereignty arguments, he defended the Republican Party against charges of radicalism and urged moderation.

Feb. 29   In the Senate, William H. Seward promised that the Republican Party would support a homestead bill, a Pacific railway, and would encourage manufacturing.

Mar.–June   **NORTH-SOUTH ECONOMIC ISSUES**

Mar.   A **free-homestead bill** passed the House, with voting almost completely sectional: only one slave-state Congressman voted yea; only one free-state member voted nay. A compromise bill finally passed both House and Senate, but on June 22 Buchanan bowed to southern pressure and vetoed it.

Apr. 11   Bill to admit **Kansas** under the freesoil Wyandotte Constitution passed the House, but no action was taken in the Senate. Kansas was finally admitted as a free state on Jan. 29, 1861.

May 10   The **tariff** bill of Congressman **Justin S. Morrill** (Vt.), increasing duties, passed the House on a sectional vote. Northerners supported it as a means of stimulating industry, while Southerners rejected it because of their low tariff tradition. Southerners blocked it in the Senate, but it became law on Mar. 2, 1861, after secession.

May The North blamed the South for sending back to committee a bill for a **transcontinental railroad** along the 41st parallel.

Apr.–Nov. Presidential campaign: Democratic Convention met at Charleston, S.C., Apr. 23–May 3. When the convention refused to adopt a plank calling on Congress to protect slavery in the territories, southern delegates withdrew and the convention adjourned.

May 9 Whigs and American Party members met in Baltimore and formed the **Constitutional Union Party,** which condemned sectional parties and recognized "no political principle other than the Constitution." The party nominated **John Bell** (Tenn.) for President and **Edward Everett** (Mass.) for Vice President.

May 16–18 The Republican Convention met in Chicago and nominated **Abraham Lincoln,** for President over William H. Seward. **Hannibal Hamlin** (Maine) was nominated for Vice President. The platform opposed slavery in the territories but defended the right of each state to "control its own domestic institutions." It included economic planks to unite East and West: free homesteads, internal improvements, a Pacific railroad, encouragement for immigration, and a vague promise to "encourage . . . industrial interests."

June 18–23 The **Democratic National Convention** in Baltimore nominated **Stephen A. Douglas** for President and **Herschel V. Johnson** (Ga.) for Vice President. South-

5-2 The Election of 1860 and Secession

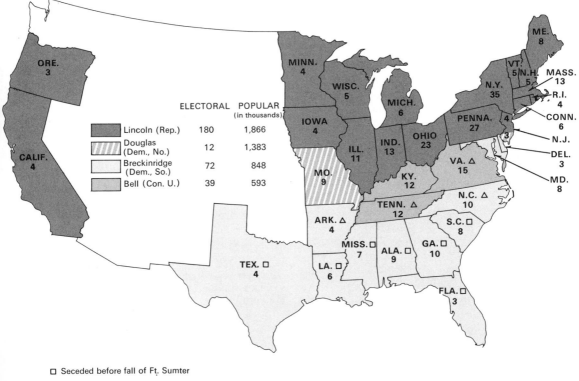

	ELECTORAL	POPULAR (in thousands)
Lincoln (Rep.)	180	1,866
Douglas (Dem., No.)	12	1,383
Breckinridge (Dem., So.)	72	848
Bell (Con. U.)	39	593

□ Seceded before fall of Ft. Sumter

△ Seceded after fall of Ft. Sumter

ern delegates again seceded. The platform promised to abide by the Dred Scott decision.

June 28   Southern Democrats met in Baltimore and nominated **John C. Breckinridge** (Ky.) for President and **Joseph Lane** (Ore.) for Vice President. The platform demanded federal protection for slavery in the territories.

Nov. 6   Presidential election: Lincoln was elected with 1,865,593 votes (180 electoral), to 848,356 for **Breckinridge** (72 electoral), 1,382,713 for **Douglas** (12 electoral), and 592,906 for **Bell** (39 electoral). Lincoln carried only free states, Breckinridge only slave states. Douglas carried Missouri and part of New Jersey; Bell carried three border states. Lincoln carried only 40 per cent of the popular vote.

Dec.-Feb., 1861   Secession The South responded violently to the Republican victory; in three weeks five states arranged conventions to vote on secession. Leading the secessionists were Robert B. Rhett and Gov. William H. Gist (S.C.), Robert A. Toombs (Ga.), Edmund Ruffin (Va.), and William L. Yancey (Ala.). Alexander H. Stephens (Ga.) and Sam Houston (Tex.) opposed secession.

Dec. 3 In his annual message President Buchanan spoke against secession but announced that the federal government could not use force to stop it.

Dec. 18 Senator **John J. Crittenden** (Ky.) proposed a constitutional amendment prohibiting slavery north of 36°-30′ but recognizing it south of that line. Lincoln refused to accept the proposal, which floundered in the Senate.

Dec. 20   South Carolina convention at Columbia voted unanimously for **secession**. Its "Declaration of Causes" called attention to the North's continued attack on slavery and the victory of the sectional Republican Party.

Dec. 26 Maj. **Robert Anderson** moved his U.S. troops from Fort Moultrie to Fort Sumter in Charleston Harbor.

Dec. 29 South Carolina demanded that the United States troops withdraw from Charleston Harbor.

Dec. 30 South Carolina seized the federal arsenal at Charleston.

1861

Jan. 9 President Buchanan sent the unarmed ship *Star of the West* to reinforce Fort Sumter, but fire from South Carolina troops forced it to turn back.

Jan. 9-Feb. 1 After a bitter struggle, particularly in Georgia and Alabama, the **Lower South seceded: Mississippi** on Jan. 9, **Florida** on Jan. 10, **Alabama** on Jan. 11, **Georgia** on Jan. 19, **Louisiana** on Jan. 26, and **Texas** on Feb. 1.

Jan.-Feb. The South seized a number of federal arsenals and barracks.

Feb. 4-27   Peace Convention in Washington, called by Virginia, proposed amendments to the U.S. Constitution similar to Crittenden's proposals, but they were rejected by the Senate.

Feb. 4 A convention of six southern states that had seceded met at Montgomery, Ala., on Feb. 8 and set up a provisional government with a constitution. The **Confederate Constitution**, which was formally adopted at Montgomery on Mar. 11, resembled the U.S. Constitution but declared the sovereignty of the states. It protected slavery but prohibited the importation of slaves.

Feb. 9 The Confederate Congress elected **Jefferson Davis** provisional President and **Alexander H. Stephens** provisional Vice President. They were formally elected Nov. 6, 1861.

Feb. 23 President-elect Lincoln arrived secretly in Washington after being warned of an assassination plot.

Mar. 4 In his **First Inaugural Address,** Lincoln announced that he had no intention of interfering with slavery where it existed; he called for peace and declared he would not accept the right of secession. Lincoln's cabinet included **William H. Seward** as Secretary of State, **Salmon P. Chase** as Secretary of the Treasury, and **Gideon Welles** as Secretary of the Navy.

The Civil War, 1861–1865

The Outbreak of War, 1861

Mar. Expectations for peace were high. In all seven seceding states vigorous minorities had supported the Union. Among the slave states still in the Union, Delaware and Missouri were clearly loyal, while the others seemed opposed to secession. Some Northerners believed that the seven cotton states would soon return in peace; some Southerners, on the other hand, believed that the North would let them go in peace.

Apr. 1 Secretary of State **Seward** proposed that the United States pick a fight with European nations in order to promote national unity and offered to take over the government. Seward believed that he alone could bring the nation together by broadening the Republican Party into a Union Party. Lincoln rejected his proposals.

Apr. 6 President **Lincoln**, who had wavered between abandoning Fort Sumter and reinforcing it with troops, finally decided to send provisions and so notified South Carolina. The naval expedition to relieve Fort Sumter got underway, Apr. 6–10.

Apr. 12 South Carolina ordered Maj. Anderson at Fort Sumter to surrender immediately, but he insisted on waiting three days. Shore batteries from Charleston, S.C., then **fired on Fort Sumter,** and the Civil War had begun. The attack ended months of northern indecision and brought immediate support for a war to restore the Union.

Apr. 13 **Fort Sumter surrendered** to South Carolina.

Apr. 15 President Lincoln called for 75,000 volunteer soldiers.

Apr. 17 When a Virginia state convention voted for secession, Col. **Robert E. Lee,** who had been offered command of the Northern army, resigned his commission in the United States Army.

Apr. 19 A riot broke out in Baltimore, Md., when a secessionist mob obstructed the Massachusetts Sixth Regiment on its way to Washington. The five-day riot, in which several were killed, cut Washington off from the North for almost a week.

May 1–20 **Arkansas, Tennessee,** and **North Carolina seceded** from the Union.

May 8 The Confederate legislature at Montgomery, Ala., authorized President Davis to enlist 400,000 volunteers and voted to shift the capital to Richmond, Va. (where it first met on July 20, 1861). The South was convinced it would win the war because it assumed that need for cotton would lead Great Britain and France to send aid, that the North would not have the will to fight, and that southern soldiers were superior to northern ones.

May 20 The Kentucky legislature voted to be neutral.

June 11 Western Virginia organized a Unionist government and eventually joined the Union as **West Virginia** (on June 20, 1863).

July 22–25 Congress resolved that the war was being fought to save the Union, not to interfere with the rights of the southern states.

North and South: In the first summer of the war, the 23 northern states were in a more advantageous position than the 11 southern states, as indicated by the following statistics:

	North	South
Population (millions)	23	9[a]
Manufacturing establishments (thousands)	110	18
Industrial workers (thousands)	1,300	110
Value of fire arms produced in 1860 (thousands)	$2,270	$73
Locomotives built in 1860 (thousands)	451	19
Horses, asses, and mules (millions)	4.6[b]	2.6
Railroad mileage (thousands)	22	9

[a] including 3.7 million slaves
[b] excluding far west

War Strategy

The North aimed to force the South to surrender by blockading the coast, by seizing Richmond, and by dividing the South through capture of the Mississippi and Tennessee rivers. The South hoped to capture Washington, move into central Pennsylvania, and force the United States to recognize its independence.

July 21   In the **First Battle of Bull Run**, the Union General-in-Chief, Winfield Scott, sent Gen. **Irvin McDowell** with 30,000 soldiers against 31,000 Confederates under Generals **Pierre G. T. Beauregard** and **Joseph E. Johnston** at Manassas Junction, Va. McDowell attacked and almost won the battle, but Gen. **Thomas J. Jackson's** great stand (which earned him the knickname of "Stonewall") turned the tide, and the Northern soldiers retreated in panic. The battle dispelled Northern assumptions that it would be a short war.

July 26   Gen. **George B. McClellan** was put in charge of the troops at Washington, D.C.

Nov. 1   McClellan replaced Scott as General-in-Chief. McClellan had carefully organized the Army of the Potomac but was so cautious that Radical Republicans began to call for action.

The Eastern Campaign, 1862–1863

1862

In spite of many different battles and generals the Eastern Campaign was indecisive. The North failed to capture Richmond, while the South was unable to win a victory north of Virginia.

Jan. 27   President Lincoln, responding to pressure for action, ordered a general move-

5-3   The Civil War

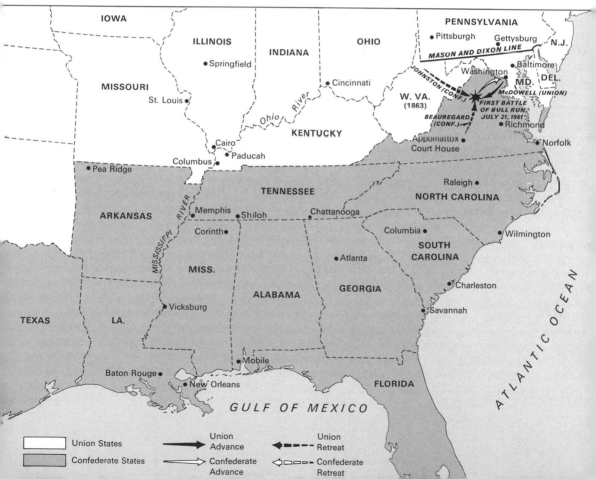

ment of all Union forces against the Confederacy, but McClellan ignored the order.

Mar. 8   Lincoln divested McClellan of all commands except that of the Army of the Potomac.

Mar. 9   The *Monitor* and the *Merrimac*: the ironclad Confederate ship *Virginia* (formerly the U.S.S. *Merrimac*), which was blocking the James River route to Richmond, on Mar. 8 sank the wooden U.S.S. *Cumberland* and burned the U.S.S. *Congress* off Hampton Roads. When it reappeared the next day to attack the *Minnesota,* the armored U.S.S. *Monitor,* with a revolving turret, engaged it in a five-hour battle and drove it off for repairs. The South burned the *Virginia* on May 10 to keep it out of Federal hands.

Mar. 17–July 2   PENINSULAR CAMPAIGN: McClellan led a force of 130,000 men down the Potomac to the peninsula between the York and James rivers in order to attack **Richmond**—where Gen. **Joseph E. Johnston** was in command—from the southeast. He advanced slowly, occupying Yorktown on May 4 and Williamsburg on May 5, and by May 21 had 115,000 troops in line along the Chickahominy River; in some cases they were only seven miles from Richmond. After Johnston attacked him at **Seven Pines** and at **Fair Oaks Station** (May 31–June 1), inflict-

ing heavy losses, McClellan awaited reinforcements and lost his chance to take Richmond.

Mar. 23–June 9   Jackson's Shenandoah Valley Campaign: Gen. Thomas J. ("Stonewall") Jackson with 16,000 men first drove Gen. Nathaniel P. Banks north out of Winchester and the Shenandoah Valley of Virginia (May 21–25). He then turned south, escaped two Union armies at Cross Keys and Port Republic (June 8–9) and rejoined Lee at Richmond on June 25. By this maneuver, he had tied up at least 54,000 Union troops, including 20,000 detached from the Richmond front.

June 1   Gen. **ROBERT E. LEE** assumed command of the Confederate Army of Northern Virginia, replacing J. E. Johnston.

June 26–July 2   The **Seven Days' Battles** began when the combined forces of Lee and Jackson attacked McClellan's right wing, forcing him to retreat to Harrison's Landing. McClellan's successful stand against Lee at **Malvern Hill** (July 1) ended the Peninsular Campaign. Union casualties in the Seven Days' Battles were 15,000; Confederate casualties were 20,000.

July 11   President Lincoln named **Henry W. Halleck** General-in-Chief of the Union Army.

Aug. 29–30   Lee and Jackson moved north from Richmond and badly outmaneuvered and defeated Gen. **John Pope** and the Army of Virginia in the **Second Battle of Bull Run** at Manassas Junction.

Sept. 17   BATTLE OF ANTIETAM: Lee and **Jackson** invaded Maryland, where McClellan (who had replaced Pope) forced them into battle on the hills near Antietam Creek, close to Sharpsburg, Md. The battle was a military draw, but it forced Lee to withdraw into Virginia. **McClellan** lost 13,000 of his 90,000 men; Lee lost 11,000 of his 40,000. The Union victory, limited as it was, removed any inclination among the British and the French to recognize the Confederacy and gave the President the occasion to issue his Preliminary Emancipation Proclamation. The Confederacy had passed its high water mark.

5-4   *The Peninsular Campaign, 1862*

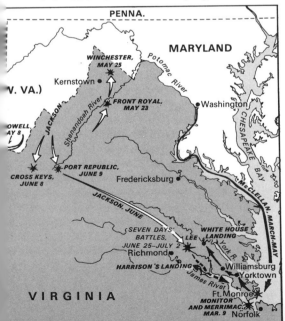

Nov. 5   Lincoln removed McClellan, who had been under severe attack from Radical Republicans because of his hesitation and his opposition to emancipation, and replaced him with Gen. **Ambrose E. Burnside.**

Dec. 13   At **Fredericksburg**, Md., **Burnside's** 120,000 troops took the offensive against **Lee's** barely 70,000 but were repulsed with heavy losses when they crossed the Rappahannock River and assaulted Lee's men on the heights beyond. Burnside lost 13,000 troops; Lee lost only 5,000.

1863

Jan. 25   Gen. **Joseph Hooker** replaced Gen. Burnside.

May 2–4   At **Chancellorsville**, west of Fredericksburg, Gen. **Hooker** with 120,000 troops attacked Lee's army of 60,000. After three days of fighting, in which **Jackson** outflanked Hooker's right and **Lee** broke through his center, the Confederate army won the battle. Each side lost over 10,000 men, but the southern losses included Gen. Jackson.

June 23   Lee moved up the Shenandoah Valley into Pennsylvania and reached Chambersburg. The Union army followed him north and took a position at Frederick, Md.

June 28   President Lincoln replaced Hooker with Gen. **George G. Meade.**

July 1–3   **BATTLE OF GETTYSBURG:** the two armies met by chance on June 30 at Gettysburg, Pa., where on July 1 the Confederates drove the North back to Cemetery Hill and Culp's Hill and took up positions facing them on Seminary Ridge. **Lee** attacked on July 2–3 and almost drove the Federals off the high ground. Gen. **James Longstreet** sent the divisions of **Pickett, Pettigrew**, and **Trimble** in a final charge only to see the troops mowed down just before they reached the Union lines. Lee's army then escaped back into Virginia. Each side suffered losses of about 25,000—more than a quarter of the men engaged. At the dedication of the battlefield cemetery on Nov. 19 Edward Everett gave the principal address, and **Abraham Lincoln** delivered his famous **Gettysburg Address.**

The Western Campaign, 1861–1863

1861

While the two armies fought to a stalemate in the East, the North won a series of decisive victories in the West that paved the way for the conquest of the South. By the end of 1863 the North had won control of the Mississippi River and all of Tennessee, thereby badly splitting the South.

Fall   The Union gathered 25,000 men under Gen. **Ulysses S. Grant** at Cairo, Ill., and 80,000 under Gen. Don Carlos Buell at Bowling Green, Ky. They faced a Confederate army of 50,000 under Gen. **Albert Sidney Johnston**, whose troops were stretched from Columbus, Ky., to Bowling Green.

1862

Feb. 6–16   Grant, aided by a gunboat flotilla, captured **Fort Henry** on the Tennessee River (Feb. 6) and **Fort Donelson** on the Cumberland River (Feb. 16), cutting Gen. Albert S. Johnston's line and forcing him to abandon Kentucky and Nashville, Tenn. (Feb. 25).

5-5   Virginia and Maryland Campaigns, 1862

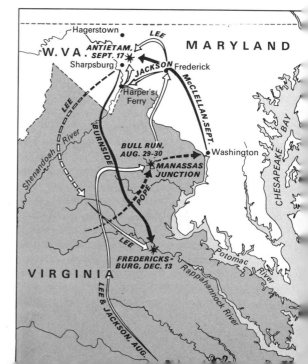

Mar. 16–Apr. 7 Gen. John Pope used gunboats to capture Confederate **Island No. 10** on the Mississippi River near southern Missouri.

Apr. 6–7 Gen. **Grant** with 40,000 troops moved south to Pittsburg Landing, Tenn., where Gen. Albert Sidney **Johnston** with 45,000 troops attacked him near **Shiloh** Church. Johnston drove Grant back but was killed in the action, and the next day Union reinforcements forced the Confederates to withdraw to Corinth, Miss., leaving the North in control of western Tennessee. Losses were heavy: 13,000 for the Union; 10,000 for the Confederacy.

Apr. 25 Flag Officer **David G. Farragut** with a Union fleet moved up the Mississippi River and captured **New Orleans**; a Union army under Gen. Benjamin F. Butler then occupied the city.

June 6 Federal gunboats defeated the Confederate fleet at Memphis, opening up most of the Mississippi River. Vicksburg (Miss.)

5-6 Eastern Campaigns, 1863

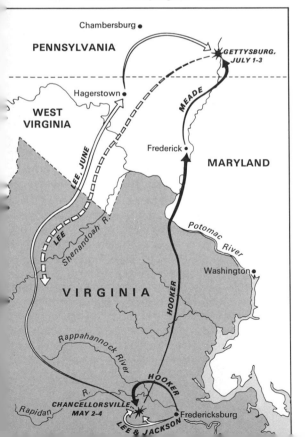

and Port Hudson (La.), however, still remained in Confederate hands.

Dec. 31–Jan. 2, 1863 Gen. **William S. Rosecrans** fought a bloody inconclusive battle with Confederate Gen. **Braxton Bragg** at **Murfreesboro** in central Tennessee, after which Bragg retreated.

1863

Mar. 29–July 4 Gen. **Grant** moved down the Mississippi River and approached **VICKSBURG** from the south with 20,000 men. After several victories he forced Gen. **John C. Pemberton**, the commander at Vicksburg, back into fortified lines. After a prolonged siege, May 22–July 4, Vicksburg surrendered. Grant inflicted 10,000 casualties on the Confederates and captured 30,000. When **Port Hudson**, La., also fell (July 9), the Mississippi River was completely open to the Union advance.

Sept. 19–20 Gen. **Rosecrans** moved east from Murfreesboro, maneuvered Gen. **Bragg** out of Chattanooga, Tenn., and met him in battle at **Chickamauga**, Ga. Bragg broke Rosecrans' line and would have won a victory had not Gen. **George H. Thomas** ("The Rock of Chickamauga") held back the Confederates.

Nov. 23–25 Bragg drove Rosecrans back into **Chattanooga**. Gen. **Grant**, now in supreme command in the west, brought reinforcements and defeated **Bragg** at Lookout Mountain (Nov. 24) and Missionary Ridge (Nov. 25), driving him out of Tennessee and paving the way for a march to the sea across Georgia. Casualties for Chickamauga and Chattanooga were 22,000 for the Union and 24,000 for the Confederacy.

The Conclusion of the War, 1864–1865

1864

Mar.–Dec. **GRANT'S RICHMOND CAMPAIGN** was one of the two major campaigns of 1864 that brought the Union victory.

Mar. 9 President Lincoln named Grant General-in-Chief of the Union armies.

May 5–6 Battle of the Wilderness: Grant and **Meade** with 100,000 men crossed the Rapidan River with the goal of destroying Lee's army and taking Richmond. They met **Lee** immediately in an indecisive battle in the Wilderness region of Virginia.

May 8–12 At **Spotsylvania Court House** (Va.) Grant suffered heavy losses but kept moving toward his goal.

June 1–3 Grant attacked Lee's entrenched forces at **Cold Harbor** and was driven off. Grant's losses May 4–June 3 were 60,000; Lee's losses were 30,000.

June 15–18 Grant lost 8,000 more men attacking **Petersburg**, south of Richmond, then settled down to a siege, having cut off Richmond from the lower south. Gloom settled over the North as reports of casualties continued to mount, and Richmond refused to fall.

5-7 Western Campaigns, 1862–1863

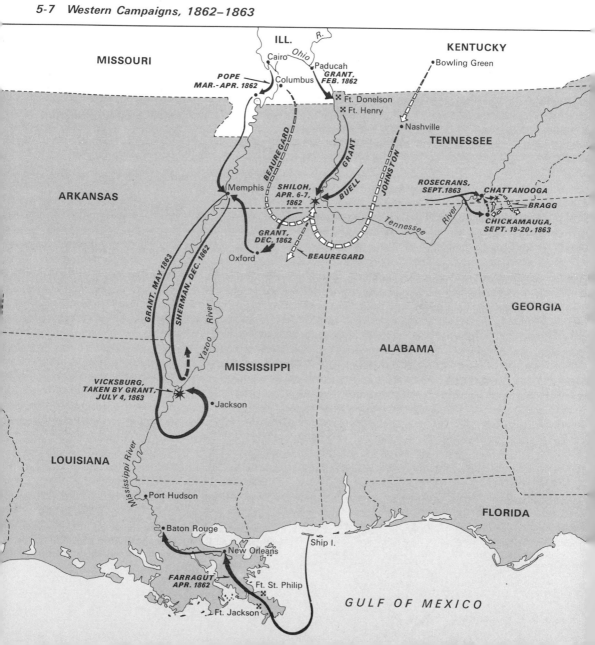

5-8 Grant's Richmond Campaign, 1864–1865

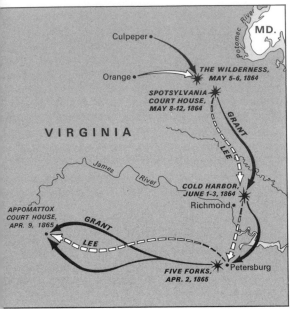

May–Dec. **SHERMAN'S MARCH TO THE SEA** through Georgia was the second campaign responsible for the southern defeat.

May 4–Sept. 2 In spite of Gen. **Joseph E. Johnston's** delaying tactics, Gen. **William T. Sherman** forced the Confederate army back to **Atlanta,** which he entered on Sept. 2.

Nov. 14–Dec. 22 Sherman's March to the Sea. Sherman led 60,000 men along a 30-mile front from Atlanta to Savannah. The famous "March to the Sea" destroyed everything in a "scorched-earth" policy and completed the split of the South into isolated sections.

Nov. 30 Gen. John M. Schofield repulsed Gen. John B. Hood's Confederate attack at Franklin, Tenn., and, with Gen. Thomas, destroyed Hood's force at Nashville (Dec. 15–16).

1865

Feb.–Apr. Gen. Sherman moved north from Georgia through South and North Carolina, devastating the countryside.

Feb. 3 In the **Hampton Roads Conference,** Confederate Vice President Stephens conferred with President Lincoln aboard a Union transport ship off Virginia but refused to surrender without recognition of southern independence.

Apr.–May The SOUTHERN SURRENDER

Apr. 2 Lee abandoned Petersburg and **Richmond** after several futile attacks on Grant's reinforced army.

Apr. 9 Lee **surrendered** to Grant at **Appomattox Court House,** Va., on terms that allowed all men to return home, officers to keep their sidearms, and soldiers to keep their own horses and mules.

Apr. 18–May 26 Final surrender: Gen. Joseph E. Johnston surrendered to Sherman near Raleigh, N.C., on April 18, while other southern troops in Alabama and Louisiana capitulated on May 4 and 26. Union forces captured Jefferson Davis in Georgia on May 10.

5-9 Sherman's Georgia Campaign, 1864–1865

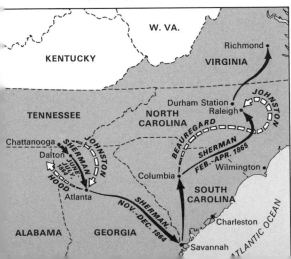

1861–65 War Enlistments and Casualties

	North	South
Enlistments[a]	1,556,678	1,082,119
Total deaths[b]	360,222	258,000
Battle deaths	110,070	94,000
Total wounded	275,175	125,000
Total casualties[c]	635,397	383,000

[a] Reduced by Livermore to the equivalent for three-year terms and taking desertion into account; the Union figure includes 178,895 Negro troops. T. L. Livermore, *Numbers and Losses in the Civil War* (Bloomington: Indiana University Press, 1958).
[b] Total for all U.S. wars before 1860 was 8,428.
[c] Total for both sides combined was almost 40 per cent of the forces.

Diplomacy

1861

Apr. 19 and 27 President Lincoln announced a **blockade** of southern ports. In spite of Confederate blockade runners from Nassau (in the Bahamas), the Union succeeded in isolating the South. Naval bases established at such places as Hatteras, N.C., Port Royal, S.C., and New Orleans made the blockade even more effective. Though Lincoln refused to recognize the existence of the Confederacy, his blockade tacitly recognized a state of **belligerency**.

May 13 Queen Victoria proclaimed British neutrality in the war, thereby recognizing Confederate belligerency.

Nov. 8 The *Trent* Affair: the U.S.S. *San Jacinto* stopped the British merchantship *Trent* and removed **James M. Mason** and **John Slidell,** Confederate commissioners who were enroute to Great Britain. The seizure made war possible with Great Britain, but Secretary of State Seward ordered the men released on Dec. 26.

Dec. The "**Cotton Famine**" in Great Britain caused by the lack of Southern cotton reached its peak, causing much unemployment among the textile workers. Even the hard times did not cause Great Britain to support the South because the British workers sympathized with the North, particularly after emancipation; Britain was able to import cotton from elsewhere; Britain depended more on northern wheat than on southern cotton; and, above all, Britain did not want to become involved in an American war.

1862

July 29 The Confederate cruiser *Alabama,* built in Great Britain, sailed from Liverpool and began a career of destroying Union shipping. The North was angry at what it considered an act of British belligerency.

Sept. Great Britain gave up any thought of recognizing the Confederacy after the northern victory at Antietam and the issuing of the Preliminary Emancipation Proclamation.

Sept. 9 In response to American protests the British government ordered the seizure of two ironclad steam warships manufactured by the Laird Company ("**Laird rams**") for use by the Confederacy in breaking the Union blockade.

Behind the Lines

Financing the War

The North was far more successful than the South in raising money and troops for the war. The North levied a **direct tax** on the states and an **income tax** (both Aug. 5, 1861), but they raised only $72 million during the war. The **internal revenue duties** (July 1, 1862) raised much more ($357 million). The U.S. government **borrowed** $2,621 million in the four fiscal years 1861–65 and issued $432 million in legal tender notes (**greenbacks,** issued on Feb. 25 and July 11, 1862, and on Mar. 3, 1863). The **National Banking Act** (Feb. 25, 1863, amended June 3, 1864) provided a system of national banks, which were required to purchase U.S. bonds to be deposited in the federal Treasury. The Comptroller of the Currency was then to issue National Bank Notes to the banks up to 90 per cent of the market value of the bonds. The **Confederacy** borrowed $115 million and printed over $1 billion of its own money, which was virtually worthless by the end of the war.

Raising the Armies

President Lincoln first called for volunteers from the **state militia** (75,000 on Apr. 15 and 42,034 on May 3, 1861). The Militia Act of July 17, 1862, proclaimed universal military liability or a state draft, but this was ineffective. The first **U.S. Conscription Act** (Mar. 3, 1863) declared that all males aged 18–45 were liable to military service but could commute service by paying $300 or by securing a substitute and gave each state a quota. The act was unfair to the poor and raised only 164,000 soldiers. The first drawing in New York City led to the **Draft Riots** (July 13–16, 1863) in which workers, mostly Irish immigrants, pillaged, attacked Negroes, and set fire to buildings. The **Confederacy** depended mostly on enlistments but passed a Conscription Act (Apr. 16, 1862) making every white man aged 18–35 eligible with numerous exemptions. Desertions were common in both armies (up to 10 per cent of the total).

Economic Development

The North passed a series of laws to stimulate the economy:

1. The **Morrill Tariff** (Mar. 2, 1861) revised tariff rates upward to an average of 47 per cent by 1865.
2. The **Homestead Act** (May 20, 1862) offered any citizen (or alien who intended to become a citizen) who was the head of a family, 160 acres after five years of continuous residence and payment of a registration fee of $10.
3. The **Morrill Land-Grant Act** (July 2, 1862) granted each Union state 30,000 acres for each Senator and Representative in Congress in order to endow an agricultural college. This led to the establishment of 69 land-grant colleges.
4. **Pacific Railway Act** (July 1, 1862) authorized a central transcontinental railroad, loaned it money, and granted it a right of way and five alternate sections of land on each side of the railroad for every mile built. The land grants were later increased by several acts.
5. **Immigration Act** (July 4, 1864) established a Commissioner of Immigration and authorized the admission of contract laborers who would work for their passage.
6. Congress established the **Department of Agriculture** (May 15, 1862).

Economists disagree over the effect of the war on the economy. Wool production expanded, but cotton production declined. The war stimulated the manufacture of uniforms, boots, and shoes but retarded the building of railroads. **Prices rose**. Between Jan., 1860, and Jan., 1865, for example, prices in New York City rose as follows: wheat flour from $4.30 a barrel to $10; English iron from $53 a barrel to $190; beef from $9.50 a barrel to $23. But the value added by manufacturing in the United States rose much more slowly in the 1860's than in the decade preceding or following. **Wages** rose only 50 per cent–60 per cent during the war compared to a 100 per cent rise in prices.

The Power of the Government in Wartime

1861

The power of the federal government, particularly that of the President, increased greatly during the war.

Apr. 15–July 12   Lincoln's use of his **war power**: by a vote of 5–4 the Supreme Court in the *Prize Cases* (1863) decided that President Lincoln's proclamations calling for the seizure of neutral shipping even though Congress had not declared war was a constitutional use of his emergency power.

Apr. 27   President Lincoln suspended the writ of *habeas corpus* on the railroad line from Philadelphia to Washington because of the Baltimore riot, and many were imprisoned.

May 25   The **Merryman Case**: when John Merryman was arrested for leading a secessionist drill company in Maryland, he appealed for a writ of *habeas corpus* to Chief Justice Roger B. Taney of the Supreme Court, who was on circuit duty. Taney tried in vain to serve the writ and in *Ex Parte Merryman* wrote an opinion denying the President's right to suspend the writ, but Merryman remained in jail.

1862

Sept. 24   President Lincoln issued a proclamation declaring that persons guilty of disloyal practices were subject to martial law, leading to the arrest of over 13,000 persons.

1863

May 1   The **Vallandigham Case**: northern opponents of the war (called Copperheads) organized groups such as the "Knights of the Golden Circle" to help the Democratic Party. On May 1, 1863, the military arrested Clement L. Vallandigham, an Ohio Democrat, for a speech denouncing the war. When a military commission ordered him imprisoned for the duration of the war, President Lincoln, embarrassed by being presented with a martyr, banished him instead to the Confederacy. Vallandigham later returned to Ohio and took part in the 1864 Presidential campaign.

June 1   Gen. **Ambrose E. Burnside** suspended the Chicago *Times*, an anti-Lincoln newspaper, but President Lincoln revoked the order. The government suspended other newspapers during the war, but Lincoln did not carry out systematic press censorship.

1864

Oct. 5   The **Milligan Case**: the army arrested Lambdin P. Milligan in Indiana for conspiracy to release "rebel" prisoners and sentenced him to hang. On Dec. 17, 1866, the Supreme Court in *Ex Parte Milligan* freed Milligan on the grounds that the President could not authorize martial law in areas where civil courts were in operation and where no emergency existed.

Politics and Emancipation in Wartime

1861

May 25   Gen. **Benjamin F. Butler** at Fortress Monroe, Va., ruled that slaves escaping to his lines were contraband of war and would not be returned.

Aug. 6   Congress passed the **Confiscation Act** that freed all slaves working or fighting for the Confederate Army.

Aug. 30   Gen. **John C. Frémont** in Missouri declared that the slaves of those fighting for the Confederacy were free and instituted martial law without consulting the President. Lincoln on Sept. 3, trying not to antagonize the border slave states of Missouri and Kentucky, modified this order to conform with the Confiscation Act. When Lincoln on Nov. 2 removed Frémont for incompetence, **Radicals,** who supported freeing the slaves, were angry.

Dec. 1   Secretary of War **Simon Cameron,** in a report to President Lincoln that was made public, recommended arming and freeing Confederate slaves. The President replaced him with **Edwin M. Stanton** on Jan. 15, 1862.

Dec. 20   **Radical Republicans** led by Rep. Thaddeus Stevens (Pa.) and Sen. Benjamin F. Wade (Ohio) set up the **Congressional Committee on the Conduct of the War.**

1862

Apr. 16   **Congress abolished slavery in the District of Columbia** and compensated the owners.

June 19   **Congress abolished slavery in the territories** without compensation.

Sept. 22   Lincoln issued his **Preliminary Emancipation Proclamation.** The official Proclamation (Jan. 1, 1863) declared that slaves in areas still in rebellion were free. Since it freed slaves only where the United States exercised no control, it actually freed not a single slave.

Dec. 17   Radical Republican Senators demanded that Lincoln replace Seward in the cabinet with Radical Republican Salmon P. Chase and set up a Radical cabinet, but Lincoln outmaneuvered them and retained his cabinet.

1864

June 7   The **Republican Party** met in Baltimore, nominated **Lincoln** for President and **Andrew Johnson** (Tenn.) for Vice President and adopted the name of **Union Party.**

Aug. 29   The **Democratic Party** met and nominated Gen. **George B. McClellan** for President and **George H. Pendleton** (Ohio) for Vice President. Copperheads wrote the platform calling for the immediate end of the war.

Summer   While McClellan repudiated the peace plank, Democrats took advantage of the nation's war weariness. The capture of Atlanta on Sept. 2 materially improved Lincoln's chances for reelection.

Nov. 8   **Presidential Election:** Lincoln was reelected with 2,206,938 votes (212 electoral) to 1,803,787 (21 electoral) for **McClellan.**

Reconstruction, 1863–1877

Presidential Reconstruction, 1863–1866

1863

Dec. 8   LINCOLN'S PLAN OF RECON-STRUCTION: President Lincoln insisted that the secessionist states had never left the Union and that he as President had the power to grant individual pardons or general amnesty to Southerners and to arrange for reconstructing the South. He therefore appointed provisional military governors for Louisiana, Arkansas, Tennessee, and North Carolina in 1862. In his plan he announced that he would pardon almost all rebels who would take an oath of future loyalty to the United States. When **10 per cent** of the 1860 voters of a state had taken the oath, they could form a government **without slavery,** which the President would then recognize.

1864

July 4   Radical Republicans in Congress, who considered Lincoln's Plan too easy, argued that the Confederate states had left the Union and that Congress alone had the power to rule them as conquered "territories" and to readmit them to the Union. Therefore, when Arkansas and Louisiana organized governments under Lincoln's plan, Congress refused to seat their representatives. Senator **Benjamin F. Wade** (Ohio) and Congressman **Henry W. Davis** (Md.) pushed through Congress their **Wade-Davis Bill** requiring a majority of the 1860 voters to take an oath of past as well as future loyalty before they could organize a state government without slavery, which Congress would then admit to the Union. **Lincoln** killed the bill with a **pocket-veto.**

Aug. 5   The **Wade-Davis Manifesto** denounced Lincoln for his pocket-veto and widened the gap between the President and the Radical Republicans.

1865

Feb. 1   Congress passed the **13TH AMENDMENT** prohibiting slavery in the United States. It went into effect on Dec. 18, 1865, when 27 states had ratified it.

Feb. 22   Slavery was abolished in the North. Maryland freed its slaves on Oct. 13, 1864, Missouri on Jan. 11, 1865, and Tennessee on Feb. 22, 1865. The 13th Amendment freed the slaves in Delaware and Kentucky.

Mar. 3   Congress established the **Freedmen's Bureau** to care for the freed slaves.

Mar. 4   In his **Second Inaugural Address** Lincoln pleaded for peace and moderation. "With malice toward none;" he said, " . . . let us strive . . . to bind up the nation's wounds . . . ."

Apr. 11   In his final public address Lincoln called for a generous reconstruction.

Apr. 14–15   THE ASSASSINATION OF PRESIDENT LINCOLN: John Wilkes Booth shot Lincoln while he was watching a play at Ford's Theater in Washington, and the President died the next morning. A fellow-conspirator also stabbed Secretary of State **Seward** in his home on Apr. 14, but Seward survived. Booth escaped but died on April 26 when he was surrounded in a barn and shot. Of nine others involved in the plot, four were hanged, four imprisoned, and one released. The assassination and the long-drawn-out funeral and burial (Apr. 19–May 4) aroused a spirit of vengeance in the North and strengthened the hand of the Radical Republicans.

May–Dec.   President Johnson's Reconstruction. Johnson adopted Lincoln's moderate position and with Congress in recess until December set about reconstructing the South. The President recognized governments set up by Lincoln in Arkansas, Louisiana, Tennessee, and Virginia, and started recognizing the remaining Confederate states as soon as provisional governors had convened **conventions** of loyal citizens that **abolished**

slavery. By December all but Texas had established governments and sent Congressmen and Senators to Washington. Texas fulfilled the requirements on April 6, 1866.

May 29   Johnson issued a proclamation of **amnesty** to most persons in the rebellion (Confederate officers and persons with assets worth over $20,000 were excepted).

Dec. 4   When Congress convened, the Republican majority refused to seat anyone sent from the Southern states. Radicals, who wanted harsh Reconstruction, were at first a minority among Republicans but after the election of 1866 were in control of the party. Leading Radicals were Senators **Charles Sumner** (Mass.), **Benjamin F. Wade** (Ohio), **Zachariah Chandler** (Mich.), and Congressman **Thaddeus Stevens** (Pa.).

Dec. 4   Congress established a **Joint Committee on Reconstruction of the South,** which Thaddeus Stevens dominated.

1865–66   Black Codes: southern legislatures elected under Johnson's reconstruction plan passed laws restricting the newly freed Negroes. The South Carolina law, which legalized marriages between Negroes but forbade interracial marriages, required a Negro to obtain a license before entering any occupation other than farming and established strict penalties for vagrancy. The harsher Mississippi law segregated Negroes on transportation facilities and discriminated against them in court procedure and in making contracts. These laws and the rise of former Confederate leaders to positions of power drove many northern moderates to the Radical side.

1866

Feb. 19   President Johnson's veto of a bill to extend the **Freedmen's Bureau** started open warfare between Johnson and Congress, which on July 16 passed a new Freedmen's Bureau bill over his veto.

Apr. 9   Civil Rights Act, passed first by Congress on Mar. 16 to grant the Negro citizenship, was passed over Johnson's veto, which declared it an invasion of states' rights.

June 16   14TH AMENDMENT: Congress sent to the states the 14th Amendment to the Constitution, which declared:

1. that "**All persons** born or naturalized in the United States," were U.S. and state **citizens,** thereby repudiating the Dred Scott decision (see p. 123);
2. that **no state** was to **"abridge the privileges"** of any citizen or "deprive any person of life, liberty, or property, without **due process of law"**;
3. that all persons (except Indians not taxed) should count for representation, thereby repealing the $\frac{3}{5}$ clause; that no federal or state office holder who supported the Confederacy was to hold any future federal or state office unless Congress removed his disability.

Most southern states rejected the amendment, but Congress declared it ratified on July 28, 1868.

July 24   Congress restored **Tennessee** to the Union after it had ratified the 14th Amendment.

July 30   A **race riot** in **New Orleans** began when whites attacked Negroes who were demanding racial equality. Thirty-seven were killed and 119 wounded. This riot and another at Memphis in May convinced Republicans of the need for strict Reconstruction.

Aug. 14   A National Union Convention at Philadelphia brought northern and southern moderates together in support of Johnson's program but had little effect.

Aug. 28–Sept. 15   Johnson's Congressional Campaigning. President Johnson took a "swing around the circle" of leading cities campaigning for Congressional candidates who supported his position. When he lost his temper and lashed back at hecklers, he only strengthened the Radicals' position.

Nov. 6   In the **Congressional elections,** the Republicans, now dominated by Radicals, won a $\frac{2}{3}$ majority in both houses.

Radical Rule, 1867–1869

1867

Jan. 22   Congress provided for a **special session** of Congress to begin on Mar. 4 following every election, thereby allowing the newly elected Congress to sit nine months earlier than it had before.

Mar. 2   Congress prescribed that all **military orders** from the President should emanate from the General of the Army in Washington, who could not be removed without approval of the Senate.

Mar. 2   **Tenure of Office Act**, passed over Johnson's veto, prohibited the President from removing any civil officer without the consent of the Senate.

Mar. 2   **FIRST RECONSTRUCTION ACT** was passed over Johnson's veto, divided the South into five **military districts** under **martial law**. In order to return to the Union a state had to call a constitutional convention (elected by universal manhood suffrage) and set up a government that would grant the **Negro suffrage** and ratify the 14th Amendment. When the South took no action to call conventions, Congress passed **supplementary acts** (Mar. 23 and July 19, 1867, and Mar. 11, 1868) allowing the military commanders to launch all statehood proceedings.

Aug. 12   President Johnson suspended Secretary of War **Edwin M. Stanton**, who was loyal to the Radicals, and made Gen. **Grant** Secretary of War *ad interim*.

1868

Jan 13   The Senate refused to accept the suspension of Stanton, and (despite an understanding with Johnson) Grant turned the office back to Stanton.

Feb. 21   President Johnson finally dismissed Secretary Stanton.

Feb. 24–May 16   **IMPEACHMENT OF JOHNSON**: on a motion by **John Covode** (Pa.) the House on Feb. 24 impeached President Johnson for violating the Tenure of Office Act and for behaving in an undignified way. After a lengthy partisan trial (Mar. 5–May 16), the Senate voted (35–19) in favor of conviction, one vote short of the necessary two-thirds. Seven Republicans voted for Johnson, including **Edmund G. Ross** (Kan.), **William P. Fessenden** (Maine), and **Lyman Trumbull** (Ill.).

5-10   Reconstruction

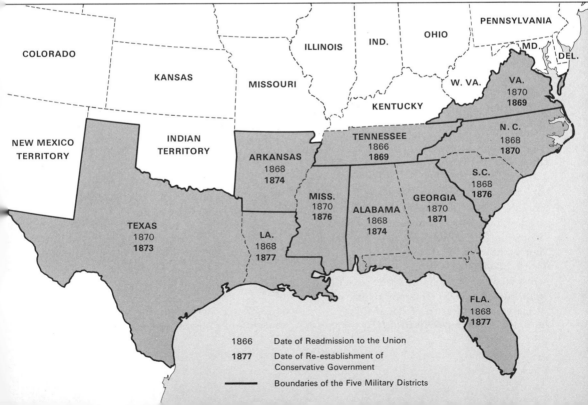

1866	Date of Readmission to the Union
1877	Date of Re-establishment of Conservative Government
——	Boundaries of the Five Military Districts

Mar. 17 THE ATTACK ON THE SUPREME COURT: Congress deprived the Supreme Court of the right to hear appeals of *habeas corpus* cases. The Radicals feared that the Court, which had agreed to hear *Ex Parte McCardle,* involving imprisonment of a Mississippi editor under the Reconstruction Act of 1867, might declare Congressional Reconstruction unconstitutional. Earlier, in *Ex Parte Milligan* (1866), the Court had ruled martial law unconstitutional where civil courts were operating; in *Mississippi v. Johnson* (1867) the Court had denied jurisdiction when asked to enjoin the President and the general in command of the military district from enforcing Congressional Reconstruction. In *Texas v. White* (1869) the Court ruled that Texas had never seceded as a state but refused to take a stand on the legality of Reconstruction. Congress in July, 1866, had **reduced the Court** to seven to prevent Johnson from making appointments (number restored to nine in 1869).

May 20 The **Republican Convention** met in Chicago and nominated Gen. **Ulysses S. Grant** for President and **Schuyler Colfax** (Ind.) for Vice President on a platform endorsing Radical Reconstruction.

June 22, 25 Congress readmitted **Arkansas** (June 22), **South Carolina, North Carolina, Florida, Alabama,** and **Louisiana** (June 25) to the Union.

July 4 The **Democrats** met in New York City and nominated **Horatio Seymour,** former governor of New York, for President and **Francis P. Blair** (Mo.) for Vice President. The platform attacked Radical Reconstruction and backed Congressman **George H. Pendleton's "Ohio Idea"** to pay off the national debt in greenbacks.

Nov. 3 **Presidential election:** the Republicans waved the **"bloody shirt"** to remind the voters that they had saved the Union. **Grant** won with 3,013,421 votes (214 electoral) to 2,706,829 (80 electoral) for **Seymour,** who carried New York, New Jersey, Delaware, Maryland, Kentucky, Georgia, Louisiana, and Oregon. (Mississippi, Texas, and Virginia did not vote).

Dec. 25 President Johnson announced **amnesty** for all involved in the Confederacy.

1869

Feb. 27 **15TH AMENDMENT,** granting the Negro the right to vote, passed Congress (ratified Mar. 30, 1870).

Black Reconstruction, 1867–1877

1867–77 Congressional Reconstruction brought 20,000 **federal troops** to the South.

1867–70 **Reconstruction governments:** new governments controlled by Negroes, whites not disfranchised, and Northerners who moved south during or after the war **("carpetbaggers")** took control of the South. Black Reconstruction disfranchised 150,000 whites and registered 700,000 Negro voters, but only in South Carolina, Mississippi, Louisiana, Alabama, and Florida did Negro voters constitute a majority. The whites not disfranchised often voted Democratic, but many (particularly those from the planter, mercantile, and industrial classes—former Whigs) turned Republican (the so-called **scalawags**). Negroes held few offices. Only in South Carolina did they dominate the legislature. There was no Negro governor during Reconstruction; only two Negroes served in the U.S. Senate and 15 in the House. The Negroes who did hold office served as well as white men. Reconstruction governments were corrupt but no more so than some governments in the North, and corruption was biracial and bipartisan. State expenditures were high partly because of new expenditures for public schools, asylums, and railroads.

1867–71 The **Ku Klux Klan,** which was founded in 1866 in Tennessee, chose former Confederate General **Nathan B. Forrest** as the first Grand Wizard. The Klan and organizations like it throughout the South used violence to try to defeat Radical Reconstruction and reestablish white supremacy. The Klan was often pitted against the **Union League,** a Radical organization that enrolled Negro voters. Congress passed the **Ku Klux Klan Acts** (the "Force Acts," May 31, 1870, and Apr. 20, 1871) to enforce the 15th and 14th Amendments. By 1871 the Klan had virtually come to an end.

1869–77 Restoration of Conservative Rule (Redemption): as troops were withdrawn and as Congress removed disability from almost all ex-Confederates (**Amnesty Act,** May 22, 1872), Conservatives gradually took over the southern states as many scalawags, disappointed in the Republican Party, shifted to the Democratic Party. By the end of 1874 Democrats had restored home rule in all states but Mississippi, South Carolina, Florida, and Louisiana. In 1875 Democrats won in Mississippi by intimidating the Negro voters through Democratic groups and acts of violence (**the "Mississippi Plan"**), thereby setting a pattern for later southern discrimination against the Negro. Conservatives gained control of the other three states in the Presidential election of 1876–77.

1870 Congress readmitted Georgia, Virginia, Texas, and Mississippi to the Union.

1873 In the **Slaughterhouse Cases,** New Orleans butchers protested against an 1869 monopoly grant to one company in the city on the grounds that the state had deprived them of their privileges and immunities as citizens under the 14th Amendment. The Court rejected their appeal by arguing that the 14th Amendment protected them only in their rights as United States citizens, which it defined very narrowly. These decisions prevented the Negro from invoking the 14th Amendment to protect his civil rights, because these were held to be rights derived from state citizenship.

1875 Civil Rights Act of 1875 (Mar. 1), proposed by Charles Sumner, gave all persons equal rights in public places. When Negroes protested that they had been denied public accommodation, the Supreme Court in the five **Civil Rights Cases** (1883) declared the Civil Rights Act unconstitutional. The Court held that the 14th Amendment protected persons from racial discrimination by states but not by individuals.

The Grant Regime, 1869–1877

1869

Mar. 18 Public Credit Act provided for payment of government bonds in gold, as the Grant Administration adopted a hard money policy.

Sept. 24 "Black Friday." When stock speculators **Jay Gould** and **James Fisk** attempted to corner the gold market, the price rose rapidly until President Grant, who refused to cooperate with the manipulators, brought the price down suddenly by selling $4 million in government gold.

1870

Feb. 7–May 1, 1871 Legal Tender Cases: in *Hepburn v. Griswold* (1870) the Supreme Court declared (4–3) that the greenbacks issued in 1862 and 1863 were not legal tender for debts contracted before the acts. After Grant appointed two new justices, who joined the minority, the Court (in *Knox v. Lee,* 1871) reversed itself by a vote of 5–4.

July 14 The Internal Revenue and Tariff Act continued tariff protection, eliminated some of the wartime excise taxes, and provided for the end of the income tax in 1872.

Sept. 20 The first editorial against Tammany boss **William Marcy Tweed** and the **Tweed Ring,** which was robbing and misgoverning New York City, appeared in the *New York Times.* The editorials in the *Times* and the cartoons of **Thomas Nast** in *Harper's Weekly* were instrumental in causing the ring to fall from power in 1871.

1872

Feb. 22 The **Prohibition Party** for the first time nominated candidates for President and Vice President. It has continued to nominate candidates since.

May 1 Liberal Republicans, who opposed Radical Reconstruction and the Grant Regime, met in Cincinnati and nominated reformer **Horace Greeley** for President and liberal governor **B. Gratz Brown** of Missouri for Vice President on a platform opposing voting disabilities for ex-Confederates and land grants for railroads and supporting civil-service reform and hard money. Other prominent Liberal Republicans included **Charles F. Adams** (Mass.), **Carl Schurz** (Mo.), and **Charles Sumner.**

June 5   Republican Convention met in Philadelphia and nominated **Grant** for President and Senator **Henry Wilson** (Mass.) for Vice President.

July 9 The **Democratic Convention** met in Baltimore and accepted the Liberal Republican slate of **Greeley** and **Brown**. On Sept. 3 "straight" Democrats nominated **Charles O'Conor** (N.Y.) for President and **John Quincy Adams II** (Mass.) for Vice President.

Nov. 5   Presidential election: Grant won with 3,596,745 votes (286 electoral) to 2,843,446 for **Greeley** (who received no electoral votes because he died shortly after the election). The remaining electoral votes were scattered.

1873

Feb. 12 "**Crime of '73**": the **Coinage Act** stopped the coinage of silver because little silver was being brought to the Treasury. Farmers and miners later called the act part of a gold conspiracy (see p. 157).

Feb. 18   Crédit Mobilier Scandal: the House censured Congressmen Oakes Ames and James Brooks for participating in the Crédit Mobilier, a dummy company whose promoters secured contracts from the Union Pacific Railroad and diverted the profits to themselves and to certain Congressmen.

Sept. 18   THE PANIC OF 1873 was brought on by the failure of **Jay Cooke and Company,** which was overinvolved in financing the Northern Pacific Railroad. The Panic was caused fundamentally by overspeculation in railroads and overexpansion in industry and agriculture. Over 5,000 businesses failed by the end of the year, and wholesale commodity prices dropped from 136 in 1872 to 90 in 1879, when the depression came to an end. Unemployment caused labor unrest during the rest of the 1870's.

1874

Nov.   In Congressional elections, the Democrats gained control of the House as the Republicans lost 85 seats.

1875

Jan. 14   Specie Resumption Act called for greenbacks to be redeemable in gold by Jan. 1, 1879, and put a limit of $300 million on the circulation of greenbacks.

May 1 The *St. Louis Democrat* exposed the "**Whisky Ring,**" a conspiracy of revenue officials and distillers to defraud the government of taxes. Hundreds were indicted including Gen. **Orville E. Babcock,** Grant's private secretary, who was saved by the President's intervention.

1876

Mar. 2 The House impeached Secretary of War **William W. Belknap** for corruption in connection with Indian trading posts, but the Senate later refused to convict him.

May 15 The House Judiciary Committee began investigation of **James G. Blaine** for allegedly accepting favors from the Union Pacific Railroad while Speaker of the House.

May 18 The **Independent or Greenback Party** met at Indianapolis and nominated **Peter Cooper,** New York philanthropist, for President and **Samuel F. Cary** (Ohio) for Vice President.

June 14   Republican Party met in Cincinnati and nominated Gov. **Rutherford B. Hayes** of Ohio for President over James G. Blaine and nominated **William A. Wheeler** (N.Y.) for Vice President.

June 27   Democratic Convention met in St. Louis and nominated Gov. **Samuel J. Tilden** (N.Y.) for President and **Thomas A. Hendricks** (Ind.) for Vice President.

Nov. 7   Presidential election: the disputed election gave **Tilden** 4,284,020 popular votes to 4,036,572 for **Hayes** and 81,737 for **Cooper.** Tilden's 184 electoral votes were one short of a majority, with the votes of **Florida, Louisiana, South Carolina,** and **Oregon** in dispute. Corruption was evident on both sides in the three southern states, where federal troops remained. When the four states in question sent in two sets of electoral returns on Dec. 6, the country lacked a constitutional means of determining who was elected.

1877

Jan. 29 Congress established an **electoral commission** of 15 members (5 each from the Senate, House, and Supreme Court) to settle the election. Since the rest of the Commission split 7–7 the decision was left up to Justice **Joseph P. Bradley** (N.J.), who wavered and then, after political pressure, declared for the Republican electors (Feb. 9–28).

Mar. 2 COMPROMISE OF 1877: the President of the Senate announced the **election of Hayes.** The Democratic House accepted the verdict because the Republicans promised Southern Democrats that they would **withdraw** the remaining federal **troops** from the South, would **appoint a Southerner** to the Cabinet, and would spend money on **southern railroads** and other improvements. President Hayes was inaugurated on Mar. 5, since Mar. 4 fell on a Sunday.

Apr. 10, 24 President Hayes removed the last federal troops from the South.

Diplomacy, 1865–1877

1863–67 The Maximilian Affair: in June, 1863, Emperor **Napoleon III** of France, sent French troops to occupy Mexico City after Mexico had been unable to repay its international debts. On April 10, 1864, he placed **Archduke Maximilian** of Austria on the Mexican throne as a puppet ruler. Seward protested mildly at first but on Feb. 12, 1866, demanded that the French withdraw. Napoleon removed his troops in the spring of 1867, and Maximilian was executed by Mexican patriots on June 19.

1867 Russia offered Alaska to the United States in order to get rid of a diplomatic and economic liability. Secretary of State Seward, an expansionist, signed a treaty on Mar. 30, 1867, to **purchase Alaska** for $7,200,000, and secured Senate ratification in spite of public ridicule of "Seward's Folly." Transfer took place on Oct. 18. On Oct. 24, Seward made a treaty to acquire the Danish West Indies (the Virgin Islands), but the treaty failed in the Senate.

1870 In June, President Grant, who was obsessed with the idea of annexing the **Dominican Republic**, submitted a treaty with the Republic to the Senate, where it was defeated.

1871 The United States demanded compensation from Great Britain for damage done Northern shipping by the British-built Confederate cruiser *Alabama.* In the **Treaty of Washington** (May 8) Secretary of State **Hamilton Fish** arranged to submit both the claims and a boundary dispute in the Northwest to arbitration. The arbitration commission later awarded the U.S. $15 million in *Alabama* claims and granted the U.S. the San Juan Islands in the northwest.

1873 The *Virginius* **Affair**: the United States refused to recognize a revolution that started in Cuba in 1868. In 1873 Spanish authorities captured the Cuban-owned *Virginius,* which was running arms into Cuba, and executed 53, including many Americans. War was averted when Spain paid an indemnity.

1875 Hawaiian Treaty: the United States made a reciprocal trade treaty with Hawaii (Jan. 30) that allowed Hawaiian sugar into the United States duty free. Hawaii also promised not to transfer territory to any other power. Though renewed in 1884, the treaty was not formally ratified until 1887.

Leading Figures of the Civil War Period

JEFFERSON DAVIS (Todd County, Ky., 1808–New Orleans, La., 1889), President of the Confederacy.

1828 Was graduated from West Point.

1828–35 Served in the army in the West, where he took part in the Black Hawk War.

1835–45 Planter in Mississippi.

1845–46 Democratic Congressman from Mississippi.

1846–47 Served in the Mexican War, in which

his regiment made a gallant stand at Buena Vista.

1847–51 Senator from Mississippi; opposed the admission of Oregon Territory and California without slavery.

1853–57 Secretary of War; brought about the Gadsden Purchase.

1857–61 Senator from Mississippi.

1861 Was elected President of the Confederacy.

1865 Captured by the Union in Georgia after the fall of the Confederacy.

1867 Released on bail after his indictment for treason was dropped.

1878–81 Wrote *The Rise and Fall of the Confederate Government*.

STEPHEN A. DOUGLAS (Brandon, Vt., 1813–Chicago, 1861), Democratic party leader and U.S. Senator.

1833–34 Journeyed west and settled in Illinois, where he began to practice law.

1835–37 Member of the Illinois legislature.

1840 Secretary of State in Illinois.

1841–43 Member of the Illinois Supreme Court.

1843–47 Member of the United States House of Representatives.

1847 Moved to Chicago.

1847–61 United States Senator from Illinois.

1850 Played a leading role in the Compromise of 1850.

1852 Leader of the "Young America" wing of the Democratic Party.

1854 Secured the passage of the Kansas-Nebraska Act, which incorporated his philosophy of popular sovereignty.

1856 Unsuccessful candidate for the Democratic Presidential nomination.

1857–58 Broke with President Buchanan over slavery in Kansas.

1858 Lincoln-Douglas Debates; defeated Abraham Lincoln for U.S. Senate.

1860 Nominated for President by the northern wing of the Democratic Party; lost the election to Lincoln.

ULYSSES SIMPSON GRANT (Point Pleasant, Ohio, 1822–Mount McGregor, N.Y., 1885), General of the Army, 18th President of the United States.

1843 Was graduated from West Point.

1846–48 Served gallantly in the Mexican War.

1852–54 Served in California and Oregon; resigned from the army when he began to drink.

1854–61 Lived as a farmer and clerk in Missouri and Illinois.

1861–63 Commanded the Union campaigns in the West.

1864 Became commanding general of the Union armies; led the Richmond campaign against Lee.

1865 Received Lee's surrender at Appomattox Court House.

1867 Was appointed Secretary of War *ad interim*.

1868 Was elected President of the United States. His Administration (1869–77) carried out Reconstruction and followed conservative hard money policies but was tainted by corruption.

ROBERT E. LEE (Westmoreland County, Va., 1807–Lexington, Va., 1870), commander of the Confederate army.

1829 Was graduated from West Point.

1846–48 Served with distinction in the Mexican War.

1852–53 Superintendent of West Point.

1859 Led the troops that put down John Brown's raid in Virginia.

1861 Resigned his commission in the U.S. Army to take command of Virginia's army.

1862 Became commander of the Army of Northern Virginia.

1862–63 Failed in two invasions of the North.

1864–65 Opposed Grant in the Richmond campaign.

1865 Was named general-in-chief of all Confederate armies.

1865 Surrendered to Grant at Appomattox Court House.

1865 President of Washington College (later renamed Washington and Lee).

ABRAHAM LINCOLN (Hardin County, Ky., 1809–Washington, D.C., 1865), 16th President of the United States.

1816 Moved to southern Indiana. Mostly self-taught, he attended school no more than one year altogether.

1830 Moved to southern Illinois, where he became clerk of a store in New Salem.

1832 Took part in the Black Hawk War.

1834–41 Served in the Illinois legislature where he became a Whig leader.

1837 Began a law career in Springfield, Ill., after reading law independently.

1847–49 Whig Congressman from Illinois, opposed the Mexican War.

1849 Resumed his law career.

1854 Denounced the Kansas-Nebraska Act in his Peoria speech.

1856 Joined the Republican Party.

1858 His "House Divided" speech attacked slavery.

1858 Lincoln-Douglas Debates; lost the race for the U.S. Senate to Douglas.

1860 Was elected President.

1863 Delivered his "Gettysburg Address."

1865 Was assassinated.

WILLIAM H. SEWARD (Florida, N.Y., 1801– Auburn, N.Y., 1872), a leading Whig and Republican statesman.

1820 Was graduated from Union College.

1822 Became a member of the New York bar at Auburn.

1830 Entered the New York senate as an Anti-Mason; served until 1834.

1839–43 As Whig Governor of New York, he supported internal improvements and opposed slavery.

1848 Was elected to the United States Senate; was reelected in 1854.

1850 Opposed the Compromise of 1850.

1855 Joined the Republican Party and took a strong antislavery position.

1856–60 Failed to win the Republican nomination for the Presidency.

1861–69 Secretary of State under Lincoln and Johnson.

1861 Was rebuffed by Lincoln when he tried to take a strong position in the Administration.

1867 Purchased the territory of Alaska from Russia.

THADDEUS STEVENS (Danville, Vt., 1792– Washington, D.C., 1868), political leader.

1814 Was graduated from Dartmouth College.

1816 Began law practice in Gettysburg, Pa.

1826 Invested in iron manufacturing.

1833–41 Served in the Pennsylvania legislature as an Anti-Mason, where he expressed a strong antislavery position.

1848 Was elected to Congress as a Whig; served until 1853.

1855 Helped form the Republican Party in Pennsylvania.

1858 Was reelected to Congress and served from 1859 until his death.

1861–65 As Chairman of the House Ways and Means Committee, he played a large role in the management of the Civil War.

1865 Became chairman of the House group on the Joint Committee on Reconstruction. As leader of the Radical Republicans, he was the strongest advocate of a harsh reconstruction.

CHARLES SUMNER (Boston, 1811–Washington, D.C., 1874), political leader.

1830 Was graduated from Harvard.

1830–40 Studied law, lectured, and traveled.

1846 Denounced the Mexican War at a public meeting in the Tremont Temple, Boston.

1851 Was elected to the United States Senate by the Free-Soilers and Democrats; became a leading Senatorial opponent of slavery.

1854 Took a strong stand against the Kansas-Nebraska Act.

1856 Delivered his "Crime against Kansas" speech.

1857 Was reelected to the Senate; reelected again in 1863 and 1869.

1861 Led the movement during the Civil War for emancipation of slaves.

1865–69 Led the Radical Republicans in the Senate against President Johnson. Headed movement to give voting rights to Negroes.

1869 Broke with Grant when he opposed the President's plan to annex Santo Domingo.

THE RISE OF AN INDUSTRIAL WORLD POWER, 1865-1900

PART 6

The Development of the South and West

The New South

POLITICS Conservative Democrats, often businessmen, who controlled the South after Reconstruction called themselves **Redeemers** because they had redeemed the South from carpetbaggers. As Republican efforts faded, politics in the one-party South became a struggle between **Conservative Democrats** and **Independents** (Greenbackers, later Populists), who represented the small farmers. The Independents opposed the Conservative Democrats' local policies of cutting school budgets, aiding railroads, and paying state debts at face value. By manipulating voting districts and using the Negro vote Conservatives, such as **Wade Hampton** in South Carolina, managed to win in the late 1870's and 1880's, but widespread corruption helped many Populists come to power in the 1890's. The former Confederate states voted solidly Democratic in Presidential elections until 1920. Nationally the South was out of power, providing no President (aside from Johnson), only 9 Supreme Court Justices, and only one Speaker of the House in the half-century after the Civil War.

THE NEGRO Redeemer governments did not disfranchise the Negroes but treated them paternalistically and exploited their votes. Segregation existed, but **extreme Jim Crow laws** and **disfranchisement** came only **in the 1890's** when the Conservatives used the issue of white supremacy to defeat Populists, who had courted Negro votes. The Populists in turn took up racism before the 1890's were over. Led by Mississippi in 1890, the South kept the Negro from voting by establishing **property or literacy qualifications for voting** (but allowed white men to squeeze through legal loopholes). The **poll tax** and the **all-white primary** were other disfranchising devices. By 1905 very few Negroes remained registered to vote (in Louisiana, for example, the number dropped from 130,334 in 1896 to 1,342 in 1904). **Lynchings** became much more frequent; the number of Negroes lynched in the U.S. rose from an annual average of 60 in 1882-86 to 128 in 1891-95. The United States Supreme Court gave constitutional backing to segregation, which became complete 1895-1915, through the **Plessy v. Ferguson** decision (1896), which decided that **"separate but equal"** facilities on a Louisiana railroad coach did not deprive the Negro of equal protection under the 14th Amendment. In *Williams v. Mississippi* (1898) the Court sanctioned Mississippi programs for keeping the Negro from voting. Almost all southern whites united behind **white supremacy,** including Populist **Thomas E. Watson** (Ga.) and Democrats **Benjamin R. Tillman** (S.C.), **Josephus Daniels** (N.C.), and **John Sharp Williams** (Miss.). Middle-class Negroes, meanwhile, took a rather conciliatory position. At the **Atlanta Exposition** in 1895 **Booker T. Washington,** the most prominent Negro in the nation, said that the Negro should seek economic gains before demanding social and political equality.

THE ECONOMY Leaders of the "**New South,**" such as **Henry W. Grady** of Atlanta, sought to transform it into an industrial society. **Railroads** in the South increased their miles of track from 16,605 in 1880 to 39,108 in 1890; between 1880 and 1900 pig-iron production multiplied four times, capital invested in **cotton manufacturing** increased seven times, and the amount of coal mined multiplied eight times. But the South remained agrarian as cotton production rose from 2.1 million bales in 1865 (it had been 5.4 million 1859) to 10.1 million 1900 and tobacco production rose from 316 million pounds in 1866 to 852 million pounds in 1900. A system of **sharecropping** replaced the plantation system. Tenants (often former slaves) received land in return for a share of the crop. Since the landowner usually advanced the tenant cash and often sold him goods on credit, the tenant fast slipped into debt. Between 1880 and 1900 the number of tenant farmers in the South rose from 553,848 to 1,231,144. Economically the South was dramatically inferior to the North with a per capita average wealth in 1900 of $509 compared to a national average of $1,165.

The Conquest of the Great Plains and the Rockies

1858   Discovery of gold in present-day Colorado led to a gold rush and the eventual entrance of Colorado as a state (1876).

1859   Prospectors discovered the **Comstock**

6-1   *The West and Admission of States, 1864–1912*

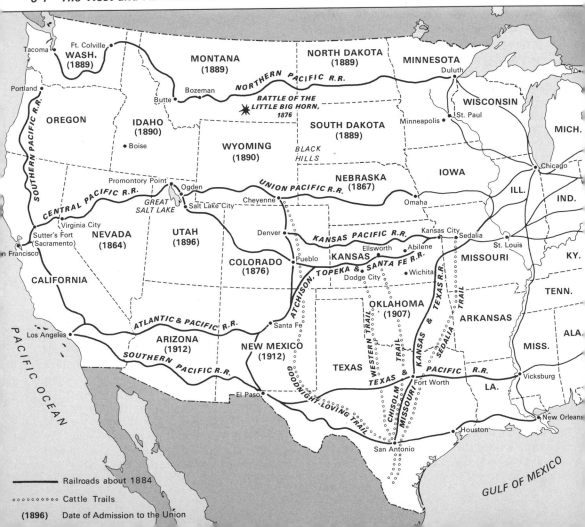

Lode in Nevada, the largest deposit of silver found in the United States. The rush that followed led to the entrance of Nevada as a state in 1864.

1860–64   Gold and silver were discovered in Idaho and Montana. After most of these discoveries in the West, rough mining towns sprang up with **vigilante committees** that kept law and order; only later were permanent local, territorial, and state governments organized. Between 1889 and 1890 Washington, Idaho, Montana, Wyoming, North Dakota, and South Dakota were admitted to the Union.

1861–65   **Cheyenne-Arapaho War** in Colorado came to a climax on Nov. 28, 1864, when Colorado militia under Col. **John M. Chivington** massacred about 450 Indians at **Sand Creek, Colo.**

1865–67   **Apache and Navaho War** ended with the establishment of reservations.

1865–68   **Sioux War** began when miners penetrated Sioux territory in Wyoming and Montana. After the Sioux had massacred 81 U.S. troops under Capt. **William J. Fetterman** in northeastern Wyoming (Dec. 21, 1866), a U.S. commission persuaded the Indians to accept confinement to reservations in the Dakotas. The **reservations** of 1867–68 marked the start of a policy of placing Indians on relatively small areas of land and training them in the ways of the white man.

1866–88   The "**CATTLE KINGDOM**" grew up when the high postwar price of cattle led Texans to start driving longhorns north to railroad points in Kansas and Nebraska, feeding them on the great Plains along the way. By 1888 cattlemen had driven 6 million head north to such cattle towns as Abilene, Kan. (1867), Cheyenne, Wyo. (1867), and Dodge City, Kan. (1875), along the Chisholm, Goodnight-Loving, and other trails. The overproduction of cattle, the fencing in of water holes, and the competition of wheat and sheep farmers on the Great Plains brought about the decline of the **long drive.** The severe winters of 1885–87 ended it, and cattlemen settled down to raise beef on the ranches. The long drives brought about the rise of the **cowboy** and an endless series of adventure stories based on his exploits.

1867–83   Hunters killed about 13 million buffalo, beginning the extermination of what had seemed an unlimited herd.

1869   The Union Pacific and Central Pacific Railroads met at Promontory Point, Utah, connecting the Atlantic and the Pacific coasts by rail for the first time.

1871–86   **Apache War** in the Southwest ended with the capture of the Apache chief **Geronimo** in 1886.

1872   Congress established Yellowstone Park, the first national park.

1873   **Timber Culture Act** granted 160 acres to anyone who would plant trees on one-quarter of it.

1874   **Joseph F. Glidden** received a patent for **barbed wire.**

1875–77   **Sioux War:** a large-scale gold rush in South Dakota sent the Sioux on the warpath. On June 25, 1876, Chief **Sitting Bull** wiped out Gen. **George A. Custer** and 264 men in the Battle of the Little Big Horn, in southern Montana, but a year later the Sioux were in flight.

1876–77   The United States subdued the **Nez Percé** Indians of Idaho under **Chief Joseph.**

1877   **Desert Land Act** offered 640 acres at $1.25 an acre to anyone who would irrigate the land within three years. In many cases cattlemen bought the land and gave false proof of irrigation.

1878   **Timber and Stone Act** allowed the purchase of 160 acres of forest or mineral land at $2.50 an acre. Lumber interests exploited the act.

1878–85   A boom in the Dakotas, stimulated by the Northern Pacific Railway, led to the settlement of the Red River Valley.

1879   In his *Report on the Lands of the Arid Regions of the United States,* Maj. **John Wesley Powell** outlined the problems of farming in the dry land west of the 100th meridian.

1881   **Helen Hunt Jackson** published *A Century of Dishonor,* condemning the brutal treatment of the Indians.

1882   Southern Pacific Railroad completed the railroad link between San Francisco and New Orleans.

1883   Northern Pacific Railroad reached Portland, Ore., from Lake Superior.

1884   Settlers known as "Boomers" moved

into closed land in Oklahoma but were driven off by Federal troops. On Apr. 22, 1889, however, the government opened the **Oklahoma District** precipitating a great land boom.

1887 Dawes Severalty Act allotted a quarter section (160 acres) of reservation land to each Indian family head and granted citizenship to those who received the land. The act marked a shift from the reservation plan and contributed to the decline of the Indian tribal culture.

1887 Congress established the Division of Forestry of the Department of Agriculture.

1890 Ghost Dance War in the Black Hills came to an end with an Indian massacre at the Battle of Wounded Knee.

1890 The U.S. Census revealed that a **frontier line** no longer existed. Between 1870 and 1890 American settlers had succeeded in settling the **GREAT PLAINS** between central Kansas and the Rockies, an area formerly passed over because it was treeless, semi-arid, and inhabited by Indians. The Great Plains offered Americans a new

environment to which they quickly adjusted. They built **windmills** to pump water from deep wells and developed special drought resistant **seeds,** used the **six-shooter** to drive off the Indians (who were surprised by a multiple-shot gun), **barbed wire** to fence in the land, and the chilled iron plow to cut through the tough plains sod.

1891 Forest Reserve Act allowed the withdrawal of public lands to establish national forest reserves and repealed the Timber Culture Act.

1894 Carey Act authorized the President to grant each state with public lands up to a million acres for reclamation, irrigation, and settlement.

1896 Congress admitted Utah to the Union.

The Farmers' Dilemma

Agriculture expanded rapidly for a number of reasons including population growth, westward expansion, railroad activity, federal land laws, and technological improvements such as the **reaper** (1831), **binder** (1850), **chilled iron plow** (1868–76) and the giant

The Revolution in Agriculture, 1860–1900

	1860	1880	1900
Population of the United States (millions)	32	50	76
Farm workers (millions)	6.2	8.6	10.9
Farmers in the work force (per cent)	59	49	38
Number of farms (millions)	2.0	4.0	5.7
Number of farms owned (millions)	—	3.0	3.7
Number of tenant farms (millions)	—	1.0	2.0
Farm acreage (millions)	407	536	839
Value of farm gross production (billions of dollars)	1.5	3.0	3.8
Value of farm property (billions of dollars)	8.0	12.4	20.4
Value of farm implements and machinery (millions of dollars)	246	406	750
Wheat production (millions of bushels)	173[a]	502	599
Average wheat price[d] (dollars per bushel)	2.06[b]	0.95	0.62
Corn production (millions of bushels)	839[a]	1,707	2,662
Average corn price[d] (dollars per bushel)	0.66[b]	0.39	0.35
Cotton production (millions of bales)	3.8	6.6	10.1
Average cotton price[d] (dollars per pound)	0.17[c]	0.10	0.09
Total exports of U.S. merchandise (millions of dollars)	316	824	1,371
Total exports of agricultural commodities (millions of dollars)	259	687	817

[a] 1859   [b] 1866   [c] 1869   [d] price received by farmers

combine harvester thresher (1888). The farmer specialized as the railroad made it possible for him to get his crop to distant markets. New centers of agriculture developed: **wheat** in the Dakotas, **corn** in Kansas and Nebraska, **cotton** in Texas. and **wool** in the mountain states. Exporting became increasingly important as the **wheat surplus** rose from 21 per cent in 1870 to 37 per cent in 1900. But the **farmer was less well off** than before the Civil War. He was forced to compete in a **world market** and yet purchased goods that were often protected by tariffs. **Farm prices dropped** drastically in 1866–1900, reaching their low in 1894–96. Farmers came to be more and more in debt as **farm mortgages** climbed to one-third of all farms by 1900, and the number of **tenant farms** grew from 25 per cent of all farms in 1880 to 35 per cent by 1900. As money contracted the farmer found it more difficult to pay off his debts, and foreclosures increased greatly in the 1890's. **Railroads** favored large shippers and charged high rates (though the farmers exaggerated these evils).

The **PATRONS OF HUSBANDRY** (Grangers), founded by **Oliver H. Kelley** in 1867, helped to bring farmers together to improve their conditions. The Grange, which by 1874 boasted a membership of 1.5 million, stressed cooperative buying and opposed monopoly. It was active politically in the Midwest, where it took part (along with other interests) in the passage of state laws regulating grain elevators and railroads. Farmers were also active in politics and joined the Greenback movement and the Farmers' Alliances (see pp. 158, 160).

The Rise of Industrialism

Reasons for Industrial Growth

Conditions were favorable for the industrial growth that made the U.S. the **world's leading manufacturing nation** by 1885. While the economy had already "taken off" before the Civil War, the war prepared the nation for large-scale operations and opened opportunities. Agricultural surpluses sold abroad provided foreign capital. With the South defeated the government stood ready to use its powers to help industry. Defenders of big business used Charles Darwin's theories of evolution **(Social Darwinism)** to justify the philosophy of **laissez-faire** and government non-interference with ruthless business practices. The climate of opinion accepted the Protestant ethic **(gospel of wealth)**, which held that "Godliness" was "in league with riches" and that with hard work anyone could become rich. The rags-to-riches stories of **Horatio Alger**, the maxims of **McGuffey's Readers** and the preaching of Protestant clergymen combined to exalt the businessman. Technological improvements and the necessary raw materials (particularly coal, oil, and iron) were available, and immigration provided a large labor force. Entrepreneurs such as **Andrew Carnegie** and **John D. Rockefeller** were able to take advantage of the situation. Later historical research has shown that these business leaders came from essentially upper or middle-class, Protestant, native, northeastern backgrounds.

The Railroads

The railroad—America's first big business—played a large role in American industrial growth. Railroad builders added 22,000 miles to the national network in the 1860's, 40,000 more in the 1870's and 74,000 miles in the 1880's. The lines brought farmers to the West, took the product of farm and mine to market, provided a market for steel, made mass production possible, and opened up the mass urban market. By 1900 railroads were capitalized at $10.3 billion compared to $8.2 billion in manufacturing and a national debt of $1.3 billion.

The **Union Pacific** Railroad (chartered 1862) received government loans and land

Industrial Growth, 1860–1900

	1860	1880	1900
Population (millions)	32	50	76
Urban populations (per cent of total)[a]	20	28	40
Immigration (thousands)	154	457	449
Value of manufactures (millions of dollars)[b]	1,886	5,370	13,000
Value added by manufacturing (millions of dollars, 1879 prices)[b]	860	1,960	6,260
Value added by agriculture (millions of dollars, 1879 prices)[b]	1,490	2,600	3,920
Railroad miles in operation	30,626	93,262	193,346
United States net international investment liabilities (millions of dollars)	377	1,584	2,501
Wholesale commodity price index (1910–14 = 100)	93	100	82
Exports of United States merchandise (millions of dollars)	316	824	1,371
Non-agricultural exports (millions of dollars, followed by per cent of total)	49(16)	122(15)	485(35)
Iron ore production (thousands of tons)	2,873	7,120	27,300
Steel ingots and castings produced (thousands of tons)	20[c]	1,247	10,188
Crude petroleum production (thousands of barrels)	500	26,286	63,621
Bituminous coal production (thousands of tons)	9,057	50,757	212,316
Workers in non-farm occupations (thousands, followed by per cent of all workers)	4,325(41)	8,807(51)	18,161(63)
General imports into the United States (millions of dollars)	354	668	850
Gross national product (billions of dollars)	9.1[d]	16.1[d]	37.1[d]

[a] persons living in places of 2,500 or more inhabitants
[b] 1859, 1879, and 1899 figures
[c] 1867
[d] annual averages, 1869–73, 1877–81, and 1897–1901

grants and using Irish labor built a line from Nebraska to Utah. There in 1869 the Union Pacific met the **Central Pacific** (chartered 1861), organized by **Collis P. Huntington** and **Leland Stanford,** who built east from San Francisco using Chinese labor. The **Northern Pacific** Railway (1864), organized first by **Jay Cooke** and later by **Henry Villard,** brought a line from Lake Superior to Portland, Ore., by 1883. The **Great Northern,** started under another name in 1878 by **James J. Hill,** built a competing line from St. Paul to Seattle, by 1893. The **Atchison, Topeka, and Santa Fe** (1863), set up by **Cyrus P. Holliday,** ran from Kansas City to Los Angeles by 1883. The **Southern Pacific** (1871), organized by Huntington, drove east toward El Paso, Tex., where in 1882 it linked tracks with the **Texas and Pacific** (1871).

Since there were too many railroads, competition was ruthless and railroads engaged in many dubious practices. Many were **overcapitalized** (issued stock far beyond the value of the assets) and consequently had to charge high rates in order to get a return on the stock. Price wars, on the other hand, led to **rebates,** by which railroads gave secret low rates to large customers, or to **pools,** in which railroads secretly agreed to divide the available business among themselves. Farmers accused railroads of charging high prices for lands granted them by the government and of charging more for a short haul than a long haul in order to attract long-distance shippers. Demand for railroad regulation arose in all parts of the country as well as in the Midwest and from many economic groups as well as from farmers.

Railroad Regulation

1869 Massachusetts established a **commission** to supervise railroads and hear complaints; within a decade at least 10 more states had followed suit.

1873 Illinois passed a law regulating the prices charged in grain storage elevators, one of a series of so-called **Granger Laws** passed by midwestern states against the railroads.

1874 **Windom Committee** of the Senate (William Windom, Minn., chairman) recommended federal construction of competitive railroads.

1874 The Senate failed to act on a House bill to regulate railroad rates.

1877 In *Munn v. Illinois,* the Supreme Court ruled that the Illinois statute regulating elevators was constitutional since the **public could control property affected with a public interest** for the common good. Since no federal law existed, the Court declared that the state could regulate interstate commerce.

1878 **John H. Reagan** (Tex.) proposed a bill in the House to eliminate railroad abuses such as rebates and overcharges, but the Senate took no action.

1886 The case of *Wabash, St. Louis, and Pacific Railway Company v. Illinois* caused the Supreme Court to **reverse part of the Munn ruling** by declaring an Illinois statute prohibiting the "long haul–short haul" abuse unconstitutional because Congress alone had power over interstate commerce.

1886 **Cullom Committee,** under Senator Shelby M. Cullom (Ill.), reported in favor of federal regulation of the nation's railroads.

1887 **INTERSTATE COMMERCE ACT** declared it illegal to issue rebates or to charge more for a short than a long haul or to make pooling arrangements; it required that all **rates be "reasonable and just"**; it also established the **Interstate Commerce Commission,** which was given power to investigate the railroads. The Act proved ineffective, however. During its first 18 years (1887–1905), the Supreme Court decided for the carriers in 15 of the 16 cases brought by the Commission.

1890 In *Chicago, Milwaukee, and St. Paul Railroad Co. v. Minnesota,* the Supreme Court ruled that railroad rate regulation was subject to judicial review.

1897 The Court decided in the **Maximum Freight Rate Case** that the **ICC did not have the power to fix rates.**

1897 In *ICC v. Alabama Midlands Railway Company,* the Court nullified the "long haul–short haul" clause of the Interstate Commerce Act.

Big Business

Steel The introduction of the **Bessemer** and **Open-Hearth** processes for converting iron ore to steel (1864 and 1868) and the exploitation of the giant iron ore fields in upper Michigan and Minnesota (Mesabi Range and others) revolutionized the iron industry. **Pittsburgh,** in the midst of the Appalachian coal fields, was the center of the industry, with iron ore floated in by barge on the Great Lakes. Here **Andrew Carnegie** built his steel mills, began to roll rails in 1875, and by 1900 controlled 40 per cent of American steel production. In 1901 **J. Pierpont Morgan** bought out Carnegie and others and set up the **United States Steel Corporation,** which controlled $\frac{3}{5}$ of the steel business and was the first billion dollar company in the United States.

Oil **Edwin L. Drake** drilled the first oil well near Titusville, Pa., in 1859; other oil fields were soon opened up in Pennsylvania, West Virginia, and Ohio. **John D. Rockefeller,** who concentrated on oil refining, established the **Standard Oil Company** of Ohio in 1870. Through ruthless practices, particularly by securing rebates from railroads, he drew oil refineries under his control. In 1879, when he set up the **Standard Oil Trust** (reorganized 1882), he controlled 90 per cent–95 per cent of all oil refined in the United States. When the Ohio Supreme Court broke the trust in 1892, Rockefeller was able (in 1899) to establish the **Standard Oil Company of New Jersey,** a holding company.

The Process of Concentration: pools (1870–87) were devices whereby competing

Total Capital in Major Branches of Manufactures, 1899

(Book value, in millions of dollars)

Food and kindred products	1,576
Textiles and textile products	1,366
Machinery, excluding transportation equipment	924
Forest products	872
Iron and steel products	870
Chemicals and allied substances	457
Nonferrous metals and products	360
Printing, publishing, and allied industries	342
Stone, clay, and glass products	336
Leather products	335

firms combined to share the market. The Interstate Commerce Act declared pools illegal in 1887, but some continued. **Trusts** (1879–90) were arrangements whereby stockholders turned their stock over to trustees who then were often able to monopolize the industry. The first large trust was the Standard Oil Company (1879–82). The Sherman Antitrust Act declared illegal in 1890 trusts in restraint of trade. In a **holding company** one corporation gained control of the stock in others until it had built up a new, purely paper corporation in the form of a pyramid of companies. The first great holding companies were Standard Oil of New Jersey and United States Steel (1901).

Trust Regulation

1886 In *Santa Clara County v. Southern Pacific Railroad,* the Supreme Court declared a **corporation to be a person** and thereby protected under the 14th Amendment.

1888 **John H. Reagan** (Tex.) introduced an antitrust bill in the House and **John Sherman** (Ohio) introduced one in the Senate.

1889 Kansas became the first state to pass an antitrust law. Fifteen other states and territories followed by 1893.

1890 **SHERMAN ANTITRUST ACT:** Senators **George F. Hoar** (Mass.), **George F. Edmunds** (Vt.), and **John Sherman** (Ohio) led in drawing up the act, which declared that "every contract, **combination** in the form of trust or otherwise, or conspiracy, **in restraint of trade** or commerce among the several states, or with foreign nations" was

illegal. The act empowered the Attorney General to institute proceedings in equity in circuit courts to prevent violations, but the act was too vague (perhaps intentionally) to be effective. Between 1890 and 1901 the federal government instituted only 18 cases under the Sherman Act, and four were against labor unions.

1895 The Supreme Court declared in *United States v. E. C. Knight Company* (Jan. 21) that the American Sugar Refining Company did not violate the Sherman Act when it acquired four Philadelphia refineries, even though the monopoly that resulted controlled 98 per cent of the sugar refined in the United States. In its decision the court **distinguished between manufacturing and commerce** and argued that a monopoly of manufacturing did not necessarily violate the Sherman Act. Attorney General **Richard Olney,** who initiated the case, was happy to see the case dismissed and the Sherman Act weakened.

1897 The Court ruled in *United States v. Trans-Missouri Freight Association* that an association of railroads to fix rates was a violation of the Sherman Act and rejected the argument that only unreasonable combinations were illegal.

1899 In *Addystone Pipe and Steel Company v. United States,* the court declared a pooling arrangement to be a violation of the Sherman Act, thereby strengthening the act.

The Labor Movement

Labor After the Civil War Workers found it difficult to adjust to the large-scale factory system that developed after the Civil War. Labor had to adjust to machinery, immigration gave America a large labor supply, and public opinion was hostile to labor organization. Workers, consequently, worked **long hours** amid **poor working conditions** and received **low wages. Few workers,** however, **joined unions** (in 1900 only 791,000 belonged to unions out of a non-farm work force of over 18 million) partly because they did not want to label themselves as "labor," partly because real wages went up after the Panic of 1873.

Workers were fundamentally capitalists and rejected socialist or anarchist programs.

1863–73   Many national trade (craft) unions developed, including the molders and the railway engineers and firemen.

1866   Reform groups as well as trade unions established the **National Labor Union** (Aug.), which had an eventual peak membership of 300,000. Led by **William H. Sylvis**, it worked for the eight-hour day, cooperatives, and the repeal of the contract labor law. In 1872 it organized the **National Labor Reform Party** and nominated Judge **David Davis** for President, but after he withdrew from the contest the entire National Labor Union collapsed.

1868   Congress passed an **eight-hour day** law for certain **federal workers**.

1873   The depression following the Panic of 1873 hurt the labor movement, and union membership dropped from about 300,000 to about 50,000 by 1877.

1875   Bad working conditions in the coal mines led a secret organization of miners known as the **Molly Maguires** to perform acts of terrorism in eastern Pennsylvania; the movement declined after the courts convicted 24 and hanged 10.

1877   **Railroad strike:** a strike against wage cuts on the Baltimore and Ohio Railway (July 16) spread to many other railroads and led to riots in Baltimore and other cities. **President Hayes** sent **federal troops** to Pittsburgh where strikers on July 21 fought a battle with state militia in which 25 people were killed.

1879   **KNIGHTS OF LABOR** (founded in 1869) grew rapidly under **Terence V. Powderly**, its president 1879–93. The Knights enrolled workers of all levels and all races and nationalities in **local assemblies**. While it called for the eight-hour day and the end of child labor, it was also concerned with cooperatives and money reform programs. The number of assemblies increased from 484 in 1882 to 5,892 in 1886, and total membership reached 700,000. Though its leaders opposed the use of strikes, it won **strikes** against the Union Pacific Railroad in 1884 and the Wabash Railroad in 1885. Hard times, the

failure of strikes, and the **Haymarket Riot** in 1886 started the downfall of the Knights, which toward the end (1893) fell under farm control.

1886

610,000 workers were involved in **strikes** in 1886, which was one of the peak strike years of the nineteenth century. The other was 1894, when 690,000 workers took part in strikes.

May 4   **HAYMARKET RIOT** took place when a bomb exploded among police who were breaking up an anarchist meeting in Haymarket Square, Chicago, killing seven and wounding seventy. Though no one identified the bomb-thrower, Judge **Joseph E. Gary** sentenced seven anarchists to death and others to prision terms. In spite of many public petitions, four were executed. In June, 1893, Gov. **John Peter Altgeld** freed three of the prisoners, maintaining that the trial had been unfair.

Dec. 8   The **AMERICAN FEDERATION OF LABOR** emerged in Columbus, Ohio, from another federation organized in 1881. The AFL was a loose **federation of craft unions** that aimed at securing gains for skilled workers. Its president, **SAMUEL GOMPERS** (1886–1924, except for 1895), was a conservative who sought higher **wages**, the **eight-hour day**, and the right to **collective bargaining** rather than vague social and political goals. By 1904 the AFL had 1,676,200 out of 2,067,000 total union members.

1888   The Union Labor Party and the United Labor Party nominated Presidential candidates.

1892

July 6   **HOMESTEAD MASSACRE** took place at the Carnegie Steel plant at Homestead, Pa., when strikers fired on Pinkerton detectives that manager **Henry Clay Frick** had imported to break up the strike. Three detectives and ten strikers were killed, and the strike ended in failure.

July 11 Fighting broke out between strikers and strike breakers at the **Coeur d'Alene silver mines in Idaho,** and federal troops were sent in on July 14.

Aug. 28 The **Socialist Labor Party** for the first time nominated a Presidential candidate and continued to do so in almost every election thereafter.

1894

June 21 The **PULLMAN STRIKE** broke out when members of the American Railway Union (**Eugene V. Debs,** president) struck against wage cuts and high rents at the company town built by **George M. Pullman** near Chicago. The entire union then struck, tying up all railroads west of Chicago.

July 4 In spite of the opposition of Gov. **John Peter Altgeld,** Attorney General **Richard Olney** secured an **injunction** under the Sherman Act against the union (July 2) and President **Cleveland** sent 2,000 federal troops to Chicago (July 4) to safeguard the mails. The strike was broken by July 20.

1895 *In Re Debs:* when Debs violated the injunction against the Pullman strike, he was jailed for contempt of court. The Supreme Court subsequently declared (May 27) that the **injunction was legitimate.** Injunctions were used against strikes over 200 times in the next quarter-century.

1898 The **Erdman Act** (June 1) allowed the chairman of the ICC and the commissioner of the Bureau of Labor to mediate in labor disputes.

Immigration to America, 1861–1910

1868 Burlingame Treaty allowed unlimited Chinese immigration to the United States.

1877 **Anti-Chinese riots** led by **Dennis Kearney,** an Irish immigrant labor leader, and unemployed workers broke out in **San Francisco.**

1880 Treaty with China (Nov. 17) allowed the United States to suspend immigration of Chinese workers.

Statistics, Total Immigration by Decades

	Thousands
1861–70	2,315
1871–80	2,812
1881–90	5,247
1891–1900	3,688
1901–10	8,795
Total	22,857

1882 **Chinese Exclusion Act** suspended Chinese immigration for 10 years. Foreign-born Chinese in the United States in 1870 numbered 63,000; in 1880, 105,000; and in 1890, 107,000. The exclusion was extended until 1943.

1882 An Act of Congress (Aug. 18) excluded from immigration criminals, paupers, the insane, and others.

1885 **Contract Labor Law** (Feb. 26) forbade the importation of contract labor.

Population by Country of Birth, 1860 and 1910

(thousands)

	Foreign-born population		Native white population of foreign or mixed parentage
	1860	1910	1910
Total	4,139	13,516	18,898
Northwestern Europe	2,472	4,239	
England	433	878	1,822[a]
Ireland	1,611	1,352	3,304
Central and Eastern Europe	1,312	6,014	
Germany	1,276	2,311	5,671
Poland	7	938	726
Austria	25	846	717
Hungary	—	496	215
Russia	3	1,314	776
Southern Europe	20	1,526	
Italy	12	1,343	772
Asia	37	191	
America	288	1,489	
Canada	250	1,205	1,651

[a] including Wales

1887 The **American Protective Association** was founded to combat Catholicism.

1890–1914 Land-holding changes, depressions, and persecution of Jews led to massive **immigration from central, eastern, and southern Europe.** The peak immigration years were 1905–14 when the median annual immigration was about one million, compared to less than one-half million in the decades immediately before and after. Immigrants concentrated in the Northeast, which had 6.6 million foreign-born whites in 1910 as compared to 4.7 million in the north-central states, 0.7 million in the South, and 1.3 million in the West. They also concentrated in cities, particularly in New York (Italians and most other groups) and in Chicago (Poles and other central and eastern European groups).

1894 The **Immigration Restriction League** was organized in Massachusetts and began to campaign for a literacy test to restrict immigration. Aristocratic Bostonians were henceforth in the forefront of the movement to preserve America for Anglo-Saxons. Cleveland vetoed a literacy test bill in 1897.

1900 In a "**Gentlemen's Agreement**" Japan agreed to limit its emigration of laborers to the United States.

1906 **San Francisco School Board** ordered Chinese, Japanese, and Korean children to attend separate public schools but abolished the order in 1907 after pressure from President Roosevelt.

1907–08 In a second "**Gentlemen's Agreement**" Japan again agreed to stop the emigration of laborers. As a result, the number of foreign-born Japanese in the United States which had increased from 25,000 in 1900 to 68,000 in 1910 was only 82,000 in 1920.

Politics, 1877–1900

From Hayes to Harrison, 1877–1890

1877

1877–88 **The two major parties,** Republican and Democratic, were so evenly balanced that Republicans won three out of four Presidential elections without a popular majority and with a plurality only in 1880. Two important Republican groups—northeastern industrialists and northwestern farmers—disagreed over the tariff and money issues. Republican leadership split among **Stalwarts** led by Senator **Roscoe Conkling** (N.Y.), **Half-Breeds** led by Sen. **James G. Blaine** (Maine), and **liberals** such as **Carl Schurz.** Democrats tried to unite southern Redeemers, southern independents, northern liberals, and northern city politicians. Their base was New York State, which provided all Democratic Presidential candidates between 1868 and 1892 excepting 1880. The Democrats did not materially differ from the Republicans on economic issues.

1877–94 After the Civil War the Treasury showed an **annual surplus,** which continued until 1894 and enabled the government to cut the federal debt from $2.8 billion in 1866 to $961 million in 1893. Debt reduction was part of a federal hard-money program that increased the value of money and lowered prices until 1896.

1878

Feb. 22 **GREENBACK LABOR PARTY** met at Toledo and wrote a platform calling for **free silver,** restrictions on immigration, and restrictions on hours of industrial labor. In the Congressional election of 1878 the Greenback-Laborites, led by **James B. Weaver** (Iowa), won 14 seats in Congress.

Feb. 28 **Bland-Allison Act** passed over Hayes' veto. Increased silver production (from $16 million in 1870 to $35 million in 1880) and a drop in the market price of silver (ratio of gold to silver rose from 15.6–1 in 1870 to 18.1–1 in 1880) led to agitation for government coinage of silver. Silver-mine operators and farmers began to refer to the Coinage Act of 1873 demonetizing silver as the "**Crime of '73.**" Congressman **Richard P. Bland** (Mo.) pushed a bill through the House calling for the **free and unlimited coinage of silver at 16–1** (1876 and again in 1877). Amended by Senator **William B. Allison** (Iowa) the final bill called for the Secretary of the Treasury to buy from $2 million to $4 million of silver a month at the market price and to issue silver certificates. Since the Secretary purchased the bare minimum, the government coined only $378 million by 1890, far below the demands of the silverites.

July 11   Hayes suspended **Chester A. Arthur** and **Alonzo B. Cornell,** in the New York custom house for violating a federal order and thereby challenged the Conkling-Stalwart faction in that state. When he secured confirmation of his own appointees, Hayes had taken a big step toward restoring the power of the executive.

1879

Jan. 1   In accordance with the Act of 1875 (see p. 143) the government **resumed specie payments for greenbacks.** Since the greenback was already circulating on a par with the gold dollar, there was no move to reclaim them.

1879–82   Prosperity came with the end of the depression in 1879 as wholesale commodity prices rose from 90 in 1879 to 108 in 1882. Times were unsettled after that, and commodity prices dropped to an index of 82 in 1890.

1880

June 2   Republican Convention met in Chicago and nominated darkhorse Congressman **James A. Garfield** (Ohio). Stalwart **Chester A. Arthur** (N.Y.) was the Vice Presidential candidate.

June 9   The **Greenback Labor Party** met in Chicago and nominated **James B. Weaver** (Iowa) for President and **B.J. Chambers** (Tex.) for Vice President and came out in support of woman suffrage, the federal in-

come tax, and regulation of interstate commerce.

June 22   The **Democrats** met in Cincinnati and nominated former Union General **Winfield Scott Hancock** (Pa.) for President and **William H. English** (Ind.) for Vice President.

Nov. 2   Presidential election: Garfield won with 4,453,295 votes (214 electoral); **Hancock** received 4,414,082 (155 electoral), and **Weaver** received 308,578 votes.

1881

May 16   Stalwart Senators **Conkling** and **Thomas C. Platt** (N.Y.) resigned from the Senate after failing to block the appointment of a Half-Breed as port collector in New York. The refusal of the New York legislature to reelect them marked the decline of the Stalwarts.

July 2   ASSASSINATION OF PRESIDENT GARFIELD: Charles J. Guiteau, an insane and disappointed Stalwart office-seeker, shot Garfield in order to make Chester A. Arthur President. Garfield died on Sept. 19.

1883

Jan. 16   Pendleton Act, sponsored by Senator **George H. Pendleton** (Ohio), established a three-member **Civil Service Commission** to administer examinations for some federal positions.

Mar. 3   The Tariff Commission (established May 15, 1882) recommended that Congress reduce certain tariffs, but the new **Tariff of 1883** carried only slight reductions and remained very protective.

1884

May 28   National Greenback Labor Party nominated **Benjamin F. Butler** (Mass.) for President and **A. M. West** (Miss.) for Vice President.

June 3   The **Republicans** met in Chicago and nominated **James G. Blaine** (Maine) for President and **John A. Logan** (Ill.) for Vice President. **Independents** ("Mugwumps"), such as **George W. Curtis** of

Harper's Weekly and **Edwin L. Godkin** of *The Nation*, bolted the party and supported the Democratic ticket.

July 8   The **Democrats** met in Chicago and nominated governor **Grover Cleveland** of New York for President and **Thomas A. Hendricks** (Ind.) for Vice President.

Nov. 4   Presidential election: in the campaign the Democrats took advantage of Blaine's alleged corruption and the Republicans pointed out that Cleveland had been the father of an illegitimate child. On Oct. 29 Blaine lost Irish-American votes in New York when Rev. **Samuel D. Burchard** called the Democrats the party of "Rum, Romanism, and Rebellion," and Blaine failed to repudiate the statement. **Cleveland** carried **New York state** by barely 1,000 votes and thereby won the election. **Cleveland:** 4,879,507 votes (219 electoral); **Blaine:** 4,850,293 votes (182 electoral); and **Butler** 175,370 votes.

1886

Jan. 19   Presidential Succession Act provided that in the event of the death or removal of both President and Vice President the members of the cabinet in order of the creation of their offices should succeed. The act replaced the act of 1792 that called for the President *pro tempore* of the Senate and the Speaker of the House to be next in line.

Aug. 3   Congress authorized the construction of two more steel ships (three had been authorized in 1883). The new Secretary of the Navy **William C. Whitney** created the **new steel navy,** 1885–89.

1887

Feb. 11   President Cleveland vetoed the Dependent Pension Bill, which provided a pension for veterans whether or not they had any military disability.

Mar. 5   Congress repealed the Tenure of Office Act, thereby strengthening the office of the President.

Dec. 6   In his annual message **Cleveland** called for **lowering the tariff** as a means of reducing the surplus and preventing the rise of trusts.

1888

June 5   Democrats met in St. Louis, and renominated **Cleveland** for President and **Allen G. Thurman** (Ohio) for Vice President.

June 19   Republican Convention met in Chicago and nominated former Senator **Benjamin Harrison** (Ind.) for President and **Levi P. Morton** (N.Y.) for Vice President.

July 21   Mills Bill, proposed by Roger Q. Mills (Tex.), calling for 7 per cent tariff reduction passed the House, but the Senate took no action on it.

Fall   Republicans promised a high protective tariff and high pensions for veterans.

Nov. 6   Presidential election: Harrison won with 5,447,129 votes (233 electoral) to 5,537,857 votes (168 electoral) for **Cleveland.**

1890

The Republican Congress, which became known as the **billion dollar Congress,** passed legislation that reduced income, raised expenses and cut away at the surplus. The first **deficit** since the Civil War occurred in fiscal 1894.

June 27   Dependent Pensions Act granted pensions to Union veterans with 90 days' service who were disabled (either in service or afterwards) and were unable to earn a living. The annual appropriation for pensions rose from $81 million to $135 million before Harrison left office.

July 14   Sherman Silver Purchase Act. The declining price of silver (ratio of gold to silver rose from 18–1 in 1880 to 20–1 in 1890) led to the Sherman Silver Purchase Act, which required the U.S. Treasury to purchase 4.5 million ounces of silver a month and issue Treasury certificates redeemable in gold. The act did not satisfy the free-silver advocates, for in three years it put only $156 million in additional money into circulation.

Oct. 1   McKinley Tariff, sponsored by Congressman William McKinley (Ohio), raised tariffs to an average of about 50 per cent.

The Farmers' Revolt, 1875–1900

Declining Prices, increasing tenancy and debt, and continued isolation drove farmers to organize in various **alliance movements**.

1875 Texas farmers formed the Texas (later **Southern**) **Alliance**, which by 1885 claimed 50,000 members.

1880 **Milton George** founded a farmers' alliance in Cook County, Ill., which grew into the **Northern Alliance,** claiming 100,000 members by 1882.

1887–89 **Dr. C. W. Macune** merged the Southern Alliance with another Texas group known as the Agricultural Wheel to form the **National Farmers' Alliance and Industrial Union.** Macune's Alliance made connections also with the Colored Farmers' Alliance, three northern state alliances, and the Knights of Labor. Macune proposed a **subtreasury plan,** by which government subtreasuries would advance legal tender notes to farmers for farm products deposited at warehouses.

1890

Nov. 4 **Congressional elections:** public reaction against the "billion dollar Congress" contributed to Democratic victories and Republican loss of the House. Farmers' candidates won ten seats in the House and two in the Senate (**William A. Peffer,** Kan., and **James H. Kyle,** S.D.). Forty-four Democratic congressmen and three senators from the South were pledged to support Alliance programs.

Dec. Farmers' groups meeting at **Ocala, Fla.,** issued a statement of grievances.

1891 A national convention of farmers' and other groups at **Cincinnati** laid plans for a third party (May 19).

1892

Feb. 22 Representatives of the National Alliance, the Northern Alliance, and the Knights of Labor, as well as Prohibitionists, Greenbackers, and others met in **St. Louis** and founded the **PEOPLE'S (POPULIST) PARTY OF THE U.S.A.**

June 7 **Republican Convention** met at Minneapolis and renominated **Benjamin Harrison** for President and nominated **Whitelaw Reid** (N.Y.) for Vice President.

June 21 The **Democratic Convention** met at Chicago and renominated **Grover Cleveland** for President and **Adlai E. Stevenson** (Ill.) for Vice President.

July 2 **Populist Party** met at **Omaha** and nominated **James B. Weaver** (Iowa) for President and **James G. Field** (Va.) for Vice President. Other important Populist leaders present were **Ignatius Donnelly** (Minn.), **"Sockless Jerry" Simpson** and **William A. Peffer** (Kan.), and **Thomas E. Watson** (Ga.). The Populist platform included the following planks:

1. a flexible **national currency** issued only by the government;
2. the **subtreasury plan** of loans to farmers;
3. an increase in the **circulating medium** to not less than $50 per capita;
4. free and unlimited **coinage of silver** at 16 to 1;
5. a graduated **income tax;**
6. **government ownership** of railroads, telephone, and telegraph; and
7. an eight-hour day for labor and immigration restriction.

Nov. 8 **Presidential election:** labor strikes during the summer and the unpopular McKinley Tariff hurt the Republicans in the election. **Cleveland** regained the Presidency with 5,555,426 votes (277 electoral) to 5,182,690 (145 electoral) for **Harrison** and 1,029,846 (22 electoral) for **Weaver.** The Populists carried Kansas, Colorado, Idaho, Nevada, and part of North Dakota and did well in the north-central, Rocky Mountain, and southern states. Populists elected five senators, ten representatives, and three governors.

1893

Cleveland's second term began with the **PANIC OF 1893.** Long-range causes included continued agricultural depression and overspeculation in trusts. The collapse of the British banking house of **Baring Brothers** in 1890 caused English investors to sell their American securities and to withdraw gold from the United States. The Sherman Silver Purchase Act also caused a **drain on the federal gold reserve,** which fell from over $190 million in 1891 to below $100 million in early 1893. The gold crisis brought on the panic, which started with a severe drop on the New York Stock exchange just before Harrison left office. The **depression** was at its worst in 1894 when **perhaps 3 million were unemployed** (perhaps 20 per cent of the working force). Recovery did not come until 1898. Wholesale commodity prices (1926 = 100): 1890, 56; 1896, 47; and 1900, 56.

Nov. 1   Repeal of the Sherman Silver Purchase Act: President Cleveland, who blamed the panic on the Silver Purchase Act, called a special session of Congress on Aug. 7 to ask for repeal. After a struggle between silver Democrats, led by farming and mining interests, and gold Democrats under Cleveland, the act was repealed.

1894

William H. Harvey published his *Coin's Financial School,* which presented the free-silver arguments and led to counter-publications by defenders of the gold standard.

Feb. 8   Congress repealed the Force Acts of 1870 and 1871, which allowed federal troops to supervise Congressional elections in the South.

Mar. 25   Populist **Jacob S. Coxey** of Ohio led a **march of the unemployed** on Washington, and about 500 of **Coxey's Army** arrived at the capital on April 30. Coxey also proposed a **federal public works** program financed by an issue of $500 million in **legal tender notes,** designed to provide relief and inflation at the same time.

Aug. 28   The Wilson-Gorman Tariff, sponsored by Senator Arthur P. Gorman (Md.) and Congressman William L. Wilson (W. Va.), lowered duties to about 40 per cent and levied an income tax of 2 per cent. On May 20, 1895, the Supreme Court in ***Pollock v. Farmers' Loan and Trust Company*** declared the income tax a direct tax and therefore unconstitutional.

Nov. 6   Congressional elections: Repub-

licans gained 117 seats in the House and five in the Senate, while Populists polled 40 per cent more votes than in 1892.

1895

Feb. 8   In order to restore the gold reserve (it was down to $41 million) Secretary of the Treasury **John G. Carlisle** made a contract with the banking syndicate of **J. P. Morgan** and **August Belmont** to purchase 3.5 million ounces of gold, one-half of which the firm would purchase abroad. This "gold deal," which brought the bankers a profit of perhaps $2 million on a loan of $62 million, led to great public criticism of President Cleveland.

Mar. 5   The **"Appeal of the Silver Democrats,"** written by Congressman **Richard P. Bland** (Mo.) and **William Jennings Bryan** (Neb.; elected in 1890) and signed by the silver Democrats in the House, called for free coinage of silver at a ratio of 16–1.

1896

June 16   Republican Convention met at St. Louis and nominated **William McKinley** (Ohio) for President and **Garret A. Hobart** (N.J.) for Vice President on a platform defending the protective tariff and the gold standard. **Silver Republicans** under Senator **Henry M. Teller** (Colo.) bolted the party and held a national convention that endorsed the Democratic ticket.

July 7   The **Democrats** met in Chicago and drew up a platform calling for **free silver** and an income tax and opposing the protective tariff. **William Jennings Bryan** (Neb.) delivered his famous **"Cross of Gold" speech** in defense of the free silver plank. The convention then nominated **Bryan** for President and **Arthur Sewall** (Maine) for Vice President. **Gold Democrats** organized the National Democratic Party in September and nominated **John M. Palmer** (Ill.) for President and **Simon B. Buckner** (Ky.) for Vice President.

July 22   The **Populist Party** met at St. Louis and endorsed **Bryan** for President and nominated **Thomas E. Watson** (Ga.) for

Vice President. Bryan, supported by many reform groups, staged an unprecedented campaign traveling 18,000 miles, but **Marcus A. Hanna,** McKinley's campaign manager, raised over $3 million (10 times what Bryan was able to spend) to oppose him. Conservative eastern groups portrayed Bryan as far more radical than he really was.

Nov. 3   Presidential election: McKinley won with 7,102,246 votes (271 electoral) to 6,492,559 (176 electoral) for **Bryan.** McKinley carried the Northeast and Midwest; Bryan carried the South, the Great Plains, and the mountain states.

1897

End of the Depression came as poor foreign wheat crops increased American exports. New discoveries of gold (the **Klondike gold rush** in Canada was that year) increased the gold supply, saved the gold reserve and brought inflation. Currency in circulation rose from $1.5 billion in 1896 to $2.1 billion in 1900 to $3.1 billion in 1908.

July 7   Dingley Tariff raised rates to an all-time high (57 per cent).

1900

Mar. 6   The Social Democratic Party was organized at Indianapolis and nominated

Eugene V. Debs (Ind.) for President and **Job Harriman** (Calif.) for Vice President. The party (renamed **Socialist** in 1901) ran candidates in almost every Presidential election after 1900.

Mar. 14   Currency Act put the United States on the gold standard with a gold reserve of $150 million to redeem legal tender notes.

May 9   Populists met in two conventions. The **Fusionists** nominated **Bryan** for President and **Charles A. Towne** (Minn.) for Vice President. The **Anti-Fusionists** nominated **Wharton Barker** (Pa.) for President and **Ignatius Donnelly** (Minn.) for Vice President.

June 19   The Republicans met at Philadelphia and nominated **McKinley** for President and governor **Theodore Roosevelt** of New York for Vice President on a platform upholding Republican foreign policy and the gold standard.

July 4   The Democratic Convention met at Kansas City, Mo., renominated **Bryan** for President and nominated **Adlai E. Stevenson** for Vice President on a platform opposing imperialism and the gold standard.

Nov. 6   Presidential election: the Republicans offset Democratic attacks on imperialism by stressing prosperity ("the full dinner pail") and won the election. **McKinley** received 7,218,491 votes (292 electoral) to **Bryan's** 6,356,734 (155 electoral).

The Rise of American Imperialism, 1881–1900

Imperialist Beginnings, 1881–1895

1881   Secretary of State **James G. Blaine** called a Pan-American conference for 1882, but when Blaine resigned the conference was called off.

1885   Josiah Strong, in his book *Our Country,* urged American expansion overseas, basing his argument on the assumed superiority of the Anglo-Saxon peoples.

1887   The Senate finally ratified the Hawaiian Treaty of 1875 when it was amended

to give the United States a naval base at **Pearl Harbor.**

1888   A *modus vivendi* with Great Britain eased a dispute over fishing rights in Canada.

1889   Berlin Conference on the **Samoan Islands** established a German-British-American protectorate over Samoa (ratified by the Senate, 1890).

1889   The first **International Conference of American States** met in Washington (Oct. 2). Secretary of State Blaine was unable to secure a customs union, but the conference established the **International Bureau of American Republics** (later the Pan-American Union).

1890   Capt. **Alfred T. Mahan's** *The Influence of Sea Power upon History, 1660–1783,* argued for increased naval power to make the United States a world force.

1891–92   The United States irritated the rebel Congressionalist Party in **Chile** in 1891 by seizing a ship that the Congressionalists had sent to San Diego for arms. Hard feeling reached a high point after the Congressionalists gained power when a mob in Valparaiso on Oct. 16, 1891, attacked American sailors on shore leave and killed two. Although both Chile and the United States made warlike gestures, war was averted when Chile tendered diplomatic apologies.

1892   **Fur sealing controversy.** In 1886, the United States started a dispute with Great Britain when it began to seize Canadian sealing vessels in the Bering Sea, which it claimed was within American jurisdiction. In 1890 Secretary of State Blaine and British Foreign Secretary Lord Salisbury made bellicose statements, but the two countries signed an arbitration treaty in 1892.

1893   **Hawaii:** the Reciprocity Treaty of 1875 (see p. 144) allowed Hawaiian sugar into the U.S. duty free. When the McKinley Tariff (1890) put sugar from all nations on the free list and gave a bounty of two cents a pound for native-grown sugar, American sugar growers in Hawaii faced ruin. Led by **Sanford B. Dole,** they started a revolt in 1893 against autocratic **Queen Liliuokalani** to bring about the annexation of Hawaii to the United States. United States Minister to Hawaii **John L. Stevens,** who favored annexation, sent the Marines ashore (Jan. 16), recognized the revolutionary government (Jan. 17), put up the United States flag (Feb. 1), and signed a **treaty of annexation** (Feb. 14). The treaty was not ratified by the time **Cleveland** came into office, and he **withdrew the treaty** (Mar. 9) and sent ex-Congressman **James H. Blount** (Ga.) to Hawaii to investigate. Blount withdrew the Marines, lowered the flag, and reported against annexation. When Cleveland tried to restore Queen Liliuokalani to power, the

Dole regime refused to step down, and Cleveland reluctantly recognized it on Aug. 7, 1894.

1895   The United States was sympathetic to **Venezuela** in its **boundary dispute** with Great Britain over the line between British Guiana and Venezuela. On Feb. 20, 1895, Congress proposed arbitration. On July 20, 1895, Secretary of State **Richard Olney** accused the British of violating the **Monroe Doctrine.** He expanded the Doctrine by stating, "the United States is practically sovereign on this continent," and "its fiat is law. . . ." British Prime Minister Lord Salisbury replied (Nov. 26) that the Monroe Doctrine did not apply and he would not agree to arbitration. Cleveland, angered by the rebuff, sent a jingoistic message to Congress (Dec. 17) asking for an American commission to draw the line. Britain, preoccupied with imperialism in Africa and elsewhere, finally gave way, cooperated with the American boundary commission, and signed a **treaty of arbitration** with Venezuela on Feb. 2, 1897. Relations between the United States and Great Britain improved greatly after 1897.

1895   Continued Spanish oppression in **CUBA** led to a revolution there in 1895. The United States sympathized with the rebels, particularly after Spanish General **Valeriano ("Butcher") Weyler** early in 1896 began to establish **concentration camps** to prevent rebel attacks on sugar plantations. The horrible conditions reported in these camps aroused humanitarian sentiment in the United States.

1896   The Senate (Feb. 28) and the House (Apr. 6) passed concurrent resolutions favoring recognition of Cuban belligerency, but President Cleveland refused to do so.

1897   **Yellow journalism:** in New York City, **William Randolph Hearst's** *Journal* and **Joseph Pulitzer's** *World* vied with each other in reporting atrocity stories of Spanish brutality in Cuba. Such reporting became known as "yellow journalism" after the two papers carried on a fight in 1895 for rights to a comic strip called "The Yellow Kid."

1897   A new liberal ministry in Spain made concessions to American sentiment about

Cuba by **recalling Gen. Weyler** (Nov. 25) and modifying the concentration camp system.

The Spanish-American War, 1898

American **business interests** (aside from those with Cuban sugar investments) opposed war with Spain from fear that it would destroy the new-found prosperity of 1897. **Humanitarians**, however, called for intervention in Cuba and **imperialists** such as Senator **Henry Cabot Lodge**, Assistant Secretary of the Navy **Theodore Roosevelt** and **Capt. Mahan** demanded war with Spain as a means of territorial conquest.

Feb. 8 Hearst's *Journal* published a **letter** written by the Spanish Minister to the United States, Senõr **Dupuy de Lôme**, and stolen from the mails, that depicted President McKinley as a spineless politician. De Lôme resigned, but the letter brought war closer.

Feb. 15 The U.S. **battleship *Maine* blew up in Havana Harbor** with a loss of 260 officers and sailors. The American public blamed the explosion on the Spanish, though it now seems unlikely that the Spanish government would have sanctioned such an act.

Feb. 25 Assistant Secretary of the Navy **Roosevelt** sent a dispatch to Commodore **George Dewey**, Commander of the Asiatic Squadron, ordering him to attack the Spanish **Philippines** in case of a war with Spain over Cuba.

Mar. 19 Senator **Redfield Proctor** (Vt.), just back from Cuba, stirred war sentiment by a speech to the Senate in which he described the miserable conditions he had observed.

Mar. 27 **President McKinley proposed that Spain** grant an armistice and remove the concentration camps and insisted on Cuban independence. Spain agreed on the first two points but not on independence.

Apr. 11 **President McKinley**, influenced by the warlike spirit in the country, sent a **war message** to Congress asking for the power to use the armed forces to end hostilities in Cuba.

Apr. 19 Congress in a **joint resolution** recognized the independence of Cuba and authorized the President to use the armed forces to force the Spanish out. The **Teller Amendment**, proposed by Senator Henry M. Teller (Col.), disclaimed any intention on the part of the United States to annex Cuba. President McKinley signed the resolution on Apr. 20.

Apr. 24 **Spain declared war** on the United States, which in turn declared war on Spain the following day.

The Military Campaigns

May 1 **Dewey's Asiatic Squadron** left Hong Kong (Apr. 27), slipped into Manila Bay, and in the **BATTLE OF MANILA BAY** destroyed the Spanish fleet of 10 ships with no damage to American ships. Over 380 Spanish were killed but no Americans. The United States attacked Manila and captured it on Aug. 13.

May 19 In spite of an American blockade, the Spanish fleet under Adm. Pasqual **Cervera** sailed from Spain and slipped into Santiago de Cuba.

June 14 Gen. **William R. Shafter** led an American force including the **Rough Riders** (a volunteer cavalry regiment under Col. **Leonard Wood** and Lt. Col. **Theodore Roosevelt**) from Tampa, Fla., to Santiago de Cuba, where it disembarked June 22–26.

July 1 In the **Land Battle of Santiago**, United States forces seized the high ground outside Santiago de Cuba in the battles of **El Caney** and **San Juan Hill** with American casualties of about 1,500. The dismounted **Rough Riders** took part in the capture of San Juan Hill.

July 3 In the **Naval Battle of Santiago**, Adm. **Cervera** tried to escape from Santiago de Cuba but Adm. **William T. Sampson's** blockading fleet destroyed the entire Spanish fleet. The Spanish lost 474 men and the United States one. The garrison of Santiago de Cuba surrendered on July 17.

July 7 President McKinley signed a treaty to annex Hawaii (June 16, 1897), and Congress adopted the treaty by joint resolution on July 7.

Dec. 10 After the peace conference opened

in Paris on Oct. 1, President McKinley on Oct. 25 instructed the peace commissioners to demand the cession of the Philippine Islands. By the **TREATY OF PARIS** Spain ceded the United States the **Philippines** (for $20 million), **Puerto Rico,** and the island of **Guam,** while giving up all title to Cuba. During the war, disease and food poisoning had been so severe that 5,462 Americans died, although only 379 were battle casualties.

The American Empire, 1899–1900

1899

Jan. In debate over the Treaty of Paris, the **imperialists** argued that the United States should expand overseas in order to build American prestige, spread Christianity and the benefits of civilization ("the white man's burden"), and protect American strategic interests. If the United States did not keep the Philippines, they argued, some foreign power would take them. The **anti-imperialists** argued that imperialism was against American traditions and inconsistent with democratic government. Though opposed to imperialism, **William Jennings Bryan** persuaded Democrats to vote for the treaty as a means of ending the war, leaving the question of Philippine independence up to the electorate in 1900. The Senate ratified the treaty, by a vote of 57–27, on Feb. 6.

Feb. 4 **Emilio Aguinaldo,** who had led the revolt against Spanish rule in the Philippines, attacked Manila as the **Filipino Insurrection** began. A United States army of some 70,000 finally succeeded in quelling the revolt in late 1899, but guerrilla warfare continued until 1902 with atrocities on both sides.

July 29 The first **Hague Conference** of 26 nations, including the United States, failed to agree on disarmament but did establish the **Permanent Court of International Arbitration** to arbitrate international disputes.

Sept. 6 **FIRST "OPEN DOOR" NOTE:**

the weakness of China during the waning years of the Manchu Dynasty became increasingly evident at the end of the century. In 1894–95 the Japanese defeated the Chinese in the **Sino-Japanese War** and annexed the island of **Formosa.** In 1898 China granted a leasehold to **Russia** at **Port Arthur** and one to **Germany** at **Kiaochow Bay.** In 1898 the British suggested that the United States join her in defending equal trading opportunities for all nations (the "open door") in China. In 1899 **Alfred E. Hippisley,** a British subject employed by the Chinese Customs service, approached **William W. Rockhill,** advisor on Far Eastern affairs to Secretary of State John M. Hay, with a proposal for an American open door note. Hay was already under pressure from American business interests that feared commercial barriers in China. He, therefore, accepted a memorandum written by Hippisley and Rockhill and issued the note on Sept. 6 as a circular letter to the United States embassies in Berlin, St. Petersburg, and London. Each of the three other major powers was asked to reassure the United States that:

1. "within its sphere of interest or leasehold in China," it **would not interfere with any treaty port** (ports open to all nations);
2. the Chinese treaty tariff would apply within its sphere of interest; and
3. within its sphere it **would not discriminate in favor of its own nationals in the matter of harbor dues.**

Americans later magnified the importance of this note, which guaranteed nothing in China and merely tried to keep the Chinese trade open to all. The replies of the three powers were evasive, but Secretary Hay announced that they had accepted the **Open Door Policy.**

Dec. 2 The United States, Germany, and Great Britain signed a **Samoan treaty** in which Great Britain gave up her claims there in return for rights elsewhere, while Germany received two of the Samoan islands, and the United States gained the rest (including Tutuila with the harbor of Pago Pago). The Senate ratified the treaty on Jan. 16, 1900.

1900

Colonial government: on April 7 President McKinley appointed a **Philippine Commission** under judge **William Howard Taft** to start civil rule in the islands. After the revolt ended, an organic act (1902) made the Philippines an unincorporated territory under the rule of the Taft Commission. The **Foraker Act** (Apr. 12) made **Puerto Rico** an unincorporated territory and gave the President the power to appoint a governor-general. On April 30, Congress gave **Hawaii** full territoral status. The Navy administered **Guam** and **Tutuila.** In the **Insular Cases** (*De Lima v. Bidwell* and *Downes v. Bidwell*, both 1901) the Supreme Court ruled that the inhabitants of the colonial empire were not automatically American citizens and had only those constitutional rights conferred on them by Congress.

June **BOXER REBELLION:** antiforeign Chinese known as The Boxers staged a revolt to oust the foreigners from China. On Aug. 14 an **international army** including American soldiers relieved the **foreign legations in Peking,** which had been under siege since June 20.

July 3 Secretary of State Hay, fearing further division of China in the wake of the Boxer revolt, issued the **second "Open Door" note** announcing an American policy of seeking to "**preserve Chinese territorial and administrative entity.**"

American Life, 1860–1900

The Rise of the City

Urban and Rural Population

| | | 1860 | | 1900 | |
| | | Population | | | Population |
	Places	(thousands)	Places		(thousands)
Urban territory	392	6,217	1,737		30,160
Places of 500,000 or more	2	1,379	6		8,075
Places of 100,000–500,000	7	1,260	32		6,134
Places of 50,000–100,000	7	452	40		2,709
Rural territory	—	25,227	8,931		45,835

Ten Largest Cities in the United States
(thousands)

1860		1880		1900	
New York[a]	1,072	New York	1,773	New York	3,437
Philadelphia	585	Philadelphia	847	Chicago	1,699
Baltimore	212	Chicago	503	Philadelphia	1,294
Boston	178	Boston	363	St. Louis	575
New Orleans	169	St. Louis	351	Boston	561
Cincinnati	161	Baltimore	332	Baltimore	509
St. Louis	161	Cincinnati	255	Pittsburgh	452
Chicago	109	Pittsburgh	235	Cleveland	382
Buffalo	81	San Francisco	234	Buffalo	352
Newark	72	New Orleans	216	San Francisco	343

[a] Manhattan and Brooklyn

Fast-growing Cities, 1860–1900

(cities with a population over 100,000 in 1890)

City	Population increase
Minneapolis	79 times
Omaha	54
Kansas City, Mo.	37
Denver	28
Chicago	16
St. Paul	16
Indianapolis	9
Cleveland	9
Jersey City	7
Pittsburgh	6
Detroit	6
Milwaukee	6
San Francisco	6

Immigrant Urban Population   Greater New York City in 1890, with four out of five residents of foreign birth or parentage, was the greatest immigrant center in the world. In Boston and Philadelphia, one-fourth to one-third of the population was foreign-born in 1890. The combined population of Chicago, Cleveland, Minneapolis, and Detroit in 1890 was two-fifths foreign-born. In the 18 largest cities in 1890, 60 per cent of all males were of foreign birth or parentage.

Urban Improvements

1866   New York City created a board to cope with epidemics.

1867   New York City built the first elevated railroad.

1870   New York and Boston incorporated museums of fine art.

1873   San Francisco built its first cable car.

1878   New Haven, Conn., opened the first telephone exchange. By 1880, 85 cities had such exchanges.

1878   Washington started the use of asphalt street paving.

1879   Cleveland and San Francisco became the first cities to install **electric street lighting**.

1880–90   The number of **public water works** increased five times.

1881   Andrew Carnegie donated a library to Pittsburgh, the first of many Carnegie libraries.

1883   The **Brooklyn Bridge** between Manhattan and Brooklyn was completed.

1884   Chicago built a ten-story building, **the first skyscraper**.

1886   The first U.S. **social settlement house** was established in New York City. Perhaps 100 were in operation by 1900.

1887   Richmond, Va., built the first electric trolley car line. By 1895, 850 such lines were in operation.

1888   Louisville, Ky., introduced the use of the Australian (secret) ballot in the United States.

1889   **Jane Addams** founded **Hull House** for social work in Chicago.

1892   Telephone connection was completed between New York City and Chicago.

1895   New York combined several libraries to form the New York Public Library.

1897   Boston opened the **first subway**.

1897   Reform administration of Samuel M. ("Golden Rule") Jones began in Toledo, Ohio.

The great increase in urban population led to a number of problems that were largely unsolved by 1900:

1. **Crime** increased rapidly. In Chicago for example, homicides rose from 25 per million people in 1881 to 107 per million in 1898.

2. The menace from fire grew as **fire losses** reached $150 million in 1893.

3. The 1880's and 1890's witnessed the rise of tenement **slum dwellings**. In New York City alone the number rose from 21,000 housing 500,000 people in 1879 to 43,000 housing over 1.5 million by 1900.

4. Sewage polluted the drinking water in almost every American city, and the **waste disposal** problem was far from solved by 1900.

5. **Child labor** was a common practice. The number of children aged 10–15 engaged in gainful work doubled during the period, to a total of approximately 2 million.

Radicalism and Reform

1869–96   **Elizabeth Cady Stanton, Susan B. Anthony,** and others founded the **National** (later National American) **Woman Suffrage**

Association in 1869. Wyoming Territory first granted women's suffrage in 1869, followed by Utah, Colorado, and Idaho by 1896.

1872–1900   Socialism: Marxian Socialists established the First International headquarters in New York City in 1872. In 1874 they formed a Workingmen's Party and in 1877 changed the name to **Socialist Labor Party.** They were particularly strong in the Cigarmakers' Union. Between 1890 and 1895 **Daniel DeLeon** of the Socialist Laborites tried unsuccessfully to get backing from the Knights of Labor and the AFL. In 1900 the **Social Democrats** (called Socialists after 1901) under **Eugene V. Debs** split from the parent party. In the Presidential election of 1904 the Socialists received over 400,000 votes to barely 30,000 for the Socialist Labor Party.

1874–1900   Prohibition: the **Women's Christian Temperance Union,** founded in 1874 and soon led by **Frances E. Willard,** took the lead in the antiliquor movement. Other groups joined in the crusade, and the **National Prohibition Party** (founded 1869) regularly ran a candidate for President. The **Anti-Saloon League of America** was founded in 1895. Progress was slight, however, as only Kansas and North Dakota joined Maine, New Hampshire, and Vermont with statewide prohibition, 1860–1900.

1877   Lewis Henry Morgan, in his *Ancient Society,* outlined his evolutionary theory of the development of culture from savagery to civilization.

1879   Henry George's *Progress and Poverty* denounced the contrast between "monstrous wealth and debasing want." He proposed a "single tax" that would appropriate all increases in the value of land (the "unearned increment") for the benefit of society as a whole. His program won such a great following that "single tax" groups sprang up, and George ran well in the 1886 election for mayor of New York City.

1881   Anarchism: revolutionaries, many of them immigrants, formed a branch of the international Working People's Association ("The Black International") in Chicago. European anarchism taught that the state could not cure the social evils of the day and hence must be destroyed. American anarchists, led by **Johann Most,** advocated the destruction of American government and the creation of a new free society but had almost no success.

1883   Lester Frank Ward, in his *Dynamic Sociology,* argued that Darwin's survival of the fittest applied to animals but not to men, who could manipulate their environment. Morgan and Ward interpreted Darwinism to justify government regulation, unlike **William G. Sumner,** whose Social Darwinism defended laissez faire (*What Social Classes Owe to Each Other,* 1883).

1885   Richard T. Ely and rebel economists formed the American Economic Association. These advocates of the "New Economics" argued that man could create a new environment through use of government power.

1888   Edward Bellamy published his *Looking Backward,* a utopian novel in which the hero looked back from the year 2000 at the 1880's. Bellamy attacked Social Darwinism and argued for the nationalization of industry for the good of society. **Nationalist clubs** supported public ownership of utilities and railroads.

1890   Jacob Riis in *How the Other Half Lives* painted a shocking picture of the slums.

1891   Hamlin Garland's *Main-Travelled Roads* described the hardships of western farm life.

1893   Stephen Crane in *Maggie: A Girl of the Streets* portrayed the evils of prostitution in a large city.

1894   William Dean Howells showed the influence of Bellamy's nationalism in his *A Traveller from Altruria.*

1894 Henry D. Lloyd attacked the Standard Oil Company in *Wealth Against Commonwealth.*

1899   Thorstein Veblen's *The Theory of the Leisure Class* condemned the values of the business class.

Education

1869–1909   Charles W. Eliot, president of Harvard, popularized the elective-course system and expanded Harvard University to include many graduate schools.

1870 Harvard and Yale organized the first American **graduate schools**. Johns Hopkins (1876) became the first institution primarily for graduate work.

1870–1900 32 states and territories adopted **compulsory attendance laws**. The number of pupils in common (public) schools increased from 9.5 million in 1878 to 15 million in 1898.

1874 The **Chautauqua Assembly** in New York State started what became a widely imitated movement for adult education on a part-time basis.

1878–98 Public **high schools** increased from 800 to 5,500; the number of pupils enrolled increased from 100,000 to over 500,000.

1880–98 States requiring communities to provide **free textbooks** rose from one (New York) to ten.

1880–1900 The national percentage of **illiteracy declined** from 17 per cent to less than 11 per cent.

1885 **Leland Stanford** endowed (Leland) Stanford University, followed by **John D. Rockefeller,** who endowed the University of Chicago, 1890. Many other philanthropists endowed American universities.

Religion

1873–96 **Evangelism: Dwight L. Moody's** career as a revivalist began in 1873. Another great revivalist preacher, **William A. ("Billy") Sunday,** began his crusade in 1896.

1874–85 **Theological Liberalism: Charles Darwin** with his *The Origin of Species by Means of Natural Selection* (1859) started a struggle between orthodoxy and theological liberalism. **John Fiske** in *Outlines of Cosmic Philosophy* (1874) and **Henry Ward Beecher** in *Evolution and Religion* (1885) attempted to reconcile evolution and Christian faith.

1875 **Mary Baker Eddy** published her *Science and Health* and organized the **Christian Scientists'** Association (1876), which spread the doctrine of healing through faith. The first Christian Science church was founded in Boston, 1879.

1876–1907 **The Social Gospel** movement was preached by **Washington Gladden** whose *Being a Christian* (1871) outlined the social responsibilities of the church. **Josiah Strong** (*Our Country,* 1885, see p. 162) and **Walter Rauschenbusch** (*Christianity and the Social Crisis,* 1907) also contributed to the movement.

1880 **Salvation Army,** first organized in England, started its social service work in the United States.

1891 Orello Cone's *Gospel Criticism* subjected the Bible to textual criticism.

Literature and Philosophy

1860–1900 **Poetry:** the poems of **Emily Dickinson,** published after her death in 1886, were filled with superb imagery; those of **Sidney Lanier,** the leading southern poet, with unusual melody. **Henry Timrod,** who wrote war poetry in Charleston, S.C., died shortly thereafter.

1865–1916 "**Local color**" writers: **Samuel Langhorne Clemens (Mark Twain),** the greatest of the local-colorists, was famous for his colloquial humor, his love of America, and his hostility to pretense. His first effort, *The Jumping Frog of Calaveras County* (1865) was set in California, while ***The Adventures of Tom Sawyer*** (1876) and ***The Adventures of Huckleberry Finn*** (1884) described life in the Mississippi Valley. **Bret Harte** wrote short stories about California, notably *The Luck of Roaring Camp* (1870). **Joel Chandler Harris** created the "Uncle Remus" stories about Negroes after the Civil War. **George Washington Cable** wrote tales of Louisiana in *Old Creole Days* (1879), and **Sarah Orne Jewett** brought rural Maine to life in *Country of the Pointed Firs* (1896).

1866–1916 **Realism: William Dean Howells,** the leading American **realist,** who also wrote for the *Atlantic Monthly* and *Harper's Monthly,* produced 36 novels, including ***The Rise of Silas Lapham*** (1885) depicting the self-made man and ***A Hazard of New Fortunes*** (1890) in which he criticized American economic conditions. **Henry James,** who settled in England in 1876, wrote novels of Americans abroad, ***The American*** (1877) and *The Ambassadors* (1903), in which he compared American and European cultures. His interest in psychology appeared in his short story *The Turn of the Screw* (1898).

1876–1918   History: Henry Brooks Adams, grandson of John Quincy Adams, was a leading historian of the day. His work ranged from the novel *Democracy* (1880), condemning American politics, to the classic nine-volume *History of the United States During the Administrations of Jefferson and Madison* (1889–91). In *The Education of Henry Adams* (1907), he explained himself and his doubts about modern scientific progress.

1878–1912   Pragmatism: Darwin's doctrine of evolution contributed to the rise of pragmatism, a new philosophy that would harmonize with the new science. **Charles S. Peirce** first described pragmatism in an essay "How to Make Our Ideas Clear" (1878). **William James** further clarified the meaning of pragmatism in his Lowell Institute Lectures (1906), in *Pragmatism* (1907), and in *A Pluralistic Universe* (1909). The pragmatists said that the difference between ideas lay in their practical application to concrete situations. The truth of any idea was not fixed but lay in its consequences.

Newspapers

1868   Atlanta *Constitution* (**Henry W. Grady**, editor), spoke for the New South.

1872   **Whitelaw Reid** succeeded Horace Greeley as editor of the New York *Tribune*.

1880   Kansas City *Star*, William R. Nelson, editor.

1881   New York *Evening Post* was sold to Henry Villard with Carl Schurz and later Edwin L. Godkin as editors.

1882   New York *Morning Journal;* sold to **William Randolph Hearst** in 1895.

1883   New York *World* was sold to **Joseph Pulitzer**. The *Journal* and the *World*, with their yellow journalism and vast circulations, marked the rise of modern journalism.

1890   Emporia, Kan., *Gazette*, was sold in 1895 to **William Allen White**, whose editorials became widely influential.

1860–1904   The number of daily newspapers rose from 387 in 1860 to 2,452 in 1904; the total number of all newspapers in 1904 was 16,459, and their total circulation was 50,464,000.

Magazines

1865   *The Nation* (New York) covered politics, literature, and the arts and was edited by **Edwin L. Godkin** to 1881.

1868   *Overland Monthly* (San Francisco), **Bret Harte**, editor.

1870   *Christian Union* (New York), later *The Outlook*, family and political.

1873   *Woman's Home Companion.*

1873   *St. Nicholas* (New York), a children's magazine.

1877   *Puck* (New York), humor.

1883   *Ladies Home Journal* (Philadelphia).

1886   *The Forum,* Walter Hines Page, editor.

1888   *Collier's* (New York).

1889   *The Arena* (Boston), muckraking.

1890   *The Literary Digest,* a compilation of comments from other publications.

1893   *McClure's Magazine,* muckraking and important fiction.

Science, Medicine, and Inventions

1862   **Gordon McKay** applied the sewing machine to making shoes, which previously had been made by hand.

1864   **George M. Pullman** patented his railroad sleeping car.

1866   Transatlantic cable opened communication with Europe.

1868   Christopher L. Scholes invented the first practical typewriter.

1869   **George Westinghouse**, air brake.

1869   Massachusetts established the first state board of health.

1873   **Josiah W. Gibbs** published his first important paper on thermodynamics.

1873–90   112 medical schools were founded in the U.S.

1876   **Alexander Graham Bell** invented the telephone.

1877   **Thomas A. Edison** developed the phonograph.

1878–80   Albert A. Michelson determined the speed of light.

1879   Thomas A. Edison, incandescent bulb for electric lighting.

1879   George B. Selden applied for the first automobile patent.

1886   Theobald Smith introduced cholera immunization.

1888   Nikola Tesla, the alternating current motor.

1888   George Eastman, hand camera.

1888   William S. Burroughs, recording adding machine.

1889   Singer Manufacturing Company, electric sewing machine.

1894   A Niagara Falls plant began the hydroelectric industry.

1895   J. Frank Duryea built the first gasoline powered motor.

1898–1904   Walter Reed's findings made possible the control of typhoid fever and yellow fever.

American Art

In painting, **John Singer Sargent** was the leading American portrait artist. **John La Farge** created exquisite stained glass windows and murals for Trinity Church, Boston. **James A. M. Whistler** was best known for his *Portrait of My Mother.* **Winslow Homer** painted rugged pictures of the Civil War, the Adirondacks, and the sea. More original was **Thomas Eakins** whose descriptive realism appeared in *The Swimming Hole.* **Albert P. Ryder,** who painted the sea and the night, displayed his symbolic mysticism in *Toilers of the Sea* and *Death on a Pale Horse.*

Towering above American **sculptors** was **Augustus Saint-Gaudens,** whose powerful sculpture is seen in his *Lincoln* in Chicago and his *Shaw Memorial* to Robert G. Shaw and his Negro Civil War regiment on Boston Common. Less powerful was **Daniel C. French,** who created the statue of Lincoln in the Lincoln Memorial.

In architecture, **Victorian Gothic** (1865–85)— which featured arches, high ceilings and jigsaw detail—became the style of many American post-Civil War homes. **French Renaissance Revival** (1865–85) with its mansard roofs, columns, cornices, and ornamentation helped give the period the name "**Gilded Age.**" **Romanesque Revival** (c.1870–90) was the work of **Henry H. Richardson,** whose integrated style appeared in Trinity Church, Boston (1877), and in numerous banks, libraries, and other buildings. The **skyscraper** (1884–   ) began in Chicago with the 10-story Home Insurance Building, designed by William L. Jenney, and the 13-story Tacoma Building (1887), the first building with an all-steel skeleton. **Louis H. Sullivan** stressed the concept that form followed function in the Wainwright Building in St. Louis (1890) and founded the school of functional architecture. The **Chicago World's Fair** in 1893 stimulated the adoption of Renaissance and classical forms and the abandonment of the Romanesque style.

Leading Figures of the Period

JAMES G. BLAINE (West Brownsville, Pa., 1830–Washington, D.C., 1893), political leader.

1847   Was graduated from Washington College.

1848–54   Taught school in Kentucky and Pennsylvania.

1854–57   Edited the Kennebec *Journal* in Augusta, Maine. Helped found the Republican Party in the East.

1859–62   Served in the Maine state legislature.

1863–76   Republican Congressman from Maine.

1869–75   Speaker of the House of Representatives. Became a leader of the "Half-Breeds."

1876–81   U.S. Senator.

1876   Was accused of graft on an Arkansas railroad scandal and failed to receive the Republican nomination for President.

1880   Again lost the Republican Presidential nomination.

1881 Secretary of State.

1884 Was defeated for the Presidency by Grover Cleveland.

1889–92 Secretary of State; convened the first International Conference of American States.

WILLIAM JENNINGS BRYAN (Salem, Ill., 1860–Dayton, Tenn., 1925), leader of the Democratic Party.

1881 Was graduated from Illinois College; in 1883, was graduated from Union College of Law, Chicago.

1883–87 Practiced law in Jacksonville, Ill.

1887 Moved to Lincoln, Neb.

1890 Was elected to Congress and was re-elected in 1892.

1893 Opposed the repeal of the Sherman Silver Purchase Act.

1894 Defeated for the Senate; became editor of the Omaha *World-Herald*.

1894–96 Lectured for free silver on the Chautauqua lyceum circuit.

1896 Received the Democratic nomination for President after delivering his "Cross of Gold" speech, but lost the election in spite of a vigorous campaign.

1900 Defeated again for President after stressing free silver and anti-imperialism during the campaign.

1901–13 Published and edited *The Commoner*.

1908 Defeated the third time for President. Continued as leader of his party until 1912, when he supported Wilson.

1913–15 Secretary of State; resigned because of what he considered Wilson's warlike policies.

1925 In the trial of J. T. Scopes, accused of teaching evolution in Dayton, Tenn., he acted for the prosecution and was subjected to a savage examination by defense attorney Clarence Darrow. He died in Dayton after the trial.

ANDREW CARNEGIE (Dunfermline, Scotland, 1835–Lenox, Mass., 1919), steel manufacturer and philanthropist.

1848 Emigrated from Scotland to the United States; became a bobbin boy in a mill in Allegheny, Pa.

1853–61 Advanced rapidly in the Pennsylvania Railroad, beginning as a telegrapher.

1861 Organized the telegraph department for the military in the East.

1865–73 Dealt in iron, oil, and railroad industries.

1873 Went into the steel business and started his first steel plant near Pittsburgh.

1888 Bought the Homestead Steel Works.

1889 Wrote the essay "Wealth."

1899 Organized his holdings as the Carnegie Steel Company. In 1900 it produced three million tons of steel at a profit of $40 million.

1901 Sold out to J. P. Morgan and associates and retired to philanthropy. Set up many trusts including the Carnegie Foundation for the Advancement of Teaching and the Carnegie Endowment for International Peace. His benefactions totalled $350 million, including over 2,800 libraries.

SAMUEL LANGHORNE CLEMENS (Florida, Mo., 1835–Redding, Conn., 1910), Mark Twain, writer, lecturer, and humorist.

1847–57 Apprentice and journeyman printer in Hannibal, Mo., and elsewhere.

1857–61 Pilot on Mississippi steamboats.

1861–62 Prospector in Nevada.

1862 Reporter for the Virginia City, Nev., *Territorial Enterprise*.

1864 Moved to California.

1865 First won fame with *The Jumping Frog of Calaveras County*.

1865–66 Newspaper reporter in the Hawaiian Islands.

1866 Began his lecturing career.

1868 Travelled to the Mediterranean.

1869 Published *The Innocents Abroad*.

1870 Settled in New York State and later in Connecticut.

1876–84 Wrote *The Adventures of Tom Sawyer, Life on the Mississippi*, and *The Adventures of Huckleberry Finn*.

1893–94 Was plunged into debt when his publishing firm failed.

1900 Wrote the pessimistic work *The Man That Corrupted Hadleyburg*.

1916 The bitter *The Mysterious Stranger* appeared after his death.

(STEPHEN) GROVER CLEVELAND (Caldwell, N.J., 1837–Princeton, N.J., 1908), 22nd and 24th President of the United States.

1859 Admitted to the New York bar.

1863   Assistant district attorney of Erie County, N.Y.

1881–82   Democratic reform mayor of Buffalo.

1883–85   Governor of New York; won the hostility of Tammany Hall.

1885–89   22nd President of the United States.

1887   Proposed tariff reduction.

1888   Was defeated by Benjamin Harrison in an attempt at reelection.

1893–97   24th President of the United States.

1893   Secured the repeal of the Sherman Silver Purchase Act.

1894   Sent federal troops into the Pullman Strike.

1895   Intervened in the Venezuela boundary dispute.

THOMAS A. EDISON (Milan, Ohio, 1847–West Orange, N.J., 1931), inventor.

1863   After being educated at home by his mother because he was a "slow learner," he became a telegraph operator.

1869   His first invention was an electrographic vote recorder.

1869   Moved to New York and founded the electrical firm of Pope, Edison, and Company.

1876   Built a plant at Menlo Park, N.J.

1876   Invented the mimeograph.

1877   Invented the phonograph.

1879   Invented the incandescent bulb.

1881–82   Developed the world's first central electric-light power plant.

1893   Produced the kinctoscope, which helped the development of the motion picture.

1896   His Vitascope gave first showing of motion pictures. The Edison laboratories took out over 1,300 patents and invented such things as the storage battery, the dictaphone, and an electric railroad.

SAMUEL GOMPERS (London, England, 1850–San Antonio, Tex., 1924), labor union leader.

1863   Emigrated to the United States.

1864–77   Member of the Cigarmakers' Union; attended Socialist meetings.

1877   President of Local 144 of the Cigarmakers' Union.

1881   Helped found the Federation of Organized Trades and Labor Unions, which in 1886 became the American Federation of Labor.

1886–1924   President of the AFL except for the year 1895. He rejected radical and Socialist programs, opposed a labor political party, and fought for better wages and hours for workers.

1900   Became vice president of the National Civic Federation under its president, Mark Hanna.

1917   Pledged the support of the AFL to the war effort; served on the Council of National Defense.

1925   His autobiography, *Seventy Years of Life and Labor,* was published posthumously.

JOHN PIERPONT MORGAN (Hartford, Conn., 1837–Rome, Italy, 1913), banker and philanthropist.

1854–56   Studied at the University of Göttingen, Germany.

1856   Entered his father's banking firm in London, England.

1857   Returned to New York, where he engaged in banking.

1871   Formed firm of Drexel, Morgan, and Company (after 1895, J. P. Morgan and Company).

1873   Broke Jay Cooke & Company's monopoly on government loans.

1894–98   Reorganized many railroads and brought them under his control.

1895   Formed a syndicate that lent the U.S. government $65 million to stop the drain on the treasury.

1901   Formed U.S. Steel Corporation, which became the first billion-dollar corporation.

1901   Organized the Northern Securities (holding) Company, which brought three northern railroads under its control. The Supreme Court declared it illegal in 1904.

1902   Helped settle the anthracite strike.

1907   Helped stop the run on New York banks during the Panic of 1907.

1913   When he died, his benefactions included the Metropolitan Museum of Art and the Morgan Library in New York City.

JOHN D. ROCKEFELLER (Richford, N.Y., 1839–Ormond Beach, Fla., 1937), industrialist and philanthropist.

1853   Family moved to Cleveland, where Rockefeller attended high school and worked as a clerk.

1858 Formed a partnership to deal in farm products.

1863 Built his first oil refinery in Cleveland; the second was built in 1865.

1867 Started an oil partnership with Henry M. Flagler.

1870 Incorporated the Standard Oil Company with himself as president. Within seven years the company had a national monopoly on oil refining and transportation.

1879–82 Established the Standard Oil Trust, which was dissolved in 1892.

1890 Founded the University of Chicago.

1897 Began his career in philanthropy; in his lifetime his benefactions amounted to more than $550 million.

1899 Established Standard Oil Company of New Jersey as a holding company (dissolved, 1911).

1901–02 Established the Rockefeller Institute of Medical Research and the General Education Board.

1913 Established the Rockefeller Foundation.

BOOKER T. WASHINGTON (Hale's Ford, Va., 1856–Tuskegee, Ala., 1915), Negro leader.

1856 Was born a slave.

1872–75 Attended and graduated from Hampton Institute for Negroes in Hampton, Va.

1875–78 Taught at a Negro school near Charleston, W. Va.

1878–79 Attended Wayland Seminary, Washington, D.C.

1879–81 Had charge of the night school at Hampton Institute.

1881 Founded the Normal and Industrial Institute for Negroes at Tuskegee, Ala., and became the first principal.

1881–1915 Became the leading Negro spokesman in the United States, urging economic progress rather than social and political rights.

1895 Delivered his famous speech at the Cotton States and International Exposition, Atlanta, Ga., in which he urged Negro-white cooperation.

1901 Wrote his autobiography, *Up From Slavery.*

Statistical Tables

Table 35.
U.S. population
(thousands)

	1870	1880	1890	1900
Total	39,905	50,262	63,056	76,094
Negro	4,880	6,581	7,489	8,834
Other non-white	89	172	357	351

Table 36.
Regional population
(thousands)

	1870	1880	1890	1900
Northeast	12,299	14,507	17,407	21,047
North Central	12,981	17,364	22,410	26,333
South	12,288	16,517	20,028	24,524
West	991	1,768	3,102	4,091

Table 37.
Wholesale commodity price index
(1860–90 index: 1900–14 = 100;
1890–1900 index: 1926 = 100)

1860	93
1865	185
1870	135
1875	118
1880	100
1885	85
1890	82
	56
1895	49
1900	56

Table 38.
Public land entries
(thousands of acres)

	1870	1880	1890	1900
Original land entries (including homesteads, not land grants to railroads)	6,663	9,152	12,666	13,391
Original homestead entries	—	—	5,532	8,478
Final homestead entries	520	1,938	4,061	3,478

6-2   Population, 1900

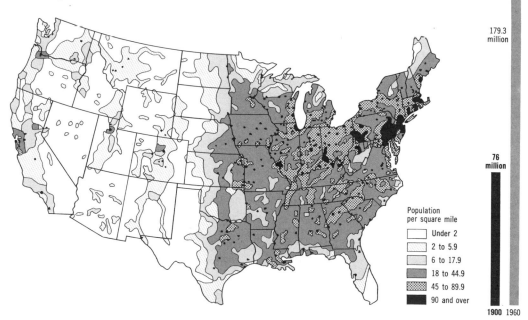

179.3 million

76 million

Population per square mile

- ☐ Under 2
- ☐ 2 to 5.9
- ☐ 6 to 17.9
- ☐ 18 to 44.9
- ☐ 45 to 89.9
- ■ 90 and over

1900 1960

Table 39.
U.S. government expenditures and
receipts
(millions of dollars)

	Expenditures	Receipts	Debt
1860	63.1	56.1	64.8
1865	1,297.6	333.7	2,677.9
1870	309.7	411.3	2,436.5
1875	274.6	288.0	2,156.3
1880	267.6	333.5	2,090.9
1885	260.2	323.7	1,578.6
1890	318.0	403.1	1,122.4
1895	356.2	324.7	1,096.9
1900	520.9	567.2	1,263.4

Table 40.
Currency stock and currency in circulation
(millions of dollars)

	1860	1870	1880	1890	1900
Total Currency in U.S.	442	900	1,186	1,685	2,366
Currency held in Treasury	7	125	212	256	285
Currency in circulation	435	775	973	1,429	2,081
Gold coin	207	81	226	374	611
Gold certificates	—	32	8	131	201
Silver dollars	—	—	20	56	66
Silver certificates	—	—	6	298	408
Treasury notes of 1890	—	—	—	—	75
Subsidiary silver	21	9	49	54	76
Minor coin	—	—	—	—	26
U.S. notes	—	325	328	335	318
National banknotes	—	289	337	182	300
State banknotes	207	2	—	—	—
Fractional and other	—	—	—	—	—
U.S. currency	—	37	—	—	—

PROSPERITY, PROGRESSIVISM, AND WORLD WAR I, 1901–1929

PART 7

The Progressive Movement, 1901–1917

The Rise of Progressivism

A variety of writers contributed to the progressive reform movement and the **literature of protest** at the turn of the century.

1899–1914   THE   SCHOLARS: jurist **Oliver Wendell Holmes, Jr.,** whose *The Common Law* appeared in 1881, and law professor **Roscoe Pound** attacked the tendency of the courts to overturn legislative reform, while **Louis D. Brandeis,** another jurist, denounced the concentration of wealth in *Other People's Money* (1914). **Charles A. Beard** reflected progressive disillusionment with the Supreme Court's conservative interpretation of the Constitution in his *An Economic Interpretation of the Constitution* (1913), which suggested that the founding fathers had economic motives in drawing up the document. **Herbert D. Croly** in *The Promise of American Life* (1909) called for national social planning by the federal government. **John Dewey,** whose "instrumentalism" was a form of pragmatism (see p. 170), advocated experimentalism in both government and education. His *School and Society* (1899) was influential in the rise of progressive education with its emphasis on the growth of the child as a good citizen.

1900–27   THE NOVELISTS: Theodore Dreiser's novels depicted the tragedy and misery that accompanied industrialization. His *Sister Carrie* (1900) described the personal corruption of a young girl in the city. In *The Financier* (1912), he turned to success in the business world. His *An American Tragedy* (1925) portrayed the central character as the victim of an urban environment. **Frank Norris** condemned the Southern Pacific Railroad in *The Octopus* (1901) and the Chicago grain market in *The Pit* (1903). In *The Jungle* (1906) **Upton Sinclair,** a Socialist, portrayed the horrible conditions in the meat packing plants of Chicago.

1902–08   THE MUCKRAKERS: Lincoln Steffens' article "Tweed Days In St. Louis" in *McClure's* magazine (Oct., 1902) initiated a wave of magazine articles that attacked corruption. Theodore Roosevelt, angry at **David Graham Phillips'** sensational article "The Treason of the Senate" (1906), branded the authors "muckrakers." **Ida Tarbell's** *The History of the Standard Oil Company* (1904) and Ray Stannard Baker's "The Railroads on Trial" also appeared in *McClure's*. *Munsey's, Cosmopolitan, Everybody's,* and other magazines hastened to publish similar attacks. By 1908 the muckrakers had stimulated reform movements in major cities from Philadelphia to San Francisco.

1897–1911   Political   progressivism achieved reforms on both the city and state levels.

In the **REFORM OF CITIES, Samuel M. ("Golden Rule") Jones** of Toledo and **James D. Phelan** of San Francisco, both elected in 1897, were among the first of the progressive mayors. Jones, who established free kindergartens and playgrounds, came to believe that public ownership of utilities and transportation was essential to urban life. **Tom L. Johnson**, a disciple of Henry George, served as mayor of Cleveland on a program of lower fares on city transportation, 1901–09. Galveston, Tex., introduced the commission form of municipal government (1900), and Staunton, Va., initiated the city manager system. Other municipal reforms included public waterworks, public contracts, the executive budget, central purchasing, and city planning. Meanwhile, Socialists gained strength in the cities, winning elections in 18 in 1911.

1900–14   STATE REFORM: the first progressive governor was **Robert M. La Follette** (Wisc., 1901–06), whose "Wisconsin Idea" included opposition to city bosses, a railroad commission, a corrupt practices act, the graduated income tax, and the direct primary. In Iowa **Albert B. Cummins** (elected governor in 1901) fought the bosses, trusts, and railroads. Though never governor, **William S. U'Ren** led the way toward the adoption by Oregon of the initiative and referendum, the direct primary and the recall. Southern reform governors **Jeff Davis** (elected 1901, Ark.), **James K. Vardaman** (1904, Miss.), and **Hoke Smith** (1906, Ga.) appealed to the "red neck" poor-white voter; in the west, progressive **Hiram W. Johnson** was elected governor of California (1910). **Woodrow Wilson** was reform governor of New Jersey (1911–12) before he was elected President. By 1914 the states had produced many important reforms.

Political reforms included:
1. Australian secret ballot (first used in Massachusetts, 1888; used in all states by 1910);
2. corrupt practices acts;
3. women's suffrage (enacted in 11 states by 1914, though Ohio and Illinois were the only ones east of the Mississippi River);
4. direct primary (Wisconsin, 1903; effective in 13 states by 1912);
5. direct senatorial primary (Oregon, 1904; 29 states by 1909);
6. initiative and referendum to allow the electorate to propose and pass laws directly (Oregon, 1902; 12 states—all west of the Mississippi—by 1912); and
7. the right of the electorate to recall an elected officer from his office (Oregon, 1908; seven states—all west of the Mississippi— by 1912).

Social and economic reforms included:
1. commissions to regulate railroads and monopolies;
2. employers' liability acts (New York, 1910; enacted in 25 states by 1914);
3. workmen's compensation laws (Maryland, 1902; enacted in 38 states by 1917);
4. minimum-wage laws for women and children (Massachusetts, 1912; passed in eight other states—all west of the Mississippi—by 1914);
5. pensions for mothers with dependent children (Illinois, 1911; 20 states by 1913);
6. maximum-hours laws (Utah law for mines, 1896; Oregon law for women, 1903); and
7. child labor laws.

Theodore Roosevelt and the Square Deal, 1901–1910

1901

Sept. 6   THE ASSASSINATION OF PRESIDENT McKINLEY: Leon Czolgosz, an anarchist, shot the President in Buffalo, N.Y. He died Sept. 14, and **THEODORE ROOSEVELT** took the oath of office that day.

Dec. 3   In his first annual message Roosevelt called for trust regulation. Otherwise the address was conservative because Roosevelt knew he must cooperate with Senators **Nelson W. Aldrich** (R.I.) and **William B. Allison** (Iowa) and Congressman **Joseph G. Cannon** (Ill.) (Speaker, 1903–11), conservative Republicans who dominated Congress.

1902

Mar. 10–Mar. 14, 1904   The **NORTHERN SECURITIES CASE**: President Roosevelt initiated a suit against a giant railroad combination, the Northern Securities Company, which led to its dissolution in 1904. Roosevelt, who instituted suits against 44 corporations, won a reputation as a trust-buster, but he was not opposed to bigness and believed in federal action only in cases of serious misbehavior.

May 12–Oct. 21   THE ANTHRACITE STRIKE: the United Mine Workers under president **John Mitchell** struck on May 12 for higher wages and union recognition. Roosevelt called a conference of operators and miners on Oct. 3 and appointed a commission to mediate (Oct. 16), whereupon Mitchell called off the strike, Oct. 21. The commission on Mar. 22, 1903, awarded the union a 10 per cent wage increase but no union recognition. Since he had not intervened on the side of the owners, Roosevelt established a pro-labor reputation, but he was always suspicious of labor radicalism.

June 17   National Reclamation Act (called Newlands Act for Democratic Congressman **Francis G. Newlands,** Nev.) set aside the proceeds from the sale of public land in 16 western states for irrigation projects.

Aug. 19   President Roosevelt left on a tour of New England and the Middle West in which he publicized his program of a **"square deal"** for all the people.

1903

Feb. 14   Congress established the **Department of Commerce and Labor** with a Bureau of Corporations to investigate trusts.

Feb. 19   Elkins Act strengthened the Interstate Commerce Act by redefining rebates and by providing for punishment of those receiving as well as those giving rebates.

1904

June 21   Republican Convention met at Chicago and nominated **Roosevelt** for President and Sen. **Charles W. Fairbanks** (Ind.) for Vice President.

July 6   Democratic Convention met in St. Louis and nominated conservative **Alton B. Parker** (N.Y.) for President and **Henry G. Davis** (W. Va.) for Vice President.

Nov. 8   Presidential election: Roosevelt won with 7,628,461 votes (336 electoral) to 5,084,223 (140 electoral) for **Parker. Eugene V. Debs,** the Socialist candidate, ran ahead of four other minor party candidates.

1905

June   Labor organization: William D. ("Big Bill") **Haywood** and **Eugene V. Debs** organized the revolutionary **Industrial Workers of the World (IWW).** After initial success in organizing lumber workers and stevedores in the West, the IWW organized the textile workers and won the Lawrence, Mass., strike (Jan.–Mar., 1912). The Triangle Fire (Mar. 25, 1911) caused the death of 146 garment workers in New York City. The fire forced the city to adopt a more rigorous building code and stimulated the growth of the **International Ladies Garment Workers' Union (ILGWU).**

1906

June 11   Employers' Liability Act made employers liable for workers' injuries on common carriers. After the Supreme Court declared it unconstitutional (1908), a new act applying only to interstate commerce became law the same year.

June 29   HEPBURN ACT strengthened the Interstate Commerce Act by giving the commission power, on appeal of the shipper, to **set maximum rates** and by placing the burden of proof on the carrier. The act also enlarged the commission to seven; allowed it to examine railroad books; extended its jurisdiction to pipe lines, express companies, bridges, and ferries; and prevented railroads from carrying most items produced by companies in which they held an interest. Roosevelt fought hard for the Hepburn Act, which was a landmark in federal regulation of interstate commerce.

June 30   Pure Food and Drug Act and **Meat Inspection Act** both became law.

1907

Oct. 22   PANIC OF 1907 began with a run on the Knickerbocker Trust Company in New York. When **J. Pierpont Morgan** organized bankers to stop the bank run, President Roosevelt allowed the U.S. Steel Corporation to acquire the Tennessee Coal and Iron Company. The panic did not lead to a serious depression.

Dec. 3   In his **annual message** Roosevelt made a number of advanced proposals, including an inheritance and income tax, fixing of railroad rates on the basis of physical valuation, postal savings banks, restriction on labor injunctions, the eight-hour day, and workmen's compensation. The message was a forerunner of Roosevelt's New Nationalism proposals in 1912.

1908

May 13–15   White House **CONFERENCE ON CONSERVATION** called public attention to the problems of conservation. The conference stemmed from the first report of the **Inland Waterways Commission** (set up in 1907) and led to the **National Conservation Commission** (appointed in 1908 with **Gifford Pinchot** as chairman), which started an assessment of national resources. Roosevelt, who believed strongly in conservation, withdrew from private entry some 1,750,000 acres of public lands during his Administration.

May 30   **Aldrich-Vreeland Act** established a **National Monetary Commission** to study banking systems. The Panic of 1907 was responsible for the act.

June 16   **Republican Convention** met in Chicago and nominated Secretary of War **William H. Taft** (Ohio) for President and **James S. Sherman** (N.Y.) for Vice President.

July 7   **Democratic Convention** met in Denver and nominated **William J. Bryan** for President and **John W. Kern** (Ind.) for Vice President; its platform pledged tariff revision.

Nov. 3   **Presidential election: Taft** with 7,675,320 votes (321 electoral) defeated **Bryan** with 6,412,294 (162 electoral).

Taft and the Election of 1912

1909

Mar. 15–Aug. 5   PAYNE-ALDRICH TARIFF: President Taft called a special session of Congress to lower the tariff. On Mar. 19, 12 **insurgent Republicans,** led by **George W. Norris** (Neb.), refused to vote for protectionist Speaker **Joseph G. Cannon,** who was nonetheless elected. A reduced tariff, proposed by **Sereno E. Payne** (N.Y.), passed the House on Apr. 9, but the **Aldrich bill** in the Senate increased the House rates in spite of opposition of Democrats and insurgent Republicans such as **Robert M. La Follette** (Wis.) and **Albert J. Beveridge** (Ind.). The Payne-Aldrich Tariff, which became law on Aug. 5, left rates on the average about the same as they had been.

July 12   Congress submitted the **16th Amendment,** permitting an **income tax,** to the states. Insurgents forced passage of the amendment after failing to get a personal income tax in the Payne-Aldrich Tariff. The amendment was ratified on Feb. 25, 1913.

Sept. 15   **President Taft** backed Secretary of the Interior **Richard A. Ballinger,** when he opened to public sale certain water-power sites, which had been previously withdrawn. Taft was strenuously opposed by Chief Forester **Gifford Pinchot.** When Pinchot later attacked Ballinger for selling Alaskan coal lands to private interests, Taft again upheld Ballinger and on Jan. 7, 1910, removed Pinchot from office. The controversy widened the gap between the President and the insurgents, who supported Pinchot.

Sept. 17   Insurgents were angry when **President Taft** in a speech at Winona, Minn., called the Payne-Aldrich Tariff the best tariff bill the Republican Party had passed.

1910

Mar. 19   The House adopted an **amendment to the rules,** proposed by **George W. Norris,** depriving the Speaker of the power to appoint the Rules Committee and removing the Speaker from the Rules Committee. The change marked a victory for the insurgents over Taft, who had supported Speaker Cannon.

June 18 **Mann-Elkins Act** extended the Interstate Commerce Act to include telephone and telegraph lines, strengthened the long haul–short haul clause, and empowered the Commission to suspend high rates.

June 25 **Postal Savings Bank System** enabled federal post offices to receive funds and pay interest.

June 25 **Mann White-Slave Act** forbade the transportation of women across state lines for immoral purposes.

Aug. 31 **Theodore Roosevelt** in his **"New Nationalism" speech** at Osawatomie, Kan., spoke strongly in favor of government regulation of business and industry and attacked the courts for their conservative decisions.

Nov. 8 **Congressional elections:** Democrats in the House and an alliance of Democrats and insurgents in the Senate gained control of Congress. Wisconsin sent **Victor L. Berger**, the first Socialist congressman, to Washington.

1911

Jan. 21 **National Progressive Republican League**, founded by **Robert M. La Follette** and other insurgents, issued a platform calling for direct election of U.S. Senators and delegates to national conventions, initiative, referendum, recall, and other progressive legislation.

May 15, 29 In **antitrust suits,** the Supreme Court dissolved **Standard Oil Company of New Jersey** and the **American Tobacco Company** after suits were initiated by the Roosevelt Administration. Taft started 90 antitrust suits, many more than Roosevelt, but never achieved Roosevelt's reputation as a trust-buster.

Aug. President Taft vetoed efforts to reduce the Payne-Aldrich Tariff, thereby further alienating insurgents.

1912

Jan.–Feb. **Roosevelt's campaign for re-nomination**: Roosevelt who sided with the insurgents and felt that Taft had failed to

continue his reform policies, decided to run for the Republican nomination. He announced his intentions in a private letter (Dec. 23, 1911). At about the same time, a Presidential boom for Senator La Follette began to lose strength (early 1912), and on Feb. 10 seven Republican governors publicly asked Roosevelt to be the Republican candidate. President Taft indicated that he would not back down by calling Progressives "neurotics." On Feb. 24, Roosevelt announced that he would accept the nomination if it were offered. Roosevelt gained considerable support in spring primaries.

May 12 The **Socialist Convention** met at Indianapolis and nominated **Eugene V. Debs** for President and **Emil Seidel**, mayor of Milwaukee, for Vice President.

June 18 The **Republican Convention** met at Chicago and renominated the **Taft-Sherman** ticket after rejecting many Roosevelt supporters in contested delegations.

June 25 The **Democratic Party** met at Baltimore and nominated Governor **Woodrow Wilson** of New Jersey for President over "Champ" Clark, Speaker of the House (1911 19), after 46 ballots. It named governor **Thomas R. Marshall** of Indiana for Vice President.

Aug. 5 The **Progressive Party** (called "Bull Moose" because Roosevelt said he felt as strong as one) met in Chicago and nominated **Roosevelt** for President and **Hiram W. Johnson** (Calif.) for Vice President. The Progressives, who included such reformers as **Jane Addams** and such businessmen as **George W. Perkins** of U.S. Steel, adopted a strong platform of progressive social reform.

May–Aug. Reform **party platforms** included the planks shown in tabular form on p. 182.

Fall In **the final campaign, Roosevelt** with his **NEW NATIONALISM** welcomed big business and asked only for a powerful federal government to regulate it. **Wilson** with his **NEW FREEDOM** demanded free competition and the end of monopolies. While he and Roosevelt were closer than the campaign rhetoric suggested, Wilson was opposed to Roosevelt's partnership of business and government.

	Democratic	*Progressive*	*Socialist*
Govern-ment and monopoly	Abolition of monopolies	Regulation of business	**Collective ownership** of railroads, grain elevators, and mines
Financial	**Tariff for revenue only,** banking reform	**Protective tariff;** government control of currency	**Government banking system**
Labor	Curb on injunctions in labor disputes	Curb on injunctions in labor disputes; no child labor; 6-day week, 8-hour day; workmen's compensation	Curb on injunctions in labor disputes; no child labor; 5½-day week; unemployment insurance, workmen's compensation; old-age pensions
Political		Direct primary; direct election of senators; state initiative, referendum, and recall	**No Senate; no Presidential veto;** national initiative, referendum and recall; **no judicial review by Supreme Court; one term for Presidents**

Nov. 5   Presidential election: Wilson, who profited from the split in the Republican Party, won with 6,296,547 votes (435 electoral); **Roosevelt** had 4,118,571 votes (88 electoral); **Taft** received 3,486,720 votes (8 electoral); and **Debs** received 900,672 votes. The Democrats also won control of both houses of Congress.

1913

Feb. 28   The **Pujo Committee Report:** the House Committee on Banking and Currency, under **Arsène P. Pujo** (La.), reported a heavy concentration of money and credit in the hands of a few bankers and blamed bank consolidation, interlocking directorates, and bank control of insurance companies, railroads, and utilities.

Mar. 1   Physical Valuation Act gave the ICC the power to establish the physical valuation of railroads in order to establish a basis for fixing rates.

Mar. 4   Congress divided the Department of Commerce and Labor into the **Department of Commerce** and the **Department of Labor.**

Wilson and the New Freedom

1913

Apr. 7   President Wilson convened a special session of Congress to revise the tariff and on Apr. 8 delivered a message in person, the first President to do so since John Adams.

May 8–Oct. 3 UNDERWOOD-SIMMONS TARIFF ACT: after the House tariff reduction bill, proposed by **Oscar W. Underwood** (Ala.) and strongly supported by Wilson, was passed on May 8, a long struggle took place. The final Underwood-Simmons Tariff lowered rates to about 25 per cent and put raw wool, sugar, iron, and steel on the free list and called for a **1 per cent tax on all incomes above $4,000,** with additional surtaxes for incomes above $20,000.

May 31   The **17th Amendment** calling for the **direct election of U.S. Senators** (sent to the states on May 15, 1912) was ratified.

June 23–Dec. 23   FEDERAL RESERVE ACT: when President Wilson on June 23 appeared before Congress to ask for banking and currency reform, there were **three plans**

in the air. The National Monetary Commission, under Sen. **Nelson W. Aldrich** (R.I.), proposed a privately controlled central bank somewhat like the Second Bank of the United States; conservative Democrats like Congressman **Carter Glass** (Va.) preferred a number of regional banks supervised by a federal board, while agrarian Democrats such as **William Jennings Bryan** wanted even more government control of banking and currency. A compromise bill sponsored by Congressman Glass and Senator **Robert L. Owen** (Okla.) was signed into law on Dec. 23 after many months of patient negotiation in which the President again played a major role. The act created a new national banking system of **12 regional Federal Reserve banks,** owned by the member banks, which would receive cash reserves from the member banks. The Federal Reserve banks were to **rediscount commercial and agricultural paper** of member banks and issue **Federal Reserve notes** as the system's currency. Each Reserve bank was to maintain a **40 per cent gold reserve** against its Federal Reserve notes that were outstanding. A **Federal Reserve Board** of seven members, including the Secretary of the Treasury and the Comptroller of the Currency, were to oversee the system, and each Federal Reserve bank was to be governed by a board of nine directors, six of whom would be appointed by the Federal Reserve Board. The Federal Reserve Board could **regulate the credit supply** by raising or lowering the rediscount rate or by manipulating the sale of government securities. The act ingeniously combined private banking features with a large measure of government control of credit and currency.

1914

May 8   Smith-Lever Act provided for agriculture extension work through land-grant colleges under the Department of Agriculture.

Sept. 26   FEDERAL TRADE COMMISSION ACT replaced the Bureau of Corporations with the Federal Trade Commission, which had the power to investigate corporations (except banks and common carriers),

receive reports, and issue **cease and desist orders** to prevent unfair business practices.

Oct. 15   CLAYTON ANTITRUST ACT, sponsored by Congressman **Henry D. Clayton** (Ala.), tried to put teeth in the Sherman Antitrust Act by defining the following as **illegal practices:** price discrimination aimed at monopoly, tying contracts, interlocking directorates of competing firms, and intercorporate stock holding (holding companies). As **remedies** it provided court injunctions, private suits, and Federal Trade Commission cease and desist orders. The act declared that **nothing in the antitrust acts should be construed to forbid labor or agricultural organizations** and forbade the use of the **injunction** in labor disputes unless necessary to prevent irreparable injury to property. The Administration brought 92 antitrust suits in eight years.

1915

Mar. 4   La Follette's Seamen's Act considerably improved conditions for sailors in the merchant marine.

1916

Jan.–Feb. 23, 1917   Wilson's advanced progressivism: partly in order to lure support in the coming campaign from Progressives, Wilson turned away from the New Freedom toward the New Nationalism. Before his first term was up, a number of social and economic reform bills, including a farm loan act and a child labor act, had become law.

Jan. 28   President Wilson nominated **Louis D. Brandeis** (Mass.), a powerful reformer, to the Supreme Court and secured confirmation in spite of conservative opposition.

June 7   The **Republican Convention** met in Chicago and nominated Supreme Court Justice **Charles Evans Hughes** (N.Y.) for President and **Charles W. Fairbanks** (Ind.) for Vice President.

June 7   The **Progressive Party** met in Chicago and nominated Theodore Roosevelt for President, but when Roosevelt withdrew in favor of Hughes, the party (June 26) endorsed the Republican candidate.

June 14   The **Democratic Convention** met in St. Louis and renominated **Wilson** for President and **Thomas R. Marshall** for Vice President.

July 11   **Federal Highway Act** authorized federal aid to states for road construction.

July 17   The **Farm Loan Act** set up 12 Farm Loan Banks to provide farm credit. Cooperative farm loan associations, which were members of the 12 banks, provided long-term farm loans at low interest rates.

Aug. 11   The **Warehouse Act** allowed farmers to deposit certain commodities at licensed warehouses and receive receipts that could be circulated as loan collateral.

Sept. 1   **Keating-Owen Child Labor Act** banned from interstate commerce goods manufactured by child labor. When the Supreme Court found it unconstitutional, in *Hammer v. Dagenhart,* Congress placed a prohibitive **tax on the products of child labor** as part of the War Revenue Act of Feb. 24, 1919. This too was declared unconstitutional in *Bailey v. Drexel Furniture Company.*

Sept. 3   **Adamson Act** provided for an eight-hour work day on interstate railroads.

Sept. 7   **Workmen's Compensation Act** brought half a million federal employees under its protection.

Sept. 8   **Emergency Revenue Act** doubled the normal rate of the income tax and added the inheritance tax.

Fall   In the **Presidential campaign,** the Democrats capitalized on the desire for peace by saying that Wilson "kept us out of war."

Nov. 7   **Presidential election: Wilson won** with 9,127,695 votes (277 electoral); **Hughes** received 8,533,507 votes (254 electoral). Hughes lost the election when he lost California and Minnesota by very narrow margins.

1917

Feb. 5   An immigration bill calling for a **literacy test** passed congress over Wilson's veto. Previously Cleveland (1897), Taft (1913), and Wilson (1915) had vetoed similar bills.

Feb. 23   **Smith-Hughes Act** provided for vocational education in conjunction with the states.

The Supreme Court and Progressivism

1898   *Holden v. Hardy* upheld a Utah law establishing an eight-hour work day in mines on the grounds that the state could regulate dangerous and unhealthy work.

1904   *Northern Securities Company v. U.S.* modified the Knight decision and ruled that the company had violated the Sherman Act by setting up an illegal combination in restraint of trade. It therefore ordered the dissolution of the Northern Securities Company.

1905   *Lochner v. New York* declared a New York law establishing a 10-hour day and a 60-hour week in bakeries illegal as a violation of the right of free contract. It ruled that bakery work was not dangerous and thus not liable to state regulation. Justice **Oliver Wendell Holmes, Jr.,** in a famous dissent, said that the Constitution was not intended to embody the theory of laissez-faire.

1908   In *Loewe v. Lawlor* (Danbury Hatters' Case), the court ruled that a secondary boycott by a labor union was a conspiracy in restraint of trade under the Sherman Act.

1908   *Muller v. Oregon* upheld an Oregon law setting a 10-hour day for laundresses on the grounds that a state could protect women. **Louis D. Brandeis,** for the state, used a famous brief based upon economic and sociological data rather than on legal precedents.

1911   *Standard Oil Company of New Jersey et al. v. U.S.* required the dissolution of the holding company and established the "rule of reason," which said that only unreasonable restraints of trade were illegal.

1918   *Hammer v. Dagenhart* declared the Keating-Owen Child Labor Act (1916) unconstitutional because it was using the interstate commerce power to interfere with local labor conditions.

1921   *Duplex Printing Press Company v. Deering* allowed the use of the injunction against a secondary boycott, in spite of the Clayton Act, on the grounds that the complainant was threatened with irreparable damage to his property.

1921 *Truax v. Corrigan* declared a state statute forbidding the use of the injunction against picketing a violation of the 14th Amendment. The Truax and Duplex decisions destroyed the Clayton Act as a defense for labor unions.

1922 *Bailey v. Drexel Furniture Company* ruled unconstitutional the 1919 act setting a tax on products of child labor.

1923 *Adkins v. Children's Hospital* ruled that a District of Columbia law setting minimum wages for women was unconstitutional as a violation of the right of free contract.

The United States as a World Power

The United States and the Americas

1901

Mar. 2–Mar. 22, 1904   Passage of the **PLATT AMENDMENT** (sponsored by Senator **Orville H. Platt**, Conn.) to the army appropriations bill (Mar. 2, 1901) authorized the President to withdraw troops from **CUBA** only after Cuba agreed:

1. not to make any treaty impairing its independence,
2. not to borrow money beyond its capacity to pay,
3. to allow the United States to intervene in Cuba to preserve Cuban independence, and
4. to sell or lease naval bases to the United States.

The Cuban constitutional convention attached the same amendment to the constitution on June 12, 1901. After the United States withdrew from Cuba (May 20, 1902), the United States-Cuba treaty (signed May 22, 1903, and ratified Mar. 22, 1904) included the Platt Amendment. Before leaving Cuba the military government under Gen. **Leonard Wood** reorganized the finances of the island and rid it of yellow fever.

Nov. 18–Feb. 23, 1904   THE PANAMA CANAL: the second **Hay-Pauncefote Treaty** with Great Britain (signed Nov. 18, ratified Dec. 16) abrogated the Clayton-Bulwer Treaty and allowed the United States to build and control an **inter-oceanic canal** across Central America. Secretary of State

John M. Hay had signed an earlier Hay-Pauncefote Treaty granting the United States the right to build a canal but not to fortify it (Feb. 5, 1900); when the Senate attached an amendment giving the United States the right of fortification (Dec. 20, 1900), the British rejected the treaty. The second treaty tacitly allowed United States fortification.

1902

Jan. 4   The **New Panama Canal Company** of France offered to sell its rights to build an isthmian canal to the United States for $40 million, a reduction from its original price of $109 million.

Jan. 18   The U.S. Isthmian Commission, which had previously favored a canal through Nicaragua, reversed itself and recommended the Panama route.

June 28   The **Spooner Act** established the Isthmian Canal Commission (1903) and authorized the President to buy the concession of the New Panama Canal Company for $40 million and arrange terms with Colombia to build a canal through Panama. Failing that, he was to build through Nicaragua.

1903

Jan. 22   By the **Hay-Herran Treaty**, the Colombian chargé to the United States, Tomás Herrán, granted the United States a 99-year lease to a canal zone in Panama in return for $10 million and an annual rent.

Aug. 12 The Colombian Senate rejected the treaty and decided to wait until the concession of the Canal Company expired in Oct., 1904, and then collect the entire $40 million.

Oct. 20 Settlement of **Alaskan Boundary Dispute**: the Klondike Gold rush in 1897 led to a dispute between the United States and Canada over the routes to the gold fields through the panhandle of Alaska. Both the United States and Canada claimed that the boundary of the panhandle gave them several important harbors. On Jan. 24, 1903, the United States and Great Britain agreed to settlement by a joint Anglo-American commission, which decided in favor of the United States.

Nov. 3–5 **Rebels in Panama**, aided by **Philippe Bunau-Varilla**, an agent of the New Panama Canal Company, staged a rebellion and announced the independence of Panama from Colombia. The commander of a United States cruiser prevented Colombian troops from landing to put down the rebellion in order—so he said—to main-tain United States right of transit under the terms of the Treaty of 1846.

Nov. 13 The United States granted full **recognition** to the republic of Panama and received Bunau-Varilla as minister.

Nov. 18 The **Hay-Bunau-Varilla Treaty** (ratified Feb. 23, 1904) gave the United States sovereign rights to a canal zone 10 miles wide in perpetuity for $10 million down and $250,000 a year. The United States received the right to keep order within Panama. Republicans loyal to Roosevelt blocked an attempt in 1914 by the Wilson Administration to pay Colombia $25 million to compensate it for the Panama affair; in 1921 the payment went through.

1904

Feb. 22–Apr. 1, 1905 ROOSEVELT COROLLARY TO THE MONROE DOCTRINE stemmed from the decision of the Hague Court (Feb. 22) in favor of Germany, Great Britain and Italy, which had used force to collect debts from Venezuela in Dec., 1902.

7-1 The United States in the Caribbean

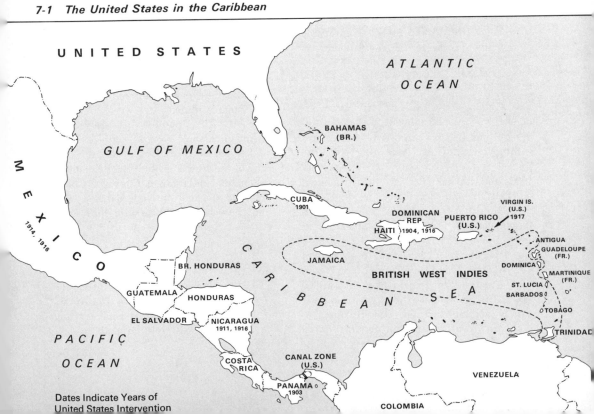

Dates Indicate Years of
United States Intervention

In his annual message (Dec., 1901), Roosevelt had indicated that he did not consider such intervention a violation of the Monroe Doctrine, but in 1902 he used his good offices to send the matter to the Hague Court. On Dec. 29, 1902, Luis M. Drago, Argentine Minister of Foreign Affairs, sent his "**Drago Doctrine**" to the United States, stating that European powers could not invade an American nation to collect debts. When he learned of the Hague verdict, Roosevelt decided to prevent similar intervention in the Dominican Republic, which owed large sums to Europe.

Dec. 6   In his annual message Roosevelt said that the Monroe Doctrine might require the United States to exercise an "**international police power**" in Latin America to prevent European intervention.

1905

Jan. 21   By executive agreement the United States took over the **Dominican customs houses** and guaranteed the territorial integrity of the republic.

Feb. 7   The Administration changed the executive agreement to a treaty in which the United States promised to "respect" rather than "guarantee" the republic's integrity. Though not ratified by the Senate until Feb. 25, 1907 (after it had been revised), the agreement went into effect as a *modus vivendi*. The United States troops withdrew from the Dominican Republic on July 31, 1907.

1906

June 29   **Building the Panama Canal**: after sanitation measures by Col. **William C. Gorgas** had eliminated much of the danger from malaria and yellow fever, Congress on June 29, 1906, authorized a lock canal. Lt. Col. **George W. Goethals** of the U.S. Army Corps of Engineers directed the construction of the 40.3-mile canal, which was completed on Aug. 15, 1914.

July 23   The Third International Conference of American States met at Rio de Janeiro and laid plans for the settlement of international claims and the payment of debts. The fourth

Conference, at Buenos Aires, 1910, completed several agreements, but many Latin American states never signed.

Sept. 29   **Cuban intervention**: after a Cuban rebellion in 1906, the United States sent troops into the island to run a provisional government until 1909. Another uprising prompted Taft to occupy the island again (July–Aug., 1912).

1907

Nov. 14–Dec. 20   Central American Peace Conference took place in Washington, drew up a treaty of peace (Mexico and the United States did not sign), and set up a **Central American Court of Justice**, which lasted until 1918.

1910

May 19–1933   "**Dollar Diplomacy**" in **Nicaragua**: the United States sent troops into Nicaragua in 1910 to protect American lives during a revolution. In an agreement of June 6, 1911, Nicaragua arranged to refund its debt through New York banks; though the Senate rejected the agreement, United States bankers gained control of the National Bank of Nicaragua. President Taft ordered 2,500 Marines into Nicaragua again in Aug., 1912, and troops remained until 1933. In the Nicaraguan affair, critics accused Taft of "**dollar diplomacy**," that is, intervening to support American investments.

1911

Jan. 21   **Canadian Reciprocity**: President Taft signed an agreement reducing rates on American commodities exported to Canada and Canadian agricultural products imported into the United States. Congress approved (Jan. 26) in spite of opposition from midwestern farm interests, but the Canadians refused to ratify the agreement.

1912

Aug. 2   The Senate adopted a resolution by **Henry Cabot Lodge** (Mass.) that the United

States disapproved of the transfer of strategic sites in the Americas to companies that might be acting for a non-American power. This **Lodge Corollary**, which extended the Monroe Doctrine, was prompted by efforts of a Japanese company to buy land in Lower California.

1913

Mar. 13–Nov. 23, 1914   Rebels in **Mexico** under **Francisco I. Madero** overthrew the 30-year reign of President Porfirio Diaz on May 25, 1911. President Taft recognized the Madero regime and embargoed arms shipments to Madero's opponents in order to protect American investments. Gen. **Victoriano Huerta** overthrew Madero, who was then assassinated (Feb. 18–22 1913). President Wilson, who disapproved of Huerta's bloody rule, announced on Mar. 11 that the United States **would not recognize the Huerta government**, thereby departing from the traditional American policy of recognizing a government actually in power.

Oct. 27   President Wilson in his **Mobile address** promised that the United States would "never again seek one additional foot of territory by conquest."

1914

Feb. 3   President Wilson lifted the arms embargo to Mexico to help the forces of **Venustiano Carranza**, who was opposing Huerta.

Apr. 9   When a few American sailors were arrested by mistake at **Tampico**, Wilson asked Congress for permission to occupy Tampico and establish a blockade against Huerta. Congress complied on Apr. 22.

Apr. 21   To prevent the landing of German arms for Huerta at **Vera Cruz**, the United States seized the customs house and by Apr. 30, 6,700 American troops were engaging Huerta's army. Wilson (Apr. 25) and Huerta (Apr. 30) accepted the mediation of Argentina, Brazil, and Chile. Huerta abdicated on July 15; Carranza occupied Mexico City on Aug. 20; and United States forces withdrew from Mexico on Nov. 23.

June 15   The **Panama Tolls Act** of 1912 had declared that United States coastal shipping would pay no tolls in the Panama Canal in spite of the Hay-Pauncefote Treaty, which stated that the canal should be open to all nations on terms of equality. When Great Britain protested, President Wilson urged Congress to repeal the clause, which it did in June, shortly before the canal opened on Aug. 15, 1914.

Aug. 5   By the **Bryan-Chamorro Treaty**, signed by Secretary of State **William J. Bryan** with **Nicaragua**, the United States leased the two Corn Islands and received the right to build a canal through Nicaragua and to establish a naval base on the Gulf of Fonseca. Before it ratified the treaty (Feb. 18, 1916), the Senate rejected efforts to include a clause giving the United States the right to intervene in Nicaragua.

1915

July 28–Sept. 16   A series of revolutions and a mounting Haitian debt led President Wilson to send marines into **Haiti**. The treaty of Sept. 16 (ratified Feb. 28, 1916) gave the United States control of the customs house and the right to take any future steps necessary to maintain Haitian independence. Marines remained in Haiti until 1934.

1916

May 15–Nov. 26   **Intervention in the Dominican Republic:** Presidents Taft and Wilson had ordered troops into the Dominican Republic briefly in 1912 and 1914, but revolts continued, and on May 15 the United States intervened again. On Nov. 26 President Wilson approved for the republic an American military regime that lasted until 1924.

Mar. 15–Mar. 13, 1917   **Pershing's Mexican Campaign:** Mexican revolutionary **Pancho Villa** on Jan. 11, 1916, murdered 16 Americans in Mexico in order to goad the United States into intervening against the Carranza regime. On Mar. 9 Villa raided Columbus, N.M., and killed 19. President Wilson, therefore, ordered Gen. **John J. Pershing** and 6,000 soldiers into Mexico, but the army clashed with Carranza's troops and was unable to keep Villa from another raid into Texas. Anticipating war with Germany, President Wilson withdrew Pershing in January and February, 1917, and when Carranza was elected President, recognized him on Mar. 13, 1917.

1917

Mar. 2 The **Jones Act** granted Puerto Ricans U.S. citizenship and manhood suffrage.

Mar. 31 **Purchase of the Virgin Islands**: fearful of a German base in the Danish West Indies, the United States on Aug. 4, 1916, signed a treaty to buy from Denmark the Virgin Islands for $25 million. The Senate consented on Jan. 17, 1917, and the United States took possession of the islands Mar. 31, 1917.

The United States and Asia

1900

Imperialism continued in China. Russia took advantage of the Boxer Rebellion to occupy Manchuria with 100,000 troops. The United States itself inquired about a leasehold in Samsah Bay opposite Formosa, but was warned off in December by the Japanese.

1902

Jan. 30 Great Britain and Japan, concerned about Russian expansion in Manchuria, signed the **Anglo-Japanese Alliance**, in which each agreed to aid the other if it became involved in a war with two powers.

Feb. 3 Secretary of State **John M. Hay**, who had admitted (Feb. 1, 1901) that the United States would not fight to back up the Open Door, protested against a Chinese plan to give a Russian bank the sole right to develop Manchuria.

Apr. 8 Russia agreed to evacuate Manchuria but by 1904 had not done so.

1904

Feb. 8 In Aug., 1903, the Japanese had asked the Russians about mutual recognition of Japanese sovereignty in Korea and Russian sovereignty in Manchuria, but no satisfaction was forthcoming. Japan thereupon delivered

a surprise attack on the Russian squadron at **Port Arthur** (Feb. 8, 1904) precipitating the **RUSSO-JAPANESE WAR**.

1905

Jan. 2–May 28 Japan completely defeated the Russians, capturing Port Arthur on Jan. 2 and sinking the Russian Baltic squadron at **Tsushima Strait** on May 27–28.

July 29 The **Taft-Katsura Memorandum**, signed by Secretary of War Taft, recognized Japanese suzerainty over Korea, while the Japanese, through Prime Minister Katsura, promised to keep out of the Philippines.

Aug. 9–Sept. 5 **Peace Negotiations**: President Roosevelt, anxious to maintain the balance of power in Asia by preventing further Japanese conquests, mediated the **peace negotiations** at a conference at Portsmouth, N.H. In the treaty, Russia recognized the Japanese position in Korea and transferred to

7-2 East Asia and the Pacific after the Treaty of Portsmouth, 1905

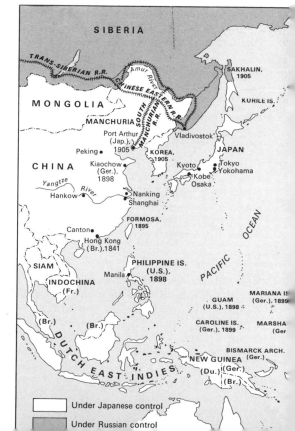

Japan the **southern half of Sakhalin Island, Port Arthur** and **Dairen** in Manchuria, and the **South Manchuria Railway.**

Nov. 18   Japan established a protectorate over Korea. Official Japanese annexation of Korea came on Aug. 22, 1910.

1907

Dec. 16–Feb. 22, 1909   President Roosevelt sent a large part of the United States fleet to the Pacific and around the world in order to strengthen the American position in the western Pacific. This was a good example of Roosevelt's use of force in diplomacy ("the big stick").

1908

Feb. 18   By the **Gentlemen's Agreement with Japan**, which followed an attempt by San Francisco to segregate Japanese in the schools, the Japanese agreed not to issue passports to laborers bound for the United States.

Nov. 30   **Root-Takahira Agreement**, stemming from an exchange of notes between Secretary of State Elihu Root and Japanese Ambassador Takahira, established agreement between the U.S. and Japan:

1. to maintain the status quo in China and the Pacific,
2. to defend the principle of the open door in China,
3. to respect each other's possessions in Asia and the Pacific, and
4. to preserve the integrity of China.

By sending out the fleet while, at the same time, making concessions to Japan, President Roosevelt completed his policy of giving way on the open door but maintaining American power in the Pacific.

1909

July 15   Dollar Diplomacy in Asia: President Taft asked for the admission of American bankers to a European pool to build a railway in China. Then in November and December Secretary of State **Philander C. Knox** asked Great Britain, Russia, and Japan to join the United States in a **Manchurian consortium** to lend money to the Chinese so that they could buy back the Manchurian railroads. The Manchurian plan failed and only drove Russia and Japan to sign a treaty (July 4, 1911) establishing southern Manchuria as a Japanese sphere and northern Manchuria as a Russian sphere. The United States did enter the Chinese railway pool on May 20, 1911, but Taft's dollar diplomacy only revealed that the European powers had tacitly given Japan a free hand in Korea and southern Manchuria.

1912–17

1912   Sun Yat-sen led and his followers carried out a revolution in China that overthrew the Manchu Dynasty and established a republic (Feb. 12).

1913   **California** damaged American-Japanese relations by passing a law (May 3) to prevent Japanese aliens from owning land. In spite of President Wilson's efforts, the law remained in effect.

1914   In August and November, Japan took advantage of World War I to seize all German holdings in Asia and the Pacific including **Kiaochow Bay** in China.

1915   The Japanese on Jan. 18 presented **21 demands** to the Chinese, most of which the Chinese accepted in a treaty of May 25, which greatly strengthened Japan's position in China and Manchuria. On May 11, Secretary of State Bryan sent a note to Japan declaring that the United States would not recognize any impairment of the territorial integrity of China.

1916   The **Jones Act** (Aug. 29) ended the commission government in the Philippines, gave the voters there the right to choose both houses of their legislature, and promised independence soon.

1917   Kikujiro Ishii led a Japanese mission to the United States to secure American recognition of Japanese expansion during World War I. In the **Lansing-Ishii Agreement** (Nov. 2), Secretary of State Robert Lansing recognized that the Japanese had **rights of propinquity** in China, while Ishii reiterated Japanese respect for the open door and the territorial integrity of China.

World War I, 1914–1920

The Background of the War, 1900–1914

1904   The *Entente Cordiale* of Apr. 8 settled Anglo-French differences and paved the way for the Anglo-French alliance in World War I.

1905–06   The **Moroccan Crisis** was brought about by the German-French rivalry in Africa that centered in Morocco, where France wanted to establish a protectorate. After German Kaiser Wilhelm II created a crisis on Mar. 31, 1905, by speaking out for Moroccan independence, President Roosevelt helped in arranging a conference at **Algeciras**, Spain (Jan. 16–Apr. 7, 1906), which guaranteed the independence of Morocco but allowed Spain and France to train the Moroccan police.

1907

June 15–Oct. 18   Second **Hague Peace Conference**, called after a suggestion by President Roosevelt, failed to stop the growing arms race.

July   Germany, Austria, and Italy renewed the **TRIPLE ALLIANCE** of 1882, which became the basis of the Central Powers' alliance at the start of World War I.

Aug. 31   Great Britain and Russia signed a convention on the Middle East. Since France had already signed an alliance with Russia (1893) and an entente with Great Britain, an informal **TRIPLE ENTENTE** had emerged to oppose the Triple Alliance.

1908   Austria annexed **Bosnia-Herzegovina** (Oct. 6), thereby antagonizing both Serbia and Russia, who resented Austrian expansion in the Balkans area.

1911   The German gunboat *Panther* arrived in Agadir on July 1 and created another **Moroccan crisis** in which Great Britain and Russia backed France.

1911–12   The United States signed **arbitration treaties** with France and Great Britain on Aug. 3, but the Senate weakened the treaties with reservations before ratifying them on Mar. 7, 1912.

1912–13   **First and Second Balkan Wars** expelled Turkey from Europe except for the area near Constantinople but left Serbia dissatisfied.

1913   On Apr. 24, Secretary of State Bryan submitted to all nations with ministers in Washington arbitration treaties calling for a **"cooling off"** period before resorting to war. The United States eventually signed and ratified treaties with 21 nations.

1914

June 28–Aug. 4   The Outbreak of World War I

June 28   A Serbian nationalist assassinated **Archduke Franz Ferdinand** of Austria and his wife at **Sarajevo**, Bosnia.

July 23   Austria delivered an **ultimatum** to Serbia, and when the response was not satisfactory declared war on Serbia (July 28).

July 30   Russia began mobilization.

Aug. 1   Germany declared war on Russia.

Aug. 3   **Germany** declared war on France and **invaded Belgium**.

Aug. 4   Great Britain declared war on Germany. World War I was underway with the **Allies** (Great Britain, France, and Russia) pitted against the **Central Powers** (Germany, Austria, and Turkey). In 1915, Italy left the Central Powers and sided with the Allies.

American Neutrality, 1914–1917

1914

Aug. 4, 19   The United States announced her **NEUTRALITY** (Aug. 4), and on Aug. 19 President Wilson urged Americans to be neutral in "thought as well as in action." His Administration and the people favored the Allies because of cultural, ethnic, and economic ties. British propaganda also turned Americans against the Germans.

Aug. 6–Oct. 20   **Contraband of war**: the United States on Aug. 6 suggested that the belligerents accept the **Declaration of London** (1909) as a naval code, but on Aug. 20 the British expanded the contraband list of the Declaration and began to intercept American ships. After protesting (Sept. 26), the United States on Oct. 20 gave up efforts to hold Great Britain to the Declaration. Britain subsequently expanded the list further and used the **continuous voyage doctrine** to seize American cargoes bound for Baltic nations but apparently headed eventually for Germany.

Aug. 15–Sept. 7, 1915   Secretary of State **Bryan** announced that **war loans** to belligerents violated neutrality, but on Oct. 15 the State Department quietly allowed such loans. President Wilson on Sept. 7, 1915, permitted New York bankers to lend $500 million to France and Great Britain. By the time the United States entered the war American bankers had loaned the Allies $2.3 billion and Germany only $27 million.

Nov. 3–Mar. 11, 1915   The **British violated neutral rights** by declaring the North Sea a **war zone** (Nov. 3) and proceeding to mine it. They also interfered with American **mail**, seized American ships, and on Mar. 11 blockaded all German ports. American protests were ineffective.

Fall   Efforts by German sympathizers, pacifists, and others to stop the **sale of munitions** failed; since the Allies controlled the seas, they imported large quantities of munitions from the United States. Total United States **exports** to Great Britain and France rose from $754 million in 1914 to $2,748 million in 1916; exports to Germany fell from $345 million to $2 million in the same period.

7-3   Europe at War, 1914

1915

Jan. 28–May 4, 1916   The German Submarine Menace

Jan. 28   A German cruiser sank an American merchant ship carrying wheat to Great Britain.

Feb. 4   Germany proclaimed a **war zone** around the British Isles and warned that neutral shipping in the zone would be in peril of submarines.

Feb. 10   The United States protested vigorously against the war zone and said it would hold Germany to **"strict accountability"** if American vessels or lives were lost.

Feb. 18   Germany announced that its submarines would sink enemy merchant vessels in the war zone without warning.

Mar. 28, May 1   One American was killed when the Germans sank the British ship *Falaba* in the Irish Sea. Three more died when the Germans by mistake torpedoed the American tanker *Gulflight.*

May 1   The German embassy warned Americans by advertisements in New York newspapers that they sailed on Allied vessels at their own risk.

May 7   A German submarine sank the British steamer *Lusitania* without warning off the Irish coast, killing 1,198 persons, of whom 128 were Americans.

May 10   President Wilson said in Philadelphia that a nation clearly in the right did not have to prove it with force. "There is such a thing," he said, "as a man being **too proud to fight.**"

May 13–July 21   In the first of the *Lusitania* notes (May 13), the United States insisted on American rights on the high seas, asked for reparations, and demanded that the Germans give up unrestricted submarine warfare, but Germany gave little satisfaction (May 28). When Wilson insisted on a second note demanding specific pledges, Secretary of State **Bryan resigned** (June 7) because he was afraid it would bring war. Wilson appointed **Robert Lansing** in his place. Neither the second nor the third notes (June 9, July 21) brought a specific German response, but secretly the Germans (June 6) ordered submarine commanders to spare passenger liners.

On Feb. 16, 1916, Germany agreed to pay an indemnity for American loss of life on the *Lusitania.*

July 24–Jan. 11, 1917   German espionage and sabotage were revealed when an American secret service agent seized documents (July 24) proving that German Ambassador **Count Bernstorff** and Capt. **Franz von Papen,** military attaché, were involved in sabotage. This led to the recall of Von Papen and of Austro-Hungarian Ambassador **Dr. Dumba.** The United States attributed two explosions with a loss of $55 million (1916–17) to the Germans.

Aug. 19   A German submarine, violating orders, sank the British passenger ship *Arabic* with a loss of two American lives. On Oct. 5, the German government promised that such an incident would not happen again.

1916

Feb. 8   The Germans declared that after Mar. 1 they would sink all armed enemy merchantmen without warning.

Feb. 22   President Wilson sent Col. **Edward M. House,** his close adviser, on two peace missions to Europe (1915–16). House's conversations with British Foreign Secretary **Sir Edward Grey,** led to the **House-Grey Memorandum,** which said that at an "opportune" moment, the United States would propose a peace conference. If the Allies accepted but the Germans refused, the United States would "probably" go to war against Germany. Wilson endorsed the memorandum, but peace efforts failed.

Feb. 17–Mar. 17   Congressman **Jeff McLemore** (Tex.), fearful that the United States would be drawn into war, introduced a resolution asking the President to prohibit Americans from travelling on armed vessels. When Wilson refused, the House tabled the resolution (Mar. 7), and the Senate tabled one by Senator **Thomas P. Gore** (Okla.) to prohibit the issue of passports to Americans travelling on belligerent ships (Mar. 3).

Mar. 24   A German submarine torpedoed the unarmed French passenger ship *Sussex* in the English Channel, injuring several Americans and violating the *Arabic* pledge.

Apr. 18 Secretary of State Lansing threatened to sever diplomatic relations if Germany did not abandon unrestricted submarine warfare.

May 4 In the *Sussex* **Pledge**, Germany promised not to torpedo any merchant vessel without warning and added a clause that the United States must insist on British observation of international rules of war. When Wilson accepted the pledge (May 8), eight months of relative German-American calm followed.

June–Sept. President Wilson at first resisted **preparedness** demands, but political pressure and the submarine sinkings forced him to change. The **National Defense Act** (June 3) called for expanding the regular army to over 200,000 men over a five-year period. A **Council of National Defense** (Aug. 29) and a **Shipping Board** (Sept. 7) were made responsible for defense planning.

July 18 The British **blacklisted** American individuals and firms suspected of doing business with the Central Powers and ordered British subjects not to trade with them.

Dec. 18 President Wilson sent notes to each belligerent asking for its peace terms. The Germans did not reply, and the Allies listed terms that were extremely unfavorable to the Central Powers.

1917

Jan. 22 In a speech before the Senate, Wilson called for an international organization to maintain world peace and demanded a **"peace without victory."**

Jan. 31 Germany announced that it was **renewing unrestricted submarine warfare** against all shipping.

Feb. 3 President Wilson **broke off diplomatic relations** with Germany.

Feb. 3–Mar. 21 Germany sank six American ships on the high seas.

Mar. 1 The State Department released a **note** from German Foreign Secretary **Alfred F. M. Zimmermann** proposing an alliance with **Mexico** if war with the United States broke out. The note, which was intercepted by British naval intelligence, suggested that when war came the Mexicans would reconquer its lost territories in Texas, New Mexico, and Arizona.

Mar. 8–15 **Revolution in Russia** led to the abdication of the Czar. The United States recognized the provisional regime on Mar. 22.

Mar. 12 President Wilson ordered American **merchant vessels in war zones to be armed** after isolationists in the Senate had filibustered to death an armed-ship bill.

Apr. 2 **WILSON'S WAR MESSAGE**, before a special session of Congress, started with an attack on German submarine warfare, calling it **"warfare against mankind."** The message concluded with a call for a crusade to make the world **"safe for democracy."**

Apr. 4–6 **Declaration of War**: after a short but bitter debate in which **Robert M. La-Follette** made a four-hour speech opposing war, the Senate voted 82–6 for war (Apr. 4), and the House voted 373–50 for war (Apr. 6). In the House minority, 34 were from the midwest.

The United States in World War I, 1917–1918

May 18 **Selective Service Act** called for the registration of all men aged 21–30 (amended Aug. 31, 1918, to ages 18–45). Of 24,234,021 men registered by Sept. 12, 1918, 2,810,296 were called for duty. The National Guard was called up and many civilians volunteered; the total number of troops serving in the war was 4,791,172, of which 2,084,000 went overseas.

June 13 Gen. **John J. ("BLACK JACK") PERSHING**, in command of the **American Expeditionary Force (AEF)** arrived in France, and the U.S. 1st Division embarked for France.

July–Nov. **The Progress of the War**: a Russian offensive in the east and a British offensive in Flanders got underway, but the Germans turned both back by fall, suffering a huge number of casualties. The French campaign on the main front was stalled. Pershing insisted on maintaining the **AEF**

as a separate force and was assigned the Toul sector east of Verdun, where elements of the 1st Division took positions in the front lines on Oct. 21. In Oct. and Nov. the Austro-German forces routed an Italian offensive.

Nov. 7 **Nicolai Lenin** led the **Bolshevik Revolution** in Russia and assumed control of the government. The Bolsheviks then made a separate peace with Germany by the **Treaty of Brest-Litovsk**, Mar. 3, 1918, which relieved Germany of the burden of a two-front war.

Nov. 24 **Leon Trotsky**, Russian foreign minister, published the Czar's secret treaties with the Allies, which revealed that the Allies had promised each other territorial gains after the war.

1918

Jan. 8 **WILSON'S 14 POINTS**: when the Allies were unable to agree on a statement of war aims, President Wilson proposed the following program before Congress:

1. **"Open covenants of peace,** openly arrived at, . . .";
2. **"freedom of navigation upon the seas, . . .";**
3. **"the removal,** so far as possible, **of all economic barriers . . .";**
4. **reduction of armaments;**
5. adjustment of colonial claims in the interests of the inhabitants as well as the powers;
6. evacuation of the Russian territory and Russian self-determination;

7-4 The United States on the Western Front, 1918

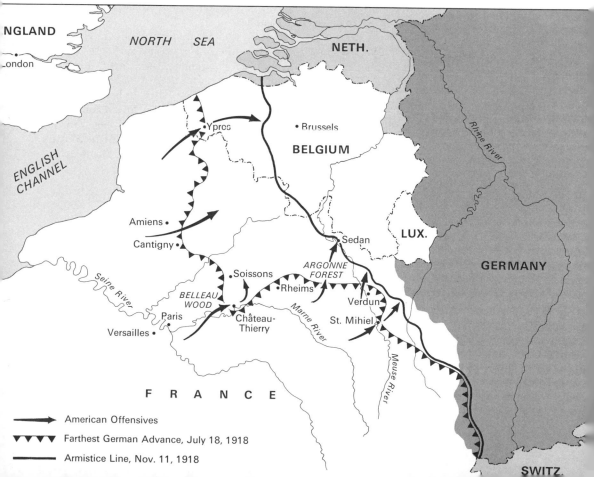

American Offensives

▼▼▼▼ Farthest German Advance, July 18, 1918

Armistice Line, Nov. 11, 1918

7. restoration of Belgium;
8. restoration of French territory, including Alsace-Lorraine, taken by Prussia in 1871;
9. readjustment of Italian boundaries along "lines of nationality";
10. self-development for the peoples of Austria-Hungary;
11. restoration of the Balkan nations including access to the sea for Serbia;
12. "autonomous development" for Turkish minorities;
13. an independent Poland; and
14. **"a general association of nations."**

Mar. 21–July 17   The German offensive, which began with the Second Battle of the Somme, was intended to reach to the English Channel.

Mar. 26 Frightened by the German success, the Allies (including the United States) established a unified command for the Western Front under Gen. **Ferdinand Foch.** American soldiers joined in the fighting near Amiens and Armentières.

May 27 The Germans started a massive offensive north of the Aisne River and on May 31 were at the **Marne River,** about 50 miles from Paris. American forces (2nd, 3rd, and 28th Divisions and 4th Marine Brigade) helped check the Germans at **Chateau-Thierry** (June 3–4) and took part in driving the Germans out of **Belleau Wood.**

June 6–July 1 The 1st Division helped stop another German drive midway between the Aisne and the Somme rivers.

July 15 The Germans started a final drive at **Rheims,** but the Allies (including 85,000 American troops) repulsed them as the tide of war began to turn.

July 18–Nov. 11 By July, a million American soldiers had arrived in France, and the great **Allied counter-offensive** (with 270,000 Americans taking part) began in the **Aisne-Marne sector** on July 18.

Aug. 20 The British, aided by 150,000 Americans, began their offensive in the Somme River valley and in Flanders.

Aug.–Aug., 1920 15,000 American troops took part in the Allied **occupation** of **Murmansk-Archangel** in Russia and **Vladivostok** in Siberia in order to protect war supplies and to aid the counter-revolutionaries against the Bolsheviks.

Sept. 12 The United States started its first independent operation at the **St. Mihiel salient,** which was captured on Sept. 16 at a cost of 7,000 American casualties.

Sept. 26 The United States committed ·1,200,000 troops to a major drive at the **Meuse River–Argonne Forest sector** and pushed the Germans back at a cost of 120,000 casualties.

Oct. 3 The Germans sent a note to the United States asking for an armistice in order to discuss peace on the basis of the 14 Points.

Oct. 20 After considerable negotiation Germany agreed to Wilson's demand to evacuate Belgium and France.

Nov. 4 After threats of a separate American peace, the Allies agreed to make **peace on the basis of the 14 Points** with two exceptions: **freedom of the seas** was left open to future definition, and Germany was to make **reparations.** President Wilson on Nov. 5 transmitted the Allied terms to the Germans.

Nov. 6 United States troops occupied Sedan. By then the Allies had pushed the Germans back to a line running from Ghent, Belgium, to Sedan, in northeastern France.

Nov. 9 After a revolution in Berlin, **Kaiser Wilhelm II abdicated,** and a German republic was proclaimed.

Nov. 11 Gen. Foch signed an **ARMISTICE** with a German commission at Compiègne.

The Peace Settlement, 1918–1920

1918

Nov. 5   Congressional elections: on Oct. 25 Woodrow Wilson appealed to the voters to return a Democratic Congress. The Republicans captured both houses after gaining about 30 seats in the House and 7 in the Senate and began to say that Wilson did not speak for the American people.

Nov. 18 President Wilson announced that he would attend the European peace conference with a **commission** consisting of

World War I Casualties

(thousands)

	Total mobilized forces	Killed or died	Wounded	Prisoners and missing	Total casualties	Per cent
United States	4,791	117	204	5	326	8
Russia	12,000	1,700	4,950	2,500	9,150	76
France	8,410	1,358	4,266	537	6,161	73
British Commonwealth	8,904	908	2,090	192	3,190	36
Italy	5,615	650	947	600	2,197	39
Germany	11,000	1,774	4,216	1,153	7,143	65
Austria-Hungary	7,800	1,200	3,620	2,200	7,020	90
Total	58,520	7,707	20,293	7,187	35,187	60

Col. House, Secretary of State Lansing, Gen. Tasker H. Bliss, and diplomat **Henry White** (the sole Republican). Republicans criticized the President for placing himself on the commission, for not appointing at least one Senator, and for ignoring prominent Republicans such as Henry Cabot Lodge and Theodore Roosevelt.

Dec. 13   Wilson arrived in France and made a **triumphant tour** of France, England, and Italy that lasted until Jan., 1919.

1919

Jan. 12–June 28   The **PEACE CONFERENCE AT VERSAILLES** was dominated by the "**Big Four**"—**Woodrow Wilson**, Prime Minister **David Lloyd George** of Great Britain, Premier **Georges Clemenceau** of France, and Premier **Vittorio Orlando** of Italy.

Jan. 25   The conference adopted the principle of the League of Nations.

Feb. 14   The conference adopted the **Covenant of the League of Nations** provisionally.

Feb. 15   President Wilson sailed for the United States, arriving Feb. 24. On Feb. 26, Wilson met with members of the Senate and House committees concerned with foreign affairs and discussed the League of Nations.

Feb. 28   Senator **HENRY CABOT LODGE** (Mass.) delivered his first speech against the League of Nations. He believed that the

League should be considered only after peace had been made.

Mar. 2   37 Republican Senators and two Senators-elect signed a "**round-robin**" letter rejecting the League in its existing form.

Mar. 4   President Wilson defiantly defended the League of Nations in a speech at New York. On the following day, he sailed again for Paris.

Mar. 28–Apr. 30   The "Big Four" made final decisions on **reparations and territorial terms** amid bitter debate. The Allied leaders forced Wilson to concede several of his 14 Points; they in turn accepted **amendments** to the League Covenant exempting the United States from the mandate system and excepting the Monroe Doctrine from the jurisdiction of the League.

June 28   The **TREATY OF VERSAILLES** was signed and included the following terms:

1. Germany was forced to admit her **war guilt** and was disarmed and forced to pay **reparations**.

2. French security. France recovered **Alsace-Lorraine** and was to occupy the **Saar Basin** for 15 years. The League was to occupy the **Rhineland** (left bank) for 15 years, while a 30-mile zone on the right **bank of the Rhine** was demilitarized.

3. **Poland** was created as an independent state and received Posen, part of Upper Silesia, and a corridor to the sea. **Danzig** became a free city.

4. German imperial possessions went to

various Allied powers under the **League mandate system**.

5. The **Covenant of the League of Nations** determined that members of the League were each to have one vote in the **General Assembly**; a **Council** composed of representatives of Great Britain, France, the United States, Italy, Japan, and four other powers was to serve as the executive. A permanent **secretariat** was to sit at Geneva. According to **Article X** members were to preserve each other's territorial integrity and **Article XVI** provided for economic sanctions against aggressors.

June 28   The United States and Great Britain signed a treaty with France in which they agreed to assist France if attacked by Germany. The Senate never ratified the treaty.

July 10–Mar. 19, 1920   THE REJECTION OF THE LEAGUE

July 10   Wilson submitted the Versailles Treaty to the Senate, where it was held up in the Foreign Relations Committee (Henry Cabot Lodge, chairman) until Sept. 10.

Sept. 3–Sept. 26   President Wilson went on a **western speaking tour** in which he defended the League before enthusiastic crowds. Republican Senators **Hiram W. Johnson** and **William E. Borah** followed him and spoke against the League. At **Pueblo, Colo.**, after making his 40th speech **Wilson collapsed** on Sept. 25 and returned to Washington.

Sept. 10–Aug. 20, 1920   Austria-Hungary, Bulgaria, and Turkey signed peace treaties. These treaties, imposed by the Allies, and independence movements during World War

7-5   Europe, 1920

I brought about the following territorial changes:

1. **Austria-Hungary** was broken into the states of Austria, Hungary, Czechoslovakia, and Yugoslavia (including Serbia).
2. Rumania annexed land from both Austria-Hungary and Russia.
3. Italy received **Trieste** and the southern Tyrol from Austria-Hungary but did not get Fiume.
4. Turkey lost Syria as a mandate to France and Palestine and Mesopotamia as mandates to Great Britain and agreed to internationalize the Straits (the Bosporus and Dardanelles).
5. Finland, Latvia, Lithuania, Estonia, and Poland became independent states.

Sept. 10   The Senate Committee on Foreign Relations reported the Versailles Treaty to the Senate with amendments and reservations. The Senate at this time consisted of three groups: **Democratic supporters of the League Covenant** led by **Gilbert M. Hitchcock** (Neb.); **reservationists,** mostly Republicans, led by Lodge, and **"irreconcilables"** led by **Hiram W. Johnson** (Calif.), **William E. Borah** (Idaho), and **Robert M. LaFollette** (Wis.), who opposed the Covenant completely. The Senate rejected all amendments but accepted a number of reservations.

Oct. 2   President Wilson suffered a **stroke** that incapacitated him completely until Oct. 20. He held no cabinet meetings until Apr. 13, 1920, and never fully recovered from the paralysis that followed the stroke.

Nov. 6   **Henry Cabot Lodge** proposed **fourteen reservations** to the League Covenant, the most vital of which said that Articles X and XVI, which required involvement to stop aggression, would be binding only when Congress so directed. While the reservations did not seriously impair the League, Wilson opposed them because he felt that the United States had a moral commitment under Article X.

Nov. 18   President Wilson instructed the Democratic majority in the Senate to vote against the Treaty with reservations. Wilson in particular opposed the reservation against Article X, which he considered the "heart of the Covenant."

Nov. 19   The Senate rejected the Treaty with the Lodge reservations by the following vote: 39 Yea (35 reservationist Republicans and 4 Democrats) and 55 Nay (42 Democrats and 13 Irreconcilable Republicans). The Senate also voted against the treaty with five mild Democratic reservations and against it with no reservations.

1920

Mar. 19   The Senate **rejected the Treaty** with fifteen reservations. The vote was 49 Yea (28 reservationist Republicans and 21 Democrats) and 35 Nay (23 Democrats and 12 Irreconcilables). President Wilson still opposed any reservations.

July 2–Oct. 18   Congress by joint resolution terminated the state of war with Germany and Austria-Hungary, and on Oct. 18 the Senate ratified separate peace treaties with Germany, Austria, and Hungary.

The Home Front During and After the War, 1917–1920

1917

Apr. 24–May 20, 1918   WARTIME ECONOMIC POLICIES

Apr. 24   The **Emergency Loan Act** ("Liberty Loan Act") authorized a bond issue of $5 billion. By Apr., 1919, loan drives had netted $21 billion, about $3/5$ of the $35 billion needed to finance the war. The public (national) debt rose from $2 billion in 1917 to $26 billion in 1919.

July 28   The **Council of National Defense** created the **War Industries Board** to coordinate government purchases and eliminate waste. Under **Bernard M. Baruch** in 1918 the Board exercised wide controls over manufacturing, price fixing, and purchase of supplies.

Aug. 10   The **Lever Act** authorized the Food Administration and the Fuel Administration to control production, cut waste, and fix prices. **Herbert C. Hoover,** Food Administrator, resorted to meatless and wheatless days to conserve food.

Oct. 3   The **War Revenue Act** doubled the income tax of 1916 and levied excise taxes so that taxation raised about 30 per cent of the cost of the war.

Oct. 6   Trading with the Enemy Act forbade commerce with enemy nations and authorized the President to put an embargo on imports. The War Trade Board licensed imports and enforced the Act.

Dec. 18   Congress approved the **18th Amendment prohibiting** the manufacture, sale, or transportation of **alcoholic liquors.** By this time 19 states had already adopted statewide prohibition. The amendment was ratified on Jan. 29, 1919, and went into effect on Jan. 16, 1920.

Dec. 26   President Wilson put the railways under the administration of Secretary of the Treasury **William G. McAdoo.** The Railroad Control Act (Mar. 21, 1918) authorized federal control of the railroads.

1918

Apr. 8   President Wilson appointed a **National War Labor Board** to serve as a final court for labor disputes during the war. The board did not allow strikes but recognized the right to collective bargaining. President **Gompers** of the AFL sat on the Council of National Defense and pledged that there would be no strikes.

Apr. 10   Webb-Pomerene Act freed foreign operations of American business from liability under the antitrust laws.

May 20   The **Overman Act** gave the President power to coordinate bureaus and agencies to promote efficiency. A total of nearly 5,000 war agencies brought considerable regimentation to American life.

Apr. 14, 1917–1920   RESTRICTIONS ON CIVIL LIBERTIES

1917

Apr. 14   The **Committee on Public Information** (the Creel Committee), headed by **George Creel,** became responsible for publicizing the war effort. The Committee published a massive amount of propaganda

to spread American war aims and to stress the supposed menace of the Germans.

June 15   ESPIONAGE ACT provided for penalties up to $10,000 and 20 years in prison for those guilty of aiding the enemy, obstructing recruiting, or causing disloyalty in the armed forces. The Court unanimously upheld this Act in **Schenck v. United States** (1919) when Justice **Oliver Wendell Holmes** declared that Schenck's pamphlets encouraging resistance to the draft created **"a clear and present danger."**

Oct. 6   Trading with the Enemy Act allowed the President to censor messages going to foreign nations.

Nov. 16   President Wilson required the registration of enemy aliens.

1918

May 16   The **SEDITION ACT** amended the Espionage Act to punish anyone who obstructed the sale of bonds, interfered with the war effort or used "disloyal, profane, scurrilous . . . language about the form of government of the United States." Officials enforced the act strictly, arresting 1,500 for seditious statements. In **Abrams v. the United States** (1919) the majority on the Court considered the distribution of pamphlets that criticized the government for sending troops to Russia a violation of the act. Justice **Holmes** dissented.

Sept. 14   A federal court sentenced **Eugene V. Debs** to 10 years in jail for interfering with recruiting. The Supreme Court upheld the sentence on Mar. 10, 1919, and President Wilson in 1920 refused to commute his sentence. President Harding released him Dec. 24, 1921, without restoring his U.S. citizenship, which had been revoked.

1919

Feb. 20   A federal court sentenced Socialist **Victor L. Berger** to 20 years in prison for violating the Espionage Act, but the sentence was later set aside.

Apr.–1920   The rise of Russian Bolshevism, the start of American communism, and the radical statements of IWW leaders contributed to the **RED SCARE**. The discovery of over 30 bombs in the mails (Apr.) and the large number of strikes only reinforced public fears. Many states passed syndicalist laws prohibiting membership in revolutionary organizations.

Sept. 1   The **Communist Party** formed an American section under the Russian International.

Nov. 10   The House refused to seat Socialist member Victor L. Berger. After his Wisconsin district reelected him, the House once again declared his seat vacant in Jan., 1920.

Dec. 21   The Department of Labor deported 249 Russians including the anarchist **Emma Goldman**.

1920

Jan. 5   U.S. Attorney General **A. Mitchell Palmer** authorized **raids** on suspected Communists; over 4,000 persons were arrested, and 556 were eventually deported.

May 5–Aug. 23, 1927   **Sacco-Vanzetti Case: Nicola Sacco** and **Bartolomeo Vanzetti**, both anarchists, were arrested on May 5 on a charge of murder in South Braintree, Mass., convicted on very flimsy evidence, (1921), and executed on Aug. 23, 1927, after widespread public debate about the case. Many attributed the conviction to the Red Scare.

Sept. 16   A bomb exploded on Wall Street in New York, killing 38 people. This was one of the last major episodes of the Red Scare.

1919–20   ECONOMIC POLICY AND POLITICS AFTER THE WAR

1919

June 4   Congress passed the **19th Amendment** calling for **women's suffrage**. It was ratified on Aug. 26, 1920.

Sept. 9   **Boston Police Strike**, which brought Gov. **Calvin Coolidge** of Massachusetts national prominence, began. In 1919 a total of 4 million workers participated in strikes.

Sept. 22   **Steel Strike** broke out in Gary,

Ind., to force the United States Steel Corporation to recognize a national committee of the AFL. President Wilson sent federal troops, who helped strikebreakers enter the plant. On Jan. 8, 1920, the AFL called off the strike, and the steel industry did not become unionized until 1937.

Oct. 28   **Volstead Act** to enforce the **prohibition** amendment was passed over President Wilson's veto. The Prohibition Act, which went into effect on Jan. 16, 1920, defined as intoxicating any beverage containing more than one-half of one per cent of alcohol and put the administration of the Act under the administration of the Bureau of Internal Revenue.

Nov. 1   The **United Mine Workers,** led by **John L. Lewis,** went on strike against the coal-mine operators. When President Wilson secured an injunction against the union, the strike was quickly ended.

1920

Feb. 28   **Esch-Cummins Transportation Act** called for the return of the railroads to private ownership instead of nationalizing them as proposed by **Glenn E. Plumb** of the Railroad Labor Brotherhoods. The Act empowered the Interstate Commerce Commission to draw up plans for consolidating the railroads into a number of groups exempt from antitrust laws and to set minimum as well as maximum rates. It also created a **Railroad Labor Board** to adjust wage disputes.

June 5   **Jones Merchant Marine Act** authorized the sale of government-built ships to private operators at low prices. The act encouraged private shipping by offering shippers government loans, lucrative mail contracts, and a monopoly on shipping between colonial territories and the United States. The **Jones-White Merchant-Marine Act** (May 22, 1928) made the terms even more attractive by giving subsidies that were thinly disguised as mail-carrying contracts.

June 8   The **Republican Convention** met in Chicago and nominated Senator **Warren G. Harding** (Ohio) for President and gov.

Calvin Coolidge of Massachusetts for Vice President. The platform rejected the League of Nations. Harding, who called for a "return to normalcy," waged a "front-porch" campaign and did little traveling.

June 10   Water Power Act created the **Federal Power Commission** to license and regulate power plants.

June 28   The Democratic Convention met in San Francisco and nominated governor **James M. Cox** of Ohio for President and Assistant Secretary of the Navy **Franklin D. Roosevelt** (N.Y.) for Vice President. The platform supported the League of Nations.

Nov. 2   The Presidential election was not the referendum on the League of Nations that Wilson had wanted. Harding talked on both sides of the issue, and a group of distinguished Republicans maintained that a vote for Harding was a vote for the League with reservations. Democratic wartime taxes and controls had alienated farmers and the middle class. Harding was elected with 16,143,407 votes (404 electoral) to 9,130,328 for **Cox** (127 electoral), and 919,799 votes for **Debs**, the Socialist candidate.

The Twenties, 1921–1929

The Republican Domestic Program, 1921–1929

1921

May, 1920–1922   A sudden drop in prices after May, 1920, was followed by a severe **RECESSION** in 1921. Partly responsible for the recession was President Wilson's postwar economic policy of suddenly balancing the budget after great wartime deficits and the speedy return of over 4 million servicemen to civilian life. Wages dropped in 1921 as almost 5 million were unemployed. The wholesale commodity price index dropped from 154 in 1920 to 97 in 1922, when prosperity returned.

June 10–Sept. 19, 1922   Economic legislation

June 10   Budget Act established the Bureau of the Budget and required the President to submit an estimate of receipts and expenditures to each regular session of Congress.

Aug. 15   Packers and Stockyards Act forbade price discrimination and other devices to create a monopoly in restraint of trade in livestock, poultry, and dairy products.

Aug. 24   Grain Futures Act forbade market manipulation and monopoly in the grain market. After the Supreme Court declared the Act unconstitutional, Congress passed a second act (Sept. 21, 1922) that controlled trading under the commerce power.

Nov. 23   Revenue Act eliminated the wartime excess profits tax and reduced the maximum surtax rate on personal incomes from 65 per cent to 50 per cent. The act was the first step in Secretary of the Treasury **Andrew W. Mellon's** program of **tax reduction** for wealthy people. By 1926 the maximum surtax on incomes was down to 20 per cent. By cutting expenses the Republicans achieved a surplus every year until 1929 and were able to reduce the national debt from $25 billion in 1919 to $16 billion in 1930.

1922

Feb. 18–Mar. 4, 1923   Farm Legislation: the **Cooperative Marketing Act** (Capper-Volstead Act) exempted agricultural cooperatives from the antitrust laws. The **Agricultural Credits Act** (Mar. 4, 1923) established 12 intermediate credit banks for farm loans.

Apr. 1, July 1   Strikes: the **coal miners' strike** began on Apr. 1 to protest wage reductions. About 500,000 miners struck before the strike ended in September. The **railway shopmen's strike** began on July 1 as a protest against a 12 per cent wage cut. Federal Judge **James H. Wilkerson** of Chicago broke the strike on Sept. 1 with a sweeping injunction that forbade the union to carry on almost any strike activity.

Sept. 19   Fordney-McCumber Tariff restored the protective rates that the Underwood-Simmons Act had reduced.

1923

Aug. 2   PRESIDENT HARDING DIED at San Francisco from an embolism. **Calvin Coolidge** took the oath of office on Aug. 3 at his family home in Plymouth, Vt.

1924

Feb. 29–June 30   THE HARDING SCANDALS: Charles R. Forbes, former director of the Veterans' Bureau, was indicted for defrauding the government through corrupt contracts and was convicted on Feb. 4, 1925. A Senate investigation headed by **Thomas J. Walsh** (Mont.) led to the indictment (June 30) of Secretary of the Interior **Albert B. Fall** and oil men **Harry F. Sinclair** and **Edward L. Doheny** for conspiracy involving federal oil reserves at Teapot Dome, Wyo., and Elk Hills, Calif. The committee discovered that Fall had secretly leased the oil fields to the oil interests in 1922 and had received "loans" of $125,000. The courts convicted Fall of bribery and Sinclair of contempt of court, but acquitted Doheny. When another investigation disclosed that Attorney General **Harry M. Daugherty** had received bribes from persons violating prohibition, President Coolidge forced him to resign (Mar., 1924).

May 19   Soldiers Bonus Act passed Congress over President Coolidge's veto. The act, supported by the American Legion and the Veterans of Foreign Wars, provided 20-year endowment policies for all veterans of the rank of Captain or below on the basis of $1.00–$1.25 for every day of wartime service.

May 26   IMMIGRATION QUOTA ACT limited annual immigration to 2 per cent of the number of each nationality resident in the U.S. by the census of 1890. The act changed the act of 1921, which had set the quotas at 3 per cent of the 1910 census, and thereby reduced the quotas from eastern

and southern Europe. The maximum total quota was set at 164,000 compared to 358,000 in 1921. The act was to be in effect until 1927 when quotas would be based on a national-origins study of the census of 1920. The second phase of the act did not go into operation until July 1, 1929, after which the quota for any nationality was the same percentage of 150,000 as the percentage of the nationality was of the total population in 1920. Since the quota laws did not apply to immigration from Canada and Mexico, immigration from those nations remained high until 1929.

June 3   McNary-Haugen Bill: agriculture made only partial recovery from the 1921 recession as farm surpluses kept prices down. The wholesale price index for farm products, which dropped from 151 in 1920 to 88 in 1921, rose to 110 in 1925 but was back down to 99 in 1927. Farmers' groups such as the **American Farm Bureau Federation** and an active farm bloc in Congress, led by Senator **Arthur Capper** (Kan.), fought hard for legislation to control the surplus. Senator **Charles L. McNary** (Ore.) and Congressman **Gilbert N. Haugen** (Iowa) introduced their Farm Relief bill in both houses on Jan. 16. It called for the federal government to buy up the annual surplus of corn, wheat, cotton, and other commodities at a relatively high price and sell it abroad at the world price. Farmers would pay an **equalization fee** to make up the government losses. The bill failed to pass the House on June 3, 1924, and on May 21, 1926; when it did pass Congress in 1927, Coolidge vetoed it on Feb. 25.

June 10   The Republican Party met at Cleveland and nominated **Calvin Coolidge** for President and **Charles G. Dawes** (Ill.) for Vice President.

June 24   The Democratic Party met at New York and nominated **John W. Davis,** a lawyer from West Virginia, for President and governor **Charles W. Bryan** of Nebraska, the brother of William Jennings Bryan, for Vice President. The nomination of Davis came on the 103rd ballot after a bitter battle between the city Democrats who wanted governor **Alfred E. Smith** of New York and the rural Democrats who preferred **William**

G. McAdoo (N.Y.), Secretary of the Treasury under Wilson. The issue of the **Ku Klux Klan** also divided the party. Revived in 1915 in Georgia, the Klan became strong again in the South and in 1920 spread to the Midwest and to the East, attacking Catholics, immigrants, Jews, and opponents of Prohibition as well as Negroes. In the early 1920's it had perhaps 5 million members, most of them rural. The Democratic platform failed to condemn the Klan by name by one vote. By 1928 the Klan had largely vanished as an issue.

July 4   The **Conference for Progressive Political Action (CPPA)** met at Cleveland and nominated Senator **Robert M. LaFollette** for President and **Burton K. Wheeler** (Mont.) for Vice President. The CPPA, organized by Progressives in 1922, had helped elect 12 governors, 13 senators, and about 25 congressmen in 1922. The railway brotherhoods, unions, farm organizations, the Socialist Party, and the Wisconsin Progressive Party all sent delegates to the CPPA convention. The platform condemned monopoly and called for the nationalization of electric power and railroads. It also demanded a lower tariff, collective bargaining, and the abolition of war.

Nov. 4   **Presidential election: Coolidge** won with 15,718,211 votes (382 electoral) to 8,385,283 (136 electoral) for **Davis** and 4,831,289 (13 electoral) for **LaFollette**. The **Communist (Workers) Party**, which ran candidates for President in the elections of 1924–40, received only 36,386 votes. In spite of its good showing the Progressive Party (CPPA) fell apart after 1924.

1925

Trade associations and holding companies Under Secretary **Herbert C. Hoover** the Commerce Department fostered industrial efficiency by gathering statistics, by seeking out foreign markets, and by encouraging competing firms in an industry to form trade associations that would share information, standardize tools and parts, and reduce competition. In 1925 the Supreme Court endorsed such activities in the **Cement Manufacturers' Protective Association case** and the **Maple Flooring Manufacturers' Association case**. At the same time the Federal Trade Commission, packed with business advocates, refused to interfere with monopolistic practices. As a result, by 1929, 93 of the 97 most powerful corporations were holding companies. Ten holding companies (of which **Samuel Insull's** was the largest) controlled almost three-fourth of all public utilities.

1928

May 25–Mar. 3, 1931   **Muscle Shoals:** Congress passed a bill sponsored by Senator **George W. Norris** (Neb.) that called for a government corporation to operate the hydroelectric station and nitrate plants at Muscle Shoals in the Tennessee River. The government built the plants in 1918 to manufacture explosives, but they were practically idle in 1928. President Coolidge gave the bill a **pocket veto**. The bill passed Congress again in 1931 only to receive a **veto** from President Herbert Hoover, who disapproved of government competition with private power interests.

June 12   The **Republican Party** met in Kansas City, Mo., and nominated **Herbert C. Hoover** for President and Senator **Charles Curtis** (Kan.) for Vice President after President Calvin Coolidge had announced in 1927 that he did "not choose to run for President in 1928."

June 26   The **Democratic Party** met at Houston and nominated governor **Alfred E. Smith** of New York for President and Senator **Joseph T. Robinson** (Ark.) for Vice President. To please the rural wing of the party the convention promised to enforce prohibition, but urban "Al" Smith said that he would work for repeal of prohibition. During the campaign critics attacked Smith as a "wet" (opponent of Prohibition), a Catholic (the first to run for President), a Tammany member, and the son of an immigrant.

Nov. 6   **Presidential election:** on Oct. 22 Hoover delivered his "rugged individualism" speech in which he denounced socialism and described free competition as the American way. In the election, **Hoover** won with 21,-391,993 votes (444 electoral); **Smith** received 15,016,169, votes (87 electoral). **Norman Thomas,** who was the Socialist candidate for President, 1928–48, received 267,835 votes. Although observers first said that Smith's **Catholicism** had hurt him, closer analysis revealed that a Protestant Democrat would probably have done no better than Smith. While Hoover did break the Democratic stranglehold on the "solid South," Smith diverted 122 northern counties from the Republican to the Democratic Party and had a slight majority of the total vote of the 12 largest cities. Democrats had laid the basis for their urban party of the 1930's. In the same election, **Franklin D. Roosevelt** was elected governor of New York.

1929

Apr. 15–June 15 President Hoover called a special session of Congress on Apr. 15 to deal with the **problem of farm relief.** Though wholesale farm prices had climbed from an index of 99 in 1923 to 106 in 1928, the economic power of farmers lagged behind the rest of the economy.

Apr. 25–June 13 The Senate passed a bill embracing the **export debenture plan,** according to which the federal government would pay the farmer a bounty for exporting his surplus crop. The government would make the payments in the form of debentures that could be used by importers to pay customs duties, thereby using receipts from the protective tariff to help the farmer. The House refused to pass the bill.

June 15 Hoover's **Agricultural Marketing Act** established a **Federal Farm Board** to stimulate the marketing of farm products by loans to cooperatives. The board was also to establish **stabilization corporations** to buy up surplus crops. The cotton, wheat, and other stabilization corporations set up by the board were unable to stem the decline in prices that followed the stock market crash of 1929.

Republican Diplomacy, 1921–1931

It is not accurate to call American foreign policy in the 1920's "isolationist." While politically the United States stood aloof from international organizations (particularly the League of Nations), economically the United States became more and more involved overseas. Whereas foreign investments in the United States were some $4 billion more than American investments abroad in 1914, by 1919 it was the other way around (not counting loans by the United States government), and by 1930 the gap was over $8 billion. The United States sought world markets and economic stability.

1921

Nov. 12–Feb. 6, 1922 After World War I the United States, Japan, and Great Britain stood on the verge of a naval arms race that none of them wanted. In addition the United States sought ways to protect American interests in the Pacific. Pressed by the British and by disarmament advocates at home such as **William E. Borah,** President Harding called a **WASHINGTON CONFERENCE** on disarmament and Pacific affairs. Secretary of State **Charles Evans Hughes,** who was chairman of the conference, startled the delegates the first day by proposing a drastic scrapping of ships already built or in construction. On Dec. 13 the United States, Japan, Great Britain, and France signed the **Four-Power Pact,** by which they agreed to respect each others' insular possessions in the Pacific. On Feb. 6, 1922, the **Nine-Power Treaty,** signed by the big four plus Italy, the Netherlands, Belgium, Portugal, and China, guaranteed China's territorial integrity and the open door policy. The **Five-Power Treaty,** signed on Feb. 6 by the big four plus Italy, set tonnage quotas for battleships after replacements as follows: United States and Great Britain, 525 thousand tons each; Japan, 315 thousand tons; France and Italy, 175 thousand tons each. The treaty also set a quota for aircraft carriers but not for other ships. A special clause of the treaty restrained the United States, Great Britain, and Japan from enlarging existing **naval bases** or creating new ones in most of their island possessions in the Pacific. In other agreements the Japanese agreed to evacuate Siberia, to return Kiaochow Bay and the Shantung Peninsula to China, and to confirm American cable rights on Yap Island. By these treaties the United States gave up a two-ocean navy but helped stabilize the Pacific and East Asia for a decade.

1922

Feb. 9–May 3, 1926   Congress established the **World War Foreign Debt Commission** on Feb. 9, 1922, to negotiate with the nations that owed the United States over $10 billion in **war debts**. In spite of the fact that the debtor nations had spent most of the money in the United States and had suffered grievously in the war, the United States insisted on repayment. Between 1923 and 1926 the Commission arranged 62-year agreements with the debtor nations by which they agreed to pay over $22 billion in principal and interest. But as the European financial situation worsened, the Commission slashed the interest rates (1925–26), canceling from 20 per cent to 80 per cent of the debts.

1923

Jan. 11–June 7, 1929   In 1921 the Allied Reparations Commission set the **German reparations** debt to the Allies at $32 billion. When the Germans were unable to pay, France and Belgium occupied the industrial Ruhr Valley (Jan. 11, 1923) but collected nothing when the German mark became worthless. An American commission headed by **Charles G. Dawes** drew up the **Dawes Plan** (Apr. 9, 1924) calling for a private loan of $200 million to enable the Germans to start reparations payments. On June 7, 1929, the **Young Plan** (drawn up by **Owen D. Young** of the United States) reduced German reparations to $8 billion and called for further reduction if the United States reduced war debts.

1924–34   Debts and Reparations: private American loans to Germany enabled her to pay part of the reparations bill, which in turn brought about $2 billion in debt repayment to the United States. The Depression after 1929 prompted President Hoover to arrange a one-year debt moratorium (Dec., 1931). At Lausanne, Switzerland, on June 16, 1932, the Allies lowered German reparations to less than $1 billion, provided the United States would revise the war debts downward. When the United States took no action, every nation except Finland defaulted on its debts (June 15, 1934).

1924–29   The United States and the League of Nations: though not a member of the League, the United States in 1924 began to send delegates and observors to special League conferences on topics such as opium, trade restrictions, and communications.

1925

Mar. 3–Jan. 29, 1935   When the League of Nations set up the Permanent Court of International Justice, known as the **WORLD COURT,** American jurists such as Elihu Root sat on the Court. On Mar. 3, 1925, the House passed a resolution urging American participation. The Senate on Jan. 27, 1926, voted to join but attached reservations, one of which the Court would not accept. In 1930 President Hoover submitted a formula for American adherence worked out by **Elihu Root** and the Court, but irreconcilables in the Senate postponed consideration until 1935. When President Roosevelt finally came out in favor of joining the Court (1935), Senator **Huey P. Long** (La.) and the Hearst newspapers succeeded in defeating the plan.

1926

May–Jan. 2, 1933   After removing all marines from **Nicaragua** in 1925, the United States sent them back in May, 1926, after a bloody revolution broke out there. President Coolidge also sent **Henry L. Stimson** as his personal representative and within a month (Apr.–May, 1927) Stimson persuaded both sides to lay down their arms. The last marines left on Jan. 2, 1933.

1927

Jan. 1–Dec. 25   In **Mexico,** a law limiting foreign concessions to 50 years went into effect on Jan. 1, thus threatening American oil rights. When President Coolidge appointed banker **Dwight W. Morrow** to negotiate with Mexico, Morrow got quick results. In Nov. and Dec. the Mexican Supreme Court and Congress guaranteed that American companies that had begun to work their property before 1917 (when a new Mexican constitution went into effect) might retain ownership.

Apr. 6–Aug. 27, 1928   **Kellogg-Briand Peace Pact:** French Foreign Minister **Aristide Briand** on Apr. 6 proposed a bilateral treaty with the United States calling for the "outlawry of war." Spurred on by Senator Borah, the National Grange and others, Secretary of State **Frank B. Kellogg** replied with a multilateral treaty that **outlawed war** as "an instrument of national policy" but did permit defensive war. Fifteen powers signed the **Pact of Paris** on Aug. 27, 1928, and eventually 62 nations signed. Secretaries of State Kellogg and Henry Stimson followed this up by negotiating bilateral **arbitration treaties** with various nations, 1928–31.

June 20–1934   Disarmament: the **Geneva Conference** (June 20–Aug. 4) failed to bring about naval restrictions. At the **London Naval Conference** (Jan. 21–Apr. 22, 1930) the United States, Great Britain, and Japan agreed to limit cruiser and submarine construction. The **World Disarmament Conference** at Geneva (Feb. 2, 1932–34) rejected American proposals for the abolition of offensive weapons.

1928

Dec. 17–Feb. 6, 1931   Latin American Conciliation: J. Reuben Clark of the State Department drafted a **memorandum** on Dec. 17, 1928, that did not renounce intervention in Latin America but did separate intervention from the Monroe Doctrine. The Hoover administration published the memorandum in Mar., 1930. President-elect **Herbert Hoover** took a **goodwill tour** of Latin America (Nov. 19, 1928–Jan. 6, 1929). Secretary of State **Henry L. Stimson** further promoted goodwill when he announced (Feb. 6, 1931) that the United States had abandoned Wilson's use of moral standards as a test for recognition in Latin America.

Leading Figures of the Period

HENRY FORD (Dearborn, Mich., 1863–1947), industrialist.
1879   Moved to Detroit.
1879–84   Machine shop apprentice and repair man.
1887   Chief engineer of the Edison Company, Detroit.
1893   Tested his first automobile.
1903   Organized the Ford Motor Company.
1909   Produced the first Model-T automobile.
1911   Won a lawsuit which freed him from the George B. Selden Patents.
1913   Introduced his successful assembly-line system of manufacturing.
1914   Introduced the eight-hour day and the $5 daily wage for workers in his manufacturing plants.

1915–16   Took his "Peace Ship" to Europe.
1918   Was defeated in an election for the United States Senate.
1919   His son Edsel succeeded him as president of Ford Motor Company.
1936   With his son Edsel, established the Ford Foundation.

OLIVER WENDELL HOLMES, JR. (Boston, 1841–Washington, D.C., 1935), Supreme Court Justice, son of Oliver Wendell Holmes, the poet.
1861   Was graduated from Harvard.
1861–64   Served in the Civil War.
1866   Was graduated from Harvard Law School.
1867   Was admitted to the bar in Boston.

1881 Published *The Common Law.*

1882 Professor of Law at the Harvard Law School.

1882–1902 Served on the Massachusetts Supreme Judicial Court; Chief Justice, 1899–1902.

1902–32 United States Supreme Court Justice.

1904 Voted against the government in the Northern Securities Case.

1905 Dissented in *Lochner v. New York.*

1918 Dissented in *Hammer v. Dagenhart.*

1919 Introduced the "clear and present danger" doctrine in *Schenck v. the United States.*

CHARLES EVANS HUGHES (Glens Falls, N.Y., 1862–Osterville, Mass., 1948), Chief Justice of the United States Supreme Court.

1881 Was graduated from Brown University.

1884 Was graduated from Columbia Law School.

1884 Started law practice in New York City.

1905–06 Counsel for the commissions investigating public utilities and insurance companies in New York State.

1906–10 Reform governor of New York State (Republican).

1910–16 Justice of the United States Supreme Court.

1916 Resigned from the Supreme Court to be the unsuccessful Republican candidate for President.

1921–25 Secretary of State; presided at the Washington Conference.

1926–30 Member of the Permanent Court of Arbitration, the Hague.

1928–30 Judge on the Permanent Court of International Justice (World Court).

1930–41 Chief Justice of the United States Supreme Court, where his position was midway between conservative and liberal.

1935 Gave the unanimous opinion in the Schechter Case declaring the NIRA unconstitutional.

1937 Opposed President Roosevelt's court reorganization plan.

WILLIAM JAMES (New York City, 1842–Chocorua, N.H., 1910), philosopher.

1860 Worked in the studio of the painter William Morris Hunt.

1861 Entered Lawrence Scientific School, Harvard.

1864–69 Attended Harvard Medical School.

1865–66 Took part in a zoological expedition to the Amazon Valley.

1867–70 Suffered ill-health and doubts about his future.

1872 Became an instructor in physiology at Harvard.

1876 Established the first psychology laboratory in America.

1878–90 Wrote his *Principles of Psychology.*

1880–1907 Taught philosophy and psychology at Harvard, where he was a professor 1885–1907.

1897 In *The Will to Believe and Other Essays,* he introduced his ideas of freedom of will and empiricism.

1907 Published his *Pragmatism,* in which he defined truth as something that "worked."

1909 Defended his philosophy of pragmatism in *The Meaning of Truth* and *A Pluralistic Universe.*

ROBERT M. LA FOLLETTE (Primrose, Wis., 1855–Washington, D.C., 1925), United States Senator and Presidential candidate.

1879 Was graduated from the University of Wisconsin after working his way through school.

1880 Began to practice law at Madison, Wis.

1885–91 United States Congressman.

1891 Broke with conservative United States Senator Philetus Sawyer, state Republican leader.

1901–05 Governor of Wisconsin; put his "Wisconsin Idea" reform program into operation.

1906–25 United States Senator.

1909 Led the insurgents opposing the Payne-Aldrich Tariff.

1911–12 Campaigned for the Progressive nomination for President but lost to Theodore Roosevelt.

1917 Voted against war with Germany.

1919 One of the "irreconcilables" who opposed the League of Nations.

1924 Unsuccessful Progressive candidate for President.

HENRY CABOT LODGE (Boston, 1850–Cambridge, Mass., 1924), United States Senator.

1871 Was graduated from Harvard.

1874 Was graduated from Harvard Law School.

1876 Received the first Ph.D. degree in political science from Harvard.

1880–86 Active in Massachusetts politics.

1882–88 Wrote biographies of Hamilton, Webster, and Washington.

1886 Was elected to the United States House of Representatives, where he supported civil service reform; served in the House until 1893.

1890 Helped draft the Sherman Antitrust Act.

1893 Was elected United States Senator from Massachusetts and served until his death; supported tariff protection and opposed reform bills.

1898–99 A strong imperialist, he joined Theodore Roosevelt in supporting the war against Spain and the acquisition of the Philippines.

1903 Assisted Roosevelt in the Panama episode.

1919–20 As Chairman of the Senate Committee on Foreign Relations, he blocked American entrance into the League of Nations.

1917–19 Opposed the prohibition and women's suffrage amendments.

THEODORE ROOSEVELT (New York City, 1858–Oyster Bay, N.Y., 1919), 26th President of the United States.

1880 Was graduated from Harvard.

1882–84 Served in the New York State Assembly.

1882–89 Wrote *The Naval War of 1812, Thomas Hart Benton,* and *The Winning of The West.*

1886 Unsuccessful candidate for mayor of New York City.

1889–95 United States Civil Service Commissioner.

1895–97 President of board of New York City police commissioners.

1897–98 Assistant Secretary of the Navy; sent the order for Commodore Dewey to proceed to Manila Bay; supported imperialism.

1898 Served as lieutenant colonel in the Rough Riders in the Spanish-American War.

1899–1900 Reform governor of New York.

1900 Was elected Vice President of the United States.

1901 Became President upon the assassination of President McKinley; served until 1909.

1908 Secured the nomination of William Howard Taft for President.

1909–10 Traveled to Africa and Europe.

1911–12 Split with Taft and ran for President on the Progressive ticket.

1915–17 Urged military preparedness and war with Germany.

WILLIAM HOWARD TAFT (Cincinnati, 1857–Washington, D.C., 1930), 27th President of the United States and Chief Justice of the United States Supreme Court.

1878 Was graduated from Yale.

1880 Was graduated from Cincinnati Law School; began to practice law in Cincinnati.

1887–90 Superior Court Justice in Ohio.

1890–92 United States solicitor-general.

1892–1900 Federal circuit court judge.

1900–04 President of the Philippine Commission and then governor of the islands.

1904–08 Secretary of War.

1909–13 President of the United States; unsuccessful candidate for reelection.

1913–21 Professor of Law at Yale Law School.

1921–30 Chief Justice of the United States Supreme Court.

1923 Dissented in the Adkins Case.

(THOMAS) WOODROW WILSON (Staunton, Va., 1856–Washington, D.C., 1924), 28th President of the United States.

1873 Entered Davidson College.

1879 Was graduated from the College of New Jersey (Princeton).

1879–80 Studied law at the University of Virginia.

1882 Started law practice in Atlanta.

1883 Entered Johns Hopkins University, where he wrote *Congressional Government* (1885) and earned a Ph.D. degree in history.

1885–90 Taught history at Bryn Mawr College (Pa.) and Wesleyan University (Conn).

1890–1902 Taught jurisprudence and political economy at Princeton University.

1902–10 President of Princeton. Resigned when his graduate school plans were defeated.

1911–13 Governor of New Jersey.

1913–21 President of the United States.

1919 Suffered a stroke from which he never fully recovered.

DEPRESSION, NEW DEAL, AND WORLD WAR II, 1929–1945

PART 8

The Depression and the New Deal, 1929–1940

Hoover and the Depression

Economic Statistics

	1920	1929	1933	1939
Population (millions)	106	122	126	131
Gross national product (billions of dollars, 1929 prices)	73	104	74	111
Per capita GNP (dollars, 1929 prices)	688	857	590	847
Federal government receipts (billions of dollars)	6.7	4.0	2.0	5.0
Federal government expenditures (billions of dollars)	6.4	3.3	4.6	8.9
National debt (billions of dollars)	24.3	17.0	22.5	40.4
Exports of United States merchandise (billions of dollars)	4.4[a]	5.2	1.6	3.1
General imports (billions of dollars)	2.5[a]	4.4	1.5	2.3
Wholesale commodity prices (1926=100)	154	95	66	77
Farm products price index (1926=100)	151	105	51	65
Wheat price per bushel (price in dollars received by farmers)	1.83	1.04	0.38[b]	0.69
Realized gross farm income (billions of dollars)	15.9	13.9	7.1	10.6
Average weekly earnings for production workers in manufacturing (in dollars)	26.30	25.03	16.73	23.86
Unemployed (millions, followed by per cent of labor force)	1.7 (4)	1.6 (3)	12.8 (25)	9.5 (17)
Index of prices of common stocks (1941–43=100)	80	260	90	121
Volume of sales on the New York Stock Exchange (millions of shares)	227	1,125	655	262
Bank suspensions	168	659	4,004	72[c]

[a] 1921   [b] 1932   [c] banks closed because of financial difficulties

The above statistics give a partial picture of the economic changes in the U.S. between 1920 and the stock market crash in 1929. The 1920's were prosperous: real per capita income in 1929 dollars rose from $543 in 1919 to $716 in 1929. But the "real" economy was not healthy, 1927–29. The GNP increased little between 1926 and 1927; after 1927 residential construction declined, and automobile production grew at a much slower rate. The capital invested in manufacturing grew far more rapidly in the 1920's than the capacity of the public to buy; in the same period, farm income declined. The productivity of industrial workers rose 43 per cent, 1919–29, but real wages rose only 26 per cent. The unequal distribution of wealth, which grew worse in the 1920's, led to a shortage of consumer purchasing power, and inventories rose. Corporate profits, meanwhile, shot up 60 per cent (1919–29), and many of the profits were reinvested in the stock market. Prices of common stock skyrocketed from an index of 80 (1920) to 260 (1929). The bull market got underway in 1924 when the index was 91, rose to 125 by 1927, and then roared onward to 260 in 1929. Investors operated on margin and were deeply in debt. The American banking system was unsound as 1929 approached. Over 5,000 banks closed their doors from 1921–28, and banks speculated too freely on the stock market. By 1929 a speculative bubble was ready to burst.

1929

The **STOCK MARKET CRASH** started when the market began to drop after Labor Day, 1929, with the heaviest selling on "**Black Thursday**," Oct. 24, and on Monday and Tuesday, Oct. 28–29. Two weeks after Black Thursday the average price of all common stocks was off 40 per cent. Between 1929 and 1932 General Motors dropped in price from 73 to 8 and United States Steel from 262 to 22; the general average was down 90 per cent.

1929–33 The **GREAT DEPRESSION** was a direct result of the market crash that turned the unhealthy economy of 1927–29 into the worst depression in American history, one that spread to all areas of American life. Bank failures, unemployment, and reduced prices all combined to create a desperate financial situation for the nation.

1930

The Gross National Product dropped from $104 billion to $59 billion in 1929–32, and Hoover took a number of steps to get the

country out of the financial depression. He used the stabilization corporations authorized by the Agricultural Marketing Act to try to raise farm prices, but they had far too little money to succeed. He urged businessmen to keep wages up, but they were unable to comply. Since he was unwilling to have the federal government bear the responsibility for relief, he appointed a committee to encourage local relief, but this was ineffective. His other efforts were also inadequate, though several foreshadowed the New Deal.

June 17   Hawley-Smoot Tariff raised rates above those of the Fordney-McCumber Tariff in spite of the opposition of economists who argued that high tariffs would sharply reduce American trade.

Nov. 4 Democrats gained 8 seats in the Senate and 53 seats in the House, where they secured a majority.

Dec. 20 Congress authorized the expenditure of over $100 million for **public works relief** after a request from President Hoover.

1931

Mar. 3 Hoover vetoed Senator Norris's bill for a federal public works project at Muscle Shoals on the Tennessee River. The administration, however, did start work on Hoover Dam on the Colorado River in 1931 (completed 1936).

1932

Jan. 22   Reconstruction Finance Corporation (RFC) was established to provide loans for banks, railroads, and insurance companies. Under **Charles G. Dawes**, RFC loaned $1.2 billion in its first six months of operation.

Feb. 27   Glass-Steagall Act made it easier for federal reserve banks to rediscount commercial paper and made $750 million in government gold available for business loans.

Mar. 23   Norris-LaGuardia Act, sponsored by Senator **Norris** and Congressman **Fiorello H. La Guardia** (N.Y.), forbade the use of injunctions to prevent strikes, boycotts, and picketing.

May–July In 1931 Congressman **Wright Patman** (Tex.) proposed a bill to pay the balance of the veterans' bonus with paper money, but Hoover opposed it as inflationary. Veterans on the West Coast organized a **BONUS ARMY,** and 15,000 members were in Washington by mid-June to demand payment. Congress rejected the bill on June 17. By mid-July about 2,000 veterans still remained in the city, and a small riot developed when the government tried to clear them out of abandoned buildings. President Hoover then called on Gen. **Douglas MacArthur,** who used tanks, cavalry, and bayonets to burn the veterans' shack town and send them out of the city.

June 14   The **Republican Party** met at Chicago and renominated President **Hoover** and Vice President **Curtis** on a platform calling for economy, a balanced budget, and the protective tariff.

June 27   The **Democratic Convention** met at Chicago and nominated governor **Franklin D. Roosevelt** of New York for President and Congressman **John Nance Garner** (Tex.) for Vice President. In his acceptance speech, Roosevelt pledged himself to a **"new deal** for the American people." The Democratic platform called for economy and a balanced budget, but it demanded a lower tariff and repeal of prohibition, as well as state unemployment and old-age insurance programs. The platform also asked for measures to aid the farmer and to control banks and the stock market.

July 21   **Relief and Construction Act** enabled the RFC to provide loans for local public works and to lend money to states for relief programs. Hoover had vetoed a **Wagner-Garner bill** to use federal employment agencies in states that had none and had blocked a **LaFollette-Costigan bill** to grant money to the states for relief.

July 22   **Federal Home-Loan Bank Act** established eight to twelve home-loan banks to rediscount home mortgages held by savings banks and insurance companies.

Summer–Fall   **Presidential campaign:** Franklin D. Roosevelt surrounded himself with advisers including **Louis Howe, James A. Farley,** his campaign manager, and **Rexford G. Tugwell, Raymond Moley,** and **Adolph A. Berle,** his so-called **"brain trust."**

In San Francisco on Sept. 23 he outlined a program to regulate business but at Pittsburgh on Oct. 19 he condemned Hoover's "reckless" spending and promised to balance the budget unless "starvation and dire need" made large appropriations necessary.

Nov. 8   **Presidential election: Roosevelt** won with 22,809,638 votes (472 electoral) to 15,758,901 (59 electoral) for **Hoover.** In spite of the desperate economic crisis, **Norman Thomas,** the Socialist candidate, received only 881,951 votes, and **William Z. Foster** of the Communist Party received only 102,785.

1933

Feb. 6   **20th Amendment,** which ended the "lame duck" session of Congress, went into effect. The amendment provided that Congress would convene each year on Jan. 3 and that the President would take office on Jan. 20 following the election.

Feb. 15   **Giuseppe Zangara** attempted to shoot President **Roosevelt** in Miami, Fla. He missed the President-elect but wounded several others and killed Mayor **Anton Cermak** of Chicago.

Feb. 20   Congress passed the **21st Amendment** repealing Prohibition. It was ratified Dec. 5, 1933.

Mar. 4   **BANKING CRISIS:** economic conditions reached an all-time low in the months between the election and the inauguration of the new President. More than 5,000 banks suspended operations in 1930–32, and hoarding and runs on banks became frequent. By Mar. 4, 24 states had declared bank holidays, and almost every bank in the nation was closed or restricted.

The First New Deal

1933

Mar. 4   In his **Inaugural Address** President Roosevelt said that "the only thing we have to fear is fear itself" and promised that he would use "broad Executive power" if necessary to combat the emergency.

Mar. 5 To meet the financial crisis, the President ordered a four-day **bank holiday** and stopped all transactions in gold and silver. At the same time, he called a special session of Congress for Mar. 9 to deal with the banking crisis. This session—the first "hundred days" of the new Administration—passed laws affecting all aspects of economic life and established the basis of the first New Deal.

Mar. 9 **EMERGENCY BANKING ACT,** which passed Congress in one day, approved Roosevelt's order of Mar. 5, arranged for the reopening of sound banks under licenses from the Treasury Department, and gave the President broad powers over money and banking. Most banks soon reopened. On Apr. 19, the President officially took the United States **off the gold standard** by forbidding gold exports.

Mar. 20 **Economy Act** called for federal salary and pension reductions in order to balance the budget.

Mar. 22 By the **Beer and Wine Revenue Act,** Congress amended the Volstead Act to legalize beer, wine, and other beverages up to 3.2 per cent alcoholic content.

Relief Measures

Mar. 31 **UNEMPLOYMENT RELIEF ACT** created the Civilian Conservation Corps **(CCC)** to provide work for men aged 18–25 in reforestation, road-building, and soil-erosion control. By 1935, 500,000 young men were living at camps and receiving wages of $30 a month, part of which was sent home.

May 12 Federal Emergency Relief Act created the **Federal Emergency Relief Administration (FERA)** under **Harry L. Hopkins** to provide outright grants to states and cities.

May 12 **AGRICULTURAL ADJUSTMENT ACT** established the **Agricultural Adjustment Administration (AAA)** to restore the farmers' purchasing power to parity with the period 1909–14. In return for reducing their acreage or crops, farmers were to receive benefit payments paid by a **processing tax** levied on the processor. The act also called for refinancing of farm mortgages through the federal land banks. The **Thomas**

Amendment allowed the President to inflate the currency by coining silver, issuing paper money, or devaluing the dollar. The **Jones-Connally Farm Relief Act** and the **Jones-Costigan Sugar Act** (Apr. 7–May 9, 1934) extended the list of crops subject to the AAA.

May 18 **TENNESSEE VALLEY AUTHORITY ACT** created the **Tennessee Valley Authority (TVA)** to construct dams and power plants to develop the Tennessee Valley region, including parts of Tennessee, North Carolina, Kentucky, Virginia, Mississippi, Alabama, and Georgia. TVA produced and sold electricity, developed a flood control program, attacked the problem of malaria, and generally raised the standard of living in the valley. TVA **electricity rates** served as a yardstick for private power companies and helped reduce the cost of electricity in the next few years. The act was a victory for Senator **George W. Norris,** who had tried in vain to get such a project at Muscle Shoals under Coolidge and Hoover.

Financial Measures

May 27 **Federal Securities Act** required that corporations register all new issues of securities with the Federal Trade Commission in order to provide investors with relevant information.

June 5 **Gold Repeal Joint Resolution** of Congress cancelled the gold-payment clause in all federal and private contracts.

June 12–July 27 The **International Monetary and Economic Conference** at London failed to reach an agreement when the United States refused to cooperate in currency stabilization. In his instructions to his delegation (July 2) President Roosevelt committed the United States to economic nationalism.

June 13 **Home Owners Refinancing Act** created the **Home Owners Loan Corporation (HOLC)** to issue bonds to refinance non-farm home mortgages. HOLC eventually refinanced 20 per cent of all mortgaged urban private dwellings in the United States.

June 16 **GLASS-STEAGALL BANKING ACT** separated commercial from investment banking, expanded the power of the Federal

Reserve Board to enable it to stop speculation, and created the **Federal Deposit Insurance Corporation (FDIC)** to insure bank deposits up to $5,000.

June 16 **Farm Credit Act** authorized the **Farm Credit Administration (FCA)** to extend credits to refinance farm mortgages.

Industrial Regulation

June 16 The **Emergency Railroad Transportation Act** placed railroad holding companies under the Interstate Commerce Commission and created the post of Federal Coordinator of Transportation **(Joseph B. Eastman)** to render the railroads more efficient.

June 16 **NATIONAL INDUSTRIAL RECOVERY ACT (NIRA)** established the **National Recovery Administration (NRA)** to supervise a program of industrial self-regulation. The act empowered industrial and trade associations to draw up **fair competition codes**, which were enforceable by law and were not liable to antitrust prosecution. The President was to approve such codes or draw up codes of his own. The codes were to be similar to those drawn up during World War I and to those encouraged by Herbert Hoover and the Department of Commerce in the 1920's. The purpose of the Act was to stimulate production and put people back to work. **Section 7a** guaranteed labor the right to **collective bargaining**. The Act also created the **Public Works Administration** (PWA) under Secretary of the Interior **Harold L. Ickes** for constructing roads, buildings, and a variety of other projects in order to reduce unemployment. NRA was ultimately unpopular and not very successful. Its administrator, Gen. **Hugh S. Johnson,** irritated many, and a review board headed by lawyer **Clarence S. Darrow** reported that big business used the codes to dominate labor and small business. Nonetheless, by limiting hours of work, it did give jobs to 2 million and contributed to the 1933 "boomlet."

June 16 Congress adjourned. During the first hundred days **President Roosevelt** had established himself as a strong leader, while his radio "**fireside chats**" (the first on Mar.

12) and frequent **press conferences** were intended to bring him close to the people.

Devaluing the Dollar

Oct. 25–Jan. 31, 1934 The Administration began to buy up gold at increasing prices in order to reduce the value of the dollar and raise farm prices. The President hoped to achieve a **commodity dollar**— with a constant buying power for all commodities—by manipulating its gold content. When gold buying proved ineffective, Congress on Jan. 30, 1934, passed the **Gold Reserve Act** to revalue the dollar at 50 per cent to 60 per cent of its original gold content. The next day the President reduced the **gold content of the dollar to 59.06 cents.**

Work Relief

Nov. 8 The President established the **Civil Works Administration (CWA)** with **Harry L. Hopkins** as administrator to create jobs for millions of unemployed. CWA, which spent almost a billion dollars, lasted until Mar., 1934, when it transferred its functions to FERA. On Feb. 15, 1934, Congress passed the **Civil Works Emergency Relief Act** providing funds for civil works and relief under the FERA. The program, which became the **WPA** in 1935, had 2,500,000 unemployed at work by Jan., 1935.

1934

June 6 **SECURITIES EXCHANGE ACT** created the **Securities Exchange Commission (SEC)** to regulate securities exchanges. The act also gave the Federal Reserve Board power to regulate margin requirements in trading securities.

June 12 The **Reciprocal Trade Agreements Act** authorized the President to negotiate with other nations agreements raising or reducing tariffs up to 50 per cent without the consent of Congress. By 1951 agreements had been reached with 53 nations.

June 19 **Communications Act** established the **Federal Communications Commission (FCC)** to regulate interstate and foreign communication by telegraph, cable, and radio.

June 19   Silver Purchase Act authorized the President to increase the Treasury's silver holdings until they reached one-fourth of the Treasury's monetary reserve. The act was in response to the demands of the inflationists and the silver bloc.

June 28   Frazier-Lemke Federal Farm Bankruptcy Act provided for a five-year moratorium on foreclosures during which time the farmer could buy back his farm at a new appraised price. When declared unconstitutional in 1935, it was replaced by the **second Frazier-Lemke Act** (Aug. 29, 1935), which called for a three-year moratorium but only with a court order.

June 28   National Housing Act set up the **Federal Housing Administration (FHA)** to insure loans to repair homes or build new ones.

Nov. 6   In Congressional elections, the Democrats gained nine seats in both the House and Senate.

Winter   After a boomlet in the spring of 1933, the economy turned down again in the fall. (The *New York Times* weekly business index was 60 in March, 99 in June, and 72 in October.) **Recovery** was brisk in the **spring of 1934** (the index rose to 86 in May), but there was little gain during the rest of the year. National income in 1934 was one-quarter higher than in 1933, and unemployment dropped 2 million, but conditions were still far worse than in 1931.

The Second New Deal, 1935–1936

The Radical Left   Throughout the land radical voices demanded extreme solutions for the nation's ills. Gov. **Floyd Olson** of Minnesota asked the government to take over key industries. Senator **Huey P. Long** of Louisiana ("The Kingfish") called for a **"Share Our Wealth" program** in which the government would confiscate all personal fortunes above a certain amount and distribute them to those in need. Father **Charles E. Coughlin** of Michigan, whose radio program had millions of listeners, demanded inflation based on silver

purchases. Dr. **Francis E. Townsend** of California publicized a plan whereby the government would pay every citizen over the age of 60 a monthly pension of $200 to be spent in the U.S. within a month. In 1934 a series of **violent strikes** took place. Taxi drivers in New York and Philadelphia, Communist-led farmers in California, copper miners in Butte, Mont., truck drivers in Minneapolis, stevedores in San Francisco, and textile workers in 20 states all struck without conspicuous success.

1935

Jan. 4   Social reform and Keynesian Economics: in his annual message **President Roosevelt** proposed a **broad program of social reform,** which marked the start of the **second New Deal,** with more emphasis on reform to help workers and farmers and less emphasis on business recovery. Some New Dealers urged the administration to adopt the countercyclical spending theories of the British economist **John Maynard Keynes.** Keynes argued that during depressions the federal budget should show a deficit of taxes over expenditures in order to stimulate the economy. When inflation returned, the government should then increase taxes over expenditures. The Administration did not follow Keynesian theories, but between 1933 and 1938 the national debt rose from $23 billion to $37 billion.

Work Relief

Apr. 8   EMERGENCY RELIEF APPROPRIATION ACT authorized the expenditure of $5 billion for a works program for the unemployed. The act was on a much larger scale than previous relief acts and marked a shift from direct relief to works programs. The **Works Progress Administration (WPA)** under **Harry L. Hopkins,** which ran most of the program, employed three million of the ten million jobless within the first year and over eight million by 1943, when it came to an end. WPA, which spent $11 billion, built thousands of buildings, roads, and bridges and established imaginative programs such as the **Federal Theater Project,** the **Federal Writers' Project,**

and the **Federal Art Project**. The **National Youth Administration (NYA)** aided over four million unemployed youths, some of them in college. Critics attacked WPA for waste and inefficiency, but it added greatly to the national purchasing power and preserved the skills and dignity of millions.

Farm Legislation

May 1–11   The **Resettlement Administration (RA)**, established May 1 under the Emergency Relief Appropriation Act with **Rexford G. Tugwell** as administrator, was authorized to resettle poverty-stricken urban and rural families and also had the power to loan money to small farmers to buy land. The RA built suburban communities for lower-middle-class city dwellers—such as Greenbelt, near Washington, D.C., and Greendale, near Milwaukee. The **Rural Electrification Administration (REA)**, established May 11 under the ERA Act, lent money to build electrical plants in areas that had no electricity. The Act revolutionized rural life. In 1935 only one farm in 10 had electricity; by 1941 it was 4 in 10, and by 1950 9 in 10.

July 5   NATIONAL LABOR RELATIONS ACT (Wagner-Connery Act) replaced section 7a of the NIRA, when the Supreme Court declared that act unconstitutional. Sponsored by Senator **Robert F. Wagner** (N.Y.) but not supported by the President, the Act required management to **deal collectively** with labor unions, while forbidding it to interfere with unions. In addition, it allowed the **closed shop** and created the **National Labor Relations Board** to judge claims of unfair labor practices.

Aug. 14   SOCIAL SECURITY ACT created a federal system of **old-age and survivors' insurance** in which employer and employee paid equal amounts (at first 1 per cent of salary but by 1967 3.9 per cent). From the fund collected the government would pay those retiring at age 65 a monthly pension ranging up to a maximum of $75 ($168 in 1967). The act also provided grants to states to help pay for pensions to the needy over the age of 65 who did not come under the federal plan. It also set up a federal-state plan of **unemployment insurance** and provided federal funds for the states to **care for dependent mothers, the crippled, the blind, and others**.

Aug. 23   Banking Act, drawn up by Federal Reserve Board Governor **Marriner S. Eccles** but partly rewritten by Senator **Carter Glass,** was a substantial revision of the Federal Reserve Act of 1913. The Act changed the Federal Reserve Board to a seven-man **Board of Governors**. The new board would have greater powers over the 12 regional banks and greater control of rediscount rates, reserve requirements, and open-market purchase of government bonds. The Act greatly increased federal power over the banking system.

Aug. 28   PUBLIC UTILITY HOLDING COMPANY ACT, supported by Senator **Burton K. Wheeler** (Mont.) and Congressman **Sam Rayburn** (Tex.), was a victory for the policy of trust-regulation advocated by Woodrow Wilson and Louis Brandeis in 1912. The Act empowered the Federal Power Commission to **regulate interstate transmission of electricity** and authorized the Securities and Exchange Commission to **restrict public utilities holding companies to one geographic area**. The New Deal meanwhile had begun many projects to develop public power: TVA, Grand Coulee, and Bonneville Dams on the Columbia River and a massive dam at Fort Peck on the Missouri River in Montana.

Aug. 30   The **Guffey-Snyder Bituminous Coal Stabilization Act** set up a commission to establish rules for the soft-coal industry based on the code drawn up under the NRA.

Aug. 30   The **Revenue Act** increased the maximum surtax on incomes to 75 per cent, raised estate taxes, and levied an excess profits tax. The Revenue Act and the New Deal spending program redistributed wealth to some degree and aroused business resentment.

1936

Jan. 27   A bill calling for immediate **payment of veterans' bonuses** passed Congress over the President's veto.

Feb. 29   Soil Conservation and Domestic Allotment Act (SCADA) continued crop restriction after the Supreme Court on Jan. 6 had declared the AAA unconstitutional. Farmers received payments not for crop control but for soil conservation.

June 9   Republican Convention met in Cleveland and nominated governor **Alfred M. Landon** of Kansas for President and Col. **Frank Knox** (Ill.) for Vice President. The platform accused the President of usurping the powers of Congress, of replacing free enterprise with regulated monopoly, and of violating the Constitution. It pledged to return relief to local agencies and to create a new system of old-age security but did not call for the repeal of New Deal legislation. **Conservative Democrats** such as **Alfred E. Smith** and **John W. Davis,** who had helped form the **Liberty League** in 1934 to oppose the New Deal, backed Landon against Roosevelt.

June 23   The Democratic Convention met at Philadelphia and renominated **President Roosevelt** and Vice President **John Nance Garner** on a platform defending the New Deal.

Aug. 14   The Union Party met at Cleveland and nominated Congressman **William Lemke** (N.D.) for President and **Thomas C. O'Brien** (Mass.) for Vice President. The party was supported by followers of **Father Coughlin, Dr. Townsend,** and **Gerald L. K. Smith** (who had replaced Huey Long as leader of the Share-Our-Wealth Clubs).

Nov. 3   Presidential election: Roosevelt gave up his efforts to represent all classes and lashed out bitterly at "the economic royalists" who opposed him. He had forged an **urban coalition** of Negroes, workers and other ethnic groups, that was the basis of the Democratic Party for the next quarter century. Since he also won the middle-class and farm votes he was able to carry every state but two, the greatest electoral victory since 1820. **Roosevelt** had 27,752,869 votes (523 electoral); **Landon** 16,674,665 (8 electoral); **Lemke** 882,479 votes. The Democratic margin in the Senate was 76–20 and in the House 331–102.

The Supreme Court and the New Deal, 1935–1939

Supreme Court Justices during the New Deal and their terms on the Court were:

Charles Evans Hughes, Chief Justice, 1930–41, moderate
Willis Van Devanter, 1911–37, conservative
James C. McReynolds, 1914–41, conservative
Louis D. Brandeis, 1916–39, liberal
George Sutherland, 1922–38, conservative
Pierce Butler, 1922–39, conservative
Harlan F. Stone, 1925–41, liberal
Owen J. Roberts, 1930–45, moderate
Benjamin N. Cardozo, 1932–38, liberal
Hugo L. Black, 1937– , New Deal
Stanley F. Reed, 1938–57, New Deal
Felix Frankfurter, 1939–62, New Deal
William O. Douglas, 1939– , New Deal

Feb. 18   *Norman v. Baltimore and Ohio Railroad Company* and *Perry v. United States* upheld the constitutionality of the joint resolution of Congress that repealed the gold clause in public and private contracts.

May 27   *Schechter* (Poultry Corporation) *v. United States* **declared the NIRA unconstitutional** by a vote of 9–0 for delegating too much power to the President and for dealing in intrastate commerce.

May 27   *Louisville Joint Stock Land Bank v. Radford* invalidated the first Frazier-Lemke Act.

1936

Jan. 6   *United States v. Butler* declared the **AAA unconstitutional** because the processing tax was not a proper use of the taxing power and because regulation of agriculture was the function of the states. Cardozo, Brandeis, and Stone dissented in the 6–3 decision.

Feb. 17   *Ashwander v. Tennessee Valley Authority* **upheld the right of TVA to build dams and to dispose of surplus power.**

May 18   *Carter v. Carter Coal Company et al.* declared that the Guffey-Snyder Bituminous Coal Act violated the commerce clause and was therefore unconstitutional.

(Cardozo, Brandeis, and Stone dissented in another 6–3 decision.)

1937

Feb. 5–Aug. 26   SUPREME COURT FIGHT: President Roosevelt, angered by the Supreme Court's reversal of part of his New Deal, proposed a bill (Feb. 5) to reorganize the judiciary by adding a new member to the Supreme Court (up to a maximum court of 15) for every justice who did not retire at 70, by adding up to 50 judges to lower courts, and by adopting other changes to speed up court business. Critics attacked the President for trying to **"pack" the Court.** In spite of evidence that his own party was against his plan, Roosevelt went on the attack and warned in a fireside chat (Mar. 9) that the Court might very well prevent the Congress from correcting the economic and social ills of the nation. The **Supreme Court Retirement Act** (Mar. 1) permitting justices to retire at 70 and the announcement by Justice Van Devanter (May 18) that he planned to retire made the need for the change less pressing. When the Court shifted ground and supported a number of New Deal measures (Mar. 29–May 24), the change seemed even less necessary. The death of Senator **Joseph T. Robinson** (Ark.), who was leading the drive to reorganize the Court (July 14), was the final blow. On July 22 the Senate sent the bill to committee, where it died. The **Judicial Procedure Reform Act** (Aug. 26) made changes in the lower courts but added no justices or judges.

Mar. 29   *West Coast Hotel Company v. Parrish* upheld a state of Washington minimum wage law for women, reversing the *Adkins v. Children's Hospital* decision of 1923. The Court denied that such a law deprived a woman of freedom of contract. **Hughes** and **Roberts** joined **Cardozo, Brandeis,** and **Stone** to form a New Deal majority, 5–4.

Apr. 12   *National Labor Relations Board v. Jones and Laughlin Steel Corporation* upheld the National Labor Relations Act by broadening the interpretation of the commerce clause. The same Justices as above supported the 5–4 decision.

May 24   *Steward Machine Company v. Davis* and *Helvering v. Davis* upheld the Social Security Act. By a vote of 5–4, with the same Justices in the majority, the Court permitted the use of the taxing power to provide for pensions.

1937–39   Deaths and retirements enabled President Roosevelt to appoint **Hugo L. Black, Stanley F. Reed, Felix Frankfurter,** and **William O. Douglas** to the Supreme Court.

The End of the New Deal, 1937–1940

1937

Strikes and union growth: the year 1937 was the worst strike year between the stock market crash and the end of World War II. The country lost 28.4 million man-days as industrial unions, encouraged by the Wagner-Connery Act, fought for union recognition, wage increases, and larger memberships. The AFL had been slow in organizing industrial workers; when it did, it ensured that the interests of the craft unions were protected. On Nov. 9, 1935, **John L. Lewis** of the United Mine Workers, **Sidney Hillman** of the garment unions, and others formed the **Committee for Industrial Organization (CIO)** within the AFL to organize industrial workers. In Nov., 1938, the CIO left the AFL and became the **Congress of Industrial Organizations** with Lewis as president.

Jan.   The **United Automobile Workers,** backed by the CIO, staged a **sitdown strike** at the **General Motors** plant at Flint, Mich. (Dec. 30, 1936–Feb. 11, 1937), and won union recognition. The "sit-down" technique, whereby workers sat down in the plant until their demands were met, spread to other industries including steel, textiles, and rubber.

Mar. 2   U.S. Steel surrendered to **John L. Lewis** and his **Steel Workers Organizing Committee (SWOC)** by granting union recognition, increased wages, and a 40-hour week. SWOC organized all the remaining steel companies by 1941.

May 30   Memorial Day Massacre occurred at the **Republic Steel** plant in South Chicago when police attacked pickets and killed 10 strikers.

Dec.   By the end of 1937 SWOC and the United Automobile Workers had each enrolled over 400,000 workers. Total **union membership** in America rose from 4.2 million in 1936 to 8.3 million in 1938—or from 14 per cent of non-agricultural employment to 28 per cent.

June   Recession: economic conditions improved considerably between 1933 and 1937: industrial production and the GNP per capita were back to the 1929 level, and unemployment had declined. The President, concerned about the mounting deficit, cut the WPA rolls and lowered PWA and other spending. These measures, together with higher taxes, almost balanced the budget. But the country suffered a severe recession from the summer of 1937 to the fall of 1938 as industrial production fell back to the 1934 level, unemployment rose, and the GNP per capita dropped. In April, 1938, Roosevelt ordered increases in spending, and conditions were better by 1939.

sponsored by Senator **Robert F. Wagner,** established the **United States Housing Authority** to promote slum clearance and housing projects through long-term loans to local agencies. By 1941, the USHA had promoted projects whose total cost was more than $750 million.

1938

Feb. 16   AGRICULTURAL ADJUSTMENT ACT authorized the Secretary of Agriculture to set **marketing quotas** for export crops on the condition that two-thirds of the farmers in a given area approved the quotas. The **Commodity Credit Corporation** was to lend money to farmers for surplus crops and store the crops until the price went up (the **ever-normal granary principle**) in order to maintain the farmers' purchasing power at the 1909–14 level (the **parity-price principle**). The act was similar to the first AAA, but payments were to be made out of the federal treasury rather than through a processing tax. The Act also set up the **Federal Crop Insurance Corporation (FCIC)** to insure crops. Prices rose under the New Deal farm program, but the farm surplus continued.

	1929	1933	1937	1938	1939
Gross national product per capita (1929 prices)	$857	$590	$846	$794	$847
Unemployment (millions)	1.6	12.8	7.7	10.4	9.5
Budget deficit (billions of dollars) (° surplus)	0.7°	2.6	2.8	1.2	3.9

The above figures indicate the nature of the 1937–38 recession. They also provide means of determining the extent to which the New Deal brought the nation out of the great depression. While production had returned to the 1929 level, unemployment remained a severe national problem.

July 22   Farm Tenant Act established the **Farm Security Administration (FSA)** to reduce tenancy by loans to tenant farmers. FSA took over the Resettlement Administration and began to regulate working conditions of migrant workers.

Sept. 1   The **NATIONAL HOUSING ACT,**

May 27   Conservatives in Congress passed the **Revenue Act of 1938** (without Roosevelt's signature), which reduced the income tax on large corporations.

June 16   A joint Congressional Resolution created the **TEMPORARY NATIONAL ECONOMIC COMMITTEE (TNEC),** made up of representatives from the executive and legislative branches, to investigate monopoly. The committee, chaired by Senator **Joseph C. O'Mahoney** (Wyo.), held hearings Dec. 1, 1938–Apr. 26, 1940, and on Mar. 31, 1941, made **recommendations** that included the following:

1. amendment of the Clayton Act to curb monopolistic practices,
2. restrictions on trade associations,
3. restrictions on mergers, and
4. repeal of the act to allow uniform prices for brand-name articles.

World War II prevented an effective follow-up on the recommendations.

June 24   Food, Drug, and Cosmetic Act required manufacturers to list the ingredients of products on the labels, prohibited misbranding, and forbade false advertising.

June 25   FAIR LABOR STANDARDS ACT established a **minimum wage of 40 cents an hour and a maximum work week of 40 hours** with time-and-a-half for overtime. The act also **forbade child labor.**

Nov. 8   Congressional elections: President Roosevelt took part in Democratic primary campaigns in order to "purge" conservative Democrats who were blocking New Deal legislation. He failed conspicuously to defeat Senators **Walter F. George** (Ga.) and **Millard F. Tydings** (Md.) but did defeat Representative **John J. O'Connor,** (N.Y.). The Democrats suffered their first setback since 1928 by losing 70 seats in the House and 7 in the Senate.

1939

Jan. 4   In his annual message President Roosevelt called particular attention to foreign affairs. The difficulties of 1937–38, culminating in the Congressional elections,

brought about the **end of the New Deal.**

Apr. 3   Administrative Reorganization Act called for regrouping government agencies in the interest of efficiency. By executive order on July 1, Roosevelt set up the **Federal Security Agency,** the **Federal Works Agency,** and the **Federal Loan Agency,** which with the **Executive Office of the President** took control of almost all the major independent agencies.

Aug. 2   Hatch Act forbade holders of federal office below the policy-making level to participate in political campaigns.

1940

June 28   The **Republican Convention,** meeting at Philadelphia, nominated **Wendell L. Willkie,** a corporation lawyer from New York, for President and Senator **Charles L. McNary** (Ore.) for Vice President on a platform attacking the New Deal but not calling for its repeal.

July 15   The **Democratic Convention** met at Chicago, renominated **Roosevelt** for President, and nominated Secretary of Agriculture **Henry A. Wallace** (Iowa) for Vice President. Both parties opposed involvement in the European war.

Nov. 5   Presidential election: Roosevelt became the first person to be elected to more than two Presidential terms when he won with 27,307,819 popular votes (449 electoral) to 22,321,018 (82 electoral) for **Willkie.**

From Isolation to Intervention, 1931–1941

The Good Neighbor Policy in Latin America

1933   In his Inaugural Address (Mar. 4) President Roosevelt dedicated the nation to **"the policy of the good neighbor,"** a policy that was applied increasingly to Latin America.

1933–Aug., 1934   United States Ambassador **Sumner Welles** mediated between rival forces in **Cuba** and helped establish the

regime of **Fulgencio Batista.** The United States **abrogated the Platt Amendment** on May 29, 1934, and Secretary Hull concluded his first **reciprocal trade agreement** with Cuba on Aug. 24, 1934.

1933   The United States signed the **Antiwar Treaty of Non-aggression and Conciliation** of the American states (Apr. 27). At the **Montevideo Conference** (Dec. 3), Secretary of State **Cordell Hull** signed a treaty renouncing the right of intervention in the western hemisphere.

1934 After the last United States **Marines left Haiti** on Aug. 15, no U.S. troops remained in Latin American nations.

1936 The United States signed a treaty (Mar. 2) with **Panama** giving up the right to intervene there.

1936 By the **BUENOS AIRES DECLARATION** of Dec. 23, the American nations including the United States pledged **never to intervene** in each other's affairs and agreed to **consult** when peace was threatened.

1938 By the **LIMA DECLARATION** (Dec. 24), 21 nations including the United States **pledged to defend republican institutions** and to consult whenever their security was endangered. The declaration was aimed at the growing Nazi menace.

1939 The **Declaration of Panama** on Oct. 3 proclaimed a **safety zone** around the Americas south of Canada and warned belligerents to stay out.

1940 The **Act of Havana** (Jul. 30), approved by the American republics including the United States, said that the republics would not allow the transfer of any European possession in the New World to any non-American power.

The United States and Europe, 1931–1941

1933 On Jan. 30, **ADOLF HITLER** became Chancellor of the Weimar Republic of Germany and soon established dictatorship by the **National Socialist (Nazi) Party**. In Italy **BENITO MUSSOLINI** had set up the dictatorship of his **Fascist Party** in 1922. Strong nationalist sentiment and dissatisfaction with the Versailles peace treaty helped bring the two dictators to power.

1933 President Roosevelt granted diplomatic **recognition of the Soviet Union** on Nov. 16 after an exchange of notes in which the Russians promised not to interfere in the domestic affairs of the United States. The expected increase in Russian-American trade did not take place.

1934–35 Strong **ISOLATIONIST SENTIMENT** was apparent in the **Johnson Debt Default Act** (Apr. 13, 1934) that forbade loans to any nation not paying its debt to the United States. On Apr. 19, 1934, the Senate appointed a committee under **Gerald P. Nye** (N.D.) to investigate the sale of munitions. The committee hearings (1934–36) maintained that pressure from munitions makers had forced the United States into World War I. Books such as *Merchants of Death* (published 1933–34) also sought to show the influence of the armament makers.

1935

Mar. 16 **Hitler** violated the disarmament section of the Versailles Treaty by reestablishing **compulsory military training** in Germany.

Aug. 31 The **Neutrality Act of 1935** was the first of several acts designed to prevent the United States from becoming involved in European affairs. The Act (which would expire in six months) authorized the President to proclaim the existence of a state of war, to prohibit the export of arms and munitions to all belligerents, and to forbid U.S. citizens to travel on belligerent vessels except at their own risk.

Oct. 3 When **Italy invaded Ethiopia,** Roosevelt proclaimed the existence of a state of war and imposed an arms embargo. Efforts to extend the embargo to oil and other items failed.

1936

Feb. 29 **Neutrality Act of 1936** extended the act of 1935 until May 1, 1937, adding a loans embargo. The Act also left it to the President to decide when a war actually existed.

Mar. 7 **Hitler** sent troops to occupy the **Rhineland,** further violating the Versailles Treaty.

July 17 **SPANISH CIVIL WAR** broke out when Gen. **Francisco Franco,** a Fascist, revolted against the republican government. By 1939 Franco had established a dictatorship over all of Spain. A number of American liberals went to Spain to fight against Franco, but on Jan. 8, 1937, Congress extended the Neutrality Act of 1936 to cover civil wars.

Oct. 25   Hitler and Mussolini formed the **Rome-Berlin axis**, establishing the alliance of Germany and Italy.

Nov. 25   Germany signed an **anti-comintern pact** with Japan. Italy joined the alliance on Nov. 6, 1937.

1937

May 1   NEUTRALITY ACT OF 1937 was designed to go into effect whenever the President proclaimed the existence of a state of war. It **forbade American citizens to export arms and munitions to a belligerent, to loan money to a belligerent, or to travel on belligerent ships.** A special clause (expiring May 1, 1939) empowered the President to prohibit the export of articles other than arms and munitions unless the buyer paid cash and took the goods away in his own vessels (the **"cash and carry"** plan).

1938

Mar. 12–13   Germany occupied **Austria** in support of a Nazi conspiracy. This *Anschluss* was the first of many aggressive moves by Hitler in Europe.

Sept. 29–30   THE MUNICH CONFERENCE: when **Hitler** demanded German annexation of the parts of **Czechoslovakia** inhabited by Germans, Great Britain, represented by Prime Minister **Neville Chamberlain,** and France agreed to let him have the Sudetenland. Reference to "Munich" has since come to symbolize appeasement.

1939

Mar. 15   **Hitler** annexed the rest of **Czechoslovakia.**

Apr. 7   Italy invaded Albania.

Apr. 15   President Roosevelt asked Hitler and Mussolini for assurances of peace but received little satisfaction.

July 10   The Senate Foreign Relations Committee refused to alter the Neutrality Act of 1937 in spite of President Roosevelt's proposal to extend "cash and carry" to arms and munitions so that the United States could aid Great Britain and France against the Axis.

Aug. 23   Germany and the Soviet Union signed a non-aggression pact, which meant that the two nations could partition Eastern Europe, each without fear of becoming involved in a second war front with the other.

Sept. 1   Germany invaded **Poland.** The **BLITZKRIEG** ("lightning war") attack was a new method of warfare and conquered Poland within a month.

Sept. 3   Great Britain and France declared **war** on Germany.

Sept. 5   The United States proclaimed its neutrality from the war.

Sept. 28   Germany and Russia partitioned **Poland** after Hitler had crushed the Polish army and captured Warsaw.

Nov. 4   Neutrality Act of 1939 amended the act of 1937 to allow the **export of arms and munitions** to belligerents on a **"cash and carry"** basis. To satisfy the isolationists the act empowered the President to establish **combat zones** into which American ships could not go.

Nov. 30   Russia invaded **Finland** and after bitter resistance gained territorial concessions in the treaty of Mar. 12, 1940.

1940

Apr. 9–June 22   In an extension of the blitzkrieg campaign, the Nazi army conquered Norway, Denmark, the Netherlands, Belgium, and France. The British army and French troops barely managed to escape to England from the port of **Dunkirk** (May 26–June 3). **Paris fell** on June 14, and **France surrendered** on June 22. On May 10, **WINSTON CHURCHILL** replaced **Neville Chamberlain** as Prime Minister of Great Britain.

The American Road to War
May 28–Oct. 16   Defense Measures: President Roosevelt named a **National Defense Advisory Commission** under **William S. Knudsen** to coordinate all economic aspects of defense. On June 15 he named Dr. **Vannevar Bush** as chairman of the **National**

Defense Research Committee. To achieve a bipartisan cabinet he appointed on June 20 two Republicans, **Henry L. Stimson** (N.Y.) and **Frank Knox** (Ill.), as the secretaries of War and Navy. Congress established the first peacetime compulsory military service program with the **Burke-Wadsworth** (Selective Training and Service) **Act** (Sept. 16), which called for the registration of all men aged 21–35. The first registration (Oct. 16) enrolled 16,400,000. **Federal expenditures** for the army and navy rose from $1.8 billion for the fiscal year 1940 to $6.3 billion for the fiscal year 1941.

June 3   The War Department began a policy of providing outdated arms and aircraft to Great Britain.

Aug. 8–Oct. 31   The **BATTLE OF BRITAIN**: the German Luftwaffe waged a great air attack on the British Isles, but against great odds the Royal Air Force destroyed some 2,000 German aircraft. The Germans gave up the assault and abandoned plans to invade Great Britain the following year.

Sept. 2   The United States transferred 50 overage destroyers to Great Britain in return for 99-year leases on bases in Newfoundland, Bermuda, the Bahamas, British Guiana, and elsewhere. The "**Destroyer Deal**" marked the end of any pretense of American neutrality.

Oct. 8   Germany invaded and conquered Rumania.

Oct. 28   Italy invaded Greece, expanding the Axis occupation of the Balkan Peninsula.

Fall   In the **Presidential campaign** both parties supported aid to Britain and France short of war.

Dec. 20   President Roosevelt established the **Office of Production Management** under **William S. Knudsen** to coordinate defense production.

1941

Jan. 6   In his annual message **President Roosevelt** recommended a **lend-lease bill** to aid the Allies and outlined the "**four freedoms**": freedoms of speech, of worship, from want, and from fear.

Mar. 11   After a two-month and very heated debate between interventionists and isolationists, Congress passed the **LEND-LEASE ACT**, which empowered the President to provide defense articles to countries whose security was vital to the defense of the United States. During the war, lend-lease aid totaled some $51 billion.

Apr.   Monthly losses of Allied and neutral shipping to German submarines rose to 654,000 tons from 320,000 tons in Jan. In Europe the Germans crushed **Greece** and **Yugoslavia,** and in **North Africa** Gen. **Erwin Rommel** started a drive (Mar. 24) to push the British east to the Nile.

Apr. 9   An American-Danish agreement allowed the United States to occupy **Greenland** for defensive purposes.

Apr. 24   The United States Navy began **patrolling to protect convoys** in the Atlantic Ocean as far as longitude 26° west.

June 22   In violation of their treaty, **Germany invaded Russia**. By Dec. 2 the Germans had reached the outskirts of **Moscow,** but through a long siege they never succeeded in taking the city.

June 24   President Roosevelt promised aid to Russia.

July 7   The United States made an agreement with **Iceland** to establish bases on the island to prevent German occupation.

Aug. 14   **THE ATLANTIC CHARTER**: President **Roosevelt** and **Prime Minister Churchill** met secretly (Aug. 9–12) at **Argentia Bay, Newfoundland,** and listed their postwar aims for the world:

1. no territorial aggrandizement,
2. self-determination for all nations,
3. easier channels of commerce and access to raw materials,
4. freedom from want and fear,
5. freedom of the seas, and
6. arms reduction.

Sept. 11   President Roosevelt ordered United States naval ships to **shoot at sight** at German submarines in American defense waters after the *U.S.S. Greer* had engaged a German submarine (Sept. 4).

Sept. 16   The United States Navy began to escort **convoys of merchant ships** from Newfoundland to Iceland.

Oct. 17, 30   German submarines torpedoed

the **U.S.S. Kearny,** killing 11, and sank the **U.S.S. Reuben James,** killing 100.

Nov. 17 Congress amended the Neutrality Act of 1939 to allow **arming of American merchant vessels and canceled the war-zones section.**

The United States and Japan, 1931–1941

1931

Sept. 18 The Japanese used an explosion on the South Manchurian Railroad near **Mukden** as an excuse to occupy **Manchuria.**

Oct. 10 President Hoover drew up a memorandum in which he agreed to cooperate with the League of Nations Council, though he was opposed to the use of economic sanctions against the Japanese.

Dec. 10 The Council sent a commission under the Earl of Lytton to report on the crisis. The **Lytton Report** of Sept., 1932, recommended the reestablishment of Chinese sovereignty over Manchuria.

1932

Jan. 7 Secretary of State **Henry L. Stimson** proclaimed his doctrine of non-recognition in notes to Japan and China saying that the United States did not recognize any agreement impairing either the territorial integrity of China or the open door.

Jan. 29 The Japanese invaded **Shanghai** but withdrew after several months.

Feb. 9 Stimson vainly sought British support for a joint protest to the Japanese.

Feb. 23 Stimson sent a letter to Senator **William E. Borah,** Chairman of the Senate Foreign Relations Committee, stating that the United States would insist on its treaty rights in Manchuria under the Nine-Power Pact.

Sept. 15 Japan established the puppet state of **Manchukuo** in Manchuria.

1933

Feb. 24 The League Assembly condemned Japanese aggression in Manchuria.

Mar. 27 Japan withdrew from the League of Nations.

1934

Mar. 24–July 4, 1946 The Tydings-McDuffie Act (Mar. 24) calling for **Philippine independence** was ratified by the Philippine legislature on May 1. The Philippine constitution was ratified on May 14, 1935, and the Philippines became officially independent on July 4, 1946.

1937

July 7–1939 War in China
July 7 Japan began a full-scale invasion of China at **Peking** and quickly occupied the coastal areas.

Sept. 14 The President refused to recognize the existence of a war because "cash and carry" would have helped Japan. In addition, the U.S. provided loans for China but otherwise took no action to stop Japanese expansion.

Oct. 5 President Roosevelt at Chicago urged an **international quarantine** of aggressors to preserve peace. The speech was a trial balloon, and its reception revealed that the public was not in favor of international involvement.

Nov. 3–Nov. 24 **Brussels Conference** to discuss the Chinese situation recessed with no agreement.

Dec. 12 *Panay* **Incident:** Japanese aircraft intentionally sank the U.S. gunboat *Panay* on the Yangtze River, killing two. When the Japanese apologized, the matter was dropped. Isolationist sentiment was so high that the **Ludlow Amendment,** which would require a public referendum before a declaration of war, almost reached the floor of the House (Jan. 10, 1938).

1938

Oct. 6 American Ambassador **Joseph C. Grew** protested against Japanese violations of the open door, but the Japanese replied that the policy could no longer be applied to the status quo.

1940

Jan. 26–Dec. 7, 1941   The Road to Pearl Harbor

Jan. 26   The United States allowed the **1911 trade treaty** with Japan to lapse as part of a policy of gradually cutting off trade with Japan. The United States gradually curtailed shipments of oil, scrap iron, and steel to Japan.

Sept. 22   Japan occupied **northern French Indo-China**.

Sept. 27   Japan, Germany, and Italy signed a three-power pact of 10 years' duration agreeing to assist one another if attacked by a power not already at war. This was aimed at the United States, as Russia was specifically exempted.

1941

July 2   An **Imperial Japanese conference** decided on expansion southward even if it meant war with the United States and Great Britain.

July 24   The Japanese occupied **southern French Indo-China**.

July 26   President Roosevelt **froze all Japanese assets** in the United States.

Aug. 6   Prime Minister **Fumimaro Konoye** of Japan proposed a **summit conference** with President Roosevelt to try to reach a settlement, but Roosevelt rejected the plan on Sept. 3.

Oct. 18   In Japan, a warlike cabinet under

Gen. **Hideki Tojo** replaced the moderate cabinet of Prince Konoye.

Nov. 20   Japanese demands presented by special envoy Saburo Kurusu and Ambassador Kichisaburo Nomura in Washington said that the Japanese would **evacuate southern Indo-China** if the United States would restore trade with Japan.

Nov. 26   In reply, a **United States ultimatum**, issued by Secretary of State Hull, demanded that the Japanese **get out of China and Indo-China** and agree to respect the open door and the sovereignty of all nations. In return, the United States would reopen trade with Japan.

Dec. 1   Japan rejected the Hull demands.

Dec. 7   Japanese naval and air forces made a surprise **ATTACK ON PEARL HARBOR** naval base in Hawaii at 7:55 A.M. The Japanese sank 5 of the 8 battleships at Pearl Harbor and damaged the others; 4 of the 8 later returned to the fleet. The attack sank or disabled 19 ships and killed 2,343 soldiers and sailors. A Presidential commission under Supreme Court Justice **Owen J. Roberts** in 1942 blamed the success of the attack on Admiral **Husband E. Kimmel** and Gen. **Walter C. Short**, who had been in command at Pearl Harbor. The attack was a severe blow to the U.S. fleet.

Dec. 8   The United States **declared war** on Japan.

Dec. 11   Germany and Italy declared war on the United States, and the United States, in turn, recognized a state of war with the Axis.

World War II, 1941–1945

The War in Europe, 1942–1945

1942

Jan.–June   German troops in Africa under Gen. **Rommel** checked a British offensive and drove east, pushing the British back toward Egypt to within 65 miles of **Alexandria**.

Jan. 26   The first United States troops for the European theater of war arrived in North Ireland.

Feb. 6   British and Americans formed the **Combined Chiefs of Staff**. Representing the United States were the Joint Chiefs of Staff —Gen. **George C. Marshall**, Army Chief of Staff; Adm. **Ernest J. King**, Chief of Naval

Operations; Gen. **Henry H. Arnold,** Commanding General, Army Air Force; and Adm. **William D. Leahy,** Chief of Staff for the President. On June 24 Gen. **Dwight D. Eisenhower** was appointed commander of the United States forces in the European Theater.

May 30 The British began sending up to 1,000 planes in **bombing attacks on Germany**; American flyers participated for the first time on July 4, and the United States carried out its first independent raid on Aug. 17. The bombing raids continued until the end of the war.

May In **the war against the submarine,** allied antisubmarine tactics became increasingly effective after May, 1942. Within a year the use of radar, "hunter-killer" teams, and improved antisubmarine missiles enabled the Allies to win the Battle of the Atlantic, making it much easier to convoy the huge

shipments of men and supplies that contributed so much to winning the war.

June–Sept. The **German offensive in southern Russia** had halted a Russian counterattack from Jan. to May; the German attack then pushed ahead until it reached **Stalingrad,** on the Volga River.

Aug. 19 American Rangers took part in a raid on Dieppe, France.

Oct.–Dec. The British under Gen. **Bernard L. Montgomery** drove the Germans out of Egypt after a great victory at **El Alamein.**

Nov. 8–May 13, 1943 The **African campaign** began with landings by Anglo-American forces under Gen. **Eisenhower** at **Casablanca, Morocco,** and at **Oran** and **Algiers, Algeria;** they were soon at the borders of Tunisia. Gen. Eisenhower recognized the French Admiral **Jean-François Darlan,** who had collaborated with the Nazis, as the ruler

8-1 The War in Europe

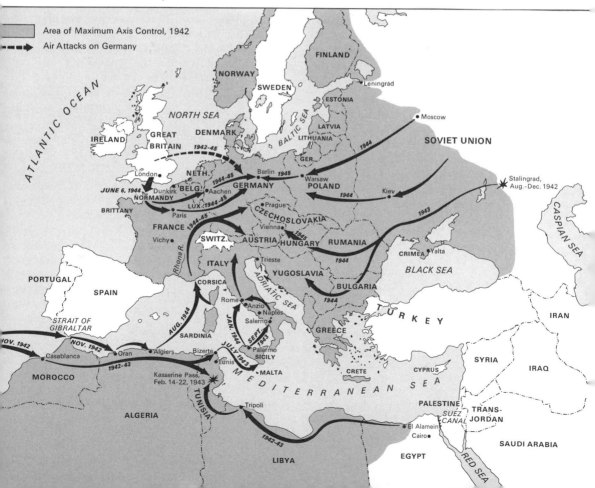

of French North Africa. After a severe set-back at **Kasserine Pass** on Feb. 14, Americans under Gen. **George S. Patton, Jr.,** drove the Germans back into Tunisia. **Gen. Montgomery** and the British pushed into Tunisia in late March, and the German and Italian North African armies surrendered on May 13. American casualties were about 20,000.

Nov. 19   A **Russian counteroffensive** began at **Stalingrad,** where a large German army was forced to surrender in February. The Russians also lifted the siege of **Leningrad.** After a brief German offensive in July, the Russians continued their drive west and reached the border of **Poland** by the end of 1943.

1943

July 9–10   The **Sicilian campaign** got under way when British General **Sir Harold R. L. G. Alexander** led Anglo-American forces into Sicily to pave the way for the invasion of Italy. The capture of **Messina** (Aug. 17) completed the conquest of the island, with American casualties of about 7,500.

Sept. 3   The **Italian campaign** began with a British invasion, under Gen. Montgomery, of southern Italy on Sept. 3; five days later Italy surrendered to the Allies. **Mussolini** escaped to German-held areas in the north, where on Apr. 28, 1945, Italian partisans captured and killed him. On Sept. 9 Americans under Gen. **Mark Clark** landed at **Salerno,** south of Naples, and soon engaged some 25 German divisions. Another landing, at **Anzio,** where the Americans were pinned down for several months, preceded the capture of **Rome** on June 4. The Allies reached **Florence** on August 12, but got little further until the last few months of the war.

1944

June 6–Sept. 11   On June 6 **Gen. Eisenhower,** Supreme Commander of the Allied Expeditionary Force, commanded an Allied force of almost 200,000 soldiers, 11,000 airplanes, and 4,000 ships of all sizes on the **invasion of Normandy.** It was the largest amphibious operation ever attempted. By July 2, the Allies had a million troops in France under British **Gen. Montgomery** and American Gen. **Omar N. Bradley** and were able to launch an offensive out of the Normandy beachhead. **Gen. Patton** led American tanks across France, and **Paris was liberated** on Aug. 25. Brussels, Antwerp, and Luxembourg were all free by Sept. 11, and by then the Allies had over 2 million men in Europe.

Aug. 15   Allied forces landed in **southern France** and began the drive north.

Sept. 12–May 8, 1945   As the **battle for Germany** began, 38 Allied divisions faced 41 German divisions. Aachen was the first German city to fall (Nov. 21), then Metz (Nov. 22). On Dec. 16 the Germans launched a fierce counterattack near **Bastogne.** The "Battle of the Bulge" was finally halted on Dec. 26 with about 77,000 American casualties. The **Russians** began a **general offensive in Poland** on Jan. 12, took **Warsaw** on Jan. 17, and reached the Oder River by Jan. 23. American troops crossed the **Rhine** on Mar. 7, and reached the **Elbe** on Apr. 11; there they halted to allow the **Russians** to take **Berlin** (Apr. 24–May 2), and American and Russian troops met at Torgau on the Elbe on Apr. 25. **Hitler committed suicide** in Berlin (Apr. 30), and **Germany surrendered** May 4–7. **V-E Day,** the formal end of the war in Europe, was on May 8.

The War in the Pacific, 1941–1945

1941

Dec. 8   The Japanese bombed the **Philippines, Wake Island, Guam, and Midway** the same day as the Pearl Harbor attack. (The date differs because of the International Date Line.) On Dec. 10 the Japanese sank the British capital ships **Prince of Wales** and **Repulse** in the South China Sea. They captured **Guam, Wake,** and **Hong Kong,** Dec. 13–25.

1942

Dec. 10, 1941–May 6   The fall of the Philippines: the Japanese invaded the Philippines Dec. 10–24 and took Manila on Jan. 2. **Gen. MacArthur's** army retreated to the **Bataan Peninsula,** and MacArthur was evacuated to Australia (arriving Mar. 17). After Bataan fell on Apr. 9, Gen. **Jonathan M. Wainwright** held out on the island of **Corregidor** in Manila Bay, where he and some 12,000 men surrendered May 6.

Jan.–Sept. 17   By Jan. 31 the Japanese had taken **Malaya; Singapore** fell Feb. 15, and most of the **Dutch East Indies** fell by Mar. 9. In the west the Japanese conquered

Thailand in December, cut the **Burma Road** supply route to China by capturing **Mandalay,** Burma (May 3), and drove the Allies out of Burma. Farther south they invaded northern **New Guinea** in March and by Sept. 17 were within 30 miles of **Port Moresby** on the south coast, where they were halted. The Japanese also bombed **Dutch Harbor, Alaska,** and seized the islands of **Attu** and **Kiska** (June 12–21) in the **Aleutians.**

Apr. 18   American carrier-based planes led by Lt. Col. (later Gen.) **James H. Doolittle** bombed Tokyo. Though it inflicted little damage, the raid gave a boost to Allied morale.

8-2   The War in the Pacific

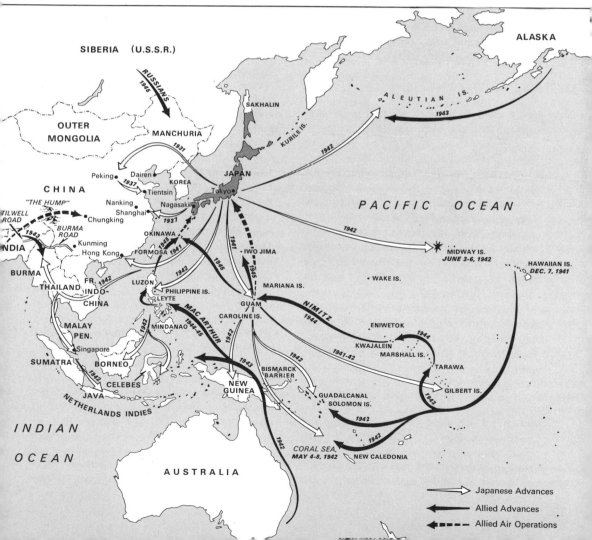

May 4–June 6 At the **Battle of the Coral Sea,** the United States checked the Japanese advance in the southwestern Pacific by sinking or damaging three Japanese carriers (May 4–8). A month later the fleet prevented the Japanese conquest of Midway Island by destroying four Japanese aircraft carriers in the **Battle of Midway** (June 3–6). These battles marked a turning point in the war in the Pacific, and within two months the United States was on the offensive.

Aug. 7–Feb. 9, 1943 The first American advance in the Pacific came in the **Solomon Islands,** where Marines landed on **Guadalcanal** and other islands on Aug. 7. The Japanese sank four Allied cruisers in the **Battle of Savo Island,** near Guadalcanal (Aug. 9), but four **American naval victories** (Aug. 23–Nov. 15) in which the Japanese lost two battleships kept Japanese reinforcements at a minimum. The Japanese abandoned Guadalcanal on Feb. 9, 1943.

1943

Jan. 2–Apr. 22, 1944 **Conquest of New Guinea and the southwest Pacific:** American ground and naval forces under the Supreme Allied Commander in the southwest Pacific, **Douglas MacArthur,** captured **Buna** in New Guinea (Jan. 2), **Lae** (Sept. 16), and completed the conquest of New Guinea by occupying **Hollandia** (Apr. 22, 1944). Amphibious forces, meanwhile, gained control of the Solomons-New Britain area by winning the **Battle of the Bismarck Sea** (Mar. 2–4) and other naval battles and by invading **New Georgia** (June 30), **Bougainville** (Nov. 1), **New Britain** (Dec. 15–26), and the **Admiralty Islands** (Mar. 1, 1944).

May 11–Aug. 15 United States and Canadian troops recaptured Attu and Kiska in the Aleutians.

1944

Nov. 21, 1943–Nov. 13 In the **central Pacific campaign,** Adm. **Chester W. Nimitz,** Commander-in-Chief of the Pacific Fleet, led the offensive that began with the capture of **Tarawa** and **Makin** in the **Gilbert Islands**

(Nov. 21–24), where losses exceeded 3,000. The **Marshalls** fell (Jan. 31, 1944–Feb. 22), followed by **Saipan** (June 15–July 9), **Guam** (July 21–Aug. 9), and **Peleliu** (Sept. 15–Oct. 13).

Jan.–May 3, 1945 Allied forces under **Lord Louis Mountbattan** and U.S. Gen. **Joseph W. Stilwell** (recalled Oct. 18, 1944, after bitter disagreements with Chinese ruler **Chiang Kai-shek**) took **Myitkyina, Burma** (Aug. 3, 1944) and enabled the Allies to open the **Ledo Road** to China by the end of the year. The capture of **Mandalay** on Mar. 20 and of **Rangoon** on May 3, 1945, completed the reconquest of Burma.

June 15 The United States began superfortress (B–29) **air attacks** on Japan with a raid on Kyushu from bases in China. The first raid from Saipan took place on Nov. 24, and the raids continued until the end of the war.

June 19–Feb. 24, 1945 The **Phillippine campaign:** in the **Battle of the Philippine Sea** (June 19–20) the Japanese lost three aircraft carriers and several hundred planes and suffered heavy damage to battleships and cruisers. When **Gen. MacArthur's** forces invaded the island of **Leyte** in the **Philippines** (Oct. 20), the Japanese made one last naval attack. In the **Battle of Leyte Gulf,** one of the greatest naval battles of all time, the United States sank three battleships, four carriers, ten cruisers, and eliminated the Japanese fleet as a factor in the war. The United States invaded **Luzon** on Jan. 9, 1945, and captured **Manila** on· Feb. 24. American casualties in the Philippine campaign amounted to about 60,000.

1945

Feb. 19–June 21 **The approach to Japan:** United States Marines captured the island of **Iwo Jima** after a month of heavy fighting and casualties of 20,000. On Apr. 1 the United States invaded **Okinawa** in the Ryukyus and conquered the island by June 21. Many of the 50,000 American casualties were the result of Japanese suicide airplane (*kamikaze*) attacks.

July 10–Aug. 9 **Bombing Japan:** a 1,000-plane raid struck Japan on July 10 as the

United States and Great Britain increased their air attacks. The United States dropped an **ATOMIC BOMB** on **Hiroshima,** Aug. 6, killing or wounding about 180,000; another bomb was dropped on **Nagasaki,** Aug. 9, with 80,000 casualties.

Aug. 10–Sept. 2   Japan surrendered and sued for peace on Aug. 10, and President Truman announced Aug. 14 as V-J day. Formal surrender took place on the U.S. battleship *Missouri* in Tokyo Bay (Sept. 2).

Casualties in World War II
(thousands)

	Total mobilized	Killed or died	Wounded
United States	16,113	407[a]	672[b]
China	17,251	1,325[c]	1,762
Germany	20,000	3,250	7,250
Italy	3,100	136	225
Japan	9,700	1,270[c]	140
U.S.S.R.	—[d]	6,115	14,012
United Kingdom	5,896	357	369

[a] 292,000 of these were killed in battle.
[b] The United States also had 124,000 captured.
[c] Killed in battle only; China, 1937–45.
[d] Total mobilization figure, including civilian population, unavailable.

The Home Front

Raising the troops: the **War Manpower Commission** under **Paul V. McNutt** controlled both military and economic mobilization. All males aged 18–38 (and temporarily those aged 18–45) were liable for military service. Selective Service classified 36,677,000, of whom 10,022,000 were finally inducted. Women served in the Army (WAACS), in the Navy (WAVES), in the Air Force (WAFS), in the Coast Guard (SPARS), and in the Marines.

Wartime economic controls: the **War Production Board** under **Donald M. Nelson** replaced the Office of Production Management as chief authority in mobilizing all resources for war. The **Board of Economic Warfare** under **Henry A. Wallace** (organized

April 14, 1942) was in charge of stockpiles of essential materials. The Rubber Administrator, the Petroleum Administrator, and the Solid Fuels Administrator for War regulated the use of rubber and oil, coal, and other fuels. Congress on Jan. 30, 1942, created the **Office of Price Administration** under **Leon Henderson** to fix prices and to ration scarce commodities. Rationing started with tires and was extended to gasoline, fuel oil, sugar, coffee, meats, butter, and other goods. Other war time agencies included: the **Office of Civilian Defense** (Mayor **Fiorello H. LaGuardia** of New York City), **Office of War Mobilization** to regulate the flow of civilian supplies, and **Office of Defense Transportation.** The **Office of Scientific Research and Development** under Dr. **Vannevar Bush** was responsible for the development of radar, rockets, and the proximity fuse.

Labor in wartime: the **National War Labor Board** under **William H. Davis** mediated labor disputes and tied wage increases to the rise in the cost of living. Strikes continued during the war, involving on the average about the same percentage of employed wage earners every year as the average for each of the three years before. President Roosevelt on May 1, 1943, took over eastern coal mines and forced **John L. Lewis** to call off the **United Mine Workers Strike** the next day. Congress on June 25, 1943, passed the **Smith-Connally War Labor Disputes Act,** which strengthened the President's power to deal with strikes that interfered with the war effort. The President seized all railroads Dec. 27, 1943–Jan. 18, 1944, to avert a strike.

The war transformed the American economy. **Federal spending** during the war exceeded $320 billion, twice the total of all previous government spending since 1789. The **national debt,** which rose $20 billion in 1933–40, went up $215 billion in 1940–45. The war practically eliminated **unemployment.** While a major share of wartime expenses was financed through the **sale of bonds,** $130 billion came from **taxation,** most of it from income taxes. The President tried in vain to **limit annual salaries to $25,000** net during the war, and the maximum surtax rose to 94 per cent. After

Financing the War

	1941	1943	1945
Federal expenditures (billions of dollars)	13.3	79.4	98.4
Federal expenditures for major national security (billions of dollars)	6.0	63.2	81.2
Federal receipts (billions of dollars)	7.1	22.0	44.5
Federal receipts from individual and corporate income taxes (billions of dollars)	3.5	16.3	35.1
Federal debt (billions of dollars)	49.0	136.7	258.7
Gross national product (billions of dollars, 1929 prices)	138.7	170.2	180.9
Wholesale commodity price index (1926=100)	87	103	106
Unemployment (millions)	5.6	1.1	1.0

prices rose in 1942, the President issued a "hold the line" order in Apr., 1943, and prices were stable until the end of the war. Prices overall rose far less during World War II than they had during the Civil War or World War I.

The atomic bomb project: Ernest O. Lawrence constructed the first cyclotron in 1930 making it possible to smash atoms. **Enrico Fermi** (who came to the United States in 1939) and others in Europe and the United States carried out experiments (1935–39) in producing nuclear energy by splitting Uranium-235 atoms. When Dr. **Arthur H. Compton**, Dr. Fermi, and others produced the first **controlled chain reaction** in unseparated uranium (Dec. 2, 1942, in Chicago), it pointed the way toward the bomb. On May 1, 1943, the Army Corps of Engineers under Gen. **L. R. Groves** took over the **"Manhattan Project"** to develop the bomb. American and British scientists under Dr. **J. R. Oppenheimer** produced a bomb at **Los Alamos**, N.M., and exploded it at Alamogordo, N.M., on July 16, 1945.

Civil liberties and internal security in wartime: even before World War II Congress created the **House Committee to Investigate Un-American Activities** (May 26, 1938) to investigate Fascist, Communist, and other organizations. On June 27, 1940, President Roosevelt revived by proclamation the Espionage Act of 1917. The **Alien Registration Act (Smith Act,** June 29, 1940) required the registration of all aliens and tightened laws for deportation. The act also made it illegal to advocate or teach the overthrow of any government of the United States by force or

to organize a group dedicated to such a purpose. On Feb. 19, 1942, President Roosevelt authorized the Secretary of War to exclude persons from restricted military areas. As a result the Secretary removed **110,000 Japanese** or Japanese-Americans from the west coast **to relocation camps** in the interior Feb.–Mar., 1942. The Supreme Court in *Hirabayashi v. United States* (1943) upheld military curfew rules on the west coast and in *Korematsu v. United States* (1944) upheld the relocation program which ended on Jan. 2, 1945.

The Election of 1944

June 26   The **Republican Convention** met in Chicago and nominated governor **Thomas E. Dewey** of New York for President and governor **John W. Bricker** of Ohio for Vice President.

July 19   The **Democratic Convention** met at Chicago and renominated **Franklin D. Roosevelt** for a fourth term and nominated Senator **Harry S Truman** (Mo.) for Vice President.

Nov. 7   Presidential election: both parties came out in favor of an international organization to keep world peace. **Roosevelt** won with 25,606,585 votes (432 electoral); **Dewey** received 22,014,745 votes (99 electoral).

The Diplomacy of World War II

1942

Jan. 1   The United States, the U.S.S.R., Great Britain, and 23 other Allied nations signed the **United Nations Declaration** supporting the principles of the Atlantic Charter. The Declaration, an executive agreement, bound the United States for the first time to a formal foreign alliance.

Jan. 15–Aug., 1944   Latin America: at the **Rio de Janeiro Conference** (Jan. 15–28, 1942) the American Republics agreed to break relations with the Axis, but **Chile** and **Argentina** did not do so until Jan. 20, 1943, and Jan. 26, 1944. During the war the United States maintained excellent relations with all Latin American nations except Argentina, which was sympathetic to the Nazis. On Aug. 16, 1944, the government froze Argentina's assets in the United States and tightened shipping restrictions after anti-American demonstrations took place in Buenos Aires.

Apr. 3   President Roosevelt appointed **Carlton J. H. Hayes** as ambassador to Spain; Hayes was charged with maintaining good relations with Franco in order to prevent **Spain** from joining the war on the side of the Axis. Liberals in the United States criticized what they considered appeasement of a dictator, but Spain never went to war.

Nov.–Oct. 23, 1944   The United States and France: after the fall of France in 1940, the United States maintained relations with the Nazi-controlled French government at **Vichy**. Liberals called the policy one of appeasement, but it made possible an easy invasion of French North Africa in Nov., 1942. After the liberation of France, the United States recognized the French government-in-exile, under generals **Charles de Gaulle** and **Henri Giraud**, as the provisional government (Oct. 23, 1944).

1943

Jan. 14–24   At a conference in **CASABLANCA**, President Roosevelt and Prime Minister Churchill announced the "**unconditional surrender**" policy but could not decide whether the second front should be in the Balkans (favored by Churchill) or in France (favored by Roosevelt).

May 12–25   Roosevelt and Churchill, meeting in Washington, agreed on a **second front at Normandy** in France.

Aug. 11–24   At the **first Quebec Conference**, U. S. Secretary of State **Cordell Hull**, British Foreign Minister **Anthony Eden**, and Russian Foreign Minister **V. M. Molotov** established a European Advisory Commission to form postwar policy on Germany. Stalin promised to go to war against Japan after Germany was defeated. The **Moscow Declaration** came out in favor of an international organization to maintain peace and security.

Nov. 22–26   At the **first Cairo Conference**, President **Roosevelt**, Prime Minister **Churchill**, and Generalissimo **Chiang Kai-shek** issued the **Declaration of Cairo** that committed the Allies to the following agreements:

1. to wage war until Japan surrendered unconditionally,
2. to return to China all the possessions Japan had taken from China,
3. to strip Japan of its Pacific Islands, and
4. to make Korea independent.

Nov. 28–Dec. 1   At the **TEHERAN** (Iran) **CONFERENCE**, President **Roosevelt**, Prime Minister **Churchill**, and Premier **Stalin** agreed to coordinate an invasion of western Europe with a Russian drive from the east.

Dec. 4–6   At the **second Cairo Conference**, Roosevelt and Churchill agreed to put **Eisenhower** in charge of the invasion of western Europe.

1944

July 1–22   The **United Nations Monetary and Financial Conference** at Bretton Woods, N.H., established the **International Monetary Fund** to stabilize national currencies. The conference also created the **International Bank for Reconstruction and Development** to lend money for postwar recovery and to provide capital for investment in underdeveloped areas.

Aug. 21–Oct. 7   At the **DUMBARTON OAKS CONFERENCE**, near Washington, D.C., representatives of the United States, Great Britain, the U.S.S.R., and China drew up plans for a **postwar international organization**.

Sept. 11–16   The **second Quebec Con-**

ference resulted in an agreement between President **Roosevelt** and Prime Minister **Churchill** on American and British zones of occupation in Germany.

Oct. 9–18   At the **second Moscow Conference, Churchill** and **Stalin** divided the **Balkans** into British and Russian spheres of influence and agreed to bound **Poland** by the Curzon line on the east and the Oder River on the west. Roosevelt, who was not present, refused to be bound by these agreements.

Social and Cultural Change, 1900–1945

Technology and Urbanization

In the twentieth century the American economy, which had heretofore concentrated on capital goods, was able to produce a greater proportion of **consumer goods. Electricity** became a part of American life; the production of electrical power increased 10 times between 1902 and 1920 and then increased 5-fold between 1920 and 1945. In 1912 one-sixth of American families had electricity in their homes; by 1927 it was almost two-thirds. The number of **telephones** in America grew from about a million in 1900 to about 13 million in 1920 and reached almost 28 million in 1945. The **radio** and the **motion picture** came into their own in the 1920's. The first important radio broadcast was made on Nov. 2, 1920, when station KDKA of East Pittsburgh broadcast the Presidential election returns. Perhaps a million families had radios by the election of 1924, 19 million in 1932, and 33 million in 1944. The motion picture industry, which was flourishing well before World War I, produced the first sound movie in 1927. Weekly movie attendance rose from 40 million in 1922 to 100 million in 1930.

Transportation also improved dramatically. The **automobile industry,** which had started in the 1890's, grew rapidly. Passenger car sales rose from about 4,000 in 1900 to 2 million in 1920 and almost 4 million in 1940. Street and electric railway revenues quadrupled between 1902 and 1922 as urban transportation expanded. The remarkable growth of **air transportation** awaited the end of World War II, but the airlines carried almost 4 million passengers in 1941 compared to 6,000 in 1926.

Urban growth accompanied the technological change. New York City alone grew from 3.4 million in 1900 to 7.5 million in 1940 and urban population increased from 40 per cent of the total in 1900 to 57 per cent in 1940.

The New Mores

The rise of the city and improved means of transportation and communication blurred the distinction between urban and rural America. The twentieth century saw the rise of **new American values**—often urban rather than rural. The writings of **Sigmund Freud** also contributed to the new mores. Freud lectured in America in 1909, and his *Interpretation of Dreams* was translated for American readers in 1913. Freudian theories, often distorted, spread rapidly and encouraged new attitudes toward behavior. A revolution in morals began to take place—for many reasons—as Americans turned their backs on the restrictions of the nineteenth century.

Women gained freedom as the twentieth century advanced. The woman suffrage amendment was but part of the movement for the emancipated woman. World War I demonstrated that women could handle almost every type of job; 10 million women were in the labor force by 1930, almost 17 million by 1950. The number of divorces per thousand rose from 1.6 in 1920 to 2.0 in 1940 and was even higher after the war.

The American Negro

1900–20   The early twentieth century was a **low point in Negro civil rights**. Jim

Crow laws in the South became more severe. Negro lynchings were somewhat less frequent than in the 1890's, but they still averaged over 60 a year, 1900–20. The period ended with the worst outbreak of interracial conflict to that point in American history. Many of these riots took place in the North, for thousands of Negroes moved north after 1900. The net **migration of Negroes out of the South** was as follows (in thousands):

1900–10	186
1910–20	495
1920–30	783
1930–40	404
1940–50	1,322
Total	3,190

These figures represent the net intercensal migration of Negroes out of the states of Virginia, North Carolina, South Carolina, Georgia, Florida, Kentucky, Tennessee, Alabama, Mississippi, Arkansas, Louisiana, Texas, and Oklahoma.

1903   Negro leader **William E. B. DuBois** published his essay "The Talented Tenth," calling on educated Negroes to uplift their race, and his militant *Souls of Black Folks*, in which he demanded civil rights for Negroes. DuBois had broken with the moderate position of Booker T. Washington.

1905   At a conference at Niagara Falls in July, **DuBois** and other militant Negroes started the **Niagara Movement**, which called for an end to all racial restrictions.

1909   The **NATIONAL ASSOCIATION FOR THE ADVANCEMENT OF COLORED PEOPLE (NAACP)** was formed by Negroes and white reformers. **DuBois** became its chief Negro leader and for 22 years served as editor of *The Crisis*, which publicized lynchings and other anti-Negro atrocities.

1917   A race riot in East St. Louis, Ill., killed 37.

1917–18   Some 360,000 Negroes who had served in the war returned home demanding additional rights.

1919   **25 race riots** took place all over the country. In Washington, D.C., white soldiers and sailors attacked Negro quarters. The most serious riot started in **Chicago** on July 27 and killed 23 Negroes and 15 whites.

1920–30   The **Negro renaissance** developed a spirit of independence in the 1920's, particularly in **Harlem**. The Negro poet and novelist **Langston Hughes**, who lived in Harlem, wrote *The Weary Blues* (1926) and *Not Without Laughter* (1930). The NAACP grew from 50 local chapters to 599 between the two wars. Negro lynchings dropped to an average of 10 per year, 1921–45. The South built more Negro schools in the 1920–30 decade than in all previous years, and by 1930 there were 15,000 Negroes with college degrees. In 1921, **Marcus Garvey** outfitted a steamship line to carry Negroes back to Africa. At its height, Garvey's **African Zionist Movement** had 500,000 members, but it collapsed when Garvey went to jail for swindling.

1930–40   The **depression** hit the Negro harder than any other group, particularly the Negro sharecropper. New Deal farm programs often forced Negroes to leave the farm and move to the city slum, but New Deal relief measures helped them to survive the depression. White CIO labor leaders treated Negroes more fairly than had any labor organizers in the past. Negroes, traditionally Republican, **went over to the Democratic Party** and helped form Roosevelt's urban coalition. Of 15 Negro wards analyzed in a special study, 4 went to Roosevelt in 1932, 9 in 1936, and 14 in 1940.

1938–44   The Supreme Court and the Negro: the NAACP entered a series of suits to gain Negroes the right to vote in southern primary elections and to attend public graduate schools. In *Missouri ex rel. Gaines v. Canada* (1938), the Court ordered Missouri to admit Negroes to the state university law school in absence of other provisions for their legal training. In *Smith v. Allwright* (1944) it held that exclusion of Negroes from Texas **primary elections** was a violation of the 15th Amendment.

1940   **Richard Wright**, one of the few Negroes to join the Communist Party, published his *Native Son*, which described the brutality of Negro slum life.

1940–45   The Negro in wartime: the movement of Negroes to the North, slowed by the depression, speeded up during the war as Negroes went to work in defense plants. 920,000 Negroes served in World

War II, 7,768 of them officers, and some military segregation practices were given up.

1941 After Negroes threatened to march on Washington, President Roosevelt issued an Executive Order (June 25) declaring that there should be no discrimination in employment in defense industries or government. His order also created the **Fair Employment Practices Committee (FEPC)** to investigate complaints of discrimination.

1943 President Roosevelt sent troops to **Detroit** June 20 to quell a **racial riot** between Negroes and whites that killed 34. On Aug. 1 Negroes in **Harlem** rioted.

Education

	1900	1946
Elementary and secondary school enrollment (thousands)	16,855	26,124
Average number of days attended, public school per pupil	99	151
High school graduates (thousands, followed by per cent of population 17 years old)	95 (6)	1,080 (48)
Enrollment in institutions of higher education (thousands)	238	1,677
Per cent of illiteracy	11	3[a]

[a] 1947

The Supreme Court and Civil Rights

1925–32 *Gitlow v. New York* and other cases extended the **14th Amendment** to cover the 1st Amendment and others in the Bill of Rights, thus reversing the Slaughterhouse Cases of 1873.

1937 In *Herndon v. Lowry*, the Court reversed the conviction of a Communist organizer in Georgia on the grounds that there was no "clear and present danger."

1938–40 The Jehovah's Witnesses cases granted religious groups the right to distribute literature and raise money without a license.

1941 *Edwards v. California* declared unconstitutional a California law excluding indigent immigrants who came from other states.

1943 *West Virginia State Board of Education v. Barnette* declared a state law requiring a flag salute to be an infringement of the First Amendment.

1944 The "**GI Bill of Rights**" provided extensive educational benefits for World War II veterans.

Religion

1900–15 **Social gospel** stressed the social responsibility of the church.

1915–25 **Fundamentalism** reached a high point in the early 1920's as a reaction to the liberal Christianity and the Social Gospel.

1925 In the **Scopes trial** at Dayton, Tenn., **William Jennings Bryan**, the fundamentalist and statesman, opposed **John T. Scopes**, who had established a test case by breaking a Tennessee law and teaching the theory of evolution. **Clarence S. Darrow**, the famous trial lawyer who defended Scopes, subjected Bryan to a severe cross-examination in which fundamentalism lost ground.

1931 Several groups that believed in the second coming of Christ united as the **Jehovah's Witnesses**.

1935–55 **Neo-Orthodoxy** stressed a return to the Bible and belief in the fall of man and God's judgment. **Reinhold Niebuhr** (*An Interpretation of Christian Ethics*, 1935, and *The Nature and Destiny of Man*, 1939) and **Paul J. Tillich** led this movement.

Literature

1893–1925 **Naturalism**: the naturalist novelists often portrayed man as the helpless pawn of his environment. In *Maggie: A Girl of the Streets* (1893) **Stephen Crane** depicted the degradation of a character caught in an American city. His *The Red Badge of Courage* (1895), which showed the unheroic side of war, was an example of naturalism applied to the Civil War. **Frank Norris** used naturalistic techniques in *McTeague* (1899), the story of a degenerate dentist in San Francisco, and also in his two reform novels, *The Pit* (1901) and *The Octopus* (1903). Perhaps the greatest naturalist was **Theodore Dreiser,** whose *An American Tragedy* appeared in 1925. **Jack London** recreated the struggle for survival in stories such as *The Call of the Wild* (1903) and *The Sea Wolf* (1904). **Sherwood Anderson** in *Winesburg, Ohio* (1919) wrote of sex-motivation in smalltown life.

1918–39   Novelists between the wars
1920–25   F(rancis) Scott (Key) Fitzgerald typified the disillusioned young men of the "lost generation" in *This Side of Paradise* (1920) and *The Great Gatsby* (1925).

1920–47   Sinclair Lewis criticized the values of small-town America in *Main Street* (1920) and those of American businessmen in *Babbitt* (1922). In *It Can't Happen Here* (1935) he warned of the possibility of a fascist state in America. He turned to the race problem in *Kingsblood Royal* (1947).

1926–52   Ernest Hemingway, who spent much of his life abroad, described the empty lives of the expatriates in Paris in *The Sun Also Rises* (1926). Later significant works included *A Farewell to Arms* (1929), *To Have and Have Not* (1937), *For Whom the Bell Tolls* (1940), and *The Old Man and the Sea* (1952).

1926–62   William Faulkner wrote of the tension within northern Mississippi society in *The Sound and the Fury* (1929), *As I Lay Dying* (1930), *Sanctuary* (1931), *Intruder in the Dust* (1948), and *The Mansion* (1959).

1930–41   John Dos Passos wrote a novel of postwar disillusionment, *Three Soldiers* (1921), and later produced *U.S.A.* (1930–36), a three-volume left-wing history of the United States in the twentieth century. He took a more positive view of America in *The Ground We Stand On* (1941).

1932   Erskine Caldwell's *Tobacco Road* recreated southern rural poverty during the depression.

1932–35   James T. Farrell's *Studs Lonigan* trilogy portrayed poverty in Chicago.

1935–52   John Steinbeck wrote powerful novels about migrant workers: *Tortilla Flat* (1935), *Of Mice and Men* (1937), *The Grapes of Wrath* (1939), *Cannery Row* (1945), and *East of Eden* (1952). *The Grapes of Wrath* aroused the nation about the plight of the "Okies" in California.

Poetry and Other Writing

1912–31   Edna St. Vincent Millay was a master of lyric poetry, particularly of the sonnet, as shown by *Renascence and Other Poems* (1917) and *Fatal Interview* (1931).

1914–46   Gertrude Stein, an expatriate who coined the phrase "the lost generation," wrote abstractionist poetry ("Tender Buttons," 1914) and a variety of experimental novels and short stories.

1915–35   Edgar Lee Masters' *Spoon River Anthology* (1915) depicted the lives of small-town people in the midwest.

1916–43   Carl Sandburg evoked the spirit of the American midwest in *Chicago Poems* (1916) and *The People, Yes* (1936) and in his biography of Lincoln (1926–43).

1919–26   Ezra Pound revolted against traditionalism by experimenting with meter in his poetry: *Cantos* (1919), *Personae* (1926).

1920–53   For more than three decades, **Eugene O'Neill** was the foremost American dramatist. He won Pulitzer prizes for *Beyond the Horizon* (1920), *Anna Christie* (1921), and *Strange Interlude* (1928) and was awarded a Pulitzer Prize posthumously for *Long Day's Journey into Night* (1956). He received the Nobel Prize for Literature in 1936. His other plays included *The Emperor Jones* (1920), *The Hairy Ape* (1922), *Ah, Wilderness!* (1933), and *The Iceman Cometh* (1946).

1922–35   T(homas) S(tearns) Eliot was an expatriate who wrote of empty lives in his epic *The Waste Land* (1922), a poem at first criticized and later much admired. His *Murder in the Cathedral* appeared in 1935.

1924–48   H(enry) L. Mencken, who in 1924 began to edit *The American Mercury,* satirized all aspects of American life, particularly its most revered institutions. His massive study *The American Language* was published in several editions, 1919–48.

1913–61 Robert Frost won the Pulitzer Prize four times for his poetry, which was based on New England farm life. Among his poems were "The Death of the Hired Man," "Mending Walls," "Birches," and "Fire and Ice."

Newspapers and Magazines

1904–47 The number of newspapers dropped from 16,459 to 10,282, but circulation rose from 50,464,000 to 119,568,000. At the same time, the number of weekly periodicals dropped from 1,493 to 892, with circulation increasing from 17,418,000 to 69,393,000.

1907 Edward W. Scripps and Milton A. McRae formed the Scripps-Rae Press Association (1897), which in 1907 became the United Press. Roy W. Howard joined the Scripps chain to form the Scripps-Howard chain of newspapers in 1922.

1913–34 The Hearst chain gained control of 30 newspapers.

1914 Herbert Croly and Walter Lippmann were instrumental in starting the *New Republic*, a magazine of social and political criticism.

1922 *Reader's Digest*, condensations of articles in other journals.

1923 *Time*, New York, Henry R. Luce, news weekly.

1933 *Newsweek*, New York, news weekly.

1936 *Life*, New York, Henry R. Luce, picture magazine.

Science, Medicine, and Inventions

1903 Orville and Wilbur Wright, first heavier-than-air flight.

1904 Thomas Edison, first sound motion picture.

1905 Albert Einstein, special theory of relativity.

1906 Lee De Forest, vacuum tube amplifier.

1909 Thomas Hunt Morgan, studies in the physical basis of heredity.

1909 Sigmund Freud and Carl G. Jung lectured, introducing their studies of psychoanalysis to the United States.

1913 Elmer A. Sperry, gyroscope stabilizer for airplanes.

1913 Schick test helped reduce the incidence of diphtheria.

1913 William D. Coolidge, improved X-ray tube.

1913 William M. Burton, cracking process for producing gasoline from petroleum.

1915 Albert Einstein, general theory of relativity.

1917 Ernst F. W. Alexanderson, high frequency alternator, making possible worldwide wireless transmission.

1922 Herbert T. Kalmus, technicolor film.

1922 Albert H. Taylor and Leo C. Young, the principle of radar.

1923 Lee De Forest, improved sound motion picture.

1931 Empire State Building, New York City, world's tallest skyscraper.

1934 Streamlined high-speed train.

1935 First British commercial television (United States, 1941).

1936 Sulfa drugs were proven effective.

1939 Discovery of antibiotics.

1939 Nylon used as a commercial fabric.

1941 Penicillin first used on humans.

1941 American Red Cross Blood Donor Service founded.

Painting

1900–17 The "Ash Can School" of painting: the realistic artists of this school turned to everyday life for subject matter and to Europe for technique. Typical artists were John Sloan (*Election Night, McSorley's Bar*), George Bellows (*Stag at Sharkey's, Day in June*), and Robert Henri (*Boy with a Piccolo*). Led by Henri, the "Ash Can" artists revolted against the conservative National Academy of Design and staged their own art show in New York in 1908.

1913 The Armory Art Show: a group of modernists led by photographer Alfred Stieglitz also broke with the Academy and presented the Armory Art Show in New York, which included French impressionist, postimpressionist, cubist, and abstractionist painting. The show aroused a great furor and drew the wrath of the conventional critics. **John Marin, Georgia O'Keeffe,** and **Charles Demuth** produced various forms of modernistic art in the 1920's.

1930–40   Social protest: many artists of the 1930's produced paintings protesting the conditions that led to the depression or showing sympathy for its victims. **Reginald Marsh** of this school was famous for *The Bowery,* as was **Edward Hopper** for *Nighthawks,* which pictured an all-night diner. The WPA Federal Art Project contributed to the art of social protest.

1930–40   Regionalists: midwestern painters **Thomas Hart Benton, John Steuart Curry,** and **Grant Wood** rebelled openly against the styles of New York and Paris. Benton often painted scenes from nineteenth-century American history, Curry depicted life on the Great Plains, and Wood's primitive style can be seen in *American Gothic.*

Architecture

1900–59   Frank Lloyd Wright, the leading innovator in American architecture, sought to integrate form with function, site, and materials. His "prairie house" style appeared about the turn of the century. His own home, Taliesin, the Imperial Hotel in Tokyo, and the Guggenheim Museum in New York were among his most famous buildings.

1918–40   International architecture: the new architecture of Europe—modern, geometrical, and unhistorical—had great influence in America between the wars. Examples of such architecture could be seen at the **Chicago World's Fair** (1933), the **San Francisco World's Fair** (1939), and the **New York World's Fair** (1939). American architecture turned to new uses of more traditional American styles in the 1940's.

Leading Figures of the Period

ALBERT EINSTEIN (Ulm, Germany, 1879–Princeton, N.J., 1955), scientist.

1900   Was graduated from the Federal Institute of Technology at Zurich, Switzerland.

1905   Received a Ph.D. degree from the University of Zurich.

1905   Presented his special theory of relativity on the electrodynamics of moving bodies, which is the basis for modern study of the atom.

1905   Developed the quantum theory of specific heat.

1912–14   Taught at the Federal Institute of Technology at Zurich.

1914   Became the first director of the Kaiser Wilhelm Institute of Physics in Berlin.

1916   Published his general theory of relativity.

1922   Received the Nobel Prize for his contributions to theoretical physics.

1933   Settled in the United States as a refugee from Nazi Germany.

1933–45   Worked at the Institute for Advanced Study at Princeton, N.J.

1939   Wrote his famous letter to Roosevelt that pointed out the possibilities of the atomic bomb and resulted in the Manhattan Project.

1949   Announced his general theory of gravitation.

1953   Completed work on his unified field theory.

HERBERT C. HOOVER (West Branch, Iowa, 1874–New York City, 1964), 31st President of the United States.

1895   Was graduated from Stanford University as an engineer.

1895–1915   Worked as a mining engineer in the United States, Australia, China, Africa, South America, and Russia.

1914   Organized and directed the American Relief Committee that helped 120,000 Americans stranded in Europe by the war to return home.

1917   United States Food Administrator.

1919   Director General of the American Relief Administration.

1921–28 Secretary of Commerce; promoted American business efficiency.

1929–33 President of the United States during the Great Depression.

1932 Was defeated for reelection.

1946 Organized famine relief in dozens of countries.

1947–49, 1953–55 Chairman of the two Hoover Commissions to reorganize the executive branch of the federal government.

1950–52 Opposed American military commitment in Europe.

JOHN L. LEWIS (Lucas, Iowa, 1880–   ), labor leader.

1880 Born in Iowa, the son of a Welsh coal miner.

1896 Went to work in the coal mines.

1909–11 Legislative agent in Illinois for the United Mine Workers of America.

1919 Acting president of the United Mine Workers; president, 1920–60.

1919–22 Called two bituminous coal strikes.

1935 Formed the Committee for Industrial Organization within the AFL and became its first president.

1936 United Mine Workers left the AFL.

1938 Organized the Congress of Industrial Organizations (CIO) outside the AFL. Became its first president.

1941 Called a national strike of the soft-coal mines.

1946 Brought the United Mine Workers back to the AFL.

1946 Led another soft-coal strike; was fined for contempt of court.

1955 The CIO merged with the AFL, but the UMW remained independent.

FRANKLIN DELANO ROOSEVELT (Hyde Park, N.Y., 1882–Warm Springs, Ga., 1945), 32nd President of the United States.

1904 Was graduated from Harvard.

1907 Was admitted to the bar in New York City after study at Columbia Law School.

1910–13 Democratic member of the New York senate.

1913–20 Assistant Secretary of the Navy.

1920 Unsuccessful candidate for Vice President.

1921 Was stricken with poliomyelitis and never regained full use of his legs.

1924, 1928 Nominated Al Smith for President at the Democratic national conventions.

1929–33 Governor of New York.

1933–45 President of the United States. Introduced the New Deal and led the free nations in World War II.

HENRY L. STIMSON (New York City, 1867–Huntington, N.Y., 1950), Cabinet member.

1888 Was graduated from Yale.

1889 Received an M.A. degree from Harvard.

1890 Was graduated from the Harvard Law School.

1891 Was admitted to the bar in New York City.

1906–09 United States attorney for the southern district of New York.

1910 Was defeated as Republican candidate for governor of New York.

1911–13 Secretary of War.

1917–18 Colonel in the American Expeditionary Force.

1927 Acted as special representative of President Coolidge to Nicaragua.

1927–29 Governor-general of the Philippines.

1929–33 Secretary of State.

1931 Announced a return to *de facto* recognition in Latin America.

1932 Announced the "Stimson doctrine" of U.S. non-recognition for Manchuria or other territories established by force.

1937–40 Led the interventionists in the United States.

1940–45 Secretary of War under Presidents Roosevelt and Truman. He was the first American to serve in the cabinets of four Presidents.

1945 Helped make the decision to drop the atomic bomb on Japan.

Statistical Tables

Table 41.
United States population
(thousands)

	1910	1920	1930	1940
Total	92,407	106,466	123,077	131,954
Negro	9,828	10,463	11,891	12,866
Immigration	1,042	430	242	71
Classification, per cent of total:				
Urban	46	51	56	57
White native-born	74	77	78	81
White foreign-born	15	13	11	9
Non-white	11	10	10	10

Table 42.
The largest cities in the United States
(thousands)

1900		1920		1940	
New York	3,437	New York	5,620	New York	7,455
Chicago	1,699	Chicago	2,702	Chicago	3,397
Philadelphia	1,294	Philadelphia	1,824	Philadelphia	1,931
St. Louis	575	Detroit	994	Detroit	1,623
Boston	561	Cleveland	797	Los Angeles	1,504
Baltimore	509	St. Louis	773	Cleveland	878
Pittsburgh	452	Boston	748	Baltimore	859
Cleveland	382	Baltimore	734	St. Louis	816
Buffalo	352	Pittsburgh	588	Boston	771
San Francisco	343	Los Angeles	577	Pittsburgh	672

Table 43.
Immigration
(thousands)

1911–20	5,736
1921–30	4,107
1931–40	528
1941–50	1,035

Table 44.
Native white population of foreign or mixed parentage, 1940

Source	*Thousands*
England and Wales	1,467
Ireland	1,839
Sweden	856
Germany	3,999
Poland	1,912
Austria	781
U.S.S.R.	1,569
Italy	2,971
Canada	1,866
Total	23,158

Table 45.
Total capital in major branches of manufacturing, 1948
(book value, in millions of dollars)

Food and kindred products	16,071
Petroleum refining	15,363
Machinery, excluding transportation equipment	14,674
Iron and steel products	13,796
Textiles and textile products	10,397
Chemicals and allied substances	9,109
Transportation equipment	8,382
Forest products	4,816
Printing, publishing, and allied industries	3,984
Paper, pulp, and products	3,692

Table 46.
Exports and imports
(millions of dollars)

	Total exports	Exports of United States merchandise	General imports
1900	1,394	1,371	850
1905	1,519	1,492	1,118
1910	1,745	1,710	1,557
1915	2,769	2,716	1,674
1920	8,228	8,080	5,278
1925	4,910	4,819	4,227
1930	3,843	3,781	3,061
1935	2,283	2,243	2,047
1940	4,021	3,934	2,625
1945	9,806	9,585	4,159

Table 47.
Industrial statistics

	1900	1920	1945
Value added by manufactures (millions of dollars, current prices)	4,647[a]	17,253[a]	74,290[a]
United States investments abroad (billions of dollars)	0.7[b]	7.0[b]	16.8
Foreign investments in the United States (billions of dollars)	3.4[b]	3.3[b]	17.6
Wholesale commodity price index (1926=100)	56	154	106
Exports of United States merchandise (millions of dollars)	1,371	8,080	9,585
Exports of finished manufactures (millions of dollars)	332	3,205	6,257
Iron ore production (thousands of tons)	27,300	67,604	88,376
Steel ingots and castings produced (thousands of tons)	10,188	42,133	71,162
Crude petroleum production (thousands of barrels)	63,621	442,929	1,713,655
Bituminous coal production (thousands of tons)	212,316	568,667	577,617
Production of electric energy (millions of kilowatt-hours)	5,969[c]	56,559	271,255
Passenger car factory sales (thousands)	4	1,906	2,149[d]
Families with radios (thousands)	0	60[e]	33,100
Workers in non-farm occupations (thousands, followed by percent of all workers)	18,161 (63)	30,985 (73)	42,986 (82)[f]
General imports into the United States (millions of dollars)	850	5,278	4,159
Gross national product (billions of dollars, 1929 prices)	37.1[g]	73.3	180.9

[a] 1899, 1921, and 1947   [b] 1897 and 1919   [c] 1902   [d] 1946   [e] 1922   [f] 1940   [g] annual average, 1897–1901

Table 48.
United States expenditures and receipts
(millions of dollars)

	Expenditures	Receipts	Debt
1900	521	567	1,263
1905	567	544	1,132
1910	694	676	1,147
1915	761	698	1,191
1920	6,403	6,695	24,299
1925	3,063	3,780	20,516
1930	3,440	4,178	16,185
1935	6,521	3,730	28,701
1940	9,062	5,144	42,968
1945	98,416	44,475	258,682

Table 50.
Wholesale commodity price index
(1926= 100)

1900	56	1925	104
1905	60	1930	86
1910	70	1935	80
1915	70	1940	79
1920	154	1945	106

Table 49.
Currency
(millions of dollars)

	1900	1920	1945
Total currency in the United States	2,366	8,158	48,009
Currency in circulation	2,081	5,468	26,746
Federal Reserve notes	—	3,065	22,867

Table 51.
Union membership
(thousands, including Canadian members of U.S. unions)

1900	791	1925	3,566
1905	1,918	1930	3,632
1910	2,116	1935	3,728
1915	2,560	1940	8,944
1920	5,034	1945	14,796

Table 52.
Farm statistics

	1900	1920	1945
Value of farm property (billions of dollars)	20.4	78.4	69.2
Wheat production (millions of bushels)	599	843	1,108
Corn production (millions of bushels)	2,662	3,071	2,869
Cotton production (millions of bales)	10.1	13.4	9.0
Number of farms (millions)	5.7	6.4	5.9
Gross domestic private farm product (billions of dollars, 1929 prices)	8.4[a]	9.5	12.2

[a] 1897–1901 annual average

PART 9

The Era of Truman and Eisenhower, 1945–1961

Post-War America, 1945–1948

1945

Apr. 12   President Roosevelt died at Warm Springs, Ga., and **HARRY S TRUMAN** became President.

Nov. 21   First post-war strike began when the United Auto Workers struck against General Motors (113 days).

1946

Jan. 21   United Steel Workers strike (3 months) started.

Jan. 25   John L. Lewis returned the United Mine Workers to the AFL.

Feb. 20   EMPLOYMENT ACT made it the government's responsibility to "promote maximum employment, production, and purchasing power."

Apr. 1   United Mine Workers strike began.

May 21   The government seized the soft coal mines when the owners would not accept a settlement and did not return them until June, 1947.

May 23–25   Railroad strike was settled when President Truman threatened to seize the railroads.

Aug. 1   ATOMIC ENERGY COMMISSION was set up. **David E. Lilienthal** became chairman in Oct.

Aug. 2   Legislative Reorganization Act reduced the number of Congressional committees and provided funds for the legislative budget.

Sept. 5–20   Maritime strike closed all U.S. ports.

Nov. 5   Republicans won control of the **80th Congress**.

Nov. 6   Wartime wage and price controls except those on rent ended.

Nov. 20   John L. Lewis called a second soft coal strike in spite of a federal injunction. The miners returned to work in December, when a federal court fined Lewis and the union.

Dec. 31   Strikes for 1946 (the worst strike year in history) involved 4,750,000 workers and 116,000,000 man days.

1947

Feb.–Mar.   Religion and the schools

Feb. 10   *Everson v. Board of Education* allowed a state to transport children to parochial schools.

Mar. 8   *McCollum v. Board of Education* declared religious instruction in Illinois public school buildings a violation of the 1st amendment. But in *Zorach v. Clauson* (Apr. 28, 1952) the Court held it constitutional to release children from school for religious instruction.

Mar. 21   22nd Amendment limiting the **tenure of future Presidents** to two full terms and less than half of another went to the states. It was ratified Feb. 26, 1951.

June 23   (Taft-Hartley) LABOR-MANAGEMENT RELATIONS ACT, sponsored by Representative **Fred Hartley** and Senator **Robert A. Taft** (both Republicans), passed

Congress over President Truman's veto. The Act:

1. empowered the President to get an **80-day injunction** to stop any strike endangering "national health or safety";
2. required unions to give 60 days' notice before starting a strike (the "cooling-off" period);
3. declared **secondary boycotts, jurisdictional strikes**, and the **closed shop** illegal but allowed the **union shop** that required new employees to join the union within 30 days;
4. declared that a union could not refuse to bargain collectively; and required unions to issue financial statements and union officials to take an **anti-Communist oath**.

July 26   NATIONAL SECURITY ACT brought army, navy, and air force under Secretary of Defense and created the **National Security Council**.

1948

Mar. 19   First government injunction under the Taft-Hartley Act was issued against a strike at the Oak Ridge Atomic Energy plant.

Apr. 20   Lewis and the United Mine Workers were fined for contempt of court during a soft coal strike.

June 21   Republican Convention met in Philadelphia and nominated **Thomas E. Dewey** (N.Y.) for President and Governor **Earl Warren** of California for Vice President.

June 25   Displaced Persons Act admitted 205,000 immigrants from Europe (increased to 341,000 in 1950).

July 12   Democratic Convention opened in Philadelphia and nominated **Harry S Truman** for President and Senator **Alben W. Barkley** (Ky.) for Vice President. When the convention passed a strong **civil rights plank**, the delegates from Mississippi and Alabama walked out.

July 17   Southern Democrats at Birmingham, Ala., formed the **States' Rights Party** ("Dixiecrats") and nominated governor **J. Strom Thurmond** of South Carolina for President and governor **Fielding L. Wright** of Mississippi for Vice President on a platform calling for racial segregation.

July 22   Progressive Party in Philadelphia nominated **Henry A. Wallace** for President and Senator **Glen H. Taylor** (Idaho) for Vice President and urged a conciliatory policy toward Russia.

July 26–Aug. 11   Truman called a **special session of Congress** to repeal the Taft-Hartley Act and to pass housing, civil rights, health, social security and anti-inflation programs. When it passed only the last, Truman called it a **"do-nothing" Congress**.

Oct.   Dewey, over-confident, waged an indifferent campaign. Truman took a 31,000-mile **whistle-stop train tour** in which he made his famous "give-em-hell" speeches calling Republicans the party of "special interests."

Nov. 2   Presidential election: in spite of the Wallace movement, which cost him New York and Michigan, and the Thurmond party, which cost him four Southern states, **Truman** won with 24.1 million votes (303 electoral) to 22 million (189 electoral) for **Dewey**, 1.2 million (39 electoral) for **Thurmond** and 1.2 million for **Wallace**. Negro, labor and farmer votes helped Truman, who ran behind the party ticket, retain office. The Democrats regained a majority in Congress.

Truman and the Fair Deal, 1949–1952

1949

Jan. 5   In his message to Congress, Truman called for a **"FAIR DEAL"** with housing, civil rights, education, and health programs. Congress defeated his compulsory health insurance program.

June 20   Government Reorganization Act, based on the work of the (Herbert) Hoover Commission, allowed the President to reorganize the executive branch with Congressional approval.

July 15   Housing Act set the long range goal of "a decent home for every . . . American family."

Oct. 26   Minimum hourly wage was raised to 75 cents.

1950

April 28   National Science Foundation Act was passed by Congress to establish a foundation to promote scientific research and teaching. In 1952–64 the NSF spent over $500 million.

Aug. 25   President Truman seized the **railroads** to prevent a strike (returned May 23, 1952).

Nov. 1   Two Puerto Rican nationalists tried to assassinate President Truman but failed.

1951

Charges of **corruption** involving Military aide **Harry H. Vaughan** and Assistant Attorney General **T. Lamar Caudle** shook the Truman Administration. Truman demanded the resignation of Caudle after widespread reports of irregularities in income-tax collections. Truman also fired Attorney General J. Howard McGrath supposedly for lack of cooperation in a "clean-up" campaign.

1952

Feb. 28   **Senate Subcommittee to Investigate Crime**, headed by **Estes Kefauver** (Tenn.), reported. Its televised hearings attracted wide public attention.

Mar. 29   President Truman announced that he would not run for reelection.

Apr. 8   The President seized the **steel industry** to prevent a nationwide strike.

May 29   President Truman vetoed a bill giving oil rights off California, Texas, and Louisiana to those states.

June 2   *Youngstown Sheet and Tube Company v. Sawyer* ruled that seizure of the steel mills did not come under the President's emergency powers and was unconstitutional.

June 3–24   **Steel strike** involved 560,000 workers.

June 27   **McCarran-Walter Immigration Bill**, sponsored by Senator Pat McCarran (Democrat, Nev.) and Representative Francis Walter (Democrat, Pa.), was passed over the President's **veto**. It retained the 1924 national-origins system and intensified the screening and deporting of aliens.

July 7   The **Republican Party** met in Chicago and nominated Gen. **Dwight D. Eisenhower** for President over Senator Robert Taft of Ohio. Senator **Richard M. Nixon** (Calif.) was nominated for Vice President.

The platform accused Democrats of "appeasement of Communism."

July 21   The **Democratic Party** convened in Chicago and nominated governor **Adlai E. Stevenson** of Illinois for President and Senator **John J. Sparkman** (Ala.) for Vice President.

Nov. 4   **Presidential election**: in the campaign the Republicans capitalized on public opposition to the Korean War. **Eisenhower** won with 33.9 million votes (442 electoral) to 27.3 million (89 electoral) for **Stevenson**.

The National Security Controversy, 1947–1957

1947

Mar. 22   Executive order set up a **Loyalty Review Board** by which the federal government could discharge employees on "reasonable grounds for belief in disloyalty."

1948

Aug.–Dec.   The **HISS CASE**: on Aug. 3, **Whittaker Chambers** testified to the House Un-American Activities Committee that he and **Alger Hiss**, formerly of the State Department, had been part of a Communist espionage group. Hiss denied all charges, and President Truman denounced the Communist investigations as a "red herring." In early Dec., Congressman **Richard M. Nixon** (Calif.) of the House Un-American Activities Committee, accused the President of withholding information in the investigation. On Dec. 15, Hiss was indicted for perjury. His first trial ended in a hung jury, but his second trial led to his conviction, Jan. 21, 1950. He served nearly four years in jail, 1951–54.

1949

Mar. 5   **Judith Coplon**, Justice Department employee, and **Valentin Gubichev**, Soviet consular official, were arrested for espionage. Both were found guilty Mar. 7, 1950.

Oct. 14   A federal court in New York convicted the 11 top leaders of the American Communist party of violating the Smith Act.

1950

Feb.–Dec., 1954   McCarthyism: on Feb. 9, Senator **Joseph R. McCarthy** (Republican, Wis.), in a speech at Wheeling, W. Va., claimed that there were 209 Communists in the State Department. He later claimed the number was 57. From Mar. through June, a subcommittee of the Senate Foreign Relations Committee, headed by Senator **Millard Tydings** (Md.), held hearings on McCarthy's charges. In Mar., McCarthy accused **Owen Lattimore** of Johns Hopkins University, an expert on China, of being a Communist "agent," but the subcommittee cleared Lattimore and nine others of being Communists (July 20).

Sept. 23   INTERNAL SECURITY ACT, sponsored by Senator **Pat McCarran**, passed Congress over the President's veto. The Act made it illegal to conspire to establish a totalitarian dictatorship in the United States. Members of Communist organizations could not hold federal appointive offices or receive passports. Communist organizations had to register with the Attorney General. Former members of totalitarian organizations were barred from the U.S.

Nov. 7   Congressional elections: charging Democrats with being "soft on Communism," Republicans gained 28 seats in the House and 5 in the Senate. Senator McCarthy helped defeat Millard Tydings (Md.) by accusing him of "whitewashing" Lattimore in the Senate hearings.

1951

July 25   Senate Judiciary Internal Security Subcommittee under Senator McCarran began investigation of Owen Lattimore and the Institute of Pacific Relations. The Committee report (July 2, 1952) condemned the IPR, but no action was taken.

Apr. 5   Julius and Ethel Rosenberg were sentenced to death after their conviction for espionage of atomic secrets. They were executed on July 19, 1953.

June 4   *Dennis v. United States* upheld the Smith Act of 1940 that made it illegal to advocate forceful overthrow of the government.

1953

Investigation of Communism: **Senate Judiciary Internal Security Subcommittee** under **William F. Jenner** (Ind.), **Senate Permanent Investigations Subcommittee** of the Government Operations Committee under **Joseph R. McCarthy** (Wisc.), and the **House Un-American Activities Committee** under **Harold R. Velde,** (Ill.) investigated Communism in government, the State Department, and American life.

Mar. 25–27   McCarthy opposed the appointment of **Charles E. Bohlen** as Ambassador to the Soviet Union, but it was confirmed nonetheless.

Apr. 27   Executive order called for another check of officials suspected of disloyalty and shifted the burden of proof to the one accused. President Eisenhower claimed that 2,200 federal employees were fired for security reasons during his first year in office.

June 14   President Eisenhower criticized Senator McCarthy indirectly by attacking "the book burners."

Oct. 12   The McCarthy Committee began an investigation of suspected communism at **Fort Monmouth, N.J.**

Dec.–Apr., 1963   The **OPPENHEIMER CASE**: the Atomic Energy Commission withdrew access to classified information from **J. Robert Oppenheimer,** chairman of the advisory committee to the Commission. He was accused of hiring and of associating with Communists. In the spring of 1954, the AEC investigating committee concluded that Oppenheimer was loyal but voted not to renew his clearance because he had disregarded the security system. The AEC on June 20 voted not to reinstate Oppenheimer. In Apr., 1963, the AEC awarded Oppenheimer the Fermi Award for contributions to nuclear physics, thus in effect reversing the 1954 ruling.

1954

Apr. 22–June 17   The so-called **ARMY-McCARTHY HEARINGS** were conducted before a special Senate committee. Army Secretary **Robert T. Stevens** charged that McCarthy's assistant, **Roy M. Cohn,** had exerted undue pressure on the Army to get special treatment for another aide, **David Schine**. McCarthy charged that Stevens had tried to pressure him into calling off the army investigations. The hearings on television, witnessed by as many as 20 million at a time, were spiced by tart exchanges between McCarthy and special Army defense counsel **Joseph N. Welch**. The Committee report cleared Cohn and Stevens, and the hearings marked the decline of McCarthy's influence.

Aug. 24   Communist Control Act added Communist-infiltrated organizations to those covered by the Internal Security Act.

Dec. 2 The Senate "**condemned**" (but did not "censure") Senator McCarthy for contempt of a Senate Subcommittee.

1957

June 17 The Supreme Court rendered two decisions to protect those unfairly accused of Communist sympathies: *Yates v. United States* interpreted the Smith Act to forbid "action" aimed at the overthrow of the government but not simply "advocacy." *Watkins v. United States* sustained refusal to name Communist Party members before the House Un-American Activities Committee because the Committee had failed to indicate the purpose of the investigations.

Eisenhower Moderation, 1953–1960

1953

Jan. 20 Inauguration of President Eisenhower. The Cabinet included Secretary of State **John Foster Dulles** and Secretary of the Treasury **George M. Humphrey**.

Apr. 1 Creation of the **DEPARTMENT OF HEALTH, EDUCATION, AND WELFARE.**

May 22 President Eisenhower signed a bill granting the tidelands to the states, thus reversing President Truman's action.

1954

Apr. 1 U.S. Air Force Academy was established in Colorado.

May 13   St. Lawrence Seaway Act was passed, reopening the Great Lakes to ocean-going ships.

June 16 President Eisenhower instructed the Atomic Energy Commission to approve a contract with a power combine headed by **Edgar Dixon** and **Eugene Yates** to build a steam generating plant in Memphis, Tenn., to feed electricity into the Tenn. Valley System. TVA authorities and public power advocates disapproved. The AEC approved the Dixon-Yates contract on Oct. 5 but was overruled by the President in July, 1955.

Aug. 2 The Housing Act of 1954 broadened the urban redevelopment program of 1949, calling it "urban renewal."

Aug. 28   Flexible price controls (75 per cent–90 per cent) for basic farm commodities replaced the rigid scale.

Aug. 30   Atomic Energy Act allowed private companies to produce electric power with their own reactors, thereby ending government monopoly of atomic energy. The act also allowed the release of atomic information to European allies.

Nov. 2   Congressional elections: Democrats regained control of Congress, and for the rest of the decade **Lyndon B. Johnson** and **Sam Rayburn,** both Texans, served as majority leader of the Senate and Speaker of the House, respectively. During the fall, Vice President Nixon campaigned vigorously, calling Democrats "soft on Communism."

1955

Aug. 4 Federal Power Commission granted the Idaho Power Company the right to build three low dams at **Hell's Canyon** in the Snake River Valley in spite of efforts in Congress to build a public-power high dam there.

Aug. 12 Minimum hourly wage was increased from 75 cents to $1.00.

July 1 Labor Department announced that 18 states had passed "**right-to-work**" **laws** banning the union shop. The Taft-Hartley Labor Act permitted the union shop only in states that did not forbid it.

Sept. 24 President Eisenhower suffered a coronary thrombosis in Denver, Col., that kept him in the hospital for two months.

Dec. 5 The CIO (Congress of Industrial Organizations, 5.2 million members) merged with the AFL (10.9 million members). **George Meany,** former president of the AFL, became president of the **AFL–CIO.**

1956

Jan. 9 President Eisenhower blocked the restoration of rigid farm price supports by calling for a **soil-bank plan** to pay farmers for retiring land used for surplus crops. It became law on May 28.

Apr. 11 The Upper Colorado Storage project passed Congress in spite of opposition from easterners, conservationists, and Californians, who feared loss of Colorado River water. According to the plan, dams and artificial lakes would store water at the head of the Colorado River, and tunnels would then deliver it to the dry eastern slope of the Rockies.

June 29 **Federal Highway Act,** the largest American road building act ever passed, called for spending over $32 billion on 41,000 miles of road in 13 years.

Aug. 13 **Democratic Convention** met in Chicago and renominated **Adlai E. Stevenson** for President. Senator **Estes Kefauver** (Tenn.) barely defeated Senator John F. Kennedy (Mass.) in the nomination for Vice President.

Aug. 20 **Republican Convention** opened in San Francisco and renominated the **Eisenhower-Nixon** ticket.

Oct.–Nov. In the Presidential campaign, Republicans defended flexible farm-price supports, private power policies and Dulles' so-called brink of war tactics. Stevenson called for a ban on nuclear testing, but the Hungarian Revolt and the Suez Crisis made the proposal untimely.

Nov. 6 **Presidential election: Eisenhower** received 35.6 million votes (457 electoral) to **Stevenson's** 26 million votes (73 electoral). Democratic control of Congress continued.

1957

Jan. 30 The Senate set up a committee to investigate labor with **John L. McClellan**

(Ark.) as Chairman and **Robert F. Kennedy** as Chief Counsel. Many of its hearings over three years were televised.

Aug. The most serious **recession** since World War II began as a result of decline in business investments and cutbacks in defense spending.

1958

Apr. The low point of the recession came when **unemployment** reached 5 million (7.5 per cent of the labor force). Industrial production dropped 13 per cent, Aug., 1957–Apr., 1958. The Administration resisted demands for both tax cuts and increased government spending until fiscal 1959. Federal administrative budget:

Fiscal year	Receipts	Expenses	Surplus
		(billions of dollars)	
1957	70.6	69.0	1.6
1958	68.6	71.4	– 2.8
1959	67.9	80.3	– 12.4

The deficit for fiscal 1959 was the largest peacetime deficit in history. Some recovery was achieved during the summer months, but unemployment remained at 6 per cent by the end of the year.

Aug. 28 **Farm Act** looked toward the eventual reduction of parity prices to 65 per cent.

Sept. 2 **NATIONAL DEFENSE EDUCATION ACT** provided $800 million over four years for loans to college and university students and for aid to states to improve science and foreign language teaching. A two-year extension for 1963–64 cost $500 million.

Nov. 4 **Congressional elections:** Republicans suffered a major setback when they lost 47 seats in the House and 13 in the Senate. Major factors were the economic recession and Republican farm policy.

1959

Sept. 14 **Labor-Management Act,** originally sponsored by Congressmen **Phil Landrum** (Democrat, Ga.) and **Robert Griffin** (Republican, Mich.), was signed by the President. The act strengthened the ban against secondary boycotts and protected workers against corruption and gangsterism in unions.

1960

Apr. 11   Government Operations Permanent Investigations Subcommittee, under Senator McClellan, was empowered to carry out investigations of labor unions.

June 16   23rd Amendment granted the **District of Columbia** the right to vote in Presidential elections. It was ratified on Mar. 29, 1961.

July 11   Democratic Convention met in Los Angeles and nominated Senator **John F. Kennedy** (Mass.) for President over Senators **Lyndon B. Johnson** (Tex.) and **Hubert H. Humphrey** (Minn.). **Johnson** was nominated for Vice President. The platform called for economic growth, civil rights, and medical care for the aged.

July 25   The Republican Party met in Chicago and nominated **Richard M. Nixon** for President and **Henry Cabot Lodge** (Mass.), Ambassador to the UN, for Vice President. The platform carried a strong civil rights plank.

Sept. 13   Health Care for the Aged Act, sponsored by Senator **Robert S. Kerr** (Democrat, Okla.) and Congressman Wilbur D. Mills (Democrat, Ark.) became law. The Act was designed to provide payments to the states to help them pay medical expenses of old persons with low incomes. Earlier the House had tabled a bill proposed by **Aime J. Forand** (Democrat, R.I.) to pay hospital costs of old people under Social Security. Earlier that year, the Senate had defeated a similar proposal by Senator **John F. Kennedy**.

Sept. 12   Kennedy, a Roman Catholic, stated before the Greater Houston Ministerial Association that he believed in separation of church and state. The speech blunted Protestant attacks on Kennedy.

Sept. 26   The first of four televised **Kennedy-Nixon debates** took place. The debates helped Kennedy by disproving the argument that he was too young.

Nov. 8   Presidential election: high unemployment and the charge that American prestige had slipped abroad helped the Democrats win a close victory. **Kennedy** received

34.2 million votes (303 electoral) to **Nixon's** 34.1 million votes (219 electoral). Democrats carried the East, the central industrial states, and the South. The Negro vote went heavily for Kennedy (68 per cent). Congress remained Democratic.

The Civil Rights Movement, 1945–1960

1945

July 1   New York Fair Employment Law, set up the first antidiscrimination commission.

1948

Jan. 12   *Sipeul v. Board of Regents of the University of Oklahoma* ruled that a state was not to deny a Negro admission to its state law school on grounds of color.

Feb. 2   President Truman proposed antilynching, anti-poll tax, antisegregation, and fair employment legislation, but no laws were passed.

May 3   *Shelley v. Kraemer* declared that a state court could not enforce a racially restrictive covenant.

July 26   Truman issued an **executive order** barring segregation in the **armed forces** and discrimination in federal employment.

1950

June 5   By the decision of *Sweatt v. Painter*, a state could not keep a Negro from its law school on the grounds that a Negro law school was available.

1953

May 4   *Terry v. Adams* held that segregated primary elections violated the 14th Amendment.

1954

May 17   In *BROWN V. BOARD OF EDUCATION OF TOPEKA*, the Supreme Court ruled, 9–0, that segregation in the elementary schools of Topeka violated the 14th Amendment, thereby ending the "separate but equal" doctrine of *Plessy v. Ferguson*.

1955

May 31 *Brown v. Board of Education* (second decision) put responsibility on local officials for implementing the first Brown decision and kept jurisdiction in federal courts. School integration was to proceed **"with all deliberate speed."**

Nov. 25 The Interstate Commerce Commission banned segregation of passengers on trains and buses in interstate travel. This ruling included railroad terminals but not bus terminals.

Dec. 5 Montgomery, Ala., Negroes led by Rev. **MARTIN LUTHER KING** began a **boycott** against segregation on buses. It ended with a federal injunction (Nov. 13, 1956) against the segregation.

1956

Feb. 1 The Virginia legislature declared the right of a state to "interpose its sovereignty" against the Brown decisions.

Feb. 3 The Supreme Court ordered the University of Alabama to admit its first Negro, **Autherine Lucy,** but she was expelled on Feb. 29 after a riot.

Mar. 11 100 southern Senators and Congressmen issued a manifesto promising to use "all lawful means" to overthrow the Brown decisions.

1957

Sept. 9 **CIVIL RIGHTS ACT** of 1957, the first since 1875, created a six-man **Civil Rights Commission**. District courts were authorized to issue injunctions to protect civil rights. Voting cases would be heard without jury.

Sept. 3 Gov. **Orval Faubus** called out the National Guard to prevent nine Negro students from entering Central High School in **Little Rock, Ark**.

Sept. 23 Faubus withdrew the troops after a federal court injunction. When the nine children approached the school, a riot broke out.

Sept. 24 President Eisenhower sent 1,000 paratroopers to Little Rock, the first federal troops in the South since Reconstruction.

Sept. 25 The Negroes entered school, but the schools were later closed until 1958.

1959

Sept. **Prince Edward County, Va.**, closed its schools to prevent integration.

1960

Feb. 1 A **"sit-in" movement** began in Greensboro, N.C., against segregation at lunch counters.

May 6 **CIVIL RIGHTS ACT** of 1960 made it a federal crime to transport dynamite across state lines in order to blow up a building. Federal courts could issue court orders empowering the Negro to vote.

Nov. 30 Federal court in New Orleans enforced desegregation of the schools after riots took place in the city.

Dec. 5 *Boynton v. Virginia* ruled that interstate bus terminals could not segregate passengers.

The New Frontier and the Great Society, 1961–1967

The Climax of the Civil Rights Movement, 1961–1967

1961

Mar. 6 An executive order established the President's **Committee on Equal Employment Opportunity** for firms with government contracts. Within the first 10 months the Administration began 14 voting-rights cases under the Civil Rights Act of 1957, compared to nine cases, 1957–60.

May 14 Negro and white **Freedom Riders** were attacked when testing segregation barriers in bus terminals in Birmingham, Ala.

Sept. The ICC prohibited segregation both on interstate buses and in terminals.

1962

Aug. 27   24th Amendment banning the **poll tax** requirement in federal elections was sent to the states; it was ratified by Jan. 23, 1964.

Sept. 30   President Kennedy sent 3,000 federal troops to the **University of Mississippi** to stop a riot and secure the admission of **James H. Meredith,** the first Negro student at the university.

Nov. 24   President Kennedy issued an **executive order** banning discrimination in federally assisted housing.

1963

Apr. 3   Martin Luther King began to lead mass demonstrations in Birmingham, Ala., to desegregate the city.

May 2–7   Police met marching Negroes in Birmingham with fire hoses and police dogs. Kennedy threatened but never sent troops.

June 11   Gov. **George Wallace** barred the registration of two Negroes at the **University of Alabama** but gave way when Kennedy federalized the Alabama National Guard.

June 11   In a television address President Kennedy referred to civil rights as a **"moral issue"** and strongly supported a civil rights act.

June 12   **Medgar W. Evers,** a leader of the NAACP in Mississippi, was shot from ambush and killed in Jackson, Miss.

Aug. 28   A massive **civil rights march** took place in Washington, D.C., and Martin Luther King gave his "I have a dream" speech at the Lincoln Memorial.

Sept. 15   Efforts to integrate schools in **Birmingham** led to violence. Bombing of a Sunday school killed four Negro girls; it was the 21st such bombing in Birmingham in eight years.

1964

May 25   *Griffin v. Prince Edward County School Board* ruled that closing public schools to avoid desegregation was unconstitutional.

June 10   The Senate voted to close off the filibuster against the civil rights bill and passed it on June 19.

July 2   CIVIL RIGHTS ACT of 1964 became law. The terms:

1. expedited law suits over voting rights;
2. barred discrimination in **public accomodations** (The Supreme Court upheld this section in *Heart of Atlanta Motel v. United States,* 1964.);
3. authorized the Attorney General to institute suits to desegregate schools;
4. barred discrimination in any program receiving federal assistance; and
5. set up an **Equal Employment Opportunity Commission.**

July 18–Aug. 30   NEGRO RIOTS, caused by ghetto living, unemployment, and hatred of the police took place in Harlem (July 18–22); Rochester, N.Y. (July 24–25); Jersey City (Aug. 2–4); Chicago (Aug. 16–17); and Philadelphia (Aug. 28–30).

Aug. 4   Three young civil rights workers were found murdered near Philadelphia, Miss. The FBI arrested 21 in connection with the murders. In Oct., 1967, seven were convicted of conspiracy to violate a person's civil rights.

1965

Feb. 21   **Malcolm X,** formerly eastern leader of the Black Muslims, was shot and killed in New York City. **Elijah Muhammed,** leader of the **Black Muslims,** who had ousted Malcolm X, denied any connection with the murder.

Mar. 21–25   A **civil rights march** took place from **Selma to Montgomery, Ala.,** to encourage greater Negro voter registration.

Aug. 6   CIVIL RIGHTS ACT of 1965 became law with the following terms:

1. **Literacy tests** were to be suspended in any county that used the test to disqualify voters and had a voter turnout of less than 50 per cent of its eligible population. (Alabama, Georgia, Louisiana, Mississippi, South Carolina, Virginia, and parts of Arizona and Idaho were included in this category.
2. Federal voting **examiners** would then be sent to register voters.
3. The Attorney General was empowered to proceed against discriminatory state poll taxes. (The Supreme Court upheld

the Act in *South Carolina v. Katzenbach,* 1966.)

Aug. 11–15 Riots broke out in **Watts** District of **Los Angeles**.

Dec. The percentage of Negroes in school with whites in the 17 southern and border states and in the District of Columbia rose as follows: 1957, 3 per cent; 1960, 6 per cent; 1963, 8 per cent; 1966, 16 per cent.

1966

May **Stokely Carmichael**, president of the **Student Non-violent Coordinating Committee** (SNCC), introduced the concept of a unified Negro community (**"BLACK POWER"**). **Roy Wilkins**, head of the **NAACP**, and **Martin Luther King**, head of the **Southern Christian Leadership Conference**, objected to the idea of Black Power, but **Floyd McKissick** of the **Congress of Racial Equality** (CORE) supported it.

June 6 **James Meredith** was wounded by a sniper while making a "march against fear" in rural Mississippi.

July Rioting occurred in the Negro West Side of Chicago and the Negro section of Cleveland.

Sept. A **civil rights bill** aimed at ending housing discrimination failed in Congress.

1967

Feb. President Johnson again called for a civil rights bill to end housing discrimination, but none was passed.

May 29 The U.S. Supreme Court ruled unconstitutional an amendment to the California constitution that gave property owners the right to discriminate in the sale and rental of housing.

June 13 Johnson appointed **Thurgood Marshall** as the first Negro to serve on the U.S. Supreme Court.

July 12–27 Severe Negro **riots** in Newark, N.J. (July 12–17) and in Detroit (July 23–27) left 63 dead. In the period 1964–67, outbreaks of racial violence occurred in 50 U.S. cities.

The Kennedy Years, 1961–1963

1961

Jan. 20 In his inaugural address President Kennedy announced the arrival of a "new generation of Americans" to power. His cabinet included **Dean Rusk** as Secretary of State, **Robert F. Kennedy** as Attorney General, and **Robert S. McNamara** as Secretary of Defense.

Jan. 30 President Kennedy called for heavy government spending to **increase the growth rate** of the **gross national product** and to reduce unemployment. He was the first President to subscribe fully to the ideas of the English economist **John Maynard Keynes**. Under Kennedy, administrative **budgets** jumped from $81.5 billion (fiscal 1961, the last Eisenhower budget) to $97.7 billion (fiscal 1964). The national **debt** climbed from $289 billion to $313 billion, **unemployment** dropped from 6.7 per cent to 5.2 per cent, and the **gross national product** grew from $520 billion to $629 billion. The 1960–61 **recession** ended Feb., 1961.

Mar. 1 Kennedy issued an executive order setting up a **PEACE CORPS** of volunteers to work in underdeveloped areas of the world. Congress made it permanent on Sept. 21.

May 1 **Area Redevelopment Act** provided $300 million to finance industrial or rural development where unemployment was high.

June 30 **Housing Act** authorized $6.1 billion for housing programs.

Sept. President Kennedy failed to get Congressional approval for a tax revision, a health care bill, a Department of Urban Affairs, and aid for secondary and elementary schools.

1962

Mar. 31 Steel unions and management agreed on contract terms with no price rise.

Apr. 10 **U.S. Steel** announced a **price increase** of $6 a ton, and most other steel companies followed suit.

Apr. 11 President Kennedy denounced the

price increase and threatened antitrust investigations.

Apr. 13 When Inland Steel and Kaiser Steel, under Administration pressure, announced that they would hold the line, U.S. Steel and the others rescinded the price increase.

May 28 The **stock market dropped** abruptly. Some business leaders blamed the drop on lack of confidence in the Administration brought about by Kennedy's pressure on the steel companies.

July 17 The Senate tabled a bill to provide health care for the aged under social security proposed by Congressman **Cecil King** (Democrat, Calif.) and Senator **Clinton P. Anderson** (Democrat, N.M.). President Kennedy blamed the defeat on the American Medical Association.

Oct. 4 **Trade Expansion Act** gave the President great power to cut tariffs.

Nov. 6 In Congressional elections, Democrats maintained their position in Congress.

1963

Jan. Kennedy proposed a tax cut, but it did not pass Congress.

Nov. 22 **PRESIDENT KENNEDY WAS ASSASSINATED** by **Lee Harvey Oswald**, a former Marine and supporter of left-wing causes, in Dallas, Tex. Governor **John B. Connally** of Texas was also shot but survived. Vice President **LYNDON B. JOHNSON** was sworn in as President on the Presidential plane.

Nov. 24 **Jack Ruby,** a Dallas night club owner, murdered Oswald in the Dallas jail in front of television cameras. Ruby died of cancer in Jan., 1967.

Nov. 25 President Kennedy was buried in Arlington National Cemetery.

Johnson and the Great Society, 1963–1967

1963

Nov. 27 President Johnson pledged to press on with President Kennedy's program, particularly the civil rights and tax cut proposals.

1964

Jan. 8 President Johnson called for a **"WAR ON POVERTY."**

Feb. 26 **Tax Cut Act** provided for a $11.5 billion reduction in taxes over two years with rates dropping from 20 per cent–91 per cent to 14 per cent–70 per cent.

July 13 **Republican Convention** met in San Francisco and nominated conservative Senator **Barry M. Goldwater** (Ariz.) for President and Congressman **William E. Miller** (N.Y.) for Vice President. The conservative platform called for a "frugal" government and demanded "victory" in foreign affairs.

Aug. 20 **Economic Opportunity Act** set up (1) a Job Corps for vocational training, (2) an Office of Economic Opportunity to organize educational and training programs, and (3) Volunteers in Service to America (VISTA) to combat poverty.

Aug. 24 **Democratic Convention** met at Atlantic City, N.J., and nominated **Lyndon B. Johnson** for President and Senator **Hubert H. Humphrey** (Minn.) for Vice President. The platform included a strong civil rights plank.

Nov. 3 **Presidential Election:** Johnson defeated Goldwater with the greatest vote of any candidate in history and the greatest percentage of the total vote (61.1 per cent as compared to 60.7 per cent for Franklin Roosevelt in 1936). **Johnson** had 43.1 million votes (486 electoral votes); **Goldwater** had 27.2 million (52 electoral).

1965

Jan. 4 President Johnson called for reforms to create the **"GREAT SOCIETY,"** including a voting rights bill, aid to schools, immigration law reform, and an attack on disease.

Mar. 3 **Appalachian Program** authorized $1.1 billion to fight poverty in an 11-state area.

Apr. 11 **ELEMENTARY AND SECONDARY SCHOOL EDUCATION ACT,** the most far-reaching in history, provided aid to school districts with a large number of poor families (over $1 billion the first year). It authorized grants to states to purchase school materials for pupils in public and private (including parochial) schools.

May 18   President Johnson called for repeal of Section 14b of the Taft-Hartley Labor Law, which permitted states to pass "right-to-work laws." Nineteen states had such laws. Repeal of 14b passed the House on July 28 but was blocked in the Senate.

July 30   Act to provide medical care for the aged **(MEDICARE)** under social security, sponsored by Congressman **Wilbur D. Mills** (Democrat, Ark.), was signed by President Johnson at Independence, Mo., in the presence of Harry S Truman, who had proposed such a bill in 1945.

Sept. 9   Congress established the **Department of Housing and Urban Development. Robert C. Weaver** became its first secretary and was the first Negro to serve in the Cabinet.

Oct. 3   IMMIGRATION ACT ended the 1924 national-origins quota system. Henceforth, immigration would be on the basis of occupational needs of the U.S.

1966

Jan. 19   President Johnson asked Congress for $12.8 billion additional for war in Vietnam.

Jan. 24   President Johnson asked Congress for a record $112.9 billion for fiscal 1967 to wage war in Vietnam and to build the "Great Society."

1967

Jan.   President Johnson asked for a record administrative budget of $135 billion for fiscal 1968. The last Kennedy budget had requested $97.7 billion, and the last Eisenhower budget had asked for a relatively modest $81.5 billion.

Feb. 11   The states ratified the **25th Amendment**, which established the conditions and order of **Presidential succession** in case of Presidential disability.

The Warren Court, 1953–1967

Earl Warren was appointed Chief Justice of the Supreme Court in 1953. The Justices who served with him, and their terms on the Court, are:

Hugo L. Black, 1937–   .
Stanley F. Reed, 1938–57.
Felix Frankfurter, 1939–62.
William O. Douglas, 1939–   .
Robert H. Jackson, 1941–54.
Harold H. Burton, 1945–58.
Tom C. Clark, 1949–67.
Sherman Minton, 1949–56.
John M. Harlan, 1955–   .
William J. Brennan, Jr., 1956–   .
Charles E. Whittaker, 1957–62.
Potter Stewart, 1958–   .
Byron R. White, 1962–   .
Arthur J. Goldberg, 1962–65.
Abe Fortas, 1965–   .
Thurgood Marshall, 1967–   .

1954–61

For cases decided by the Warren Court involving civil rights and national security, see pp. 249 and 251–54.

1962

Mar. 26   *Baker v. Carr* ruled that the failure of Tennessee to reapportion its state legislature since 1901 violated the 14th amendment. This case opened the subject of **state apportionment** to judicial review.

June 25   In *Engel v. Vitale* New York officials were forbidden to require an official church **prayer in the public schools**.

1963

Mar. 18   In *Gideon v. Wainwright*, the Court declared that a state must provide a **defense counsel** for indigent defendants.

June 17   *Abington Township School District v. Schempp* declared that recitation of the Lord's Prayer or the reading of passages from the Bible were violations of the 1st amendment, applied to the states by the 14th amendment.

1964

Feb. 17   *Wesberry v. Sanders* instructed states to realign their **Congressional districts** so that the districts would be substantially equal in population (the principle of "one man, one vote").

June 15   In *Reynolds v. Sims* and 13 other cases, the court decided that both houses of a state legislature must be apportioned on the basis of population.

June 22   *Escobedo v. Illinois* declared the right of a suspect to have a lawyer when being **interrogated** by the police.

1965

June 7   *Griswold v. Connecticut* declared unconstitutional an 1879 Connecticut law fining a person for offering **birth control** information.

1966

June 13   *Miranda v. Arizona* ruled that statements made by a prisoner under interrogation could not be used as evidence unless legal safeguards were used in obtaining them.

American Policy in Europe, 1945–1967

World War II to Cold War, 1945–1946

1945

Feb. 4–11   The **YALTA CONFERENCE** determined the postwar map of **eastern Europe**:

1. **Poland** east of the Curzon line (at about the 24th meridian) went to the U.S.S.R.
2. German territory east of the **Oder** and **Neisse** Rivers went to Poland.
3. Poland was to be governed by the government at **Lublin** with leaders from the London government-in-exile added. The Polish government would be "democratic."
4. **Unconditional surrender** of Germany was required.
5. "**Democratic**" governments were promised for the liberated states of Europe.

For the **United Nations,** it was agreed that:

1. The UN Conference was to meet in **San Francisco** in April.
2. The **Ukraine** and **Byelorussia** would have separate votes in the UN. The Big three could **veto** all important matters before the Security Council.

Mar.   A Communist regime in **Rumania** marked the start of Russian subjugation of eastern Europe. The U.S. recognized governments there and in **Hungary** and **Bul**-garia without condoning the suppression of democracy.

Apr. 25–June 26   At the **UNITED NATIONS CONFERENCE** at San Francisco, delegates of 50 nations unanimously approved a **UN charter:**

1. The UN was to take collective measures to maintain peace and security and to settle disputes.
2. In the **General Assembly** each member nation was to have one vote. A two-thirds vote was required on important matters, a majority on all others.
3. The 11-member **Security Council** was to determine action when a breach of the peace had taken place and could call on member nations for military support. The five permanent members of the Council (U.S., U.S.S.R., Great Britain, France, and China) could **veto** non-procedural matters.
4. The **Secretariat** headed by a Secretary General would carry on routine work.
5. An **Economic and Social Council** was to deal with human welfare and rights.
6. An **International Court of Justice** at the Hague was to handle international disputes.

May 7   UNCONDITIONAL GERMAN SUR-RENDER was announced.

June 5   German occupation zones were

established by the European Advisory Commission at London: Germany east of about the 11th meridian was to be occupied by Russia. West Germany was divided among the U.S., Great Britain, and France. Berlin (within east Germany) was to be occupied by all four powers.

June 12   U.S. troops withdrew into the U.S. zone in Germany.

June 29   Lt. Gen. **Lucius Clay** reached agreement with the Russians allowing U.S. troops into **Berlin**. The right of access through east Germany to Berlin was never formally guaranteed.

July 17–Aug. 2   At the **POTSDAM CONFERENCE** in a suburb of Berlin, **President Truman, Premier Stalin**, and **Prime Minister Churchill** (who was replaced by the new British Prime Minister, **Clement Attlee,** on July 28) agreed that:

1. The Council of Foreign Ministers of the Big Five would prepare **peace treaties** and would deal with a central German government whenever it came into being.
2. **Polish-German borders** would be determined by the final peace treaties.

3. Occupation authorities would **democratize** and **denazify** Germany.
4. Germany would be a **single economic unit** during occupation.
5. Russia was to take capital equipment from Germany in place of reparations.

July 28   The Senate accepted the UN Treaty.

Aug. 21   **End of Lend-Lease:** total American aid 1941–45 was $50.6 billion (Great Britain received $31.4 billion; the U.S.S.R. received $11.3 billion). The Allies gave the U.S. $7.8 billion in reverse lend-lease (the U.S.S.R. gave $2.2 billion). Settlement with Great Britain and six other nations (not the U.S.S.R.) was made by July, 1948.

Oct. 24   The UN charter went into effect.

Nov. 20–Oct. 1, 1946   **International Military Tribunal at Nuremberg,** Germany, tried 23 Nazi officials for crimes against humanity, convicted 18, and sentenced 11 to be hanged. The U.S. prosecutor was Supreme Court Justice **Robert H. Jackson.** The U.S. tried over 800,000 former Nazis in the U.S. zone and convicted more than 500,000 with no executions.

Dec. 6   The U.S. loaned $3.7 billion to Great Britain.

Dec. 17   The **UN Relief and Rehabilitation Administration** (UNRRA) received $1.4 billion from the U.S. By 1947 the U.S. had granted $11 billion to UNRRA and other relief agencies.

Dec. 20   The Senate defeated amendments to the UN Participation Act requiring Congressional permission for the use of U.S. troops.

1946

Jan. 10   The first meeting of the UN General Assembly was held in London. The Security Council met a week later. **Trygve Lie** of Norway became the first Secretary General. In Oct., the UN met in New York City, where permanent quarters were completed in 1951.

Jan. 19   **Iran** charged in the Security Council that the U.S.S.R. had kept troops in Iran after the agreed-upon withdrawal date. Russia agreed to remove the troops by May 6.

Jan. 24   The UN created its **Atomic Energy Commission.**

9-1   German Partition

Occupied by U. S.	Occupied by U.S.S.R.
Occupied by France	Transferred to Poland
Occupied by Gr. Britain	

Feb. 28   Secretary of State **James F. Byrnes** announced a "get tough with Russia" policy.

Mar. 5   Winston Churchill in a speech at Fulton, Mo., referred to an **"IRON CURTAIN"** running through eastern Europe.

Apr. 25   Russia rejected Byrnes's plan, involving inspection, to unite Germany.

June 14   Bernard Baruch, U.S. delegate to the UN Atomic Energy Commission, proposed an International Atomic Development Authority that would own all hazardous atomic energy activities and would have unlimited power of inspection. The U.S.S.R. rejected the plan.

June 19   The U.S.S.R. demanded the destruction of all atomic bombs (all American) before any agreement could be reached.

July 1 and 25   The U.S. exploded its fourth and fifth atomic bombs at **Bikini Atoll** in the Pacific.

July 29–Oct. 15   PARIS PEACE CONFERENCE, with **Byrnes** and · Senators **Thomas Connally** and **Arthur H. Vandenberg** representing the U.S., agreed on treaties with Axis **satellites** (signed in New York on Feb. 10, 1947).

Sept. 6   Byrnes accused the U.S.S.R. of stripping eastern Germany for reparations and pledged that the U.S. would stay in the western zone. Secretary of Commerce **Henry Wallace** criticized Byrnes for this but was dismissed by President Truman for his opposition to American policy toward Russia.

Containment of Russia, 1947–1952

1947

Feb. 21   Britain announced that it must end all economic and military aid to Greece.

Mar. 10–Apr. 24   Foreign Ministers' Conference met in Moscow with **George C. Marshall** of the U.S., **Ernest Bevin** of Great Britain, and **Vyacheslav Molotov** of the U.S.S.R. present. Russia insisted on a centralized government for a united Germany, while the U.S. preferred a federal system. No action was taken.

Mar. 12   The **TRUMAN DOCTRINE** called for the **containment of Soviet expansion;** President Truman asked Congress for $400 million to aid Greece and Turkey, in danger

of falling to armed Communist minorities.

Apr. 23   The Senate endorsed the Truman Doctrine; the House endorsed it on May 9.

June 5   Secretary of State George C. Marshall announced the **MARSHALL PLAN** for European recovery by which the United States would grant money to bring about the economic and social recovery of Europe from its wartime devastation.

July 3   Molotov walked out of a Paris meeting of the U.S., Britain, France, and the U.S.S.R. on the Marshall Plan, charging an "imperialist" plot. The Soviet Union later refused to take part in any program of European recovery.

July   Article by **George Kennan,** head of the planning staff of the State Department, signed "Mr. X," outlined the policy of containment of the U.S.S.R. that was followed for the next decade.

July 12–Sept. 22   At the **Marshall Plan Conference** at Paris, 16 nations set up the **Committee for European Economic Cooperation:** Great Britain, France, Ireland, Iceland, Denmark, Norway, Sweden, Belgium, Netherlands, Luxembourg, Portugal, Switzerland, Italy, Greece, Turkey, and Austria. Spain and Germany were not invited. Nations behind the Iron Curtain declined to attend.

Sept.   The **Cominform** (Communist Information Bureau) was set up to promote worldwide revolution.

1948

Feb. 25   Communists took over the government of **Czechoslovakia.**

Apr. 3   FOREIGN ASSISTANCE ACT called for spending $5.4 billion in the **European Recovery Program** (ERP) the first year. About $15 billion was spent in the program's first four years. The **Economic Cooperation Administration** (ECA) administered the act.

Mar. 6   Ambassadors of the U.S., Great Britain, France, Luxembourg, Belgium, and the Netherlands met in London and agreed on the formation of a federal government in West Germany and the participation of Germany in ERP.

Mar. 17   Britain, France, and the Benelux countries signed the **Brussels Pact** for collective self-defense.

June 24–May 12, 1949   BERLIN BLOCK-ADE: the Russians cut off surface traffic through East Germany to Berlin. The immediate cause given was a dispute over the currency used in Berlin.

June 25   The U.S. and Great Britain began the **Berlin Airlift,** which carried up to 4,500 tons of supplies a day to Berlin for 321 days.

Oct. 4   The West took the Berlin matter to the UN, but Russia blocked a compromise.

1949

Jan. 20   In **Point Four** of his inaugural address, President Truman called for a program of economic aid to underdeveloped countries.

Jan. 25   The U.S.S.R. set up a Council of Mutual Economic Assistance that included the U.S.S.R., Poland, Czechoslovakia, Bulgaria, Rumania, and Hungary.

Apr. 4   The **NORTH ATLANTIC PACT** was signed by the U.S., Great Britain, France, Iceland, Denmark, Norway, Belgium, Nether-lands, Luxembourg, Portugal, Italy, and Canada. The Pact established the **North Atlantic Treaty Organization (NATO)** with each nation pledged to defend all others against attack. Greece and Turkey joined in 1952 and West Germany in 1955. France withdrew its troops from NATO in 1966 but remained a member of the North Atlantic Pact.

Apr. 8   The U.S., Great Britain, and France merged their German zones of occupation.

May 4   Russia announced that it would reopen the routes to Berlin if the Foreign Ministers would reopen discussions on Germany.

May 8   A federal government for **West Germany** was formed at Bonn.

May 12   The Berlin blockade ended.

May 23–June 20   At the Foreign Ministers' Conference at Paris, Russia demanded the withdrawal of western troops from Germany, and the West urged extension of the Bonn constitution to East Germany. No agreement was reached, and the conference ended with no guarantee of access routes to Berlin.

9-2   Berlin and East Germany

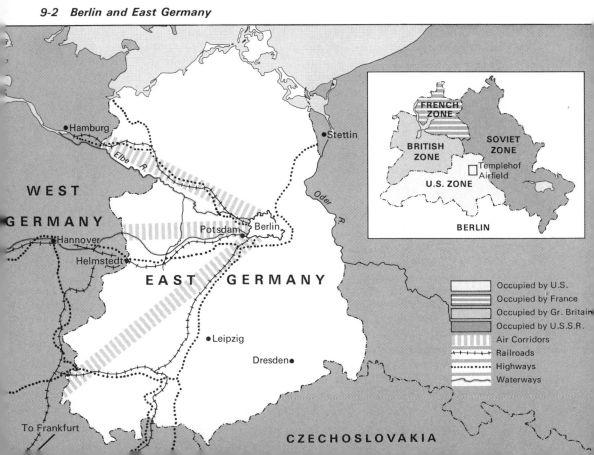

July 21 The Senate ratified the NATO treaty after debate in which Senator **Arthur H. Vandenberg** (Mich.) defended the treaty.

Sept. 23 The U.S. disclosed that an **atomic explosion** had taken place in **Russia** within recent weeks.

Oct. 7 **East Germany** announced the formation of the **German Democratic Republic.**

Oct. 28 **MUTUAL DEFENSE ASSISTANCE ACT** authorized $1.3 billion in military aid to NATO nations, and to Greece, Turkey, Iran, Korea, the Philippines, and Nationalist China. This marked the start of a shift in emphasis from economic to military aid.

Fiscal years	Economic aid	Military aid
	(billions of dollars)	
1945–50	26.5	2.0
1951–55	11.6	14.5
1956–60	12.0	11.3
1961–65	15.9	7.9

Dec. 15 West Germany was admitted to ECA.

1950

Jan. 31 President Truman ordered the development of the **HYDROGEN BOMB.**

June 5 **Act for International Development** put Truman's Point Four Plan into operation.

Dec. 19 NATO appointed **Dwight D. Eisenhower** as Supreme Commander of its forces.

1951

Mar. 19 **Schuman Plan** for pooling the European coal and steel market was agreed upon by France, West Germany, Italy, and Benelux (Belgium, the Netherlands, and Luxembourg). This was part of the movement that led to the **European Common Market.**

Apr. 4 The Senate endorsed a plan to send four divisions of troops to Europe for NATO.

Oct. 10 **MUTUAL SECURITY ACT** combined funds for the Marshall Plan, the Mutual Defense Act, and Point Four.

Oct. 19 Congress officially ended the state of war with Germany.

9-3 *Europe, North Africa, and the Middle East*

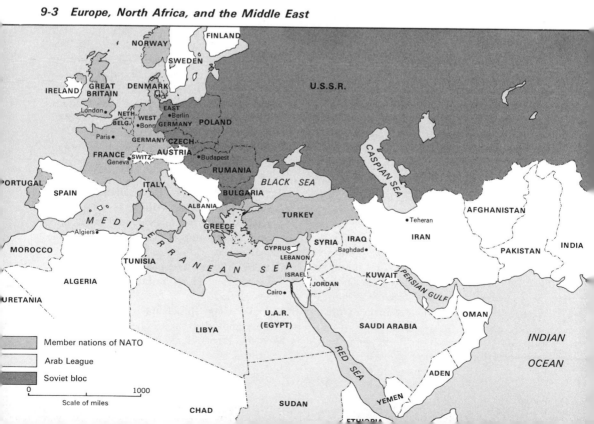

1952

May 26   The Allies abolished the German High Commission.

May 27   European Defense Community was drawn up by France, Benelux, Italy, and West Germany to provide an army to be linked with NATO. The U.S. ratified the treaty on July 1, but France delayed ratification of EDC.

Oct. 3   First British atomic explosion took place.

Nov. 16   The U.S. exploded its first **hydrogen bomb**.

Republican Foreign Policy in Europe, 1953–1961

1953

Jan. 20.   President Dwight D. Eisenhower and Secretary of State John Foster Dulles took office.

Jan. 27   Dulles pledged steps to "**liberate**" the captive peoples behind the Iron Curtain.

Mar. 5   The **death of Joseph Stalin** was announced. **Georgi Malenkov** became Premier of the U.S.S.R.

Apr. 10   Dag Hammarskjöld of Sweden became Secretary General of the UN.

June 17   Anti-Russian riots broke out in **East Berlin** and **East Germany**, but the U.S. took no action to help the revolts.

Aug. 20   The Soviet Union announced the successful explosion of a hydrogen bomb.

Dec. 14   Dulles tried to frighten France into joining EDC by threating an "**agonizing reappraisal**" of American foreign aid.

1954

Jan. 12   Dulles explained to the nation the new defense policy based on "**massive retaliation**" by the **Strategic Air Command**.

Feb. 26   The Senate rejected an amendment by Senator **John W. Bricker** (Ohio) to restrict the power of the President in foreign policy.

Aug. 30   France refused to join EDC, thereby killing it.

Oct. 23   Western European Union was set up in place of EDC. Consisting of France, Britain, Benelux, Italy, and West Germany, WEU provided West German troops for NATO with enough controls to satisfy France.

1955

Feb. 8   Nikolai A. Bulganin replaced Malenkov as Soviet Premier, but first party secretary **NIKITA S. KHRUSHCHEV** held the real power.

May 5   West Germany became sovereign and joined NATO.

May 14   Warsaw Pact, the Russian equivalent of NATO, bound Albania, Bulgaria, Czechoslovakia, East Germany, Hungary, Poland, and Rumania to the U.S.S.R.

June 24   The U.S., Britain, France, and the U.S.S.R. signed a treaty granting **Austrian independence**.

July 18–23   Geneva Summit Meeting with President **Eisenhower,** Prime Minister **Anthony Eden** of Great Britain, and Premier **Bulganin** of the U.S.S.R. failed to agree on unification of Germany.

1956

Jan. 11   Secretary Dulles claimed that the U.S. was willing to go to the "**brink of war**" in order to win the "Cold War."

Feb.   Russian leaders began systematic attacks on the policies of Stalin ("de-Stalinization") and adopted a policy of "**peaceful co-existence**" with the West.

Oct. 21   Revolt in Poland led to the establishment of a nationalist Communist government.

Oct. 23   REVOLT IN HUNGARY was begun by students, writers, and politicians against the Russian Communist rule. Imre Nagy, a nationalist Communist, became Premier.

Oct. 29   Suez crisis began as Israel invaded Egypt, followed by Britain and France on Oct. 31.

Nov. 1   Nagy proclaimed Hungarian neutrality and asked for UN help.

Nov. 4   Russian tanks crushed the Hungarian revolt.

Nov. 6   Suez Crisis ended when Russia threatened to defend Egypt, the U.S. refused to back Great Britain, and a cease-fire was established.

Nov. 6   President Eisenhower was reelected.

Nov. 12   President Eisenhower announced that the U.S. did not advocate open rebellion behind the Iron Curtain.

Dec. 12   The UN General Assembly condemned Russian action in Hungary.

1957

May 15   Great Britain exploded its first hydrogen bomb.

Oct. 2   **Adam Rapacki**, Polish Foreign Minister, proposed a ban on nuclear weapons in Germany, Poland, and Czechoslovakia. George Kennan later proposed disengagement (removal of troops) in central Europe but was opposed by Dean Acheson. The U.S. rejected the **Rapacki Plan** on May 3, 1958.

Oct. 4   The U.S.S.R. put the 1st artificial **satellite, Sputnik I**, into orbit. Meanwhile the Russians had perfected an **intercontinental ballistic missile**. Concern arose over a "missile gap" between the U.S.S.R. and the U.S.

Dec. 16–19   NATO decided to set up missiles in Europe to offset Russian missiles. By Mar., 1959, Great Britain, Turkey, and Italy had agreed to supply bases.

1958

Mar. 27   Nikita S. Khrushchev became Premier of the U.S.S.R.

June 1   France, Benelux, West Germany, and Italy formed the **EUROPEAN ECO-NOMIC COMMUNITY (Common Market)**.

Nov. 4   U.S., U.S.S.R., and Great Britain agreed to a **moratorium** on nuclear testing.

Nov. 10   **Berlin crisis** began when Khrushchev announced that the U.S.S.R. was about to turn over its Berlin zone to East Germany and demanded that the western powers do likewise. If they refused, he said, they would have to deal with the East German government on all Berlin matters.

Nov. 27   Khrushchev threatened to sign a peace treaty with East Germany if the West did not get out of Berlin within six months.

Dec. 16   NATO announced that it would not accept a Soviet "ultimatum."

1959

Jan. 8   **Charles DeGaulle** became first president of the Fifth French Republic.

May 11–Aug. 5   Foreign Ministers' Conference met at Geneva. No agreement was reached on Berlin. Khrushchev, anxious for a summit conference, allowed the deadline on Berlin to pass without any action.

Sept. 15   **Khrushchev** began a tour of the U.S. On Sept. 23, he conferred with President Eisenhower on the issue of Berlin at **Camp David**, Md. The Berlin ultimatum was removed, and a summit conference was planned between the two leaders for 1960.

1960

May 1–16   **U–2 CRISIS**: on May 1, a U.S. U–2 photo-reconnaissance plane was shot down 1,300 miles within Soviet territory. When the U.S. said that a meteorological plane might have been forced down within the U.S.S.R. by mechanical difficulties, the U.S.S.R. countered with the claim of shooting down a photography plane. Khrushchev announced on May 7 that the pilot, **Francis Gary Powers**, was alive and had confessed to high level photography spying. Four days later, President Eisenhower admitted that he had authorized the flights that had been going on for four years. Never before had a chief of state admitted espionage. On May 16, Khrushchev used the U–2 incident as an excuse for refusing to attend the summit talks in Paris.

Oct. 18   Khrushchev stated that he would await the election of a new American President before settling the Berlin crisis.

Democratic Foreign Policy in Europe, 1961–1967

1961

Jan. 20   Inauguration of President **JOHN F. KENNEDY**. **Dean Rusk** became Secretary of State.

June 1 Kennedy met with DeGaulle at Versailles.

June 3–4 Kennedy and Khrushchev met in Vienna to discuss Germany. Khrushchev threatened to sign a treaty with East Germany and to declare West Berlin a "free city."

July 25 President Kennedy made plans to call out the **reserves** because of the Berlin crisis.

Aug. 13 Khrushchev broke agreements for free access within Berlin by erecting a **wall between East and West Berlin.** He thereby cut off the great exodus taking place from East Berlin to the West.

Aug. 31 The U.S.S.R. announced that it would resume **nuclear testing** in the atmosphere.

Sept. 5 The U.S. resumed underground nuclear testing. It started atmospheric testing again on Apr. 25, 1962.

1962

Oct. 14 **CUBAN CRISIS** began as the U.S. discovered that the Russians were installing missile sites on Cuba with a range covering most of the U.S.

Oct. 22 President Kennedy ordered the U.S.S.R. to withdraw its missiles and imposed a **quarantine** by naval blockade on Cuba.

Oct. 26 With a possible nuclear war threatened, Khrushchev offered to remove the missile bases if Kennedy would promise not to invade Cuba.

Oct. 28 Kennedy and Khrushchev agreed on the substance of Khrushchev's offer to withdraw the armaments.

Nov. 21 Kennedy lifted the blockade after the U.S.S.R. gave assurances that the missiles had been removed.

1963

Aug. 5 **Nuclear Test Ban** treaty was signed by which the U.S., the U.S.S.R., and Great Britain agreed not to test nuclear weapons in the atmosphere. France, which had exploded its first nuclear bomb in Feb., 1960, did not sign.

Aug. 30 The U.S. and the U.S.S.R. opened a **"hot line" communications link** to lessen the risk of accidental war.

1963–65 **President DeGaulle** of France adopted an independent anti-American foreign policy:

1. He signed a cooperation treaty with West Germany (Jan. 22, 1963).
2. He vetoed the admission of Great Britain to the European Common Market.
3. He opposed American plans for a NATO nuclear force.
4. He had already developed France's own nuclear bomb and refused to sign the nuclear test ban.
5. He gave diplomatic recognition to Communist China.
6. He opposed American participation in the Vietnam War.
7. He insisted (Sept., 1965) that NATO withdraw all troops and bases from France by 1967.

1964

Oct. 15 In the U.S.S.R., Khrushchev was replaced by **Leonid Brezhnev,** who became party secretary, and by **Aleksei Kosygin,** who became premier.

1966

June 6 NATO decided to move its headquarters to **Belgium.**

July 1 France officially removed its troops from NATO.

1967

Jan. 27 U.S., U.S.S.R., and Great Britain signed a pact barring nuclear weapons in space.

Mar. 31 NATO withdrew all troops and bases from France.

May 15 Fifty nations, including the U.S. and the members of the European Common Market, agreed to reduce tariffs by about one-third. The agreement came after four years of "Kennedy Round" international financial negotiations in Geneva.

American Policy in Asia, 1945–1967

The Communist Takeover of China, 1945–1949

1945

Feb. 4–11 At the **YALTA CONFERENCE, President Roosevelt, Prime Minister Churchill,** and **Premier Stalin** agreed to the following terms for Japan and China:

1. In two or three months after the German surrender, the U.S.S.R. would **enter the war** against Japan.
2. The southern half of **Sakhalin Island** and the **Kurile Islands** would go to Russia.
3. A joint Sino-Soviet company would operate the **Chinese Eastern** and **South Manchurian railroads.**
4. The Soviet lease of **Port Arthur** would be renewed.
5. The U.S.S.R. would recognize the **Nationalist** government of China.

Apr. 1 The U.S. invaded the Japanese-held island of Okinawa.

July 16 First atomic bomb test took place at the Alamogordo Air Base, N.M.

Aug. 6 The U.S. dropped the **first atomic bomb** on **Hiroshima,** Japan, which suffered 180,000 casualties.

Aug. 8 The U.S.S.R. declared war on Japan.

Aug. 9 The second **atomic bomb** was dropped on **Nagasaki,** Japan.

Aug. 14 By the **Sino-Soviet Treaty,** Chiang Kai-shek agreed to concessions granted at Yalta.

Aug. 14 The **surrender of Japan** was announced.

Aug. 17 General MacArthur temporarily divided **Korea** between the U.S. and the U.S.S.R. at the **38th parallel.**

Aug. 27 The American **OCCUPATION OF JAPAN** began. Under the Supreme Allied Commander, Gen. Douglas MacArthur, the U.S. carried out thoroughgoing policies of "democratizing," reforming, and rebuilding Japan. The occupation ended in 1951.

Sept. 2 The Japanese formally surrendered in ceremonies on board the U.S.S. *Missouri.*

Oct. War broke out between Communists and Nationalists in China. Russia failed to evacuate Manchuria. The U.S. helped Chiang move troops to Manchuria.

Dec. 15 President Truman sent Gen. George C. Marshall to China to help establish a "united democratic China."

1946

May 8 The joint U.S.-U.S.S.R. commission in Korea disbanded.

June 7–30 Communist and Nationalist Chinese made a truce in Manchuria.

1947

Jan. 6 U.S. peace mission to China under Marshall ended as the war there expanded.

July 11–Aug. 24 Mission by Lt. Gen. **Albert J. Wedemeyer** to China resulted in a report (made public in 1949) that urged U.S. military aid to the Nationalists but suggested that Chiang give up Manchuria.

1948

Apr. 3 **Foreign Aid Act** provided $500 million for China.

May 10 A UN Commission held elections in South Korea but was not allowed north of the 38th parallel.

Aug. 15 The **Republic of Korea** was established in South Korea.

Nov. 1 Chinese Communists capped victories in Manchuria with the capture of Mukden.

1949

Jan. 31 Chinese Communists occupied Peking.

Apr. 20 Communists crossed the Yangtze River and captured Nanking (Apr. 24).

Aug. 5 The U.S. State Department issued

a **white paper** that blamed the corruption of the Chiang Kai-shek regime for the Communist victory and said that the U.S. had done all it could to save China.

Aug. 7   House Speaker **Joseph W. Martin, Jr.** (Mass.), accused the Democratic Administration of giving insufficient aid to Chiang Kai-shek.

Oct. 1   Communist regime under Chairman **Mao Tse-tung** was established in China.

Oct. 2   The U.S.S.R. recognized the Mao regime. Great Britain followed suit on Jan. 5, 1950, but the U.S. refused recognition.

Nov. 30   Chungking, the last Nationalist stronghold, fell to the Communists.

Dec. 8   Chiang Kai-shek declared Taipei, **Formosa**, the capital of Nationalist China. Chiang and several hundred thousand troops had moved there toward the end of the Communist conquest.

The Korean War, 1950–1953

1950

Jan. 12   Secretary of State Dean Acheson announced that the U.S. **defense perimeter** did not include Korea and Formosa.

Feb. 14   U.S.S.R.-China 30-year mutual defense pact was concluded by Stalin and Mao.

June 25   **North Korean Communists invaded South Korea.** The last U.S. troops had been withdrawn from Korea a year earlier, and Soviet troops had left in 1948.

June 25   UN Security Council (U.S.S.R. not present) declared North Korea the aggressor and demanded a cease-fire in Korea. The Council also called on members for military aid to repel the North Korean attack.

June 27   **President Truman** sent the U.S. **Seventh Fleet** to the Formosa Straits to prevent the Chinese Communists from invading Formosa or the nationalists from invading the mainland.

June 29   Truman ordered the U.S. army into South Korea.

July 7   UN Security Council ordered a UN Command under a U.S. Commander **(Gen. Douglas MacArthur).**

July–Aug.   North Koreans drove South Koreans and Americans to the **Pusan beachhead**.

Sept. 15   **U.S. counteroffensive** began with the invasion of **Inchon** by sea.

Oct. 1   Allied forces crossed the 38th parallel.

Oct. 7   UN General Assembly called for **unification** of Korea.

Oct. 11   China warned that it might invade North Korea.

Oct. 27   **Chinese troops** were discovered to be fighting in Korea.

Nov. 7   The Joint Chiefs of Staff refused to let MacArthur bomb Chinese bases in Manchuria because they did not want to risk having the U.S.S.R. enter the war.

Nov. 26   UN troops were turned back by **Chinese counterattack** after reaching the **Yalu Valley**.

Dec. 24   American troops were evacuated from the **Hungnam** beachhead.

Dec. 30   Truman rejected MacArthur's plan to use Chiang's troops in Korea.

1951

Jan. 25   The UN retreat halted south of the 38th parallel. By April 21, the UN forces had moved back across the parallel in many places, and the front was stabilized.

Mar. 24   MacArthur exceeded his authority and contradicted Truman by ordering the Chinese to surrender.

Apr. 5   Representative Joseph W. Martin, Jr., published a letter from MacArthur calling for a more aggressive policy in Korea.

Apr. 11   **President Truman recalled Gen. MacArthur.**

Apr. 19   Gen. MacArthur addressed Congress and called for all-out war in Korea.

June 27   After a two-month debate on foreign policy, the Senate committees investigating Asian policy urged a continuation of Truman's policy of **limited-war**.

July 10   UN negotiators began truce talks in Korea, but problems such as that of the North Korean **prisoners** in the hands of the UN prevented a settlement for two years. Many of the prisoners did not want to return to North Korea, but the Communists insisted on compulsory repatriation. When the Communists gave way, an **ARMISTICE** was concluded (July 27, 1953); it provided for a demilitarized zone near the 38th parallel and called for a political conference, which has never been held.

Sept. 1 ANZUS Mutual Assistance Pact was signed by the U.S., Australia, and New Zealand.

Sept. 8 Japanese Peace Treaty was signed by 49 nations. The U.S. was granted **military bases** in Japan.

Republican Foreign policy in Asia, 1953–1961

1953

Feb. 3 The Administration removed the Seventh Fleet from the Formosa Straits and "**unleashed**" **Chiang Kai-shek** to invade the mainland. It was soon apparent that Chiang was not capable of an invasion.

1954

Jan. 26 U.S. ratified a mutual defense treaty with **South Korea**.

Mar. 8 **U.S.-Japanese** Mutual Defense Agreement was signed.

Mar. 20 The U.S. refused a French request to intervene in the Vietnam War.

Apr. 26–June 15 Geneva Conference met. The conference divided Vietnam and failed to unite Korea.

Aug. 11 First **Formosa Crisis** began as Chinese Foreign Minister **Chou En-lai** stated that Formosa must go to the Chinese Communists.

Aug. 17 President Eisenhower promised to use the Seventh Fleet to defend Formosa.

Sept. 3 Chinese Communists began to shell the offshore island of **Quemoy**.

Sept. 8 **SOUTHEAST ASIA TREATY ORGANIZATION** (SEATO) was established at Manila. The U.S., Great Britain, France, Australia, New Zealand, the Philippines, Thailand, and Pakistan signed.

Dec. 2 The U.S. signed a mutual defense pact with **Nationalist China** to defend Formosa.

1955

Jan. 29 Joint **Congressional Resolution** gave the President authority to defend Formosa and the Pescadores Islands in Taiwan Strait.

Apr. 18–24 **Afro-Asian Nations** meeting at Bandung, Indonesia proclaimed their opposition to colonialism. The Chinese began to expand their political influence in Southeast Asia and Africa.

Apr. 23 Chou En-lai offered to negotiate over Formosa. The shelling of **Quemoy** and **Matsu** gradually ceased.

1957

June 28 Secretary Dulles defended the American policy of not recognizing Communist China and of blocking its entrance to the UN. The U.S. succeeded in keeping Communist China from gaining membership in the UN.

Aug. 1 The U.S. removed its combat troops from Japan.

9-4 The Korean War

1958

SINO-SOVIET SPLIT: The Chinese began new policies:

1. **The "Great Leap Forward"** was an effort to catch up with the West, which failed after initial success.
2. The **commune system** of large collective farms was instituted but was cut back later.

These policies, and the Stalinist line of the Chinese, irritated the Russians. The Chinese, on the other hand, looked upon the Russian policy of "coexistence" as capitulation to the West.

Aug. 23   Second **Formosa Crisis.** Communists renewed the shelling of Quemoy and Matsu. The U.S. gave Chiang military aid.

Sept.   The U.S. debated the wisdom of defending the offshore islands.

Sept. 11   President Eisenhower announced that the U.S. would defend the offshore islands if a Communist attack was part of an assault on Formosa.

Oct. 23   Dulles and Chiang announced that the Nationalists had given up any possible conquest of China. The Administration returned to the Truman policy of **"leashing" Chiang Kai-shek.** Shelling of offshore islands tapered off.

1959

Apr. 2   Tibet's Dalai Lama escaped into India as China crushed the autonomous Tibet.

9-5   East Asia and the Pacific

Member Nations of SEATO

Nations that have Bilateral Treaties with the U.S.

Communist Bloc

July The Communist Pathet Lao endangered the government of **Laos**. Prince **Souvanna Phouma** had earlier encouraged the entry of Communists into the neutral government.

Nov. 27 Anti-American riots, led by student and left-wing groups, broke out in Japan because of fear that the U.S. would arm Japanese forces with atomic weapons.

1960

June 16 Further riots in Japan forced that government to withdraw its invitation to President Eisenhower to make a state visit.

June 18 In a new treaty the U.S. retained its military bases in Japan, but agreed to consult with Japan before changing its military position there.

Dec. The U.S. supported the right-wing government of Prince **Boun Oum** in Laos against the **Pathet Lao**.

The Vietnam War, 1945–1967

1945

Aug. Allied Commission, primarily British, arrived in Saigon to take control of French Indo-China.

Sept. 2 Communist leader **Ho Chi Minh** set up the Democratic Republic of Vietnam (North Vietnam).

Dec. The British withdrew, leaving Vietnam in French hands.

1946

Mar. 6 France recognized the **Democratic Republic of Vietnam** as part of the Indochinese Federation and the French Union.

Nov. 23 Guerrilla warfare between France and the Democratic Republic of Vietnam began.

1948

June 5 France established the state of **Vietnam** as part of the French Union (which included Cambodia and Laos). War continued between Vietnam and the regime of Ho Chi Minh.

1950

Jan. 31 The U.S.S.R. recognized the Democratic Republic of Vietnam under Ho Chi Minh.

Feb. 7 The U.S. recognized Laos, Cambodia, and Vietnam as independent states within the French Union.

May 8 The U.S. began economic and military aid to the Vietnam government.

Dec. 23 The U.S. drew up a mutual defense agreement with France, Vietnam, Laos, and Cambodia.

1954

Mar. 20 France asked for U.S. military intervention.

Apr. 3 Secretary of State **Dulles** asked a group of Congressmen to support the use of American air forces in Vietnam, but his request was refused.

Apr. 26 A **Geneva Conference** began to determine the fate of Indo-China with the U.S., France, Great Britain, the U.S.S.R., Communist China, Vietnam, Democratic Republic of Vietnam, Laos, and Cambodia represented.

May 8 The beseiged French garrison at Dienbienphu fell to the North Vietnamese. The defeat marked the end of effective French military strength in Southeast Asia.

July 7 **Ngo Dinh Diem** became Prime Minister of South Vietnam.

July 21 **DECLARATION OF THE GENEVA CONFERENCE,** not signed by the U.S. or Vietnam, divided Vietnam at the **17th parallel** into the northern **Democratic Republic of Vietnam** and the southern **Republic of Vietnam**. Unification would depend upon elections scheduled for 1956 but never held. France withdrew its troops.

Sept. 8 **Protocol** to the SEATO Treaty included Laos, Cambodia, and South Vietnam under the area protected by the Southeast Asia Treaty Organization.

Oct. 24 The U.S. promised aid to South Vietnam.

1955

Feb. U.S. military advisors began to train the South Vietnamese Army.

Oct. 26 The Republic of South Vietnam was established, and Ngo Dinh Diem was installed as President.

1960

Dec. 20 **National Liberation Front** of Communists, peasants, and Buddhists opposed to Ngo Dinh Diem was set up in South Vietnam. **Viet Cong** was the military arm of the NLF. By then, U.S. military advisers to South Vietnam numbered about 350.

1961

May 5 President Kennedy warned that the U.S. was considering use of American troops in Vietnam.

Dec. 8 A U.S. **white paper** warned that South Vietnam was in danger of Communist conquest from North Vietnam.

1962

Feb. 7 U.S. military forces in South Vietnam had increased to about 4,000.

9-6 Vietnam

1963

Jan. 26   12,000 U.S. troops were in Vietnam.
May 8   Buddhist riots against the Catholic regime of Ngo Dinh Diem began.
Nov. 1   A **military coup** overthrew Ngo Dinh Diem.

1964

June 20   Lt. Gen. **William C. Westmoreland** became commander of U.S. forces in Vietnam.
Aug. 2   North Vietnamese torpedo boats attacked the American destroyer *Maddox* in the **Gulf of Tonkin**. Torpedo boats attacked U.S. destroyers again on Aug. 4.
Aug. 5   U.S. planes bombed torpedo boat bases in North Vietnam.
Aug. 11   **SOUTHEAST ASIA RESOLUTION** by Congress pledged U.S. support to peace and security in Southeast Asia.
Aug. 19   U.S. military strength in Vietnam reached 17,000 troops.

1965

Feb. 7   Viet Cong attack on U.S. forces at **Pleiku** led to U.S. air raids on North Vietnam. **Bombing of North Vietnam** continued on a regular basis. The U.S. presented evidence of North Vietnamese infiltration of South Vietnam.
Apr. 7   President Johnson, in a speech at Johns Hopkins University, announced that the U.S. was ready to start "unconditional discussions" to end the war.
Apr. 8   Hanoi announced the **peace requirements** it would consider in ending the war:
1. withdrawal of U.S. troops;
2. end of foreign bases in Vietnam;
3. recognition of the National Liberation Front in South Vietnam;
4. reunification of Vietnam without foreign intervention.

May 25   The U.S.S.R. began to build anti-aircraft missile sites in North Vietnam.
June 19   A military regime under **Nguyen Cao Ky** was established in South Vietnam.
Oct. 23   The U.S. had about 150,000 troops in Vietnam.

Nov. 20   The number of U.S. troops killed in Vietnam since 1961 reached 1,095.
Dec. 24–Jan. 31, 1966   U.S suspension of the bombing of North Vietnam failed to bring about peace talks with the government of Ho Chi Minh.

1966

Jan.   Senator **J. William Fulbright**, who opposed the war in Vietnam, began **hearings** before the **Senate Foreign Relations Committee** on the war. Debate started in the U.S. over the American role in Vietnam. "**Hawks**" supported intervention to prevent the spread of Chinese Communism in southeast Asia. "**Doves**" attacked the war as a threat to world peace.
Feb. 6–8   President Johnson met Premier Ky in **Honolulu**. The President pledged to fight for social reform in Vietnam.
Sept. 11   South Vietnam held elections for an assembly to write a constitution. In spite of terrorist tactics of the Viet Cong, 81 per cent of registered voters cast ballots.
Oct. 17   President Johnson began 17-day **tour of the Pacific**, including Australia, New Zealand, the Philippines, and Korea.
Oct. 23–25   Johnson took part in the **Manila Conference** on the Vietnam war. Representatives of South Vietnam, South Korea, Thailand, the Philippines, Australia, and New Zealand also participated. In a communiqué, the U.S. and its allies pledged to continue fighting while seeking a "just peace."
Oct. 26   Johnson visited U.S. troops in Vietnam. At that time, there were about 400,000 American forces there. From 1961 to the end of 1966, American casualties numbered 44,402 (6,664 dead); losses of combat aircraft were 1,750.

1967

Jan.   Efforts to bring about peace talks between the U.S. and North Vietnam failed.
Mar.   The U.S. further intensified its war effort.
Sept. 3   South Vietnam held elections for a civil government and elected the presi-

dential slate of Nguyen Van Thieu and Nguyen Cao Ky.

Democratic Foreign Policy Elsewhere in Asia, 1961–1967

1962

May 15   President Kennedy sent 4,000 troops to **Thailand** in order to strengthen the anti-Communist position in Laos.

June 11   Geneva Conference on Laos set up a **neutralist** government under **Souvanna Phouma**. An armistice among conflicting factions had been agreed upon in May, 1961.

Oct. 20   Chinese **Communists invaded India** at Ladakh in Kashmir and in Assam Province. In response, the U.S. sent military aid to India.

Nov. 21   After reaching the Brahmaputra River, the Chinese withdrew. The invasion gained China favorable boundaries along the Himalayas.

1964

Feb.–Mar.   A dispute arose in the UN between Pakistan and India over the province

of Kashmir, which India had annexed in 1957 and continued to occupy.

Oct. 16   Communist China exploded its first atomic bomb.

1965

May 14   Communist China exploded a second atomic bomb.

Summer   An attempted Communist coup in **Indonesia** failed amid mass slaughter of Communist supporters. President Sukarno, who had ruled since the end of World War II, fell from power in Oct.

Sept. 2   Chinese Defense Minister **Lin Piao** declared that the rural areas of Africa and Asia would in time conquer the city areas of North America and Europe.

1966

May   The U.S. sent additional troops to Thailand to prevent Communist infiltration.

Aug.   Mao Tse-tung and Lin Piao created the **Red Guard movement** to arm Chinese youth to maintain the ideals of the Communist revolution. Mao continued to maintain power in China through 1967 in spite of widespread opposition.

American Policy in Latin America, 1945–1967

1945

Feb. 21–Mar. 8   Inter-American Conference met at Chapultepec Castle, Mexico City. All American nations except Argentina were represented. By the **Act of Chapultepec** (Mar. 3), a threat of war against one country was considered a threat against all.

Mar. 27   Argentina declared war on the Axis.

Apr. 9   The U.S. recognized the government of Argentina.

1946

Feb.   In spite of American opposition, **Juan D. Peron** was elected president of Argentina and established a dictatorship that lasted until 1955.

1947

Counterrevolutions began against many of the Latin American reform governments of the 1940's; the first of these occurred in Ecuador.

Sept. 2   Inter-American Conference at Rio de Janeiro drew up a **Treaty of Reciprocal Assistance**. An Organ of Consultation would determine the necessary response to aggression. The treaty was ratified by the U.S. Senate on Dec. 8.

1948

Mar. 30–May 2   Conference of American States at Bogota drew up the charter of the **ORGANIZATION OF AMERICAN STATES**, to become effective Dec. 13, 1951:

1. **International Conference of American States** would be the supreme organ.
2. Ministers of Foreign Affairs would serve as the **Organ of Consultation**.
3. A **Council** would handle executive affairs at the headquarters at Washington.

1954

The High point of the counterrevolutionary movement was reached with 13 military rules in Latin America. A new reform movement then began against the dictators.

Jan. Pro-Communist regime of **Jacobo Arbenz Guzmán** in **Guatemala** began to spread Communism to neighboring countries.

Mar. 1–28 At the Inter-American Conference at **Caracas**, Secretary of State John Foster Dulles succeeded in getting only a mild anti-Communist resolution passed.

May Guatemala labor leaders, supplied with Czechoslovakian armaments, started strikes in Nicaragua.

June 18 Guatemalan exiles in Honduras, supported by the U.S. Central Intelligence Agency (CIA), entered Guatemala, forced

9-7 Central and South America, 1954–1962

Arbenz to resign (June 29), and set up an anti-Communist government.

June 19–25   Guatemalan and Russian protests at the UN accomplished little.

1958

Jan. 23   Dictator **Marcos Perez Jiménez** was overthrown in Venezuela.

Apr. 27–May 15   Vice President **Nixon**, on a Latin American good-will tour, encountered hostile demonstrations in **Peru** and **Venezuela**. In response, the U.S. moved troops into the Caribbean.

Dec. 7   Election of Romulo Betancourt as president brought political stability to Venezuela.

1959

Jan. 1   President **Fulgencio Batista**, dictator in Cuba, resigned after two years of revolution led by **Fidel Castro**.

Feb. 16   Castro became Premier of Cuba, executed many Batista supporters, and announced his alliance with communism and the U.S.S.R.

Aug. 12–18   OAS meeting at Santiago, Chile, took no action to prevent the spread of Communism from Cuba.

Nov. 3   Mobs attacked the U.S. embassy in **Panama City**.

1960

Feb. 13   **U.S.S.R.-Cuban trade agreement** was established.

June 29   Castro seized a U.S. oil refinery.

Oct. 12   The U.S. ended sugar purchases from Cuba and cut off almost all exports to Cuba.

Nov. 17   The U.S. ordered its navy to prevent a Communist invasion of Guatemala.

1961

Jan. 3   U.S. broke off diplomatic relations with Cuba.

Jan. 9   U.S. training of anti-Castro forces in Guatemala was revealed.

Mar. 13   President Kennedy called for an **ALLIANCE FOR PROGRESS** to raise living standards in Latin America. Congress voted funds for it on July 2.

Apr. 17   **INVASION OF CUBA** by 1,400 Cuban refugees was crushed at the **Bay of Pigs**. The CIA trained and equipped the invaders, who failed partly from lack of promised air-force support.

May 30   **Rafael Trujillo**, dictator of the **Dominican Republic**, was assassinated.

Aug. 17   The U.S. and all Latin American countries except Cuba signed the charter of the Alliance for Progress at **Punta del Este, Uruguay**.

1962

Jan. 31   Cuba was expelled from membership in the OAS.

Oct. 22–28   The U.S. forced the U.S.S.R. to withdraw **missiles** from Cuba but promised not to invade Cuba.

1964

Jan. 9–10   **Panama Crisis**: mobs clashed with U.S. troops in the **Canal Zone** over the issue of flying American and Panamanian flags.

Apr. 4   Diplomatic relations between the U.S. and Panamá were resumed with an agreement to discuss revision of the Canal treaty.

Dec. 18   President Johnson announced that the U.S. would make a new treaty that would give Panama sovereignty over the Canal Zone.

1965

Apr. 24   Civil War broke out in the Dominican Republic between the Dominican Revolutionary Party under **Juan Bosch** and military conservatives led by Gen. **Elías Wessin y Wessin**.

Apr. 28   The **U.S. landed troops** near Santo Domingo to prevent a Communist takeover. The OAS organized a peace force to join the U.S. troops.

1966

June 2   **Joaquín Balaguer,** a rightist, defeated the leftist Bosch and became president of the Dominican Republic.

June 28   U.S. troops began leaving the Dominican Republic.

1967

Apr. 12–14   **Punta del Este (Uruguay) Conference** of the heads of state of Latin America and the U.S. laid plans for a Latin American **common market.** President Johnson was present; Cuba was not included.

American Policy in the Middle East, 1945–1967

1946

Apr. 20   British and American Committee of Inquiry recommended transfer of British mandate in Palestine to a UN trusteeship, the creation of a state protecting both Arabs and Jews, and the admission of 100,000 European Jews into Palestine. Arabs and Jews rejected the plan.

1947

Nov. 29   UN plan of **partition,** supported by the U.S., called for independent Jewish and Arab states in Palestine with the city of Jerusalem to be administered by the Trusteeship Council.

Dec. 17   The **Arab League** (Egypt, Iraq, Saudi Arabia, Lebanon, Syria, Trans-Jordan and Yemen) announced that it would stop the division of Palestine.

1948

May 14   Jews in Palestine announced the formation of the state of **Israel.** Immediate **U.S. recognition followed.**

May 14–Nov. 30   **War** between Israel and the Arab League. A UN cease-fire ended the fighting.

1949

Feb.–July   Peace treaties gave Israel most of Palestine except the land west of the Jordan River, the Gaza Strip, and east Jerusalem. Israel was not recognized by the Arab League states.

May 11   Israel was admitted to the UN.

1953

June 18   The monarchy of Egypt was abolished by a coup d'état, and Egypt was proclaimed a republic with Gen. **Mohammed Naguib** as premier and president.

1954

Apr. 18   Col. **Gamal Abdel Nasser** became premier of Egypt.

Oct. 19   Great Britain gave up its base in the Suez Canal area.

Nov. 14   President Naguib was deposed, and Nasser took full control of the Egyptian government.

1955

Feb. 24   **Baghdad Pact** to defend the northern Middle East was signed by Turkey and Iraq, with Great Britain, Pakistan, and Iran joining by the end of the year.

Sept. 27   Egypt made a pact with Czechoslovakia for arms.

1956

Jan.   Nasser rejected an American loan for a dam at Aswan on the Nile and turned to Moscow.

June 13   The last British troops left Egypt.

June 23   Nasser was elected president of Egypt and in mid-July finally accepted the U.S. offer for Aswan. The U.S., however, withdrew its offer (July 19) after rumors of a Russian loan to Nasser.

July 26   Nasser **nationalized** the **Suez** Canal Company.

July 27–Oct. 13   Prime Minister **Anthony Eden** of Great Britain and U.S. Secretary of State Dulles failed to arrive at a common Suez policy.

Oct. 29   **Israel** invaded the Egyptian-held Gaza Strip. Two days later, **Great Britain and France** invaded Egypt.

Nov. 2   The UN General Assembly called for a cease-fire in Egypt, and Russia threatened to defend Egypt (Nov. 5).

Nov. 6   The U.S. urged a peaceful settlement, and the war ended in a stalemate.

1957

Mar. 7   The **EISENHOWER DOCTRINE** passed Congress, empowering the President to use armed force to defend the independence of a Middle Eastern country from Communist aggression.

Apr. 25   The U.S. sent the Sixth Fleet to the eastern Mediterranean to bolster the regime of **King Hussein** in **Jordan** against Egyptian pressure.

1958

Feb. 1   Syria and Egypt merged as the United Arab Republic, which became the center for pro-Russian influence in the Middle East.

May 9   Syria supported a revolt in **Lebanon** against pro-U.S. **President Chamoun**.

May 22   Lebanon complained of interference by the U.A.R.

July 14   Revolt carried out by a group sympathetic to Nasser established a neutralist government in **Iraq**.

July 15   The U.S. sent the **Marines** into Lebanon at the request of President Chamoun.

Oct. 25   U.S. troops left Lebanon, which gradually resumed a neutral position.

Dec. 27   Nasser accepted a Russian loan for the Aswan Dam.

1959

Mar. 5   The U.S. agreed to support Turkey, Iran, and Pakistan in case of aggression directed against them.

Aug. 19   The Baghdad Pact became the Central Treaty Organization. Iraq had resigned on March 24, and the U.S. had not joined the pact.

1961

Sept. 28   Syria withdrew from the United Arab Republic and reestablished its independence.

1967

May 18   UN Secretary-General U Thant, in compliance with Egypt's request, ordered the withdrawal of UN troops from the Israeli-Egyptian border. Tension in the Middle East was increased markedly during the early months of the year by frequent skirmishes on the border.

May 22   The United Arab Republic (Egypt) began a blockade of the Strait of Tiran at the mouth of the Gulf of Aqaba, preventing Israeli ships leaving the port of Eilath from entering the Red Sea.

June 5   The **ARAB-ISRAELI WAR** broke out between Israel and Syria, Egypt, and Jordan. While the United States remained neutral, the Arab states considered the U.S. position to be in support of Israel. The U.S.S.R. supported the Arabs with armaments and diplomatic maneuvering.

June 7   The war ended abruptly after Israel completely routed the Arab forces and occupied the remainder of the divided city of Jerusalem (which had been a source of friction for years). Israel also took land on the Syrian and Jordanian borders as well as the Sinai Peninsula as far west as the bank of the Suez Canal. The General Assembly of the United Nations met in emergency session in an attempt to settle the war but was not able to exert any decisive influence on the conflict.

June 23, 25   U.S. President **Johnson** and Soviet Premier **Alexei Kosygin** met near New York City to discuss the sources of world tension while the UN continued to debate possible solutions to the crisis in the Middle East.

American Policy in Africa, 1954–1967

1954

The United States assumed a neutral position when a guerrilla war of independence broke out against France in **Algeria**. The war was concluded when Algeria gained its independence in 1962.

1958

Nov. 1   When the U.S. delayed diplomatic recognition of **Guinea**, the Russians advanced loans to the new nation.

1960

June 30   Rioting broke out in the **Congo** as

soon as Belgium granted it independence. Premier **Patrice Lumumba** asked for UN aid.

July 11   The Congro province of **Katanga** seceded under the leadership of **Moïse Tshombe**.

Sept.   **Joseph Kasavubu** and the Congo army ousted Premier Lumumba, who was supported by the U.S.S.R.

July 14   The UN asked Belgium to withdraw its troops and authorized a peace force to help the Congo. The UN forces remained in the Congo until after Katanga had been restored to the nation in 1964.

Nov. 22   The UN seated the delegates of Kasavubu, not Lumumba. Kasavubu was subsequently deposed (1965).

American Civilization, 1945–1967

Changes in American Life

Population: the American annual **growth rate** rose to 1.8 per cent in the 1950's, but dropped to 1.2 per cent in 1965. Almost 4 million **immigrants** entered the country 1951–65 with the largest numbers coming from Canada and Germany (about 600,000 each).

The Affluent Society: the economy grew so rapidly that by 1965 the **gross national product** per capita (1958 prices) had risen to $3,133 from $2,342 in 1950. Median **family income** rose from $4293 in 1950 to $5,904 in 1960 (1964 prices). The average **wage** in manufacturing in 1965 was $2.61 an hour compared to $1.78 in 1945 (1965 prices). By 1956 the number of white-collar workers had grown larger than the number of blue-collar workers.

Poverty, the City, and the Negro: in spite of affluence poverty remained a serious problem. In 1960 almost one-third of American fami-

lies lived on less than $4,000 a year. The standard of living was particularly low in the cities, where 70 per cent of Americans lived in 1960. The urban **crime rate** was far higher than elsewhere: in 1964 there were over 4,000 arrests in cities per 100,000 population compared to 2,000 in suburban and 1,500 in rural areas. From 1949–65 federal **urban renewal** grants totaled almost $5 billion, and the policy of slum clearance was partly replaced by one of urban renewal. By 1960 the percentage of dilapidated housing units or units without basic plumbing dropped to 18 per cent from 37 per cent in 1950. **Negroes** did not share in the national affluence. In 1960–61, Negro families averaged an income of $3,838 before taxes compared to $6,508 for white families.

Mass Culture, Conformity, and Rebellion: the **paperback revolution** doubled receipts from the sale of books 1954–63. **Television** began to dominate American life as the number of families with television sets rose from 8,000 in 1946 to 46 million in 1960. The percentage of advertising spent on television rose from 3 per cent in 1950 to 17 per cent in 1965. The importance of television was further shown by the furor over TV quiz-show scandals in 1959 and the Kennedy-Nixon television debates in 1960. **Advertising** became a business in itself; the money spent on advertising rose from $3 billion in 1945 to $15 billion in 1965. Although the 1950's were known as a decade of conformity, critics such as **William H. Whyte, Jr.** (*The Organization Man*) and **Jack Kerouac** (*On the Road*) were heard. Young people who felt alienated from traditional values joined the **"Beatnik"** revolt in the late 1950's and the **"Hippie"** movement in the mid-1960's. In the mid-1960's the "new left," particularly the **Students for a Democratic Society** (SDS), demanded the end of the war in Vietnam and the start of a drive to end poverty in America.

Transportation: in 1956, for the first time, railroads carried less than 50 per cent of inter-city freight traffic. The percentage carried by **motor vehicles** rose from 9 per cent in 1940 to 17 per cent in 1961. Passenger car factory sales jumped from 6.7 million in 1950 to 9.3 million in 1965. Americans were more **mobile** than before; in 1960 only half of the families were living in the same houses they had occupied in 1955.

Technology: the impact of the new technology was shown in **electronics** where sales increased from $2.5 billion in 1950 to over $10 billion in 1960. The development of **computers** had important economic results. Data on inventories, production, and other economic statistics were so quickly available, for example, that the stock market responded more quickly than before to economic and political changes.

Education: between 1945 and 1965 the **money spent** on education by state and local governments rose from $2.9 billion to $23.7 billion. Federal money spent on education jumped from $0.2 billion to $4 billion during the same period. Public school **integration** developed slowly until 1965. Then the percentage of Negroes in school with whites in the deep South rose from 2 per cent in 1965 to 16 per cent in 1967.

Government: both state and local governments as well as the federal government grew after World War II. Money spent on state and local government increased seven times between 1944 and 1965; federal civil expenses increased only four times.

Philanthropy: foundations grew rapidly after World War II. Of all foundations in 1960, 88 per cent had been founded after 1939. In 1955–56 the **Ford Foundation** granted a billion dollars to colleges, universities, and hospitals.

Health insurance: medical care for the aged was provided by the federal government in 1965. At the same time the majority of the population was already enrolled in private health insurance programs; the percentage covered by private medical insurance rose from 4 per cent in 1945 to 57 per cent in 1964.

Literature

American writers after World War II did a superb job of identifying the problems of postwar America. In a nation eager above all to establish its identity, J. D. Salinger caught the desperation of the new generation, while Mary McCarthy and Norman Mailer portrayed examples of an older generation. Scores of social scientists dissected American society: C. Wright Mills portrayed the fears of the middle class; W. H. Whyte outlined the dangers of the organization. As awareness of discrimination increased, more and more writers, many of them Negro, tried to explain the role of the Negro in America. None interpreted the Negro's dilemma more thoroughly than Swedish sociologist Gunnar Myrdal. And while no giant—such as a Hemingway or a Faulkner—emerged, American literature in the two decades after Hiroshima was vigorous, creative, and above all relevant.

Selected Writing, War Novels

1948 James Gould Cozzens, *Guard of Honor*.

1948 Norman Mailer, *The Naked and the Dead*.

1951 James Jones, *From Here to Eternity*.

1951 Herman Wouk, *The Caine Mutiny*.

The Search for Identity

1951 J. D. Salinger, *The Catcher in the Rye*.

1953 Saul Bellow, *The Adventures of Augie March*.

1955 Mary McCarthy, *A Charmed Life*.

1957 James Gould Cozzens, *By Love Possessed*.

1959 Norman Mailer, *Advertisements for Myself*.

The Beat Generation

1956 Alan Ginsberg, *Howl, and Other Poems*.

1957 Jack Kerouac, *On the Road*.

Poetry and Drama

1946 Robert Lowell, *Lord Weary's Castle*.

1947 Tennessee Williams, *A Streetcar Named Desire*.

1947 W. H. Auden, *Age of Anxiety*.

1949 Arthur Miller, *The Death of a Salesman*.

1949 Robert Frost, *Complete Poems of Robert Frost*.

1953 Tennessee Williams, *Cat on a Hot Tin Roof*.

1953 Arthur Miller, *The Crucible*.

1957 Eugene O'Neill, *Long Day's Journey into Night*.

1957 Archibald MacLeish, *J.B.*

American Society and Technology

1948 Alfred C. Kinsey *et al.*, *Sexual Behavior in the Human Male*.

1948 Norbert Wiener, *Cybernetics*.

1950 David Riesman, *The Lonely Crowd*.

1951 C. Wright Mills, *White Collar: American Middle Classes*.

1956 W. H. Whyte, *The Organization Man*.

1957 Vance Packard, *The Hidden Persuaders*.

1958 John K. Galbraith, *The Affluent Society*.

1960 Paul Goodman, *Growing Up Absurd*.

1962 Donald N. Michael, *Cybernation: The Silent Conquest*.

1962 Michael Harrington, *The Other America, Poverty in the United States*.

1964 Marshall McLuhan, *Understanding Media*.

1965 Kenneth Keniston, *The Uncommitted: Alienated Youth in American Society*.

The American Negro

1944 Gunnar Myrdal, *An American Dilemma*.

1952 Ralph Ellison, *The Invisible Man*.

1963 James Baldwin, *The Fire Next Time*.

1965 Claude Brown, *Manchild in the Promised Land*.

1965 Kenneth Clark, *Dark Ghetto*.

Religion and Intellectual History

1944 Reinhold Niebuhr, *The Children of Light and the Children of Darkness*.

1946 Joshua L. Liebman, *Peace of Mind*.

1949 Fulton J. Sheen, *Peace of Soul*.

1952 Reinhold Niebuhr, *The Irony of American History*.

1952 Norman Vincent Peale, *The Power of Positive Thinking*.

1953 Russell Kirk, *The Conservative Mind*.

1959 Daniel Bell, *The End of Ideology*.

Religion

1950 **National Council of Churches** was formed in Nov. by Protestant and Eastern Orthodox denominations; it marked the start of extensive mergers among Protestant churches. In 1957 the Congregational-Christian Church merged with the Evangelical and Reformed Church to form the United Church of Christ. In 1960 the **United Presbyterian, Methodist, Protestant Episcopal**, and **United Church of Christ** organizations began to discuss the possibilities of merger.

1957 Evangelist **Billy Graham** held a campaign in New York City, part of his crusade that had started in 1946 and was still going strong in 1967.

1964 The conclusion of the **Ecumenical council** of the Roman Catholic Church in

Rome led to increased cooperation between Catholics and Protestants in the U.S.

1964 Church **membership** was found to have doubled since 1940 from 64.5 million to 123.3 million.

1966 The Roman Catholic Church ended the requirement that Catholics abstain from eating meat on Fridays.

1967 Reformers among Roman Catholics demonstrated an interest in birth control, marriage of priests, and lay control of Catholic universities.

Science and Technology

The U.S. became the **research center** of the world. One of the by-products of Naziism and World War II was the migration of scientists from Europe to the U.S. (**Enrico Fermi**, nuclear research, **Albert Einstein**, relativity, **Fritz Albert Lipmann**, cell structure, for example). This movement, together with the rapid rise of American science, made the U.S. the most important center of research in the world after 1945. A large number of Nobel Prize winners in science and medicine 1946–65 were from the U.S. In physics, 18 of 36 winners were American.

Medicine: great progress was made, 1947–52, in the development of **antibiotics** for the treatment of disease, including the discovery of aureomycin, terramycin, and streptomycin (for use against tuberculosis).

1949 **Antihistamines**, discovered earlier, were advertised for the treatment of colds.

1951 **Robert B. Woodward** announced the total synthesis of **cortisone**. He also synthesized cholesterol and chlorophyll.

1953 The American Cancer Society published a report linking smoking and cancer.

1954–55 Treatment of **poliomyelitis**. In 1954, **John F. Enders** and two others received the Nobel Prize for research in poliomyelitis virus. In 1955, **Dr. Jonas Salk** announced that his vaccine was effective against polio. Polio cases in the U.S. which numbered almost 40,000 in 1955, were only 3,277 in 1960. The polio death rate dropped from 1.3 per 100,000 population in 1950 to almost zero in 1964.

1964–65 The birth-control pill came into widespread use.

1964 Arteriosclerotic **heart disease** and **cancer** increased during the 1950's in spite of research in both fields.

Death Rate per 100,000 Population

	1950	1964
Malignant neoplasms	140	151
Arteriosclerotic heart disease	213	285

1964 Jan. 11 The U.S. Public Health Service Report announced that cigarette-smoking helped cause lung cancer. On Apr. 27 leading cigarette manufacturers adopted an advertising code in which they agreed not to use health arguments in support of cigarettes.

1965 The **death rate** dropped to 9.4 per 1,000 population, down from 10.6 (1945) and 17.2 (1900). Life expectancy at birth in 1964 was 68 for white males (62 in 1940) and 75 for white females (67 in 1940). For non-white males, life expectancy at birth in 1964 was 61 (52 in 1940), and for non-white females it was 67 (55 in 1940).

Physics: transistors were invented in 1948 at the Bell Telephone Laboratories by Drs. **Walter H. Brattain, John Bardeen,** and **William B. Shockley,** for which they were awarded the Nobel Prize in 1956. Transistors led to the development of the **computer,** to which **John von Neumann** made great contributions.

1955 **Enrico Fermi** and **Leo Szilard** recieved a patent for a nuclear reactor as **nuclear research** became more advanced. In 1954 the first **atomic powered submarine,** the *Nautilus,* was commissioned at Groton, Conn. Such submarines were equipped with **Polaris missiles** with nuclear warheads in 1960.

1964 **Charles H. Townes** and two Russians received the Nobel prize in physics for developing the **maser-laser** principle of producing high intensity light rays.

Chemistry and Biology: in 1954, **Linus C. Pauling** was awarded the Nobel prize for his study of the forces holding proteins and molecules together.

The Conquest of Space: in 1949, an Air Force jet bomber crossed the U.S. in a new record time of 3 hours and 46 minutes at an average speed of 607 miles per hour.

1957 The U.S.S.R. announced on Aug. 26 that it had tested an intercontinental ballistic missile. On Oct. 4, the U.S.S.R. launched the **first artificial satellite,** *Sputnik I,* into orbit around the earth.

1958 The U.S. launched its first satellite, *Explorer I,* on Jan. 31. **The National Aeronautics and Space Administration** (NASA) was set up in July. The U.S. sent up its first lunar probe from Cape Canaveral, Fla., in Oct. and tested its first intercontinental ballistic missile in Nov.

1959 The U.S.S.R. put the first satellite (*Lunik I*) into orbit about the sun on Jan. 2, and, in Sept., *Lunik II* became the first manmade missile to hit the moon.

1961 On Apr. 12, the U.S.S.R. put the first **man in space** when Maj. **Yuri A. Gagarin** went into orbit in *Vostok I.* About a month later, Lt. Comm. **Alan B. Shepard, Jr.,** became the **first American in space**.

1961 On Nov. 9, Maj. **Robert White** reached a speed of 4,105 miles per hour in an X–15 rocket-propelled airplane.

1962 Lt. Col. **John H. Glenn, Jr.,** in the *Friendship 7,* was the first American to orbit the earth.

1963 **Telstar II** transmitted the first television pictures to be sent around the curvature of the earth (May 7). In Aug., Maj. **Joseph A. Walker** took an X–15 airplane about 67 miles above the earth.

1964 *Ranger VI,* launched from **Cape Kennedy** (formerly Cape Canaveral), made contact with the moon. In July, *Ranger VII* sent back more than 4,300 pictures of the moon before crashing on the lunar surface.

1965 A Russian cosmonaut walked in space for the first time (Mar. 18).

1966 *Luna IX* (Russian) made **first "soft" (controlled) landing on the moon** (Feb. 3). This was followed in June by *Surveyor I,* which made the first American soft landing on the moon.

Architecture

American architecture since World War II has been original in concept, practical in design, and often outstanding in execution. New forms of architecture for public and private buildings have evolved with styles ranging from impersonal architecture stressing such modern materials as glass and steel to warm personal architecture stressing the texture of more traditional wood, brick, and stone. A few of the many outstanding new structures are listed below.

Office Buildings

Lever House in New York City, designed by Skidmore, Owings & Merrill, was the first of the "glass tower" office buildings; its design has been widely imitated and even improved upon. The John Hancock Center in Chicago, also a design of Skidmore, Owings & Merrill, is, at 100 stories, the tallest office building constructed since the Empire State Building was completed.

Eero Saarinen's design for the CBS Building in New York combined form and function; the architect integrated the interior and the furnishings of the building with its external design.

New York's Seagram Building, designed by **Ludwig Mies Van Der Rohe,** was innovative for American design in its use of an open plaza in front of the building.

Apartment Buildings

I. M. Pei's Society Hill Towers in Philadelphia and his Kips Bay Apartments in New York proved that urban redevelopment need not follow convention or lack imagination. Both are complexes of modern apartment buildings and open plazas built in place of city tenements and slum areas.

Public Structures

Saarinen's design for the John Foster **Dulles International Airport** at Chantilly, Va., and his **Gateway Arch** in St. Louis both display ingenious use of structural materials used in complete harmony with their form.

Leading Figures of the Period

DWIGHT D. EISENHOWER, (Denison, Tex., 1890–   ), general, 34th President of the United States.

1909 Was graduated from high school, Abilene, Kan.

1915 Was graduated from West Point.

1935–39 Assistant to Gen. MacArthur in the Philippines.

1942 Commander of U.S. forces in Europe.

1944 Led the Normandy invasion of France, June 6.

1945 Commander of American occupation zone of Germany.

1945 Appointed as U.S. Chief of Staff.

1948 President of Columbia University.

1950 Commander of Allied Powers in Europe.

1952 Won election to the Presidency as a Republican candidate.

1953–61 Served two terms as President. Took part in summit diplomacy, resisted Russian expansion in the Middle East, and followed a conservative policy in domestic affairs.

1955–57 Suffered a heart attack, underwent an operation for ileitis, and had a stroke, but recovered from all.

LYNDON B. JOHNSON, (Stonewall, Tex., 1908–   ), 36th President of the United States.

1930 Was graduated from Southwest State Teachers College, Texas, and taught school.

1932 Secretary to Congressman Richard M. Kleberg.

1935 Was appointed Texas administrator of the National Youth Administration.

1937–49 Democratic Congressman.

1941–42 Naval officer in the Pacific.

1949–61 U.S. Senator.

1955–61 Majority Leader of the Senate.

1955 Suffered heart attack but recovered.

1960 Was defeated for Democratic nomination for President but accepted Vice Presidential nomination.

1961–63 Vice President.

1963 Became President after the assassination of President Kennedy.

1964–65 Secured passage of a broad program of domestic reform.

1964 Was elected President by the largest popular vote of any candidate. Proposed the "Great Society" programs for domestic reform.

JOHN F. KENNEDY, (Brookline, Mass., 1917–Dallas, Tex., 1963), 35th President of the United States.

1940 Was graduated from Harvard.

1941–45 PT-boat officer in the Pacific.

1946 Was elected as a Democratic Congressman from Massachusetts.

1952 Defeated Henry Cabot Lodge for the U.S. Senate.

1956 Was narrowly defeated for Democratic Vice Presidential nomination.

1960 Was elected President, the first Catholic and the youngest person to be elected.

1961 Introduced the "New Frontier."

1961 Peace Corps and Alliance for Progress programs were established.

1961 Bay of Pigs invasion of Cuba failed (Apr.).

1961 Russians constructed wall dividing Berlin (Aug.).

1962 Forced the U.S.S.R. to withdraw missiles from Cuba.

1963 Nuclear-test ban treaty was signed.

1963 Assassinated in Dallas, Tex.

MARTIN LUTHER KING, JR. (Atlanta, Ga., 1929–Memphis, Tenn., 1968), civil rights leader.

1948 Was graduated from Morehouse College, Atlanta, Ga.

1951 Received B.D. from Crozer Theological Seminary.

1955 Received Ph.D. from Boston University.

1955 Led Negroes in a boycott of segregated public transportation, Montgomery, Ala.

1957 Organized the Southern Christian Leadership Conference to fight for Negro rights and became its president.

1958 Published *Stride Toward Freedom*.

1963 Started non-violent demonstrations against segregation in Birmingham, Ala.

1963 Led civil rights march to Washington (Aug. 28).

1964 Was awarded Nobel Peace Prize.

1965 Led civil rights march to Montgomery from Selma, Ala.

1968 Was assassinated in Memphis, Tenn.

DOUGLAS MACARTHUR, (Little Rock, Ark., 1880–Washington, D.C., 1964), General of the Army.

1903 Was graduated from West Point.

1903–06 Served in the Philippines and Japan.

1906–07 Aide-de-camp to President Roosevelt.

1917–18 Served with the 42nd ("Rainbow") Division in World War I, was twice wounded, and in 1918 became commander of the division.

1919–22 Superintendent of West Point.

1922–25 United States commander of Manila in the Philippines.

1928 Commander of the Philippine Department.

1930–35 Chief of Staff of the United States Army.

1935–37 Military adviser to the Philippine Commonwealth.

1937–41 Retired from the United States Army; served as Field General of the Philippine army.

1941 Was recalled to active U.S. service as commander of U.S. forces in the Far East.

1941–45 Conducted the Pacific campaign in World War II.

1945–50 Supreme Commander of the occupation of Japan.

1950–51 Commanded the United Nations forces in the Korean War.

1951 Was relieved of his command by President Truman because of a dispute over policy (Apr. 10).

GEORGE C. MARSHALL (Uniontown, Pa., 1880–Washington, D.C., 1959), General of the Army, Secretary of State.

1901 Was graduated from Virginia Military Institute.

1902 Received a commission in the U.S. Army.

1917–19 Served with the U.S. Army in Europe in World War I.

1919–24 Aide-de-camp to Gen. John Pershing.

1924–27 Served in China.

1938 Chief of the War Plans Division of General Staff.

1939–45 Chief of Staff of the Army during World War II.

1945 Special Ambassador to China; failed to bring peace in civil war there.

1947 Secretary of State; responsible for the Marshall Plan to help rebuild Europe.

1950–51 Secretary of Defense.

ADLAI E. STEVENSON, (Los Angeles, 1900–London, 1965), Presidential candidate, U.S. Ambassador to the United Nations.

1922 Was graduated from Princeton.

1926 Was graduated from Northwestern Law School.

1927–33; 1935–41 Practiced law in Chicago.

1933–34 Counsel to the AAA.

1941–44 Assistant to the Secretary of the Navy.

1945 Assistant to the Secretary of State.

1945 Served on the U.S. delegation to the UN Conference.

1948 Was elected as Democratic governor of Illinois.

1952–1956 Was defeated for the Presidency by Dwight D. Eisenhower.

1961–65 U.S. Ambassador to the UN.

ROBERT A. TAFT, (Cincinnati, Ohio, 1889–New York City, 1953), Senator, son of President William Howard Taft.

1910 Was graduated from Yale.

1913 Received LL.B. degree from Harvard.

1913 Began to practice law in Cincinnati.

1921–26, 1931–32 Served in the Ohio legislature.

1939–53 U.S. Senator (Republican) from Ohio. An expert on finance.

1939–41 Isolationist in foreign policy.

1945 Supported U.S. entrance into the UN.

1946–53 Leading conservative Republican in the Senate.

1947 Co-author of the Taft-Hartley Act.

1936, 1940, 1948 Unsuccessful candidate for the Republican Presidential nomination.

1952 Was defeated by Dwight D. Eisenhower for Republican Presidential nomination.

1953 Majority leader of the Senate.

HARRY S TRUMAN (Lamar, Mo., 1884–   ), 33rd President of the United States.

1901 Was graduated from high school and became a bank clerk.

1906–17   Operated a farm near Independence, Mo.

1917   Served in the field artillery in World War I as a first lieutenant and captain.

1919–22   Unsuccessfully ran a haberdashery shop in Kansas City, Mo.

1922–24   Backed by Democratic boss Thomas Pendergast, he became judge of Jackson County Court.

1926–34   Presiding judge of Jackson County Court.

1935–45   Served as Democratic Senator from Missouri.

1941–44   Chairman of Senate Committee to investigate government defense expenditures.

1944   Was elected Vice President.

1945   Became President after the death of President Roosevelt.

1945   Authorized the dropping of the atomic bomb on Japan.

1945   Attended the Potsdam Conference.

1947   Truman Doctrine began policy of containment of communism.

1948   Defeated Thomas E. Dewey in Presidential election.

1949   Called for a Fair Deal reform program.

EARL WARREN, (Los Angeles, 1891–   ), Chief Justice of the Supreme Court.

1912   Was graduated from University of California Law School.

1914   Received a degree in law and began his practice.

1925–39   District Attorney of Alameda County, Calif.

1939–43   Attorney General of California.

1943–53   Governor of California.

1948   Republican candidate for Vice President.

1953   Was appointed Chief Justice of the U.S. Supreme Court (Sept.).

1954   *Brown v. Board of Education* declared segregation of Negro students in schools to be unconstitutional.

1962   *Engel v. Vitale* declared state school prayer unconstitutional.

1963   *Gideon v. Wainwright,* first of several decisions protecting the rights of prisoners.

1964   *Wesberry v. Sanders* required states to realign Congressional districts.

1963–64   Chairman of Presidential commission to investigate the assassination of President Kennedy.

Statistical Tables

Table 53.
Population of the United States[a]

(millions)

	1940	1950	1960
Total	132.0	151.2	180.0
Increase over preceding census (per cent)	7	15	19
Urban[b]	74.4	96.5	125.3
Rural	57.2	54.2	54.1
White	118.2	134.9	158.8
Negro	12.9	15.0	18.9
Other races	0.6	0.7	1.6

[a] Does not include members of the armed forces overseas or populations of outlying areas. Includes Alaska and Hawaii in 1960.
[b] The definition of urban changed between 1940 and 1950. By the new definition, the figure for 1940 would be over 80.0.

Table 54.
Immigration to the United States

(thousands)

	Total
1946–50	864
1951–60	2,515
1961–65	1,450

By country of origin, 1951–65

Europe	1,860
Germany	597
Great Britain	306
Italy	264
Asia	252
The Americas	1,792
Canada	621
Mexico	528
South America	230
West Indies	243
Total	3,966

Table 55.
Per cent distribution of families by income level
(by color of head of family)

White families	Under $2,000	$2,000–$5,999	$6,000–$9,999	Over $10,000
1950	22.2	62.6	11.6	3.5
1955	15.3	54.1	23.8	6.8
1960	11.0	41.3	32.5	15.3
1964	8.1	33.2	34.5	24.1
Non-white families				
1950	53.4	43.2	3.2	0.3
1955	39.7	51.7	7.9	0.6
1960	31.7	47.9	15.4	4.9
1964	21.7	50.3	19.7	8.3

Table 56.
Share of aggregate U.S. income received by families
(per cent)

	1950	1955	1960	1964
Lowest 1/5 of families in income	4	5	5	5
Second 1/5	12	12	12	12
Middle 1/5	17	18	23	18
Second highest 1/5	24	23	23	24
Highest 1/5	43	42	42	41
Top 5 per cent	17	17	17	15
Median income of families[a]	$4,293	$5,143	$5,904	$6,569

[a] Based on constant (1964) dollars.

Table 57.
Ten leading cities, 1960
(millions)

	Total population	Negro population[a]	
1. New York	7.8	1.1	(14)
2. Chicago	3.6	0.8	(23)
3. Los Angeles	2.5	0.3	(12)
4. Philadelphia	2.0	0.5	(25)
5. Detroit	1.7	0.5	(29)
6. Baltimore	0.9	0.3	(34)
7. Houston	0.9	0.2	(23)
8. Cleveland	0.9	0.3	(30)
9. Washington, D.C.	0.8	0.4	(54)
10. St. Louis	0.8	0.2	(28)

[a] Figures in parentheses indicate percentage of the total population made up by Negroes.

Table 58.
Consumer price indexes
(1957–59 = 100)

1945	62.7	1960	103.1
1948	83.8	1965	109.9
1950	83.8	1966	114.7
1955	93.3		

Table 59.
Employment and unemployment
(millions)

	1945	1950	1955	1960	1965
Civilian labor force	53.9	63.1	65.8	70.6	75.6
Unemployed	1.0	3.4	2.9	3.9	3.5
Per cent unemployed	1.9	5.3	4.4	5.6	4.6

Table 60.
Employed persons by occupation and color
(percentage of group employed in types of occupations)

White	1950	1955	1960	1965	Non-white	1950	1955	1960	1965
White-collar workers	40.3	42.1	46.4	47.5	White-collar workers	10.2	12.0	16.0	19.5
Blue-collar workers	39.3	39.0	35.9	36.2	Blue-collar workers	37.5	41.8	39.8	40.7
Service workers	8.5	9.0	10.2	10.7	Service workers	33.8	31.6	31.8	31.7
Farm workers	11.7	9.9	7.6	5.6	Farm workers	18.4	14.5	12.4	8.1

Table 61.
School integration
(per cent of Negro students in school with whites in 11 southern states; figures based on enrollments in the spring of the year)

	1965	1966	1967
Alabama	—	0.4	4.4
Arkansas	0.8	6.0	15.1
Florida	2.7	9.8	22.3
Georgia	0.4	2.7	8.8
Louisiana	1.1	0.9	3.4
Mississippi	—	0.6	2.5
North Carolina	1.4	5.2	15.4
South Carolina	—	1.7	5.6
Tennessee	5.3	16.3	28.6
Texas	7.3	17.2	44.9
Virginia	5.1	11.0	25.3
Total	2.1	6.1	15.9

Table 62.
Federal administrative income and expenditures
(billions of dollars, current prices)

Fiscal year	Receipts	Expend- itures	Public debt	Gross national product
1945	44.4	98.3	259.1	213.6
1950	36.4	39.5	257.4	284.6
1955	60.2	64.4	274.4	397.5
1960	77.8	76.5	286.5	503.8
1965	93.1	96.5	317.9	676.3

Table 63.
School enrollment
(millions)

	Total	Elementary School	High School	College and University
1950	30.3	21.4	6.7	2.2
1955	37.4	27.1	8.0	2.4
1960	46.3	32.4	10.2	3.6
1965	53.8	35.1	13.0	5.7

Table 64.
Health insurance programs
(per cent of population covered)

	Hospital plan	Surgical plan	Medical Plan
1945	25.1	10.1	3.7
1950	51.0	36.1	14.4
1955	66.3	56.6	34.2
1960	74.1	67.9	49.1
1964	79.2	73.7	57.0

Table 65.
Labor union membership

	Millions	Percentage of non-agricultural employment
1945	14.3	35.8
1950	14.3	31.9
1955	16.8	33.6
1960	18.1	31.4
1964	16.8	28.9

Table 66.
Work stoppages
(thousands)

	Work stoppages	Workers	Man-days idle	Per cent of working time
1946	5.0	4,600	116,000	1.4
1950	4.8	2,410	38,800	0.4
1955	4.3	2,650	28,200	0.3
1959	3.7	1,880	69,000	0.6
1963	3.4	941	16,100	0.1

Table 67.
Manufacturing summary

	1947	1950	1955	1960	1964
All employees (millions)	14.3	14.8	16.8	16.8	17.3
Salaries and wages (billions of dollars)	39.7	47.9	72.1	88.1	106.0
Value added by manufacture (billions of dollars)	74.3	89.8	135.0	164.0	206.0

Table 68.
Exports and imports by country
(billions of dollars)

Exports (including re-exports)				
	1950	1955	1960	1965
North America	3.4	5.0	5.4	7.7
South America	1.4	1.7	2.1	2.1
Europe	3.0	4.2	6.5	8.9
Asia	1.5	2.1	3.6	5.5
Total	10.3	15.5	20.6	27.3

Imports				
	1950	1955	1960	1965
North America	3.1	4.0	4.4	6.6
South America	2.0	2.2	2.4	2.6
Europe	1.4	2.5	4.3	6.3
Asia	1.6	1.9	2.7	4.5
Total	8.9	11.4	14.7	21.4

Table 69.
Foreign assistance net
(billions of dollars)

Fiscal years	Total	Economic	Military
1945–50	28.5	26.5	2.0
1951–55	26.0	11.6	14.5
1956–60	23.3	12.0	11.3
1961–65	23.8	15.9	7.9
Total, 1945–65	101.2	65.5	37.7

Table 70.
Foreign assistance net by area and country, 1945–65
(billions of dollars)

	Economic aid	Military aid
Western Europe	23.8	16.2
France	4.2	
West Germany	3.1	
Italy	2.9	
United Kingdom	6.4	
Yugoslavia	1.9	
Eastern Europe	1.6	
Near East and South Asia	15.4	6.0
Greece	1.7	
India	5.2	
Pakistan	2.6	
Turkey	1.8	
Africa	2.2	0.2
Far East and Pacific	14.5	12.0
China (Taiwan)	2.1	
Japan	2.5	
Korea	3.9	
Vietnam	2.3	
Western Hemisphere	5.6	1.0
Brazil	1.7	
Other	2.3	0.4
Total	65.5	35.7

Table 71.

U.S. balance of payments

(billions of dollars)

	1945	1950	1955	1960	1965
Receipts	16.3	14.2	20.6	28.2	40.1
Payments	19.0	17.8	22.3	31.1	40.7
Including U.S. travel abroad	0.3	0.8	1.2	1.7	2.5
Balance of payments	− 2.7	− 3.6	− 1.1	− 3.9	− 1.3
U.S. gold reserves	20.1	22.7	21.7	17.8	13.7

Table 72.

Federal, state, and local social welfare expenditures

(billions of dollars)

Total expenditures	Social welfare				Per cent of gross national product made up by social welfare expenditures
	Total	Social insurance	Health and medical services	Education	
1945	8.9	1.4	2.3	3.0	4.2
1950	23.0	4.9	2.1	6.7	8.7
1955	32.3	9.9	3.1	11.3	8.5
1960	52.4	19.3	4.5	18.0	10.6
1965	77.7	28.1	6.7	27.7	12.0
Federal					
1945	4.1	0.8	1.8	0.2	1.9
1950	10.0	2.0	0.6	0.2	3.8
1955	14.2	6.4	1.2	0.5	3.7
1960	24.7	14.3	1.7	1.0	5.0
1965	40.0	21.9	3.1	4.0	6.2
State and local					
1945	4.8	0.7	0.6	2.9	2.3
1950	13.0	2.8	1.5	6.5	4.9
1955	18.1	3.5	1.9	10.8	4.8
1960	27.7	5.0	2.7	17.0	5.6
1965	37.8	6.2	3.6	23.7	5.8

APPENDIX

The Declaration of Independence*

The unanimous Declaration of the thirteen United States of America.

When, in the Course of human events, it becomes necessary for one people to dissolve the political bands which have connected them with another, and to assume, among the Powers of the earth, the separate and equal station to which the Laws of Nature and of Nature's God entitle them, a decent respect to the opinions of mankind requires that they should declare the causes which impel them to the separation.

We hold these truths to be self-evident, that all men are created equal, that they are endowed by their Creator with certain unalienable Rights, that among these, are Life, Liberty, and the pursuit of Happiness. That, to secure these rights, Governments are instituted among Men, deriving their just Powers from the consent of the governed. That, whenever any form of Government becomes destructive of these ends, it is the Right of the People to alter or to abolish it, and to institute new Government, laying its foundation on such Principles, and organizing its Powers in such form, as to them shall seem most likely to effect their Safety and Happiness. Prudence, indeed, will dictate that Governments long established should not be changed for light and transient causes; and, accordingly, all experience hath shewn, that mankind are more disposed to suffer, while evils are sufferable, than to right themselves

° Reprinted from Worthington C. Ford, ed., *Journals of the Continental Congress, 1774–1789* (Washington, D. C., 1904–37), Vol. 5, pp. 510–15. The original spelling, capitalization, and punctuation have been retained.

by abolishing the forms to which they are accustomed. But, when a long train of abuses and usurpations, pursuing invariably the same Object, evinces a design to reduce them under absolute Despotism, it is their right, it is their duty, to throw off such Government, and to provide new Guards for their future Security. Such has been the patient sufferance of these Colonies; and such is now the necessity which constrains them to alter their former Systems of Government. The history of the present King of Great Britain is a history of repeated injuries and usurpations, all having in direct object the establishment of an absolute Tyranny over these States. To prove this, let Facts be submitted to a candid world.

He has refused his Assent to Laws the most wholesome and necessary for the public good.

He has forbidden his Governors to pass Laws of immediate and pressing importance, unless suspended in their operation till his Assent should be obtained; and when so suspended, he has utterly neglected to attend to them.

He has refused to pass other Laws for the accommodation of large districts of People, unless those People would relinquish the right of Representation in the legislature; a right inestimable to them and formidable to tyrants only.

He has called together legislative bodies at places unusual, uncomfortable, and distant from the depository of their Public Records, for the sole Purpose of fatiguing them into compliance with his measures.

He has dissolved Representative Houses repeatedly, for opposing, with manly firmness, his invasions on the rights of the People.

He has refused for a long time, after such dissolutions, to cause others to be elected; whereby the Legislative Powers, incapable of Annihilation, have returned to the People at large for their exercise; the State remaining in the mean time exposed to all the dangers of invasion from without, and convulsions within.

He has endeavoured to prevent the Population of these States; for that purpose obstructing the Laws for Naturalization of Foreigners; refusing to pass others to encourage their migrations hither, and raising the conditions of new Appropriations of Lands.

He has obstructed the Administration of Justice, by refusing his Assent to Laws for establishing Judiciary Powers.

He has made Judges dependent on his Will alone, for the tenure of their offices, and the amount and payment of their salaries.

He has erected a multitude of New Offices, and sent hither swarms of Officers to harrass our People, and eat out their substance.

He has kept among us, in times of Peace, Standing Armies, without the Consent of our legislatures.

He has affected to render the Military independent of and superior to the Civil Power.

He has combined with others to subject us to a jurisdiction foreign to our constitution, and unacknowledged by our laws; giving his Assent to their Acts of pretended Legislation:

For quartering large bodies of armed troops among us:

For protecting them, by a mock Trial, from Punishment for any Murders which they should commit on the Inhabitants of these States:

For cutting off our Trade with all parts of the world:

For imposing Taxes on us without our Consent:

For depriving us, in many cases, of the benefits of Trial by Jury:

For transporting us beyond Seas to be tried for pretended offences:

For abolishing the free System of English Laws in a neighbouring province, establishing therein an Arbitrary government, and enlarging its Boundaries, so as to render it at once an example and fit instrument for introducing the same absolute rule into these Colonies:

For taking away our Charters, abolishing our most valuable Laws, and altering fundamentally the Forms of our Governments:

For suspending our own Legislatures, and declaring themselves invested with Power to legislate for us in all cases whatsoever.

He has abdicated Government here, by declaring us out of his protection, and waging War against us.

He has plundered our seas, ravaged our Coasts, burnt our towns, and destroyed the Lives of our People.

He is at this time transporting large Armies of foreign Mercenaries to compleat the works of death, desolation and tyranny, already begun with circumstances of Cruelty and perfidy scarcely paralleled in the most barbarous ages, and totally unworthy the Head of a civilized nation.

He has constrained our fellow Citizens, taken Captive on the high Seas, to bear Arms against their Country, to become the executioners of their friends and Brethren, or to fall themselves by their Hands.

He has excited domestic insurrections amongst us, and has endeavoured to bring on the inhabitants of our frontiers, the merciless Indian Savages, whose known rule of warfare, is an undistinguished destruction of all ages, sexes and conditions.

In every stage of these Oppressions, We have Petitioned for Redress, in the most humble terms: Our repeated Petitions, have been answered only by repeated injury. A Prince, whose character is thus marked by every act which may define a Tyrant, is unfit to be the ruler of a free People.

Nor have We been wanting in attentions to our British brethren. We have warned them from time to time of attempts by their legislature to extend an unwarrantable jurisdiction over us. We have reminded them of the circumstances of our emigration and settlement here. We have appealed to their native justice and magnanimity, and we have conjured them by the ties of our common kindred, to disavow these usurpations, which, would inevitably interrupt our connexions and correspondence. They too have been deaf to the voice of justice and consanguinity. We must, therefore, acquiesce in the necessity, which denounces our Separation, and hold them, as we hold the rest of mankind, Enemies in war, in Peace Friends.

WE, THEREFORE, the Representatives of the UNITED STATES OF AMERICA, in GENERAL CONGRESS assembled, appealing to the Supreme Judge of the World for the rectitude of our intentions, DO, in the Name, and by Authority of the good People of these Colonies, solemnly

PUBLISH and DECLARE, That these United Colonies are, and of Right, ought to be FREE AND INDEPENDENT STATES; that they are Absolved from all Allegiance to the British Crown, and that all political connexion between them and the State of Great Britain, is and ought to be totally dissolved; and that, as FREE and INDEPENDENT STATES, they have full Power to levy War, conclude Peace, contract Alliances, establish Commerce, and to do all other Acts and Things which INDEPENDENT STATES may of right do. AND for the support of this Declaration, with a firm reliance on the protection of divine Providence, we mutually pledge to each other our Lives, our Fortunes, and our sacred Honour.

The Constitution of the United States of America*

We the people of the United States, in Order to form a more perfect Union, establish Justice, insure domestic Tranquility, provide for the common defence, promote the general Welfare, and secure the Blessings of Liberty to ourselves and our Posterity, do ordain and establish this CONSTITUTION for the United States of America.

ARTICLE I

SECTION 1. All legislative Powers herein granted shall be vested in a Congress of the United States, which shall consist of a Senate and House of Representatives.

SECTION 2. The House of Representatives shall be composed of Members chosen every second Year by the People of the several States, and the Electors in each State shall have the Qualifications requisite for Electors of the most numerous Branch of the State Legislature.

No Person shall be a Representative who shall not have attained to the Age of twenty-five Years, and been seven Years a Citizen of the United States, and who shall not, when elected, be an Inhabitant of that state in which he shall be chosen.

Representatives and direct Taxes† shall be apportioned among the several States which may be included within this Union, according to their respective Numbers, which shall be determined by adding to the whole Number of free Persons, including those bound to Service for a Term of Years, and excluding Indians not taxed, three fifths of all other Persons.‡ The actual Enumeration shall be made within three Years after the first Meeting of the Congress of the United States, and within every subsequent Term of ten Years, in such Manner as they shall by Law direct. The Number of Representatives shall not exceed one for every thirty Thousand, but each State shall have at Least one Representative; and until such enumeration shall be made, the State of New Hampshire shall be entitled to chuse three, Massachusetts eight, Rhode-Island and Providence Plantations one, Connecticut five, New-York six, New Jersey four, Pennsylvania eight, Delaware one, Maryland six, Virginia ten, North Carolina five, South Carolina five, and Georgia three.

When vacancies happen in the Representation from any State, the Executive Authority thereof shall issue Writs of Election to fill such Vacancies.

The House of Representatives shall chuse their Speaker and other Officers; and shall have the sole Power of Impeachment.

SECTION 3. The Senate of the United States shall be composed of two Senators from each State, chosen by the Legislature thereof, for six Years; and each Senator shall have one Vote.°

Immediately after they shall be assembled in Consequence of the first Election, they shall be divided as equally as may be into three Classes. The Seats of the Senators of the first Class shall be vacated at the Expiration of the second Year, of the second Class at the Expiration of the fourth Year, and of the third Class at the Expiration of the sixth Year, so that one-third may be chosen every second Year; and if Vacancies happen by Resignation, or otherwise, during the Recess of the Legislature of any State, the Executive thereof may make temporary Appointments until the next Meeting of the Legislature, which shall then fill such Vacancies.†

No Person shall be a Senator who shall not have attained to the Age of thirty Years, and been nine Years a Citizen of the United States, and who shall not, when elected, be an Inhabitant of that State in which he shall be chosen.

The Vice President of the United States shall be President of the Senate, but shall have no vote, unless they be equally divided.

The Senate shall chuse their other Officers, and also a President pro tempore, in the absence of the Vice President, or when he shall exercise the Office of the President of the United States.

---

* Original spelling, capitalization, and punctuation have been retained.
† Modified by the Sixteenth Amendment.
‡ Replaced by the Fourteenth Amendment.

° Superseded by the Seventeenth Amendment.
† Modified by the Seventeenth Amendment.

The Senate shall have the sole Power to try all Impeachments. When sitting for that purpose, they shall be on Oath or Affirmation. When the President of the United States is tried, the Chief Justice shall preside: And no person shall be convicted without the Concurrence of two thirds of the Members present.

Judgment in Cases of Impeachment shall not extend further than to removal from Office, and disqualification to hold and enjoy any Office of honor, Trust, or Profit under the United States: but the Party convicted shall nevertheless be liable and subject to Indictment, Trial, Judgment, and Punishment, according to Law.

SECTION 4.   The Times, Places and Manner of holding Elections for Senators and Representatives, shall be prescribed in each state by the Legislature thereof; but the Congress may at any time by Law make or alter such Regulations, except as to the Places of Chusing Senators.

The Congress shall assemble at least once in every Year, and such Meeting shall be on the first Monday in December, unless they shall by Law appoint a different Day.°

SECTION 5.   Each House shall be the Judge of the Elections, Returns and Qualifications of its own Members, and a Majority of each shall constitute a Quorum to do Business; but a smaller number may adjourn from day to day, and may be authorized to compel the Attendance of absent Members, in such Manner, and under such Penalties, as each House may provide.

Each House may determine the Rules of its Proceedings, punish its Members for disorderly Behavior, and, with the Concurrence of two thirds, expel a Member.

Each House shall keep a Journal of its Proceedings, and from time to time publish the same, excepting such Parts as may in their Judgment require Secrecy; and the Yeas and Nays of the Members of either House on any question shall, at the Desire of one fifth of those Present, be entered on the Journal.

Neither House, during the Session of Congress, shall, without the Consent of the other, adjourn for more than three days, nor to any other Place than that in which the two Houses shall be sitting.

SECTION 6.   The Senators and Representatives shall receive a Compensation for their Services, to be ascertained by Law, and paid

° Superseded by the Twentieth Amendment.

out of the Treasury of the United States. They shall in all Cases, except Treason, Felony, and Breach of the Peace, be privileged from Arrest during their Attendance at the Session of their respective Houses, and in going to and returning from the same; and for any Speech or Debate in either House, they shall not be questioned in any other Place.

No Senator or Representative shall, during the Time for which he was elected, be appointed to any civil Office under the Authority of the United States, which shall have been created, or the Emoluments whereof shall have been increased, during such time; and no Person holding any Office under the United States shall be a Member of either House during his continuance in Office.

SECTION 7.   All Bills for raising Revenue shall originate in the House of Representatives; but the Senate may propose or concur with Amendments as on other bills.

Every Bill which shall have passed the House of Representatives and the Senate, shall, before it become a Law, be presented to the President of the United States; If he approve he shall sign it, but if not he shall return it, with his Objections, to that House in which it shall have originated, who shall enter the Objections at large on their Journal, and proceed to reconsider it. If after such Reconsideration two thirds of that House shall agree to pass the bill, it shall be sent, together with the objections, to the other House, by which it shall likewise be reconsidered, and if approved by two thirds of that House, it shall become a Law. But in all such Cases the Votes of both Houses shall be determined by Yeas and Nays, and the Names of the Persons voting for and against the Bill shall be entered on the Journal of each House respectively. If any Bill shall not be returned by the President within ten Days (Sundays excepted) after it shall have been presented to him, the Same shall be a Law, in like Manner as if he had signed it, unless the Congress by their Adjournment prevent its Return, in which Case it shall not be a Law.

Every Order, Resolution, or Vote to which the Concurrence of the Senate and House of Representatives may be necessary (except on a question of Adjournment) shall be presented to the President of the United States; and before the Same shall take Effect, shall be approved by him, or being disapproved by him, shall be repassed by two thirds of the Senate and House of Representatives, according to the Rules and Limitations prescribed in the Case of a Bill.

SECTION 8. The Congress shall have Power To lay and collect Taxes, Duties, Imposts and Excises, to pay the Debts and provide for the common Defence and general Welfare of the United States; but all Duties, Imposts and Excises shall be uniform throughout the United States;

To borrow money on the credit of the United States;

To regulate Commerce with foreign Nations, and among the several States, and with the Indian Tribes;

To establish an uniform Rule of Naturalization, and uniform Laws on the subject of Bankruptcies throughout the United States;

To coin Money, regulate the Value thereof, and of foreign Coin, and fix the Standard of Weights and Measures;

To provide for the Punishment of counterfeiting the Securities and current Coin of the United States;

To establish Post Offices and post Roads;

To promote the Progress of Science and useful Arts, by securing for limited Times to Authors and Inventors the exclusive Right to their respective Writings and Discoveries;

To constitute Tribunals inferior to the Supreme Court;

To define and punish Piracies and Felonies committed on the high Seas, and Offenses against the Law of Nations;

To declare War, grant Letters of Marque and Reprisal, and make Rules concerning Captures on Land and Water;

To raise and support Armies, but no Appropriation of Money to that Use shall be for a longer Term than two Years;

To provide and maintain a Navy;

To make Rules for the Government and Regulation of the land and naval forces;

To provide for calling forth the Militia to execute the Laws of the Union, suppress Insurrections and repel Invasions;

To provide for organizing, arming, and disciplining the Militia, and for governing such Part of them as may be employed in the Service of the United States, reserving to the States respectively, the Appointment of the Officers, and the Authority of training the Militia according to the discipline prescribed by Congress;

To exercise exclusive Legislation in all Cases whatsoever, over such District (not exceeding ten Miles square) as may, by Cession of particular States, and the acceptance of Congress, become the Seat of the Government of the United States, and to exercise like Authority over all Places purchased by the Consent of the Legislature of the State in which the same shall be, for the Erection of Forts, Magazines, Arsenals, dock-Yards, and other needful Buildings; —And

To make all Laws which shall be necessary and proper for carrying into Execution the foregoing Powers, and all other Powers vested by this Constitution in the Government of the United States, or in any Department or Officer thereof.

SECTION 9. The Migration or Importation of such Persons as any of the States now existing shall think proper to admit shall not be prohibited by the Congress prior to the Year one thousand eight hundred and eight, but a tax or duty may be imposed on such Importation, not exceeding ten dollars for each Person.

The privilege of the Writ of Habeas Corpus shall not be suspended, unless when in Cases of Rebellion or Invasion the public Safety may require it.

No Bill of Attainder or ex post facto Law shall be passed.

No capitation, or other direct, Tax shall be laid unless in Proportion to the Census or Enumeration herein before directed to be taken.

No Tax or Duty shall be laid on Articles exported from any State.

No Preference shall be given by any Regulation of Revenue to the Ports of one State over those of another: nor shall Vessels bound to, or from, one State, be obliged to enter, clear, or pay Duties in another.

No Money shall be drawn from the Treasury, but in Consequence of Appropriations made by Law; and a regular Statement and Account of the Receipts and Expenditures of all public Money shall be published from time to time.

No Title of Nobility shall be granted by the United States: And no Person holding any Office of Profit or Trust under them, shall, without the Consent of the Congress, accept of any present, Emolument, Office, or Title, of any kind whatever, from any King, Prince, or foreign State.

SECTION 10. No State shall enter into any Treaty, Alliance, or Confederation; grant Letters of Marque and Reprisal; coin Money; emit Bills of Credit; make any Thing but gold and silver Coin a Tender in Payment of Debts; pass any Bill of Attainder, ex post facto Law, or Law impairing the Obligation of Contracts, or grant any Title of Nobility.

No State shall, without the Consent of the Congress, lay any Imposts or Duties on Imports or Exports, except what may be absolutely necessary for executing its inspection Laws: and the net Produce of all Duties and Imposts, laid by any State on Imports or Exports, shall be for the Use of the Treasury of the United States; and all such Laws shall be subject to the Revision and Control of the Congress.

No State shall, without the Consent of Congress, lay any duty of Tonnage, keep Troops, or Ships of War in time of Peace, enter into any Agreement or Compact with another State, or with a foreign Power, or engage in War, unless actually invaded, or in such imminent Danger as will not admit of delay.

ARTICLE II

SECTION 1. The executive Power shall be vested in a President of the United States of America. He shall hold his Office during the Term of four years, and, together with the Vice-President, chosen for the same Term, be elected, as follows:

Each State shall appoint, in such Manner as the Legislature thereof may direct, a Number of Electors, equal to the whole Number of Senators and Representatives to which the State may be entitled in the Congress: but no Senator or Representative, or Person holding an Office of Trust or Profit under the United States, shall be appointed an Elector.

The Electors shall meet in their respective States, and vote by Ballot for two persons, of whom one at least shall not be an Inhabitant of the same State with themselves. And they shall make a List of all the Persons voted for, and of the Number of Votes for each; which List they shall sign and certify, and transmit sealed to the Seat of the Government of the United States, directed to the President of the Senate. The President of the Senate shall, in the Presence of the Senate and House of Representatives, open all the Certificates, and the Votes shall then be counted. The Person having the greatest Number of Votes shall be the President, if such Number be a Majority of the whole Number of Electors appointed; and if there be more than one who have such Majority, and have an equal Number of Votes, then the House of Representatives shall immediately chuse by Ballot one of them for President; and if no Person have a Majority, then from the five highest on the List the said House shall in like Manner chuse the President. But in chusing the President, the Votes shall be taken by States, the Representa-

tion from each State having one Vote; a quorum for this Purpose shall consist of a Member or Members from two-thirds of the States, and a Majority of all the States shall be necessary to a Choice. In every Case, after the Choice of the President, the Person having the greatest Number of Votes of the Electors shall be the Vice President. But if there should remain two or more who have equal votes, the Senate shall chuse from them by Ballot the Vice-President.°

The Congress may determine the Time of chusing the Electors, and the Day on which they shall give their Votes; which Day shall be the same throughout the United States.

No person except a natural-born Citizen, or a Citizen of the United States, at the time of the Adoption of this Constitution, shall be eligible to the Office of President; neither shall any Person be eligible to that Office who shall not have attained to the Age of thirty-five years, and been fourteen Years a Resident within the United States.

In Case of the Removal of the President from Office, or of his Death, Resignation, or Inability to discharge the Powers and Duties of the said Office, the same shall devolve on the Vice President, and the Congress may by Law provide for the Case of Removal, Death, Resignation, or Inability, both of the President and Vice President, declaring what Officer shall then act as President, and such Officer shall act accordingly, until the disability be removed, or a President shall be elected.†

The President shall, at stated Times, receive for his Services a Compensation, which shall neither be increased nor diminished during the Period for which he shall have been elected, and he shall not receive within that Period any other Emolument from the United States, or any of them.

Before he enter on the execution of his Office, he shall take the following Oath or Affirmation: —"I do solemnly swear (or affirm) that I will faithfully execute the Office of President of the United States, and will, to the best of my Ability, preserve, protect, and defend the Constitution of the United States."

SECTION 2. The President shall be Commander in Chief of the Army and Navy of the United States, and of the Militia of the several States, when called into the actual Service of the United States; he may require the Opinion, in writing, of the principal Officer in each of

° Superseded by the Twelfth Amendment.
† Modified by the Twenty-fifth Amendment.

the executive Departments, upon any subject relating to the Duties of their respective Offices, and he shall have Power to Grant Reprieves and Pardons for Offenses against the United States, except in Cases of Impeachment.

He shall have Power, by and with the Advice and Consent of the Senate, to make Treaties, provided two thirds of the Senators present concur; and he shall nominate, and by and with the Advice and Consent of the Senate, shall appoint Ambassadors, other public Ministers and Consuls, Judges of the supreme Court, and all other Officers of the United States, whose Appointments are not herein otherwise provided for, and which shall be established by Law: but the Congress may by Law vest the Appointment of such inferior Officers, as they think proper, in the President alone, in the Courts of Law, or in the Heads of Departments.

The President shall have Power to fill up all Vacancies that may happen during the Recess of the Senate, by granting Commissions which shall expire at the End of their next Session.

SECTION 3.   He shall from time to time give to the Congress Information of the State of the Union, and recommend to their Consideration such Measures as he shall judge necessary and expedient; he may, on extraordinary occasions, convene both Houses, or either of them, and in Case of Disagreement between them, with respect to the Time of Adjournment, he may adjourn them to such Time as he shall think proper; he shall receive Ambassadors and other public Ministers; he shall take Care that the Laws be faithfully executed, and shall Commission all the Officers of the United States.

SECTION 4.   The President, Vice President and all civil Officers of the United States, shall be removed from Office on Impeachment for, and Conviction of, Treason, Bribery, or other high Crimes and Misdemeanors.

ARTICLE III

SECTION 1.   The judicial Power of the United States, shall be vested in one supreme Court, and in such inferior Courts as the Congress may from time to time ordain and establish. The Judges, both of the supreme and inferior Courts, shall hold their Offices during good Behaviour, and shall, at stated Times, receive for their Services, a Compensation, which shall not be diminished during their Continuance in Office.

SECTION 2.   The judicial Power shall extend to all Cases, in Law and Equity, arising under this Constitution, the Laws of the United States, and treaties made, or which shall be made, under their Authority;—to all Cases affecting ambassadors, other public ministers and consuls;—to all cases of admiralty and maritime Jurisdiction;—to Controversies to which the United States shall be a Party;—to Controversies between two or more States;—between a State and Citizens of another State;°—between Citizens of different States,—between Citizens of the same State claiming Lands under Grants of different States, and between a State, or the Citizens thereof, and foreign States, Citizens or Subjects.

In all Cases affecting Ambassadors, other public Ministers and Consuls, and those in which a State shall be Party, the supreme Court shall have original Jurisdiction. In all the other Cases before mentioned, the supreme Court shall have appellate Jurisdiction, both as to Law and Fact, with such Exceptions, and under such Regulations as the Congress shall make.

The trial of all Crimes, except in Cases of Impeachment, shall be by Jury; and such Trial shall be held in the State where the said Crimes shall have been committed; but when not committed within any State, the Trial shall be at such Place or Places as the Congress may by Law have directed.

SECTION 3.   Treason against the United States, shall consist only in levying War against them, or in adhering to their Enemies, giving them Aid and Comfort. No Person shall be convicted of Treason unless on the Testimony of two Witnesses to the same overt Act, or on Confession in open Court.

The Congress shall have power to declare the Punishment of Treason, but no Attainder of Treason shall work Corruption of Blood, or Forfeiture except during the Life of the Person attainted.

ARTICLE IV

SECTION 1.   Full Faith and Credit shall be given in each State to the public Acts, Records, and judicial Proceedings of every other State. And the Congress may by general Laws prescribe the Manner in which such Acts, Records and Proceedings shall be proved, and the Effect thereof.

° Modified by the Eleventh Amendment.

SECTION 2. The Citizens of each State shall be entitled to all Privileges and Immunities of Citizens in the several States.

A Person charged in any State with Treason, Felony, or other Crime, who shall flee from Justice, and be found in another State, shall on demand of the executive Authority of the State from which he fled, be delivered up, to be removed to the State having Jurisdiction of the crime.

No Person held to Service or Labour in one State, under the Laws thereof, escaping into another, shall, in Consequence of any Law or Regulation therein, be discharged from such Service or Labour, but shall be delivered up on Claim of the Party to whom such Service or Labour may be due.

SECTION 3. New States may be admitted by the Congress into this Union; but no new State shall be formed or erected within the Jurisdiction of any other State; nor any State be formed by the Junction of two or more States, or parts of States, without the Consent of the Legislatures of the States concerned as well as of the Congress.

The Congress shall have Power to dispose of and make all needful Rules and Regulations respecting the Territory or other Property belonging to the United States; and nothing in this Constitution shall be so construed as to Prejudice any Claims of the United States, or of any particular State.

SECTION 4. The United States shall guarantee to every State in this Union a Republican Form of Government, and shall protect each of them against Invasion; and on Application of the Legislature, or of the Executive (when the Legislature cannot be convened) against domestic Violence.

ARTICLE V

The Congress, whenever two-thirds of both Houses shall deem it necessary, shall propose Amendments to this Constitution, or, on the Application of the Legislatures of two-thirds of the several States, shall call a Convention for proposing Amendments, which, in either Case, shall be valid to all Intents and Purposes, as part of this Constitution, when ratified by the Legislatures of three-fourths of the several States, or by Conventions in three-fourths thereof, as the one or the other Mode of Ratification may be proposed by the Congress;

Provided that no Amendment which may be made prior to the Year One thousand eight hundred and eight shall in any Manner affect the first and fourth Clauses in the Ninth Section of the first Article; and that no State, without its Consent, shall be deprived of its equal Suffrage in the Senate.

ARTICLE VI

All Debts contracted and Engagements entered into, before the Adoption of this Constitution, shall be as valid against the United States under this Constitution, as under the Confederation.

This Constitution, and the Laws of the United States which shall be made in Pursuance thereof; and all Treaties made, or which shall be made, under the Authority of the United States, shall be the supreme Law of the Land; and the Judges in every State shall be bound thereby, any Thing in the Constitution or Laws of any State to the Contrary notwithstanding.

The Senators and Representatives before mentioned, and the Members of the several State Legislatures, and all executive and judicial Officers, both of the United States and of the several States, shall be bound by Oath or Affirmation to support this Constitution; but no religious Test shall ever be required as a qualification to any Office or public Trust under the United States.

ARTICLE VII

The Ratification of the Conventions of nine States shall be sufficient for the Establishment of this Constitution between the States so ratifying the same.

Done in Convention by the Unanimous Consent of the States present the Seventeenth Day of September in the Year of our Lord one thousand seven hundred and Eighty seven, and of the Independence of the United States of America the Twelfth. In Witness whereof We have hereunto subscribed our Names.

Articles in Addition to, and Amendment of, the Constitution of the United States of America, Proposed by Congress, and Ratified by the Legislatures of the Several States, Pursuant to the Fifth Article of the Original Constitution.

AMENDMENT I°

Congress shall make no law respecting an establishment of religion, or prohibiting the free exercise thereof; or abridging the freedom of speech, or of the press; or the right of the people peaceably to assemble, and to petition the Government for a redress of grievances.

AMENDMENT II

A well regulated Militia, being necessary to the security of a free State, the right of the people to keep and bear Arms shall not be infringed.

AMENDMENT III

No Soldier shall, in time of peace, be quartered in any house, without the consent of the Owner, nor in time of war, but in a manner to be prescribed by law.

AMENDMENT IV

The right of the people to be secure in their persons, houses, papers, and effects, against unreasonable searches and seizures, shall not be violated, and no Warrants shall issue, but upon probable cause, supported by Oath or affirmation, and particularly describing the place to be searched, and the persons or things to be seized.

AMENDMENT V

No person shall be held to answer for a capital or otherwise infamous crime, unless on a presentment or indictment of a Grand Jury, except in cases arising in the land or naval forces, or in the Militia, when in actual service in time of War or public danger; nor shall any person be subject for the same offence to be twice put in jeopardy of life or limb; nor shall be compelled in any criminal case to be a witness against himself, nor be deprived of life, liberty, or property, without due process of law; nor shall private property be taken for public use, without just compensation.

° The first ten amendments were passed by Congress September 25, 1789. They were ratified by three-fourths of the states December 15, 1791.

AMENDMENT VI

In all criminal prosecutions, the accused shall enjoy the right to a speedy and public trial, by an impartial jury of the State and district wherein the crime shall have been committed, which district shall have been previously ascertained by law, and to be informed of the nature and cause of the accusation; to be confronted with the witnesses against him; to have compulsory process for obtaining witnesses in his favor, and to have the Assistance of Counsel for his defence.

AMENDMENT VII

In suits at common law, where the value in controversy shall exceed twenty dollars, the right of trial by jury shall be preserved, and no fact tried by a jury, shall be otherwise reexamined in any Court of the United States, than according to the rules of the common law.

AMENDMENT VIII

Excessive bail shall not be required, nor excessive fines imposed, nor cruel and unusual punishments inflicted.

AMENDMENT IX

The enumeration in the Constitution, of certain rights, shall not be construed to deny or disparage others retained by the people.

AMENDMENT X

The powers not delegated to the United States by the Constitution, nor prohibited by it to the States, are reserved to the States respectively, or to the people.

AMENDMENT XI°

The Judicial power of the United States shall not be construed to extend to any suit in law or equity, commenced or prosecuted against one of the United States by Citizens of another State, or by Citizens or Subjects of any Foreign State.

° Passed March 5, 1794. Ratified January 8, 1798.

AMENDMENT XII°

The Electors shall meet in their respective States and vote by ballot for President and Vice-President, one of whom, at least, shall not be an inhabitant of the same State with themselves; they shall name in their ballots the person voted for as President, and in distinct ballots the person voted for as Vice-President, and they shall make distinct lists of all persons voted for as President, and of all persons voted for as Vice-President, and of the number of votes for each, which lists they shall sign and certify, and transmit sealed to the seat of the government of the United States, directed to the President of the Senate;—The President of the Senate shall, in the presence of the Senate and House of Representatives, open all the certificates and the votes shall then be counted; —The person having the greatest number of votes for President, shall be the President, if such number be a majority of the whole number of Electors appointed; and if no person have such majority, then from the persons having the highest numbers not exceeding three on the list of those voted for as President, the House of Representatives shall choose immediately, by ballot, the President. But in choosing the President, the votes shall be taken by states, the representation from each state having one vote; a quorum for this purpose shall consist of a member or members from two-thirds of the states, and a majority of all the states shall be necessary to a choice. And if the House of Representatives shall not choose a President whenever the right of choice shall devolve upon them, before the fourth day of March next following, then the Vice-President shall act as President, as in the case of the death or other constitutional disability of the President.—The person having the greatest number of votes as Vice-President, shall be the Vice-President, if such number be a majority of the whole number of Electors appointed, and if no person have a majority, then from the two highest numbers on the list, the Senate shall choose the Vice-President; a quorum for the purpose shall consist of two-thirds of the whole number of Senators, and a majority of the whole number shall be necessary to a choice. But no person constitutionally ineligible to the office of President shall be eligible to that of Vice-President of the United States.

° Passed December 9, 1803. Ratified September 25, 1804.

AMENDMENT XIII°

SECTION 1.　Neither slavery nor involuntary servitude, except as a punishment for crime whereof the party shall have been duly convicted, shall exist within the United States, or any place subject to their jurisdiction.

SECTION 2.　Congress shall have power to enforce this article by appropriate legislation.

AMENDMENT XIV†

SECTION 1.　All persons born or naturalized in the United States, and subject to the jurisdiction thereof, are citizens of the United States and of the State wherein they reside. No State shall make or enforce any law which shall abridge the privileges or immunities of citizens of the United States; nor shall any State deprive any person of life, liberty, or property, without due process of law; nor deny to any person within its jurisdiction the equal protection of the laws.

SECTION 2.　Representatives shall be apportioned among the several States according to their respective numbers, counting the whole number of persons in each State, excluding Indians not taxed. But when the right to vote at any election for the choice of electors for President and Vice-President of the United States, Representatives in Congress, the Executive and Judicial officers of a State, or the members of the Legislature thereof, is denied to any of the male inhabitants of such State, being twenty-one years of age, and citizens of the United States, or in any way abridged, except for participation in rebellion, or other crime, the basis of representation therein shall be reduced in the proportion which the number of such male citizens shall bear to the whole number of male citizens twenty-one years of age in such State.

SECTION 3.　No person shall be a Senator or Representative in Congress, or elector of President and Vice-President, or hold any office, civil or military, under the United States, or under any State, who, having previously taken an oath, as a member of Congress, or as an officer of the United States, or as a member of any State legislature, or as an executive or judicial officer of any State, to support the

° Passed February 1, 1865. Ratified December 18, 1865.

† Passed June 16, 1866. Ratified July 28, 1868.

Constitution of the United States, shall have engaged in insurrection or rebellion against the same, or given aid or comfort to the enemies thereof. But Congress may by a vote of two-thirds of each House, remove such disability.

SECTION 4. The validity of the public debt of the United States, authorized by law, including debts incurred for payment of pensions and bounties for services in suppressing insurrection or rebellion, shall not be questioned. But neither the United States nor any State shall assume or pay any debt or obligation incurred in aid of insurrection or rebellion against the United States, or any claim for the loss or emancipation of any slave; but all such debts, obligations, and claims shall be held illegal and void.

SECTION 5. The Congress shall have the power to enforce, by appropriate legislation, the provisions of this article.

AMENDMENT XV°

SECTION 1. The right of citizens of the United States to vote shall not be denied or abridged by the United States or by any State on account of race, color, or previous condition of servitude—

SECTION 2. The Congress shall have power to enforce this article by appropriate legislation.

AMENDMENT XVI†

The Congress shall have power to lay and collect taxes on incomes, from whatever source derived, without apportionment among the several States, and without regard to any census or enumeration.

AMENDMENT XVII‡

The Senate of the United States shall be composed of two Senators from each State, elected by the people thereof, for six years; and each Senator shall have one vote. The electors in each State shall have the qualifications requisite for electors of the most numerous branch of the State legislatures.

When vacancies happen in the representation of any State in the Senate, the executive

authority of such State shall issue writs of election to fill such vacancies: *Provided,* That the legislature of any State may empower the executive thereof to make temporary appointments until the people fill the vacancies by election as the legislature may direct.

This amendment shall not be so construed as to affect the election or term of any Senator chosen before it becomes valid as part of the Constitution.

AMENDMENT XVIII°

SECTION 1. After one year from the ratification of this article the manufacture, sale, or transportation of intoxicating liquors within, the importation thereof into, or the exportation thereof from the United States and all territory subject to the jurisdiction thereof for beverage purposes is hereby prohibited.

SECTION 2. The Congress and the several States shall have concurrent power to enforce this article by appropriate legislation.

SECTION 3. This article shall be inoperative unless it shall have been ratified as an amendment to the Constitution by the legislatures of the several States, as provided in the Constitution, within seven years from the date of the submission hereof to the States by the Congress.

AMENDMENT XIX†

The right of citizens of the United States to vote shall not be denied or abridged by the United States or by any State on account of sex.

Congress shall have power to enforce this article by appropriate legislation.

AMENDMENT XX‡

SECTION 1. The terms of the President and Vice-President shall end at noon on the 20th day of January, and the terms of Senators and Representatives at noon on the 3d day of January, of the years in which such terms would have ended if this article had not been ratified; and the terms of their successors shall then begin.

SECTION 2. The Congress shall assemble at

° Passed February 27, 1869. Ratified March 30, 1870.
† Passed July 12, 1909. Ratified February 25, 1913.
‡ Passed May 16, 1912. Ratified May 31, 1913.

° Passed December 17, 1917. Ratified January 29, 1919.
† Passed June 5, 1919. Ratified August 26, 1920.
‡ Passed March 3, 1932. Ratified January 23, 1933.

least once in every year, and such meeting shall begin at noon on the 3d day of January, unless they shall by law appoint a different day.

SECTION 3.   If, at the time fixed for the beginning of the term of the President, the President elect shall have died, the Vice-President elect shall become President. If a President shall not have been chosen before the time fixed for the beginning of his term, or if the President elect shall have failed to qualify, then the Vice-President elect shall act as President until a President shall have qualified; and the Congress may by law provide for the case wherein neither a President elect nor a Vice-President elect shall have qualified, declaring who shall then act as President, or the manner in which one who is to act shall be selected, and such person shall act accordingly until a President or Vice-President shall have qualified.

SECTION 4.   The Congress may by law provide for the case of the death of any of the persons from whom the House of Representatives may choose a President whenever the right of choice shall have devolved upon them, and for the case of the death of any of the persons from whom the Senate may choose a Vice-President whenever the right of choice shall have devolved upon them.

SECTION 5.   Sections 1 and 2 shall take effect on the 15th day of October following the ratification of this article.

SECTION 6.   This article shall be inoperative unless it shall have been ratified as an amendment to the Constitution by the legislatures of three-fourths of the several States within seven years from the date of its submission.

AMENDMENT XXI°

SECTION 1.   The eighteenth article of amendment to the Constitution of the United States is hereby repealed.

SECTION 2.   The transportation or importation into any State, Territory, or possession of the United States for delivery or use therein of intoxicating liquors, in violation of the laws thereof, is hereby prohibited.

SECTION 3.   This article shall be inoperative unless it shall have been ratified as an amendment to the Constitution by conventions in the several States, as provided in the Constitution,

° Passed February 20, 1933. Ratified December 5, 1933.

within seven years from the date of the submission hereof to the States by the Congress.

AMENDMENT XXII°

No person shall be elected to the office of the President more than twice, and no person who has held the office of President, or acted as President, for more than two years of a term to which some other person was elected President shall be elected to the office of the President more than once.

But this Article shall not apply to any person holding the office of President when this Article was proposed by the Congress, and shall not prevent any person who may be holding the office of President, or acting as President, during the term within which this Article becomes operative from holding the office of President or acting as President during the remainder of such term.

AMENDMENT XXIII†

SECTION 1.   The District constituting the seat of Government of the United States shall appoint in such manner as the Congress may direct:

A number of electors of President and Vice President equal to the whole number of Senators and Representatives in Congress to which the District would be entitled if it were a State, but in no event more than the least populous State; they shall be in addition to those appointed by the States, but they shall be considered, for the purposes of the election of President and Vice President, to be electors appointed by the State; and they shall meet in the District and perform such duties as provided by the twelfth article of amendment.

SECTION 2.   The Congress shall have power to enforce this article by appropriate legislation.

AMENDMENT XXIV‡

SECTION 1.   The right of citizens of the United States to vote in any primary or other election for President or Vice President, for electors for President or Vice President, or for Senator or Representative in Congress, shall

° Passed March 12, 1947. Ratified March 1, 1951.
† Passed June 16, 1960. Ratified April 3, 1961.
‡ Passed August 27, 1962. Ratified January 23, 1964.

not be denied or abridged by the United States or any State by reason of failure to pay any poll tax or other tax.

SECTION 2. The Congress shall have power to enforce this article by appropriate legislation.

AMENDMENT XXV°

SECTION 1. In case of the removal of the President from office or of his death or resignation, the Vice President shall become President.

SECTION 2. Whenever there is a vacancy in the office of the Vice President, the President shall nominate a Vice President who shall take office upon confirmation by a majority vote of both Houses of Congress.

SECTION 3. Whenever the President transmits to the President pro tempore of the Senate and the Speaker of the House of Representatives his written declaration that he is unable to discharge the powers and duties of his office, and until he transmits to them a written declaration to the contrary, such powers and duties shall be discharged by the Vice President as Acting President.

SECTION 4. Whenever the Vice President and a majority of either the principal officers of the executive department or of such other body as Congress may by law provide, transmit

° Passed July 6, 1965. Ratified February 11, 1967.

to the President pro tempore of the Senate and the Speaker of the House of Representatives their written declaration that the President is unable to discharge the powers and duties of his office, the Vice President shall immediately assume the powers and duties of the office as Acting President.

Thereafter, when the President transmits to the President pro tempore of the Senate and the Speaker of the House of Representatives his written declaration that no inability exists, he shall resume the powers and duties of his office unless the Vice President and a majority of either the principal officers of the executive department or of such other body as Congress may by law provide, transmit within four days to the President pro tempore of the Senate and the Speaker of the House of Representatives their written declaration that the President is unable to discharge the powers and duties of his office. Thereupon Congress shall decide the issue, assembling within forty-eight hours for that purpose if not in session. If the Congress, within twenty-one days after receipt of the latter written declaration, or, if Congress is not in session, within twenty-one days after Congress is required to assemble, determines by two-thirds vote of both Houses that the President is unable to discharge the powers and duties of his office, the Vice President shall continue to discharge the same as Acting President; otherwise, the President shall resume the powers and duties of his office.

Presidential Elections (1789–1964)

Year	Number of states	Candidates	Parties	Popular vote	Electoral vote	Percentage of popular vote
1789	11	GEORGE WASHINGTON	No party designations		69	
		John Adams			34	
		Minor Candidates			35	
1792	15	GEORGE WASHINGTON	No party designations		132	
		John Adams			77	
		George Clinton			50	
		Minor Candidates			5	
1796	16	JOHN ADAMS	Federalist		71	
		Thomas Jefferson	Democratic-Republican		68	
		Thomas Pinckney	Federalist		59	
		Aaron Burr	Democratic-Republican		30	
		Minor Candidates			48	
1800	16	THOMAS JEFFERSON	Democratic-Republican		73	
		Aaron Burr	Democratic-Republican		73	
		John Adams	Federalist		65	
		Charles C. Pinckney	Federalist		64	
		John Jay	Federalist		1	
1804	17	THOMAS JEFFERSON	Democratic-Republican		162	
		Charles C. Pinckney	Federalist		14	
1808	17	JAMES MADISON	Democratic-Republican		122	
		Charles C. Pinckney	Federalist		47	
		George Clinton	Democratic-Republican		6	
1812	18	JAMES MADISON	Democratic-Republican		128	
		DeWitt Clinton	Federalist		89	
1816	19	JAMES MONROE	Democratic-Republican		183	
		Rufus King	Federalist		34	
1820	24	JAMES MONROE	Democratic-Republican		231	
		John Quincy Adams	Independent Republican		1	
1824	24	JOHN QUINCY ADAMS	Democratic-Republican	108,740	84	30.5
		Andrew Jackson	Democratic-Republican	153,544	99	43.1
		William H. Crawford	Democratic-Republican	46,618	41	13.1
		Henry Clay	Democratic-Republican	47,136	37	13.2
1828	24	ANDREW JACKSON	Democratic	647,286	178	56.0
		John Quincy Adams	National Republican	508,064	83	44.0
1832	24	ANDREW JACKSON	Democratic	687,502	219	55.0
		Henry Clay	National Republican	530,189	49	42.4
		William Wirt	Anti-Masonic	33,108	7	2.6
		John Floyd	National Republican		11	
1836	26	MARTIN VAN BUREN	Democratic	765,483	170	50.9
		William H. Harrison	Whig		73	
		Hugh L. White	Whig	739,795	26	49.1
		Daniel Webster	Whig		14	
		W. P. Mangum	Whig		11	
1840	26	WILLIAM H. HARRISON	Whig	1,274,624	234	53.1
		Martin Van Buren	Democratic	1,127,781	60	46.9

Candidates receiving less than 1 per cent of the popular vote have been omitted. For that reason the percentage of popular vote given for any election year may not total 100 per cent.

Before the passage of the Twelfth Amendment in 1804, the Electoral College voted for two presidential candidates; the runner-up became Vice-President. Figures are from *Historical Statistics of the United States, Colonial Times to 1957* (1961), pp. 682–83; and the U.S. Department of Justice.

Presidential Elections (cont.)

Year	Number of states	Candidates	Parties	Popular vote	Electoral vote	Percentage of popular vote
1844	26	JAMES K. POLK	Democratic	1,338,464	170	49.6
		Henry Clay	Whig	1,300,097	105	48.1
		James G. Birney	Liberty	62,300		2.3
1848	30	ZACHARY TAYLOR	Whig	1,360,967	163	47.4
		Lewis Cass	Democratic	1,222,342	127	42.5
		Martin Van Buren	Free Soil	291,263		10.1
1852	31	FRANKLIN PIERCE	Democratic	1,601,117	254	50.9
		Winfield Scott	Whig	1,385,453	42	44.1
		John P. Hale	Free Soil	155,825		5.0
1856	31	JAMES BUCHANAN	Democratic	1,832,955	174	45.3
		John C. Frémont	Republican	1,339,932	114	33.1
		Millard Fillmore	American	871,731	8	21.6
1860	33	ABRAHAM LINCOLN	Republican	1,865,593	180	39.8
		Stephen A. Douglas	Democratic	1,382,713	12	29.5
		John C. Breckinridge	Democratic	848,356	72	18.1
		John Bell	Constitutional Union	592,906	39	12.6
1864	36	ABRAHAM LINCOLN	Republican	2,206,938	212	55.0
		George B. McClellan	Democratic	1,803,787	21	45.0
1868	37	ULYSSES S. GRANT	Republican	3,013,421	214	52.7
		Horatio Seymour	Democratic	2,706,829	80	47.3
1872	37	ULYSSES S. GRANT	Republican	3,596,745	286	55.6
		Horace Greeley	Democratic	2,843,446	°	43.9
1876	38	RUTHERFORD B. HAYES	Republican	4,036,572	185	48.0
		Samuel J. Tilden	Democratic	4,284,020	184	51.0
1880	38	JAMES A. GARFIELD	Republican	4,453,295	214	48.5
		Winfield S. Hancock	Democratic	4,414,082	155	48.1
		James B. Weaver	Greenback-Labor	308,578		3.4
1884	38	GROVER CLEVELAND	Democratic	4,879,507	219	48.5
		James G. Blaine	Republican	4,850,293	182	48.2
		Benjamin F. Butler	Greenback-Labor	175,370		1.8
		John P. St. John	Prohibition	150,369		1.5
1888	38	BENJAMIN HARRISON	Republican	5,447,129	233	47.9
		Grover Cleveland	Democratic	5,537,857	168	48.6
		Clinton B. Fisk	Prohibition	249,506		2.2
		Anson J. Streeter	Union Labor	146,935		1.3
1892	44	GROVER CLEVELAND	Democratic	5,555,426	277	46.1
		Benjamin Harrison	Republican	5,182,690	145	43.0
		James B. Weaver	People's	1,029,846	22	8.5
		John Bidwell	Prohibition	264,133		2.2
1896	45	WILLIAM MCKINLEY	Republican	7,102,246	271	51.1
		William J. Bryan	Democratic	6,492,559	176	47.7
1900	45	WILLIAM MCKINLEY	Republican	7,218,491	292	51.7
		William J. Bryan	Democratic; Populist	6,356,734	155	45.5
		John C. Wooley	Prohibition	208,914		1.5

° Greeley died shortly after the election; the electors supporting him then divided their votes among minor candidates.

Candidates receiving less than 1 per cent of the popular vote have been omitted. For that reason the percentage of popular vote given for any election year may not total 100 per cent.

Presidential Elections (cont.)

Year	Number of states	Candidates	Parties	Popular vote	Electoral vote	Percentage of popular vote
1904	45	THEODORE ROOSEVELT	Republican	7,628,461	336	57.4
		Alton B. Parker	Democratic	5,084,223	140	37.6
		Eugene V. Debs	Socialist	402,283		3.0
		Silas C. Swallow	Prohibition	258,536		1.9
1908	46	WILLIAM H. TAFT	Republican	7,675,320	321	51.6
		William J. Bryan	Democratic	6,412,294	162	43.1
		Eugene V. Debs	Socialist	420,793		2.8
		Eugene W. Chafin	Prohibition	253,840		1.7
1912	48	WOODROW WILSON	Democratic	6,296,547	435	41.9
		Theodore Roosevelt	Progressive	4,118,571	88	27.4
		William H. Taft	Republican	3,486,720	8	23.2
		Eugene V. Debs	Socialist	900,672		6.0
		Eugene W. Chafin	Prohibition	206,275		1.4
1916	48	WOODROW WILSON	Democratic	9,127,695	277	49.4
		Charles E. Hughes	Republican	8,533,507	254	46.2
		A. L. Benson	Socialist	585,113		3.2
		J. Frank Hanly	Prohibition	220,506		1.2
1920	48	WARREN G. HARDING	Republican	16,143,407	404	60.4
		James N. Cox	Democratic	9,130,328	127	34.2
		Eugene V. Debs	Socialist	919,799		3.4
		P. P. Christensen	Farmer-Labor	265,411		1.0
1924	48	CALVIN COOLIDGE	Republican	15,718,211	382	54.0
		John W. Davis	Democratic	8,385,283	136	28.8
		Robert M. La Follette	Progressive	4,831,289	13	16.6
1928	48	HERBERT C. HOOVER	Republican	21,391,993	444	58.2
		Alfred E. Smith	Democratic	15,016,169	87	40.9
1932	48	FRANKLIN D. ROOSEVELT	Democratic	22,809,638	472	57.4
		Herbert C. Hoover	Republican	15,758,901	59	39.7
		Norman Thomas	Socialist	881,951		2.2
1936	48	FRANKLIN D. ROOSEVELT	Democratic	27,752,869	523	60.8
		Alfred M. Landon	Republican	16,674,665	8	36.5
		William Lemke	Union	882,479		1.9
1940	48	FRANKLIN D. ROOSEVELT	Democratic	27,307,819	449	54.8
		Wendell L. Willkie	Republican	22,321,018	82	44.8
1944	48	FRANKLIN D. ROOSEVELT	Democratic	25,606,585	432	53.5
		Thomas E. Dewey	Republican	22,014,745	99	46.0
1948	48	HARRY S TRUMAN	Democratic	24,105,812	303	49.5
		Thomas E. Dewey	Republican	21,970,065	189	45.1
		J. Strom Thurmond	States' Rights	1,169,063	39	2.4
		Henry A. Wallace	Progressive	1,157,172		2.4
1952	48	DWIGHT D. EISENHOWER	Republican	33,936,234	442	55.1
		Adlai E. Stevenson	Democratic	27,314,992	89	44.4
1956	48	DWIGHT D. EISENHOWER	Republican	35,590,472	457	57.6
		Adlai E. Stevenson	Democratic	26,022,752	73	42.1
1960	50	JOHN F. KENNEDY	Democratic	34,227,096	303	49.9
		Richard M. Nixon	Republican	34,108,546	219	49.6
1964	50	LYNDON B. JOHNSON	Democratic	43,126,506	486	61.1
		Barry M. Goldwater	Republican	27,176,799	52	38.5

Candidates receiving less than 1 per cent of the popular vote have been omitted. For that reason the percentage of popular vote given for any election year may not total 100 per cent.

Population of the United States (1790–1967)

Year	Total population (in thousands)	Number per square mile of land area (continental United States)	Year	Total population (in thousands)	Number per square mile of land area (continental United States)
1790	3,929	4.5	1835	15,003	
1791	4,056		1836	15,423	
1792	4,194		1837	15,843	
1793	4,332		1838	16,264	
1794	4,469		1839	16,684	
1795	4,607		1840	17,120	9.8
1796	4,745		1841	17,733	
1797	4,883		1842	18,345	
1798	5,021		1843	18,957	
1799	5,159		1844	19,569	
1800	5,297	6.1	1845	20,182	
1801	5,486		1846	20,794	
1802	5,679		1847	21,406	
1803	5,872		1848	22,018	
1804	5,065		1849	22,631	
1805	6,258		1850	23,261	7.9
1806	6,451		1851	24,086	
1807	6,644		1852	24,911	
1808	6,838		1853	25,736	
1809	7,031		1854	26,561	
1810	7,224	4.3	1855	27,386	
1811	7,460		1856	28,212	
1812	7,700		1857	29,037	
1813	7,939		1858	29,862	
1814	8,179		1859	30,687	
1815	8,419		1860	31,513	10.6
1816	8,659		1861	32,351	
1817	8,899		1862	33,188	
1818	9,139		1863	34,026	
1819	9,379		1864	34,863	
1820	9,618	5.6	1865	35,701	
1821	9,939		1866	36,538	
1822	10,268		1867	37,376	
1823	10,596		1868	38,213	
1824	10,924		1869	39,051	
1825	11,252		1870	39,905	13.4
1826	11,580		1871	40,938	
1827	11,909		1872	41,972	
1828	12,237		1873	43,006	
1829	12,565		1874	44,040	
1830	12,901	7.4	1875	45,073	
1831	13,321		1876	46,107	
1832	13,742		1877	47,141	
1833	14,162		1878	48,174	
1834	14,582		1879	49,208	

Figures are from *Historical Statistics of the United States, Colonial Times to 1957* (1961), pp. 7, 8; *Statistical Abstract of the United States: 1962*, p. 5; and *Current Population Reports*, Series P-25 (September 1966), pp. 12, 15.

Population of the United States (cont.)

Year	Total population (in thousands)	Number per square mile of land area (continental United States)	Year	Total population (in thousands)°	Number per square mile of land area (continental United States)
1880	50,262	16.9	1925	115,832	
1881	51,542		1926	117,399	
1882	52,821		1927	119,038	
1883	54,100		1928	120,501	
1884	55,379		1929	121,770	
1885	56,658		1930	123,188	41.2
1886	57,938		1931	124,149	
1887	59,217		1932	124,949	
1888	60,496		1933	125,690	
1889	61,775		1934	126,485	
1890	63,056	21.2	1935	127,362	
1891	64,361		1936	128,181	
1892	65,666		1937	128,961	
1893	66,970		1938	129,969	
1894	68,275		1939	131,028	
1895	69,580		1940	132,122	44.2
1896	70,885		1941	133,402	
1897	72,189		1942	134,860	
1898	73,494		1943	136,739	
1899	74,799		1944	138,397	
1900	76,094	25.6	1945	139,928	
1901	77,585		1946	141,389	
1902	79,160		1947	144,126	
1903	80,632		1948	146,631	
1904	82,165		1949	149,188	
1905	83,820		1950	151,683	50.7
1906	85,437		1951	154,360	
1907	87,000		1952	157,028	
1908	88,709		1953	159,636	
1909	90,492		1954	162,417	
1910	92,407	31.0	1955	165,270	
1911	93,868		1956	168,174	
1912	95,331		1957	171,229	
1913	97,227		1958	174,882	
1914	99,118		1959	177,830	
1915	100,549		1960	179,992	60.1
1916	101,966		1961	183,057	
1917	103,414		1962	185,890	
1918	104,550		1963	188,658	
1919	105,063		1964	191,372	
1920	106,466	35.6	1965	193,795	
1921	108,541		1966	195,857	
1922	110,055		1967	197,836	
1923	111,950				
1924	114,113				

° Figures for 1960–67 include Puerto Rico but do not include Armed Forces abroad.

Admission of States

Order of admission	State	Date of admission	Order of admission	State	Date of admission
1	Delaware	December 7, 1787	26	Michigan	January 26, 1837
2	Pennsylvania	December 12, 1787	27	Florida	March 3, 1845
3	New Jersey	December 18, 1787	28	Texas	December 29, 1845
4	Georgia	January 2, 1788	29	Iowa	December 28, 1846
5	Connecticut	January 9, 1788	30	Wisconsin	May 29, 1848
6	Massachusetts	February 6, 1788	31	California	September 9, 1850
7	Maryland	April 28, 1788	32	Minnesota	May 11, 1858
8	South Carolina	May 23, 1788	33	Oregon	February 14, 1859
9	New Hampshire	June 21, 1788	34	Kansas	January 29, 1861
10	Virginia	June 25, 1788	35	West Virginia	June 30, 1863
11	New York	July 26, 1788	36	Nevada	October 31, 1864
12	North Carolina	November 21, 1789	37	Nebraska	March 1, 1867
13	Rhode Island	May 29, 1790	38	Colorado	August 1, 1876
14	Vermont	March 4, 1791	39	North Dakota	November 2, 1889
15	Kentucky	June 1, 1792	40	South Dakota	November 2, 1889
16	Tennessee	June 1, 1796	41	Montana	November 8, 1889
17	Ohio	March 1, 1803	42	Washington	November 11, 1889
18	Louisiana	April 30, 1812	43	Idaho	July 3, 1890
19	Indiana	December 11, 1816	44	Wyoming	July 10, 1890
20	Mississippi	December 10, 1817	45	Utah	January 4, 1896
21	Illinois	December 3, 1818	46	Oklahoma	November 16, 1907
22	Alabama	December 14, 1819	47	New Mexico	January 6, 1912
23	Maine	March 15, 1820	48	Arizona	February 14, 1912
24	Missouri	August 10, 1821	49	Alaska	January 3, 1959
25	Arkansas	June 15, 1836	50	Hawaii	August 21, 1959

INDEX

Numbers in **boldface** type refer to statistical tables.